D0128300

Introduction to

Politics

Canadian Edition

Introduction to
Politics

Robert Garner
Peter Ferdinand
Stephanie Lawson
David B. MacDonald

OXFORD
UNIVERSITY PRESS

OXFORD
UNIVERSITY PRESS

Oxford University Press is a department of the University of Oxford.
It furthers the University's objective of excellence in research, scholarship,
and education by publishing worldwide. Oxford is a registered trade mark of
Oxford University Press in the UK and in certain other countries.

Published in Canada by
Oxford University Press
8 Sampson Mews, Suite 204,
Don Mills, Ontario M3C 0H5 Canada

www.oupcanada.com

Library and Archives Canada Cataloguing in Publication

Introduction to politics/Robert Garner ... [et al.].—1st Canadian ed.

Includes bibliographical references and index.
ISBN 978−0−19−544303−5

1. Political science—Textbooks.
2. International relations—Textbooks.
I. Garner, Robert, 1960–

JA66.I582 2012   320   C2012-904068-1

Cover image: Justin Case/Digital Vision/Getty Images

This book is printed on permanent (acid-free) paper ∞.

Printed and bound in the United States of America
3 4 — 16 15 14

Contents Overview

Detailed Contents

PART I   Political Concepts and Ideas

1 | Politics and the State   21

2 | Political Power, Authority, and the State   45

3 | Democracy and Political Obligation   60

4 | Freedom and Justice   76

PART II   ## Comparative Politics

8 | Law, Constitutions, and Federalism   160

9 | Legislatures and Legislators   182

10 | Bureaucracies, Policy-Making, and Governance   204

PART III

International Relations

List of Boxes

KEY CONCEPT BOXES

BIOGRAPHY BOXES

List of Tables

Welcome! We hope you enjoy this Canadian edition of *Introduction to Politics*. The work of four political scientists, from the United Kingdom, Australia, and Canada, it is truly an international effort. Retaining the structure of the original text (Introduction and Part 1 by Robert Garner; Part 2 and Conclusion by Peter Ferdinand; Part 3 by Stephanie Lawson), David B. MacDonald has made this thought-provoking work more accessible for Canadian students while adding a wealth of Canadian examples and references to recent events (such as the Arab Spring) and current issues (such as the rising profile of women in politics around the world).

Comprehensive coverage of foundational concepts is accompanied by a variety of learning features designed to help you navigate the text material, hone your critical skills, and deepen your understanding of how politics affects your life. Part 1 explores political concepts and ideas, from theories of the state, power, freedom, and justice to ideologies both traditional and alternative. Part 2 examines political institutions in historical and comparative perspective. Part 3 offers an overview of international relations, a subfield of politics that is increasingly crucial in the era of globalization.

© Xinhua/Shen Hong/Corbis

Political Culture

13

CHAPTER OVERVIEW

We begin this chapter by presenting some of the ideas and objectives behind the concept of political culture. Then we look at some of the problems that have arisen in applying it. A case study of Russia illustrates the difficulty of establishing exactly how political culture influences political change. We then argue that despite these problems, political culture remains an important field of study in political science. We conclude by suggesting a more realistic approach to political culture that takes into account the centrality of institutions in political life and the multiplicity of political cultures that may influence the political climate in any particular nation.

A Guided Tour

A variety of learning features will help you navigate the text material and reinforce your comprehension of it. To get the most out of this book, take advantage of these features:

Chapter Overviews at the beginning of every chapter indicate the scope of coverage in the chapter, including the key concepts and debates that the chapter discusses.

KEY CONCEPT BOX 17.2
UN Peacemaking, Peacekeeping, and Peacebuilding

The UN has been engaged in **peacekeeping** since 1956. The idea of using forces from UN member states to defuse conflict was introduced by Canadian diplomat (and later Prime Minister) Lester B. Pearson, who proposed that an international police force supervise the ceasefire between the combatants in the Suez Crisis (a conflict pitting the UK, France, and Israel against Egypt over control of the Suez Canal). For his efforts Pearson was awarded the Nobel Peace Prize in 1957. Former UN Secretary-General Boutros Boutros-Ghali, in his 1992 report to the Security Council, described peacekeeping as

> the deployment of a United Nations presence in the field, hitherto with the consent of all the parties concerned, normally involving United Nations military and/or police personnel and frequently civilians as well. Peacekeeping is a technique that expands the possibilities for both the prevention of conflict and the making of peace.

These forces are coordinated by the UN Department of Peacekeeping Operations.

Early peacekeeping missions were military, but over time peacekeepers' activities have become more complex, partly because many conflicts are now internal, and therefore the parties to conflict are often non-state actors (e.g., militia groups). The UN mission in Cambodia from 1991 to 1993 was one example of non-traditional peacekeeping. Other examples include the missions in Somalia (1992–3) and the former Yugoslavia (1992–5), in which the role of peacekeepers was to distribute relief supplies and promote stability. Other missions in Haiti, Kosovo, and East Timor have focused more on monitoring peace agreements and training police forces.

© Niko Guido/istockphotos.com

PHOTO 17.2 UN soldiers in Haiti provide crowd control as relief workers distribute rice following the earthquake of 2010.

17

"Key Concept Boxes" provide additional information and discussion of important ideas.

---

6 | Challenges to the Dominant Ideologies   131

KEY QUOTE BOX 6.5
Prime Minister Pierre Trudeau Announces Canada's Multiculturalism Policy (1971)

. . . [T]here cannot be one cultural policy for Canadians of British and French origin, another for the original peoples and yet a third for all others. For although there are two official languages, there is no official culture, nor does any ethnic group take precedence over any other. No citizen or group of citizens is other than Canadian, and all should be treated fairly. . . . The individual's freedom would be hampered if he were locked for life within a particular cultural compartment by the accident of birth or language. It is vital, therefore, that every Canadian, whatever his ethnic origin, be given a chance to learn at least one of the two languages in which his country conducts its official business and its politics.

A policy of multiculturalism within a bilingual framework commends itself to the government as the most suitable means of assuring the cultural freedom of Canadians. Such a policy should help to break down discriminatory attitudes and cultural jealousies. National unity if it is to mean anything in the deeply personal sense, must be founded on confidence in one's own individual identity; out of this can grow respect for that of others and a willingness to share ideas, attitudes and assumptions. A vigorous policy of multiculturalism will help create this initial confidence. It can form the base of a society which is based on fair play for all. . . . In implementing [this] policy, the government will provide support in four ways.

First, resources permitting, the government will seek to assist all Canadian cultural groups that have demonstrated a desire and effort to continue to develop a capacity to grow and contribute to Canada, and a clear need for assistance, the small and weak groups no less than the strong and highly organized. Second, the government will assist members of all cultural groups to overcome cultural barriers to full participation in Canadian society. Third, the government will promote creative encounters and interchange among all Canadian cultural groups in the interest of national unity. Fourth, the government will continue to assist immigrants to acquire at least one of Canada's official languages in order to become full participants in Canadian society (Trudeau, 1971: 8545–8).

SOURCE: Pierre Elliott Trudeau (1971), "Announcement of Implementation of Policy of Multiculturalism Within Bilingual Framework," *House of Commons Debates*, 8 Oct.: 8545–8. http://www.abheritage.ca/albertans/speeches/trudeau.html

6

"Key Quote Boxes" allow for the inclusion of longer quotations without interrupting the flow of the discussion.

"Biography Boxes" provide background information on selected thinkers and political figures.

BIOGRAPHY BOX 5.3
Tommy Douglas (1904–86)

Tommy Douglas is generally regarded as the father of the modern Canadian welfare state. A Baptist minister, he combined religious conviction with a dedication to social justice. He was among the founders of the Cooperative Commonwealth Federation (CCF) in 1932, and after 17 years as premier of Saskatchewan (1944–61), during which he introduced Canada's first universal health care system, he was elected to lead the CCF's successor, the New Democratic Party, on its founding in 1961. Douglas saw himself as a champion of working families.

PHOTO 5.2 Tommy Douglas fires up a crowd in 1963.

Conservatism

Elements of conservative thought can be fo…
philosopher Plato, who defended the rule …
kings"—can be regarded as the first conserva…
the Enlightenment that conservative thought …
and socialism promoted the progressive an…
conservatism provides a negative response t…
attack on the French Revolution of 1789, first …

Case Studies demonstrate how political ideas, concepts, and issues manifest themselves in the real world.

CASE STUDY
Gender and Genocide in the Bosnian War, 1992–5

With the end of the Cold War, the Socialist Federative Republic of Yugoslavia (created in 1945) began to disintegrate, generating bitter conflict. First, in 1991, the republics of Slovenia and Croatia held referenda on their future status within the SFRY. Slovenia managed to leave the federation relatively peacefully, but Serbia, ruled by the nationalist leader Slobodan Milosevic (former president of both Yugoslavia and Serbia at various times), refused to recognize Croatian independence, since more than 10 per cent of Croatia's population was ethnically Serbian. The next Yugoslav republic to hold a referendum on independence, in 1992, was Bosnia–Herzegovina. With a multiethnic population of Catholic Croats, Orthodox Serbs, and Bosnian Muslims who had lived in relative harmony for years, Bosnia became the scene of gruesome bloodshed. Many Bosnian Serbs (a minority in the republic) refused to support the separation plan and held their own counter-referendum. They were supported by nationalists in Serbia, including Milosevic, who backed the Bosnian Serb separatist political party, and various Serbian militia groups (MacDonald, 2002: 78–82; 98–106; 220–4).

The war that ensued saw several notorious episodes of "ethnic cleansing," among them the slaughter of an estimated 8,000 Bosnian Muslim men and boys in Srebrenica in July 1995, carried out by units of the Army of Republika Srpska (VRS). At the subsequent trial of one Serbian leader, Radislav Krstic, a statement before the International Criminal Tribunal for the former Yugoslavia (ICTY), summed up the character of the Srebrenica massacre:

PHOTO 16.4 In July 1995, some 30,000 Muslim refugees fled the city of Srebrenica as the Bosnian Serb army overran the area.

Key Points throughout highlight the essential ideas and arguments.

Former Yugoslav Republic of Macedonia). At the same time, the deepening and widening of the EU is a project in **regionalization** that raises questions about the future of the traditional sovereign state in its original heartland.

KEY POINTS

- Largely because of the global reach of the European empires and their political legacies, the European state system became the basis for the current international state system and international order.
- Formal sovereign statehood has not always delivered significant benefits, especially in the Third World, where weak or failing states are unable to meet the needs of their citizens.
- Jackson's concept of the "quasi state" highlights the fact that some Third World states depend so much on the international community for their continuing existence that their sovereignty is essentially "negative."

14

Conclusion

In this chapter we have provided a broad overview of key aspects of the study of International Relations, from its foundations as a discipline and its basic terminology to sovereignty, the state, and rnational systems, includ-esent era of globalization. inst this world historical and international systems me systems have achieved e. It would therefore be a ly remain as it is over the

See Chapter 1, page 25, for an exploration of different theoretical conceptions of the state.

See Chapter 20, page 417, for an exploration of states in a globalizing world.

7

See Chapter 14, page 291, for a more detailed discussion of the rise of the modern state system.

See Chapter 10, page 208, for a discussion of theories of bureaucratic policy-making.

responsible for paying them; even in states that did impose taxes, a great deal of the cost of maintaining officials came from the ruler's own income. Eventually, when a salaried bureaucracy began to develop, beginning in the seventeenth century, one of its most important functions was to collect and administer taxes. Gradually what emerged was a system for extracting taxes from more and more property owners, especially to pay for war. As Tilly put it: "War made the state and the state made war" (Tilly, 1975: 42). Time and again, the need to raise funds for fighting drove governments to devise new ways of raising money. The US, for instance, introduced income tax in 1861 to pay for the American Civil War then raging between North and South. Canada introduced income tax in 1917, to help pay for its contributions to the First World War. Gradually this capacity to extract taxes, coupled with access to a modernizing and industrializing commercial economy and a large rural population, enabled some states to dominate others (Tilly, 1990: 15). They in turn became the models that others had to deal with and, if possible, surpass.

The French Revolution transformed the capacity of the state, leading to a level form of taxation for all its citizens, as well as the principle of the modern citizen army, which helped France to dominate continental Europe until 1814. Britain was forced to emulate France in order to raise enough money and create a large enough armed force to resist it. By the beginning of the nineteenth century, bureaucracies had become central to the state's operation (van Creveld, 1999: 143). This was a key development, for it laid the foundations of the modern state. First, state officials were expected to advance the state and the public good, rather than any individual ruler. Second, officials developed rules and patterns of administration that separated them from the rest of society. In the late nineteenth century, the German sociologist Max Weber would lay out the key characteristics of the new bureaucracies: impersonal, rule-based, goal-oriented activity, with promotion of officials based exclusively on merit and performance. Weber saw bureaucracy as an ideal type of social organization, which he identified with the ongoing rationalization of social life. He emphasized the technical superiority of bureaucratic organization over any other form, although he was often critical of bureaucracies' power and the way they operated.

As the European states grew stronger, new institutions and legal principles had to be established to constrain their rulers, particularly through constitutions. Finer emphasizes two events that were crucial in this respect: the American revolution and the French revolution.

Cross-references in the margins make connections between the chapters deepen your understanding of particular topics and themes. Page references and colour coding aid navigation.

- **Key Questions** at the end of every chapter help you assess your comprehension, and may also be used as topics for seminar discussions and coursework.

- **Further Reading** lists at the end of each chapter include annotations that can help you find the most useful sources for particular topics.

- **Web Links** at the end of each chapter guide you to relevant learning material on the Web.

- **Key Terms** (bolded on their first appearance in each chapter) are defined at the end of the book in a glossary that will be especially useful when you're preparing for exams.

- **Online Resource Centre** This book is the central element of a complete learning and teaching package. Online supplements for instructors and students – including a test generator, links to major news networks, and interviews with Canadian politicians – extend learning opportunities beyond the page. These ancillary materials are available on the companion website www.oupcanada.com/Garner.

For Students

Student Study Guide

- Detailed chapter outlines are accompanied by questions that will help you test your grasp of the ideas discussed in the text.

Links to News Clips

- An online guide to links of news clips demonstrates how politics plays out in different events and settings.

For Instructors

Instructor's Manual

- This online guide includes detailed outlines of the various parts and chapters, along with additional questions designed to encourage class discussion for each chapter.

PowerPoint Slides

- A suite of customizable PowerPoint slides, arranged by chapter, provides an array of summary pages that can be presented as part of a lecture or distributed as handouts.

Test Generator

- A comprehensive set of multiple choice, true/false, short-answer, and essay questions, with suggested answers, allows instructors to create customized tests for each chapter.

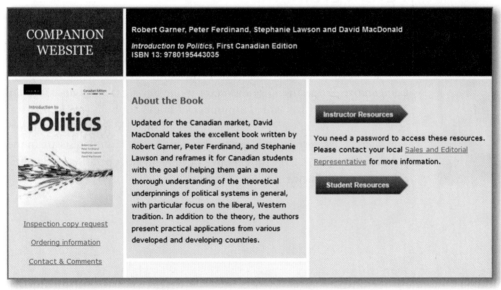

 www.oupcanada.com/Garner

About the Authors

Robert Garner

Robert Garner is Professor of Politics at the University of Leicester in the UK. He was previously at the Universities of Buckingham and Exeter. He has published widely in the area of environmental politics in general and the politics and philosophy of animal rights in particular. His books include *Environmental Politics* (2000), *Animals, Politics and Morality* (2004), *The Political Theory of Animal Rights* (2005), and *Animal Ethics* (2005).

Peter Ferdinand

Peter Ferdinand is Reader in Politics and International Studies and former Director of the Centre for Studies in Democratization at the University of Warwick in the UK. A former Head of the Asia-Pacific Program at the Royal Institute of International Affairs, he is the author of *Communist Regimes in Comparative Perspective: The Evolution of the Soviet, Chinese and Yugoslav Models* (1992) and has edited a number of books on politics and political economy in Taiwan, Central Asia, and Hong Kong. He is also the editor of *The Internet, Democracy and Democratization* (2000). His interests are in the politics of Pacific Asia, the former Soviet Union, democratization, and political economy, and new rising world powers.

Stephanie Lawson

Stephanie Lawson is Professor of Politics and International Relations at Macquarie University, Sydney. She has also held teaching and research appointments at the University of Birmingham, the University of East Anglia, the Australian National University, and the University of New England. Her main research interests focus on culture, ethnicity, nationalism, and democracy, and combine comparative and normative approaches to the study of world politics. She is the author of many book chapters and articles dealing with these issues in the Asia-Pacific region as well as globally. Her recent books include *Culture and Context in World Politics* (2006), *Europe and the Asia-Pacific: Culture, Identity and Representations of Region* (2003), *International Relations* (2003), and *The New Agenda for International Relations: From Polarization to Globalization in World Politics?* (2002).

David B. MacDonald

David B. MacDonald is Associate Professor of Political Science at the University of Guelph, Ontario. He received his PhD in International Relations from the London School of Economics and has also held posts as Senior Lecturer at Otago University, New Zealand, and Assistant Visiting Professor at the ESCP-Europe Graduate School of Management, Paris. He is the author of three books—*Balkan Holocausts? Serbian and Croatian Victim—Centred Propaganda and the War in Yugoslavia* (2002); *Identity Politics in the Age of Genocide* (2008); and *Thinking History, Fighting Evil* (2009)—and co-editor of two: *The Ethics of Foreign Policy* (2007) and *The Bush Leadership, the Power of Ideas and the War on Terror* (2012). He has also written many articles and book chapters on his areas of interest: colonialism and genocide, comparative indigenous politics, US foreign policy, and the comparative politics of western settler societies. His website is www.davidbmacdonald.com. (Photo credit: Gulliver MacDonald.)

Acknowledgements

Several members of the OUP editorial teams deserve special thanks from the authors. In the UK, Ruth Anderson, the Commissioning Editor, got three of us together in the first place and ensured that the project ran smoothly. Monika Faltejskova took on the difficult job of coordinating the writing schedule in the early stages and was succeeded by Emily Medina-Davis. In Canada, Kate Skene, Katie West, Patti Sayle, and Sally Livingston deserve special thanks for overseeing the adaptation process. Finally, we are grateful to Janni Aragon of the University of Victoria, as well the various reviewers, in Canada and the UK, who preferred to remain anonymous. Their constructive criticisms of draft chapters have made the final product that much stronger. Our thanks to them all.

The Nature of Politics and Political Analysis

CHAPTER **OVERVIEW**

We begin this introduction by considering the nature of politics and whether it is an inevitable feature of all human societies. Then we examine two fundamental questions that arise whenever we try to establish the "boundaries of the political." First, should politics be defined narrowly, so as to exclude everything but the institutions of the state, or should the definition be broad enough to include other social institutions and relationships? Second, is politics by definition a matter of cooperation and consensus-seeking, as some theorists maintain? Moving on to the study of politics, we distinguish three forms of political analysis—empirical, normative, and semantic. Finally, we ask whether politics is a science in the sense that the natural sciences are.

Why Is Politics So Hard to Define?

Politics is an exciting and dynamic area of study, but it is so vast and many-sided that it is difficult to define precisely. The challenge of definition appears even greater when we recognize that, at the popular level, politics is often seen in a negative light, associated with conflict and corruption of the sort typified in Canada by the "sponsorship scandal" that helped to bring down the Liberal government in 2006. However, politics can also be seen in a positive light, as a calling to improve the lives of the people that politicians represent; remember the groundswell of hope that carried US presidential candidate Barack Obama to the White House in 2008. Some political thinkers, including Jean-Jacques Rousseau (1712–78) and J.S. Mill (1806–73), have considered participation in political life to be a noble calling.

To the extent that those contrasting perspectives suggest conflict, they actually give us a clue to what politics is about. We might even argue that politics is associated with conflict precisely because all societies of any complexity contain many different interests and values. In fact, one popular definition of politics identifies it as the process by which groups representing divergent interests and values make collective decisions. There are two assumptions here. The first is that all complex societies will always a need a mechanism to sort out those different interests and values and try to reconcile them. The second is that economic scarcity is an inevitable characteristic of all societies. If there are not enough goods to go around, a society needs some mechanism to determine how those limited goods will be distributed.

Political decisions about how economic goods will be distributed—what the American political scientist Harold Lasswell (1936) called "Who Gets What, When, How"—help to determine both the nature of society and the well-being of those who live in it. As we will see in Chapter 4, competing theories of justice focus on a particular ordering of economic goods. However, these are not the only goods that humans value.

The study of politics before the nineteenth century was almost entirely concerned with the study of values. What is the good life? What is the best kind of society for us to live in? Political philosophers have offered many conflicting answers. For the last two centuries, however, as Stoker points out, one "central divide . . . has been between those who prefer liberty over equality and those who prefer equality over liberty" (2006: 6). In the twenty-first century, the conflict between liberty and security is of growing importance; this will be a constant theme in the chapters that follow.

→
See Chapter 3, page 67 for a discussion of the classical theory of democracy.

→
See Chapter 4, pp. 84–90 for a discussion of theories of justice.

Is Politics Inevitable?

If we define politics in terms of differences, conflicts, and scarcity, then we might say that it is an inevitable feature of all societies. Not everyone will agree, of course. For some, such a claim underestimates the possibility of achieving greater social cohesion based on

◀ The Saskatchewan Legislative Building in Regina (Dennis Macdonald/Getty Images).

agreement around core values. Marxists, for example, argue that differences of interests in society centre on the existence of competing social classes, and hence that the elimination of class distinctions would offer the prospect of a society based on consensus and coopera- tion, one in which there would be no need for either politics or the state.

If, as Karl Marx and Friedrich Engels famously argued in the *Communist Manifesto* (1976 [1848]: 105), politics is "merely the organized power of one class for oppressing another," it follows logically that once conflict is ended through the overthrow of capitalism, there will be no competing classes and therefore, by definition, no politics. For others, this Marxist vision is unrealistic—"ideal fancy," in the words of the British philosopher Isaiah Berlin (1969: 118)—because it fails to take into account the human tendencies towards difference, ambition, and competition. A modern version of the Marxist end-of-conflict thesis is the "end of history" thesis proposed by Francis Fukuyama (1992): that since 1945, liberal democratic ideology had proven its superiority over all rivals, and though it might still be challenged, it would ultimately prevail around the world. In other words, by "the end of history" Fukuyama meant the end-point of ideological evolution. It is true that when he was writing, the Cold War had just come to an end, communism in Eastern Europe was being dismantled, and the growing affluence of the West was making it difficult for left-of-centre parties to attract political support.

However, even a quick glance at world affairs raises serious questions about Fukuyama's thesis. As this book will reveal, a number of alternatives to the liberal democratic model are in use in various parts of the world (Heywood, 2004: 71–2). Some of these alterna- tives have similarities with Western liberal democracy but also significant differences. The post-communist regimes of Eastern Europe, for instance, operate very differently from Western democracies because of their limited experience with democratic practices and ideas. Many East Asian regimes (such as China, Malaysia, and Singapore) emphasize economic development over democracy, sometimes at the expense of civil liberties and democratic procedures. The difficulty of establishing democracy in Afghanistan also casts doubt on the "end of history" notion. Finally, some alternatives have nothing in common with the Western liberal democratic model. The military regimes of some African coun- tries fall into the latter category, as do fundamentalist Islamic regimes that put religious norms before liberty and democracy.

Certainly, many fundamental conflicts require political resolution. Some are based on territory, others on political values; the most insoluble contain elements of both. Conflict continues even in Western Europe, as recent debates over multiculturalism show (in 2010 Chancellor Angela Merkel went so far as to announce that multiculturalism in Germany had failed "utterly"). As the British political theorist Andrew Gamble (2000: 108) points out, "The notion that there are no longer any great ideological issues in the world . . . becomes bizarre in relation to the vast populations . . . in Africa, in Asia, in Latin America and in the former territories of the Soviet Union."

Gamble (2000) also challenges the pessimistic assumption that politics is irrelevant because the human "ability to change [the] world . . . has been lost, and lost irrevocably" to the forces of "bureaucracy, technology and the global market" (14). Some globalization theorists, for example, believe that it no longer matters what supposedly sovereign governments do because we are controlled by global economic forces that no one can change (see Chapters 1 and 20). As a result, according to Gamble, the "space for politics is shrinking, and with it the possibility to imagine or to realize any serious alternative to our present condition" (2000: 2–3).

See Chapter 1, pages 35–42, for a discussion of human nature.

See Chapter 6, pages 129–133, for a discussion of multiculturalism.

Gamble argues that this view is too pessimistic, and we agree. It's true that there are many constraints on human will. We have to deal with the realities of the global market and dehumanizing technology; but this does not mean that human agency has no impact. Rather, there is a tension between impersonal forces and human will, a tension "between politics and fate," that must be recognized and tackled.

Political Questions

If we all had the same interests and values, and if there were enough of everything to go around, there would be no need for a mechanism to make decisions about "Who Gets What, When, How." We could have everything we wanted. But politics is based on the assumption that this is not the case. As a result, students of politics ask a number of questions about the decisions that are taken.

In the first place, they ask what values such decisions serve. Do they serve the values of justice or liberty? If so, what do we mean by justice and liberty? Is a just decision one that is made in the interests of the few, the many, or all? The second basic set of questions concerns who makes the decisions, and who should make them. Does one person do the decision-making, or a few, or many, or all? Is there anything special about democratic forms of government? Are we under a greater obligation to obey decisions taken in a democratic way than in other ways? These are the kinds of question that formed the basis of Aristotle's famous six-fold classification of **political systems**; see **Box 0.1**.

KEY CONCEPT BOX 0.1
Aristotle's Classificatory Schema

The Greek philosopher Aristotle (384–322 BCE) argued that a government could be judged by the degree to which it ruled in the interests of all, as opposed to the interests of some small section of the population. Accordingly, he developed a six-part classification containing three "proper" forms of government and three "deviant" forms. His preferred form was a monarchy. He classified democracy as a deviant form on the grounds that the rule of the many in their own interests would be little better than mob rule. However, he also considered democracy to be (as British Prime Minister Winston Churchill was to put it, many centuries later) the least bad form of government (Cunningham, 2002: 7).

TABLE 0.1

Number ruling	Rulers rule in the interest of . . .	
	. . . all	. . . themselves
One	Monarchy	Tyranny
Few	Aristocracy	Oligarchy
Many	Polity	Democracy

SOURCE: R. Dahl (1991), *Modern Political Analysis* (Englewood Cliffs, NJ: Prentice-Hall): 59.

The third basic question that students of politics ask is how those who make the decisions are able to enforce them. Here we need to distinguish between **power** and **authority**, two concepts that are central to politics. We could say that rulers are able to enforce their decisions either because they have the power to do so, or because they have the authority to do so. The former implies some form of coercion: those with power are able to force those without power to behave in ways they would not choose. Clearly, regimes that rely exclusively on the exercise of power in that sense are likely to be inefficient and unstable. Such regimes will survive only if they are able to impose coercion continually—a difficult exercise. As Libya's Moammar Gadhafi found out, even the most coercive regime cannot hold on to power once the people decide to revolt.

By contrast, a regime with authority has no need of force, because the people recognize that the ruler has a legitimate right to exercise power and therefore they consent to be ruled. In other words, authority is defined in terms of legitimacy. Converting power into authority is the goal of most regimes, because it makes ruling far easier and less costly. It also makes leadership more stable.

→
See Chapter 2, pages 46–48 for an exploration of the concepts of power and authority.

KEY POINTS

- In societies of any complexity, politics is usually predicated on the existence of competing interests and values.
- Most commentators believe that politics is inevitable because all societies contain differences that have to be managed in some way.
- The "end of history" thesis suggests that liberal democratic values are the only legitimate values left in the modern world after the defeat of fascism and communism, but this view is seriously mistaken. Ideological conflicts persist throughout the world and liberalism itself has faced challenges to its legitimacy.
- Given competing values and interests, the study of politics becomes the study of which values and interests dominate, who is responsible for the decisions that are made, and on what grounds they can or cannot be justified.

Boundaries of the Political 1: State, Society, and the International Community

So far, then, we can say that politics is rooted in differences of interests and values, and that it seeks to manage those differences in a world where scarcity is inevitable. But this takes us only so far in a definitional sense, because it says nothing about the boundaries of "the political." Where does politics begin and end? Those who prefer a narrow definition would exclude all institutions other than those of the state. Others believe that to draw the boundaries so narrowly is to miss much of importance that should fairly be described as political. This narrow definition sets politics apart, however artificially, from other social sciences with which we believe it is intimately connected. In this book, therefore, we will refer to subfields of politics such as political sociology and political economy, which focus on the relationships between the state and society and the economy respectively.

Why has political analysis traditionally centred on the state? Because, in the words of the German sociologist Max Weber (1864–1920), the state has a "monopoly of the legitimate use of physical force in enforcing its order within a given territorial area" (Gerth and

Mills, 1946: 77–8). In other words, the state is the highest authority in a society, and as such is **sovereign**. As the supreme law-making body within a particular territory, the state ultimately has the power of life and death over individuals. It can put people to death for crimes they have committed and it can demand that its citizens fight for their country in wars with other sovereign states. Defined in this way, the state can be distinguished from the government in the sense that it is a much larger entity, containing not just political offices but also bureaucratic, judicial, military, police, and security institutions. The state can also be distinguished from **civil society**: the body non-governmental institutions that link the individual and the state; see **Box 0.2**.

→
See Chapter 12, pages 239–243, for a discussion of civil society.

KEY CONCEPT BOX 0.2
Civil Society

The term "civil society" usually refers to the many private groups and institutions that operate between the individual and the state, from business organizations and trade unions to religious institutions, voluntary organizations, **non-governmental organizations** (NGOs), and **interest groups** of all kinds. The German philosopher G.W.F. Hegel (1770–1831) distinguished between the family and civil society, but other theorists include the family as an institution within civil society.

→
See Chapter 3, pages 72–74, for a discussion of political obligation.

Discussions of political power usually focus on the state. However, some scholars argue that politics operates at many levels, and therefore they extend the boundaries of the political realm to include everything from the family to the international community. Today many are particularly interested in the study of politics at the supranational level. Arguably too, the focus of politics has begun to shift as national economies become increasingly interdependent and the forces of globalization place increasing constraints on what individual "sovereign" states can do on their own.

Certainly, the academic study of international relations has expanded enormously in the past few years. The fact that a third of this book is devoted to relations between states is a reflection of the growing importance of this field. However, we also need to recognize that the traditional "**realist**" approach to international relations still sees the state as the key actor. In this model, the difficulty of securing agreement between states can be a significant barrier to the successful resolution of supranational problems.

→
See Chapter 15, pages 303–307, for a discussion of realism.

Another dent in the argument of those who draw tight boundaries around "the political" comes from those who argue that politics exists in the institutions of society below the state. Colin Hay (2002: 3), for instance, makes this abundantly clear when he insists that "the political should be defined in such a way as to encompass the entire sphere of the social." Leftwich (1984) substantially agrees, arguing that "politics is at the heart of *all* collective social activity, formal and informal, public and private, in all human groups, institutions and societies." The term **governance**, which is increasingly preferred to "government," draws the boundaries of the governmental process much wider. It includes not only the traditional institutions of government but all the other inputs that may influence decisions affecting society, such as the market, interest groups. Indeed, references to the politics of business organizations, universities, churches, sport, and the family have become part of everyday discourse.

→
See Chapter 6, pages 119–124, for a discussion of feminism.

Some ideological traditions concur with this wider view of politics. Many feminists, for instance, believe the personal realm to be acutely political as a result of the dominance of patriarchy in personal relationships and the family; hence the slogan "the personal is the political." And classical Marxists insist that political power comes from dominance in the economic realm. Similarly, whatever its internal divisions—and there are many—Islam's scripture-based tradition governs all aspects of Muslim life, including relations within the family. To deny the political nature of this tradition is to further limit our ability to address issues of importance in the contemporary world.

Although Leftwich specified "human . . . societies," we can even ask whether the boundaries of the political should stop at our species. There might be a strong case for recognizing at least some non-human animals as beings whose interests should be taken into account in the political process (Garner, 2005). In general, according to Jamieson (2002), proponents of animal rights have advanced three main arguments:

1. "Animals and humans are similar in ways that count. They are conscious beings capable of enjoying life or experiencing pain and suffering.
2. Animals are innocent. They have done nothing to deserve human mistreatment or cruelty.
3. Treating animals well helps create a more benevolent society, whereas cruelty and abuse leads to moral bankruptcy" (2002: 149–151).

An even more radical school of thought (sometimes described as "dark green" ecology) would extend the boundaries of the political to encompass the whole of the natural world.

See Chapter 6, pages 124–129, for a discussion of environmentalism.

It has been suggested that to expand the boundaries of the political beyond the state is to run the risk of diluting the study of political science to the point that we could no longer distinguish between the work of, say, the sociologist and that of the political analyst. Hay's response to this concern is that it confuses politics as an *arena* with politics as a *process* (2002: 72). For Hay, the distinctiveness of politics lies not in the arena within which it takes place, but in "the emphasis it places on the political aspect of social relations." This "political aspect" is defined in terms of the "distribution, exercise and consequences of power." In other words, politics is about power, and it occurs wherever power is exercised. Of course, Hay is not suggesting that politics explains everything there is to know about social relationships; or even the most important things. Other disciplines—sociology, economics, psychology, cultural studies—have important roles too. "Though politics may be everywhere," Hay (2002: 75) continues, "nothing is exhaustively political."

Boundaries of the Political 2: What Kind of Activity Qualifies?

Some commentators suggest that politics as the art of negotiating peaceful resolutions to conflict, through cooperation, compromise, and the building of consensus. When efforts to reach consensus don't succeed and the parties concerned resort to other means (coercion, suppression of dissent, violent protests, etc.), proponents of this view say that politics has either failed or been rejected. The best-known advocate of this position was Bernard Crick (1962). For Crick, politics was "only one possible solution to the problem of order" (18), the best way to resolve conflict, a "great and civilizing human activity" associated with such admirable values as toleration, respect, and fortitude (15).

Crick argued that politics is most likely to succeed when power is widely distributed across the society, so that no single group can impose its will on others. Unfortunately, as he recognized, political approaches are too often rejected in favour of force. He therefore called for promotion of the values he associated with politics.

A similar argument is put forward by Gerry Stoker. In a book that restates many of Crick's arguments, Stoker (2006) writes that politics is "one of the ways we know of . . . to address and potentially patch up the disagreements that characterize our societies without recourse to illegitimate coercion or violence" (7). He further argues that much of the current discontent regarding democratic politics is misplaced: our expectations are too high, and we need to understand that politics is by nature messy, muddled, and "designed to disappoint" (10).

The arguments put forward by Crick and Stoker represent a particular kind of politics, not politics per se. Yes, the reconciliation of differences and the resolution of conflict are at the heart of politics, but we cannot restrict discussion of politics to situations where compromises are made and agreements reached. We also need to be able to talk about force, violence, and military conflict as "politics by other means" (to borrow the famous dictum of the military strategist Carl von Clausewitz).

It's worth noting that both Crick and Stoker have been criticized for associating politics too closely with liberal democracies, in which power is commonly assumed to be widely dispersed. It would seem strange if our definition of politics forced us to argue that countries governed undemocratically by economic, religious, or military elites do not practise politics, but should, as Crick and Stoker recommend, aspire to it. For an assortment of definitions of politics, see **Box 0.3**.

KEY QUOTE BOX 0.3
The Nature of Politics

A political system is "any persistent pattern of human relationships that involves, to a significant extent, control, influence, power or authority" (Dahl, 1991: 4).

Politics is the "the art of governing mankind by deceiving them." (Isaac D'Israeli, quoted in Crick 1962: 16).

Politics "can be simply defined as the activity by which differing interests within a given unit of rule are conciliated by giving them a share in power in proportion to their importance to the welfare and the survival of the whole community" (Crick, 1962: 21).

"Politics is a phenomenon found in and between all groups, institutions (formal and informal) and societies, cutting across public and private life. It is involved in all the relations, institutions and structures which are implicated in the activities of production and reproduction in the life of societies. . . . Thus, politics is about power; about the forces which influence and reflect its distribution and use; and about the effect of this on resource use and distribution . . . it is not about Government or government alone" (Held and Leftwich, 1984: 144).

"Politics is designed to disappoint—that is the way that the process of compromise and reconciliation works. Its outcomes are often messy, ambiguous and never final" (Stoker, 2006: 10).

KEY POINTS

- Defining politics is complicated by questions about where the boundaries should be drawn.
- Some argue that the boundaries of the political should be drawn narrowly, recognizing the state as the key political institution. Others argue that politics needs to be defined far more broadly, to encompass power relations in social institutions such as the family or political institutions at the supranational level.
- The second boundary problem concerns the kind of activity that may be described as "political." Some, like Crick, define politics solely in terms of cooperation, negotiation, and consensus-building. Others find this definition too limiting and argue that politics is also practised in undemocratic regimes or in periods of civil or international strife.

The Study of Politics

The study of politics dates back to at least the fifth century BCE and the Greek philosophers Plato and Aristotle, who are considered the "founding fathers" of the discipline. Yet politics did not become an independent discipline in higher education before the beginning of the twentieth century; until then it had been studied only in the context of law, philosophy, and history. The American Political Science Association, the body of academics specializing in political studies, was formed in 1903 and its British equivalent, the Political Studies Association, in 1950 (Stoker and Marsh, 2002: 2).

The teaching of politics has traditionally distinguished between the study of political ideas (sometimes referred to as political theory or philosophy), the study of political institutions and processes within states, and the study of relations between states. This book is structured around these distinctions, but the three areas are far from mutually exclusive; in fact, they overlap regularly. As Part 1 of this book will show, the study of political ideas combines conceptual analysis, coverage of the key figures in the history of political thought, and discussion of ideologies. The study of institutions and processes, covered in Part 2, can take a number of forms, including examination of the institutions of a single state, comparison of institutions and processes in various states, political history, electoral politics, and public administration. Finally, students of international politics, the subject of Part 3, often examine the role of states as well as supranational actors and institutions, either historically or contemporaneously.

The Rise and Fall of Normative Analysis

In all three branches of political science, at least three major kinds of political analysis are undertaken: normative, empirical, and semantic. The first, normative analysis, asks questions of a valuational kind: whether, when, and why we ought to value freedom, or democracy, or equality, for example, or under what circumstances we should or should not obey the state. The goal is to identify what is good, what we ought to want, or which alternative is better. For millennia, normative analysis was the core of political philosophy, and many of the "classics" in the history of political thought, from Plato's *Republic* through Thomas Hobbes's *Leviathan* to major twentieth-century works such as John Rawls's *Theory of Justice*, have been devoted to determining what constitutes the "good life," the kind of society and polity within which it would be desirable for us to live.

For much of the twentieth century, however, normative analysis was pushed into the background by two newer types of analysis: empirical and semantic (see the next section). Both arose during the "behavioural revolution" of the 1950s, a time when number-crunching, particularly in relation to the study of electoral behaviour, was the gold standard (see **Box 0.5**, on page 13). In this period, philosophizing about what kind of society and polity we ought to have—the basis of normative analysis—was regarded as unnecessary at best and at worst meaningless.

A variety of intellectual and practical political reasons have been put forward to explain what Peter Lasslett (1956: vii) described as the "death of political philosophy," ranging from the growth of secularism (Dahl, 1991: 120) to the emergence, in the West at least, of consensus politics (that is, widespread agreement on the fundamental political principles). In the academic world, the decline of normative analysis was partly a product of the rise positivism, whose proponents sought to apply the scientific methodology of the natural sciences to social phenomena (see **Box 0.4**). Positivism was associated in particular with the French social scientist Auguste Comte (1798–1856), who argued that the development of the scientific method represented the culmination of human evolution.

An extreme variation on that theme was logical positivism, a school of thought developed in the 1920s by a group of philosophers known as the "Vienna Circle" (see Ayer, 1971). For logical positivists, the only legitimate statements were those that (1) were empirically verifiable and (2) sought to say something about the meaning of concepts and the relations between them. Normative or valuational statements were considered meaningless.

KEY CONCEPT BOX 0.4
Positivism

Positivism is a philosophical system that sees the scientific or "positive" stage of human intellectual evolution as the last of three major stages in our history. It holds that science must limit itself to what is observable, and insists on a clear separation between fact and value. At the extreme, the doctrine known as logical positivism holds that normative claims are meaningless: the only meaningful statements are those that can be either investigated empirically, by observation, or examined semantically.

Normative political philosophy began to make a comeback in the latter part of the twentieth century, partly as a result of the decline in consensus politics, and partly in response to new and innovative political philosophy, notably Rawls's *A Theory of Justice* (1971). Nevertheless, a great deal of contemporary political philosophy is much more cautious and tentative than the grand narratives of the past. In part, this reflects a recognition that normative questions present certain problems for the political philosopher. As we shall see below, empirical facts can play a part in the resolution of normative questions. However, for most scholars it remains impossible to derive normative statements from empirical facts—in other words, to derive an *ought* from an *is*. Consider the premise "she is old and lonely and her health is frail," followed by the conclusion "you ought to help her" (Thomas, 1993: 14). Clearly, the conclusion does not follow from the premise unless we add another clause to the effect that "we ought to help those who are old, lonely, and frail." This, of course, is another normative statement, not capable of empirical confirmation.

If we cannot resolve normative questions by invoking empirical facts, how can we judge the validity of a normative statement? Were the logical positivists right to believe that normative statements are meaningless and that the effort to judge between competing values is worthless? If so, as Dahl (1991: 118) points out, this means that asking whether democracy is better than dictatorship is equivalent to asking whether "you like coffee better than tea." The problem is that different ideologies are based on different foundational values. Socialism and liberalism, for instance, are based on the foundational values of equality and freedom respectively. How can we judge between them?

There is no easy answer to this normative conundrum. Dworkin (1987: 7–8) offers a possible solution when he cleverly argues that it is a mistake to regard modern political theories as representing different foundational values. Rather, he suggests that they all have a commitment to egalitarianism in the sense that they all hold that humans are worth the same and have an equal value.

Even if Dworkin is right, however, not all political ideologies hold that all humans are of equal value. Does this mean that we committed to saying that slavery is as good as freedom, or racism as good as racial tolerance? Intuitively, most of us would not want to accept this kind of relativism. So how are we to judge between competing political and moral values?

In the first place, a relativist position exaggerates the difficulty of passing judgment on the validity of competing belief systems. Nagel (1987: 232), for instance, argues convincingly that it is possible to dismiss a particular belief "in terms of errors in . . . evidence, or identifiable errors in drawing conclusions from it, or in argument, judgment and so forth." Moreover, there *are* some conceptions of the good—health, bodily integrity, wealth, even liberty—to which everyone might aspire (Waldron, 1989: 74–5), as well as "conceptions of the good which are manifestly unreasonable" (Arneson, 2000: 71). Of course, we may never be certain about the competing value of many conceptions of the good; nevertheless, as Arneson (2000: 77) points out, "if one sets the threshold of supporting reasons for public policy at the level of certainty, it is doubtful that any proposed policy can pass."

Empirical and Semantic Analysis

The second type of analysis common to politics, and to most other academic disciplines as well, is empirical. **Empirical analysis** seeks to identify observable phenomena in the real world with a view to establishing what is, as opposed to what ought to be. Empirical analysis is the basis of the natural sciences, and many *positivist* political analysts seek to bring what they see as the impartial and value-free methods of the natural sciences to the study of political phenomena.

The third type of analysis commonly used in politics is semantic. **Semantic analysis** is concerned with the meaning of the concepts we use, where these concepts came from, and why and how we use them. Semantics has an important function in political studies, given that so many of the concepts used in politics have no commonly accepted definition and are, as Gallie (1955–6) put it, "essentially contested." Defining what we mean by terms such as "democracy" and "freedom" is a crucial starting point.

In reality, none of the three forms of political analysis outlined above are practised in isolation. As Wolff (1996: 3) points out, "studying how things are helps to explain how things can be, and studying how they can be is indispensable for assessing how they ought to be." Thus normative claims are based largely on empirical knowledge. In the case of

→

See pages 35–42 for a
discussion of human
nature.

Hobbes, for instance, the normative claim that society ought to rely on an all-powerful sovereign was supposedly rooted in the empirical observation that human nature was brutally competitive and that only a "Leviathan" could provide the necessary security. Conversely, a great deal of empirical analysis presupposes some normative assumptions. This can be seen in the topics that students of politics choose to explore. Thus we might choose to investigate the causes of war because we assume that war is undesirable and therefore that we should try to eliminate it. For the early theorists of international relations, in the years just after the First World War, researching past wars with a view to ending future ones was a priority.

It may be useful at this point to consider the differences between what we might call empirical and normative political theory. For positivists, creating theory involves the generation of testable hypotheses about political phenomena; for example, the hypothesis that democracy can flourish only in societies with market economies and private ownership. By contrast, normative theory involves the formation of judgments about our political goals: for example, whether a democratic political framework (or a capitalist economic framework, etc.) is desirable in the first place.

We noted earlier that the study of political "theory" has traditionally been separated from the study of political institutions and processes. To those who would maintain this separation there are two responses. First, those who study government without recognizing the key normative questions raised by political philosophers will receive only a partial picture of their discipline. Systems of government created by human beings reflect normative beliefs. The American Constitution, for example, is a product of the Founding Fathers' vision of what a modern state ought to be like, and amendments made since their time—for example, extending the right to vote to women in 1920—reflect more recent normative thinking.

Alongside normative theorizing, theorizing of an empirical kind is also a central part of the study of political institutions and processes. Theories are used in empirical work to organize and make sense of the masses of information that political researchers unearth, and to identify and explain relationships between observable phenomena. A key element of the empirical approach is the comparative method, in which political analysts develop testable generalizations by comparing political phenomena across different political systems or historically within the same system. To test the hypothesis posed above—that democracy requires a free market and private ownership—would require a comparative examination of different regimes in order to understand the relationship between political and economic variables. It would also require semantic analysis of the concept of democracy— a concept that, as we shall see in Chapter 3, is subject to many different interpretations. To take another example, the proposition that countries with electoral systems that use a form of **proportional representation** tend to experience more political and economic instability than those that use the first-past-the-post system could be tested by undertaking an empirical comparison of countries that use one or the other.

Deductive and Inductive Theories of Politics

Stoker and Marsh (2002: 3) point out that there are "many distinct approaches and ways of undertaking political science." Arguably, however, the most important approaches to the empirical study of politics can be divided into two groups: those using deductive reasoning and those using inductive reasoning. The deductive method is associated with rational-choice theories of politics, and the inductive approach with **behaviouralism** (see **Box 0.5**). Together, these newer approaches moved politics away from the formal, legalistic study of institutions and, in particular, constitutions, which had been more prevalent in the nineteenth and early twentieth centuries.

KEY CONCEPT BOX 0.5
Behaviouralism

This approach was developed, particularly in the United States, in the post-1945 period. It stressed the importance of the scientific method in the study of social phenomena. Objective measurement of the social world was the goal, and values were to be completely eliminated from social enquiry. Behaviouralism assumed that human behaviour is capable of being measured in a precise way, and that generalizations can be derived from it. This school of thought reached the height of its influence in political studies in the 1960s. Since then it has been increasingly challenged by those who question the idea that political science and social enquiry in general are value-free.

Rational-choice analysis, which was first developed in the field of economics, has become increasingly important since the 1970s. Treating politics as a response to the problem of collective action, this approach has applications both in the study of political institutions and processes, and in the study of international relations. In general, rational choice analysis starts with certain fundamental assumptions about human behaviour from which hypotheses or theories are deduced, before being tested against facts in the "real world": specifically, it is assumed that humans are essentially rational beings, "utility maximizers" who will follow the path of action most likely to benefit them. This approach has been used in "game theory," where individual behaviour is applied to particular situations. Game scenarios reveal how difficult it can be for rational individuals to reach optimal outcomes, not least because "free-riders" reap the benefits of collective action without paying any of the costs. In political science, the best-known applications of rational-choice theory can be found in the fields of voting and party competition, and in interest group politics.

One problem with the deductive method is that its fundamental assumptions remain just that: assumptions. Many regard those assumptions as simplifications at best and at worst as entirely inaccurate descriptions of human behaviour. Moreover, rational choice theory has generated a large number of hypotheses about various aspects of the political process, but is short on empirical tests of those hypotheses (Hay, 2002: 39–40). Rational choice theory is better at predicting outcomes on the basis of certain stated premises than it is at developing accurate empirical theories of the real world.

Inductive approaches to politics, by contrast, start with empirical observations and draw explanatory generalizations from them. Whereas in deductive approaches, theory is deduced from first principles before being tested, in inductive approaches theory follows observation and generalization. This is the classic method of scientific inquiry. A classic example of inductivism is behaviouralism. The topics that behaviouralists focused on

See Chapter 1, pages 25–28, and Chapter 10, pages 213–216, for more on interest groups.

were quantifiable (e.g., voting behaviour). Thus empirical data on British voting behaviour during the 1960s gave rise to the generalization that voting is class-based (the working class tended to vote Labour and the middle and upper classes tended to vote Conservative).

The weaknesses of the inductive method mirror those of the deductive method. Whereas the latter is strong on theory but weak on empirical testing, the reverse is true of the former. The inductive approach focuses more on gathering empirical data than it does on the generation of theory. This traditional positivist approach was famously critiqued by the philosopher of science Karl Popper (1902–94). Popper argued that instead of generating empirical data from which a hypothesis can be derived, theorists should seek to falsify existing hypotheses: that is, they should focus on testing earlier studies to see if they are correct or incorrect. "Falsification" is simply the process of testing, and its results may either disprove or support the existing theory. If the previous theory can't be disproved, the earlier conclusion stands until such time as another study proves it wrong; then political science moves on to a new theory. For example, if I hypothesize that *I only like chocolate ice-cream*, the only way to sustain this hypothesis is to try other flavours and reject them. Falsification occurs if I sample another flavour—say, bubblegum—to see if my original hypothesis holds. If I find that I also like bubblegum ice-cream, then I have just disproved my theory and need to generate a new one: *I only like chocolate and bubblegum ice-cream.*

In this way truth claims became temporary, only as good as the next successful attempt to refute them. Verification can never be conclusive, but falsification can be. More to the point, positivists have tended, since Popper, to show less interest in the inductive method and more in the generation of hypotheses to be refuted.

Another weakness of the inductive method is that the hypotheses it generates tend not to be explanatory: that is, they don't identify a causal link between generalizations. Rather, they tend to involve patterns of statistical correlation (Hay, 2002: 79). Finding correlations between phenomena is not the same as finding that one explains the other. For example, the fact that a statistical correlation is found between social class and voting behaviour does not, in itself, explain why the correlation exists. Perhaps working-class people feel a greater ideological affinity with the Labour party, or think that Labour MPs, many of whom come from working-class backgrounds, will be better able to represent their interests in Parliament. Alternatively, it might be the case that working-class people are just as likely to vote Conservative as Labour if each party advertises to the same extent in all neighbourhoods, but Labour puts more money and effort into working-class neighbourhoods while the Conservatives focus their campaigns on middle- and upper-class neighbourhoods.

KEY POINTS

- Political analysis involves three main approaches; empirical, normative, and semantic.
- Theorizing normatively about politics is difficult and often contentious. On the other hand, the difficulties should not be exaggerated. Moral relativism is not the inevitable consequence of political philosophy.
- In practice, these three forms of political analysis are not mutually exclusive. We need to know what *is* before we can talk sensibly about what *ought* to be. Similarly, empirical analysis presupposes some normative assumptions.
- Empirical political analysis tends to use either inductive or deductive reasoning. Behaviouralism uses the former, rational choice theory the latter.

Can Politics Be a Science?

Whether a social science such as politics can be, or should be, scientific is an open question. The debate, as Hay argues, is a "complex, voluminous and multi-faceted" one (2002: 75), and we can cover only its major themes here. To a certain extent, the answer depends on whether our definition of science is loose or strict. Politics is a science in the sense that it "offers ordered knowledge based on systematic enquiry" (Stoker and Marsh, 2002: 11). In fact, according to this definition even normative analysis can be scientific as long as it is undertaken in a systematic way. A more rigorous definition would require that the methodology of the natural sciences be applied to the political realm, as the behaviouralists tried to do. Here an appropriate definition of science might be "the ability to generate neutral, dispassionate and objective knowledge claims" (Hay, 2002: 87).

The attractions of an objective, value-free account of politics, one that would allow us to identify the "truth" about political phenomena, are obvious. However, there is reason to think that a truly scientific account of politics is unlikely. First, we can question whether the methods of natural science can be transferred to any social science. Human beings are unpredictable, and their political behaviour is not consistent with unbending scientific laws in the way that, say, the workings of molecules are. As Hay (2002: 50) points out, the social sciences "deal with conscious and reflective subjects, capable of acting differently under the same stimuli."

The only way of avoiding the conclusion that the unpredictable nature of human beings makes a science of society impossible is to assume that human behaviour can be determined. As we saw in the case of rational choice theory, it's doubtful that assumptions about human behaviour can stand the test of empirical observation. Furthermore, the study of politics is not value-free, since we impose our own assumptions and norms on our work from the very start of a research project. The questions we ask and the ways in which we frame them have a crucial bearing on the answers we get back. We might want to argue, too, that politics should be about values and norms. To attempt to exclude them is to miss much of what is valuable in the study of the political.

KEY POINTS

- Behaviouralists, in particular, suggest that the study of politics can have the scientific rigour of the natural sciences.
- Opponents of this view argue that political behaviour is inconsistent with scientific "laws," and that the study of politics neither is nor should be "value-free" in the way that the natural sciences are.

Conclusion

In this chapter we have introduced some basic definitions and themes current within political analysis. We have also suggested keeping an open mind as to what is "political"; to define the boundaries too narrowly would be to miss much that is important in the real world. The rest of this book will reflect that broad orientation.

Part 1, Chapters 1–6, continues the exploration of political ideas and ideologies, focusing on the state, power and democracy, freedom and justice, and traditional and new political ideologies. Part 2, Chapters 7–13, focuses on political institutions and processes, with chapters on all the main elements of the political system: constitutions, executives and legislatures, bureaucracies, parties and elections, the media, and political culture. Part 3, Chapters 14–20, examines relations between states, moving from a historical account of the development of the states system to discussions of international relations theory, international security, diplomacy and foreign policy, international organizations and, finally, international political economy.

? KEY QUESTIONS

- What is politics?
- Is politics synonymous with the state?
- Is politics an inevitable feature of all societies?
- Distinguish between normative and empirical analysis in the context of political theory.
- Can politics be a science?
- What is the case for defining politics narrowly?
- How can we evaluate between competing normative claims?
- Evaluate the claims made by inductive and deductive approaches to political studies.
- "Politics is generally disparaged as an activity which is shrinking in importance and relevance" (Gamble: 2000). Discuss.

📖 FURTHER READING

Crick, B. (1962). *In Defence of Politics*. London: Weidenfeld & Nicolson.
A classic argument for a positive interpretation of politics as a matter of building consensus.

Dahl, R. (1991). *Modern Political Analysis*. Englewood Cliffs, NJ: Prentice-Hall.
A classic account of the study of politics by a legendary American academic.

Gamble, A. (2000). *Politics and Fate*. Cambridge: Polity Press.
A spirited critique of the idea that impersonal forces such as globalization have destroyed our ability to control our own futures. Gamble argues that we are not prisoners of "fate," and in fact have considerable control over our political destinies.

Hay C. (2002). *Political Analysis*. Basingstoke: Palgrave Macmillan.
A comprehensive and accessible account of different approaches to political science.

Marsh, D. and G. Stoker, eds (2002). Theory and Methods in Political Science. Basingstoke: Palgrave.
An extremely useful collection of articles setting out the field.

Stoker, G. (2006). *Why Politics Matter*. Basingstoke: Palgrave.
A modern version of Crick's work, defining politics in terms of consensus and democracy.

📱 WEB LINKS

www.cpsa-acsp.ca
The Canadian Political Science Association is the major Canadian professional society for students of politics and government. It also publishes the *Canadian Journal of Political Science*.

www.apsanet.org
The American Political Science Association performs the same role as above in the United States.

www.psa.ac.uk

The Political Studies Association (PSA) of the United Kingdom, founded in 1950, is the British equivalent of the APSA.

www.politicsresources.net

Political Science Resources is a web gateway with more than 17,000 links to major politics and government sites around the world, created by Richard Kimber.

www.library.vanderbilt.edu/romans/polsci

Vanderbilt University maintains this extensive web gateway, which offers hundreds of links, including overviews of the discipline of political science and its subfields.

www.hyperpolitics.net

An innovative online dictionary of political terms.

PART I

Political Concepts and Ideas

"POLITICAL THEORY" might sound dull and dry to some people, but it is the stuff that revolutions are made of. Ideas about justice, equality, and freedom; power and morality; war and peace, are not the exclusive domain of the ancient Greeks and nineteenth-century Germans with enormous moustaches. Around the world, these concepts and ideas inspire people to think creatively about life and how to improve it, both inside their own societies and outside them, in the global society in which all of us are increasingly united. At the same time, political philosophers revisit the work of earlier theorists and reinterpret it in the light of the present. In this way political theory, far from remaining static, keeps pace with the changing world. In 2011, when hundreds of thousands of people joined forces to protest against long-standing dictatorships and demand a better life for themselves, they were inspired by centuries of political ideals.

In principle, political philosophers ask just two kinds of questions about political phenomena: semantic and normative. As we saw in the Introduction, however, empirical observation does have an important role to play in the normative realm, and in any case "political theory" is a broader category than "political philosophy." In Chapters 1 and 2, therefore, in addition to introducing the central concept of the state, we look at a number of empirical observations regarding the location of power in it.

Among the fundamental questions that political theorists ask is what gives a state legitimacy: in other words, why should we obey it? This question of political obligation is discussed in Chapter 3. Questions of freedom and justice—what limits should be placed on the state, and how state goods ought to be distributed—are the subjects of Chapter 4. Finally, Chapters 5 and 6 explore political ideologies, traditional and contemporary.

Political philosophy has a checkered history. Some have argued that its last great age was the nineteenth century, and have blamed its decline on the rise of secularism. As the political scientist Robert Dahl (1991: 120) pointed out, "values could no longer be successfully justified by basing them on divinely revealed religious truths." Some have questioned the worth of philosophy in the light of the Holocaust, all the more so given that Germany was widely considered to be the most philosophically sophisticated country in Europe (Horton, 1984: 115). Another challenge was posed by the school of thought known as logical positivism, which (as we saw in the Introduction) questioned the value of normative analysis of any kind. Finally, by the early 1960s much of the Western world had enjoyed more than a decade of economic prosperity and consensus politics, and there seemed little reason to look at alternative political arrangements when the existing ones—based on a mixed economy, the welfare state, and nuclear deterrence—were working so well.

That consensus was about to change radically, however. First there were the protests against the war in Vietnam in the mid-1960s; then came the massive economic problems of the 1970s. Suddenly it seemed that longstanding certainties were open to question, and political ideologies were becoming polarized. At the same time, the influence of logical positivism began to decrease. An important factor here was the appearance of significant new works of political philosophy in the 1970s, most notably John Rawls's *A Theory of Justice*, which we will discuss in detail in Chapter 4.

By the beginning of the twenty-first century political theory was facing yet another challenge. To the extent that globalization throws into question the centrality of the sovereign state, it casts doubt on the political theory that has developed with the latter as its focal point. But political theorists have been grappling with the impact of globalization for some time now. Thus we consider cosmopolitan theories of democracy and justice, for instance, in Chapters 3 and 4. And among the newer ideas that we examine in Chapter 6 are two whose growth reflects the increasing interconnectedness of peoples and nations around the world: environmentalism and multiculturalism.

Politics and the State

CHAPTER OVERVIEW

We begin this chapter by stressing the importance of the sovereign state to the study of politics. A brief survey of the basic state types is followed by a discussion of four schools of thought regarding the distribution of power in the state: pluralism, elitism, Marxism, and the New Right. We then look at several views on the proper role of the state, from the classic liberal insistence on minimal intervention to the communitarian idea that the state should work to unite the community around specific social objectives. Finally, we consider the challenges—both empirical and normative—that confront the sovereign state today.

1

The Political Importance of the State

The state is a difficult concept to define, and there is considerable debate about what a good definition should include (Gallie, 1955–6). As we have seen, Weber defined the state as an institution claiming a "monopoly of the legitimate use of physical force in enforcing its order within a given territorial area" (Gerth and Mills, 1946: 77–8). Certainly the state has been inextricably linked with **sovereignty** since the sixteenth century, when the French political philosopher Jean Bodin (1529–96) defined the latter as "the most high, absolute, and perpetual power over the citizens and subjects in a Commonwealth." As the highest form of **authority** in a particular territory, the sovereign state is in theory above any challenge: there is no higher authority within that territory, and—equally important—no external challenge to it. The first sovereign states emerged in Europe in the fifteenth and sixteenth centuries, replacing the feudal societies in which authority had been shared between the aristocracy (emperors, kings, princes, dukes, etc.) and the Roman Catholic Church (Tilly, 1975). Since that early period, most countries in the world have adopted the sovereign state model; today, virtually the only stateless societies are small communities of nomadic peoples.

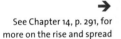

See Chapter 7, p. 143, for a discussion of the rise of the European state system.

How useful is the concept of sovereignty as a description of political reality? In constitutional theory the state is sovereign; but in practice it inevitably faces challenges from both inside and outside its borders—challenges that limit its autonomy. In this sense, sovereignty has always been something of a myth. There is a crucial distinction between *de jure* sovereignty (the legal right to rule supremely) and *de facto* sovereignty (the actual distribution of political power). As David Held (1989: 216) points out, "Sovereignty has been an important and useful concept for legal analysis, but it can be a misleading notion if applied uncritically as a political idea." For example, the concept of sovereignty is of little relevance when discussing a "failed state" such as Somalia, which is unable to perform the basic functions of sovereignty: controlling the territory, enforcing the laws collecting taxes, and so on.

See Chapter 14, p. 291, for more on the rise and spread of the state system.

See Chapter 7, p. 151, for a discussion of weak states.

A Typology of the State

A common way of classifying states is according to how much they intervene in society and the economy. At one end of the continuum is the so-called **night-watchman state** in which the government concentrates on ensuring external and internal security, plays little role in **civil society** and allows the economic market to operate relatively unhindered. For such a state, the primary duty is to protect the individual's rights to life, liberty, and property against any threat, external or internal. The idea of the state as night-watchman was central to classical liberal thought and played a large part in shaping nineteenth-century politics not only in Britain but throughout the Western settler countries, including Canada and the United States.

Emphasizing the individual's right to private property, the night-watchman model continues to be popular with **libertarians**. Libertarians believe that the state's role should be minimal, and most are very critical of large state bureaucracies. They also object to the maintenance of a large military force, especially when it is deployed to fight overseas. Thus most American libertarians opposed the 2003 invasion of Iraq, since foreign intervention exceeds the mandate of the government. The only time military force should be used is in self-defence when the country is under attack. Nor do libertarians approve of **welfare**

◀ Political graffiti in Caracas, Venezuela (© Hanquan Chen/Istock).

state programs such as universal health care. Libertarians believe that local governments and private enterprise are the most efficient providers of the services that citizens really want and need. The basis of libertarianism is an almost utopian belief that individuals know what is best for themselves and are capable of living their lives ethically and responsibly without undue interference from government (Machan 2005: 38).

In fact, the minimal state is an ideal that has probably never existed in reality. (Perhaps the closest approximation to it was Hong Kong under British colonial rule, when government activity was limited to basic services such as policing and garbage removal; but of course Hong Kong was a colony, not an independent state.) Nevertheless, the degree and character of state intervention in the world today vary enormously.

Towards the interventionist end of the continuum is what has been called the **developmental state**. States that adopt this hands-on model forge strong relationships with private economic **institutions** in order to promote economic development. This approach has been particularly prevalent in East Asia, where it has developed rapidly since 1945. The prime example of a developmental state is Japan (Johnson, 1995), but the model is also relevant to South Korea and even Malaysia—a so-called **illiberal democracy** (see below).

Developmental states are associated not just with economic development but with government efforts to secure greater social and economic equality. A common criticism of Britain's post-1945 political and economic development has been that the country embraced **social democracy**, with its emphasis on the welfare state, but neglected the

See Chapter 20, p. 422, for an exploration of the relationship between the state and economic institutions.

PHOTO 1.1 US Vice-President Joe Biden (centre left) meets with Chinese President Hu Jintao (centre right) at the Great Hall of the People in Beijing in 2011. While China continues to develop positive relationships with Western countries, it remains an authoritarian regime controlled by a small and unelected elite.

Official White House Photo by David Lienemann

developmental aspect (Marquand, 1988), limiting the economic growth that would have helped to further the social democratic project. The same criticism was levelled at Canadian and American governments when they were establishing their welfare state programs during the 1950s and 1960s. This issue remains important today, especially in the wake of the 2008 economic crisis.

We can also define states in terms of the degree to which their political leaders are subject to the will of the people. Here we can make a useful distinction between **liberal democracies**, illiberal democracies, and **authoritarian** regimes (Hague and Harrop, 2007: 7–9). Liberal democracies such as Canada, the United States, and India are characterized by free and fair elections, universal suffrage, a relatively high degree of personal liberty, and protection of individual rights. None of these democracies is ideal: all experience some corruption, election fraud, lack of transparency, and economic inequality. For the most part, though, voters, elected officials, and international organizations such as the Organization for Economic Co-operation and Development (**OECD**) are satisfied that their governments are effective and accountable to the people they represent.

Illiberal democracies such as Russia and Malaysia do hold regular elections, but they give relatively little protection to rights and liberties. Furthermore, these states control the means of communication—television, radio, newspapers—and may even attempt to control internet content and access. This creates a situation in which opposition leaders and parties are disadvantaged, and as a result there are relatively few transfers of power through elections.

Authoritarian regimes do not have fair elections and their political rulers lack accountability. About a third of the world's people live under regimes that can be described as authoritarian. China—with just under 20 per cent of the world's population—is a good example, as are many states in the Middle East, such as Saudi Arabia. In such regimes the political elite may centre on a royal family, the military, the ruling party, or an individual dictator such as Iraq's former leader Saddam Hussein. However, recent events in Egypt, Libya, and other Arab states have shown that even the most repressive governments can be overthrown if the popular will is strong enough.

The degree to which authoritarian regimes intervene in economic and social life varies widely. At the extreme end is the totalitarian state; here intervention is often total. Totalitarian regimes use brutal and oppressive state police to try to control all aspects of life. Whereas liberal states give priority to civil society and seek to intervene in it relatively rarely, under **totalitarianism** civil society is severely repressed. Totalitarianism is very much a twentieth-century phenomenon, associated with Nazi Germany, the Soviet Union under Stalin, East Germany, China under Mao Zedong, and North Korea under Kim Il Sung, Kim Jong-Il, and Kim Jong-un. Iran has acquired a number of totalitarian features since the Islamic revolution of the late 1970s. The rise of totalitarianism is strongly associated with the advent of modern communications technology. Beginning in the early twentieth century, the development of mass media made it increasingly easy to spread state propaganda (Curtis, 1979: 55); radio broadcasts of leaders' speeches were especially useful, encouraging listeners to feel a sense of personal connection with dictators such as Adolf Hitler in Germany and Benito Mussolini in Italy. At the same time, these states were able to spy on opposition groups using surveillance technology, monitor foreign radio broadcasts, and discourage plots against the regime by imposing severe punishments for any communication (including conversations and letters as well as publications) critical of the government.

KEY POINTS

- However difficult it is to define, the state is a central institution for students of politics.
- Sovereignty is a defining feature of the state, although it is arguably more important in the legal context than the political one.
- An empirical typology of the state would run from the minimalist night-watchman state typical of nineteenth-century capitalist regimes at one end of the spectrum to the totalitarian state of the twentieth century at the other.

Theories of the State

Another crucial dimension of the state involves **power**. Although we will examine the concept of power at length in Chapter 2, it's important at this stage to note that different theories of the state tend to centre on different accounts of power distribution. In this chapter we will look at three major theories of the state (pluralism, elitism, and Marxism) and one that is slightly more peripheral (that of the New Right).

See Chapter 6, p. 119, for a discussion of feminist perspectives on the state.

Pluralism

Until the mid-twentieth century, **governance** was generally assumed to be the business of government and elite decision-makers. Beginning in the 1960s, however, North American political scientists increasingly focused on a pluralist theory of the state; many of your older professors will be familiar with this tradition. There are several varieties of **pluralism**, some more accurate than others. According to proponents of **classical pluralism** such as Robert Dahl (1963, 1971), society is composed of thousands of groups of all shapes and sizes pursuing thousands of activities and competing for political, social, and economic influence. For pluralists, the existence of competing groups is a natural feature of all societies of any complexity. The only way to prevent the formation of groups is through suppression, as under the old Soviet system.

For pluralists the role of the state can also be defined in terms of the activities of groups. In this *political* pluralism, the state's role is to regulate and mediate between these groups. Some pluralists see the state as a neutral arbiter in this system; others see it as a group in itself, competing against other groups in society. The outputs of government are the result of group pressure. What governments do will reflect the balance of power among the groups that make up the society, all of which are able to make their voices heard in the political process, and all of which will get at least some of the things they want. This is not to say that all groups or interests are equal; however, competition ensures that none of them can become predominant.

As Chapter 12 will explain in more detail, an **interest group** is an organization set up to promote or defend a particular interest or cause. We can distinguish between two sorts of interest groups. First, sectional groups are concerned with protecting the (usually economic) interests of their members. Examples include unions such as the Canadian Union of Public Employees and the Public Service Alliance of Canada, and business organizations such as the Canadian Council of Chief Executives. Second, cause (or promotional) groups promote the interests of a particular group of people (for example, the homeless or an ethnic group) or an ideal (such as environmental protection or opposition

See Chapter 12, p. 243, for a detailed discussion of interest groups.

1

to pornography). Some political scientists argue that business organizations often have a stronger influence on government policy than environmental or other groups. This is particularly true when it comes to key economic issues, as we can see in **Box 1.1**.

Pluralists argue that power in society is diffuse or fragmented. In pluralist theory, most interest groups will be able to influence public policy outcomes, at least to some extent. Thus Dahl defines modern liberal democratic politics in terms of "minorities rule" rather than majority rule, or **polyarchy** rather than democracy. The idea here is that politics is based on the permanent interplay of numerous groups, each of which constitutes only

KEY QUOTE BOX 1.1
Competing for Influence: The Oil and Gas Industry versus Environmentalists

This article by Münster and Davis appeared in *The Hill Times* (an Ottawa weekly) in February 2010.

> Canada's leading environmentalists say they're losing interest in lobbying federal Environment Minister Jim Prentice because the government has locked itself into an environmental policy "bunker" and is not giving their ideas serious consideration. . . .
>
> According to the communications log in the Registry of Lobbyists, since Mr. Prentice was appointed to the ministry on Oct. 30, 2008, environmental NGOs have met 10 times with him and industry has had 90 meetings with Mr. Prentice. The purpose for six of the industry meetings was stated to be for either the Alaska or the MacKenzie Valley gas pipelines.
>
> Bill Rodgers, Mr. Prentice's director of communications, said the minister has been diligent in meeting with both environmentalists and the energy industry. He said the minister is meeting with so many energy sector lobbyists in part because he is the minister responsible for the MacKenzie Valley gas pipeline project, requiring many meetings on the issue. . . .
>
> Some say energy interests have an inordinate influence on Canada's national policy, something which is symptomatic of a deeper "corruption" in Canada. Among them is Thomas Homer-Dixon, who holds the Centre for International Governance Innovation Chair of Global Systems at the Balsillie School of International Affairs in Waterloo, Ontario. In a December interview, Mr. Dixon asserted that "our political processes in Canada are being corrupted by narrow energy interests." He said some policy options—such as major constraints on oil sands development—have become third-rail issues for politicians, and are virtually beyond discussion within elite political circles in Canada. "It's not overt corruption in a money-passing-under-the-table kind of way, it's subtle, in that democratic conversation becomes radically constrained," he said. "That's the role of power and money speaking in political system." Politicians who raise such options, he said, can be seen as "almost treasonous . . . and are declared to be almost persona non grata" (Münster and Davis, 2010).

© Dan Barnes/istockphoto.com

PHOTO 1.2 An oil refinery in Alberta. Some worry that Canada's political elites have been heavily influenced by the oil and gas industry, while environmentalists have been largely excluded from the conversation.

a minority within the society. Successful political parties are the ones that are able to forge a majority coalition of minority groups. In other words, political parties operate as umbrella organizations, uniting many groups with different ideas and interests.

The pluralist conclusion that power is fragmented is based on a number of related arguments. The first is that political influence is not dependent on one particular resource. In fact, there are many important resources—among them wealth, organization, public support, a group's position in the economy, the ability to exercise (or threaten to exercise) sanctions—and none of them is the preserve of a single interest group. Rather, different groups have different strengths and weaknesses. For example, key workers such as nurses or doctors may not be particularly wealthy or even have much public support, but they can gain influence through the crucial functions they perform.

Second, even though it may seem that one group or small set of groups is influential in a particular issue area, the same groups are not influential in other issue areas. To give a classic example, the Saskatchewan Wheat Pool was traditionally influential in setting agricultural policy, at least for grain prices (Watts 1990: 191). The power of the Wheat Pool (known as Viterra after merging with several other organizations) is still considerable. However, it confirms the pluralist position because it has little or no influence in other policy areas such as education or health care; different groups are important in those areas.

Bruce MacDonald

PHOTO 1.3 A former Wheat Pool grain elevator in Kronau, Saskatchewan. Hundreds of these once dotted the prairies.

Third, the influential groups in various policy areas are almost always challenged by some "countervailing influence." In the economic sphere, for instance, the influence of business groups is checked by the influence of trade unions (Watts 1990).

A Continuum from Pluralism to Elitism

The position we have just described is **classical pluralism**. But we can see a number of other theories of the state on a continuum between classical pluralism and classical elitism. The first, elite pluralism or **elitism**, was developed in the late 1950s and early 1960s after the classical form was systematically challenged by critics such as the American sociologist C. Wright Mills, who argued in his 1956 book *The Power Elite* that power in American society is concentrated in the hands of a powerful elite that dominates the economic, military, and governmental spheres. (This critique is echoed in Homer-Dixon's comments on Canada's oil and gas industry, quoted in **Box 1.1**.)

→

See Chapter 3, p. 66, for a discussion of democratic elitism.

The pluralist response, led by Dahl (1958), was to agree that participation in decision-making was not as balanced as pluralists had initially assumed, to accept the existence of political elites, and to concede that the latter played a disproportionate role in groups. Far from abandoning pluralism, though, Dahl suggested that it still existed because political elites compete with each other to achieve their aims. Politics may be hierarchical, but there is no single homogeneous elite group. Thus pluralists would see business as divided between, say, the financial and the manufacturing sector, or between major industries with competing interests.

Further down the continuum between pluralism and elitism is **corporatism** (see the case study below). Traditionally, "corporatism" referred to a top-down model in which the state incorporated economic interests, coordinating policy with trade unions

CASE STUDY
Corporatism: Europe Versus North America

Corporatism, more specifically neo-corporatism, has been quite common in certain European states, but far less so in North America. A study of 18 industrialized countries published in 1991 ranked Austria, Norway, Sweden, and the Netherlands as the most corporatist political systems and New Zealand, Canada, the UK, and the US as the least, hence closer to the pluralist model. The same study examined the factors explaining the existence of corporatism and found the influence of social democracy in government to be the most important variable, followed closely by the degree of consensus in the political system (Lijphart and Crepaz, 1991).

The Austrian system of "social partnership" remains the most corporatist structure, with trade unions and employers organized in four institutions: a trade union organization (OGB), and three "chambers" established by law with compulsory membership and the power to consider government bills before they are put before parliament: one Chamber of Labour (BAK) and two employer chambers, the Economic Chamber (WKO), and the Chamber of Agriculture (PKLWK). This structure has traditionally been characterized by informal relationships between the various actors (Talos and Kittel, 2002), but its key features are the centralization and hierarchical character of the peak associations of labour and business.

Until the 1970s corporatism was applauded for its economic success. Since then, however, it has been losing favour. A survey of Scandinavian corporatism, for instance, reveals a decline both in the number of corporatist actors in public bodies and in the degree to which governments base decisions on corporatist-style agreements (Blom-Hansen, 2000). Even in Austria, corporatism has begun to weaken. Although the structure remains intact, public support for it is decreasing, opposition from some rank-and-file organizations is growing, and relations between the chambers are becoming more adversarial. As a result, government has become more autonomous, relying less on the peak associations of economic interests (Talos and Kittel, 2002: 44–8).

Although this form of corporatism does not have the negative connotations associated with the top-down variety practised by fascist and authoritarian regimes, it has not escaped criticism. First, many argue that neo-corporatist governments tend to be unduly influenced by business interests. Even if trade unions are successfully integrated, neo-corporatism is still regarded as less open and democratic than pluralist systems because it is hierarchically organized and gives disproportionate power to economic elites. Second, from the perspective of the New Right (see below), it fails to allow the market free rein, and gives in to "unrealistic" demands by unions and social pressure groups.

and industries, in order to control them and civil society in general. Corporatism was attempted in Spain, Portugal, and Greece during the early part of the twentieth century, and was a staple of Mussolini's Fascist regime. From 1922 to 1939 Mussolini maintained the illusion that the government consulted widely with labour unions and corporations, but in reality he centralized power in his own hands and merely pretended to consult with other sectors of society (Wiarda 1997: 40).

Modern societal or **neo-corporatism** reflects a more genuine attempt by governments to incorporate economic interests into the decision-making process (Held, 1989: 65). This version of corporatism shares with pluralism the belief that groups are a crucial part of the **political system**. But it rejects the pluralist notion that the various groups theoretically have an equal opportunity to be heard. Instead, corporatism attributes a special role to economic elites, arguing that government outputs are the product of a tripartite relationship between elites in government, business, and trade unions. The state sanctions the insider role of economic elites in return for their cooperation in securing their members' support for government policy.

Elitism

At the other end of the spectrum we find the elite theory of the state. While classical pluralists hold that in Western liberal democracies a multitude of groups compete to influence the government, elite theorists argue that all societies, regardless of their democratic rhetoric, are ruled by a single, unified, and self-conscious elite. A diagram of elite pluralism would show a series of pyramids, whereas a diagram of **elitism** would show one pyramid containing the elite on top and the masses at the bottom.

Elitism is particularly associated with a group of scholars writing in Italy at the turn of the twentieth century (in particular, Robert Michels, Gaetano Mosca, and Vilfredo Pareto), although their work was built on by later writers, mainly American. Rejecting Marx's vision of a future egalitarian society, the original elite theorists believed that a ruling elite was an inevitable feature of all complex societies, whether capitalist democracies or communist systems based on the working class. They claimed to have discovered what Michels (1962 [1911]) called the "iron law of oligarchy": in all organizations of any complexity, whether political parties or interest groups, there will always be one dominant group that for some reason—whether because of the resources it can muster, its psychological characteristics, or its position within society—is able to take control. In this system, unlike Marxism (see below), no one resource is necessarily crucial: thus it is possible to conceive of elites based on military, administrative, or religious factors as well as economic ones.

Later scholarship on elitism came from the United States. Whereas the original Italian version saw elite rule as inevitable (and preferable to Marxist egalitarianism), modern thinkers such as James Burnham (1941) and Mills (1956) argued that it is illegitimate and should be challenged.

Marxism and the State

For much of the twentieth century, a large proportion of the world's population lived under regimes inspired, at least in part, by the ideas of Karl Marx (1818–83); Marxist thought also played a role in the development of the social democratic principles that

→
See Chapter 5, p. 109, for a discussion of fascism.

inspired the Cooperative Commonwealth Federation and the New Democratic Party in Canada. Marxism shares with elitism the recognition that every modern capitalist society is dominated by a united, self-interested ruling group and that, despite elections, the influence of the mass of citizens in such societies is minimal.

There are two crucial differences between elitism and Marxism, however. First, unlike elitists, Marxists are very specific about the character of the ruling group in capitalist societies. As we saw, the elitists argued that the power of the ruling group could derive from any of several sources. For Marx, by contrast, the power of the ruling group in capitalist societies was always based on its control of the primary economic resource: the means of production. In Marxist terminology, the dominant class was the **bourgeoisie** and the dominated class was the proletariat (or working class).

Marx produced an enormous and disorganized body of literature that has been interpreted in a number of ways. The dominant interpretation holds that it is pointless for the working class to seek **emancipation** by gaining the vote and winning power through elections, since the real base of political and economic power is not the elected government. Rather, power lies in the economic sphere of society: those who have economic power also have political power. It is not Prime Minister Harper and his government who are in charge, but the bankers on Toronto's Bay Street. Likewise, President Obama is constrained by Wall Street. To win power, therefore, the working class needs attack its source in the economic sphere.

The second difference between Marxism and elitism is that Marxists believe a communist revolution will bring about a truly egalitarian society, one that will abolish hierarchical power. By contrast, elite theorists argue that a hierarchical system of power is an inevitable feature of all complex societies, and that it is unrealistic to think otherwise.

See Chapter 2, p. 57, for a discussion of Marxist ideas on state power.

BIOGRAPHY BOX 1.2
Milovan Djilas (1911–95)

Milovan Djilas fought alongside Yugoslav communist leader Josip Broz Tito in the Second World War and played a key role in creating the Yugoslav federal state in 1945, which Tito led until his death in 1980. But Djilas soon experienced the reality of the scenario proposed by elitist theorists in the US: in any complex society, the leaders will form a tight-knit oligarchic group with firm control of power. Communist leaders, Djilas found, were just as likely as bourgeois capitalists in other countries to seek to concentrate power for themselves. He spoke out openly against Tito's corruption and elitism, and suffered as a result: stripped of his party positions, he was imprisoned for several years and lived the remainder of his life as a dissident intellectual. Having contributed to the creation of communist Yugoslavia, towards the end of his life he witnessed its fall in civil war as Serbian and Croatian nationalisms split the country apart. Among his many books, *The New Class: An Analysis of the Communist System*, published in 1955, remains a classic dissident account of the excesses of communist rule. It cautions us that in any society, we have to pay close attention to how state power is exercised, not just how leaders say it is exercised.

AP Photo/Harry Koundakjian

PHOTO 1.4 Dictators old and new: Tito welcomes Libyan leader Moammar Gadhafi to Belgrade in 1973. Like Tito, Gadhafi was welcomed as a breath of fresh air when he first took power, but both regimes degenerated into authoritarian rule and corruption.

The New Right Theory of the State

A different theory of the state was promoted from the 1970s onwards by members of the New Right who credited their ideas to liberal free-market advocates such as Thomas Hobbes, John Locke, and Adam Smith (see below). According to the New Right, the state has a tendency to expand its activities far beyond what is healthy for society, for two reasons. First, competitive electoral politics encourages politicians to offer ever-increasing benefits in order to attract votes, but once elected, governments find it very difficult to meet their promises and as a result sometimes sail perilously close to bankruptcy; Britten (1977) referred to this pattern as the "economic consequences of democracy."

The second force, according to New Right thinkers, is the tendency of the state bureaucracy to expand because it is in its interest to do so (Niskanen, 1971). To increase intervention and "big" government, bureaucrats will create relationships with interest groups. Both the bureaucrats and the groups have an interest in governments offering more, mainly financial, benefits. Dunleavy and O'Leary (1987: 117–19) call this the "over-supply thesis."

For the New Right, the pluralist theory of the state is wrong on two counts. First, the state is not neutral, but serves its own interests. Second, the interplay of competing interests in a democracy does not encourage stability and equilibrium, as pluralists suggest, but leads to "a hyperpluralism of powerful groups confronting weak governments," which can result in legislative paralysis (Dearlove and Saunders, 2000: 220). These New Right perspectives reached the height of their popularity in Canada, the US, and the UK during the 1980s, when the Mulroney, Reagan, and Thatcher governments began cutting taxes and rolling back the welfare state while promoting the privatization of state assets and increased contracting-out to private companies for services formerly provided by government. In Canada, Mulroney created a "privatization secretariat" that sold off a number of Crown corporations (state-owned enterprises) including Teleglobe Canada, Canadair, and De Havilland (Donner 2011). New Right policies also involved promoting freer trade and looser restrictions on the flow of foreign capital into and out of the country.

Many of these policies were controversial, but Mulroney remained proud of his government's accomplishments in privatizing state industries and opening Canada to foreign investment. Reflecting on those accomplishments in a speech in China in 2009, he said that when he became prime minister,

> [f]ormidable protective trade barriers, a maze of opaque and restrictive foreign investment barriers and heavy handed regulation hobbled the Canadian economy. There was no choice but to grasp the nettle of change and that is what we did. We implemented a free trade agreement with the US, extended it to Mexico and created the North American Free Trade Agreement. We converted a foreign investment review agency into a foreign investment promotion agency and declared that "Canada was open for business." We now offer binding guarantees for the fair treatment of foreign investment in our country, embedded in our free trade agreements or foreign investment protection and promotion agreements. Domestically, we moved to free the economy through deregulation, the privatization of government-owned companies and substantial tax reform (Mulroney, 2009).

The Empirical Dimension of the State

The theories of the state outlined above have two dimensions, empirical and normative. We will examine the normative dimension in the next section. First, though, it's important to consider the degree to which each of those theories reflects the reality of any particular political system.

An **empirical analysis** of pluralism might say that it exaggerates the extent to which power is fragmented in liberal democratic societies and too readily assumes that all groups have a reasonable chance of influencing policy-making. Unfortunately, there is strong evidence to suggest that certain interests are much more powerful than others. The elitist and Marxist theories of the state can also be challenged on empirical grounds. Do ruling elites remain *entirely* untroubled by elected bodies in liberal democracies? Do economic elites *always* control politicians? Certainly we can challenge many, if not all, Marx's claims about the future direction of capitalism; indeed, as we shall see in Chapter 5, post-Marxian Marxists adapted the classical theory to circumstances very different from the ones Marx imagined.

See Chapter 2, p. 51, for a more developed critique of pluralism.

See Chapter 5, p. 96, for a discussion of the development of socialist ideas.

1

PHOTO 1.5 US President George H. Bush talks with British Prime Minister Margaret Thatcher and Canadian Prime Minister Brian Mulroney before the start of the 1989 NATO Summit in Brussels. Mulroney and Thatcher in particular were seen as embodying New Right ideals of the state, increasing privatization and corporate influence in government.

KEY POINTS

- We can arrange empirical theories of the state on a continuum from classical pluralism at one end to elitist theory and Marxism at the other.
- While pluralism sees the power structure as diffuse and fragmented, both elitism and Marxism see it as concentrated.
- One key difference between Marxism and elitism is that for the former the dominant group is always the class that owns the means of production, distribution, and exchange, whereas the latter recognizes that the sources of power can be diverse. Another is that Marxism looks forward to a future egalitarian society, while elitist theory sees elitism as an inevitable feature of all societies.
- All three of the theories outlined above can be criticized on empirical grounds as failing to adequately describe the reality of the world as it is.

The Role of the State: What Should the State Do?

We can also assess theories of the state on normative grounds. Here the question is how well they represent how the state *should* be organized. We will spend some time discussing what constitutes the ideal polity and the good society in Chapters 3 and 4, particularly in the context of the crucial question of **political obligation**. First, though, we will sketch out some of the major answers to this normative question.

Pluralism and Elitism: A Normative Critique

Two main normative critiques can be made of pluralism. First, in emphasizing the differences in society, it tends to devalue the idea of the general or public interest. It simply accepts the pessimistic view that society consists of a diverse range of competing, sometimes hostile interests, ignoring the possibility of common interests and values, as well as the human capacity for cooperation and desire to work together. Similarly, the revised elite version of pluralism can be criticized from a normative perspective for dismissing the importance of political participation. Is competition between political elites really the best outcome that democracy can achieve? Political philosophers have argued that it is not, and that opportunities to participate should be enhanced.

As for elite theory, it makes no value judgment about the validity of elite rule. It simply asserts that, like it or not, modern societies are dominated by a ruling elite: that's just the way it is. However, students often confuse this empirical claim for a normative one. It is possible to justify elite rule on the grounds that the best should rule, without interference from the less able masses. Plato offered just such an argument to justify the rule of "philosopher kings." Similarly, the modern theory of democratic elitism, examined in Chapter 3, is based in part on the normative claim that elites should be left alone to govern because the masses tend to have authoritarian values and therefore mass participation in politics is likely to lead to instability and crisis (Dye, 2000). In these circumstances, one might assume that apathy would be encouraged. Nevertheless, proponents of this theory are not arguing against public participation so much as they are trying to give a realistic overview of how society operates.

See Chapter 3, p. 66, for a discussion of elitism.

The Liberal Social Contract Tradition

A classic way of determining what the role of the state should be is provided by the liberal **social contract** tradition associated with the seventeenth-century liberal political thinkers Hobbes and Locke, along with Jean-Jacques Rousseau (1717–78; see also Chapter 4). The social contract tradition is based on a fairly narrow idea of an imaginary **state of nature**, in which individuals exist without government. These philosophers reasoned that to find out what form of government is justified and why, we should try to imagine what life would be like without the state. Social contract theorists envision individuals coming together to decide the nature of the political system under which they will live. This approach was also adopted by the twentieth-century liberal political philosopher John Rawls, whose ideas we will consider in Chapter 4.

See Chapter 4, p. 85, for an exploration of Rawls's theory of justice.

Although both start from the idea of a social contract, Hobbes and Locke present very different versions of an ideal state. Much of the difference has to do with **human nature**— a key variable in political thought (see Plant, 1991, Chapter 1). Hobbes famously paints a picture of human nature as self-serving and competitive; as he famously put it, life in the state of nature (i.e., without government) is "solitary, poor, nasty, brutish and short" (1992 [1651]: 186). Under these circumstances, a political system is necessary in order to impose order and ensure security against the risk of both external threat and internal conflict. The ideal political system for Hobbes, then, is rule by an all-powerful sovereign, the "Leviathan."

1

Locke, writing a little later, appeared much less pessimistic about human nature and the ability of human beings to live together. Because, in his view, there were no immediate security considerations, individuals should choose to live under political rule only when it protects the **natural rights** that they have in the state of nature (1988 [1690]); see **Box 1.3**. Locke promotes what became known as negative rights. These rights—to life, liberty, and property—are rights against societal and state interference.

KEY CONCEPT BOX 1.3
Natural Rights

Many philosophers draw a distinction between natural rights and legal rights. Legal rights are those that exist in a particular society at a particular time. They are simply statements of what the existing law is. Natural rights, by contrast, are rights that humans are considered to possess no matter what legal and political system they live under. They are said to derive from **natural law**, a higher law handed down from nature or God. During the Nuremberg trials (1945–6) that brought many German Nazi leaders to justice, the concept of natural law played a key role. Although none of the people prosecuted in Nuremberg had broken the laws of their own state, they were judged to have violated higher natural laws against causing war and systematically killing civilians. Such laws were more legitimate than any state law and applied to all humanity. In other words, a strong distinction was drawn between legal and moral wrongs (Washington 2008: 111).

Modern liberal thinkers, particularly since 1945, have argued for the existence of positive rights. These are rights to social goods, such as free education and health care, and they have been enshrined in the United Nations Convention on Human Rights, established in 1948. Positive rights have the potential to conflict with the negative rights promoted by Locke. In particular, the right to own property conflicts with the positive rights to basic food and shelter. Some political thinkers, including the Canadian political scientist C.B. Macpherson, have criticized Locke for defending a possessive individualism that justifies selfishness, greed, and vast inequalities (1962).

Another distinct view of social contract theory and democracy comes from Mary Wollstonecraft (1759–97), an influential political commentator. In her book *A Vindication of the Rights of Woman* (1978 [1792]), she argued that liberty was virtually impossible without equality. A society free from both poverty and inherited wealth would make it possible for everyone, including women, to participate in the running of society. She took particular aim at the British aristocracy, led by "voluptuous tyrants" and their "cunning envious dependents." For her, human reason and the ability to participate in political life are skills that have to be developed. If women were excluded from the public sphere, it was not because they were naturally inferior, but because men dominated society and refused to extend the same rights and privileges to them. Women had less protection under the law than men, and little if any formal education. Social mores prevented them from being equal members of society. If Hobbes attacked the "divine right of kings," Wollstonecraft attacked the "divine right of husbands" (Held, 2006: 49–51).

Following on Wollstonecraft's critique of social contract theories, J. Ann Tickner (1992; see **Box 1.5**) observed that the assumptions about human nature held by figures such as

KEY QUOTE BOX 1.4
David Held on Mary Wollstonecraft

Until the twentieth century, there were few if any writers who traced as perceptively as she did the relation between public and private spheres and the ways in which unequal gender relations cut across them to the detriment of the quality of life in both. The radical thrust of her argument posed new questions about the complex conditions under which a democracy, open to the participation of both women and men, can develop (Held, 2006: 53).

KEY QUOTE BOX 1.5
State of Nature or State of Man? J. Ann Tickner on How Women Can Change Perceptions and Bring Peace

I shall suggest an alternative story, which could equally be applied to the behavior of individuals in the state of nature. Although frequently unreported in standard historical accounts, it is a true story, not a myth, about a state of nature in early nineteenth-century America. Among those present in the first winter encampment of the 1804–1806 Lewis and Clark expedition into the Northwest territories was Sacajawea, a member of the Shoshone tribe. Sacajawea had joined the expedition as the wife of a French interpreter; her presence was proving invaluable to the security of the expedition's members, whose task it was to explore uncharted territory and establish contact with the native inhabitants to inform them of claims to these territories by the United States. Although unanticipated by its leaders, the presence of a woman served to assure the native inhabitants that the expedition was peaceful since the Native Americans assumed that war parties would not include women: the expedition was therefore safer because it was not armed.

This story demonstrates that the introduction of women can change the way humans are assumed to behave in the state of nature. Just as Sacajawea's presence changed the Native American's expectations about the behavior of intruders into their territory, the introduction of women into our state-of-nature myths could change the way we think about the behavior of states in the international system. The use of the Hobbesian analogy in international relations theory is based on a partial view of human nature that is stereotypically masculine; a more inclusive perspective would see human nature as both conflictual and cooperative, containing elements of social reproduction and interdependence as well as domination and separation. Generalizing from this more comprehensive view of human nature, a feminist perspective would assume that the potential for international community also exists and that an atomistic, conflictual view of the international system is only a partial representation of reality (Tickner, 1992: 62–3).

Hobbes, Locke, and Rousseau were extremely partial, based on a narrow male-centred perspective that considered cooperation and optimism to be more vices than virtues, and violence and competitiveness to be natural for all human beings. Carole Pateman has also produced some ground-breaking work on social contract theories. Her innovative book *The Sexual Contract* (1998) offers a gendered critique not only of liberal and conservative traditions but also of socialist and other left-leaning traditions. It's important to keep Pateman's and Tickner's arguments in mind, because if we assume that human nature favours cooperation and peace, the powers we are willing to give up to a powerful state may diminish considerably.

→

See Chapter 15, p. 307, for Hobbes's influence on international theory.

The Night-Watchman State

Both Locke and Hobbes are often used by the New Right to legitimate the excesses of the free market. Another classical liberal tradition revived by the New Right is the principle of limited state interference. Until the end of the nineteenth century, classical liberals advocated a minimal state in order to maximize freedom. The political popularizers of the New Right, as we have noted, were political leaders such as Mulroney, Thatcher, and Reagan, but academic support for these ideas was provided by political economists such as Friedrich Hayek (1899–1992) and Milton Friedman (1912–2006), as well as political philosophers such as Robert Nozick (1938–2002). Similar views have more recently been are expounded by the Fraser Institute in Calgary, which helped to shape the New Right policies introduced in the provinces of Alberta and Ontario in the 1990s, and has an influence on the current Conservative government in Ottawa.

→

See Chapter 5, p. 94, for a discussion of liberalism.

→

See Chapter 4, p. 87, for a discussion of Nozick and the minimal state.

The New Right criticized the state interventionism that had become standard in liberal democracies after 1945. Intervention took several forms: welfare programs, market regulation and demand management as prescribed by the British economist John Maynard Keynes (1883–1946): increasing state spending on public works and the welfare state to stimulate public demand when it falls too low and reducing it when increasing demand threatens to create inflationary pressures. Different models of interventionism had been adopted in the UK, the US, Canada, and throughout Western Europe. The New Right argued that state intervention was counter-productive because it encouraged excessive reliance on the state, stifling self-reliance, individual initiative, and the entrepreneurial spirit, and was inefficient, propping up unprofitable businesses and large bureaucracies while failing to reward individual effort appropriately.

Utilitarianism

Another strand of liberal thought is **utilitarianism**, a theory of the state associated with the British political thinker Jeremy Bentham (1748–1832). Bentham argued that the legitimacy of a government should be judged by the degree to which it promoted the greatest happiness, or, as he sometimes put it, the greatest happiness of the greatest number (1789 [1948]). Happiness, for Bentham, was associated with pleasure. If governments maximize happiness they are valid; if they fall short of this goal they are not. Bentham argued that only if rulers were accountable to the electorate would they seek to maximize the happiness of all, rather than their own happiness. This forms the basis of

→

See Chapter 3, p. 65, for a discussion of the utilitarian theory of democracy.

the utilitarian theory of democracy. The main advantage of utilitarianism is that by focusing on the happiness of the community rather than the protection of individual rights, it promotes the kind of collective goals associated with the welfare state. On the down side, utilitarianism, or at least the classical version associated with Bentham, has been criticized for ignoring the risk that the human rights of minorities might be overridden by the majority.

Liberalism and Communitarianism

The classical liberal theory of the state, which is closely associated with pluralism, holds that the state should remain neutral in debates over different conceptions of the good. A liberal society's function, Arblaster (1984: 45) suggests, "is to serve individuals, and one of the ways in which it should do this is by respecting their autonomy, and not trespassing on their rights to do as they please as long as they can do so without harm to others." This **harm principle**, associated with J.S. Mill, is central to the liberal emphasis on freedom and toleration. It is also the central theme of Rawls's later work as laid out in his *Political Liberalism* (1993).

See Chapter 4, p. 81, for further discussion of the harm principle.

For much of its history, the major ideological opposition to liberalism came from the left, from Marxism in particular. In more recent years, liberal theory has been challenged by a body of thought known as **communitarianism**. The label "communitarian" embraces a wide variety of views, but in general communitarians call for the state to play a role in uniting society around a common set of values. This contrasts with the liberal insistence that the state should allow multiple belief systems to coexist (see **Box 1.6**).

KEY CONCEPT BOX 1.6
Communitarianism

Since the 1970s, communitarianism has offered a potent ideological challenge to liberalism. The essence of the approach is an attack on the asocial individualism of liberalism. This attack is both methodological and normative (Avineri and de-Shalit, 1992: 2):

- Methodologically, communitarians argue that human behaviour is best understood in the context of an individual's own social, historical, and cultural environments. Thus "it is the kind of society in which people live that affects their understanding both of themselves and of how they should lead their lives" (Mulhall and Swift, 1996: 13).
- Some communitarians critique liberalism on the normative grounds that liberal theory accurately reflects liberal society and therefore should be transformed. Others suggest that liberal theory misrepresents the reality of modern societies where social ties are more important in determining the belief-systems of individuals than liberal theory has realized (Walzer, 1990).

Normatively, communitarians emphasize the value of communal existence and the importance of being bound together by a shared vision of the good promoted by the state. This tradition can be traced back to Aristotle (MacIntyre, 1985).

The State and the General Will

Political philosophers such as Rousseau and Hegel have inspired communitarians by suggesting that the state and morality are inextricably linked. For Rousseau, the state should be judged by the degree to which it upholds the **general will**. This is the will that binds people together and can be contrasted with the selfish or partial will that exists in everyone.

Rousseau felt that the general will could emerge only in small-scale communities. Hegel, however, thought that modern nineteenth-century Prussia could achieve a very similar objective. Hegel distinguished between the state, civil society, and the family. He saw the state as the embodiment of the general interest, in which the partiality and self-interest of **civil society** and the family would be overcome. This optimistic view of the state stands in sharp contrast to Marx's wholly negative view of the state as an instrument of exploitation. In fact, Marx began as a follower of Hegel but later argued that the reality of the state in Prussia was very different from the glorified version of it that Hegel presented; see **Box 1.7**.

BIOGRAPHY BOX 1.7
Georg Wilhelm Friedrich Hegel (1770–1831)

Hegel was born in Stuttgart in 1770. After a varied career as a personal tutor and a school principal, he was appointed Professor of Philosophy at the University of Heidelberg in 1816. Two years later he was invited to take the prestigious chair of philosophy at the University of Berlin, where he stayed until his death in 1831.

Hegel's main work of political theory was the *Philosophy of Right*, published in 1821 (1942). His starting point is the political and social dissatisfaction that characterized the Prussia of his day, social fragmentation being the major difficulty. He moves from suggestions for reforms designed to create a more homogeneous society to, in the *Philosophy of Right*, a philosophical understanding of the modern world. Very basically, he argues that if we appreciate the unifying role played by the state, transcending the partial unity provided by the family and civil society, then we can be happy with our world.

Hegel has often been seen as an apologist for the repressive Prussian regime. Marx turns Hegel's philosophy on its head by arguing, first, that human history can be explained by the developing of material forces rather than, as Hegel had argued, by the development of the mind or the realm of ideas. Second, Marx argued that the point of philosophy was not merely to explain the world, but to change it. In other words, Marx argued that in order to achieve the goal Hegel had set—a unified and inclusive polity—it was necessary to change the existing world by abolishing the divisive class system.

KEY POINTS

- A normative critique of pluralism focuses on its downgrading of the public or general interest, while a normative critique of elitism focuses on its insistence that elites alone should rule.

- The liberal social contract tradition, represented notably by Hobbes and Locke, offers two distinct arguments justifying the existence of the state, the former focusing on security, the latter on the protection of natural rights.
- Wollstonecraft argued that greater economic equality and the emancipation of women were preconditions for creating a fair and equitable democratic system.
- Tickner and Pateman rightly demonstrate that there is more than one view of human nature, and that social contract theorists often confuse their own Western male views for the views of human beings in general.
- Other normative theories propose a limited role for the state (the New Right), the pursuit of happiness or preference satisfaction as the ultimate goal (utilitarianism), the upholding of moral pluralism (liberalism), and a critique of the state in general (anarchism).
- A key debate in modern political theory is the one between liberal and communitarian theories of the state. The former upholds a version of moral pluralism, whereas the latter seeks moral uniformity. The antecedents of the communitarian position lie in the efforts of political philosophers such as Rousseau and Hegel to justify obedience to a state promoting the general will.

→

See Chapter 5, p. 113, for an exploration of anarchism.

The Future of the State?

The concept of the state is now under attack by various scholars who challenge not only its utility but its very existence. There are empirical and normative dimensions to this debate. Empirical arguments suggest that certain modern developments, such as globalization, are making the state increasingly redundant. From the normative perspective, the state is an exploitative institution that should be done away with.

Is the State Being "Hollowed Out"?

The "hollowing out" thesis (Jessop, 1990) suggests that the state no longer plays the significant role that it used to. The **globalization** thesis, for example, suggests that the world has become so economically and politically interdependent that there is little room for states to manoeuvre; that currency speculators like George Soros have more power than Canada's Minister of Finance or the Secretary of the Treasury in the US; and that the power of government is far less than it was historically. If this thesis is true, there is a significant gap between the reality of politics in the modern world and both political theory, with its focus on the sovereign nation-state, and the **realist** tradition in international relations, which centres on a system of autonomous and competing sovereign states. Globalization challenges both assumptions.

See Chapter 20, p. 422, for a discussion of the relationship between the state and international economic institutions.

   We will consider globalization in greater detail later in this book. For now, let's look at it from our two perspectives, empirical and normative. From an empirical perspective, the major impetus behind globalization is the internationalization of the economy. With the growth of multinational corporations—whose power now rivals the power of states—and the liberalization of world trade, the economic policies of individual states have come to be determined elsewhere (Ohmae, 1995). Partly as a result of greater economic **interdependence** (together with improved communication technology and the emergence of global environmental problems) supranational institutions have emerged to challenge the power of states.

As a result, critics argue, realists who believe in the primary role of sovereign states in the international system are behind the times. World politics has changed fundamentally since the end of the Cold War. We are now living in a period of "new Medievalism," where "as in medieval Europe, sovereignty is shared among societies that interact in an ongoing way" (Cunningham, 2002: 203; see also Slaughter, 2003: 190). In other words, state borders are no longer rigid; they are porous, and state governments compete for authority with a variety of transnational and international institutions that includes the United Nations, multinational corporations, and **non-governmental organizations** such as Greenpeace and Human Rights Watch. Others argue that the globalization thesis exaggerates the reality, that sovereign states still have a great deal of autonomy, and that in any case they were never as self-contained as is often supposed (Robertson, 1992).

For those in favour of this type of globalization, the liberation of world markets is a positive development, facilitating greater prosperity. Furthermore, global environmental problems require global solutions that are beyond the reach of sovereign states. Other problems such as terrorism and human trafficking also require high levels of cooperation. Finally, globalization promotes the **cosmopolitan** goals of peace, toleration, and justice in a world where we owe our allegiance not to a single state but to humanity at large—a form of global **citizenship** (Heater, 1999). Others do not see the nation-state as an obstacle to **cosmopolitanism**, and suggest that a system of markets unencumbered by the state is a negative phenomenon, exacerbating inequality in the world and increasing exploitation, particularly in developing countries.

A Critique of the Marxist Theory of the State

Marxists regard the state as an exploitative institution that must be transcended. For classical Marxists, the state is nothing more than a vehicle for the exercise of power by the dominant class. Once the class system is abolished, the state itself is abolished; in the words of Marx's collaborator Friedrich Engels, it "withers away." A communist society will not require an enforcing state because the demise of capitalism will fundamentally transform human nature. In other words, once classes are abolished, significant conflict between individuals will become a thing of the past.

Many scholars argue that this vision of the future is overly optimistic (see Plamenatz, 1963: 351–408). Why? First, complex societies contain many different sources of division or conflict. Getting rid of classes may eliminate one source of conflict, but other conflicts—based on differences of religion, culture, language, types of work—will still exist and have to be dealt with by an institution such as the state. The experience of the communist states of Eastern Europe supports this critique: with the collapse of communist rule, numerous interests that had been suppressed for decades re-emerged. Among the consequences were civil conflict in many countries such as Yugoslavia, as well the rise of organized crime.

Moreover, the transformation of human nature envisaged by Marx is overly simplistic. There may be some truth in the claim that reducing economic inequality will have an impact on the behaviour of individuals, reducing crime based on acquisitiveness. However, this does not mean that society can exist effectively without the need for differential rewards as incentives. People who work harder or who generate more creative ideas may demand more money or more recognition than those who contribute less. Some argue that an overly egalitarian state would have the effect of suppressing the natural urge that individuals have to be different from and better than others. Others might counter that this is an acceptable price to pay to bring about a fairer and more equal society.

Conclusion

We began this chapter by noting the difficulty of defining the state. We then considered various ways of classifying states and saw that one of the most important centres on the distribution of power. We identified a range of empirical theories along a continuum from the open and diffuse picture painted by classical pluralism to the closed and hierarchical picture painted by elitists and Marxists.

Overall, theories of the state, with the possible exception of Marxism, do not give enough emphasis to the external constraints operating on the state in the modern world. By this we mean globalizing tendencies, which will be a recurring theme of this book. In Chapters 3 and 4 we will resume our exploration of how the state should be organized and what it should do. First, though, in Chapter 2 we will look closely at the concept of power, because this will help us to understand how difficult it is to determine which of our theories of the state is the most accurate description of a particular political system.

❓ KEY QUESTIONS

- What is the state?
- What functions should the state perform?
- Can we do without the state?
- Compare and contrast the pluralist, elitist, and Marxist theories of the state.
- How adequate is the pluralist theory of the state?
- Provide a normative critique of pluralism and elitism.
- What might a feminist version of the social contract look like?
- How effective is the communitarian critique of liberalism?
- Are the state's days numbered?

📖 FURTHER READING

Hall, Anthony J. (2010). *Earth Into Property: Colonization, Decolonization, and Capitalism.* Montreal: McGill–Queens University Press.
> A thought-provoking overview of the development of the modern globalizing world, through a history of colonialism, the dispossession of indigenous peoples, and the spread of global capitalism.

Held, David (2006). *Models of Democracy.* Stanford, CA: Stanford University Press.
> An excellent book on the history of democracy and its many models that also discusses the contributions of many female writers, including Wollstonecraft.

Hoffman, J. (1995). *Beyond the State: An Introductory Critique.* Cambridge: Polity.
> A normative critique of the state that also outlines the different approaches considered in this chapter.

James, A. (1986). *Sovereign Statehood: The Basis of International Society*. London: Allen & Unwin.

A detailed conceptual account of sovereignty; argues that the concept remains useful in understanding modern politics.

Pateman, Carole (1998). *The Sexual Contract*. Stanford, CA: Stanford University Press

A classic and robust critique both of social contract theorists such as Locke, Hobbes, and Rousseau and of the way their gendered ideas were implemented by the Founding Fathers of the United States.

WEB LINKS

www.political-theory.org

On political theory in general, see the homepage of the "Foundations of Political Theory" section of the American Political Science Association. Among other things, it will give you access to a wide range of key journals.

www.politicaltheory.info

The Political Theory Daily Review is a portal weblog that provides links to the latest news, publications, and reviews covering all fields of political theory and political philosophy.

www.marxists.org

For Marxist literature.

www.ucl.ac.uk/Bentham-Project

The best source on Bentham, this is the website of the Bentham Project at University College London.

Political Power, Authority, and the State

2

CHAPTER OVERVIEW

In this chapter we explore the concept of power. We start by defining power in the context of authority, before going on to discuss the classic threefold typology of authority put forward by Max Weber. We then pose some conceptual questions. Is power the same thing as force? Must it be exercised deliberately? Is it a good thing? Can we ever eliminate it? In the rest of the chapter we look at some of the methodological problems that arise when we try to measure power, particularly in relation to the theories of the state discussed in Chapter 1.

Power and Authority

We noted in the Introduction that **power** and **authority** are central concepts in politics. Politics is largely about competing interests and values, and in practice most of us want to see our own interests and values come out on top. Since those who have power can often determine the agenda that will be adopted by political decision-makers, it's important to understand how power works.

We also saw that a common way of distinguishing between power and authority is to equate the former with coercion and the latter with consent. Authority may be defined as legitimate power in the sense that rulers gain the acceptance of the ruled not through coercion but by persuading them to recognize the rulers' right to exercise power. Converting power into authority, then, is highly desirable (see the case study on the next page). As Goodwin (2007: 328) points out, "Where coercion creates obedience at a high cost in manpower and equipment, authority can control both the minds and the behaviour of individuals at a very low cost."

With respect to the exercise of power, there are two possible alternatives to the use of coercion. One is to rule through ideological control. In this case the ruler maintains control by manipulating the preferences of the ruled so that they reflect the interests of the ruler. Such control—associated with elitist thought and Marxist critiques of capitalist society (see below)—is much more effective than coercion because it eliminates the need for permanent surveillance. But to believe this is possible, we have to believe that individual preferences can be manipulated in such a way.

Some political theorists link authority with philosophy, and power with sociological analysis (Barry, 2000: 83). Here authority is linked with right, or what *should be*. By contrast, power is understood as an empirical concept, linked with what *is*. This distinction, unfortunately, is problematic. As we noted above, authority can be a product of manipulation; hence not all authority is legitimate.

There is no doubt, for example, that Hitler had a great deal of authority within German society, yet few would claim that the Nazi regime was legitimate. At the very least, we can agree with Goodwin's (2007: 331) assertion that "a state's authority in the eyes of the people is not necessarily an indicator of its justice." One could even argue that power is preferable to authority because, while authority can be based on imperceptible manipulation, power is based on coercion, which at least can be recognized and resisted (Goodwin, 2007: 331).

The second alternative to the use of coercion is to make the ruler legitimate in the eyes of the ruled—in other words, to convert power into authority. To understand how that might be done we need to consider what the basis of authority is, and how one can judge whether a political system is legitimate or not. The best-known analysis of legitimate authority was provided by Weber (Gerth and Mills, 1946). He regarded so-called "legal–rational" authority as the main basis for authority in the modern world. For example, the president of France is obeyed not because she or he is charismatic or claims to have a divine right to rule, but because she or he holds the office of the president. In the modern Western world, and in many other parts of the world as well, political institutions are accepted because they are subject to democratic principles. Indeed, the president remains the only part of the French polity whose **constituency** is the entire French electorate; see **Box 2.1**.

◀ Security personnel patrol the Great Hall of the People in Beijing (© Imaginechina/Corbis)

CASE STUDY
The Supreme Court of Canada: Authority, Power, and Legitimacy

© Tony Tremblay/istockphoto.com

PHOTO 2.1 The Supreme Court of Canada, Ottawa

One useful example of the distinction between power and authority is the role of the Supreme Court. The Supreme Court has very important powers in the Canadian political system because of its established right to determine whether or not the laws made by the elected members of the federal parliament and the provincial legislatures are constitutional. But members of the Supreme Court themselves are not elected: they are appointed by the prime minister, and (unless they choose to retire early or are removed for wrongdoing) they remain on the bench until they reach the age of 75.

Many commentators ask whether the Supreme Court's apparent power is worrying in a democratic polity. The court has made many important political decisions relating to such controversial issues as abortion, same-sex marriage, and Holocaust denial; yet its members are not accountable to the people in the way that elected legislators are.

One way to understand the sort of power the Supreme Court has is by reference to the distinction between power and authority. The Court itself has no army or police force to enforce its decisions. As a result, in order for its decisions to be accepted without the threat of coercion, the court relies on its authority. Arguably, the Supreme Court would almost certainly lose its authority, and therefore its legitimacy, if too many of its decisions were too far out of line with public opinion. Supreme Court justices are therefore constrained by the need to maintain the legitimacy of the Court as an authoritative institution in the Canadian polity.

2

See Chapter 3, p. 72, for a
discussion of the problem
of majority rule.

KEY CONCEPT BOX 2.1
Weber on Authority

Max Weber proposed a three-fold classification of authority. He recognized that these were ideal types, and that all societies were likely to contain elements of all three:

- **Traditional authority** is based on traditional customs and values. A major example would be the principle of the divine right of kings, according to which monarchs were ordained by God to rule.
- **Charismatic authority** is based on the personal traits of an individual. It is often associated with the leaders of authoritarian or totalitarian regimes, since charismatic leaders tend to emerge at times of crisis. This form of authority may be less important in modern liberal democracies, where authority tends to be based on status of the office rather than personal qualities. But charisma still plays some part, particularly now that the media image of leaders is central to their approval ratings, their fund-raising ability, and their power to pass legislation. In Weber's view, charismatic authority is unreliable, since the disappearance or discrediting of this individual will immediately lead to instability.
- **Legal–rational authority** is based on the status of either the ruler's office as part of a system of constitutional rules (in a democratic country) or a religious text such as the Koran (in Islamic regimes).

Weber argued that the tendency of the modern world is towards legal–rational authority.

As Hoffman and Graham (2006: 5–11) rightly point out, we can define power and authority separately, but in practice all governments use both. Some exercise of power is necessary even in a **democracy**, since the decisions taken by a majority will always leave a minority who may be resentful that their views did not prevail. Thus, even though democratic states rely much more on the exercise of authority than do **authoritarian** states, which rely more on the exercise of power, the former have to exercise power at least some of the time and the latter always have some authority.

Unfortunately, the distinction between authority and power is further clouded by the reality that in many cases authority is granted to institutions or individuals precisely because they have power. Even **totalitarian** regimes usually have some degree of authority, if only the charismatic authority associated with political leaders such as Stalin and Hitler.

Conceptual Questions about Power

The meaning of power can be teased out a little further if we consider the following questions.

Is Power the Same as Force?

It is often argued that there is a conceptual difference between power and force or coercion (Barry, 2000: 89–90). Although power can be, and usually is, exercised through the threat of force, we might argue that the actual use of force means that power has failed.

For example, the US clearly used a great deal of force in Vietnam and, more recently, Iraq. Yet it failed to win the war in Vietnam; by 1975 that country was reunited under a communist government and it remains a communist state today. As the sociologist Steven Lukes (2005: 70) points out, "having the means of power is not the same as being powerful."

Must Power Be Exercised Deliberately?

There are some who argue that power must be exercised deliberately. The British philosopher Bertrand Russell (1872–1970), for example, insisted that power is "the production of *intended* results: the unforeseen effects of our influence on others cannot be called power" (1938: 25). Few of us would attribute power to someone who has benefited from a situation that he or she didn't do something to create. As Polsby (1980: 208) points out, taxi drivers benefit when it rains, but the increase in business they experience is merely an unplanned effect of the weather, which they do nothing to cause. To show that taxi drivers benefit from the rain is not to show "that these beneficiaries created the status quo, act in a meaningful way to maintain it, or could, in the future, act effectively to deter changes in it." As a result, "Who benefits? . . . is a different question from who governs?" (209).

Is Power a Good Thing?

Some political thinkers would argue that whether or not power is good depends on how it is used. Using power to achieve certain outcomes is obviously good. As Lukes (2005: 109) put it, there are "manifold ways in which power over others can be productive, transformative, authoritative and compatible with dignity." By contrast, using power to harm others is bad. From a liberal perspective, however, the exercise of power is always undesirable because it "involves the imposition of someone's values upon another" (Barry, 2000: 99). This is why liberals recommend limitations on power, often through separation of powers, to prevent one branch of government from exercising too much power over another.

Can We Eliminate Power?

A related question is whether it is ever possible to eliminate power. Can there ever be a society in which no one exercises power over anyone else? Here the French philosopher Michel Foucault (1926–84) is instructive. Foucault is usually understood to offer a challenge to thinkers such as Jürgen Habermas (1929–), Herbert Marcuse (1898–1979) and Lukes, who imply that power is illegitimately exercised and therefore ought to be curtailed. For Foucault, power is everywhere, and power relations between individuals are inevitable.

In his work *Discipline and Punish* (1977), Foucault argues that the history of legal punishment in France seems progressive at a superficial level because extremely violent punishment eventually gave way to regimented incarceration; in reality, though, these are two ways of achieving the same goal. Both involve power relations and the domination and dehumanization of prisoners. History, for Foucault, is "an endlessly repeated play of domination" (quoted in Hay, 2002: 191). Because power is everywhere, there is no way to liberate ourselves from it, although we can, as Foucault shows, change its focus and implementation. Lukes (2005: 107) disputes Foucault's conclusion that power and domination

2

AP Photo/Michel Lipchitz

PHOTO 2.2 Michel Foucault and others demonstrate in Paris against the death of an Algerian worker in the central police station in 1972. Though best-known as a theorist, Foucault argued that his work also had important moral implications.

are inescapable, and argues that it is possible, as he puts it, for people to be "more or less free from others' power to live as their own nature and judgment dictate." In his view, people can work to free themselves from domination: first, though, they have to recognize that domination exists.

KEY POINTS

- The concepts of power and authority often diverge over the issue of legitimacy, the former implying the use or threat of sanctions, the latter reflecting rulers' right to rule.
- A key question is the degree to which power is converted into authority. Weber's threefold classification remains useful. He argues that modern political authority is based on legal–rational factors rather than on tradition or charisma.
- Common questions asked about power include whether power is the same as force, whether power can be said to be exercised without the intention of doing so, whether the exercise of power can ever be good, and whether power relationships can be eliminated.

Power and Theories of the State

In the face of so many different theories of power, how do we figure out which of them most accurately describes the reality in, say, Canada, or the US? In his book *Power: A Radical View*, first published in 1974, Lukes identified three dimensions or "faces" of power. The first face is universally acceptable: "A exercises power over B when A affects B in a manner contrary to B's interests" (Lukes, 2005: 30); an alternative definition comes from Dahl: "A has power over B to the extent that he can get B to do something that B would not otherwise do" (quoted in Lukes, 2005: 16).

Pluralism and Lukes's Three Dimensions of Power

How power is conceptualized has an important bearing on the validity of theories of the state. To see why, we need to return to the pluralist theory of the state. Pluralists measure power in terms of decision-making; this corresponds to Lukes's first dimension, above.

Pluralist researchers look at the decisions made and the preferences of the groups involved in decision-making in a particular set of policy domains. If a group's aims are met even in part, then it is judged to have power (see Hewitt, 1974). If no one group gets its way on all occasions, then the pluralist model is confirmed. The advantage of this approach, based on the first face of power, is that it is easy to research. Indeed, numerous "community power" studies were undertaken in the US in the late 1950s and 1960s, most of which confirmed the pluralist theory of the state (Dahl, 1963; Polsby, 1980).

Clearly this approach could lead to non-pluralist conclusions; it's possible that one group, or one small set of groups, will be found to get its way, in which case the pluralist model will not be confirmed. However, critics of pluralism suggest that the pluralist **methodology** is more than likely to generate pluralist conclusions (Moriss, 1975). In the first place, the pluralist methodology makes no attempt to rank issues in order of importance: it would treat a debate over where to put a school-crossing sign as no less important for the overall community than a debate over the minimum wage, for example. This approach makes no allowance for the fact that some issues are more important than others. Nor does it consider the possibility that an elite group may allow a small local group to have its school-crossing sign in order to ensure that the elite gets its way on more important issues such as the minimum wage; see **Box 2.2**.

Second, pluralists assume that the barriers to entry for groups in the political system are low: if a group has a case to argue or a grievance to express, all it has to do is enter the decision-making arena and speak out. But this is a dubious assumption. Some groups—such as the unemployed or the homeless—may not have the resources or the expertise to organize effectively. Landed immigrants who do not have citizenship have no right to vote, even for their school trustees or city councillors, and are thus entirely disenfranchised from the political system. Until 1960, the same was true of First Nations people in Canada: they had to give up their official status as "registered Indians" to become citizens and gain the right to vote. Other groups may not even bother to organize because they are convinced that they have no chance of succeeding. By focusing on the groups that are active in the decision-making arena, pluralists may miss a range of interests that for various reasons never appear in that arena.

Third is the related assumption that the issues discussed in the decision-making arena are the most important ones. In other words, the pluralist approach ignores the possibility that an elite group, or even a ruling class, has determined what will and will not be discussed.

2

KEY CONCEPT BOX 2.2
The First Face of Power and its Critics

The decision-making approach to measuring power, which corresponds to what Lukes (2005) calls the first face of power, is illustrated in Table 2.1. The table shows the outcome of four issues on which three groups took positions. All three groups got their way at least some of the time: Groups A and B got their way on Issues 1 and 2, while Group C achieved its goal on Issue 4. Pluralists would conclude from this that no one group was able to get its way on all issues, and that power is therefore widely dispersed.

TABLE 2.1 The Pluralist Decision-Making Approach

	Issue 1	Issue 2	Issue 3	Issue 4	Total
Group A	WON	WON	LOST	LOST	2
Group B	WON	WON	WON	LOST	3
Group C	LOST	LOST	LOST	WON	1

SOURCE: Adapted from Hay (2002: 174)

The decision-making approach can generate non-pluralist conclusions. Group A might have got its way on all four issues and groups B and C might have lost out. However, the critics of pluralism suggest that the decision-making approach is likely to generate pluralist conclusions. One reason is that pluralists tend to assume that all issues are of the same political importance. As Table 2.2 illustrates, this assumption can distort the political reality. What it misses is the possibility that an elite group will win on the most important issue or issues, while other groups will win only on the less important ones. Thus, in the example below, Group C wins on fewer issues but still gets its way on the issue weighted most heavily (Issue 4).

Imagine, for instance, that groups A and B are trade unions and Group C is a business organization. Further imagine that Issues 1–3 give workers an extra 15-minute coffee break at various times in the work day, while Issue 4 grants employers the right to prohibit strike action. Clearly, Issue 4 is much more important for business interests and is a serious restriction on trade unions; yet a pluralist methodology would fail to count this as an exercise of power by one group.

TABLE 2.2 Pluralism and Issue Preferences

	Issue 1	Issue 2	Issue 3	Issue 4	Total
Weighting	1	1	1	5	
Group A	WON	WON	LOST	LOST	2
Group B	WON	WON	WON	LOST	3
Group C	LOST	LOST	LOST	WON	5

SOURCE: Adapted from Hay (2002: 177)

This is where the "second face" of power comes into play. First identified in the 1960s by Peter Bachrach and Morton Baratz, this face recognizes that the pluralist decision-making approach (the "first face") measured only the *public* exercise of power. They argued that power is also exercised in less obvious ways: for example, when a dominant elite keeps issues that might threaten its interests off the public agenda, limiting contestation to relatively unimportant "safe" matters (Bachrach and Baratz, 1962: 948). Thus elites may create "barriers" to the public airing of certain grievances, or mobilize social "bias" to freeze out some options while privileging others. For Lukes, this kind of agenda-setting clearly *is* a form of power, and Bachrach and Baratz don't go far enough, simplistically assuming that "interests are consciously articulated and observable" (Lukes, 2005: 5, 20–4).

Although difficult, it is possible to identify cases of non-decision-making, where issues of importance to some groups have not appeared on the political agenda. A number of empirical studies (Crenson, 1971; Blowers, 1984) have attempted to show how the third face of power can be observed in situations of seeming inaction. A starting point is to identify covert grievances—grievances that clearly exist but are never openly discussed. The next step is to identify reasons they might have been excluded from public discussion. There are a number of possibilities. For example, those who would have brought certain issues forward might have been prevented by force or coercion, or perhaps politicians have reached a consensus and decided that there is no need to offer the electorate a choice. Rules or procedures can also be used to exclude certain issues. For example, if an issue is referred to a legislative committee or, in the Canadian context, a royal commission, decision-making will be postponed until more evidence has been collected.

Other examples of non-decision-making might include cases where anticipation of failure discourages a group from entering the decision-making arena in the first place, or decision-makers themselves decide not to oppose certain powerful interests because of the anticipated costs. A study by the American political scientist Charles Lindblom (1977) found that business interests are powerful in the decision-making arena because of their position in the economy. Governments recognize that businesses help deliver desirable economic scenarios, such as economic growth and low unemployment rates. As a result they are likely to accede to business demands. The power of business is enhanced even further when governments have to deal with multinational companies that have the option of taking their business to another country if they don't get what they want.

The crucial point here is that business interests don't need to lobby decision-makers or demonstrate on the street in order to be heard. Thus pluralist researchers using the decision-making approach to measure power may not identify business interests among the various interests with a stated position. Yet governments will automatically consider business interests because they anticipate business's influence.

The first two dimensions of power assume that political actors are aware of their own interests. This is not the case with the third. A much more insidious way in which an elite group or ruling class can set the political agenda is through its ability to shape the demands that groups articulate in the decision-making arena. As Lukes explains this third dimension of power (2005: 27), "A may exercise power over B by getting him to do what he does not want to do, but he also exercises power over him by influencing, shaping or determining his very wants." For additional comments on this subject by Lukes, see **Box 2.3**; for a critique see **Box 2.4**.

Official White House Photo by Pete Souza

PHOTO 2.3 Who wields power in the US? Even though President Obama's health care plan was a long way from the sort of state-funded health care seen in Canada, the UK, France, and Germany, powerful business interests were able to persuade many Americans that "Obamacare" was the next thing to "socialism"—a term of abuse on the American right.

Pluralists are criticized for assuming without much evidence that the preferences expressed by individuals and groups are in their interests. No attempt is made to figure out how individuals and groups come to hold the preferences they do. For elitists and Marxists this is a serious omission, since the ability of dominant groups to exercise ideological control is a key aspect of their power. For those studying the third face of power, elites, by shaping individual preferences—through control over the means of communication and socialization—can ensure that demands that would pose a threat to its interests never reach the political agenda (for example, see the discussion of the power of the media in Chapter 12). Thus a seemingly pluralistic country—with freedom of association, free elections, and so on—may in reality be nothing of the kind if most people suffer from some form of **false consciousness**.

→
See Chapter 12, p. 249, for a discussion of the power of the media.

CASE STUDY
Crenson, Lukes, and Air Pollution

As an example of how individuals can be manipulated so that the wants they express do not reflect their actual interests, Lukes (2005: 44–8) cites a well-known study by the political scientist Matthew Crenson (1971). Crenson asks why the issue of air pollution was raised in some American cities but not in others. He looks in detail at two cities in the state of Indiana. One, East Chicago, introduced air pollution controls in 1949; the other, Gary, waited until 1962. Crenson's explanation is that Gary was dominated by a powerful steel company. Its reputation for power prevented the issue from being raised, and when it was impossible to ignore, US Steel influenced the content of the legislation. It was not just that the industry prevented supporters of pollution control from getting a hearing (an example of non-decision-making), although that was part of the story. Support for pollution controls was weak because, Crenson (1971: 27) claims, there was an element of ideological power in which "local political institutions and political leaders" exercised "considerable control over what people choose to care about and how forcefully they articulate their cares."

For Lukes, Crenson's study reveals a genuine case where the real interests of people are different from the wants they express. As he remarks, "there is good reason to expect that, other things being equal, people would rather not be poisoned," and yet it appears that in this case they were prepared to accept it (Lukes, 2005: 48).

Unfortunately, using this study in support of the third face of power is problematic. Both Crenson and Lukes assume that it was in the interests of the people in both East Chicago and Gary to have pollution control legislation, but whereas in East Chicago, the people articulated their "real" interests and achieved pollution control legislation, in Gary they did not. However, this assumption is dubious. Why? Because it could equally be argued that residents of Gary were well aware of the benefits that air pollution legislation might bring but were equally aware of the economic drawbacks. Paying the costs of such legislation would make US Steel less profitable and might lead to high unemployment and low wages.

It may or may not be the case that pollution control legislation has economic consequences. Arguably, at the level of the individual industrial unit, pollution control would lead to unemployment and reduced pay, even if the benefits to society as a whole (including economic benefits) did outweigh those costs. The latter would have been little consolation to those whose livelihoods depended on employment at US Steel in Gary, which dominated the local economy.

KEY QUOTE BOX 2.3
The Third Face of Power

> Is it not the most insidious exercise of power to prevent people, to whatever degree, from having grievances by shaping their perceptions, cognitions, and preferences in such a way that they accept their role in the existing order of things, either because they can see or imagine no alternative to it, or because they see it as natural or unchangeable, or because they value it as divinely ordained and beneficial? (Lukes, 2005: 28).

KEY POINTS

- Determining the empirical validity of the theories of the state requires an analysis of power.
- Pluralists focus on the decision-making arena, or what Lukes calls the first face of power.
- This approach, though capable of producing non-pluralist conclusions, does not provide the complete picture. It misses the possibility that a political elite or ruling class can prevent decision-making on certain key issues (the second face of power) and ensure that the wants expressed by political actors are not the kind that will damage the interests of the ruling group (the third face).

2

Interests and Power

Despite the force of their arguments, critics of pluralism face methodological difficulties of their own. If power is exercised in more subtle ways, how do we go about measuring it? We saw that it is possible (though not easy) to identify non-decision-making; but how do we figure out if individual preferences have been shaped by dominant forces in society?

Lukes's third face of power assumes that it is possible to distinguish between what individuals or groups *perceive* to be in their interests and what is *actually* in their interests. We might be able to recognize when people are acting against their best interests, but this is rarely simple. Take the issue of smoking, for example (Dearlove and Saunders, 2000: 368). Can we say that smokers who understand the danger are acting against their best interests? Some people would have given up smoking if they had been aware of the damage it was going to do to their health. Others, however, well aware of the potential health costs, may insist that they want to continue smoking because of other benefits. They may argue that it relaxes them, prevents them from putting on weight, provides an ice breaker in social situations—or that they value other things more than a long life. In these situations, are we still to say that these people are acting against their best interests?

A more morally complex example of conflict over "real interests" can be seen in the battles over enfranchisement of First Nations in Canada. Until 1960, Aboriginal people had to renounce their status as members of their particular nations in exchange for the right to vote in federal and provincial elections. In this situation, First Nations people were faced with a choice. In order to vote and have the same "legal" status as other Canadians, they had to renounce their cultural identity and their membership of a group that had signed a treaty with the Crown (Fleras and Elliot, 1999: 180). According to Fleras and Elliot, First Nations

> prefer to define themselves as a people whose collective rights to self-determination are guaranteed by virtue of their ancestral occupation, not because of difference, need, or disadvantage. There is little enthusiasm to being integrated as an ethnic component into a Canadian multicultural mosaic, with a corresponding diminishment of their claims (1999: 189).

Although social contract theorists from Hobbes to Pateman take it for granted that people want to vote and be equal citizens, this case should make us question that assumption.

As we hope these examples illustrate, there is an ever-present danger of taking a patronizing attitude towards individuals and promoting a "we know best" mentality. As Colin Hay points out in **Box 2.4**, researchers must take care to prevent their own subjective preferences from intervening.

Another innovative critique of the "third face of power" argument is provided by James C. Scott (1990). He argues that researchers tend to mistakenly assume that dominated groups will always comply with those who try to manipulate them ideologically. This is not the case; in fact, some dominated groups will pretend to absorb and articulate the dominant world-view of the rulers, while promoting a below the surface counter-culture that challenges these dominant norms. This kind of strategy, Scott argues, is apparent in cases of slavery, serfdom, caste domination, and, at a micro level, in relations between prisoners and guards, or teachers and students. Although Lukes (2005: 127–8) casts doubt on the correctness of Scott's interpretation, arguing that the evidence "does not show

> **KEY QUOTE BOX 2.4**
> ## Colin Hay on the Third Face of Power
>
> The problem [with the third face of power] . . . is the deeply condescending concep-
> tion of the social subject as an ideological dupe that it conjures up. Not only is this
> wretched individual incapable of perceiving her/his true interests. . . . But rising above
> the ideological mists is the enlightened academic who from his/her perch in the ivory
> tower may look down to discern the genuine interests of those not similarly blessed
> (Hay, 1997: 47–8).

there is also not widespread consent and resignation" (2005: 131), in fact both scenarios are possible. The problem is that without inside knowledge, it may not be possible to know what the group's goals and strategy actually are.

Marxism and Power

The methodological problems we noted with studies of the third face of power can also be seen in Marxist accounts. In emphasizing the ability of the ruling class to exercise ideological control over the proletariat, Marxists too can have trouble distinguishing "real" interests from perceived interests. Following Marx's dictum that "the ideas of the ruling class are in every epoch the ruling ideas" (McLellan, 1980: 184), Marxists may take it for granted that the proletariat's lack of revolutionary fervour is the result of a "false consciousness" imposed by the ruling class. Marx assumed that a revolutionary class consciousness would arise spontaneously in response to objective economic developments. But (as we will see in Chapter 5), later Marxists such as Lenin were not so confident: despairing of a spontaneous revolution, they argued that a revolutionary party was required to articulate and promote the "real" interests of the proletariat.

See Chapter 5, p. 96, for an exploration of the development of socialism.

The concept of false consciousness was developed by many post-Marxian Marxists. The Italian Marxist Antonio Gramsci (1891–1937), for instance, emphasized the ability of the ruling class to manipulate the proletariat ideologically through their "hegemony." In any society, the elites had the power to determine not only what would be legal and illegal, but also what would be considered normal and abnormal. In this way they shaped the character of everyone living in a particular territory. Gramsci believed that intellectuals had a crucial role to play in challenging this domination, because they could step outside social conventions and see how people were brainwashed into thinking one way or another (1971). Similarly, the neo-Marxist thinker Herbert Marcuse observed that capitalist states created a situation where a large part of the population was led to believe that the state was benign, if not beneficial, whereas in reality the state was exerting its power against their interests. For Marcuse, writing during the 1960s, the evidence was obvious: the state was increasingly forced to react violently to public protests against its policies (1964).

Marxists, like elitists, have struggled to explain why the ruling class continues to rule despite universal suffrage and competitive elections. Marx himself, of course, did not face this problem; he was writing at a time when suffrage was limited to a small number of wealthy men. Later Marxists such as Ralph Miliband (1924–94) have tended to fall back on three arguments (Miliband, 1978). First, they note the similar social and educational backgrounds of state and economic elites.

Second, Marxists such as Miliband argue that business constitutes a particularly powerful interest group. Third, Marxists (as well as elitists) argue that we should focus not on the way decisions are made and who is involved in the decision-making arena, but on the outcomes of decision-making. Who wins and who loses as a result of the decisions that are made? From the Marxist perspective, we have only to look at the inequalities in most societies, including liberal democracies, to see that the same groups win and lose every time. As Westergaard and Resler (1975: 141) put it in their classic Marxist account of the class structure:

> Power is visible only through its consequences: they are the first and the final proof of the existence of power. The continuing inequalities of wealth, income and welfare that divide the population are . . . the most visible manifestations of the division of power in a society such as Britain.

Now, it is true that a great deal of inequality exists in most capitalist societies. Yet to claim that universal suffrage and the rise of left-of-centre governments have had no impact on the distribution of resources would clearly be false. The creation of the welfare state and the introduction of free education have improved the lives of many people in modern liberal democracies. In response to this argument, Marxists contend that the creation of the welfare state was instrumental for the owners of capital because good health care and education are essential to produce and maintain a productive workforce. They also argue that reforms benefiting the working class are made only when concessions are necessary to prevent social unrest.

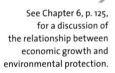

See Chapter 6, p. 125, for a discussion of the relationship between economic growth and environmental protection.

Both of these arguments are problematic, however. First, not all social benefits are necessarily in the interests of the dominant economic class. This might be the case with measures designed to improve industrial productivity, but it's hard to see low-cost higher education in the humanities and social sciences in that light. Second, the argument that reforms have prevented social unrest and even revolution is weak because it is impossible to disprove. We cannot possibly know what the consequences of not granting concessions would have been. Finally, we have to ask whether a class that is constantly making concessions to public demands can still be described as a "ruling" class.

KEY POINTS

- Marxists have difficulty explaining how a ruling class can still be said to control a liberal democracy in which universal suffrage has long been the norm and a welfare state has been established for decades.
- Marxists argue that universal suffrage does not dent the power of business interests, and that social welfare reform is in the interests of the dominant class.

Conclusion

We have seen that semantic, normative, and empirical questions about power abound: What is it? Is it a good thing? How is it distributed? The answers to all these questions are contested, the answer to the last above all. In fact, here we reached something of an impasse. On the one hand, the pluralist answer, although quantifiable and research-able, is incomplete. On the other hand, the answer favoured by Marxists, although persuasive, is problematic because it appears unresearchable. This helps to explain why the debate between competing theories of the state continues without any clear victor.

? KEY QUESTIONS

- What is the difference between power and authority?
- Must power always be exercised deliberately?
- Would it be desirable to eliminate the exercise of power?
- What methodological problems make it difficult to determine the empirical validity of theories of the state?
- What are the implications for the pluralist theory of the state of Lukes's second and third faces of power?
- Is power as thought control a viable concept?
- What does the character of political elites tell us about the distribution of power?
- Is there anything of value today in the Marxist theory of the state?

FURTHER READING

Bachrach, Peter, and Morton Baratz (1963). "Decisions and Non-Decisions." *American Political Science Review* 57: 632–42.
   A much-cited critique of the pluralist theory of the state, emphasizing the importance of non-decision-making.

Crenson, Matthew (1971). *The Un-Politics of Air Pollution*. Baltimore, MD: Johns Hopkins University Press.
   A study that attempts to put into operation Lukes's critique of the pluralist decision-making methodology.

Dahl, Robert (1963). *Who Governs? Democracy and Power in an American City*. New Haven, CT: Yale University Press.
   The classic example of the decision-making methodology associated with pluralism.

Lukes, Steven (2005). *Power: A Radical View*. 2nd edn. Basingstoke: Palgrave Macmillan.
   A celebrated account of power; this second edition includes an essay defending the original account (published in 1974) against critics.

Miliband, Ralph (1978). *The State in Capitalist Society*. New York: Basic Books.
   The best-known modern defence of the Marxist theory of the state.

WEB LINK

http://stevenlukes.com/
   Steven Lukes's website offers a selection of his articles and chapters.

3 Democracy and Political Obligation

CHAPTER OVERVIEW

We have two major aims in this chapter: to introduce the key aspects of democratic theory and to examine the strength of the argument that democracy is the most important grounding for political obligation. We will begin by exploring the historical evolution of the term democracy and the debate between advocates of the protective and participatory theories of democracy, as well as the cases for deliberative and cosmopolitan democracy. We will then outline why democracy is seen as the major grounding for political obligation and consider the implications for minorities of the majoritarian principle.

What Is Democracy?

As with many political concepts, it's difficult to find a definition of "democracy" that everyone can agree with. Certainly most people feel that democracy is a "good" thing. Today, some two decades after the collapse of the Soviet Union and its satellites, "Around two-thirds of all the countries in the world have a basic set of democratic institutions built around competitive elections that enable all adult citizens to choose and remove their government leaders" (Stoker, 2006: 7).

With the expansion of competitive elections has come an expansion in the numbers of **illiberal democracies** or, as they are also known, competitive authoritarian regimes or semi-democracies (Zakaria, 2003; Levitsky and Way, 2002). These are regimes in which, although elections are not blatantly rigged, elected rulers, once in power, have little interest in protecting individual rights such as free speech. This make it difficult for those who oppose the rulers to organize, because the latter are able to manipulate electoral outcomes through their control of the media and state institutions. For this reason the turnover of political leaders through competitive elections is small. In 2005, roughly thirty of the world's countries were described as only partly free (Hague and Harrop, 2007: 52); see the case study on the next page.

While it is true that democracy may mean different things to different people, we might still agree on a core meaning. Very basically, "democracy" refers to a regime in which political power is widely distributed and power in some way rests with the people. Thus democracy has something to do with political equality. As Arblaster (2002: 7) points out, this definition is sufficiently vague to allow for a number of interpretations. Lively (1975: 30) suggests seven possibilities:

See Chapter 1, p. 23, for a description of illiberal democracy.

1. That all should govern in the sense that all should be involved in legislating, in deciding on general policy, in applying laws, and in governmental administration.
2. That all should be personally involved in crucial decision–making (i.e., in deciding on general laws and matters of general policy).
3. That rulers should be accountable to the ruled (i.e., be obliged to justify their actions to the ruled and be removable by the ruled).
4. That rulers should be accountable to the representatives of the ruled.
5. That rulers should be chosen by the ruled.
6. That rulers should be chosen by the representatives of the ruled.
7. That rulers should act in the interests of the ruled.

Lively argues that interpretations 1 to 4 can justifiably be described as democratic, whereas interpretations 5 to 7 cannot (33–42). The key issue is accountability: the latter three include no provisions for the rulers to be removed by the ruled.

Furthermore, number 7 allows for the inclusion of regimes (such as those subscribing to communism) that, even though they lack competitive elections, claim to be democratic on the grounds that their rulers act in the real interest of the many by promoting social and economic equality (Macpherson, 1966: 12–22). This claim, however, is a logical mistake. The outcomes of a **political system** are separate from the means by which its rulers are chosen. It may be, as we will see below, that democracy (in the sense of a political system requiring regular competitive elections) is the most effective way of ensuring that rulers do act in the interests of the ruled. It may also be that achieving political equality requires

◀ Police clash with protestors during the G20 summit in Toronto in June 2010 (Scott Olson/Getty Images).

3

CASE STUDY
Singapore as an Illiberal Democracy

Singapore declared independence from Britain in 1963. Since then, its political institutions have been impeccably democratic, with **plurality**-based elections and a Westminster system of parliament, cabinet, and prime minister. Yet one party, the People's Action Party (PAP), has won control of Parliament in every election, and one individual, Lee Kuan Yew, was prime minister from 1959 to 1990, making him the longest-serving PM in the world. The current prime minister, Lee Hsien Loong, is the eldest son of Lee Kuan Yew. As a result, opposition parties have argued that it is essentially a one-party state. Of course, the fact that one party has remained in power for decades is not necessarily inconsistent with liberal democracy. However, elements of Singapore's politics suggest that it is a classic example of an illiberal democracy, containing elements of both democracy and authoritarianism.

© Chris Pritchard/istockphoto.com

PHOTO 3.1 Singapore is an extremely wealthy and ultra-modern city state, but its democratic credentials are questionable.

Although elections are not rigged, the PAP has been accused of manipulating the political system through censorship (the broadcasting media are state-owned, newspapers are heavily controlled, and the use of satellite receivers is illegal), gerrymandering (where constituency boundaries are altered to benefit the ruling party), and use of the judicial system against opposition politicians. As for liberal democratic values, freedom of speech is heavily curtailed and the penal system (which includes capital punishment) is draconian. In general, economic development (where there has been huge progress) is given a higher priority than democratic development.

SOURCES: Mauzy and Milne (2002); Worthington (2002); BBC News (2011).

a degree of economic equality. Ultimately, a benign dictatorship with the interests of her people at heart is not impossible. Many one-party communist states, of course, were far from benign, precisely because their leaders were not accountable. We can also question whether illiberal democracies like Singapore uphold the accountability rule and can be described as truly democratic. To add an extra layer of complexity, **liberal democracies** do not escape criticism from a democratic perspective because of the potential for conflict between majoritarian decision-making and the protection of individual rights.

Focusing on the first four of Lively's types, we are still left with a lot of variation. The first two are forms of **direct democracy**, whereas the latter two are forms of **representative democracy**. Direct democracy is a system in which the people rule directly, and it may be possible only in a very small-scale society. Representative democracy may be a more realistic proposition. Here, the people choose others to represent their interests. There can also be stronger and weaker versions of representative democracy, depending on a country's political culture and the history of its institutions. British MPs, invoking the eighteenth-century parliamentarian Edmund Burke, have long insisted on their independence from their constituents, so that on certain issues (mainly moral ones such as capital punishment and abortion) they vote according to their conscience. To enforce discipline, party whips are on constant patrol. Of course, it's unlikely that MPs can entirely ignore their constituents' views without suffering negative consequences at a future election.

See Chapter 9, p. 186, for a quotation from Burke on the relationship between MPs and their constituents.

KEY POINTS

- The concept of democracy is about popular rule, or the rule of the people.
- Lively suggests that democracy requires that the people either make decisions directly or choose, and be able to remove, those who make decisions on their behalf.

Historical Background

"Democracy" is a compound of two Greek words: *demos*, meaning the citizens within a city-state, and *kratos*, meaning power or rule (Arblaster, 2002: 15). The term was originally used to describe the ruling practices of the ancient Greek city-states. Many contemporary democratic theorists and activists look back to that era with great affection. They see in the city-states a model for participatory democracy that modern liberal democracies fall far short of achieving. But in fact the Greek system was possible only because it excluded a large number of people—notably women, slaves, and foreigners. It was because those non-citizens did a great deal of the work that those with the privilege of citizenship were able to engage in politics.

The Greek city-states practised direct democracy. More specialized and time-consuming tasks were allocated to a smaller number of office holders. Office holders were subject to regular rotation, chosen by the rest of the citizens. Jury service was also a feature of Greek city-states, so that all citizens had a chance to exercise justice. Plato and Aristotle argued that democracy basically amounted to mob rule, and was an aberrant form of government, although, as we saw in the Introduction, Aristotle did consider democracy less bad than tyranny and oligarchy (Cunningham, 2002: 7). Later political thinkers took a similarly negative view. Neither Hobbes nor Locke—the two most important English political theorists of the seventeenth century—regarded democracy as a desirable form of government.

3

Is democracy strictly a European concept? We should not assume that there was only one source of democratic ideas. Indeed, much of what we take to be democratic today originated in North America *before* colonization, not after. Ronald Wright (1992) has suggested that the indigenous Six Nations were very influential in creating the basis for democratic norms of government in North America. The Mohawk, Oneida, Onondaga, Cayuga, Seneca, and Iroquois nations lived together in peace for some two centuries under their "Great Law of Peace." US "Founding Father" Benjamin Franklin was so taken with the idea of the Great Law that he wrote in 1751: "It would be a very strange thing if Six Nations of ignorant savages should be capable of forming a scheme for such a union, and be able to execute it in such a manner as that it has subsisted ages, and appears indissoluble; and yet that a like union should be impracticable for ten or a dozen English Colonies" (Wright, 1992: 115–16). Note the central role of women in the Confederacy as Wright describes it:

> The Peacemaker's Great Law was an inspired blend of elective and heredity rights, of checks and balances. He established a Confederacy Council of fifty *royaneh* (sachems, or lords) chosen by clan mothers—the Iroquois, like the Cherokees, being matrilineal and partly matriarchal. . . . The *royaneh* reach their decisions through a series of small caucuses (an Amerindian word, by the way) until all are of one mind. Though sachems are male and elected in life, women have the right to depose them. In addition, anyone of outstanding merit may be elected to the council as a Pine Tree Chief (Wright, 1992: 119).

Accounts of the Confederacy's origins—"part constitution, part mythology" (119)—were transmitted orally for centuries until they were collected and translated by people such as

© SF photo/istockphoto.com

PHOTO 3.2 A reconstructed Iroquois longhouse in southern Ontario. Villages were made up of many longhouses, and the Six Nations population numbered in the tens of thousands.

the Seneca ethnologist Arthur C. Parker around the turn of the twentieth century. In his introduction to a collection of the texts, Parker wrote:

> Here . . . we find the right of popular nomination, the right of recall and of woman suffrage, all flourishing in the old America . . . centuries before it became a clamor of the new America of the white invader. Who now shall call Indians and Iroquois savages? (quoted in Wright, 1992: 120).

The French and American Revolutions

The French and American revolutions of the eighteenth century turned the tide of world history in favour of democracy. Both proclaimed democracy to be one of their goals, based on European and First Nations models. The framers of the US Constitution, most notably James Madison (1751–1836), were very keen to rid themselves of the absolute monarchy of King George III. But they were equally concerned about the consequences of introducing majoritarianism. The potential for the ignorant masses to be swayed by a powerful orator meant that majority tyranny was an ever-present threat. Therefore the Founding Fathers established a directly elected legislature, the House of Representatives, but at the same time set strict limits on its power. First, they required that legislative power be shared between the House and the Senate, whose members were to be appointed by state legislatures. Second, they created two other branches of government, each with its own specific powers: the executive, headed by the president, and the judiciary, headed by the Supreme Court, made up of judges appointed for life by the president and approved by the Senate. In reality, then, only half of one of the three branches of government was truly democratic.

The Nineteenth-Century Move Towards Democracy

By the nineteenth century, democracy was becoming more popular in both theory and practice. Many countries began the long journey towards universal suffrage. In theoretical terms, the utilitarian theory of democracy was extremely influential; see **Box 3.1**.

KEY CONCEPT BOX 3.1
The Utilitarian Theory of Democracy

The utilitarian theory of democracy was developed in the nineteenth century by Jeremy Bentham in association with his disciple James Mill (1773–1836; the father of the liberal philosopher J.S. Mill). At first Bentham was not concerned about democracy, feeling that an enlightened despot was just as likely to pursue the utilitarian aim of the greatest happiness. But he changed his mind after the British government failed to implement any of his schemes for reform.

Bentham and Mill argued that, left to their own devices, members of a government will simply work to maximize their own pleasure; they will not pursue the greatest happiness of all unless their positions in power depend on it. It was on these grounds that utilitarians argued for democracy: to ensure that the government would remain accountable to the people. From the utilitarian perspective, therefore, elections are protective devices designed to ensure that decision-makers take the preferences of the people into account.

As C.B. Macpherson (1977: 23–43) pointed out, utilitarian theory represented the first attempt to apply democracy to a class-divided capitalist industrial society. Utilitarianism gave rise to liberal democracy, which links democracy with the kind of liberal principles originally associated with the industrial middle class. The linking of democracy and capitalism raised the crucial question of how to reconcile political equality with economic inequality. Many property owners in the nineteenth century feared that universal suffrage would result in pressure for greater economic and political equality and put their privileges at risk.

In fact, the advent of universal suffrage in 1928 did not produce any significant move towards a socialist political program. Macpherson (1977: 62) and other left-wing academics such as Miliband (1972) blamed trade-union and left-of-centre political leaders for betraying the revolutionary potential of the working class. As we have seen, however, there are several factors that might explain why universal suffrage did not bring about political equality, let alone economic equality. Classical Marxism, for example, emphasizes that power lies in the economic base, of which the political realm is a mere reflection; thus as long as this base of power remains in place, universal suffrage will have little impact. Even from a non-Marxist perspective, the difficulty of establishing political equality in an economically unequal society is clear. Furthermore, political equality is not achieved by universal suffrage alone: free and fair competition between organized groups in society is even more important. A multiplicity of pressure groups means a multiplicity of democratic claims, creating what Dahl (1971) calls a **polyarchy** in which "minorities rule."

In the last three decades, the democratic landscape has been transformed with a doubling of the number of states holding competitive elections. This is partly a reflection of the collapse of the Soviet bloc and the emergence of independent states in Eastern Europe, but the trend can also be seen in southern Europe (Greece, Portugal, and Spain), Latin America (e.g., Chile), parts of Africa (e.g., Botswana), and Asia (e.g., Malaysia).

KEY POINTS

- For much of its history, democracy was seen in a negative light.
- The turning point came in the late eighteenth century. Following the French and American Revolutions, democracy was cast in a more positive light, partly because of the influence on the US Constitution of the "Great Law" of the Six Nations confederacy. Democratic ideals and models today represent a fusion of European and indigenous ideas.
- The nineteenth century saw a sustained effort to achieve universal suffrage in practice and to justify it in theory. The utilitarian theory of democracy developed by Bentham and Mill was the first attempt to justify the introduction of democracy into a class-divided society.
- The final quarter of the twentieth century saw a major increase in the numbers of regimes holding competitive elections and proclaiming themselves democratic.

Competing Theories of Democracy

By the mid-twentieth century the most important dispute in academic political theory was between two competing theories of democracy. On one hand is what has come to be known as the "participatory" theory. On the other is **democratic elitism**, also known as "protective" theory. This theory became prominent in the post-1945 period and is associated with the Austrian economist and sociologist Joseph Schumpeter (1883–1950), who articulated it in his widely cited book *Capitalism, Socialism and Democracy*, originally published in 1942.

Schumpeter was reacting to what he saw as the inevitable role played by elites in modern polities. He recognized the importance of the arguments advanced by the Italian elite theorists, whom we encountered in Chapter 1. However, far from agreeing with their conclusion that democracy is a sham, Schumpeter argued that it could be reconciled with **elitism**. In his view, the classical model of democracy, emphasizing the active participation of citizens in the making of political decisions, was both unrealistic and undesirable; see **Box 3.2**.

The classical model is unrealistic, Schumpeter argued, because mass participation is not a characteristic of modern democratic societies: empirically, most people seem happy to leave politics to the class of political elites. It is also undesirable because the masses are often irrational, tend to have authoritarian values, and can be seduced by charismatic and dictatorial leaders. It was no accident that Schumpeter was writing during the rise of fascism in Germany and Italy, where Hitler and Mussolini appeared to have the consent, some of it enthusiastic, of a large proportion of the masses. In such circumstances, far from threatening democracy, elites became the protectors of democracy against the authoritarian values of the masses.

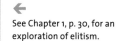

← See Chapter 1, p. 30, for an exploration of elitism.

KEY CONCEPT BOX 3.2
Advocates of the Protective and Participatory Theories of Democracy

Protective theory	Participatory theory
Bentham	Greek city-states
James Mill	Rousseau
Schumpeter	J.S. Mill
Downs	G.D.H. Cole
	Bachrach
	Pateman

Thus Schumpeter sought to replace the classical theory of democracy with what he believed to be a more desirable alternative. In a well-known passage, he redefined democracy as "that institutional arrangement for arriving at political decisions in which individuals acquire the power to decide by means of a competitive struggle for the people's vote" (Schumpeter 1961: 269). Note that this definition makes no reference to participation: it leaves decision-making in the hands of a political elite. What makes the system democratic, for Schumpeter, is the competition between elites. The voters do not even choose between different sets of policies; they simply choose between different teams of leaders who then decide what policies to carry out.

Schumpeter's account has been built on by other political scientists, who have also factored in the role of intermediary groups such as trade unions and business organizations that compete with each other to persuade the political leadership to adopt their policies. Kornhauser (1960) argued that this system safeguards liberal democracies from both totalitarianism and "mass society." Without intermediary groups, atomized individuals can easily be mobilized by elites with totalitarian intentions who seek to overthrow the existing regime and replace it with themselves.

This elite theory of democracy, which held sway in political science circles for roughly twenty years after the end of the Second World War, was reinforced by an "economic theory of democracy" that built on the earlier utilitarian model; see **Box 3.3**. Theories of the latter kind can be classified as "protective" models of democracy in that they seek to hold political leaders accountable to the wishes of the voters. They are concerned with democracy as a tool for voter utility maximization.

KEY CONCEPT BOX 3.3
The Economic Theory of Democracy and its Critics

This version of the protective theory is associated with the American political scientist Anthony Downs, whose hugely influential book *An Economic Theory of Democracy* (1957) is a good example of the rational choice approach to political science (see Introduction). Developed to explain the nature of voter choice and party competition, Downs's theory is labelled economic because it shares certain fundamental principles with economics, in particular the assumption that humans are individualistic utility maximizers whose aim is to achieve the most benefits for themselves at the least possible cost.

For Downs, the behaviour of politicians and voters is analogous to the behaviour of producers and consumers in the economy:

- Political parties and politicians are equivalent to producers. Just as producers seek to maximize profit, politicians seek to maximize votes. Their only goal is to win power.
- Likewise, just as consumers seek the best buy for their money, voters seek to "buy" at the lowest possible price the set of policies that will best serve their interests. As a result, parties must offer the voters what they want or they will not win enough votes to gain power.

Based on these simple principles, Downs constructed a model of competitive party politics in which voters are located on an ideological continuum from left to right, and political parties seek to place themselves at the point where the majority of the voters are situated. This is the vote maximization position.

While Downs's theory was certainly popular, it has attracted a number of criticisms that are worth considering.

- It is overly simplistic. For example, to focus on just one ideological continuum is inadequate, since that does not take into account the complexities of voter preferences. Moreover, voter choice is not simply about competing ideologies. A crucial dimension of voter choice is voters' perception of politicians' competence. This is not easily located on the kind of spectrum that Downs uses (Stokes, 1963).

- It is by no means certain that voters and politicians behave in the way that Downs tells us they do. Evidence suggests that at least some voters use their votes altruistically, on grounds of principle, rather than in their own self-interest. Similarly, to describe politicians as mere vote maximizers is too simplistic. Parties know that they have to win votes in order to gain power, but this does not necessarily mean that they have no principles they want to promote.
- Even more devastating for the economic theory of democracy is the evidence suggesting that many voters lack the sophistication that the economic theory demands (Robertson, 1976: 177–81). According to the alternative party identification model, many voters make their electoral choices not on the basis of their perceptions of the various policies on offer, but on the basis of a long-standing psychological identification with one or another of the parties. In other words, their support for a party does not change when the party's policies change.
- The economic theory of democracy also finds it difficult to explain why most people bother to vote at all (Barry, 1970: 13–22). For the economic theory, voting is a cost that is worth paying only if the benefits outweigh the costs. Under these circumstances, there is no point in voting unless one's vote makes a difference to the result. The chances that one vote will make that much difference are minimal.
- The economic theory of democracy takes voter preferences as given. Thus it ignores the possibility that these preferences are shaped by powerful forces in society—not least by the political parties themselves, particularly when they have governmental power (Dunleavy and Ward, 1981).

The alternative, of course, is the classic "participatory" model invented by the ancient Greeks. More concerned with democracy as an end in itself, this model sees participation in itself as enriching. Whereas the protective theory sees participation as a burden that individuals accept only in order to ensure that politicians are accountable, the classic theory values participation for the positive effect it has on those individuals. Citizens who participate become more virtuous and intelligent, they understand the need for cooperation, and their own self-worth increases, as does their status in the eyes of others.

The roots of this participatory model can be found in the practice of the Greek city-states and in the political philosophy of Rousseau, J.S. Mill, and the British socialist thinker G.D.H. Cole (1889–1959) (Wright, 1979). Support for it began to re-emerge in the 1960s, when a new breed of radical democratic theorists (Bachrach, 1967; Duncan and Lukes, 1964; Pateman, 1970) began to argue that, in abandoning participation, the elite theorists had lost sight of the true meaning of democracy and abandoned the principle of rule by the people. What was needed was a revival of participation in the political process. These theoretical insights coincided with the rise of mass movements in both North America and Europe in the 1960s: for example, the movements against nuclear weapons and the war in Vietnam, and in favour of grassroots environmentalism.

Assessing the validity of these competing theories is difficult, not least because the meaning of the concept of democracy is disputed. Lively (1975: 40–1) argues that Schumpeter's theory is not democratic, primarily because it does not fulfil the accountability criterion.

3

Schumpeter makes no recommendation about the frequency of elections, and his position could even be seen as justifying the election of a monarch for life.

We can make two observations about these competing models of democracy. First, if democracy can be defined as political equality, then the elite theory stretches that definition to its absolute limits. Second, advocates of the participatory model must be able to show that their version of democracy is neither undesirable nor unrealistic. In fact, this is what much of the literature in the area seeks to do. For example, advocates say that people can be encouraged to participate more, and that once they start they will get better at it. They also argue that political apathy is in part a reflection of the lack of participation in decision-making in the working environment; thus industrial democracy is extremely important (Pateman, 1970). As Lively (1975: 38) astutely remarks, "it does not follow from the fact that 'classical' democracy does not exist that it cannot ever exist; nor does it force us to redefine democracy, for it might just as well lead us to the conclusion that Western systems are not democracies or are only imperfect democracies."

Finally, advocates of the participatory model have to show that participation is possible (Arblaster, 2002: 84–5). Technological developments may facilitate involvement in politics through use of the Internet, mobile phones, and interactive television technology. Another way of increasing participation might be through greater use of referendums, in which electors vote on particular issues. This form of direct democracy has been used in many countries, including Canada, but has been particularly common in Switzerland and the US.

Deliberative Democracy

A recent offshoot of the idea of democratic participation is "deliberative democracy" (Bessette, 1994; Dryzek, 2000). Heavily influenced by the ideas of Jürgen Habermas, this model suggests that it is not enough for voters to have an opportunity to exercise a political choice: "true" democracy must allow for choices to be developed through discussion and reflection. Supporters maintain that the process of public debate and argument increases both the rationality and the legitimacy of the decisions that are made. This means that political choices are never set in stone. As Cunningham (2002: 165) points out, "democracy on the deliberative conception should be more than voting, and it should serve some purpose other than simply registering preferences."

To describe deliberative democracy as another version of direct participatory democracy would be a mistake. In fact, its advocates are skeptical about the possibilities of direct democracy in large-scale modern societies. They may also doubt whether direct democracy can necessarily produce the kind of reflective deliberation they seek. David Held, for example, argues that the quality of participation may be more important than its quantity (Held, 2006: 236–7). One suggestion for putting deliberative democracy into practice is through deliberative polling, in which a small group of people would be polled for their views on certain issues before engaging in debates about them. Then, after the deliberation, they would be polled again to see if their views have altered; the results would then be disseminated to a wider audience (Held, 2006: 247–8).

Supporters of deliberative democracy regard it as a way of promoting altruism in liberal democracies currently dominated by private interests. They expect it to increase toleration of other people's views in divided societies and thereby lead to greater consensus. Moreover, decisions made following deliberation are more likely to be rational (because

PHOTO 3.3 Stevie Wonder, the acclaimed singer-songwriter and UN Messenger of Peace, speaks to students at a forum called "Peace and Democracy: Make Your Voice Heard" in 2011.

they were not taken in haste) and to be considered legitimate. The downside is that real substantive deliberation on important issues takes a lot of time. Extensive debate on an issue such as free trade, or an oil pipeline from Alberta to Texas, may result in delays, or even paralysis, in decision-making. In addition, the theory has been criticized for exaggerating the degree of consensus that can be reached as a result of deliberation (Cunningham, 2002: 166).

KEY POINTS

- Since the 1960s, debates have focused on two basic models of democracy: participatory and elitist.
- In the post-1945 period, Schumpeter's theory of democratic elitism held sway. The classical theory, associated with participation and citizen involvement in decision-making, was widely considered undesirable and unrealistic.
- Beginning in the 1960s, elite theory was challenged by a new breed of participationists who were eager to pursue the possibilities of greater citizen involvement. The success of their enterprise depends on showing that greater participation is both desirable and realistic.
- Participatory theory has been built on by exponents of deliberative democracy who suggest that political discussion is likely to produce better and more legitimate decisions.

Why Is Democracy Thought to be Special?

Today "democracy" is almost synonymous with "politics" not just in the West but in much of the world: an indispensable part of good governance. Why is this? The usual answer is that democracy is the main reason we are obliged to accept and obey the laws of our state. In other words, if we ask why should obey the law, the answer would be "because it is democratically made."

This question of **political obligation**—why we should obey the laws of the state—is one of the central preoccupations of political theory. It is crucial because of the compulsory nature of the state. If we join a voluntary organization, such as an activist group or a church, we have to accept the rules of that organization; if we don't like them, we have the option of leaving. The situation is different when it comes to the state. Some people may be able to go and live somewhere more to their liking, but most people don't have that option. Most of us have no choice but to accept the laws of the state; if we choose not to obey them, then we can expect sanctions to be applied against us.

Democracy seems to offer the ideal grounding for political obligation, because laws that we make are likely to be in our interests: therefore we get what we want and don't lose anything by belonging to our particular political community. Thus democracy has a strong claim to be the political system that (as **social contract** theorists would say) people in the **state of nature** would choose, since it would give all of them a say in the making of the laws under which they were to live. In other words, the freedom of the state of nature would be maintained in a democratic political system.

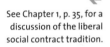

See Chapter 1, p. 35, for a discussion of the liberal social contract tradition.

Is Democracy Special? The Problem of Majority Rule

The principal advantage of democracy, then, is that it allows us to participate in the making of the laws we live under; therefore those laws are likely to be in our interests. The principal problem with democracy is that we will rarely arrive at unanimous decisions. As a result, democratic government means accepting the will of the majority.

There are a number of problems with the majoritarian principle, however. In the first place, it is well documented that if there are more than two alternatives on which voters can have preferences, then it is difficult to reach a majority decision (Lively, 1975: 14–15). Canadians are only too familiar with what happens when there are more than two parties running for election in a first-past-the-post electoral system: in two of Canada's last three federal elections, the Conservatives formed the government even though the Liberals and the New Democrats together won more seats in the House of Commons.

Even if majority rule can be established, we can't be certain that it is the most appropriate political mechanism. For one thing, majority rule leaves open the possibility that a government elected with majority support will deny the principle of majoritarianism in the future, passing legislation to impede or even prevent the practice of democracy in the future. Furthermore, if the principle of majoritarianism is upheld, every decision will leave some people in a minority. Some political philosophers suggest that we cannot expect people to obey a law they did not support. Robert Paul Wolff, in his book *In Defense of*

Anarchism (1970), argues that those who find themselves in a minority are not obliged to accept the law; furthermore, because there is no solution to the majority rule problem, no government can ever be considered fully legitimate. For Wolff, the only legitimate society would be one that preserves individual autonomy: an anarchist society, without government.

In practice, we may have to console ourselves with the thought that at least a majority rule decision ensures that more people are on the winning side than are not. Most of us can also feel confident that we will not be on the losing side of every decision, and that—since everyone can expect to be in a minority from time to time—the majority in any particular instance is not likely to do any fundamental harm to the minority's interests.

Nevertheless, there are situations in which the same people make up a permanent minority. The classic case is Northern Ireland, where traditionally most issues have been decided on ethno-nationalist lines with Protestants in the majority and Catholics in the minority on key issues. It was the persistent discrimination faced by the minority Catholic community that led to the resurgence of the troubles in the late 1960s. A form of rule known as **consociational democracy**, involving the sharing of power in divided societies, is one possible solution to the problem of entrenched minorities.

Cosmopolitan Democracy

In this chapter we have focused exclusively on democracy in connection with the city-state and, in more recent times, the nation-state. Nevertheless, in this era of globalization we should also mention the idea of **cosmopolitan democracy**. Held, for example, suggests (2006: 304–9) that since citizens of nation-states are increasingly affected, if not dominated, by forces beyond their home countries, political leaders need to ensure that global forces are controlled by democratic means.

Democratic theorists should therefore ensure that international institutions can both effectively control global developments and be accountable to democratic control. Held (2006: 306) suggests the creation of regional parliaments with the power to make decisions binding in international law, and the use of referendums across national boundaries. He points to the European Union as an example, though where the existing sovereign state fits into the EU model is not clear. As Hoffman and Graham (2006: 119) point out, this undermines the radical force of Held's argument. For them (123), the "concept of a 'cosmopolitan democracy' can only be coherently sustained if the international community ceases to be composed of states."

See Chapter 8, p. 175, for a further discussion of consociationalism.

An alternative approach to the undemocratic implications of globalization is to "urge *strengthening* the sovereignty of [democratic] states by defending their internal political structures against external constraint and interference" (Cunningham, 2002: 201). Of course, the cosmopolitan model is based on the assumption that globalization is a reality—a position challenged by the realist school of international relations, which puts the nation state at the centre of political analysis.

KEY POINTS

- The problem with democracy as a source of a political obligation is that few, if any, decisions are unanimous. As a result, there is always a minority of people whose freedom is reduced by the fact they have to accept decisions with which they disagree.

3

- Some political philosophers, most notably Wolff, argue that because of the minority rule problem, no state can ever be legitimate.
- As long as different groups form the minority on different decisions, the problem is relatively minor. However, permanent minorities are likely to suffer oppression at the hands of the majority.
- In recent years, the impact of globalization has led some political theorists to discuss ways of democratizing supranational institutions and processes to create a cosmopolitan democracy.

Conclusion

However democracy is defined, it is almost universally supported. Yet when we examine its claims to be the most important grounding for political obligation, we come up against the fact that majoritarianism has consequences for minorities. The obvious solution to the problem of minorities is to create some mechanism to protect their interests against those of the majority. Many political systems have done this by including protection for individual rights in their constitutions. In Canada today that protection is provided by the Charter of Rights and Freedoms (1982). In the US it takes the form of the first ten amendments to the Constitution, also known as the "Bill of Rights," which the Founding Fathers created precisely because they were concerned about the potential for what they called "the tyranny of the majority."

The problem of minorities leads us to conclude that democracy may not provide an adequate theory of political obligation after all, and that other principles, such as the protection of individual rights, may be equally important. Perhaps the key to a successful democratic system is to balance the ability of the majority to express its will with protections for minorities.

? KEY QUESTIONS

- What is democracy?
- Is it possible to reconcile elitism with democracy?
- Distinguish between direct democracy, democratic elitism, and representative democracy. Which is to be preferred?
- Is democracy special?
- Are we obliged to obey decisions taken democratically?
- Why should we obey the state?
- Critically examine the economic theory of democracy.
- Is democracy consistent with a class-divided society?
- Discuss the relationship between democracy and majority rule.
- Is cosmopolitan democracy possible? Is it desirable?

📖 FURTHER READING

Held, David (2006). *Models of Democracy*. 3rd edn. Cambridge: Polity.
    Probably the best general text on democracy, coupling comprehensive descriptions with astute evaluation.

Macpherson, C.B. (1977). *The Life and Times of Liberal Democracy*. Oxford: Oxford University Press.

> A contentious account of the development of democratic thought and practice. Compelling reading.

Shapiro, Ian (2003). *The Moral Foundations of Politics*. New Haven, CT: Yale University Press.

> An admirably concise account of the answers given by political theorists to the question of political obligation.

WEB LINKS

www.chinadaily.com.cn/english/doc/2005-10/19/content_486206.htm.

> The full text of the Chinese White Paper on Democracy.

www.freedomhouse.org.

> A useful site that rates countries according to their degree of freedom and democracy.

4 Freedom and Justice

CHAPTER OVERVIEW

Freedom and justice are distinct political concepts, but they are both fundamental to democracy. Since freedom is most obviously defined as the absence of constraints, we begin by examining a variety of constraints that may be relevant to political freedom. Then we explore the degree to which freedom is desirable by considering other values (such as equality, concern for others, and the maximization of happiness) that might conflict with freedom, mainly in the context of the political thought of John Stuart Mill. In the second part of the chapter we turn to the concept of justice and examine various criteria for determining its meaning through readings of Rawls and Nozick. We conclude with a look at three alternative theories of justice that challenge conventional liberal assumptions about justice: cosmopolitan, communitarian, and Green.

Constraints on Freedom

Like most political concepts, freedom (or liberty; the two terms are used interchangeably) is difficult to define. Like democracy, it is regarded as a "good" that all governments should strive for. In practice, though, we might have grounds for limiting freedom in order to protect or pursue other "goods" that we value. A common-sense starting point might be to say that freedom is the absence of constraints. But this only takes us so far, because political theorists disagree about what counts as a constraint.

Non-Democratic Government

To what extent is freedom restricted by living in a non-democratic society? There may be no necessary relationship between freedom and the absence of democracy. It's possible to imagine a benign dictatorship that grants considerable freedom to its people. Conversely, a democratic polity could conceivably limit freedom in a variety of ways. As Berlin (1969: 130) correctly points out, 'The answer to the question "'Who governs me?" is logically distinct from the question "How far does government interfere with me?"'

Physical Coercion

Perhaps the most obvious example of a constraint on individual freedom is a situation in which others physically prevent us from doing what we want to do; imprisonment and slavery are two extreme examples. Unfair or discriminatory laws may also fall into this category, since, as Barry (2000: 196) points out, the costs of breaking the law—such as a long prison sentence or even the death penalty—are so high that they are often equivalent to physical constraints.

Physical Incapacity

We might want to add *physical incapacity* to the list of constraints, in the sense that we are unfree when physical impairment prevents us from doing what we want. One example would be a condition that deprives an individual of an ability that others have, such as the ability to walk; but another might be a condition that affects all humans, such as the inability to fly. Such constraints, though clearly impediments, may have to be accepted if the situation is unalterable or beyond the control of human **agency**. It's different, however, when a disability could be altered or accommodated and all that stands in the way is a lack of the resources required for, say, corrective surgery or a powered wheelchair. In that case, the argument for using the language of freedom is compelling. In other words, human agency is necessary for an impediment to count as a constraint on our freedom.

Rationality

Some political theorists also say that freedom can justifiably be limited according to how rational we are. Thus we would not see the supervision and direction of children, or of adults with senile dementia, as constraints on their freedom in the way that we would in the case of

◀ Free Tibet campaigners in Paris demonstrate against Beijing during the Olympic Torch Relay in April 2008 (© P Deliss/ Godong/Corbis).

healthy adults. Restrictions on the freedom of children or people with dementia are justified in the pursuit of other goals, such as protecting their safety. There are dangers in the claim that only rational behaviour is free, since it is by no means clear what rational behaviour is.

Psychology

Another set of constraints worth considering are psychological influences on our behaviour. If we can be constrained by physical coercion, we might also be constrained psychologically: that is, we can be driven to behave in certain ways by external influences that affect the way we think. A powerful example is commercial advertising, which is designed to create wants that otherwise would not exist. There is no genetic or natural desire to own an iPad or a Blu-ray player, for example; yet effective marketing has ensured that these products are in hot demand. In the same way, tobacco advertising has fuelled a demand for cigarettes. In response, the UK government banned such advertising on the grounds that it encourages smoking, which is addictive and life-threatening. Canada and Australia have also instituted large warning labels as well as photos of the damage that cigarette smoking can cause. Interestingly, both tobacco advertising and governmental counter-advertising campaigns can be seen as efforts on the part of elites to influence, if not determine, the way the masses think. Both are examples of Lukes's "third dimension" of power, and also reflect Gramsci's work on hegemony.

← See Chapter 2, p. 51, for an exploration of the three dimensions of power.

Economic Impediments

If we see freedom as the absence of externally imposed physical coercion, we seem to be saying that freedom is best achieved if the state and society leave people alone. However, some political thinkers argue that the state can do a great deal to increase freedom by intervening in the lives of individuals. As Wollstonecraft and many later Marxist theorists pointed out, a person is not fully free to develop as a human being if she does not have enough to eat, or a roof over her head. By intervening to provide a basic standard of living below which no one can fall, the state can increase the freedom of individuals to make something of their lives. This idea has been at the root of the modern welfare state in many countries, including Canada.

KEY POINTS

- Since freedom is defined as the absence of constraints, the identification of constraints on our freedom is a useful starting point.
- Possible constraints can be divided into those that are external to us, and those that are internal to us, the latter including characteristics such as rationality.

Negative and Positive Freedom

The theoretical distinction between negative and positive freedom dates back to the ancient Greeks (Gray, 1991: 7) but was also heavily influenced by John Locke and Jean-Jacques Rousseau. Locke argued in favour of negative rights: that is, rights to be free from government interference, particularly in economic matters. Rousseau, by contrast, argued that the state had an obligation to provide its citizens with a decent standard of living (Forsythe, 2009: 91).

In modern times, the distinction between these two forms of rights has been associated with the political theorist Isaiah Berlin (1909–97). Berlin famously argued that these represent the two main conceptions of freedom. In the simplest terms, he defined **negative liberty** as "freedom from" and **positive liberty** as "freedom to." According to Berlin, "liberty in the negative sense involves an answer to the question: 'What is the area within which the subject . . . is or should be left to do or be what he is able to do or be, without interference by other persons?'" The positive conception, by contrast, is concerned with the question "What, or who, is the source of control or interference that can determine someone to do, or be, this rather than that?" (Berlin, 1969: 121–2). Berlin distinguishes between the *area* of control (negative freedom) and the *source* of control (positive freedom). The ability of individuals to be self-governing is crucial for advocates of the latter. Although influential during the 1960s, Berlin's view was later criticized, in part because theorists such as Tim Gray were able to show that there were multiple versions of freedom, not just the two that Berlin identified (Gray, 1991: 8–11).

Another way of looking at this issue is to compare the approaches to rights of the US and the Soviet Union. The US, through its Constitution and first ten amendments (the Bill of Rights), promoted negative freedoms: the right to freely assemble, the right to free speech, the right to practise one's own religion without state interference, and the right to a free press, unrestricted by the government. Such rights give priority to individual autonomy— in effect, the right to be left alone by the state to pursue one's own goals (Janda, Berry, and Goldman, 2008: 457–8). By contrast, more positive rights were generally mistrusted as threats to the capitalist system (Forsythe, 2009: 92–3). Economic rights to a minimum wage or workplace protection, for example, could constrain business practices, while social

© Joel Carillet/istockphoto.com

PHOTO 4.1 The flags of Tunisia, Libya, and (in the background to the left) Egypt fly at a crowded demonstration in Cairo's Tahrir Square on 25 February 2011.

and cultural rights such as government-funded heath or child care, or higher education, were widely rejected on the grounds that they would represent either a burden on state resources or an impediment to free enterprise and consumer "choice." Meanwhile, communist countries in general promoted positive rights, including the right to employment, the right to education, the right to health care, and, in many cases, the right to state-funded child care, on the grounds that the state had a responsibility to take care of its citizens.

In international law, these two types of rights are protected in two separate covenants, both adopted by the UN in 1966: the International Covenant on Civil and Political Rights (CCPR) and the International Covenant on Economic, Social, and Cultural Rights (CESCR) (Robertson, 1997: 256–72). These two main types of rights *can* be seen as complementary if we argue that the state should try to promote equality in society to a limited extent, while still safeguarding individual liberty to a limited extent. The key is to find a balance between the US and Soviet extremes. Pierre Trudeau is a good example. On the one hand he promoted state-run health care, and on the other, he removed the Criminal Code provisions that prohibited same-sex acts between consenting adults. Trudeau saw no contradiction between the idea that that the state had a role to play in health care and the idea that it had "no place in the bedrooms of the nation'" (Ricci, 2009: 111).

Is Freedom Special?

Justifying freedom is different from defining it, although justification and definition are linked in that our assessment of the value of freedom depends on what we think it is. We might argue that we can limit freedom in order to increase equality. But if we define freedom in such a way that it requires state intervention to equalize resources, then the two concepts are not diametrically opposed. There are a number of justifications for freedom. Some political theorists argue that there should be a presumption in favour of freedom (Benn, 1971): that is, those who want to limit freedom need to make a strong case. However, we might ask why freedom should be valued so highly.

One argument is that freedom is a basic human right (Hart, 1967). But this argument also depends on a prior argument in favour of rights in general, and a right to freedom in particular. Ronald Dworkin argues that the freedoms necessary to ensure that individuals are treated with equal concern and respect (so-called "strong" liberties) should be inviolable. But Dworkin takes it for granted that equality is a good thing. Moreover, his argument for upholding strong liberties has been criticized as biased. Is it not a matter of opinion which liberties count as strong ones that uphold the right to equal concern and respect? (Gray, 1991: 106). This is particularly problematic if we believe that cultural pluralism—where competing norms of behaviour are regarded as acceptable—is desirable; see **Box 4.1**.

Mill, Utilitarianism, and Freedom

One of the best-known defences of freedom was put forward by John Stuart Mill in his essay *On Liberty* (in Mill 1972), originally published in 1859. True to the utilitarian principles of his father James, Mill argues that freedom is conducive to the greatest amount of happiness. For Mill certain types of pleasure are more valuable than others and should be pursued both by individuals and by the state. These "higher pleasures" are associated with cerebral activities—literature, music, art, and so forth—as opposed to physical ones.

KEY CONCEPT BOX 4.1
Freedom and Cultural Pluralism

"Cultural pluralism" refers to situations in which different cultures follow different norms of behaviour within a single society. Consider the following cases:

1. In 2004 the French National Assembly banned religious symbols in schools. In addition to the *hijab* (headscarf) worn by some Muslim girls, the ban covered Jewish skullcaps, Sikh turbans, and conspicuous Christian crosses. The legislation was designed to promote the secularism that has been a prized element of French national identity for more than two hundred years. Nevertheless, fear and hostility towards Muslim immigrants are also at play here (Winter, 2008: 1–5).

2. It is estimated that well over 100 million women have been subject to circumcision, which is also called female genital mutilation (FGM). This practice (involving the removal of either some of or of the entire clitoris) can lead to serious physical and psychological problems. Yet it is justified on cultural and religious grounds and is still widely practised in Western and Southern Asia, the Middle East, and large parts of Africa. It has also been estimated that several thousand girls are circumcised every year in Britain. In Canada, FGM is prohibited under two sections of the Criminal Code, because it is seen as assault (Weir, 2000: 1344).

These examples bring cultural pluralism into the debate about the limits of freedom. Should we seek to limit cultural pluralism even if that means reducing freedom? Or should we allow cultural diversity even if that means allowing practices that cause harm and deny freedom to certain groups?

Presenting the case for the maximum possible freedom of thought and discussion, Mill argues that even beliefs that are obviously false or hurtful to the sensibilities of others should not be censored, since true beliefs will gain support when they have to be upheld against objections, and false beliefs are more likely to be denounced if they are open to public challenge. The wider the variety of opinions and lifestyles that are tried and tested, the stronger the society will be. In this way freedom of thought and expression is a means to social progress.

In the same essay Mill argues that freedom of action should be subject to only one limitation, known as the **harm principle**: only those actions that harm others ("other-regarding actions") should be prevented by public opinion or the state. Self-regarding actions—that is, actions affecting only oneself—are not to be interfered with. We are entitled to warn someone of the dangers of pursuing a particular path, according to Mill, but we may not physically restrain that person unless his or her action would harm somebody else. Actions that others find offensive, but that do not cause them physical or financial harm are not to be understood as other-regarding.

Freedom, Happiness, and Paternalism

Mill's thoughts on liberty have been very influential in determining the nature of state intervention in modern liberal societies. Laws legalizing homosexuality between consenting adults, for instance, owe much to Mill's distinction between self- and other-regarding actions.

4

CASE STUDY
Smoking and Liberty

In 2003, Prince Edward Island became the first Canadian province to ban smoking in public places. The main justification for the ban—that smoking harms non-smokers who are forced to passively inhale the smoke produced by others—recalls Mill, who would argue that smoking in private where no one else will be harmed is legitimate but smoking in public is not.

There are two criticisms of Mill's harm principle, however, that suggest the smoking ban does not go far enough. The first criticism points out that it is difficult to distinguish between self- and other-regarding actions. Is it not the case that smoking, even in private, has the potential to harm others? If I become ill through smoking, then this will have an impact on family members who will be harmed—financially and emotionally—by my death or illness. My poor health will also have wider financial consequences, for the health care system that has to treat me and for the social system that has to support me if I am unable to work.

The second criticism posits that there are good reasons for the state to intervene to prevent individuals from harming themselves. In the case of smoking, then, my health and well-being may not be served by liberty, and indeed my happiness might be enhanced by restricting my freedom. You could even argue that the state should step in to ban smoking in order to improve the health of those who choose to smoke and thereby increase overall levels of happiness.

Much of the debate about Mill has focused on his arguments for freedom of action. In the first place, it is regularly argued that the distinction between self- and other-regarding actions is unsustainable: surely there are few, if any, actions that affect the actor alone. Some have challenged Mill's view that actions which offend others but do not cause them physical harm should be seen as self-regarding. For instance, the British judge Lord Devlin (1905–92) argued that there is no such thing as private immorality because even private behaviour will have public consequences. Widespread drug-taking, for instance, will affect economic performance and put pressure on health resources. For Devlin (1965), society is held together by shared moral values, and excessive moral pluralism will be catastrophic for social stability.

As we saw in the case study on smoking, we can also challenge Mill's assumption that freedom of action is conducive to happiness or well-being. Utilitarians, committed to maximizing happiness in society, would have to think hard about behaviour that others find offensive but that do not directly harm them physically or financially. They would have to assess the merits of allowing that behaviour to continue, versus the merits of putting a stop to it; see **Box 4.2**. Such decisions are very important in the age of the Internet, when the exercise of freedom of expression can so easily have unintended consequences. In 2005, for instance, violent protests broke out around the world when conservative Muslims learned that a Danish magazine had published a series of cartoons mocking the prophet Mohammad. In November, 2011, the offices of the French magazine *Charlie Hebdo* were firebombed after the magazine issued a spoof edition supposedly "guest edited" by the founder of Islam (Jolly, 2011).

4

> **KEY CONCEPT BOX 4.2**
> Liberalism, Morality, and Freedom
>
> It is a central liberal principle that offensive behaviour should not be prohibited by society or the state merely because it causes offence. Consider the following legal case reported in the British newspaper the *Guardian*:
>
> Court of Appeal (Criminal Division)
> Regina v Brown et al.
> Before Lord Lane, Mr Justice Rose and Mr Justice Potts
> 9 February 1992
>
> The defendants belonged to a group of sado-masochist homosexuals who had, over 10 years, willingly and enthusiastically participated in acts of violence against each other for the sexual pleasure engendered in the giving and receiving of pain. The acts took place in private at different locations including a room equipped as a torture chamber. The acts of genital torture involved the use of pain inflicting instruments—whipping with a cat-o'nine tails, caning, burning with a blow torch, branding with hot metal, hitting with a spiked glove, applying stinging nettles to the genital area . . . All the activities were carried out with the consent of the passive partner or victim. There was . . . no permanent injury . . . and no complaints to police.
>
> Unfortunately for the participants, their activities were filmed on video and it was this evidence that resulted in the case being brought. In an original trial they were found guilty (under the Offences Against the Person Act 1861) and prison sentences were imposed.
>
> A number of questions can be asked about this case.
>
> 1. Are there paternalistic grounds for prohibiting these activities?
> 2. Are these activities self- or other-regarding?
> 3. Is your reaction determined by the nature of the activities or a general principle?
> 4. Does such behaviour threaten the moral fabric of society?

To be fair to Mill, remember that racially motivated writing and speech could be prohibited on the grounds that they are other-regarding. This was the principle behind the prosecution in 2006 of Nick Griffin, the leader of the British National Party leader, and the radical cleric Abu Hamza, both of whom were charged with inciting racial hatred. Action was taken against them not because their comments were offensive, but because they were seen as inciting their followers to cause harm to others.

See Chapter 1, p. 39, for more on the liberal theory of the state.

Mill, Marx, and Socialism

Mill put forward a liberal theory of freedom, justifying limited state intervention and maximizing personal autonomy, that did much to shape the modern liberal theory of the state, with its emphasis on neutrality and moral pluralism. However, Mill was well aware of the poverty and squalor in which so many people lived in nineteenth-century England.

→
See Chapter 5,
p. 94–95, for a discussion
of the difference between
classical and new liberalism.

4

Indeed, he recognized the challenge and, to some extent, the value of the socialist critique of liberalism that emerged in the second half of the century. Mill can therefore be located on the cusp between the old **classical liberalism** and the **new liberalism**, emphasizing social reform, that came to dominate British politics.

KEY POINTS

- Why do we value freedom? Various reasons have been proposed: because it is a basic human right, a means to happiness, a means to self-development, and so on.
- J.S. Mill argues for maximizing freedom; only "other–regarding" actions should be subject to state or societal intervention.

The Meaning of Justice

Justice is another political concept that is difficult to define. In its most basic sense, justice requires us to give to others what they are entitled to. This differentiates justice from charity: although it may be morally good for us to give to the poor, we are under no obligation to do so. In the modern world, justice is concerned with how different resources—wealth, income, educational opportunities, and so on—should be distributed. This distributional concept implies that resources are scarce, because if we had enough resources to go around, there would be no need to agonize over who should have them and who should not.

Theorists distinguish between **procedural justice** and **social justice**. The first focuses on the fairness of the process by which an outcome is reached, whereas the second focuses on the fairness of the outcome itself. Modern theories of social or distributive justice have identified a number of criteria that we might use as guides to distribution (Miller, 1976: 24–31). We could say that resources should be distributed according to *need*, or according to *merit* (or *desert*), or according to a principle of pure equality. All theories of justice involve equality, not in the sense that resources should be distributed equally, but in the sense suggested by the principle of equality before the law: treatment should be consistent. Once we have accepted that equals should be treated equally, we may decide that some humans are not equal with others in various respects and that differential treatment can be justified on those grounds. For instance, we might decide that since some people work harder than others, or are more talented than others, they should receive more of the resources that are available for distribution.

A theory of justice based on need is closely associated with socialism, as in the slogan "from each according to his ability, to each according to his needs." Nevertheless, the existence of the welfare state indicates that modern liberal democracies also recognize that meeting needs is just (though most of them limit the needs they recognize to the most basic).

A theory of justice based on merit or desert advocates distributing resources according to what individuals deserve, whether because of natural talent, willingness to do hard work, or general contribution to society. A **meritocratic theory of justice** considers it just to reward people differentially, according to merit, and recognizes the social advantages of using incentives to encourage the development and use of talent. It also recognizes the importance of equal opportunity: if rewards are to depend on merit, the playing field must be levelled so that no one starts out with an insurmountable structural disadvantage. It therefore would seem to demand educational and welfare opportunities for all.

KEY POINTS

- Justice is a distributional concept. Where different theories of justice diverge is over the criteria for distributing resources.
- A distribution principle based on need is problematic because (a) it is not always clear what qualifies as need and (b) it denies any role to the importance of desert.
- A distribution principle based on merit allows for incentives, but would seem to seem to require considerable state intervention to ensure the equality of opportunity that the principle demands.

Rawls's Theory of Justice

The meaning of justice becomes clearer if we look at a particular account. The best-known is John Rawls's *A Theory of Justice*, published in 1971; see **Box 4.3**. Rawls's account can be divided into two parts: first the *method* he used to arrive at his principles of justice and then the *principles* themselves.

Drawing from the **social contract** tradition, Rawls devises a method for arriving at principles of justice to which everyone can consent. The problem with competing theories of justice is that they are based on judgments about values that cannot be resolved. So how do we choose between a theory of justice emphasizing merit and one emphasizing need? Our choice will probably depend on our values and our vision of the kind of society that we want: one that emphasizes equality or one that emphasizes achievements.

Rawls devises a hypothetical situation in which there will be unanimous support for particular principles of justice. Imagine, he says, an **original position** in which individuals are asked to meet and decide how they want their society to be organized. In this original position, the members will be under a "veil of ignorance." They will have no idea what their own position in society will turn out to be: they don't know if they will be rich or poor, black or white, male or female, disabled or able-bodied. Rawls also assumes that individuals in the original position will be self-interested, wanting the best for themselves. Finally, he also suggests that they will desire what he calls "primary goods," such as wealth, good health, education, and so on.

See Chapter 1, p. 35, for more on the social contract tradition.

BIOGRAPHY BOX 4.3
John Rawls (1921–2002)

John Rawls was an American philosopher who spent most of his career at Harvard University. Despite his reluctance to engage in political debate, his book *A Theory of Justice* (1971) is widely regarded as one of the most influential works of political theory in the twentieth century. His rights-based theory of justice not only rejuvenated a discipline in apparent decline but also presented a major challenge to the utilitarian tradition that was dominant at the time in North America and Western Europe.

In his second book, *Political Liberalism* (1993), Rawls argued that his theory of justice applied only to the political realm. In the wider sphere of ethics he advocated the greatest possible freedom for people to pursue different conceptions of the good life. This moral pluralism has become a central feature of the liberal creed.

In the second part of the theory, Rawls outlines the principles he thinks would emerge when the individuals in the original position had imagined the perfect society. There are two:

1. Each person is to have an equal right to the most extensive total system of equal basic liberties compatible with a similar system of liberty for all.
2. Social and economic inequalities are to be arranged so that they are both:
   (a) to the greatest benefit of the least advantaged . . . and
   (b) attached to offices and positions open to all under conditions of fair equality of opportunity (Rawls, 1971: 302).

Rawls adds that 1 (the liberty principle) has priority over 2, and that 2(b) (the fair opportunity principle) has priority over 2(a) (the difference principle): thus liberty cannot be sacrificed in order to achieve economic improvement. This rules out slavery, in which it is possible that individuals without liberty could still have a high degree of economic and social well being.

Critiques of Rawls

Rawls's work has generated a huge literature (see, for instance, Daniels, 1975; Wolff, 1977; Kukathas and Pettit, 1990). Some critics focus on his method, others on his principles. First, some theorists question whether people in the original position would in fact have chosen the principles of justice that Rawls describes. Wolff (1996: 177–86), for example, questions the assumption that, because they don't know where they will end up in the social system, individuals behind the veil of ignorance will make the conservative choice to minimize their risks by adopting what Rawls refers to as the "maximin" strategy (maximizing the minimum): ensuring that the worst possible scenario is as good as it can be. Certainly it would be extremely risky to adopt a "maximax" strategy and create a society in which the rich would be very rich and the poor very poor, but is there not a middle way between the two extremes? For example, we could choose a society that would have more inequality but that would also provide the worst-off with some basic protection. In this scenario, the average position in society would be considerably improved, and though life at the bottom of the social pile would be less good, it would not be a total catastrophe.

Rawls's reluctance to sanction the "middle way" leads some to suggest that he created his model specifically to produce the outcomes he wanted. There is some evidence for this. Rawls admits that he is not totally reliant on the heuristic device of the social contract to derive his principles of justice. Rather, he adopts what he calls a "reflective equilibrium," where the principles he imagines coming from the original position are checked for consistency with our moral intuitions (Rawls, 1971: 20). Inevitably, the principles of justice arrived at will be, at the very least, influenced by already existing moral conventions.

Rawls's principles of justice have been criticized from the left and the right, and it is worth looking at these criticisms further. From the left, Wolff (1977) argues that Rawls's difference principle is not as egalitarian as it seems. He is particularly suspicious of the priority given to liberty. Should liberty always be protected against any alternative? Rawls takes it for granted that most people can afford the basics required to survive. Yet there are many parts of the world where this is not the case: in such places, Wolff argues, liberty is, and in many cases should be, sacrificed to achieve a basic standard of living.

From the right, Rawls's major critic has been the American philosopher Robert Nozick (1938–2002). Nozick was writing from a libertarian perspective, which calls for a minimal state focused on protection of property rights. He put forward a procedural theory of justice in which the main concern is not the outcome (e.g., meeting needs) but the way in which property (in the broad sense, meaning anything possessed by an individual) is acquired. It is therefore a historical theory in which "past circumstances or actions of people can create differential entitlements or differential deserts to things" (Nozick, 1974: 155). Provided that the property was acquired fairly, then the owner has a just entitlement to it. Nozick considered any attempt to redistribute property, even through taxation, to be unjust.

For Nozick, therefore, Rawls's end-state theory—that inequality is justified only when it benefits everyone, and in particular the worst-off—is illegitimate. He notes that Rawls's principles are inconsistent. How can one hold that liberty should be prized and yet advocate a major redistribution of resources? For Nozick, any attempt to impose a particular pattern—such as an outcome that meets a particular need—will require enforcement and hence restriction of liberty.

Nozick's entitlement theory comes with two provisos. First, the original acquisition of property has to have been fair; if it involved force or fraud, then compensation is due. As critics point out, it is clearly the case that much property has, in the past, been unfairly acquired. The levels of compensation that might be required to provide redress, and the difficulty of establishing how much is due, represent huge problems for Nozick's theory (Barry, 2000: 151). This is particularly true in North America, where much of the territorial landmass was simply taken from indigenous people without their consent, and many legal treaties between First Nations and the Crown were never fully honoured. The second proviso is that acquisition must not go against the essential well-being of others. This rules out any attempt to buy up all the water or food supplies in a community and then deny them to others.

Intuitively, one might doubt that the consequences of Nozick's theory are just. For example, his principles could result in such inequalities that the poorest members of society would be at risk of starvation. Moreover, it can be argued that redistributing resources actually increases liberty because it increases choices for the poor (Wolff, 1996: 194–5).

KEY POINTS

- Rawls's theory of justice has been criticized both for his principles of justice themselves and for the way he arrives at them.
- Some argue that individuals in the original position would not necessarily choose the principles that Rawls says they will. Some theorists accuse Rawls of manipulating the method in order to produce the outcome he desires.
- Rawls has been criticized from the left and the right. From the left, his principles are seen as not egalitarian enough; from the right, they are seen as too egalitarian.
- Nozick provides the best-known critique of Rawls from the right. He argues that the kind of redistribution that Rawls calls for is illegitimate. Individuals should be entitled to hold the property they own without intervention by the state, provided they have acquired it fairly.

Alternative Theories of Justice

Rawls and Nozick, although different in many ways, both put forward theories of justice based on liberal ideas. Both of them also limited their focus to relationships between human beings within sovereign states. Other theories of justice are not limited in these ways.

Cosmopolitan Theories of Justice

The growing interconnectedness of peoples and sovereign states suggests there are grounds to argue for an extension of justice beyond national boundaries. To limit discussion of justice to the internal affairs of wealthy Western states seems trivial, given the staggering inequalities between different parts of the world, particularly in light of the claim that the rich states of the global North are at least partly responsible for the poverty in the South. This has led political theorists to develop theories of justice that are global in scope; see the case study below.

This **cosmopolitan** approach is based on the principle that our loyalties should lie with human beings as a whole, not just with those who happen to live within our country. The idea that human beings are equal members of a global citizenry has a long history in political thought. However, the growing inequality between North and South in recent decades, and the increasing recognition of this inequality, has made **global justice** "one of the great moral challenges of the age," as the international relations theorist Andrew Linklater has argued (2008: 555).

There is little agreement on what our moral obligations should be to those who do not belong to our own community. At one extreme, Peter Singer (2002) has argued in favour of an unlimited obligation, whereby we (in the rich North) are obliged to help others (in the poor South) even to the point of seriously eroding our own standards of living. A less extreme position, adopted by Thomas Pogge, calls for application of Rawls's principles on a global scale, to increase redistribution between the rich and poor parts of the world (Pogge, 1989).

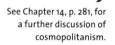

See Chapter 14, p. 281, for a further discussion of cosmopolitanism.

CASE STUDY
Climate Change and Justice

Cosmopolitan theories of justice try to impose a duty on individuals and states to act positively to end injustices in the world, or at least to refrain from doing harm. Both approaches feature in the politics of climate change. Cosmopolitans insist that rich industrialized countries must stop burning fossil fuels at the rate they currently do. Equally, since these countries are held responsible for climate change, they should help states in the developing world. Bangladesh, with its massive flooding problems, is a well-known example of a country in serious peril from climate change. Although it did little if anything to cause climate change, it suffers from its effects, and also lacks the money to deal with its problems.

Communitarianism and Justice

An alternative to cosmopolitan theories of justice, and to liberal theories of justice in general, is **communitarianism**. Communitarians do not accept the idea, implicit in both Rawls's and Nozick's theories, that liberal theories can apply in all social settings, whatever their individual historical or cultural features. They reject this universalism in favour of culturally specific justice claims. In other words, principles of justice should take into account the particular social and cultural character of the society for which they are intended. Principles designed in this way will differ from society to society (Walzer, 1985).

The communitarian position offers an important critique of the cosmopolitan theory of justice. Communitarians see the cosmopolitan notion of global citizenship as naïve, since our loyalties develop, and our identities are forged, within our own particular communities (Walzer, 1994). They also see it as undesirable and illegitimate to impose our own liberal conceptions of justice on other cultures.

Green Political Thought and Justice

In recent years Green political thought has challenged the view that justice can be applied only to currently living humans. There are a number of positions in this debate that are worth looking at. At the more moderate end, many philosophers have raised the question of whether justice should be applied to future generations of humans (see Barry, 1999). Of course, this **intergenerational** justice might clash with **intragenerational** justice. To put it starkly: can we really justify cutting back on economic development to save the environment for future generations when there are so many people in the world starving today?

See Chapter 6, p. 124, for more on the philosophy of environmentalism.

© Josef Friedhuber/istockphoto.com

PHOTO 4.2 Two polar bears caught on a shrinking ice floe. Global warming is having a severe effect on the Actic, where sea ice is melting at an unpredecented rate.

A number of Green political theorists and moral philosophers want to extend the recognition of justice claims beyond those of human beings. Many, for example, have tried to apply justice to at least some non-human animals (Garner, 2005). Some Green political theorists would further and include the whole of nature as deserving of justice. Some draw the line after living things (Taylor, 1986); others want to include inanimate phenomena too, arguing that it is possible to conceive of applying justice to ecosystems, or biodiversity (Fox, 1984).

KEY POINTS

- The conventional liberal understanding of justice has been challenged by at least three alternative understandings.
- Cosmopolitan theories of justice argue that we have obligations towards all humans, not just those residing within our own national boundaries.
- Communitarian theories argue that principles of justice depend on particular social, cultural, and historical experience and should not be considered universal.
- Green theories challenge the assumption that justice applies only to humans.

Conclusion

In this chapter we have examined the meaning of liberty and justice (semantic analysis) and tried to assess the values central to competing theories of liberty and justice (normative analysis). As our examination of freedom and justice reveals, political concepts are interconnected. We cannot properly evaluate freedom without considering how it relates to justice. This exercise also requires us to consider the merits of freedom and equality, which most, if not all, theorists conflicting. At the same time we have seen that the essentially contested nature of political concepts makes it difficult to move beyond an exercise in semantics. For example, freedom has been regarded as a source of inequality, on the one hand, and as a prerequisite for equality, on the other.

There is no doubt that theorists of freedom and justice now have to engage with the impact of **globalization**. Our growing knowledge of different cultures—made possible both by technological developments that give us a clearer picture of how different societies operate, and by the increasing mobility that has led to the emergence of multicultural communities—makes us more circumspect about the value of freedom and the restrictions on freedom that may be considered legitimate. Likewise, there are increasing calls for the principle of justice to be applied globally to address the shocking inequalities between different parts of the world. These developments represent important challenges for political theorists, challenges they will have to grapple with for some time to come.

? KEY QUESTIONS

- What constraints exist on our freedom?
- Are there only two types of liberty, negative and positive?
- Is Mill's distinction between self- and other-regarding actions a viable principle?
- Should freedom of thought and expression be maximized?
- For what values, if any, would you want to limit freedom?
- Can justice exist without freedom?

- How valid is a needs-based theory of justice?
- Critically examine Rawls's theory of justice.
- How viable is a cosmopolitan theory of justice?
- Can justice apply to non-humans?

📖 FURTHER READING

Mill, J.S. (1972). *Utilitarianism, On Liberty, and Considerations on Representative Government.*
London: Dent.
> The classic argument for individual freedom.

Dobson, A. (1998). *Justice and the Environment.* Oxford: Oxford University Press.
> A wide-ranging consideration of the relationship between justice and the environment by a
> leading Green political theorist.

Dower, N. (1998). *World Ethics: The New Agenda.* Edinburgh: Edinburgh University Press.
> A useful survey of the international ethics literature.

Ignatieff, Michael (1998). *Isaiah Berlin: A Life.* London: Metropolitan Books
> An accessible biography of Isaiah Berlin that introduces readers to his philosophy as well as some
> of his critics.

MacCallum, G. (1967). "Negative and Positive Freedom." *Philosophical Review* 76.
> An influential article seeking to provide a universal definition of freedom.

Rawls, John (1971). *A Theory of Justice.* Cambridge, MA: Harvard University Press.
> There is no substitute for this hugely important book.

📱 WEB LINKS

www.freedomhouse.org
> This site attempts to measure freedom in different countries.

www.utilitarian.net/jsmill
> A useful site on Mill.

http://plato.stanford.edu/entries/original-position
> On Rawls.

5 Traditional Ideologies

CHAPTER OVERVIEW

No ideology can be understood outside the economic, social, and political environment in which it emerged. All the ideologies we will examine in this chapter were shaped by the European Enlightenment. Liberalism, socialism, nationalism, and anarchism, as we will see, reflected key Enlightenment principles, while conservatism and fascism resisted them. Almost all of the ideologies reviewed in this chapter have had an extraordinary impact on the development of world politics in the last two centuries, and it is fair to say that the world would have been a very different place had they not existed.

What Is an Ideology?

Both this chapter and the next focus on political ideologies. Ideologies are central to this book because they help to shape the political landscape, domestic and international. Many of the themes we will encounter will be familiar to you, because each ideology consists of a set of political ideas. Liberalism, for instance, centres on the concept of liberty, whereas socialism centres on the concept of equality. In this chapter we will examine traditional ideologies associated with the **Enlightenment** (see **Box 5.1**). Liberalism, socialism, **nationalism**, and **anarchism** all emerged as aspects of Enlightenment thought, whereas conservatism and fascism tried to challenge its assumptions. In the next chapter we will examine more contemporary ideologies that challenge the claims of the traditional ideologies outlined in this chapter.

The term "ideology" was coined at the time of the French Revolution by Antoine Destutt de Tracey (1754–1836), who used it to refer to a science of ideas that could be discovered in the same way that truths are discovered in the natural sciences. Others, however, soon recognized the **normative** character of ideology. For some the word itself has a negative meeting, and an "ideologue" is someone with an uncompromising devotion to a certain set of ideas even if they have little practical use. An ideology might be defined as a set of ideas designed to describe the existing political order, present a vision of what the ideal political order should look like, and, if necessary, prescribe a means to transform the former into the latter. An ideology therefore contains empirical, semantic, and normative elements.

KEY CONCEPT BOX 5.1
Enlightenment

The Enlightenment was an intellectual and cultural movement of the seventeenth and eighteenth centuries that emphasized the application of reason in the search for knowledge and human progress. It was both a cause and an effect of the decline in the authority of religion that accompanied it. A notable critic of the Enlightenment within political philosophy was the British conservative philosopher Edmund Burke (1729–97), who railed against what many have seen as its high point, the French Revolution (Burke, 1968 [1790]).

A number of features of ideologies are worth noting. First, ideologies are more often than not action-oriented: they seek to promote a particular social and political order for which they urge people to struggle. Second, it is sometimes said that ideologies are less rigorous and sophisticated than "proper" political philosophy. In reality, as Vincent (1995: 17) points out, "ideological themes can be found on a continuum from the most banal jumbled rhetoric up to the most astute theorizing."

Third, the twentieth century has been described as the age of ideologies because of the havoc wreaked during it by regimes based on two particular ideological traditions—communism and fascism. However, it would be more appropriate to say that the twentieth century was the age of ideologies with which liberalism profoundly disagreed. The liberal critiques of fascism and communism as ideologies reflect a tendency among some liberals to regard liberalism itself as somehow above the ideological fray. As Goodwin (2007: 35) points out, "Liberalism appears as a necessary truth, the basis of reality, rather than as one political ideology among many."

◀ The hammer and sickle symbol on a wall in the South Indian state of Kerala, where communism has had a strong presence since the 1950s (Olaf Krüger/Getty Images).

Fourth, ideologies tend to combine concepts that political philosophers look at individually. We can try to identify the core characteristic of a particular ideology, but this is difficult, if not impossible, because all ideologies have different strands or schools, and sometimes there is considerable overlap between one ideology and another. Ideologies are, then, in the words of Festenstein and Kenny (2005: 4), "internally pluralistic, contested, complex, and overlapping."

One final general point about political ideologies is worth making here. Ideologies reflect, as well as shape, the social and historical circumstances in which they develop. For example, since the nineteenth century the two most influential ideologies have been liberalism and socialism. It was no accident that these ideologies emerged during the industrial revolution and reached their height in the nineteenth century. In the first place, both liberalism and socialism reflected the optimism of the time, when it was thought that there was nothing that human beings could not understand rationally and achieve politically and economically. Human beings could be masters of all they surveyed. Second, liberalism and socialism became dominant ideologies because they were associated with new social groups created by the industrial revolution. Liberalism was largely promoted by the industrial middle class; socialism, by the industrial working class.

KEY POINTS

- Traditional ideologies were shaped by the Enlightenment.
- Ideologies are action-oriented.
- It is usually possible to identify the core concepts of an ideology, but all ideologies combine a variety of concepts and therefore their meanings are disputed.
- Ideologies reflect as well as shape the social and historical circumstances in which they exist.

Liberalism

Liberalism is an important ideology because it has been the dominant political tradition in the West for many centuries. We have already encountered various facets of liberalism throughout this book, and many of the key Western political thinkers—Hobbes, Locke, Bentham, Mill, Rawls, and Nozick—are in the liberal tradition.

The Historical Development of Liberalism

The origins of liberalism are often traced to the rise of a capitalist political economy in the seventeenth and eighteenth centuries, during which time theorists developed a philosophical defence of private property. The individualistic political philosophy of Hobbes and Locke is crucial here (Macpherson, 1962). Liberalism is difficult to pin down, not least because of its longevity and the range of forms it has taken. "Liberal" has been used to describe parties of the right, such as in Australia, with John Howard's coalition government in the 1990s, and the centre-left, such as the Liberal Party of Canada. In some countries it is associated with the free market; in others, most notably the US, with state intervention.

Classical liberalism draws in particular on the economic theory of Adam Smith (1723–90) and the social theory of Herbert Spencer (1820–1907). Emphasizing limitation of the state's role, it calls for the state to do little apart from ensuring internal and external security, and enforcing private property rights. This view is partly justified on the grounds that the market is the most effective means of meeting human needs. There is also a moral dimension in that a limited state maximizes individual freedom and rewards those who work hardest.

Classical liberalism was challenged towards the end of the nineteenth century, when the extent of poverty was beginning to be recognized and socialism was emerging as an alternative. In response to these challenges, liberal thinkers such as T.H. Green (1836–82), L.T. Hobhouse (1864–1929) and J.A. Hobson (1858–1940) called for a **new liberalism** emphasizing social reform. New liberals saw a more positive role for the state in correcting the inequities of the market. Social liberals argued that, far from reducing liberty, state intervention actually increased it by expanding the opportunities for individuals to achieve their goals. The new liberalism influenced the direction of Liberal Party politics in the UK; the British Liberal government elected in 1906 introduced a range of social–reform measures, including old-age pensions.

The new liberalism dominated the political landscape for much of the twentieth century, although not always under the "liberal" name; in Britain, for example, its main vehicle was the social democratic Labour party. In the 1970s, however, a revised version of classical liberalism emerged to challenge it under the guise of the New Right, and right-wing governments, particularly in Britain, the US, and Canada, were elected on platforms that reflected, in part, the classical liberal agenda. The academic support for this popular movement was provided by thinkers such as Friedrich von Hayek and Robert Nozick.

See Chapter 20, p. 407, for a discussion of liberal political economy.

See Chapter 4, p. 87, for Nozick's critique of Rawls's theory of justice.

Liberal Thought

One of the key questions about liberal ideology is the degree to which the two types of liberalism identified above are compatible. Arguably, the core meaning of liberalism is found in the concepts of liberty, tolerance, individualism, and a particular kind of equality. Liberty is *the* concept at the centre of liberal thought, "the primary value in the liberal creed" as Goodwin (2007: 41) puts it. For some liberal thinkers liberty is an intrinsic good; for others, such as John Stuart Mill, it is a means to an end: its value lies in the possibilities for self-development it produces.

The classical liberal tradition emphasizes **negative liberty**: individual freedom from external constraints, including constraints imposed by the state. The new liberal tradition emphasizes **positive liberty**: freedom to pursue self-development, which is assumed to require state intervention to protect rights, promote equality of opportunity, and so on. Critics of the new liberalism charge that in shifting the emphasis from the individual to society, it has abandoned "true" liberalism. Advocates of the new liberalism respond that liberty cannot be maximized without state intervention to create the necessary conditions.

Central to liberty is a focus on the individual. In the **social contract** tradition of Hobbes and Locke, the individual exists before society is created. The notion of rights is prominent in liberal thought precisely because of the centrality of the individual. Individuals should be protected against society and the state. At its libertarian extreme, individualism denies that the state has the right to intervene in any aspect of the individual's life. As we have seen, however, even classical liberalism sees some role for the state; thus extreme libertarianism is closer to anarchist than to liberal thought (see below).

The liberal focus on the individual reflects the belief that individuals are rational and hence able to determine their own best interests, which they will always pursue. Thus, in the economic realm, individuals are best left to their own devices as consumers and producers. The "hidden hand" of the market will ensure that economic utility is achieved.

See Chapter 4, p. 79, for a discussion of the distinction between positive and negative liberty.

See Chapter 1, p. 35, for discussion of the liberal social contract tradition.

← See Chapter 1, p. 39, for a discussion of communitarianism.

The pre-eminence of the individual in liberal thought downgrades the community from a unified entity to a mere aggregate of individuals with competing interests and values. This distinction between the community and the individual is the source of the modern debate between liberals and **communitarians**. Communitarian thinkers criticize the liberal social contract tradition for basing its principles on a notion of humans in a pre-social state. For communitarians, political principles must be derived from the actual societies that provide identity and meaning for individuals.

The liberal approach to equality is distinctive. Liberals hold individuals to be of equal value, but reject any notion that outcomes should therefore be equal. Rather, liberals look to equality of opportunity to ensure fairness on the principle that if individuals start from the same position, then they will be rewarded according to their merit. Of course, the free market does not allow for genuine equality of opportunity, because individuals don't start out in life from the same position. Thus it might be argued that the state intervention advocated by the new liberals actually makes equality of opportunity more of a reality. The introduction of free education and health care, in particular, has helped to equalize life chances.

KEY POINTS

- Liberalism is the dominant political tradition in the West.
- Liberalism has two main strands, classical and "new" or social reforming.
- The core concept of liberalism is liberty, with the classical tradition emphasizing negative liberty and the social reforming tradition emphasizing positive liberty.
- The priority attributed to the individual in liberal thought entails a downgrading of the community.
- Liberals advocate equality of opportunity rather than equality of outcome.

Socialism

The word "socialism" first appeared in print in the *Co-operative Magazine* in 1827. Socialism as an ideology developed with the emergence of an industrial working class in the course of the industrial revolution. Although it has been closely associated with working-class parties, socialism differs from trade unionism in that it has much broader goals, focused not just on workers but on the whole of society, which it seeks to transform in cooperative and egalitarian directions. Somewhat ironically, many of the advocates of socialism have come from the middle classes, and they have always faced some hostility from working-class organizations.

Historical Development

Although the pivotal figure in the historical development of socialism is Karl Marx, three pre-Marxian thinkers—Claude-Henri Saint-Simon (1760–1825), Charles Fourier (1772–1837), and Robert Owen (1771–1858)—are usually regarded as the founders of socialism. Marx considered these thinkers utopian in that they had no practical vision of how the necessary political change would come about. Marx, by contrast, developed a "scientific" theory according to which socialism was not only ethically desirable but historically inevitable.

← See Chapter 1, p. 30, for a discussion of Marxist ideas on the state.

Marx's ideas have had a huge impact on world politics in general. Lenin and the Bolsheviks revised them to suit Russia's circumstances, and after the Russian Revolution in 1917 they established the Soviet state on the foundations provided by Marxist ideas.

Thereafter world socialism was divided between two camps: communism, centring on the "Third International" of world communist organizations, and social democracy.

Means and Ends in Socialist Thought

We have already noted that every ideology seems to encompass more than one strand. This is particularly true of socialism. In order to understand the key divisions within the socialist tradition, it is useful to distinguish between *means* and *ends*: between the methods that socialists have thought appropriate to achieve their objectives, and the end goals. In terms of means, the key distinction has been between revolutionary and evolutionary socialism. In the revolutionary camp we need to make a further distinction. Some, including Marx, believed that the inevitable revolution would take the form of a popular uprising. Others, including Lenin and his supporters, called for a coup led by a disciplined band of revolutionaries. It was Lenin's advocacy of a disciplined party—the Bolsheviks—that led to the creation of the Communist Party, a **political party** that dominated the Soviet Union from 1917 until its collapse in 1991.

The main alternative to revolution has been offered by evolutionary socialism. Based on the belief that universal suffrage would make it possible to achieve socialism through political democracy, this school of socialist thought assumes that the state can be responsive to working-class interests. Its advocates formed an important strand of socialist thought outside the USSR after the Russian Revolution.

Socialists have often disagreed about the objectives of socialism. Two issues are most important here. First, some socialists see a crucial role for the state in a socialist society, whereas others envisage a decentralized communal society. Again, the contrast between Marx and Lenin is useful here. Marx suggested that once class conflict had been eliminated, there would be no need for a state, since the capitalist state was merely a vehicle for the ruling class; see **Box 5.2**. At times, Marx's vision of a future communist society lacked any centralized administrative structure. By contrast, Lenin recognized the need for a

---

KEY QUOTE BOX 5.2
Marx's Vision of Communism

Marx wrote very little about what a future communist society would look like. In the *Communist Manifesto*, however, he did say this:

> When, in the course of development, class distinctions have disappeared, and all the production has been concentrated in the whole nation, the public power will lose its political character. . . . If the proletariat during its contest with the bourgeoisie is compelled, by the force of circumstances, to organize itself as a class, if, by means of a revolution, it makes itself the ruling class, and, as such, sweeps away by force the old conditions of production, then it will, along with these conditions, have swept away the conditions for the existence of class antagonisms and of classes generally, and will thereby have abolished its own supremacy as a class. (Marx and Engels, 1976: 105).

AFP/Getty Images

PHOTO 5.1 Marxist leader Biman Bose addresses a press conference in Kolkata, India, in May 2011 following the defeat of the world's longest-serving democratically elected communist government. The Left Front had governed the state of West Bengal for 34 years.

state—a "dictatorship of the proletariat"—after the communist revolution, at least for a time, to ensure the defeat of the enemies of the revolution. Of course, the Soviet state remained in place long after that goal had been achieved.

The second major issue on which socialists have differed is the form that public ownership should take. Since the 1960s in particular, theorists have advanced more decentralized models involving worker's cooperatives and even a "market socialism" (Miller, 1990). The key question is: where to draw the line? When does a particular balance between public and private ownership cease to be socialist? This debate became particularly vociferous in Britain after the 1945 Labour government had undertaken extensive nationalization. Many wanted to go further along the public ownership route, while others were prepared to settle for the mixed economy as a permanent state of affairs. These debates continue to animate Labour circles in Britain in terms of both philosophy and practical politics.

We can see echoes of the same debates in Canada, where the welfare state was greatly expanded under the various Trudeau governments. Although state-funded health care remains almost sacred in Canada, debates over the scope and size of other government programs are renewed with every election.

Key Socialist Principles

Despite some agonized debates, we can identify a number of core socialist principles that remain more or less consistent. The first is *a generally optimistic view of* **human nature**.

Socialists tend to see human nature as capable of being shaped by social, economic, and political circumstances. Whereas liberals and conservatives regard human beings as inherently self-seeking and individualistic, socialists believe that those characteristics are socially conditioned, not innate. Ideally, a socialist society would shape the values of its citizenry by promoting cooperation, fellowship, and compassion.

The second core socialist principle is *equality*. Unlike liberals, socialists do advocate equality of outcome, because they understand inequality to be the result of different locations in a social structure rather than differences in ability; education is a classic example, because it is heavily influenced by social class. Whereas liberals consider inequality to be a necessary incentive, socialists believe that human nature can be moulded to the point where individuals would be willing to work for the good of society even in the absence of material incentives.

The third core principle of socialism is *community*. There is an emphasis on cooperation and collective rather than individual goals. Community is linked to the other two core socialist values in that common ownership and equality support communal values.

Utopianism and Authoritarianism

Many liberals and conservatives suggest that the socialist vision is utopian, unrealistic, and unrealizable. According to this argument, the ideal socialist society, in which human beings can achieve genuine **emancipation** and fulfilment as members of a community, demands too much of its citizens. Such a society might be acceptable if all its effects were benign, but the egalitarianism it demands results in an **authoritarian** state that must continually intervene to prevent different levels of talent and effort from changing the egalitarian balance of society (Popper, 1962).

The overbearing Soviet state was seen as a direct product of socialist ideas. Stalin killed millions of his own people during his decades in power, and later Soviet leaders showed little respect for human rights. But the authoritarian label cannot be attached to social democracy as it evolved in most Western developed countries, where it draws from liberalism as much as it does from Marxism and often has an explicitly religious dimension; see **Box 5.3**.

KEY POINTS

- Socialist thought is dominated by the work of Karl Marx, who described his socialism as scientific, as opposed to the utopian variety of the socialist thinkers who preceded him.
- In the early twentieth century, socialism divided into two camps, with the communists on one side and the revisionists (later social democrats) on the other.
- To classify different varieties of socialism, it is useful to distinguish between means and ends.
- Core socialist principles include an optimistic view of human nature, equality of outcome, and community and cooperation.
- Some liberal and conservative theorists argue that socialism is utopian and has authoritarian tendencies. They point to Stalin's long time in power as an example.

See Chapter 4, p. 87, for Nozick's libertarian critique of Rawls's theory of justice.

5

Tommy Douglas is generally regarded as the father of the modern Canadian welfare state. A Baptist minister, he combined religious conviction with a dedication to social justice. He was among the founders of the Cooperative Commonwealth Federation (CCF) in 1932, and after 17 years as premier of Saskatchewan (1944–61), during which he introduced Canada's first universal health care system, he was elected to lead the CCF's successor, the New Democratic Party, on its founding in 1961. Douglas saw himself as a champion of working families.

Barry Philp/GetStock.com

PHOTO 5.2 Tommy Douglas fires up a crowd in 1963.

Conservatism

Elements of conservative thought can be found throughout history. Indeed, the Greek philosopher Plato, who defended the rule of the intellectual elite—the "philosopher kings"—can be regarded as the first conservative thinker. However, it was as a response to the Enlightenment that conservative thought gained a popular following. Where liberalism and socialism promoted the progressive and rationalistic values of the Enlightenment, conservatism provides a negative response to it. The classic text here is Edmund Burke's attack on the French Revolution of 1789, first published in 1790 (1968). See **Box 5.4**.

BIOGRAPHY BOX 5.4
Edmund Burke (1729–97)

Burke was born in Dublin, Ireland, in 1729. After studying at Trinity College he moved to England in 1750 where he qualified as a lawyer before settling on a career in politics. He became a Member of Parliament in 1765.

Burke's fame came from his writing and speeches on important political issues of his day. He is best known for his vitriolic *Reflections on the Revolution in France,* but he also wrote and spoke on the British constitution, as well as Britain's relations with India and the North American colonies. The fact that he opposed the French Revolution but supported the American Revolution and the Indian opposition to British colonial rule has been much discussed.

Some put this apparent contradiction down to a fear that the French Revolution threatened the emerging capitalist class in Britain. Others argue that there was no inconsistency since Burke was applying his political principles in a logical way. He opposed the French revolutionaries because they were overthrowing an established order on the grounds of abstract rational principles. But he supported the Americans and the Indians because they were upholding long-held traditions against British encroachment.

Conservative political movements have not been ideologically uniform. In much of Europe they have historically been anti-liberal and reactionary, whereas in Britain, conservatism has been tinged with liberalism. The nineteenth-century Conservative Party was notable for the social reforming administrations of Robert Peel and Benjamin Disraeli. After 1945, the Conservative Party largely accepted the dominance of social democratic ideas until the 1970s, when it came heavily under the influence of the New Right. A similar shift to the right was noticeable in North America with the election of Ronald Reagan in the US and Brian Mulroney in Canada.

See Chapter 1, p. 32, for a discussion of the New Right theory of the state.

With its emphasis on the loosening of state controls on the free market, the New Right had more in common with classical liberalism than with conservatism. Certainly, the strongly ideological character of Margaret Thatcher's leadership in Britain was inimical to the pragmatism of conservative thought. However, the New Right also promoted a number of traditional conservative values—law and order, respect for authority, patriotism and civic virtue—and the Thatcher government was prepared to use the state to enforce them. This ideological mix was described by one commentator as a combination of "the free economy and the strong state" (Gamble, 1994).

Conservative Thought

Determining the nature of conservative thought is not easy, because conservatives generally claim to be non-ideological, preferring practical principles over abstract reasoning. As a result, conservative thinkers have been reluctant to stake out clear platforms or ideological positions. This is unfortunate, partly because the term "conservatism" can be interpreted as signifying nothing more than a desire to defend existing privilege and power, and partly because conservative thought has come to be identified with "certain fundamental convictions . . . which constitute a distinct political standpoint" (Goodwin, 2007: 174).

Foremost among these convictions is an *aversion to rationalism*. This rationalism was very much a product of the Enlightenment. It celebrated the ability of human beings to construct societies on the basis of rational principles such as—in the case of France—"liberty, equality, and fraternity." There was no limit to the progress possible in human societies. For Michael Oakeshott (1901–90), a notable twentieth-century conservative, a rationalist "stands . . . for independence of mind on all occasions, for thought free from obligation to any authority save the authority of reason" (1962: 1).

It was the rationalist character of the French Revolution that Burke so savagely attacked. In trying to create a new society based on abstract principles, the French revolutionaries had destroyed traditions and institutions that had evolved over the centuries. For Burke and conservatives in general, the social and political world is too complex to be explained in catch phrases: far better to rely on tried and tested traditions, which reflect the collective wisdom of a society gained over many generations.

A number of other conservative positions derive from this anti-rationalist stance. First, the conservative model of society is organic rather than mechanical. Society cannot be taken apart and rearranged like the parts of a machine. Rather, it is a complex organism composed of a multitude of interdependent parts. Thus changing one part may have an unpredictable and undesirable impact on other parts. Burke is not saying that change is impossible: only that it should be gradual and moderate, and care must be taken care to preserve what is valuable. There is an assumption here that what exists has value and works for the well-being of society.

A second conservative characteristic, related to anti-rationalism, is a tendency to resist change. Conservatives don't believe that we can fully understand our contemporary social and political environment. At the very least, the collective wisdom developed over centuries is preferable to the abstract reasoning of a few: we should stick with what we know. The same skepticism regarding human capacities is reflected in the conservative *advocacy of hierarchy*. As Plato recognized, effective self-government is a myth. Some people are more capable of governing than others. This is the reason behind Burke's well-known argument justifying the right of MPs to retain their autonomy from their constituents.

Social and Cultural Conservatism

Many conservatives are also anxious to preserve traditional values against the threats posed by an increasingly global culture. The desire to cling to the past is an important ingredient in social and cultural conservatism. Thus in the US "values voters" support candidates who promise to maintain traditional moral values. Many conservatives, such as Patrick Buchanan, argue that religion needs to play a more important role in social morality. Secularism is condemned as a dangerous, amoral trend that will fragment society and reduce social harmony. The *If it ain't broke don't fix it* principle resonates with many conservatives, who find little wrong with society as it is and are wary of any change, even when it is necessary to address serious problems in society. An early Canadian example was a 1891 Conservative campaign poster featuring the country's first prime minister, John A. Macdonald, and the slogan "The old flag, the old policy, the old leader." Conservatives argue that "new" and "different" do not necessarily mean "better." What is tried and true is often worth preserving, if only because it is what many people are comfortable with.

CASE STUDY
Canadian Social Liberalism Versus American Conservatism

In 2003, the Liberal government of Jean Chrétien refused to join the Bush administration in invading Iraq. In an open letter to US National Security Advisor Condoleeza Rice, Foreign Minister Lloyd Axworthy contrasted what his left-of-centre Liberal government felt were Canada's priorities with the priorities of the conservative American administration:

> If we're going to spend money . . . it will be on day-care and health programs, and even on more foreign aid and improved defence. Sure, that doesn't match the gargantuan, multi-billion-dollar deficits that your government blithely runs up fighting a "liberation war" in Iraq, laying out more than half of all weapons expenditures in the world, and giving massive tax breaks to the top one per cent of your population while cutting food programs for poor children. Just chalk that up to a different sense of priorities about what a national government's role should be when there isn't a prevailing mood of manifest destiny (Axworthy, 2005).

At a theoretical level, the differences between Canadian and American political cultures were explored at length by the American scholar Seymour Martin Lipset. In *Continental Divide* (1990), for example, he drew out distinctions between Tory and Liberal traditions in the two countries:

> One was Whig and classically liberal or libertarian—doctrines that emphasize distrust of the state, egalitarianism, and populism—reinforced by a voluntaristic and congregational religious tradition. The other was Tory and conservative in the British and European sense—accepting of the need for a strong state, for respect for authority, for deference —and endorsed by hierarchically organized religions that supported and were supported by the state (Lipset, 1990, 2).

Critics who found Lipset's argument reductionist might have felt vindicated two decades later, when the US elected Barack Obama, a left-of-centre Democrat, while Canada elected Stephen Harper, a right-of-centre Conservative. Clearly, political cultures are neither homogeneous nor unchanging.

KEY POINTS

- Conservatism is a reaction to the Enlightenment tradition of political thought.
- The New Right has liberal as well as conservative elements.

- The underlying characteristics of conservatism are an aversion to rationality, an organic view of society, skepticism regarding human capacities, and a preference for hierarchy.
- Social and cultural conservatism tends to be suspicious of change, and prefers the status quo to the uncertainty of new and unexplored policy options.

Neoconservativism

In the US, **neoconservatism** became very influential during the presidency of George W. Bush (2001–9), and there is a direct link between neoconservative ideas and the 2003 invasion of Iraq (MacDonald, 2009). It is useful to outline the differences and similarities between traditional conservatives and neoconservatives, as these groups are sometimes confused. There are overlaps, certainly, but also some important distinctions. The first major difference, as the prominent neoconservative Irving Kristol argues, is that most neoconservatives started out on the left. They were "liberals mugged by reality," who began as Democrats and gravitated towards the Republicans, particularly in the late 1970s under Jimmy Carter's presidency. Moreover, neoconservative policies rarely reflected conservative values such as "tradition, ritual, hierarchy, small government, fiscal austerity, devotion to place, [and] homage to the past" (Bacevich, 2005: 70-1).

Kristol defines American neoconservatism with reference to four main principles. First, "patriotism is a natural and healthy sentiment and should be encouraged by both private and public institutions"; there is something morally wrong with those who cast aspersions on their own country. Second, "world government is a terrible idea since it can lead to world tyranny"; America should not have its ability to do good constrained by international bodies such as the United Nations. Third, "statesmen should, above all, have the ability to distinguish friends from enemies" (Kristol, 2003); the world is composed of good and evil actors, and the latter must be treated with firm resolve, not appeasement or compromise. What unified the neoconservatives, according to Fukuyama (2006: 15–16), was their hatred of communism and their condemnation of liberals who criticized their country and undermined American resolve at a time when it was most sorely needed.

Finally, Kristol's fourth principle maintains that, as a superpower, the US is subject to special rules in international politics. "[T]he 'national interest' is not a geographical term, except for fairly prosaic matters like trade and environmental regulation," Kristol argues. Rather, "A larger nation has more extensive interests," and these include "ideological interests." Helping fellow democracies or "friends" such as Israel is crucial to furthering US goals. (Kristol, 2003). Neoconservatives promote the use of military power to advance American goals, with a focus on the Middle East as the primary locus of US interests.

Neoconservatives have seen themselves as "hard Wilsonians," promoting what they believe to have been the ideals of President Woodrow Wilson at the end of the First World War: to spread democracy as a necessary condition for global stability and peace. Like neoconservatives, Wilson saw America as a crusading nation with a global mission. Yet, even though he had a strong moral, even self-righteous streak, Wilson was quite different from today's neoconservatives. First, he was a keen promoter of international institutions, and considered it his greatest failure as president that he had not managed to persuade the US to join the League of Nations. Furthermore, having seen the carnage of war, Wilson detested the armaments industry. Thus neoconservatives who borrow Wilson's expansive vision of America's power conveniently ignore his warnings about militarization and unilateral solutions to complex problems. The fact that Wilson distrusted big business has also been ignored by the many neoconservatives who are often enthusiastic participants in America's corporate capitalist system (MacDonald, 2009: xv; Bacevich, 2005: 10–12).

Not all neoconservatives supported the Iraq war. Francis Fukuyama parted company with his former colleagues by 2004. Jeanne Kirkpatrick was never in favour of the war, and had serious reservations about the "Bush Doctrine" of pre-emptive attack and spreading democracy by force, although her criticisms were far more muted than Fukuyama's (Podhoretz, 2006). Further, while neoconservatism influenced the Bush administration, it was not the be-all and end-all of American foreign policy. President Bush played to a variety of constituencies, including "country club Republicans, realists, representatives of oil and other corporate interests, evangelicals, hardball political strategists, right-wing Catholics, and neoconservative Jews allied with Israel's right-wing Likud party" (Cole, 2005).

A detailed examination of the defence industry before and after 9/11 makes it clear that major contractors such as Lockheed Martin and Boeing pushed for war, helped by the revolving door between government officials and industry. Spending on weapons systems and military equipment, which had fallen significantly with the Cold War, could once again be justified to fight a war that was virtually limitless in its global scope (Scheer, 2008: 14–15, 54–8). The oil-producing states of the Persian Gulf, particularly Saudi Arabia, also influenced the Bush administration's policies (Woodward, 2006: 3; MacDonald, 2009: xvi).

Historians and political scientists have judged neoconservatives critically, viewing their vision for the US as an exercise in imperial hubris, mixed with naive optimism. Certainly there were strategic miscalculations. For instance, many neoconservatives saw Iraq's Saddam Hussein as a modern-day Hitler and pushed for his removal on moral rather than strategic grounds, without regard for the consequences. Similarly, many neoconservatives wrongly assumed that US models of democracy and capitalism could be imposed on very different societies such as Iraq and Afghanistan. They will also be remembered for contributing to the worst financial crisis their country has seen since the Great Depression (MacDonald, 2009: xiv-xvii).

Nationalism

Perhaps the best concise definition of nationalism to date comes from the Canadian political scientist and former Liberal party leader Michael Ignatieff:

As a political doctrine, nationalism is the belief that the world's people are divided into nations, and that each of these nations has the right to self-determination, either as self-governing units within existing states, or as nation states of their own.

As a cultural ideal, nationalism is the claim that while men and women have many identities, it is the nation which provides them with their primary form of belonging.

As a moral ideal, nationalism is an ethic of heroic sacrifice, justifying the use of violence in defence of one's own nation against enemies, internal or external. These claims—political, moral and cultural—underwrite each other. The moral claim that nations are entitled to be defended by force of violence depends on the cultural claim that the needs they satisfy for security and belonging are uniquely important. The political idea that all peoples should struggle for nationhood depends on the cultural claim that only nations can satisfy these needs. The cultural idea in turn underwrites the political claim that these needs cannot be satisfied without self-determination (Ignatieff 1994: 34).

The Academic Study of Nationalism

The study of nations and nationalism is commonly divided among three schools: the primordialists, the modernists and perennialists, and the ethno-symbolists. **Primordialists** see the nation as a natural phenomenon, a normal and understandable aspect of human relationships. In the 1950s and '60s, the sociologists Clifford Geertz and Edward Shils emphasized the power of "primordial attachment" to the nation as a community with unique characteristics that must be preserved (Smith, 2010: 55–8).

By contrast, the **modernists** see the nation as an invented or constructed form of social organization. They argue that nations are often created by elites who seek to gain power within a state and use nationalism as a tool to control and manipulate the masses. According to this view, the idea of nationalism was a product of the industrial revolution, when rural people began leaving their homes to seek work in the growing cities. Modernists such as Ernest Gellner argue that, having left their village identities, local dialects, and cultural traditions behind, these people had a deep need for a new identity that could be shared with people very different from themselves. Nationalism became a way of bringing disparate peoples together under the umbrella of an overarching "high culture" that had some similarities with traditional folk cultures but was also substantially different. The dislocation of urban spaces, the loss of former identity, and a sense of vulnerability all helped to make the national symbols and narratives promoted by the elites attractive (Gellner, 1983: 57).

The precise content of national narratives is relatively unimportant. Gellner famously argued that "[t]he cultural shreds and patches used by nationalism are often arbitrary historical inventions. Any old shred and patch would have served as well" (1983: 56). Other well-known Modernists include Paul Brass, Benedict Anderson (who coined the term "imagined communities" to describe nations), and Tom Nairn, who developed an economic modernist model based on Marxism (see Ozkirimli, 2000).

A related group called the **Perennialists** share the Modernists' opinion that nations are constructed but do not necessarily associate their origins with the industrial revolution. Liah Greenfeld, in her book *Nationalism: Five Roads to Modernity* (1993), asserts that nations in some cases was created before industrialization. In England she traces the birth of the nation to the creation of the Protestant Church of England under King Henry VIII. Later nations developed in the pre-industrial rural Germany of the early nineteenth century and the agrarian Russia of the eighteenth and nineteenth centuries. In these cases, other forms of association such as religion and kingship helped to bind individuals together as coherent "peoples" (Greenfeld, 1993).

The third group of nationalism theorists are the **ethno-symbolists**, who argue that nations are constructed and invented, but not necessarily by elites. According to Anthony D. Smith, many nations are based on pre-existing ethnic groups, with their own sense of identity and their own history. Arguably, Smith's main contribution to the discipline of nationalism studies is his privileging of what he called "ethnies": "named human populations with shared ancestry myths, histories and cultures, having an association with specific territory, and a sense of solidarity" (Smith 1998: 191). Not all ethnies become nations, but most nations are derived from ethnies, particularly "ethnic cores" that have the characteristics required to absorb and assimilate other ethnies and make them part of an emerging nation. Unlike the nation it may later become, a core ethnie needs to selectively borrow new elements from foreign groups through "controlled culture contact" (Smith 1990: 35–9). As the ethnic core expands and absorbs other ethnies, it incorporates their elements within its growing ethnic (and ultimately proto-national) culture.

In time the ethnic core forms a coherent nation, with a national homeland, a unified economy, and unified myths and symbols (Smith 1990: 40, 64–5). It is at this point that foreign elements and cultural borrowings may be perceived as threatening the authenticity and purity of the nation. Diversity is abandoned in favour of a more unified identity, and a process of purging and exclusion begins. For Smith, nations are based on "an ideal of authenticity which presupposes a unique culture-community, with a distinct and original character." Each nation possesses its own "peculiar historic 'genius,'" which the nationalists are tasked with rediscovering and possessing (Smith, 2001: 442; see also Smith, 1998: 194). Clear-cut territorial boundaries need to be established, and a "keen eye" is required to determine the identity of "'alien' objects throughout trade and exchange, as well as for successive migrations, invasions and colonisation." Throughout, images of cultural purity, "distinctiveness," and "originality" play a crucial part in identity construction (442–3).

For Smith, local history and identity are crucial elements in the construction of national myth. The communal past of a nation forms a "repository or quarry from which materials may be selected in the construction and invention of nations" (Smith, 1996: 37). History is fragmented into diverse elements; in this way a "useable past" is created, from which nationalists can choose the myths they need in order to rally the people and together reclaim national greatness (37). Different elements may be chosen at different times, depending on the era and the state of the nation. Heroic myths may be chosen in times of defeat, myths of peace and reconciliation in times of war (37). The only requirement is that such myths belong properly to the nation: that they are rooted in the nation's own past.

History and Further Distinctions

The search for national identity was initially a European phenomenon, centring first on the Italian and German quests for unification, achieved in 1871 and 1861, and then, after the First World War, on national **self-determination** as set out by the US President Woodrow Wilson in the peace settlement. After the Second World War, European colonies in Asia, Africa, and the Middle East sought, and largely secured, their independence. In more recent times there has been a resurgence of nationalism, particularly in Eastern Europe following the collapse of the Soviet Union.

The political scientist Hans Kohn (1944) made a useful distinction between civic and ethnic nationalism. **Civic nationalism** is loyalty to the institutions and values of a particular political community. **Ethnic nationalism**, by contrast, is loyalty to a shared inheritance based on culture, language, or religion. Where the first type is inclusive, open to anyone who wishes to sign on to the values and institutions of a particular community, the second is exclusive in the sense that membership is inherited and is not the product of rational choice.

© Stephan Zabel/istockphoto.com

PHOTO 5.3 Swiss flags adorn traditional buildings.

Because of its inclusive character, civic nationalism seems to present less of a threat to political order than exclusive ethnic nationalism. This distinction can be exaggerated, however, because even a political community based on loyalty to institutions and values has borders that must be protected. Even if inclusion is not based on religion or race, it must be based on something, and this has the potential to cause conflict. On the other hand, despite its negative image, nationalism need not necessarily result in division and conflict. Liberal nationalism, for instance, though too romantic for some, sees nations as the source of internal unity and envisages cooperation between nations.

KEY POINTS

- Nationalism has had an enormous impact on world politics since the nineteenth century.
- Primordialists argue that nations are natural, ancient, and a central part of the social community.
- Modernists trace the emergence of nations to the industrial revolution and the need for new identities during periods of urban dislocation and social change.
- Perennialists look farther back, to pre-industrial societies.

- Ethno-symbolists draw a more complex picture. For Smith, ethnic groups or "ethnies" develop over time to form the core of modern nations. Myths and symbols are central to this process.
- A useful distinction can be made between civic nationalism and ethnic nationalism.

Fascism

Unlike the other ideologies we have discussed in this chapter, fascism is a twentieth-century phenomenon. It is particularly associated with the relatively short-lived regimes led by Benito Mussolini (1883–1945) in Italy, and Adolf Hitler (1889–1945) in Germany. Indeed, some commentators regard fascism as a distinctly interwar phenomenon (Trevor-Roper, 1947). Others disagree with this limitation (Kitchen, 1976). Various scholars have attributed the rise of fascism to particular political and historical circumstances, to a flaw in human psychology, or to moral decay (Vincent, 1995: 145–50).

Fascism represents an extreme form of nationalism accompanied (unlike other forms of nationalism) by a set of racial, social, and moral ideas, most of which are simply unacceptable in a modern liberal democracy. In addition, fascism rejects abstract intellectualizing in favour of action, instinct, and emotion. For this reason scholars looking for texts to use as primary sources have had to rely mainly on the works of the Italian fascist Giovanni Gentile (1875–1944) and Hitler's *Mein Kampf* (1969 [1926]).

Fascism is, above all, anti-Enlightenment, opposing ideas such as liberalism, democracy, reason, and individualism. It is also profoundly anti-Marxist, although Nazism was seen as a form of nationalized (as opposed to international) socialism. Although certain elements of fascism recall conservatism, in particular its emphasis on the organic state, fascism is also revolutionary.

Fascism's opposition to liberalism and individualism stems from the belief that the community creates individuals: without it, they are nothing. It therefore rejects the liberal notion that humans can be imagined living in a pre-social state; rather, it maintains that identities are forged through membership in a community. In fascist theory, the state gives meaning to individual lives; hence individuals should be subservient to it. This is what justifies the **totalitarian** state, in which the individual is subsumed in the interests of the state's goals.

At the same time, fascism embraces the elitist position that some individuals are superior to others; see **Box 5.5**. The masses are perceived as largely ignorant and in need of elite leaders, particularly one all-powerful leader, a Führer or Duce. In German fascism, this emphasis on inequality and hierarchy took on a "racial" character: thus German "Aryans" were considered superior to all other groups but in particular Jews, Roma ("Gypsies"), and Africans. Belief in the superiority of German nation or *Volk* fed into a militant, aggressive, and expansionist nationalism whose aim was to establish the dominance of the "master race" around the globe. Ironically, although **social Darwinism** would suggest that subjugating the "inferior races" should have been relatively easy for the Aryans, there was a constant fear that the former would dominate and destroy the Aryans if they were not eliminated first. War was seen as virtuous and character-building, while also serving the goal of establishing racial supremacy; see **Box 5.6**.

See Chapter 1, p. 30, for a discussion of the elite theory of the state.

5

KEY CONCEPT BOX 5.5
Elitism in Political Thought

The concept of **elitism** has played a role in a number of the ideological traditions we have discussed in this chapter. It's important to recognize the different ways in which the concept is used. The classical elite theorists discussed in Chapter 1 put forward an empirical theory, arguing that elites will always exist, whatever the claims of democracy; they did not claim that elite rule was desirable. By contrast, both fascism and conservatism often use the term in a normative sense, arguing that rule by an elite is not only inevitable but desirable. In National Socialism (Nazism) this elitism took on racial connotations; however, this has not been the case with conservatism.

KEY CONCEPT BOX 5.6
Nazism and the Biological State

Racist and anti-Semitic musings predate the Nazi era. They can be traced back at least as far as the nineteenth century, when Houston Stewart Chamberlain (among others) identified an enduring history of deep racial antagonism between "Aryans" and "Semites" (Haas, 1992: 28). The French racist aristocrat Joseph-Arthur, Comte de Gobineau, expressed similar ideas in his *Essay on the Inequality of the Human Races* (1967 [1853–5]). Eugenic theories (promoting the gradual "perfection" of humanity [a highly skewed and unrealizable goal] through the sterilization of certain groups and the "judicious mating" of those with desirable physical and mental traits) were advanced by many others, including Sir Francis Galton, his American disciple Charles Davenport, and the German theorist Wilhelm Schallmeyer.

What was unique about Nazi anti-Semitism was the German state's unprecedented ability to "redefine evil"—to re-conceptualize race relations by pitting one group in stark competition with another (Haas, 1992: 2). If Germans were the apogee of human development, Jews were dangerous "racial aliens" (Burleigh and Wippermann, 1991: 305). Ethics were so twisted in the Nazi era that good and evil took on entirely new definitions. According to Peter Haas, the regime was able to commit "what we judge to be heinous crimes" not because the Germans were quintessentially evil and brutal," but because they "simply came to understand ethics in different terms" (Haas, 1992, 2). Claudia Koonz's work on the "Nazi conscience" explores how the regime rejected universal forms of morality. Instead the state promoted biased ethical values, "appropriate to their Aryan community." In their racialized view of the world, Nazis became "ethnic fundamentalists" (Koonz, 2003: 1, 13).

Yehuda Bauer describes the Nazi project as "the most radical attempt at changing the world that history has recorded to date: the most novel and the most revolutionary" (2001: 52–3). Even though Jews posed no threat whatever, a racial ethic cast them in a demonic light, making their destruction inevitable. As Bauer puts it: "No genocide to date has been based so completely on myths, on hallucinations, on abstract, nonpragmatic, ideology—which then was executed by very rational, pragmatic means" (2001: 48).

Part and parcel of this unique ethical system was the obsession with racial hygiene and biological purity. Lifton (1986) describes the Nazi system as a "biocracy":

> The model here is a theocracy, a system of rule by priests of a sacred order under the claim of divine prerogative. . . . Just as in a theocracy, the state itself was no more than a means to achieve [what Hitler claimed to be] "a mission of the German people on earth": that of "assembling and preserving the most valuable stocks of basic racial elements in this [Aryan] people . . . [and] . . . raising them to a dominant position (Lifton, 1986: 17).

This was a world view unique to the Nazis. Though they were not the first to hypothesize on the importance of racial purity and justify the killing of those they deemed inferior, they were the first to construct an entire worldview based on these concepts (Proctor, 1988: 10–45; Burleigh and Wippermann, 1991: 30–1; Lifton, 1986: 46). National Socialism was soon dubbed "applied biology," with biology figuring as "one of the defining features of the Nazi world view" (Proctor, 1988: 30, 45, 47, 64). Of course Jews were not the only victims of the biocracy. Mentally and physically handicapped Aryans were also killed, and Roma and Sinti ("Gypsies") were exterminated. Nevertheless, Jews were the chief victims of Nazi biocratic principles and the most obvious target of the state (Bauman, 1989: 70).

© David Klein/istockphoto.com

PHOTO 5.4 The annual "March of the Living" commemoration held on Holocaust Memorial Day at the infamous Auschwitz–Birkenau death camps in Poland. The building in the background is the gatehouse of the Auschwitz II-Birkenau camp.

5

CASE STUDY
Neo-Nazism and Holocaust denial

Since the end of the Second World War there have been many neo-Nazi organizations and movements, although their adherents rarely use that term. Their goal has been to revive the ideology of National Socialism, or some variant of it, and promote white power. The neo-Nazi phenomenon exists in many countries, including Canada and the US, but it is perhaps most notable in Austria, Russia, Belgium, Croatia, France, and Germany, where it re-emerged in the 1990s, following reunification. Typical activities include promotion of Nazi regalia, efforts to gain support in student organizations, and violence against immigrants, Jews, and Muslims, sometimes including murder. In some places neo-Nazis compete in elections, and Holocaust denial is common. In Canada neo-Nazi activity has centred on two organizations—the Nationalist Party of Canada and the Heritage Front—and a few individuals, notably Holocaust deniers Ernst Zundel and Fred Leuchter. A series of court cases against Zundel brought to light a new pseudoscientific aspect to Holocaust denial, epitomized by the infamous *Leuchter Report*, which alleged that the gas chambers at Auschwitz and Maidenek were never used on human victims (Lipstadt, 1993: 162–9; Shermer and Grobman, 2000: 128–33).

Deniers seek to rehabilitate Hitler, depicting him as a man of peace who was pushed into war either by the Allies or by the dangers of Soviet expansion. The fact that Germany's wartime leaders admitted their guilt is explained away as a matter of strategic self-sacrifice intended to gain Germany's re-admittance to the "family of nations" from which they had been expelled even though they were "innocent" of any wrongdoing. Deniers frequently accuse Jews of using the Holocaust to gain international sympathy and support for the State of Israel (Lipstadt, 1993: 22–3; Najarian, 1997: 1).

What is the end goal for deniers? Alexander, among others, believes that the denialist project is to rehabilitate Nazism. Removing the Holocaust from the equation allows deniers to draw attention to the "positive" aspects of National Socialism (Alexander, 2001: 454; Miller, 1995). Another motivation for some deniers is to discredit Israel. Claiming that Israel was built on a lie is a way for some Middle Eastern leaders to justify strong anti-Israel policies, which help to deflect public attention away from their own despotic practices and ensure domestic support for their continued rule.

SOURCE: Schain, Zolberg, and Hossay (eds) (2002); MacDonald (2008).

KEY POINTS

- Fascists reject abstract intellectualizing in favour of action.
- Fascism is best understood in terms of its oppositional mentality.
- Central fascist themes are the state's role in creating meaning for individuals, and an elitist view of humans.
- In Germany, belief in the superiority of some humans took on a strong racial dimension, to the extent that Nazi Germany was known as the "racial state."
- Neo-Nazism emerged as a problem in Europe and North America in the 1960s.
- Holocaust denial has had two main goals: rehabilitating the Nazi state (and Hitler) and discrediting Israel.

Anarchism

Anarchism has many similarities with the liberal and socialist traditions. Whether it has had any lasting impact on the development of modern politics is questionable, however. Anarchist thought dates back to the nineteenth century and has come in a number of varieties, although it is most closely associated with the socialist tradition (Goodwin, 2007: 151). Anarchists such as Pierre-Joseph Proudhon (1809–65), Mikhail Bakunin (1814–76), and Peter Kropotkin (1842–1921) were all involved in the socialist International, regularly engaging in debate, and falling out, with Marx.

What anarchists share is their abhorrence of the state, which they regard as an illegitimate, even criminal, organization, illegitimately exercising force over individuals and society, and reducing the liberty of the people. But what do anarchists actually oppose? Is it just the state, or is it the state, government, and any form of authority structure? If the latter, then anarchism takes an optimistic view of human nature. In fact, though, anarchist thinkers have differing views on this topic. Some say that human nature is intrinsically good; others, that it is socially determined and can be shaped by the social and political environment. Whatever the exact form of the theory, anarchists all tend to argue that in an anarchist society, the people will be morally correct and do what is required of them.

Compared to the other ideologies we have considered, anarchism has had little influence on modern politics. Strong anarchist movements existed between the 1880s and the 1930s, and anarchists briefly held power during the Spanish Civil War (Vincent, 1995: 117). Since then, anarchist tendencies have appeared in the 1960s counter-culture, student protest movements and, more recently, in the environmental and anti-globalization movements. Nevertheless, it has remained a peripheral ideology, tainted (however unjustly) with the charge that it is a recipe for confusion and chaos.

Conclusion

In this chapter we have examined a variety of traditional ideologies. Clearly, they have exercised an extraordinary influence on world politics, though not always in the way their adherents intended. Indeed, such has been the negative impact of at least some of them that since the middle of the twentieth century, political theorists have been much more circumspect about offering the kind of overarching interpretations of the world, or "meta narratives," that ideologies traditionally offered.

Ideologies have become much less ambitious and much less certain. We will discuss the ideologies that have emerged in this different climate—such as **postmodernism** and environmentalism—in the next chapter. For now, we will simply note that it is easy to see why these new ideologies have become more important in recent years. The twenty-first century, unlike the nineteenth, is deeply skeptical about the ability of human beings to master the world; therefore we are much more cautious about universal ideologies that proclaim to understand the world and how to put it right.

? **KEY QUESTIONS**

- What is an ideology?
- Does new liberalism develop or depart from classical liberalism?

- What are the core principles of liberalism?
- Is modern social democracy socialist?
- Is socialism utopian and authoritarian?
- To what extent can conservatism be considered an ideology?
- Is nationalism an ideology?
- Did fascism die with Hitler and Mussolini?
- Assess the claim that fascism is concerned more with political action than political ideas.
- Is anarchism naive and unrealistic?

📖 FURTHER READING

Bellamy, R. (2000). *Rethinking Liberalism*. London: Pinter.
  A collection of essays on the development of liberal thought by a noted scholar.

Browning, Christopher (1992). *The Path to Genocide: Essays on Launching the Final Solution*. Cambridge: Cambridge University Press.
  A highly detailed and skillfully executed account of the rise of Nazism and the Holocaust.

Freeden, Michael (1996). *Ideologies and Political Theory*. Oxford: Oxford University Press.
  This monumental work not only covers ideology in depth but also offers an innovative way of thinking about them.

Goodwin, B. (2007). *Using Political Ideas*. 5th edn. Chichester: John Wiley & Sons.
  An excellent introduction to the ideologies discussed in this chapter

MacDonald, David B. (2008). *Identity Politics in the Age of Genocide: The Holocaust and Historical Representation*. London: Routledge.

O'Sullivan, N. (1976). *Conservatism*. London.
  A well-regarded account of conservative thought.

Wright, A. (1996). *Socialisms: Old and New*. 2nd edn. London: Routledge.
  Reflects the diversity of socialist thought.

📱 WEB LINKS

plato.stanford.edu/entries/liberalism/
  On liberalism and its varieties.

www.kirkcenter.org/burke/ebsa.html
  On Edmund Burke's conservatism.

www.nationalismproject.org
  The key site on nationalism, with case studies, book reviews, and discussion.

specialcollections.library.wisc.edu/exhibits/Fascism/Intro.html
  On life under fascism in Italy.

www.publiceye.org/eyes/whatfasc.html
  A discussion of contemporary fascism with links to articles.

www.anarchistfaq.org
  On anarchism.

Challenges to the Dominant Ideologies

6

CHAPTER OVERVIEW

This chapter explores a variety of more contemporary ideologies, most of which represent direct challenges to the traditional ideologies discussed in Chapter 5. Many of them doubt the ability of any ideology to provide an overarching explanation of the world. This is not surprising, since they emerged amid the catastrophic consequences of some traditional ideologies. Some of them emphasize respect for difference and diversity, recognizing the importance of powerful identity groups based on gender, culture, and ethnicity. In addition, environmentalism raises questions regarding the sustainability of our industrialized, consumerist way of life.

The End of History?

The neoconservative theorist Francis Fukuyama first explored the "end of history" thesis in 1989, in an essay entitled "The End of History?" By the time he published the book based on that essay (*The End of History and the Last Man*) in 1992, the question mark had disappeared. Ideological struggle was over, Fukuyama argued, because the ideals of liberalism had spread throughout the world and now stood unchallenged. Understood in the context of the **Cold War**, where the key ideological battle was between communism and liberalism, the thesis has some merit. Daniel Bell (1960) had famously declared the "end of ideology," meaning that the challenge of socialism was dead, at least in Western Europe. With the collapse of communism in Eastern Europe, which occurred very soon after the original essay appeared, the ideals of the market and individual freedom quickly established themselves in its place.

Fukuyama interpreted these events to mean that the ideological narrative of liberalism had displaced its communist rival. As we saw in the introduction to the present book, however, this interpretation underestimates the degree of political and institutional variety in the world. Another interpretation is that history can no longer be understood in the terms of the grand ideological artefacts that sought to explain the past, present, and future, and saw the human condition as one of unremitting progress (Gamble, 2000: 20–3). Given the history of the twentieth century, such scepticism is not surprising.

State Dept Image/4 May 2011

PHOTO 6.1 The US Department of State uses its Office of Broadcast Services to promote the merits of American-style democracy and diplomacy to people in other parts of the world. In the wake of the wars in Iraq and Afghanistan, the US is no longer as popular abroad as it once was.

◀ Kenza Drider of Avignon travelled to Paris to demonstrate against the ban on the public wearing of the niqab on the day the law came into effect in April 2011 (Pascal Le Segretain/Getty Images).

The experience of Soviet-style communism appeared to demonstrate the futility of attempting to organize complex societies according to an ideological system.

The contemporary ideologies explored in this chapter should be seen in the context of growing scepticism about the utility of the "modern" ideologies rooted in the **Enlightenment**. **Postmodernism** offers the most fundamental challenge to modernism, questioning the idea that any single ideology can encompass all facets of the social and political worlds. Postmodernism celebrates difference, accepting the subjective nature of political ideologies. For postmodernists there are, in the words of Andrew Gamble (2000: 116), "no foundations, no objective standards, no fixed points, above all no universalism and no knowledge which is not constructed and relative."

Similarly, much modern feminism rejects monolithic value systems and considers the differences between men and women to be politically important. We also explore the politics of difference in the context of multiculturalism, as a potential antidote to the ethnic nationalism discussed in the previous chapter. Another contemporary ideology, environmentalism, reflects a growing scepticism about the desirability of human efforts to master and control nature. They question both the goal of dominating nature and the end results of those efforts. Finally, the idea that liberal values are now dominant in the world as a whole is clearly at odds with the political and social importance of religious fundamentalism, which—regardless of belief system—is very different from the largely **secular** Enlightenment ideologies we looked at in the previous chapter.

See Chapter 5, p. 107, for a discussion of ethnic nationalism.

KEY POINTS

- Contemporary ideologies challenge the metanarrative character of traditional ideologies.
- Traditional ideologies are regarded as too homogeneous and certain in their orientation.

Postmodernism

For many theorists postmodernism is not an ideology itself but a critique of ideologies, or at least of particular types of ideology. Thus some major accounts of ideologies (Vincent, 1995; Heywood, 2007; Goodwin, 2007; Hoffman and Graham, 2006) do not feature separate chapters on postmodernism. "Postmodern" is a label attached to a wide variety of theories in a wide variety of disciplines, not just in the social sciences but also in art, architecture, and cultural studies. It is also associated with a wide variety of academics and authors, although the two with the biggest impact on political theory have been Michel Foucault and Jacques Derrida (1930–2004). It is difficult to provide one all-embracing definition of postmodernism, as the term encompasses so many different emphases and nuances. At the very least, though, the postmodern approach recognizes that the limitations inherent in any supposed "master narrative." In that sense, postmodernism is a direct challenge to the modernist approach.

See Chapter 16, p. 331, for a discussion of postmodernism's contribution to international relations.

The Enlightenment had a clear influence on modernism's belief in the omnipotence of reason: the confidence (shared by all modernist ideologies except conservatism) in the ability of reason to penetrate to the essential truth of things and to achieve progress; and the belief, based on the natural sciences, that "a real world exists independently of our knowledge of it" (Stoker and Marsh, 2002: 11). Postmodernism, by contrast, suggests that the search for ultimate answers is futile: the world is too diverse and fractured to be captured by any grand explanatory scheme or theory. Instead, difference and variety should

6

be celebrated. At the same time, postmodernism promotes an "anti-foundationalist ontology" according to which the world cannot be objectively observed but is socially constructed in a variety of ways. See **Box 6.1.**

KEY CONCEPT BOX 6.1
Ontology, Epistemology, and Foundationalism

An ontology describes what we think there is to know about the world, while epistemology asks what can we know about what exists. A key ontological question is whether there is an objectively observable "real world" out there that is separate from our knowledge of it. Such a question cannot be answered by collecting "facts." Whereas foundationalists argue that there is an observable real world and set about trying to understand it, "anti-foundationalists" argue that the world is socially constructed and therefore focus on understanding that process of social construction.

For some theorists of postmodernism the term merely identifies the historical period that has followed the age of **modernity**. In other words, postmodernism is not a **normative** theory; it simply describes the world as it is, increasingly fractured and uncertain. In politics, for instance, the homogeneous Soviet bloc in Eastern Europe has collapsed and been replaced by a plurality of democratic regimes. Similarly in the West, regimented class politics, in which voting behaviour was largely determined by class, has declined significantly. There is now room for a greater plurality of issues, such as environmentalism and feminism; voting behaviour is more individualistic, and electoral choices are determined by a wider array of factors. The decline in class politics is, in part, a product of the decline in manufacturing industry and the rise of a greater variety of employment patterns, marking the end of the **Fordist** era; see **Box 6.2.**

Postmodernism is also associated with relativism: no political or moral commitment is absolute. Clearly, this position goes against much of what we have been trying to do in the opening few chapters of this book. A postmodernist would probably reject the effort to build a rational case for democracy or freedom, or to decide between the liberty claims of liberalism against the equality claims of socialism. The postmodern outlook discourages

---

KEY CONCEPT BOX 6.2
Fordism

Named after the American auto manufacturer and innovator Henry Ford (1863–1947), Fordism is a form of large-scale mass-production that is homogeneous in terms of both the products made and the repetitive jobs that it requires workers to perform. The social structure that came with Fordism consisted mainly of unionized blue-collar workers who lived similar life-styles and tended to vote en bloc for left-of-centre parties. We are now supposedly in a "post-Fordist" era, in which the manual working class has declined and a more varied economic structure, based on global service industries, has emerged.

commitment, and for this reason it is often criticized as destructive. According to Hay (2002: 217), part of the problem is that "by confining itself to deconstruction post-modernism never risks exposing itself to a similar critique by putting something in place of that it deconstructs." In other words, postmodernism is seen as simply opposing what is around us, without offering any solutions or alternative visions of the world to take its place. According to Gamble (2000: 116), it offers "no guidance as to what should be done about all the modernist processes which are in full flow."

We see two responses to this charge. First, we can say that the deconstruction in post-modernism is a valid corrective to the illegitimate "certainties" so common in modernist political analysis. It is not the postmodernist's fault that the world is not as modernists depict it; indeed, postmodernism may give us a more realistic picture of how the world works. In addition, we should be wary of oversimplifying and making postmodernism out to be concerned only with opposing the world as it is. Hay (2002: 226) argues that postmodernism can be understood in a more sympathetic way, as questioning existing beliefs in a sceptical fashion, rather than ruling them out completely. Indeed, he proposes that "postmodernism is perhaps best seen as a heightened sensitivity to the opinions and worldviews of others—a respect for others and other perspectives."

KEY POINTS

- Postmodernism is not so much an ideology as a critique of particular ideologies.
- The postmodern attitude recognizes the limitations of all master narratives.
- Postmodernism celebrates diversity and difference.
- Postmodernism has been criticized for focusing on deconstruction and not offering any guidance to positive action.

Feminism

Feminism starts from the assumption that the status of women in society is unequal to that of men; therefore women are oppressed in a variety of ways, and this oppression needs to be clearly identified if it is to be eradicated. Feminists generally (and correctly) point out that until recently political theory has either failed to recognize the fact of this oppression or has actively sought to justify it (Pateman, 1988). It has been common since the 1980s to divide academic feminism into liberal, socialist/Marxist, and radical strands, although since then, as Bryson (1999: 8) points out, feminism has been further divided into several different categories, some of which are mentioned below

See Chapter 16, p. 324, for feminism's contribution to international relations.

Liberal Feminism

Liberal feminism is often described as "first wave" feminism in the sense that it was characteristic of feminist thought in the late nineteenth and early twentieth centuries. It argues that women should have the same formal rights as men in the public sphere, where equality is demanded in the worlds of politics and work. Two key liberal feminist texts, advocating political and legal rights for women, are Mary Wollstonecraft's *Vindication of the Rights of Women*, which we have already discussed, and *The Subjection of Women,* by J.S. Mill (possibly co-authored by his wife Harriet Taylor Mill), originally published in 1792 and 1869 respectively.

There is no doubt that substantial ground has been made in securing greater equality for women in the public arena. Women have legal and political rights in Western liberal democracies. After lengthy campaigning by the suffrage movement, women in New Zealand were the first to vote, in 1893, although they could not run for the country's legislature until 1918. Canada and Britain granted women limited voting rights in 1917 and 1918 respectively; Canada extended the vote to all women in 1919, but Britain waited until 1928 before recognizing women's right to vote on the same terms as men. Other **liberal democracies** followed suit; the US enfranchised women in 1920, following passage of the Nineteenth Amendment to the US Constitution.

In the workplace, legislative initiatives against gender discrimination, such as the British Equal Pay Act of 1970, have helped to reduce the pay gap and equalize working conditions. Marriage laws, too, have become more enlightened. Women are no longer regarded as essentially the property of men. However, first-wave feminism did not make it a priority to change the political and economic arenas in which women and men interacted. Rather, it focused on increasing access and representation for women in the world as it then was.

Without doubt, greater strides are needed both in the workplace and in the political arena. Women still lag far behind men when it comes to participation in government (see Tables 6.1 and 6.2). In addition, despite equal pay legislation, women's average earnings remain less than men's, not least because women do different jobs that tend to be valued less. Large numbers of women have part-time and low-paid employment. Moreover, women remain the primary care-givers in many families and as such are often disadvantaged in the workforce. As a result of this continuing inequality, some feminists argue for the introduction of **positive discrimination** to redress the unfair competition between men and women.

Liberal feminists, though, still regard the state as the "proper and indeed the only legitimate authority for enforcing justice in general and women's rights in particular" (Jaggar, 1983: 200). Thus they argue for the elimination of sexist attitudes in society through education, and the application of pressure on the state through interest representation and political parties.

TABLE 6.1 The Political Representation of Women in British Government, 1992–2001

Government Office-Holding 1992, 1997 and 2001					
Election	Governing party	Office	Women	Men	Women as % of total
1992	Conservative	Cabinet	2	20	9
		Junior Minister	5	62	7
1997	Labour	Cabinet	5	17	22
		Junior Minister	14	56	20
2001	Labour	Cabinet	7	16	30
		Junior Minister	23	44	34

SOURCE: Duncan Sutherland and Yvonne Galligan, Centre for Advancement of Women in Politics, Queen's University Belfast. www.qub.ac.uk/cawp/UKelectionhtmls/elec-shuffle.html

Second-Wave Feminism

Second-wave feminism is a relatively recent development, dating from the 1960s. It has taken many forms, but they all emphasize that the exploitation of women is more central and universal than liberal feminists think. In other words, the problem is not merely one of inequality in the public realm: it is the nature of the public realm itself, which is seen to be "patriarchal" and therefore antithetical to the real interests of women. Patriarchy exists not only in the public realm but also in family life and in relationships between men and women at all levels of society; see **Box 6.3**. In short, men's oppression of women is all-pervading (Millett, 1971). Therefore second-wave feminists argue that "it is not equality that women should want, but liberation" (Hoffman and Graham, 2006: 329).

Some second-wave feminists emphasize the sexual repression of women under **patriarchy**, arguing that women have been effectively "castrated" by a patriarchal culture that requires them to be passive and submissive. This was the theme of Germaine Greer's book *The Female Eunuch*, published in 1970. Women have also suffered physical injury and even death at the hands of patriarchal societies, not least in the practices of female circumcision in Africa and the Islamic world and female infanticide in China and India (Goodwin, 2007: 213–14).

TABLE 6.2 Political Representation of Women in Parliaments, 2011

Rank	Country	Lower or Single House				Upper House or Senate			
		Elections	Seats	Women	% W	Elections	Seats	Women	% W
1	Rwanda	09 2008	80	45	56.38	09 2011	26	10	34.6
2	Andorra	04 2011	28	14	50.0	-	-	-	-
3	Cuba	01 2008	586	265	45.2	-	-	-	-
4	Sweden	09 2010	349	156	44.7	-	-	-	-
5	Seychelles	09 2011	32	14	43.8	-	-	-	-
6	Finland	04 2011	200	85	42.5	-	-	-	-
7	South Africa*	04 2009	400	169	42.3	04 2009	53	17	32.1
8	Netherlands	11 2006	150	55	36.7	05 2007	75	26	34.7
9	Nicaragua	11 2011	92	37	40.2	-	-	-	-
10	Iceland	04 2009	63	25	39.7	-	-	-	-
40	Canada	05 2011	307	76	24.8	N/A	98	36	36.7
53	United Kingdom	05 2010	650	145	22.37	N/A	827	181	21.9
68	United States *	11 2010	434	73	16.8	11 2010	100	17	17.0

*South Africa: The figures on the distribution of seats do not include the 36 special rotating delegates appointed on an ad hoc basis, and all percentages given are therefore calculated on the basis of the 54 permanent seats.
*United States of America: The total refers to all voting members of the House.

SOURCE: Inter-Parliamentary Union. www.ipu.org/wmn-e/classif.htm

Whereas Marxist feminists (see below) consider patriarchy to be a product of the organization of economic classes in the capitalist system, second-wave feminists regard it as an independent explanatory variable rooted in biology. This gender-based sphere of domination, they argue, is largely ignored by conventional political theory in its focus on the state. As Carole Pateman (1989: 3) points out, "the public sphere," in conventional political theory "is assumed to be capable of being understood on its own, as if it existed . . . independently of private sexual relations and domestic life." By upholding patriarchal domination in families and **civil society**, the state contributes to gender-based oppression. MacKinnon (1989: 80) puts this eloquently when she writes:

> However autonomous of class the liberal state may appear, it is not autonomous of sex. Male power is systemic. Coercive, legitimized, and epistemic, it is the regime.

The feminist project, therefore, is to ensure that this form of oppression is understood and eliminated. Only then can the state be made equally representative for both men and women.

KEY QUOTE BOX 6.3
Kate Millett on Patriarchy

What goes largely unexamined, often even unacknowledged . . . in our social order, is the birthright priority whereby males rule females. . . . It is one which tends moreover to be sturdier than any form of segregation, and more rigorous than class stratification. . . . However muted its present appearance may be, sexual dominion obtains nevertheless as perhaps the most pervasive ideology of our culture and provides its most fundamental concept of power (Millett, 1971: 25).

Race, Class, and Feminism

A number of feminist criticisms have been directed at second-wave feminism. One is that in politicizing all aspects of our lives, it displays a **totalitarian** tendency to hold "feminists . . . accountable to their 'sisters' for every aspect of their behaviour" (Bryson, 1999: 28). Another is that it falsely creates an image of women as helpless victims and men as their enemies, thus undervaluing what women have achieved and reducing the likelihood that men will support feminism (Jaggar, 1983: 115).

Perhaps the most important critique is that second-wave feminism has a tendency to ignore the oppression of women based on race and class. In terms of the former, it has been argued that feminism has universalized the experiences of white (usually middle class) women, neglecting the specific oppression that women of colour have been subject to. It must be recognized that the particular life experiences of African, Indian, Asian, and Middle Eastern women cannot be subsumed under one all-encompassing feminist critique.

In terms of class, Marxist and socialist feminists put a different slant on women's exploitation (Mitchell, 1971; Barrett, 1988). The reality is that capitalism exploits working-class people regardless of gender, but particularly working-class women, whom (they say) feminists

PHOTO 6.2 Women often bear a much larger share of the burden for raising children and supporting the household than men do. Here women in Timor-Leste comb a garbage dump for metal cans to sell, 2009.

often ignore. Socialist feminists argue that a transformation of society is required to improve working life for men and women alike and ensure that domestic life ceases to have an economic function. This will necessarily involve changing the state so that it has a central role to play in improving women's lives.

Marxist feminists are less sanguine than socialist feminists about the prospect that the state can be relied on to improve women's position. One influential version of the Marxist theory of the state holds that women's domestic labour serves a crucial function in the capitalist economy because it frees men to work. Thus the capitalist system has an interest in ensuring that women remain subservient to men (McIntosh, 1978).

See Chapter 2, p. 57, for an exploration of Marxist ideas on power and the state.

Varieties of Feminism

Between liberal and second-wave feminism and even within the second wave itself, there have been many divisions. One major issue has been the importance of biological differences. While Firestone (1972) regards these differences as the source of women's oppression, Pateman (1989) rejects this position as "implicitly accept[ing] the patriarchal claim that women's subordination is decreed by nature" and argues that biology, in itself, is neither oppressive nor liberating; [it] becomes either a source of subjection or free creativity for women only because it has meaning within specific social relationships (Pateman 1989: 126).

Other feminists focus their efforts on ensuring that women have the right to control their own bodies. Some feminists have violently opposed pornography (Dworkin, 1981), while others (notably liberal feminists) have sought to reclaim it for women (McElroy, 1995).

Finally, it is worth noting that some feminists have embraced elements of postmodern theory, in part because postmodernism's celebration of difference encourages recognition of women's particular roles and values as equally important to those of men, as well as appreciation of the differences among women based on class, race, and culture.

KEY POINTS

- Feminism starts from the assumption that women's position in society is subordinate to that of men.
- Liberal feminism focuses on the public sphere, seeking to ensure that women enjoy the same formal rights that men do.
- Although significant progress has been made in the securing of legal and political rights for women, serious inequalities remain.
- Socialist feminists insist that more attention should be paid to working-class women, whose plight is inextricably linked to the capitalist system.
- Second-wave feminists seeks to focus attention on patriarchal relationships in the private sphere.
- Feminist thought has been fragmented by divisions over many issues, including objectives and political strategy.

Environmentalism

Concern for the natural environment is not new. Legislation designed to control pollution dates back to the nineteenth century, and there are earlier examples. As a distinctive political issue, however, the environment was not a focus of attention until the 1970s, and it did not become a mainstream issue for another decade. The rise of environmentalism is partly a consequence of severe environmental problems, including air pollution, the use of pesticides in agriculture, the depletion of non-renewable resources, the extinction of many species of plants and animals, and the problems of ozone depletion and climate change. International gatherings such as Stockholm Conference of 1972 and the Earth Summit held in Rio de Janeiro twenty years later helped to establish the state of the environment as a key issue of our time. Meetings in Kyoto, Japan, in 1997 attempted to tackle the problems of global warming. Later conferences in Copenhagen and Mexico City have so far produced few concrete agreements, let alone results.

Ideologically, environmental thought can be divided into two main categories. On the one hand is the reformist approach (sometimes described as light green or shallow environmentalism). On the other is the radical (dark green or deep) approach. For some political theorists only the latter can be properly described as an ideology (Dobson, 2007). To distinguish the two, we might refer to the former as environmentalism and the latter as **ecologism**. Environmentalism can be seen as a single-issue concern not necessarily inconsistent with a range of ideologies such as socialism or liberalism, whereas ecologism is a separate ideology with its own distinct ideas. The differences between the two can be illustrated if we examine their major characteristics.

The Economic Realm

One major distinction between the reformist and radical accounts can be seen in their approaches to economic growth. Radical greens see economic growth as incompatible with environmental protection. The critique of economic growth is in a part a normative claim to the effect that individuals would lead much more fulfilled lives in a non-materialistic society. Above all, though, it makes the empirical claim that there are natural limits to growth, and that unless production and consumption levels and population size are reduced to sustainable levels, the result will be economic and political collapse.

This empirical claim received its impetus from a report by a group of American scientists that was published as *The Limits to Growth* (Meadows, 1972). The report was based on a series of computer models showing the consequences of population and economic growth while factoring in potential solutions to a variety of environmental problems. In each case, the authors argued, there was a need to cut economic growth to slow down environmental degradation. They concluded that if economic activity was not curtailed, then the point of no return would be reached not far into the twenty-first century.

There have been many criticisms of the *Limits to Growth* report (Martell, 1994: 33–40). Not least, some suggest that there is no necessary trade-off between economic growth and environmental protection. Reformist critics argue that as long as growth is sustainable, then it is permissible from an environmental perspective. Sustainable development is therefore the centrepiece of a reformist alternative. There have been numerous definitions of **sustainable development.** The best-known defines it as development that "meets the needs of the present generation without compromising the ability of future generations to meet their own needs" (World Commission on Environment and Development, 1987).

As a concept, however, sustainable development is often vague. A more precise formulation is the principle known as **ecological modernization** (Hajer, 1997) which suggests a number of scenarios in which growth could be sustainable. First, growth need not depend on the use of non-renewable resources such as coal and gas. The use of renewable energy, such as wind, wave, and even nuclear power, coupled with energy conservation, could help to ensure that growth remains sustainable. Second, the production of environmental goods—such as catalytic converters for cars or scrubs for removing the pollution from power stations—can itself be a source of economic growth. Finally, environmental damage is not cost-free economically: thus there are strong economic reasons to protect the environment. This was the major finding of a 2006 British government report on climate change, which estimated that if temperatures rise by 5°C, up to 10 per cent of global output could be lost, and the poorest countries would lose more than 10 per cent of their output.

The Philosophical Realm

Reformists take an **anthropocentric** (human-centred) view of the world; see **Box 6.4**. Thus from their point of view the value of **non-human** nature is extrinsic to humans:

KEY CONCEPT BOX 6.4
Anthropocentrism

Anthropocentrism is a human-centred ethic according to which only humans have intrinsic value; non-humans have only extrinsic value. It is challenged by those who consider non-human animals to merit moral consideration because of their sentiency, and also by eco-centric thinkers who believe that all of nature should have moral standing.

CASE STUDY
Whaling and Environmental Ethics

Whaling provides an interesting case study of environmental ethics in action. When the International Whaling Commission (IWC) was set up by the whaling nations (most notably Japan, Norway, and Iceland) in 1946, its purpose was to protect whale stocks so that they could continue to be hunted. The motivation behind this move, then, was clearly anthropocentric. Whales were regarded as a human resource with only extrinsic value.

Protecting whales became an important part of the environmental movement in the 1970s. The symbolism of Greenpeace activists risking their lives by sailing close to whaling ships in order to obtain documentary evidence had a significant impact on Western public opinion. By the 1980s, the whaling nations were outnumbered at deliberations of the IWC, and in 1986 commercial whaling was put under a moratorium in an effort to prevent a number of whale species from becoming extinct. Since then, the whaling nations, consistent with their ethical position, have argued that whale stocks have recovered and therefore commercial whaling should be allowed to resume. The nations opposing the hunt follow a very different ethic. With the backing of public opinion, they object to whaling not because it is unsustainable, but because the practice is cruel and damages the interests of whales. In other words, they regard whales as having intrinsic value that should be taken into account. Since the two sides are arguing past each other, the debate is unlikely to be resolved amicably.

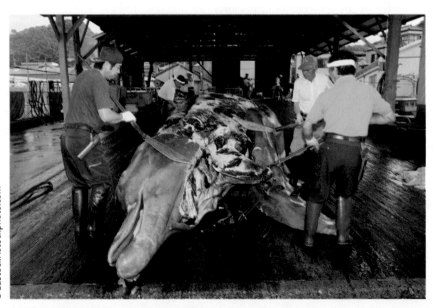

© EdStock/istockphoto.com

PHOTO 6.3 Japanese whalers with a Baird's beaked whale in 2003. Although the IWC banned the commercial hunt in 1986, Japanese whaling operations continue under the guise of scientific research. Iceland and Norway also continue whaling despite the ban.

it has no real value in our social world. We protect the environment because it is in our interests to do so, not because we think that nature has any worthwhile interests of its own. Some radical greens, by contrast, embrace an **ecocentric** ethic (Leopold, 1949; Fox, 1995; Eckersley, 1992) that recognizes intrinsic value both in humans and in non-human nature. In other words, they believe that nature has moral worth independent of human beings.

The difficulties of philosophically justifying an ecocentric ethic are considerable from the perspective of the European traditions we have discussed so far. For many philosophers sentiency—the capacity to experience pain and pleasure—is the benchmark for moral standing. It's easy to believe that damage to the interests of a human or other animal matters to that individual, less easy to believe that damage to a tree matters to the tree. Clearly it is possible to harm a tree's interests, but, as Frey argues (1983: 154–5), it does not seem sensible to talk about wronging the tree. Thus to pollute a river is to harm it, but since it has only extrinsic value, it cannot be wronged: only those sentient beings who benefit from the river can be wronged by polluting it.

The key question seems to be whether it is necessary to establish an ecocentric ethic in order to protect the environment. Increasingly, green thinkers argue that there are sufficient prudential grounds for protecting nature (Barry, 1999). For example, we should protect forests because it is in our interests to do so—not least because they provide crucial sinks for carbon dioxide and therefore help to control rises in the temperature of the planet. The question of whether they have intrinsic value is not relevant. See the case study on whaling.

The Political Realm

There is now a considerable body of green political thought (Dobson, 2007). Reformists believe that environmental problems can be solved within existing political structures, while radicals argue that far-reaching social and political changes are required. Many radical greens have advocated decentralized, small-scale, self-sufficient anarchist-type communities linked together by loose authority structures (Schumacher, 1973; Bookchin, 1971). Although a loose alliance of such communities might be able to reduce or eliminate large-scale industrial production, bring people closer to nature, and facilitate political participation and social cohesion, some green thinkers have questioned the environmental utility of this approach (Goodin, 1992). International agreements are difficult enough to achieve in the existing state system, even though are recognized as essential for effective environmental protection; it seems unlikely that a variety of small, self-governing communities would be able to ensure effective coordination.

Finally, in the political realm, critics raise the question of **agency**. Which social class or grouping is most likely to bring about change? Various candidates have been suggested, ranging from the middle class (Porritt, 1984) to the unemployed (Gorz, 1985). The issue of agency is linked to questions of justice, since those worst affected by environmental degradation are the very same people one might expect to campaign for action to deal with it. This is the rationale of the environmental justice movement. Of course, justice remains separate from practical politics, and this is particularly the case for ecocentric thinkers who attach moral worth to non-human life that is unable to secure its own liberation.

A Distinct Ideology?

Does radical environmentalism or ecologism represent a distinct ideology, separate from the other ideologies we have considered? A quick glance at the literature reveals that thinkers representing a number of traditional ideological positions have sought to ally those positions with environmentalism. Thus there are works of eco-socialism (Pepper, 1993), eco-liberalism (Wissenburg, 1993), and eco-feminism (Mellor, 1982). There has even been an attempt to claim the green label for fascism (Bramwell, 1989).

On the other hand, the existence of Green political parties throughout the world suggests that ecologists regard their position as distinct. Clearly, the limits to growth position adds an extra dimension to political thinking. In particular, it challenges the optimistic notion, shared by liberals, socialists, and Marxists, that humans can master their environment for their own infinite economic ends. Similarly distinct is the ecocentric ethic adopted by some radical greens. All traditional ideologies are anthropocentric, regarding the natural world as a resource for humans to exploit.

Aboriginality and Green Ideals

Green approaches to the natural world often recall Aboriginal traditions that stress the interconnected and cyclical nature of life. For example, some Canadian green theorists draw attention to the Anishinaabe teaching that we should always think in terms of seven generations: contemplating the consequences of our actions seven generations into the future (Borrows 2008: 9). Time is understood to move be circular; thus there is no expectation of evolution towards some utopian future (Graveline, 1998: 59). Kidwell, Noley, and Tinker posit that the primary symbolic paradigm of indigenous individuality and community is the circle, "a polyvalent symbol signifying the family, the clan, the tribe, and eventually all of creation." The core teaching of the circle is equality. "No relative is valued more than any other. A chief is not valued above the people; nor are humans valued above the animal nations, the birds, even the trees and rocks." Because circles have neither beginning nor end, "There is no hierarchy in our cultural context, even of species. . . . all the createds participate together, each in [its] own way, to preserve the wholeness of the circle" Thus "American Indians are driven by their culture and spirituality to recognize the personhood of all things in creation" (Kidwell et al., 2001: 47, 50).

Justice Murray Sinclair—chair of the Truth and Reconciliation Commission charged with documenting the experiences of those affected by Canada's infamous Indian Residential School system—has underlined a fundamental difference between his people and those of European background when it comes to perceptions of "one's relationship with the Creator." The classic Judeo-Christian belief that humans occupy an exalted position "just below God and the angels, but above all other earthly creation" is anathema to Aboriginal traditions, according to which human beings are the least powerful and least important element in creation. They cannot influence events, and are disrespectful and unrealistic if they try. Human interests are not to be placed above those of any other part of creation (Sinclair, 1994: 22–3).

In short, indigenous and Western perceptions of the "relative hierarchy and importance of being in creation" (Sinclair, 1994: 23) are at opposite ends of the spectrum, with indigenous peoples focused on living in harmony with the natural world of which humans are but a small part, and Western traditions stressing human domination of the natural world from which they are separate.

Because they see humans as part of the natural world, Aboriginal traditions maintain that humans can tap into its power, but only through careful study and constant respect. As Graveline (1998: 53) explains it, "Power is understood as all-pervasive and consistent. Through knowledge of it, we can come to understand it and thus utilize it to advantage." Understood in this way, knowledge of the natural world is a kind of power in itself. As humans we depend on this natural power, whether or not we choose to acknowledge it (Graveline, 1998: 53–5)

Daniel Wildcat expresses a similar view. The "holistic or complex integrative thinking" promoted by Aboriginal traditions offers a useful complement to Western thought. Indigenous perspectives "promote problem solving and action outside the dualisms and dichotomies that so typify the Western worldview—for example, material versus spiritual, science versus religion, objective versus subjective, nature versus culture, and so on" (Wildcat, 2009: 301). "Indigenous knowledge" systems go back thousands of years and can help us gain insight into both the natural world and our place in it.

KEY POINTS

- The rise of environmentalism is in part a reflection of the severity of the environmental problems in the world today.
- Environmental thinkers can be divided into two camps: reformist and radical.
- In economic terms, reformists support "sustainable development," whereas radicals argue that growth cannot be sustained indefinitely: if humans do not voluntarily limit development, natural limits will be imposed, with disastrous consequences.
- In philosophic terms, the reformist ethic is anthropocentric, while the radical ethic is ecocentric. In political terms, radicals advocate far-reaching change while the reformist position can coexist with a variety of ideologies.
- Aboriginal thought holds that humans are interconnected with the natural world, and that we have a duty to consider the impact of our actions on generations to come.

Multiculturalism

Multiculturalism has emerged as a direct challenge to nationalist demands for states based exclusively on ethnicity. The traditional model of **citizenship**, associated above all with the work of T.H. Marshall (1950), emphasized the need to "promote a . . . common national identity among citizens" (Kymlicka, 2002: 327). By contrast, the multicultural model advocates pluralistic states encompassing many different religious, cultural, and ethnic identities. Multiculturalism has become a particularly pressing issue, in theory and in practice, precisely because modern societies are becoming increasingly multicultural in a literal sense. We will consider two key questions here. First, what is the correct ideological location for multiculturalism? Second, is it a positive or negative phenomenon?

Multiculturalism and Ideology

From a theoretical perspective, multiculturalism is often associated with **communitarianism**. As we saw in Chapter 1, communitarianism focuses on group rights, identity,

See Chapter 1, p. 39, for a discussion of communitarianism.

and community cohesion; hence it poses a direct challenge to the liberal focus on the autonomous individual. As Will Kymlicka (2002: 337) points out, "Communitarians . . . view multiculturalism as an appropriate way of protecting communities from the eroding effects of individual autonomy, and of affirming the value of community,"

This opposition between multiculturalism and liberalism might seem somewhat odd. From the beginning, liberals have emphasized freedom, religious toleration, and state neutrality with respect to competing conceptions of the good. These principles all seem to suggest that liberals would support minority rights and multiculturalism. It is not surprising, therefore, that, since the 1960s, liberals have sought to accommodate multiculturalism.

However, accommodation presents problems for liberals when the minority cultural rights they want to uphold would require the violation of individual rights. It would be difficult for liberals to sanction practices such as forced marriage or female genital mutilation. These are of course extreme examples, and stereotypical ones at that. But they are issues often raised by critics of multiculturalism, and it is worth considering how liberals deal with them.

One way out of the dilemma is to offer limited support for multiculturalism, affirming it only when it does not infringe on individual rights (Kymlicka, 2002: 340–1). Rawls (1993) argues for only a "reasonable pluralism"; thus he does not require liberals to accept a practice such as slavery as morally legitimate. Kymlicka (1995) goes further than Rawls in promoting multiculturalism, arguing that the degree to which we should expect a minority group to assimilate depends on how it came to be part of the society: people who have chosen to immigrate should be prepared to adapt, whereas indigenous peoples who have not chosen to be cultural minorities, such as Canada's First Nations, New Zealand's Maori or Australia's Aborigines and Torres Strait Islanders, should have differentiated rights, even when they conflict with liberal principles. In Canada, Australia, and New Zealand, the key issue here is that indigenous peoples had pre-existing rights before the colonizers came, thus giving them a distinct legal status which other groups cannot claim.

Kymlicka has some supporters, but other theorists argue that multiculturalism and liberalism cannot be reconciled. Thus the political theorist Brian Barry (2001) rejects multiculturalism as a threat to liberal values. On the other hand, some political theorists argue that the liberal multiculturalism of those such as Rawls and Kymlicka is heavily weighted toward liberalism, and that a convincing multiculturalism would have to transcend the liberal objection to the infringement of individual rights. Parekh (2000), for instance, argues that we should adopt a much more pluralistic morality and be prepared to jettison liberalism when it conflicts with multiculturalism. In effect, he recognizes a separate ideological status for multiculturalism, distinct from both liberalism and communitarianism.

Is Multiculturalism a Good Thing?

A related question is whether multiculturalism is a positive principle that liberal states should adopt. This has become a politically important issue, particularly in the context of 9/11, and the later terrorist attacks carried out in London, Madrid, Bali, and elsewhere. One concern, obviously, is that moral pluralism opens the door to potential infringement of individual rights. Another is the idea that multiculturalism is "corrosive of long-term political unity and social stability" (Kymlicka, 2002: 366); it is for this reason that France insists on assimilation—a policy that has caused serious controversy in the context of religious dress.

KEY QUOTE BOX 6.5

Prime Minister Pierre Trudeau Announces Canada's Multiculturalism Policy (1971)

. . . [T]here cannot be one cultural policy for Canadians of British and French origin, another for the original peoples and yet a third for all others. For although there are two official languages, there is no official culture, nor does any ethnic group take precedence over any other. No citizen or group of citizens is other than Canadian, and all should be treated fairly. . . . The individual's freedom would be hampered if he were locked for life within a particular cultural compartment by the accident of birth or language. It is vital, therefore, that every Canadian, whatever his ethnic origin, be given a chance to learn at least one of the two languages in which his country conducts its official business and its politics.

A policy of multiculturalism within a bilingual framework commends itself to the government as the most suitable means of assuring the cultural freedom of Canadians. Such a policy should help to break down discriminatory attitudes and cultural jealous-ies. National unity if it is to mean anything in the deeply personal sense, must be found-ed on confidence in one's own individual identity; out of this can grow respect for that of others and a willingness to share ideas, attitudes and assumptions. A vigorous policy of multiculturalism will help create this initial confidence. It can form the base of a soci-ety which is based on fair play for all. . . . In implementing [this] policy, the government will provide support in four ways.

First, resources permitting, the government will seek to assist all Canadian cultural groups that have demonstrated a desire and effort to continue to develop a capa-city to grow and contribute to Canada, and a clear need for assistance, the small and weak groups no less than the strong and highly organized. Second, the government will assist members of all cultural groups to overcome cultural barriers to full partici-pation in Canadian society. Third, the government will promote creative encounters and interchange among all Canadian cultural groups in the interest of national unity. Fourth, the government will continue to assist immigrants to acquire at least one of Canada's official languages in order to become full participants in Canadian society (Trudeau, 1971: 8545–8).

SOURCE: Pierre Elliott Trudeau (1971), "Announcement of Implementation of Policy of Multiculturalism Within Bilingual Framework," *House of Commons Debates*, 8 Oct.: 8545–8. http://www.abheritage.ca/albertans/speeches/trudeau.html

On the other hand, multiculturalism is often defended as a way of assimilating people into a national polity by offering them token cultural rights in return for their loyalty to the state and its institutions. In Canada, many Aboriginal peoples reject multiculturalism precisely because the official policy was designed to slowly but steadily assimilate minorities, including themselves, into the mainstream. The same is true of some Muslim immigrants who feel that despite its emphasis on multiculturalism, Canada, like the US, remains a deeply Christian society. What Canadian society should and should not tolerate became a matter of vocal debate in December 2011, when immigration minister Jason Kenney announced that new Canadians would not be allowed to wear the niqab (a face-covering veil) while taking the oath of citizenship. Kenney argued that veiling is a cultural tradition, not a requirement of Islam; that it is contrary to Canadian values of equality; and that it presents a legal difficulty: "I don't know how we can verify that someone whose face is covered is actually taking the oath that the law requires of them." While some people supported this move, others felt that this was an unnecessary affront to Canadian Muslims (Blatchford, 2011).

Furthermore, though some mainstream Westerners may feel that minority cultures are less advanced than their own, this is often little more than xenophobia. Indeed, some Western practices that we take for granted might themselves seem uncivilized or retrograde to other people. For example, Hindus who adhere to a strict vegetarian diet may find Western-style meat consumption offensive and unnatural as well as unhealthy. And many Aboriginal peoples in Canada have strenuously objected to the Alberta oil sands and other environmentally dubious projects designed for short-term economic gain. The idea that Western society has nothing to learn (and possibly much to lose) from minorities is arguably a liberal conceit that needs to be critically examined.

In defence of multiculturalism, there is little evidence that it leads to social conflict. Indeed, it might be regarded as a force for social inclusion, since minority groups are

© Stacey Newman/istockphoto.com

PHOTO 6.4 An RCMP officer congratulates a new citizen following a swearing-in ceremony held at the Milton, ON, fairgrounds on Canada Day, 1 July 2011.

more likely to feel accepted in their new societies if they are allowed to continue practising their cultural traditions (Kymlicka, 2002: 367). Moreover, cultural diversity can enrich otherwise homogeneous lives, encourage toleration of difference, and allow individuals to develop a sense of belonging.

Finally, at a time when most Western countries have aging populations, it's also important to recognize that the West's economic future will increasingly depend on new immigrants to work and to pay the taxes required to support their adoptive countries' welfare states.

KEY POINTS

- Multiculturalism promotes pluralistic societies that encompass many different religious, cultural, and ethnic identities.
- Multiculturalism was initially aligned with communitarianism but was eventually adopted by liberals.
- Liberal advocacy of multiculturalism can be problematic if it means accepting illiberal cultural practices.
- Some liberals reject multiculturalism as a threat to liberal rights; some seek to qualify their support; and some, writing from outside of the liberal tradition, argue that liberalism should be sacrificed in favour of multiculturalism.
- Multiculturalism has been criticized as threat to social unity as well as liberal rights. It has also been defended as a means of accommodating diversity and the richness it brings.

Religious Fundamentalism

Religion is not ideological as long as it remains a private concern among individuals and groups. It becomes ideological when it organizes political principles along religious lines and seeks political influence or power in order to achieve it. There are, of course, many times in world history when religion has played a political role, not least in the conflicts between Catholics and Protestants in Europe in the sixteenth and seventeenth centuries.

Since then, however, many societies, influenced by the Lockean principle of religious toleration, have moved to separate the church from the state, not least in the US, where this separation is enshrined in the Constitution. In these secular regimes, religion is a private matter and the state remains neutral between competing faiths, unless one of them infringes on the rights of any citizen. Nevertheless, there are many places where conflict has centred on religion, including Northern Ireland (between Protestants and Catholics), particularly in the 1970s; Iraq (between Sunni and Shia Muslims), since the American and British invasion of 2003; and Darfur in the Sudan (between Muslims and Christians). As Goodwin (2007: 427) notes, "religious differences have, for millennia, led to a waste of human life and to the undermining of the imperatives of human toleration."

The fundamentalist religious groups that emerged in the twentieth century are ideological precisely because they do seek to enter the political realm. To be a fundamentalist is to believe that your doctrine alone is true (in the case of religious groups based on a particular interpretation of a sacred text) and should be the guiding force in your society. Since the 9/11 terrorist attacks, Islamic fundamentalism has received the most media attention, but in earlier periods Basque and Irish Republican terrorism were much more prominent (Schechter, 2003, 115). The political scientist Samuel Huntington argued, in a controversial study during the 1990s, that the world faced by a "clash of civilisations" in which societies upholding Western values are under attack from non-Western civilizations, particularly those dominated by Islam.

Of the seven civilizations that Huntington identified, he argued that the most militaristic and prone to violence was that of Islam, which he held responsible for the majority of both inter- and intra-civilization conflicts in modern history (Huntington, 1997: 256–8). The end of history, it seemed, was little more than wishful thinking. Although Huntington's work was dismissed for its ethnocentric tone and dubious conclusions, his theory of world politics increased in popularity following 9/11.

A number of important caveats need to made about fundamentalism in general, and religious fundamentalism in particular. First, most Muslims, Hindus, Christians, and Jews are tolerant and peaceful, and are content for religion to remain separate from politics. Turkey, for instance, has retained secular political framework created in the 1920s, which has maintained political stability for many decades, even though the governing party today is explicitly Islamic. All religions—Christianity, Islam, Judaism, Hinduism, Sikhism, and even Buddhism—have their fundamentalist elements, although they are generally a minority (Heywood, 2007: 281). For this reason one critique of Huntington has suggested that it would be preferable to talk about a clash between fundamentalist Muslims and fundamentalist Christians rather than a "clash of civilisations" (Ali, 2002).

Many theorists have argued that this clash argument is exaggerated and bears little resemblance to reality. It also downplays internal divisions within Islam, while overplaying conflicts with the West. In the Muslim world, for example, the Sunni–Shia split has often been more significant than the division between Islam and Christianity, and periods of Islamic–Christian cooperation have been significant. This view is most notably advanced by Fawaz Gerges, who has criticized the "clash of civilizations" theory for failing to distinguish between Islamic culture and Islamism's putative hatred of the West. Such essentialist arguments made it nearly impossible to understand that Muslim grievances might have more to do with local conditions or responses to American power than with any hatred of the West as such. Gerges and others also discount the view that the Muslim world should be approached as a homogeneous entity. For example, the eight-year war between Iraq and Iran (1980–8) was motivated in part by the Sunni–Shia split (see MacDonald, 2009: 110).

We might also argue that fundamentalism is not limited to religion—that all ideologies have their fundamentalist elements. The obvious candidates here would be Stalinist communism and fascism in interwar Germany and Italy; but even liberalism can be fundamentalist about its belief in the value of liberty and the idea that it must be protected at all costs.

A defining characteristic of Islamic fundamentalism is its desire to create a theocracy (a regime based on religious principles). It is undoubtedly a potent religious force, particularly in the Middle East and Africa. It received a boost when the Shah of Iran was deposed by a fundamentalist Shia group, led by the Ayatollah Ruhollah Khomeini, in 1979. Following on from the Muslim Brotherhood, formed in Egypt in 1928, a number of new militant Islamic groups have emerged, most notably al-Qaeda (literally "the base"), formed by Osama bin Laden in Afghanistan in 1988 and held responsible for the attacks on the World Trade Center and the Pentagon in 2001.

In some ways Islamic fundamentalism is opposed to modernity. It is anti-democratic and morally conservative, regarding modern Western values as corrupt and licentious.

Nevertheless, it is "best described . . . as a modern movement opposed to modernity" (Hoffman and Graham, 2006: 397). This is because Islamic fundamentalists (and those of the Christian variety too) have not been slow in adopting modern communication technologies such as the Internet to propagate their ideas and mobilize activists. Videos, chat rooms, and online anti-Western video games are just some of the tools Islamic fundamentalist groups have used to attract recruits around the world. It is noticeable, too, that an Islamic regime such as Iran is fully prepared to use the products of scientific research, including nuclear weapons' technology, to defend itself against perceived threats from the West.

Adverse social and economic circumstances, often coupled with the mistakes of Arab dictatorships such as the Ba'athist regimes in Iraq and Syria, have also contributed to the strength of these movements. It has also been claimed that the Islamic terrorist threat has been largely provoked by the actions of the US, which themselves have been influenced by Christian fundamentalism: hence the label "clash of fundamentalisms."

Given that Christianity is the world's biggest religion, it would be surprising if it did not include fundamentalist elements. Christian fundamentalism is particularly associated with the Christian New Right that emerged in the US in the 1970s. There has been a variety of loosely connected groupings, of which perhaps the best known was the Moral Majority, formed by the Reverend Jerry Falwell in 1979 and active through the 1980s. The Christian New Right has campaigned for conservative moral values—particularly against issues such as gay rights and women's right to abortion. Christian fundamentalists have sought to influence Republican politicians, usually through campaign contributions. Fundamentalists gained some measure of influence during the eight years of Ronald Reagan's presidency (1980–8) and again during the tenure of George W. Bush (2000–8), who claimed to be a born-again Christian himself.

KEY POINTS

- Religious fundamentalism seeks to organize politics along religious lines.
- Fundamentalism occurs not only in all religions but, arguably, in all ideologies.
- Religious fundamentalists, both Muslim and Christian, are anti-modernist in that they are morally conservative (and, in the case of the former, anti-democratic), but they are also modernist in that they use modern communication media and campaigning strategies.

Conclusion

The ideologies discussed in Chapter 5 were focused on the state; by contrast, the ideologies discussed in this chapter all represent challenges to the state. This is seen first in the emphasis on the supranational dimension observed, in particular, in environmentalism, multiculturalism, and religious fundamentalism (Hoffman and Graham, 2006: 317–18). All have been affected by **globalization**, a central theme of this book. The new ideologies are also products of social and economic change, in particular the decline of class as a major fault-line in world politics. This has resulted, as Goodwin (2007: 425) notes, in the "rise of ideas and ideologies which transcend classes but focus on other group characteristics such as ethnicity, gender or religion." Finally, environmentalism is a product of the deterioration of the natural environment, which has resulted in an ideological world that, though more dynamic and pluralistic than it was in the past, is also less sure of itself and more open to change.

The final point to note here is that the traditional ideologies we considered in the preceding chapter have responded to the challenges presented by those examined in this one. We have seen, for instance, how liberalism and socialism have contributed to the debates about feminism, environmentalism, and multiculturalism. Indeed, it is not clear whether the latter two do exist as distinct ideologies; they might be more accurately described as particular issues to which the traditional ideologies have responded. All this suggests that the modernist project, though not in perfect health, remains convincing for many people around the world.

? KEY QUESTIONS

- Account for the emergence of challenges to the traditional ideologies.
- What has been the impact of postmodernism on ideologies?
- Has feminism achieved its objectives?
- Does feminism have a theory of the state?
- Is there a distinct ideology of environmentalism?
- How justifiable is a non-anthropocentric ethic?
- Is multiculturalism consistent with liberalism?
- What are the strengths and weaknesses of multiculturalism?
- Under what circumstances does religion become ideological?
- Is modernism dead?

FURTHER READING

Bryson, V. (2003). *Feminist Political Theory: An Introduction.* 2nd edn. Basingstoke: Palgrave.
An excellent introduction.

Dobson, A. (2007). *Green Political Thought.* 4th edn. London: Unwin Hyman.
The standard introduction to the subject.

Gray, J. (2003). *Al Qaeda and What It Means to be Modern.* London: Faber & Faber.
A typically incisive account of religious fundamentalism by a key thinker.

Kymlicka, W. (2002). *Contemporary Political Philosophy.* 2nd edn. Oxford: Oxford University Press.
Chapter 8 covers the multicultural debate in which Kymlicka is a key participant.

Moussalli, A. (ed.) (1998). *Islamic Fundamentalism.* Reading: Ithaca Press.
A good collection of articles by leading experts in the field.

WEB LINKS

www.ipu.org/wmn-e/classif.htm
For information on women's political representation.

www.erraticimpact.com/ecologic/
For a list of environmental links.

http://multiculturalism.aynrand.org/
A website against multiculturalism.

PART II

Comparative Politics

I N MAY 2010 THE British Conservative party returned to power for the first time since 1997 and Conservative leader David Cameron put together one of Britain's few coalition governments. A year later, in Canada, Stephen Harper's Conservatives managed to win their first majority. In both cases media commentators suggested that the Conservative victory marked a move towards the centre right, while expressing concern at the low voter turnouts. In Canada the Liberal Party suffered a debilitating defeat, the worst in its long history as a political force, and the New Democratic Party became the official opposition for the first time. Meanwhile, the separatist Bloc Québécois seemed to have imploded.

What explains these changes in electoral politics? Why do some parties surge forward while others seem to fade into the background? Can we identify any common factors that might account for the Conservative victories in both Canada and Britain, or are there simply too many variables to allow for generalization? In 2011 Vancouver exploded in a riot after a Canucks hockey game, and a few months later Britain was rocked by unprecedented rioting in many major cities. Did these events have any causes in common? Were they somehow connected with the shift towards the right? With the slow recovery from the 2008 economic crisis? With some other factor? These are just a few of the questions that comparative politics tries to tackle.

So what is comparative politics? Historically, this subfield of political science, which emerged in the 1950s, has sought to understand political phenomena by comparing across regions, countries, or time periods. Comparison reveals similarities and differences that allow us to understand individual cases better, and comparison across a broad range of cases can help us with theory-building. Among the phenomena that may be compared are political institutions and systems (legislatures, political parties, interest groups); political behaviour (voting, mass demonstrations, contesting election); and political ideas (liberalism, conservatism, communism). The field is a large and interesting one, with plenty of scope for most students of political science.

In the next seven chapters we will move from political theory to political institutions, from more normative to more empirical analysis. A central goal of the social sciences is to look beneath the surface of reality for underlying general trends and patterns. Knowing about particular political institutions (or sets of them) is only part of the story. To get a fuller sense of the political world, we also need to understand where those institutions fit within a larger social and political framework. There are many questions we can ask. Why do political parties exist? Why does coalition politics work better in Europe than it does in North America? Can we identify general patterns in the ways parties behave? What are the general principles at the root of electoral systems? How can we explain the behaviour of interest groups? And how best can we understand the countless decisions of individuals who involve themselves in politics? Are rational choice theories the most useful, or should we look elsewhere, to questions of culture, or national identity? In the case of Quebec separatism, or the rise of the Tea Party movement in the US, culture and emotions often seem more important than cool, rational calculations.

Political science has its own books and journals, but it also borrows from other disciplines. In this section and the next (on international relations) we will integrate insights from other fields of study. History is particularly important for political analysis. For example, a long historical perspective on the rise of the state in Europe and its spread to other parts of the world can help us to understand why states around the world today closely resemble each other in terms of structures, or why they interact in the ways they do. Other disciplines are also very useful. Economics plays a big role in explaining the division of resources within and between states, while law is key to understanding the place of constitutions, justice systems, and police forces in the decision-making process. Sociology too contributes to our understanding of the relationship between classes and ethnic communities on the one hand, and the decisions taken by political authorities on the other.

Finally, we emphasize the comparative approach. In this part of the book we will introduce you to politics from all regions of the world. Many political studies concentrate on the Western developed world, and we will devote later chapters to the study of the US party system, contrasting this with approaches to policy-making in the UK and France. We will also include some Canadian examples. Other students are more attracted to politics in the developing world or in other regions. We discuss Islamic understandings of justice, the challenges posed by weak states in Africa, and examine why presidentialism is popular but often problematic in Latin America and the Philippines. Throughout this section we will use consistent and compatible approaches to the analysis of institutions, because institutions that seem similar may function very differently depending on whether they operate in the developed or the developing world. There is no doubt that general institutions such as presidencies or political parties look different in Europe and the US, Mexico and Iran.

Chapter 7 will analyze the emergence and spread of the modern state. Chapter 8 will look at constitutions, the relationship between law and politics, and federalism. Chapter 9 will concentrate on legislatures; Chapter 10, on bureaucracies and policy-making. Chapter 11 will deal with elections and political parties, while Chapter 12 will explore political activity around core institutions: civil society, interest groups, the media, and new technologies such as the Internet. Finally, Chapter 13 will discuss the significance of political culture.

Institutions and States

CHAPTER OVERVIEW

This is the first in a series of chapters focusing on domestic institutions. As you will see, political scientists spend a lot of time analyzing the behaviour of institutions and theorizing about them. Following brief introductions to the concept of the institution and the different factors that structure political behaviour, we will examine the state from a variety of perspectives. A brief historical account of the development of the European state and the spread of that model to other parts of world is followed by an introduction to the European state system (an interdependent series of sovereign states) and its spread between the seventeenth and twentieth centuries. We will then look at the basic functions of the modern states and draw some distinctions between types of state: strong, weak, and democratic.

Understanding Institutions: Informal and Formal

What is an **institution**? Perhaps we can best understand the concept if we think in terms of *regular patterns of behaviour that give stability and predictability to social life.* Some institutions are informal, with no clear written rules. Examples include the family, social classes, or ethnic groups. In each of these cases individuals internalize "codes of behaviour" as a result of socialization as members of the group. What makes someone feel like an Acadian or a Québécois will have a lot to do with his or her personal upbringing and the emotional and other forms of belonging that identity confers. Other institutions are more formalized, with codified rules and organization. Examples include governments, political parties, bureaucracies, legislatures, constitutions, and law courts. To the extent that institutions structure behaviour, we might see them as constraints, limiting what people can do; on the other hand, those who understand how they work can use them as tools or resources to achieve specific political or other goals.

Students of politics tend to concentrate on formal institutions, which are the basis of political systems. Many theorists try to identify regularities that can be elevated to the level of "laws." A good example is Duverger's Law, which (as we will see in Chapter 11), states that first-past-the-post electoral systems produce two-party systems.

→

See Chapter 11, page 231, for a discussion of Duverger's Law.

At the same time, political scientists examine the environment in which political systems are located. Environmental pressures, whether they come from within the state or from the international arena, can rock any political system, leading to domestic political disruption or even breakdown. The Libyan revolution is a recent example; see **Box 7.1**. In most cases, however, states adapt in one way or another and carry on. Political scientists attempt to identify regular patterns of adaptation as a way of generalizing more widely about the behaviour of political institutions.

As Steinmo rightly puts it: "Institutions define the rules of the political game and as such they define who can play and how they play. Consequently, they ultimately can shape who wins and who loses" (Steinmo, 2001: 7555). Still, it is also important to grasp the relationships between political institutions and the environmental forces—political, social, economic—forces that surround them. In this chapter we will use a simplified version of Anthony Giddens' **structuration theory** to clarify those relationships. Giddens distinguished between "system," "structure," and "structuration" (1979: 66). We use the term "system" to mean "political system"—the large arena within which institutions such as parties or bureaucracies compete or cooperate for influence. We use the term "structure" to mean "political institution." And by **structuration**, we mean the factors that both hold back and also provide resources for changes in the operation of institutions and the system as a whole. These can range from levels of economic development, regional or class group activity, to the behaviour of individual political actors. In studies of politics, big events or changes are virtually never caused by just one factor: there are multiple, overlapping causes, and it is often an enormous challenge to sort out which ones are the most important.

For example, George W. Bush did not lead the US into war with Iraq in 2003 only to destroy (alleged) weapons of mass destruction, to oust Saddam Hussein, or to gain control of Iraqi oil reserves. The reasons were far more complex, and included Bush's own

◀ A demonstrator waves a composite Libyan, Syrian, and Egyptian flag in Cairo's Tahrir Square in May 2011 (Peter Macdiarmid/ Getty Images).

KEY CONCEPT BOX 7.1
The Libyan Revolution of 2011

In 2011, after more than four decades under the rule of Colonel Moammar Gadhafi, the North African nation of Libya was rocked by protests and violent counter-attacks by government forces. A month after the protests began in mid-February, the United Nations authorized a coalition of nations including the US, UK, France, and Canada to enforce a "no-fly" zone across the country, to protect civilians. Gadhafi's forces cracked down hard, but in August the capital, Tripoli, fell to anti-government militias and in October Gadhafi was found and killed by enraged protesters. Although an interim government has been established and promises multiparty democratic elections, as of January 2012 it was struggling to gain control of the militias, which have refused to give up their arms.

SOURCE: "Libya—Revolution and Aftermath," *New York Times*. Updated 4 Jan. 2012.

© EdStock/istockphoto.com

PHOTO 7.1 Libyan leader Colonel Moammar Gadhafi at a meeting of G8 development ministers in Rome in 2009.

7

perceptions of reality, the counsel he received from his advisors, his personal belief that the US could spread democracy to the Middle East, and a wide variety of domestic and foreign pressures (MacDonald, 2009). As well, Jean Chrétien's decision not to take Canada into the same war was motivated by a host of considerations, not the least of which was a ground-swell of popular feeling against the Bush administration. We can also contrast Australia's decision to join the US effort in Iraq with New Zealand's decision to condemn the US invasion as illegitimate. Some theorists felt that the differences boiled down to political culture: New Zealanders and Canadians were far more interested in international law and the United Nations than it seemed were the Australian and US governments. Others pointed to differences in the security environments that the various countries faced. Australia felt threatened by Indonesia, and the US by the Middle East, whereas Canada and New Zealand perceived their security environments to be relatively benign (MacDonald, O'Connor, and Katzenstein, 2008). Most political decisions result from the interplay of many factors, and it is the relative weight of those factors that determines the outcome. When we, as observers, try to explain what those factors were, this is often a matter of our own interpretation of the information we have, which may not be complete.

A basic distinction that political scientists often find useful is the difference between "structure" and "agency." "Structure" refers to the impact of a particular group of institutions. To what extent did a certain structure determine the outcome, or at least help make a particular outcome more likely? Sometimes outcomes are explained in terms of "path-determined" outcomes; once a particular decision was taken, other decisions along the same path became easier to follow, while turning away became harder. Thus once Bush had publically announced that war was a serious option, and got approval from the US Congress (a powerful institution), it became much harder to back down. The same is true of Prime Minister Helen Clark in New Zealand. Once she had announced that her country would not go to war without a UN Security Council resolution, it would have been hard for her to join the "Coalition of the Willing."

By contrast, "agency" refers to the impact of actions taken by one or more agents, either individuals or groups of them. Since politics is a social activity, it is rare that a particular political outcome is determined by structure alone. Nor do agents have complete freedom, since their options are always constrained by structures of one kind or another. We might liken this situation to a game of hockey. Although individual players like Sidney Crosby have tremendous agency to score goals, they (like their teammates) are constrained by the National Hockey League, which makes the rules that govern the games between the 30 franchised teams of the NHL.

→

See Chapter 20 for an exploration of the relationship between the state and economic institutions.

KEY POINTS

- Institutions play a vital role in structuring political behaviour.
- Political, economic, and social factors all provide structuration in political life and determine particular outcomes.
- "Structure" and "agency" perform complementary and contrasting functions in determining outcomes.

States

In Chapter 1 we explored some of the defining elements of the state. Among those elements were sovereignty, legitimacy, and a monopoly on the use of force in a particular territorial area. In addition, states claim a monopoly on law-making. At its most basic level, then, "the state" is the structure of rule and authority within a particular geographical area. In that sense the state is abstract; as the political theorist Barry Buzan notes, "In some important senses, the state is more an idea held in common by a group of people, than it is a physical organism" (1991: 63). Thus we refer to the nation-state, the welfare state, and so on.

In the rest of this chapter we will look at the rise of the European state and its spread across the world, often through **colonialism**; the European state system; the modern state; strong and weak states; and, finally, the democratic state.

In ancient times tribes and small communities around the world had their own forms of rule. We can trace the roots of European thought about government to classical Greece and Rome, the great civilizations whose ideas were rediscovered during the Renaissance after centuries of near-oblivion. The modern European state model developed gradually between the seventeenth and nineteenth centuries, after which it was carried to other parts of the world. This is not to say that the European model is not contested. People who were subject to European colonialism do not necessarily consider the European model of government better than what they had before.

KEY POINT

- The term "the state" is used in a great variety of ways, some concrete and some abstract. This can make detailed analysis difficult and contentious.

The Rise of the European State

State capacity may be defined as "the ability of a government to administer its territory effectively" (Wang 1995: 90). It takes four basic forms, as Wang explains:

> the capacity to mobilize financial resources from the society to pursue what the central policymakers perceive as the "national interest" (extractive capacity); the capacity to guide national socioeconomic development (steering capacity); the capacity to dominate by using symbols and creating consensus (legitimation capacity); and the capacity to dominate by the use or threat of force (coercive capacity). These four capacities are conceptually distinct but interrelated in practice. For instance, the legitimation of a regime is dependent on its performance. If the state is able to produce and deliver economic and social goods at the level its subjects expect, or at least as its rulers promise, it should have no legitimacy problem. On the other hand, if the state apparatus cannot adequately steer the economic system, this is likely to result in a decline in its legitimacy. With legitimation capacity, the state can effectively steer activities without the necessity of constantly deploying coercion. Without legitimacy, however, the state would find it much more difficult to extract resources from the society, and would have to bear much higher costs for maintaining law and order. . . . (Wang, 1995: 90)

The development of state capacity is a fascinating story. As the well-known theorist Charles Tilly (1990: 96) put it, over the last thousand years the European state has evolved from a wasp to a locomotive: what was once a small inconvenience to the people it ruled over has become a powerful driver of social and economic development. And while locomotives can pull heavy loads, they can also crush anything that gets in their way.

Until the seventeenth century it was impossible to separate the state from the ruler. The officials who ran the affairs of state were personally appointed by the ruler, who was also

See Chapter 1, page 25, for an exploration of different theoretical conceptions of the state.

→
See Chapter 20, page 417, for an exploration of states in a globalizing world.

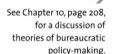

→
See Chapter 14, page 291, for a more detailed discussion of the rise of the modern state system.

→
See Chapter 10, page 208, for a discussion of theories of bureaucratic policy-making.

responsible for paying them; even in states that did impose taxes, a great deal of the cost of maintaining officials came from the ruler's own income. Eventually, when a salaried bureaucracy began to develop, beginning in the seventeenth century, one of its most important functions was to collect and administer taxes. Gradually what emerged was a system for extracting taxes from more and more property owners, especially to pay for war. As Tilly put it: "War made the state and the state made war" (Tilly, 1975: 42). Time and again, the need to raise funds for fighting drove governments to devise new ways of raising money. The US, for instance, introduced income tax in 1861 to pay for the American Civil War then raging between North and South. Canada introduced income tax in 1917, to help pay for its contributions to the First World War. Gradually this capacity to extract taxes, coupled with access to a modernizing and industrializing commercial economy and a large rural population, enabled some states to dominate others (Tilly, 1990: 15). They in turn became the models that others had to deal with and, if possible, surpass.

The French Revolution transformed the capacity of the state, leading to a level form of taxation for all its citizens, as well as the principle of the modern citizen army, which helped France to dominate continental Europe until 1814. Britain was forced to emulate France in order to raise enough money and create a large enough armed force to resist it. By the beginning of the nineteenth century, bureaucracies had become central to the state's operation (van Creveld, 1999: 143). This was a key development, for it laid the foundations of the modern state. First, state officials were expected to advance the state and the public good, rather than any individual ruler. Second, officials developed rules and patterns of administration that separated them from the rest of society. In the late nineteenth century, the German sociologist Max Weber would lay out the key characteristics of the new bureaucracies: impersonal, rule-based, goal-oriented activity, with promotion of officials based exclusively on merit and performance. Weber saw bureaucracy as an ideal type of social organization, which he identified with the ongoing rationalization of social life. He emphasized the technical superiority of bureaucratic organization over any other form, although he was often critical of bureaucracies' power and the way they operated.

As the European states grew stronger, new institutions and legal principles had to be established to constrain their rulers, particularly through constitutions. Finer emphasizes two events that were crucial in this respect: the American revolution and the French revolution. For Finer,

> the transcendent importance of the American Revolution is that it demonstrated for ever that quality of the Western European government we have called "law-boundedness." Here is a government which draws its powers from and can only act within a framework of fundamental law—the Constitution—which is itself interpreted by judges in the ordinary courts of the country. Could law-boundedness . . . receive a more striking affirmation? (Finer, 1997: 1485)

From this "law-boundedness" followed six innovations, listed in **Box 7.2**.

Although it was the American constitution that introduced the "separation of powers" as a formal principle, its framers were influenced by the British practice of constitutional monarchy, under which absolute power rested not with the monarch but with Parliament, which could even oblige the king or queen to step down if required. Whereas in Britain (and various states in continental Europe) the parliament was divided between two houses based explicitly on social class (the House of Commons and the House of Lords), in the

KEY CONCEPT BOX 7.2
The Governmental Innovations of the American Revolution

Finer (1997: 1485) identifies six innovations associated with the American Revolution:

1. the deliberate formulation of a new frame of government by way of a popular Convention;
2. a written constitution;
3. a bill of rights enshrined within it;
4. guaranteed protection for these rights through judicial review;
5. the separation of powers along functional lines; and
6. the division of powers between national and state governments.

US the division between the House of Representatives and the Senate was not class-based. The logic was similar, though, since the Senate was indirectly elected by state legislatures and its members were largely insulated from mass politics.

At the time, the combination of new institutions and principles was an experiment: no one knew whether they would all work together. Nevertheless, the American Constitution proved a model and a starting point for most subsequent writers of constitutions. Just over a decade after the American Revolution, the revolution in France further transformed the theory and practice of government. In Finer's view,

> The French Revolution is the most important single event in the entire history of government. The American Revolution pales beside it. It was an earthquake. It razed and effaced all the ancient institutions of France, undermined the foundations of the other European states, and is still sending its shock-waves throughout the rest of the world (Finer, 1997: 1517).

The governmental legacy of the French Revolution can be summarized in four main points: see **Box 7.3**.

Not all the points listed in Box 7.3 can be reconciled with each other. The French Revolution celebrated the "rights of man," making all men equal (it said little about women); yet it inaugurated an era of populist dictatorship. Although the revolution was at first widely praised, Napoleon's military expansionism provoked a backlash among other peoples, especially in the German states, that led to the creation of nation-states throughout Europe in the nineteenth century. And although it preached universal harmony, the revolution also led to a new form of military organization—the mass citizen army—that became the model for military organization throughout Europe. Yet in their different ways, these diverse elements influenced various forms of modern government in Europe and throughout the world. Elements of modern democracies and modern dictatorships, rule by law and by force, can be seen in the French Revolution. Although it began as an attempt to establish checks on the absolutist monarchy, it led to greater government intrusion into the lives of ordinary people than ever before. As Finer puts it: "all four [of these elements] are still alive, working like a leaven throughout the globe. In that sense the revolution is a Permanent Revolution. Nothing was ever like it before and nothing foreseeable will turn this Revolution back" (Finer, 1997: 1566).

> ### KEY CONCEPT BOX 7.3
> #### The Governmental Legacy of the French Revolution
>
> Finer (1997: 1538–66) highlights four elements of the French Revolution that left a lasting legacy:
>
> 1. The Declaration of the Natural Rights of Man and the Citizen established the legal basis for the sovereignty of the democratic state, based on the General Will.
> 2. The revolution laid down the national unity of all French citizens and their primary obligation of loyalty to the state. When Napoleon attempted to extend French power throughout Europe, deposing traditional rulers, he provoked nationalistic responses from the peoples of other nations, who rose up against French power.
> 3. In defence of the Revolution the French state mobilized vast numbers of citizens to fight on its behalf, forcing its enemies to mobilize comparable citizen armies.
> 4. The Committee of Public Safety followed by the Napoleonic dictatorship marked the rise of neo-absolutism.

7

KEY POINTS

- A milestone in the development of the European state was the separation of state officials from the ruler.
- Another key development was the separation of the state from the rest of society through institutionalization and bureaucratization.
- Warfare was a catalyst for raising funds from society and increasing the state's reach.
- The American and French Revolutions helped to develop some of the better known modern principles of government.
- New institutions such as national constitutions and legislatures helped to check the power of rulers.

The Spread of the European State Model

Colonialism

In the eighteenth and nineteenth centuries, the economic and military might of the dominant European powers, supported by superior technology, helped them develop **empires** overseas. The primary purpose of colonialism was exploitation—to take the riches of Asia, Africa, the Middle East, and the Americas to Europe—but one of its legacies was the spread of the European-style state to other continents, albeit in simplified versions. Administrative arrangements in the colonies were never as sophisticated as in Europe, because the colonizing powers had no interest in doing anything more than maintaining order. They also invested the minimum in infrastructure, apart from the roads, canals, and railway lines needed to transport goods from the interior of colonies to the coasts for shipping to Europe.

The former Spanish colonies in Latin America gained their independence in the nineteenth century, the former British, French, German, and Italian colonies in the twentieth. At that point, most of the newly independent states simply took over the structures and institutions put in place by their European colonizers. This is hardly surprising, since those were the structures and institutions that the post-independence elites, trained in the colonial centres of power, were familiar with. To change everything overnight would not have been realistic: thus most leaders were forced to start working with what was in place and make what changes they could over time.

Among the institutions that the former colonies adopted was the bureaucratic machine that extracted resources from the people to pay for government. India is a prime example: it inherited its large bureaucracy from the British, along with the small elite cadre of specialized administrators who form the prestigious Indian Civil Service. In some cases the separation between ruler and officials that had marked the rise of the modern state was now reversed. In what have been called **patrimonial states**, some rulers came to use the state to extract resources from the rest of society for their own benefit; this practice has been associated with African states in particular, although it is not exclusive to them.

Another legacy that has been a major problem for former colonies is the European insistence on undivided sovereignty. Pre-colonial borders tended to be fluid and changeable, reflecting the nomadic lifestyles of the indigenous peoples, but Western states imposed formal boundaries. Designed in colonial capitals such as Paris, London, and Berlin, the new borders took little account of local social and cultural relations. The main goal had been to divide up territory according to the interests of the colonial powers. Thus members of the same ethnic or religious group were often split between two or more colonies, while traditionally hostile groups were sometimes forced together within the same boundaries. The consequences for state legitimacy and viability in South America, North America, and sub-Saharan Africa are still with us today. When the colonies became independent, the arbitrary boundaries created by the colonial powers made it extremely difficult to create cohesive nation-states on the European model. Had all the African colonies gained their independence at the same time, for example, the colonial borders could theoretically have been reconsidered in light of pre-colonial linguistic, tribal, religious, and other distinctions. But the fact that decolonization took place over several decades, starting in the late 1940s, made a wholesale reconfiguration of borders nearly impossible. Thus in many parts of the world the state has had to create the nation, whereas in Europe the nation had generally created the state

Pragmatic Adoption of the Western Model

The spread of the European state model was not limited to former colonies, however. Other countries pragmatically adopted the Western model in order to compete with the West. Among them was Japan. In 1854, when Commodore Matthew Perry of the US Navy led a number of warships into Tokyo Bay and demanded that Japan open up to international trade, the Japanese had been cut off from the outside world for nearly three centuries. They had no ships that could challenge the Americans, so they were forced to comply. What followed was a series of transformations of Japanese society and the Japanese state. Impressed by American power, Japan sought to modernize so that it could compete with the West and become "rich and strong" itself (Terry, 2002: 38).

In 1867 the shogunate that had kept Japan in isolation fell and the imperial family was restored to power. The new government adopted a more centralized and coercive system of rule, based largely on the Prussian model, and set out to establish a civilian bureaucracy capable of developing resources for the state. The samurai—traditionally a class of independent warriors—were forced to serve the state as part of either the bureaucracy or the new national army.

© sack/istockphoto.com

PHOTO 7.2 Traffic congestion on the Yaskuni dori in the Shinjuku district of Tokyo during rush hour. One of the busiest and most important shopping and sightseeing streets in Tokyo, the Yasukuni dori is world-famous for its neon signs.

In addition, the new government sent representatives abroad to study the political, legal, and technological strengths of the West. In 1890 the first Japanese constitution came into force, setting limits (albeit ambiguous ones) on the powers of the emperor and establishing a parliament (the Diet) as well as an independent judiciary. Together, these reforms had a tremendous impact. From a technologically backward, inward-looking, ostensibly feudal society Japan transformed itself into a modern industrial state. By 1895 it was able to defeat its greatest regional rival, China, in war, and a decade later it became the first non-European state to win a war against a European imperial power—Russia. Then it set out to establish its own empire, beginning with the annexation of Korea in 1910. For the next 35 years Japan ruled with an iron fist, forcing Koreans to embrace the Shinto faith, change their names to more Japanese-sounding ones, and swear allegiance to the Emperor. Korean men were drafted into the Imperial army, and several hundred thousand Korean women were forced into sexual slavery (Dudden, 2006: 117–22). Within a few decades the new Japanese state had accomplished what had taken European nations centuries.

Turkey is another example of country that was never colonized but adopted Western forms of rule in order to compete with the West. It had been the core of the Ottoman Empire since its inception in 1299, but by the nineteenth century the empire was in decline and many of its components, such as Greece and Bulgaria, were seeking independence. Significantly, the military took the lead in looking to the West for ideas and models that would enable Turkey to compete. Military considerations drove increasingly radical reforms of the state in the late nineteenth and early twentieth centuries. When the empire finally collapsed following the First World War, the long history of Western-style reform culminated in the creation of a secular republic in 1923. The new president, Mustafa Kemal Ataturk (the name means "father of the Turks"), pushed through a series of reforms, based mainly on principles borrowed from France, that included complete separation of state and religion (Starr, 1992: 8–15). The new Turkey then became a model for promoters of democracy in other countries; see the case study below.

CASE STUDY
A Turkish Model for Iraq?

In 2002 many presidential advisors were already interested in invading Iraq and deposing its dictator, Saddam Hussein. Accordingly, the Bush administration discussed what form of government should be put in place in a post-occupation Iraq. Among the more significant influences promoting regime change was the Princeton University historian Bernard Lewis, a friend of Vice President Dick Cheney who was strongly influenced by Ataturk's transformation of Turkey into a modern secular republic. The process had been dictatorial, but the democratic system it established had proved more stable than any of its counterparts in the Middle East.

The idea of a Turkish-style redemption for the Arab world was a powerful one that Lewis had been promoting since the 1960s. According to Michael Hirsh (2004), the "Lewis Doctrine" called for "a Westernized polity, reconstituted and imposed from above like Kemal's Turkey . . . a bulwark of security for America and a model for the region." The Turkish model helped many US policy-makers conceptualize what a democratic Iraq could ideally look like. Unfortunately, it did not take into account Iraq's complex, multi-ethnic identity and history. While Iraq is now a more or less functional democracy, the process of transformation has been longer and more painful than US officials expected, and the democratic future of the country remains uncertain.

SOURCES: MacDonald, 2009: 130; Michael Hirsh, "Bernard Lewis Revisited," *Washington Monthly*, November, 2004, http://www.washingtonmonthly.com/features/2004/0411.hirsh.html (accessed 2 Sept. 2006).

KEY POINTS

- The European state model spread to other continents.
- War and colonial expansion were the key elements in much of this spread, but some countries, such as Japan and Turkey, chose to adopt the Western model.

The European State System

The modern European state system is widely considered to have originated in the Peace of Westphalia, which ended the Thirty Years' War in 1648. That treaty established the paradigm of the state as

a sovereign, territorially delimited political unit, facing other similar units, each striving for supremacy but never achieving it owing to their rapidly adopted skill of forming combinations that would defeat such a purpose, that is, the techniques of the "**balance of power**" first developed by the Italian city-states in the fourteenth and fifteenth centuries (Finer, 1997: 1306).

The Treaty of Westphalia established three principles:

1. the **sovereignty** of states and their fundamental right to self-determination;
2. legal equality between states;
3. non-intervention of one state in the affairs of another.

See Chapter 14, page 282, for details on the Montevideo Convention.

See Chapter 14, page 295, for a detailed discussion of the globalization of the modern state system.

Although the criteria that states use for mutual recognition today were agreed under the Montevideo Convention of 1933, they are based on principles that were first established in the Treaty of Westphalia.

Today the state is the universal form of political organization around the world. In 2011 South Sudan joined the United Nations as its 193rd member state. Ranging in size from China, with a population of over 1.3 billion, to Tuvalu, with a population estimated at 12,000, the UN's members range in area from more than 17 million sq. km (Russia) to 2 sq. km (Monaco). The newest aspirant for recognition as a state is Palestine.

KEY POINTS

- The principles that govern relations between states today were established in 1648 in the Peace of Westphalia.
- The European state model spread to other continents and became the basis of the international system of states.
- War and colonial expansion were the key elements in much of this spread, but some countries, such as Japan and Turkey, chose to adopt the Western model.

The Modern State

Basically, states today have two sets of roles or functions, internal and external. The former are the functions they perform with respect to their own populations; the latter are the functions they perform with respect to other states.

Internal Functions

See Chapter 10, page 208, for a discussion of bureaucratic policy-making.

See Chapter 1, page 23, for a description of the developmental state.

The internal role of the state, according to Graeme Gill (2003), has been understood through three quite distinct lenses. First, some theorists have cast the state in the role of partisan: every state, strong or weak, "is seen as pursuing its own institutional interests or those of the officials who work within it" (Gill 2003: 8). The state is supported in this role by a Weberian state bureaucracy with its own structure and procedures that help it resist pressures from the rest of society.

The second role is that of guardian. Here the state is seen as working in the interests of the society as a whole, stabilizing and maintaining a healthy balance between the various, sometimes conflicting, interests in society. Examples would include **federal** or **consociational** political systems designed to counter fundamental cleavages such as those posed by the Catalan and Basque separatist movements in Spain. Another example would be the kind of **developmental state** seen in East Asia, where the state directs the development of society and the economy along the path that it believes to be most favourable to the **national interest**; for example, industrialization and economic modernization.

The third view sees the state as a tool—"a pliable instrument" (Gill, 2003: 9), lacking autonomy—in the hands of one or more groups in the society. This could describe a genuine **liberal democracy**, where the people control the state's actions. But it could also describe a state controlled by one section of society, such as "big business," or one particular ethnic group; it could even describe a patrimonial state, in which power flows directly from the leader and political elites take advantage of their connections to enrich themselves and their clients. Marxists certainly believed that the state was controlled by the bourgeois class, and thus hardly autonomous. Elite theorists as well argue that the state is controlled by powerful interests who may use it to further their own power (Gill, 2003: 10)

In practice, modern states often perform all three roles at the same time. Most state bureaucracies operate to some extent on the basis of their own institutions and codified procedures that help to protect them from outside interference. Most states develop some perspective on the desirable path of development for their societies and attempt to mobilize the resources necessary to achieve it, and most states are to some extent responsive to groups outside themselves. Dictators, such as former President Suharto of Indonesia, favoured "loyal" businessmen who did their bidding and in return enjoyed special favours. What is important is which of the three roles is predominant in a particular state.

KEY POINTS

- Modern states can be characterized according to whether they function primarily in their own interest (the "partisan" role); in the interest of the society as a whole (the "guardian" role); or in the interest of some particular segment of the society (the "instrument" role).

External Functions

States have two external functions: to manage relations with other states and to protect their people and territory against attacks from outside. By recognizing one another as sovereign, states reinforce each other's authority as the legitimate rulers of defined territories. In this way they reduce the threat of **anarchy** posed by the lack of a global government. Diplomatic recognition gives governments some reassurance against incursions by other states, although it is not an iron-clad guarantee: other states could still choose to attack, and sometimes do. On the other hand, it also means that states expect their counterparts to interact with them in familiar and predictable ways, mainly through diplomatic means. Bureaucratic agencies such as foreign ministries in one state expect to find equivalent agencies in other states. This strengthening **international society** contributes to the proliferation of government agencies in individual states.

Strong States and Weak States

The state today is more powerful than ever before. The twentieth century witnessed the most extreme manifestations of state power that the world has ever seen. **Totalitarian** states such as Hitler's Germany and Stalin's Russia murdered tens of millions of people and intruded into the private lives of their citizens to an unprecedented degree, both through pervasive state propaganda and through enormous networks of secret police and informers that closed off virtually all avenues for self-expression. Now that the archives of some of these states are open, we can get a clearer perspective on the reach of such state bureaucracies. For example, at the time of its collapse in 1989, the German Democratic Republic had what has been described as a "honeycomb" state, in which one sixth of the adult population were involved in one way or another in the state's "micro-systems of power." One out of every 180 citizens was a full-time employee of the secret police—the highest ratio in any of the communist states (Fulbrook, 2005: 236, 241).

We can view these regimes as extreme versions of the modern state. As its powers have increased, so too have people's expectations of what it can do. Rotberg (2004) provides a long list of the political goods or functions that a modern state might be expected to provide its citizens. Typically the most important are:

1. human security;
2. predictable and recognizable methods of adjudicating disputes, and regulating both the norms and the prevailing values of a particular society or polity;
3. freedom to participate in politics and compete for office, respect and support for national and regional political institutions, such as legislatures and courts, tolerance of dissent and difference, and fundamental civil and human rights.

Among the many other services expected by citizens are healthcare, schools and educational institutions, infrastructure such as roads, railways, and harbours, communication networks, a banking system with a national currency, space for the flowering of **civil society**, and policies regulating the way the money made within the state is shared out (Rotberg, 2004: 2–3). States in the developed world usually perform these functions to the satisfaction of their citizens, even if not perfectly. They are "strong" or "robust" states.

However, many states clearly don't function as well as they could. Most of these weak states are in the developing world. Chabal and Daloz have argued that the state in Africa is "not just weak, but essentially vacuous, with virtually none meeting the Weberian criteria" (1999: 1). The French historian Jean-Francois Bayart, described the situation in much of sub-Saharan Africa as follows:

> The frontiers of the state are transgressed, the informal sector is a canker on the official economy, taxes are not collected, poaching and undisciplined exploitation of mineral resources becomes endemic, weapons circulate, resettled villages split up, the people appropriate the legitimate use of force to themselves and deliver summary justice, delinquency spreads, businesses suffer from languor induced by underproductivity, delays and absences (Bayart, 1993: 258).

Table 7.1 presents a list of the world's "weakest" states in 2007, according to the *Brookings* magazine. The country in first place, Somalia, has effectively been without a central state since 1991; the consequences are discussed in the case study on page 155.

Even though the structures of modern states are fairly similar, then, they vary considerably in capacity. This raises the question of what makes a state strong and what makes it weak.

PHOTO 7.3 Poverty in the midst of prosperity: shacks in Soweto, South Africa

It is possible to identify a series of factors. Obviously, one is size. Although Monaco has the same international legal status in the UN General Assembly as China, in practice there is an enormous difference in their capacity to pursue their goals in the world. Another factor is economic strength. As the largest economy in the world, the US has the power to finance a high level of domestic public services and respond to the preferences of its people. a poor state such as Burma is much less capable of providing adequate services for its people. A third factor is military might. Again, the US, as the only remaining military superpower, is better able than most to protect its people and territory, as well as pursue foreign policy goals, although its failures in Iraq suggest that even American power is not unlimited.

So far we have looked primarily at external factors related to the strength of states, but domestic factors are equally important. First there is the issue of legitimacy. If a state lacks its people's consent to rule, it must rely on force to achieve acquiescence, and this can be a source of weakness. In some cases lack of legitimacy is the result of disagreement over its borders. Many post-colonial states have international boundaries that were imposed more or less arbitrarily, with the consequence that some ethnic or tribal communities do not think of themselves as citizens of the states whose borders they straddle; often they wish to establish their own homelands. In other cases lack of legitimacy reflects lack of support for the dominant ideology of the state. Ultimately, what brought down the regimes in Eastern Europe and the Soviet Union was the lack of popular support for the official ideology of communism. Without popular legitimacy states are brittle, however strong they may look on the surface. They are vulnerable to new challenges because they lack flexibility and are slow to adapt.

TABLE 7.1 Index of State Weakness in the Developing World

Rank	Country	Overall Score	Economic	Political	Security	Social Welfare	GNI Per Capital
1	Somalia	0.52	0.00	0.00	1.37	0.70	226
2	Afghanistan	1.65	4.51	2.08	0.00	0.00	271
3	Dem. Rep. Congo	1.67	4.6	1.80	0.28	0.52	130
4	Iraq	3.11	2.87	1.67	1.63	6.27	1134
5	Burundi	3.21	5.01	3.46	2.95	1.43	100
6	Sudan	3.29	5.05	2.06	1.46	4.59	810
7	Central African Rep.	3.33	4.11	2.90	5.06	1.25	360
8	Zimbabwe	3.44	1.56	1.56	6.81	3.84	350
9	Liberia	3.64	3.39	3.91	6.01	1.25	140
10	Côte d'Ivoire	3.66	5.23	2.12	3.71	3.56	870
11	Angola	3.72	5.42	2.67	5.32	1.45	1980
12	Haiti	3.76	3.90	2.62	5.21	3.31	480
13	Sierra Leone	3.77	5.01	3.87	5.43	0.76	240
14	Eritrea	3.84	3.09	2.78	7.01	2.48	200
15	North Korea	3.87	0.52	0.95	7.28	6.73	n/a
16	Chad	3.90	5.80	2.42	6.18	1.21	480
17	Burma	4.16	4.72	0.89	3.96	7.07	n/a
18	Guinea-Bissau	4.16	5.22	3.83	5.96	1.69	190
19	Ethiopia	4.46	6.14	4.03	5.91	1.75	180
20	Rep. Congo	4.56	5.08	2.77	6.45	3.95	1100

SOURCE: http://www.brookings.edu/~/media/Files/rc/reports/2008/02_weak_states_index/02_weak_states_index_basket_scores.pdf

A second crucial factor in the strength of states is the robustness of state institutions. To what extent can they withstand turbulence in the rest of society? Bayart, Chabal, and Daloz repeatedly suggest that the weakness of many African states is the result of the interpenetration of state, society, and the economy. Individual African politicians expect to use the state to become rich as a way of impressing others and redistributing resources to their "clients." They note: "Rich men are powerful and powerful men are rich" (Chabal and Daloz, 1999: 52). Ethnic and tribal communities expect "their" representatives, whether democratically elected officials or lowly members of the government bureaucracy, to channel resources to them, because if they don't do so, no one will. Thus state institutions in many parts of Africa are far less robust than in Europe or North America, because they do not stand above or apart from society in the same way. In such

CASE STUDY
Somalia as a Failed State

With a landmass as large as France, Somalia has a relatively small population, estimated at just under 10 million in 2011—roughly 15 per cent of its French counterpart. Unlike many post-colonial states, especially in sub-Saharan Africa, Somalia is not particularly ethnically heterogeneous, and the main divisions between Somalis are based on clans and sub-clans rather than ethnic differences. Nor are its boundaries much disputed, though Somalis have also traditionally lived in what are now Ethiopia, Kenya, and Djibouti. The colonial and post-colonial states have all hung above the rest of society, only partially integrated into it.

In 1960 the post-independence state was formed from former British and Italian colonies. Nine years later the civilian president was assassinated and General Siad Barre seized power. Barre tried to create a modern state by suppressing traditional clan ties, but gradually the army broke up along clan lines. Barre's regime became notoriously corrupt and its domestic support shrank to his own clan.

In 1991 Barre was overthrown by his former intelligence chief, Mohamed Farah Aidid. This incident led to a bloody civil war between rival militias. Hundreds of thousands of people died, either from the ferocious fighting or from starvation, and in 1993 the UN, led by the US under President Bill Clinton, set out to impose a peace. The members of Operation Restore Hope, as it was called, were initially welcomed into the capital, Mogadishu, but after a few months their unsuccessful efforts to arrest Aidid and his supporters led to widespread civilian casualties. These events united Somalis against outsiders. Even the Red Cross had to be protected. Mogadishu was devastated by withering American firepower and retaliation (Peterson, 2000). The brutal deaths of 18 US servicemen turned American popular opinion against the intervention, and the UN later withdrew.

Even now there is no central authority in Somalia. In 2003 Kenya took the lead in organizing a conference that established a Transitional Federal Government, but little progress has been made towards national legitimacy. In late 2006, forces from Ethiopia intervened to frustrate a movement for national unity, based on several Islamic parties.

Menkhaus (2007: 86–7) writes of "a loose constellation of commercial city-states and villages separated by long stretches of pastoral statelessness." One part of the country (Puntland) has declared autonomy, while another (Somaliland) in the north is effectively independent. The only effective administrations are at the local level, and public services (education, healthcare, welfare) have collapsed. In the absence of a functioning nation-wide judicial system, clans and sub-clans rely on the traditional practice of recompense for injuries or damage suffered by their members, but heavily armed militias can still demand resources from civilians with impunity.

Under these conditions, life in Somalia might be expected to resemble the state of nature as Hobbes described it: "poor, nasty, brutish and short." Yet average life expectancy is estimated at 48 years—higher than in many other African countries and about the same as in Nigeria. Somaliland is said to be as safe as anywhere in the Horn of Africa. It has even established a basic democratic system with elections and political parties. While insecurity is a major problem, and there are over 450,000 Somali refugees abroad, the extreme violence of the early 1990s has subsided.

← See Chapter 1, page 35, for more on Hobbes and the social contract tradition.

The traditional economy based on trade in herds of cattle is flourishing as compared with the pre-1991 period, since the state cannot extract usurious taxes (Little, 2003). Private enterprise has found ways of providing services such as the transfer of money within and outside the country, despite the lack of banks. Businessmen also buy off militiamen to provide security for their trade, so there is no state monopoly on the means of violence. Mobile phone companies prosper, while the landline service decays. The private sector provides public services that allow for quick profits (e.g., running ports and airports, electricity supply), but not public sanitation. Transnational corporations such as Total and GM have found ways of doing business in the country despite the lack of a stable institutional and legal system. Somalis abroad send back anywhere between US$500 million and 1 billion per year, which helps support the domestic economy, especially in the cities.

In short, Somalis have found ways of coping with the lack of a state, which they regard as "an instrument of accumulation and domination, enriching and empowering those who control it and exploiting and harassing the rest of the population" (Menkhaus, 2007: 86–7). Yet they are disadvantaged because they have no navy to protect their maritime resources, are unable to defend their businesses against foreign competition, and cannot even provide the veterinary services required to qualify their cattle for export to places like Saudi Arabia. Meanwhile, insecurity in urban areas has made any significant investment in infrastructure or industry very difficult. Whether the presidential elections scheduled for August 2012 will lead to the establishment of an effective national government remains to be seen.

cases a strong, autonomous, rule-based bureaucracy is almost impossible to achieve. State institutions are not really institutionalized, and the state is more easily penetrated by outside forces as a result.

On the other hand, the African states are still relatively young, and they may well become more robust in time. Van Creveld (1999: 306) reminds us that in the nineteenth century newly independent states in South America were similarly fragile. Colombia had 30 civil wars; Venezuela had 50 revolutions and Bolivia 60. Coronil describes Venezuela at the beginning of the twentieth century:

> the state was so weak and precarious as a national institution that its stability and legitimacy were constantly at risk. Without a national army or an effective bureaucracy, in an indebted country that lacked a national road network or an effective system of communication, the state appeared as an unfulfilled project whose institutional form remained limited to localized sites of power with but partial dominion over the nation's territory and sway over its citizens (Coronil, 1997: 76).

As we shall see in Chapter 11, Venezuela looks quite different today.

In general, European and North American states are strong, while those in the developing world are comparatively weak. Western theorizing about the state has tended to focus on issues associated with the strong. Recently, though, the problems of weakening states in the developed world have begun to attract more attention, largely because of increasing globalization. States in the developed world now increasingly see their sovereignty eroding as multinational corporations and other transnational actors and forces leach power from

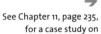

See Chapter 11, page 235, for a case study on Venezuela.

their governments (Marsh, Smith, and Hothi, 2006: 176). The level of erosion is certainly far less than what we see in the developing world. Nevertheless, state autonomy appears to be declining throughout the world.

KEY POINTS

- There is an enormous range in the capacity of states in different regions of the world.
- Some states are at best "quasi" states.
- States need legitimacy and robust institutions to be considered strong.
- Globalization is limiting state capacity around the world.

See Chapter 20, page 417, for an exploration of the impact of globalization on the study of politics.

The Democratic State

What is a democratic state? Initially, the answer might seem obvious: a democratic state is one that holds elections for some or all of the leading positions in the state or government. The problem is that that the same can be said of authoritarian states, which hold elections in which the outcome is determined in advance. We could instead say that a democracy has genuinely free and fair elections. But is that enough? We could say that a democratic state must have political parties; but there are exceptions (Uganda is one, as we will see in Chapter 11).

The question of election aside, perhaps we could define a democratic government as one that is genuinely accountable to elected representatives. Accountability is presumed to be an essential element of a democratic state. Parties are elected to parliament in some authoritarian states, but they cannot exercise any effective check on the government. Perhaps we should specify extra conditions that would ensure such accountability, such as a provision requiring that governments (or ministers) lose office if they fail to do what "the people" want. But is that all democracy is about? What about the representation of major social groups in elected bodies? Should there be roughly equal representation for men and women? Do ordinary citizens have a role to play beyond voting in elections? Is civil society an essential requirement for a functioning democracy? Is a democratic **political culture** also needed to make democracy work?

These questions explore dimensions of democratic political systems. Yet, as we argued at the beginning of this chapter, a democratic system is not the same as a democratic *state*. To understand what a democratic state entails, we need to ask wider, more abstract questions about conceptions of authority. Do views about authentic democracy vary from one country to another, or from one region of the world to another (Paley, 2002)? Bell and others have identified a different sort of democracy in East and Southeast Asia, one they call **illiberal democracy**. Illiberal democracies, like liberal ones, have elections and political parties, but they operate on the basis of more definite views about appropriate forms of social harmony. The main priority of the legal system is to control society rather than to protect rights and liberties (Bell et al., 1995). The Chinese government produced a White Paper that promotes a different understanding of democracy (*White Paper on Political Democracy*, 2005). In what ways does it differ from the standard understanding in liberal democracies? Are the citizens of a given state the only ones who can fairly judge whether their state is democratic, or can foreigners have a legitimate view?

See Chapter 11, page 227, for a case study on Uganda.

See Chapter 3, page 61, for a discussion of the meaning of democracy.

See Chapter 12, page 239, for a detailed exploration of the concept of civil society.

See Chapter 1, page 23, for a brief discussion of illiberal democracy.

7

KEY QUOTE BOX 7.4
Hilary Clinton Compares Electoral Corruption in Nigeria and the US

During a state visit to Nigeria in 2009, US Secretary of State Hillary Clinton recalled how George W. Bush won the presidency because of a disputed electoral outcome in Florida:

> In a democracy there have to be winners and losers. And part of creating a strong democratic system is that the losers, despite how badly we might feel, accept the outcome. Because it is for the good of the country we love. Our democracy is still evolving. You know, we had all kinds of problems in some of our past elections, as you might remember. In 2000, our presidential elections came down to one state where the brother of the man running for president was the governor of the state. So we have our problems, too (Sky News, 2009).

These remarks were controversial, because as Secretary of State, Clinton was supposed to be an impartial voice for US foreign policy. However, she could not resist suggesting a similarity between her own country and one of the world's most corrupt states.

These are just some of many dimensions that might contribute to the assessment of a "democratic state". We encourage you to try to carry out a democratic audit of a state with which you are familiar, whether your own or another. International IDEA, a democracy promotion institute, offers a checklist of questions designed to help citizens assess their own countries (International IDEA, 2002a). Use this as a starting point for your audit. You can also get an idea of how such an audit might work in practice from the examples presented in the accompanying publication (International IDEA, 2002b).

KEY POINTS

- There are multiple dimensions to a democratic state.
- A democratic political system and a democratic state are different concepts.

Conclusion

This chapter has established the framework for the next six chapters. These will explore various dimensions of the state both as organization and as authority structure. We have also illustrated the great disparities in capacity that exist among the world's states today. The next three chapters will focus on the most important institutions of states, while the following two will deal with broader forces that give structure to the context of political life.

? KEY QUESTIONS

- What is a nation-state? Does it matter whether the nation or the state came first?
- Does the state require moral authority to enjoy domestic legitimacy?

- Is state capacity simply a reflection of the country's level of economic development?
- How applicable are theories of the modern Western state to states in the developing world?
- After carrying out a democratic "audit" of your chosen a country, what are your conclusions?
- Did internal dissension or external destabilization play a bigger role in destroying the Somalian state?
- How would you try to strengthen a weak state in the developing world? Would democracy help?
- Are some states simply too weak or too arbitrarily constructed to justify continued international recognition? Should the international community simply let them disintegrate? What would be the consequences?
- Is the state entering a period of decline? How would you measure its effectiveness compared with earlier periods?

📖 FURTHER READING

Buzan, Barry (1991). *People, States and Fear*. 2nd edn. London: Harvester International.
    A widely-read study that considers both the internal and external roles of the state; see Chapter 2 in particular.

Chabal, Patrick, and Daloz, Jean-Pascal (1999). *Africa Works: Disorder as Political Instrument*. Oxford: The International Africa Institute in association with James Currey.
    A vivid account of the distinctive features of states in Africa.

Noah Feldman (2008). *The Fall and Rise of the Islamic State*. Princeton, NJ: Princeton University Press.
    A sophisticated introduction to the history of the Islamic state and its contemporary evolution.

Gill, Graeme (2003). *The Nature and Development of the Modern State*. Basingstoke: Palgrave.
    A good survey of theories of the state in the aftermath of the collapse of communism.

Hay, Colin, Michael Lister, and David Marsh, eds (2006). *The State: Theories and Issues*. Basingstoke: Palgrave.
    A collection of articles that discuss contemporary issues in theories of the Western state.

Nelson, Brian (2006). *The Making of the Modern State*. London: Macmillan.
    A sweeping historical survey of the rise and spread of the Western state.

📱 WEB LINKS

www.pbs.org/ktca/liberty
    Devoted to the American Revolution.

http://chnm.gmu.edu/revolution/
    Devoted to the French Revolution.

www.magnacartaplus.org
    Contains links to many human rights documents.

www.foreignpolicy.com/story/cms.php?story_id=3865
    The most recent of regular lists of failed states.

www.china.org.cn/english/features/book/145941.htm
    The Chinese government's 2005 White Paper on democracy.

8 Law, Constitutions, and Federalism

CHAPTER OVERVIEW

In this chapter we discuss the role that constitutions play in determining the basic structure of the state and establishing the fundamental rights of citizens. Then, as a reminder that the rule of law may not always be interpreted uniformly, we explore different ways in which states may attempt to realize justice in the application of the law, focusing in particular on differences between Islamic and Western practices. After a look at the importance of constitutional courts we will turn to federalism, a system of government that, in addition to accommodating diversity, offers a way of containing the powers of the state. Then we explore consociationalism as an alternative approach to managing diversity. We conclude with a brief discussion of the increasing legalization of political life.

Law and Politics

Chapter 7 emphasized the power of the modern state. It also underlined the importance of controlling that power. According to Finer, one of the main Western innovations in the theory of the state was the concept of "law-boundedness." In other words, the decisions of the ruler(s) had to be codified and published in order to limit the exercise of arbitrary power and provide predictability in public affairs. Fareed Zakaria, a former editor of *Foreign Affairs* and CNN commentator, concurs:

> For much of modern history, what characterized governments in Europe and North America and differentiated them from those around the world, was not democracy but constitutional liberalism. The "Western model" is best symbolized not by the mass plebiscite but the impartial judge (Zakaria, 1997: 27).

The spread of Western conceptions of law around the world is a consequence of the spread of Western ideas of the state. In traditional societies in other parts of the world, rule-making had not been the exclusive domain of political rulers: binding rules on human conduct could also be imposed by other sources of authority, such as clans or religious leaders. Although these rules may not have been called "laws," they had the same force. Moreover, traditional societies in Africa and Asia tended to rely on self-regulation and internalized norms of harmony to achieve order, rather than formal legal adjudication (Menski, 2006: 547). The same is true of decision-making in pre-colonial North America (see **Box 8.1**).

KEY QUOTE BOX 8.1
Indigenous Governance Models in Canada

Does the forward march of the European state model mean that indigenous ways were somehow less effective or backward? Mohawk political theorist and professor Taiaiake Alfred has argued that "Traditional government is the antidote to the colonial disease and its corruptions and abuses of power, and to the disempowerment of our people and communities." Alfred defines the indigenous concept of governance this way:

> There is no central or coercive authority, and decision-making is collective. Leaders rely on their persuasive abilities to achieve a consensus that respects that autonomy of individuals, each of whom is free to dissent from, and remain unaffected by, the collective decision. The clan or family is the basic unit of social organization, and larger forms of organization, from tribe through nation to confederacy, are still predicated on the political autonomy and economic independence of clan units through family-based control of lands and resources.
>
> A crucial feature of the indigenous concept of governance is its respect for individual autonomy. This respect precludes the notion of "sovereignty"—the idea that there can be a permanent transference of power or authority from the individual to an abstraction of the collective called "government." The indigenous tradition sees government as the collective power of the individual members of the nation; there is no separation

---

◀ A banner carried by "Occupy Wall Street" demonstrators on the Brooklyn Bridge recalls the opening words of the US Constitution (© Julie Dermansky/Corbis).

between society and state. Leadership is exercised by persuading individuals to pool their self-power in the interest of the collective good.

Governance in an indigenist sense can be practised only in a decentralized, small-scale environment among people who share a culture. It centres on the achievement of consensus and the creation of collective power, bounded by six principles:

- Governance depends on the active participation of individuals.
- Governance balances many layers of equal power.
- Governance is dispersed.
- Governance is situational
- Governance is non-coercive.
- Governance respects diversity (Alfred, 2009: 49–51).

In Alfred's view, indigenous governance can be practised only in small, homogeneous communities. What do you think would happen if a country with millions of people were to adopt this form of governance?

All Canada Photos: Chris Cheadle

PHOTO 8.1 Mungo Martin House, outside the Royal British Columbia Museum in Victoria, was built by the Kwakwaka'wakw carver Mungo Martin in 1953 on the model of a traditional "big house." The potlatch that marked its opening was the first to be held in public after the ban on the practice was lifted in 1951. The house is still used today for First Nations gatherings.

SOURCE: Alfred, T. (2008). *Peace, Power, Righteousness: An Indigenous Manifesto*. 2nd edn. Don Mills, ON: Oxford University Press.

Gradually, however, Western states arrogated to themselves the exclusive responsibility for issuing such rules in the form of laws, and codified them for the sake of consistency of application. Then, as legislatures became more common, law-making became their primary function. Gradually, as Western states spread around the world, so did these practices. Law-making was associated with the "civilizing mission" that Western states set for themselves, and as Alfred's analysis shows, it was radically contrary to some indigenous conceptions of governance. This monopoly on legislative activity is another essential feature of modern states, which often claim that the legitimacy of binding rules for society depends on approval by the legislature. Sometimes this position is described as **legal positivism**, which means that law is what the state says it is. It has become widely accepted in Western states that because other types of rule lack this legitimacy, they also lack the authority of state laws. As Twining (2000: 232) put it:

> [O]ver 200 years Western legal theory has been dominated by conceptions of law that tend to be monist (one internally coherent legal system), statist (the state has a monopoly of law within its territory), and positivist (what is not created or recognized as law by the state is not law).

Legal positivism is perhaps best exemplified in the principle of **secularism** embraced by France. Here civil state authorities assert their precedence over all competing sources of rule-making authority, especially religious ones. Ataturk was heavily influenced by this example: the reforms that he introduced in the 1920s asserted the supremacy of the Turkish state over Islamic religious authorities. The Turkish state's Directorate of Religious Affairs controls the mosques by employing all Muslim clerics on salaries and subjecting them to an administrative hierarchy, which supervises their pronouncements. The most striking demonstration of the state's claim to authority was the announcement in 2008 that it would seek to establish which of the Prophet's sayings or *hadith* were genuine.

The extent to which this claim to legal **monism** has been accepted can be seen in the UK. There was heated opposition to the Archbishop of Canterbury's suggestion, in 2008, that British Muslims should have access to *shariah* law in matters regarding family life. Although the Archbishop, who leads the Anglican Church, did not propose the establishment of a parallel legal system, his suggestion was seen as a challenge to the primacy of state-approved and state-codified law. A number of states in other parts of the world permit greater legal pluralism. India, Pakistan, and Bangladesh, for example, allow different religious communities the right to establish their own rules to regulate matters of faith and family. (India has a significant Muslim minority, while Pakistan and Bangladesh are majority Muslim.)

There is a close connection between legal and political systems. "Establishing laws to regulate human conduct has been one of the most basic functions performed by states since earliest times. To ensure that citizens accept those laws as legitimate, they must be established according to rules of procedure that are themselves legitimate and must be approved by the legislature (a subject to which we shall return in Chapter 9). Almost all states have legislatures, although their powers and procedures may vary widely.

Key functions performed by law include determining criminal behaviour, prescribing punishments for criminals, and providing impartial rules for binding adjudication in disputes. These functions are encapsulated, especially in the West, in the concept of the **rule of law**: the principle that everyone in a society, whether ruler, minister, or ordinary

© Peter Turnley for Harper's/Corbis

8

PHOTO 8.2 East meets West: Young Turkish women in Istanbul smoke both traditional water pipes and American cigarettes. Although its population is 99% Muslim and the country could have adopted Islam as its official religion, Turkey has been a secular democracy since the days of Ataturk.

citizen, is expected to obey the law and (at least in theory) everyone is equal before it. For such a system to enjoy legitimacy, Fuller laid down eight conditions that must prevail in order for laws to be just; see **Box 8.2**. These conditions have been widely understood to make up the necessary basis for the rule of law.

The idea that the legal system can help prevent the abuse of power by the executive was enshrined in the American **Constitution** and has been included in other constitutions since then. One prerequisite for the courts to perform that function is independence from the state: in other words, the state must accept that judges are free to determine the merits of legal cases, no matter what the implications might be for the government. Although an impartial legal system is a check on legislators' freedom to manoeuvre, the rule of law is one of the essential elements of **good governance**. It is also an integral feature of **liberal democracy**. We will return to the adjudication function of legal systems and their relationship with political systems towards the end of this chapter.

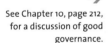
See Chapter 10, page 212, for a discussion of good governance.

KEY CONCEPT BOX 8.2
Eight Requirements for Just Laws

To be just, a law must be: (1) general in scope; (2) public; (3) prospective rather than retroactive; (4) clear; (5) consistent; (6) relatively constant; (7) capable of being obeyed; and (8) enforced as written (Fuller, 1969: 33–94).

Constitutions

The term "constitution" can be used in two ways, one general and one more narrow. In the broad sense it denotes the overall structure of a state's political system; see **Box 8.3**. In this broad sense, the term may also be understood to refer to a nation's **political culture**; thus a decision that is said to be contrary to the nation's "constitution" may infringe the "spirit" of the constitution rather than its precise terms.

KEY QUOTE BOX 8.3

Anthony King Defines "Constitution"

[T]he set of the most important rules and common understandings in any given country that regulate the relations among that country's governing institutions and also the relations between that country's governing institutions and the people of that country (King, 2007: 3).

The second, narrower sense of "constitution" refers to a specific document that lays down the basic institutions of state and the procedures for changing them, as well as the basic rights and obligations of the state's citizens. This document also serves as the basic source of national law, so that individual laws and legal codes are expected to conform to it. It is, or should be, the core of the legal system. Ensuring that this demanding requirement is met demands continual monitoring, and most states have a special constitutional court to adjudicate in cases of apparent conflict, although in Canada and the US this role is fulfilled by the Supreme Court. This responsibility is particularly onerous in Islamic states, where secular civil codes must be harmonized with divinely inspired, universal *shariah* law. For an example of one attempt to devise an Islamic constitution, see Moten (1996: Appendix B). For the more practical difficulties facing a constitutional court (in this case in Egypt) trying to cope with these problems, see Lombardi (1998).

In practice, the difference between the two senses of the term "constitution" is not nearly as great as it used to be. Only three western states—the UK, New Zealand, and Israel—now do not have written constitutions. Recent decades have seen a surge of constitution-writing around the world, including in Canada. With the patriation of the Canadian constitution in 1982 Canada gained the right to make its own laws without the approval of the British sovereign. The Liberal government of Pierre Trudeau invited Queen Elizabeth II to sign the document, relinquishing what until then had been an important aspect of her formal power.

At least 81 states have adopted new constitutions, while a further 33 have carried out major constitutional reforms. In many countries, including the states that made up the former Soviet Union and Yugoslavia, constitution-making was a consequence of the collapse of communism, but they were not the only ones to do; Saudi Arabia adopted a constitution in 1992, Algeria in 1989 (amended 1996), and Morocco in 1996. A written constitution makes legitimate patterns of political behaviour both more transparent

AP Photo/Canadian Press, Ron Poling

8

PHOTO 8.3 Queen Elizabeth II signs the Canadian Constitution in 1982 as Prime Minister Pierre Trudeau looks on.

and more regularized. But as King (2007) reminds us, no single written document can cover all of even the most fundamental elements of the political system. For example, virtually no state establishes a particular electoral system in its constitution; yet the electoral system plays a vital role in determining how power can change hands.

In addition to the details of specific constitutions, you should also bear in mind the related notion of **constitutionalism**. This term too can mean two things. It can refer to a normative outlook on the political values in particular country's constitution (i.e., doing things according to its "spirit"); or it can refer to a broader normative view according to which the constitution is the most fundamental principle of political life. At its most extreme, this could mean that constitutions, once codified, should never change. In practice, no state makes this an absolute principle: constitutions are amended or even replaced. However, states generally make such change very difficult by insisting on special procedures for changing them so that such change takes place without haste and after due reflection. The notion that the constitution has a special status is part of constitutionalism.

Respect for the primacy of the constitution remains a core element of North American political systems. Amending the Canadian constitution was particularly difficult because, for political reasons, the government of Quebec refused to sign the constitution on the grounds that the Canada Act, which created the constitution, did not recognize Quebec's distinct society. This thorny issue still has not been resolved, despite many efforts (Laforest, 1995: 161–4). Thus almost 8 million of Canada's roughly 34 million have been excluded from the constitution (see Statistics Canada 2011). Some Aboriginal leaders also objected, based on the fact that their treaties were signed with the British crown and not the Canadian government. Constitutions are equally difficult to amend in continental Europe, where the memory of disastrous dictatorships has made a robust constitutional order look very positive. A great deal of the advice on good governance offered to developing countries by the West involves the rule of law, which provides greater governmental transparency and predictability for foreign investors as well as for local citizens.

KEY POINTS

- Common usage of the term "constitution" is ambiguous, sometimes referring to a legal document and sometimes a pattern of rule.
- Constitutions may embody aspirations for future patterns of rule, in addition to regulating how governance is exercised now.
- Constitutionalism is a normative doctrine giving high priority to the observance of a constitution's provisions and efforts to ensure that it is effective.
- Even if a constitution excludes a large segment of the population, as in the case of Quebec, it is likely to be very difficult to change.

Fundamental Rights

A basic feature of most constitutions is a list of the fundamental rights of citizens. The first such lists were contained in the American Constitution and the Declaration of the Rights of Man and the Citizen in revolutionary France. The Universal Declaration of Human Rights, adopted by the UN in 1948, was based on a draft prepared by a commission whose chair was Eleanor Roosevelt, the widow of President Franklin D. Roosevelt.

Comparison of the two Declarations shows an evolution in the thinking about the range of rights to which citizens are entitled. The French document concentrates mainly on the establishment of a legal basis for the relations between the citizen and the state, so most of the rights it specifies involve legal due process. But it does include more specific political rights vis-à-vis the state: freedom apart from what the law specifically forbids (Articles 4, 5) freedom of expression (Article 11), and the citizens' right, either personally or through their representatives, both to determine the contributions that are made to the state and to expect an account from the state of how those resources have been used (Articles 14, 15).

KEY QUOTE BOX 8.4
Canada's Charter of Rights and Freedoms (1982)

The Charter of Rights and Freedoms is part of Canada's constitution. The role of interpreting it falls to the Supreme Court of Canada, which can strike down as unconstitutional laws that it deems to violate the Charter. Among the protections guaranteed by the Charter are the following:

Fundamental Freedoms

2. Everyone has the following fundamental freedoms:
   (a) freedom of conscience and religion;
   (b) freedom of thought, belief, opinion and expression, including freedom of the press and other media of communication;
   (c) freedom of peaceful assembly; and
   (d) freedom of association.

Democratic Rights

3. Every citizen of Canada has the right to vote in an election of members of the House of Commons or of a legislative assembly and to be qualified for membership therein.

...

Mobility Rights

6. (1) Every citizen of Canada has the right to enter, remain in and leave Canada.
   (2) Every citizen of Canada and every person who has the status of a permanent resident of Canada has the right
      (a) to move to and take up residence in any province; and
      (b) to pursue the gaining of a livelihood in any province. . . .

Legal Rights

7. Everyone has the right to life, liberty and security of the person and the right not to be deprived thereof except in accordance with the principles of fundamental justice.
8. Everyone has the right to be secure against unreasonable search or seizure.
9. Everyone has the right not to be arbitrarily detained or imprisoned.
10. Everyone has the right on arrest or detention
      (a) to be informed promptly of the reasons therefor;
      (b) to retain and instruct counsel without delay and to be informed of that right; and
      (c) to have the validity of the detention determined by way of habeas corpus and to be released if the detention is not lawful.

...

12. Everyone has the right not to be subjected to any cruel and unusual treatment or punishment.
13. A witness who testifies in any proceedings has the right not to have any incriminating evidence so given used to incriminate that witness in any other proceedings, except in a prosecution for perjury or for the giving of contradictory evidence.

...

15. (1) Every individual is equal before and under the law and has the right to the equal protection and equal benefit of the law without discrimination and, in particular, without discrimination based on race, national or ethnic origin, colour, religion, sex, age or mental or physical disability.

SOURCE: "Canadian Charter Of Rights And Freedoms' Being Part I of the Constitution Act, 1982 www.efc.ca/pages/law/charter/charter.text.html

In the twentieth century, citizens' rights extended beyond the purely "political" to include broader social rights. In constitutions, these additions usually relate to welfare provisions, but they may specify other conditions as well. For example, many states (especially in Catholic or Islamic societies) lay particular emphasis on the family as the basic unit of society and assign it a privileged position. The Universal Declaration of Human Rights (UDHR) was one of the first documents to establish social rights. Everyone has the right to social security (Article 21), to work and equal pay for equal work

(Article 23), to rest and leisure with reasonable limits on working hours (Article 24), to a standard of living "adequate for the health and well-being of himself and of his family" (Article 25), to education (Article 26), and to participation in the cultural life of the community (Article 27). The UDHR also includes a number of additional political rights that were not mentioned in the Rights of Man. Thus every individual has the right to freedom of thought, conscience, and religion, including the right to change them (Article 18); the right to freedom of opinion and expression, including the freedom to receive and impart information and ideas through any media and regardless of frontiers (Article 19); and the right to freedom of peaceful assembly and association (Article 20). In theory, all states that have accepted the Declaration have also committed themselves to observing it, whether or not its provisions are specifically incorporated in their constitutions.

In principle all these rights are "justiciable" within individual states. Thus citizens should be entitled to go to a court of law to seek redress if they feel that any of these rights are being infringed by their government. Of course, this depends on the willingness (and financial ability) of individual citizens to pursue their own claims in the courts.

Clearly, this extension of rights leaves a great deal of room for judicial interpretation. Welfare and cultural rights do not lend themselves to a simple "yes" or "no." They leave open the questions of amount or degree. Is a citizen of a developing country entitled to the same level of welfare as one in Europe? The same level of healthcare? Of education? It all depends on the priorities of the sovereign government in question. Should the courts become involved in determining the levels of welfare spending as opposed to other claims on the budget? This is a sensitive issue in democracies. In the US, the Supreme Court simply refuses to hear cases it deems to be "political." Even in the case of explicitly "political" rights, such as freedom of expression and association, where a yes/no judgment by the courts is more likely, recent experience has shown that such rights are often balanced against other public priorities. For example, the right to freedom of expression may have to be weighed against the "right" to public safety from racial hatred or terrorism.

Although the twentieth century saw a dramatic expansion in the range of rights to which citizens are supposedly entitled, there is still scope for individual legal systems to come up with a great variety of interpretations. This explains why, in democracies perhaps even more than in **authoritarian** regimes, the court system is increasingly limiting elected governments' freedom of manoeuvre.

Increasingly, alongside provisions regulating the operation of specific institutions, the constitutions of nation-states contain aspirations about the directions in which their political systems should develop. This has always been a feature of constitutions of states in Latin America, but it is increasingly prominent in Europe and also in Islamic societies. Insofar as they contain provisions for aspirations that are not yet realized, they also give the courts scope to contribute to the realization of those aspirations. In that sense they allow for greater legalization of the political process. In fact, they will contribute to it.

KEY POINTS

- Over the last two centuries the number of universal rights has increased.
- New rights include rights to welfare, cultural protection, and cultural respect.
- There is potential for conflict between the courts' duty to enforce rights and the sovereignty of parliament.

Constitutional Courts and Judicial Review

Because of the sensitivity of the issues they are called on to determine, all states have a constitutional court of some kind. As we shall see, this is particularly true of federal states where constitutional guarantees to subnational units are a crucial reassurance that their interests will not be repressed. Some courts are actually designated constitutional courts, while others may assume that role as part of a wider range of judicial functions. Even Britain, which does not have a formal constitution, entrusted the function of interpreting the legality of laws to the Appellate Committee of the House of Lords. It did so until 2010, when a new Supreme Court was established.

In most countries the judges who serve on such courts are trained lawyers, either academic or professional. France is an exception, however. It does not require that a member of its Conseil constitutionnel be a lawyer; some of them have been distinguished politicians. In addition, the Conseil's powers are limited by the fact that in France, a law that has been promulgated cannot be changed except by parliament.

In Canada, the US, and the UK, the courts have been willing to challenge government decisions through judicial review, on the grounds that fundamental rights have been infringed, or that administrators have failed to observe due process. While this kind of intrusion has often been regarded as embarrassing or irritating for governments, the courts have justified it on the grounds that human rights must be respected, even those of condemned criminals. Although this tendency appears to be spreading to other countries, France again is an exception. There the state takes the view that challenges to the constitutionality of potential human rights abuses are better raised in parliament, which has the duty of holding the government to account, than by the courts. British judges used to share this view until the 1970s, but no longer (King, 2007: 115–49).

KEY POINTS

- States establish special courts, or legal arrangements, to safeguard constitutions.
- There is increasing pressure for executive policy-making to be subject to standards laid down by judicial review.

Legal Adjudication of Political Problems

As these examples show, despite the increasing legalization of political life, there is still much scope for variation in the way the courts of different nations interpret and implement even universal human rights. This is not only because of the interests, or self-interest, of particular nation-states, but also because of different approaches to the ultimate objective of the justice that legal systems are expected to dispense. Approaches to the function and purpose of law also vary from one country to another. As Montada (2001) put it, the concern for justice seems universal, but it takes many faces, because there are divergent views on what is meant by the term and how it is realized in particular legal jurisdictions. Four basic differences revolve around different interpretations of the meaning of "justice."

The first can be summarized as a kind of legal positivism. The law of a particular country is neither more nor less than the sum of the laws it has established. A phrase often used by French lawyers is "La loi est la loi." This means that the wording of every law approved by parliament is almost sacred. It is inappropriate for judges to enquire whether any law is phrased inadequately. Their task is simply to enforce it.

This approach to constitutional issues is replicated in France's former colonies, but it also resonates more widely. In pre-modern China there was a school of legal thinking called the Legalists. Their main concern was to ensure that the Chinese obeyed the law. As long as they did, this would ensure order and harmony in society and prevent **anarchy**. The Legalists were not especially interested in "justice" per se. For them, an orderly society was a just one. It was order and harmony that was just, not necessarily any particular law. They wanted to deter law-breaking, as that would be unjust. Therefore extreme punishment was "just," however brutal for the individual law-breaker, as it would ensure justice for the rest of society. This was rule by law, but it was aimed at making people fear rulers and officials. It was law designed for **deterrence.**

A second approach to the social function of law was typified by communist states. Here the function of law was subordinated to a higher, non-legal goal: communism itself. Universal human rights were of less concern, except in the indefinite future. Judges had to be members of the Communist party, which meant that they had to defer to the party leadership. So appeals to the courts to defend the human rights of political dissenters were bound to fail. Even today officials of the Chinese Communist party can be prosecuted for criminal offences only after the party leadership has agreed. Thus, even though there is increasing talk of "rule of law" replacing "rule by men" in China, there is still a long way to go, at least by Western standards.

A third approach to law and society can be seen in Islamic states, where in general there is no doubt about the traditional importance of justice and the law. According to Rosen (1989: 74), "Everywhere one encounters in Islamic life the idea of justice." For Lewis (2005: 39), "the traditional Islamic ideal of good government is expressed in the term 'justice'." And according to Hallaq (2005: 193), "if ever there was any pre-modern legal and political culture that maintained the principle of the rule of law so well, it was the culture of Islam." Of course, this rule of law had more to do with Islamic practice than with any separation of the powers of rulers and judges, as in the West: it existed because both rulers and judges were supposed to defer to the revealed law of the *shariah*. In general, rulers appointed judges and could dismiss them. There was no notion of ordinary people having rights vis-à-vis their rulers, unless the rulers broke divine law.

On the other hand, an Islamic state would not claim the same monopoly over law-making that Western states do. Islamic law is made by religious scholars, not rulers; and there is not the same insistence on consistency between the decisions of judges and on binding precedents. Judges try to do justice according to the particular circumstances of an individual case, rather than forcing the facts to fit a set of orthodox decisions. There is no systematic codification of legal precedents. Traditionally in Islamic societies there was a tendency for political monism but legal pluralism. In the West we find the reverse: a greater tendency towards political pluralism and legal monism, with legal systems expected to deliver consistent authoritative verdicts.

By contrast, the fourth approach to legal justice—what we can loosely term the Western approach—emphasizes **procedural justice**. This means making sure that verdicts are similar and consistent in similar sets of circumstances. It requires a greater legal bureaucracy to ensure consistency of verdicts, with one or two higher layers of appeal courts, as well as ministries of justice to administer them. It also risks delivering verdicts that are not well tailored to individual circumstances. Nevertheless, it does provide relatively high predictability about likely outcomes in court cases. The Western approach gradually spread more widely around the world in the nineteenth and twentieth centuries, partly a result of the spread of the Western state. However, it also took root in countries that had never been Western colonies.

One of the best examples is Japan. As the Japanese state sought to respond to challenges from the West in the second half of the nineteenth century, it sent scholars to Europe to study alternative national legal systems, particularly those of Britain, Germany, and France. The scholars assessed the merits of different legal codes and created a mixed system. Japan turned to the principles of German administrative law to provide the basis of its new code of administrative law, while it looked to Germany and France for its commercial law. Turkey responded in similar ways. From the 1870s onwards, Turkey too began to produce legal codes that grafted Western legal principles and justice on to its own well-established forms of jurisprudence and courts, and these spread throughout its empire in the Middle East. Civil courts assumed greater authority over religious ones. Gradually the state took control of the legal process as Turkey embarked on Western-style modernization.

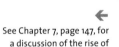

See Chapter 7, page 147, for a discussion of the rise of the Western state model.

Although Western legal practices and norms have spread around the world, this does not mean that they have become universal and fully consistent. The decision of President Pervez Musharraf of Pakistan to "correct" his country's Supreme Court in 2007 by dismissing most of the judges and replacing them with more pliant ones was a striking example of persisting differences. It resonated with earlier traditions of Islamic rulers; and in Islamic states in general, there remains a shifting tension between the prescriptions and reasoning of *shariah* law and civil codes.

We should also remember that other elements in the context of national legal systems may have a significant bearing on the way law is practised. Epp has shown how the pursuit of civil rights in a number of states with quite similar legal frameworks—the US, India, the UK, and Canada—has varied considerably according to the legal infrastructure of individual countries. In particular, what matters is the availability of public resources to help poorer litigants pursue cases. Litigants in the US and Canada find this much easier than do those in the UK or India. In consequence, there has been a much stronger movement to pursue rights-related cases in North America, with Canada in particular undergoing what Epp describes as "a vibrant rights revolution" since 1960. He explains this in part by the 1982 Charter of Rights and Freedoms, but also in part by a growing support structure for legal mobilization (advocacy organizations; government aid for litigants; lawyers and legal scholars who changed the previous prevailing conservative mindset of the legal system) (Epp, 1998: 156, 195–6). The availability of resources for litigation has an important impact on the pursuit of rights. What this shows is that there is a close connection between a country's legal system and the evolution of its political system. The two interact with and influence each other.

Even the number of lawyers in a country will have a big impact on the place of law in a nation's public life and therefore on citizens' ability to access the law. The United States has almost one million qualified lawyers—about 0.3 per cent of the population. The UK has half that percentage, Germany a quarter, and France an eighth, while Japan and India have only roughly one twenty-fifth. No doubt this also played a part in the limited pursuit of rights in India that Epp mentioned above. These figures help to explain the widespread perception that the Japanese are reluctant to go to the courts when they have a problem and try to find alternative ways of resolving disputes.

- Orientations on appropriate functions for legal systems have traditionally varied from country to country.
- This can lead to different interpretations of even universal rights.
- Western jurisprudence emphasizes procedural justice through greater consistency and bureaucratic organization.

Federalism, Consociational Democracy, and Asymmetrical Decentralization

The American Constitution was explicitly designed to restrain the power of the state. One way was through the establishment of checks and balances, with the threefold division of power between executive, legislature, and judiciary. A second way was through the establishment of a federal system. The territorial decentralization of power was designed as a further check on any possible oppression. But federalism also recognized the reality that individual states in the US saw themselves as at first as sovereign entities who entered the union as a "voluntary compact." Canada too was formed by representatives of individual provinces that agreed to cede some aspects of their sovereignty to a federal government. Clashes between member units and the centre are common, especially when the former feel that the federal government is intruding on their jurisdiction.

AP Photo/Adrian Wyld, The Canadian Press

PHOTO 8.4 Leaders of three federal states meet at the 2011 G20 Summit in Cannes to discuss policy: Canadian Prime Minister Stephen Harper, Australian Prime Minister Julia Gillard, and Indian Prime Minister Manmohan Singh.

Ever since the nineteenth century, **federalism** has been touted as a solution to the risks of potential dictatorship. The importance of this idea can be seen in the federal constitution that was imposed on West Germany after the Second World War. It was intended to undermine the remaining roots of Nazi dictatorship, and it has worked. Once reunified in 1990, the new German state divided its federal power between 16 *Länder* ("lands"). These institutions have taken root in the German political system and have made Germany a reliable democratic partner in the heart of Europe.

In general, what is federalism? According to Robertson (1993: 184), it is a form of government in which power is constitutionally divided between different authorities in such a way that each exercises responsibility for a particular set of functions and maintains its own institutions to discharge those functions. In a federal system each authority therefore has sovereignty within its own sphere of responsibilities, because the powers that it exercises are not delegated to it by some other authority.

This definition emphasizes how a constitution safeguards equality between the national government and the member units, and demarcates responsibility for performing particular functions. It reassures the provinces or states that their decisions cannot be overridden by some higher authority.

To provide substance for that protection, federal systems usually establish two institutions. First, there is normally a two-chamber parliament, with the upper chamber composed of representatives from the provinces or states. The latter are given specific powers to ensure that their constitutional prerogatives cannot be legislated away without their consent. Second, there is usually a constitutional court to rule on the constitutionality of legislative proposals, again to reassure member units that they cannot be coerced into submission.

Generally, since the American Revolution, federalism has provided a constitutional framework for states facing two other challenges. One is simply territorial size. As **Table 8.1** shows, eight of the ten largest states in the world by area are federations.

TABLE 8.1 Federalism among the Ten Largest States in the World by Territory

State	Federal/Unitary
Russia	F
Canada	F
US	F
China	U
Brazil	F
Australia	F
India	F
Argentina	F
Kazakhstan	U
Sudan	F

Australia is a classic example. The federation was originally created in 1900 to allow significant devolution of power to individual states because of the difficulties of trying to run the whole country centrally, given the communication technologies that were available at that time. Of course many federations are also heterogeneous in terms of population. This was not a significant factor in Australia, but in Canada the French–English division, coupled with the vast size of the growing country, made federalism the obvious choice.

Federalism offers a way of accommodating diversity by guaranteeing minority communities—usually ethnically based—that there will be no political challenge to their particular way of life, culture, language, and religion. In fact, not all federations are large, and some are very small indeed (see **Table 8.2**).

TABLE 8.2 | List of Federations

Argentina	Germany	Pakistan
Australia	India	Russia
Austria	Iraq	St Kitts and Nevis
Belgium	Malaysia	Sudan
Bosnia and Herzegovina	Mexico	Switzerland
Brazil	Micronesia	United Arab Emirates
Canada	Nepal	US
Comoros	Netherlands	Venezuela
Ethiopia	Nigeria	

The experience of federations is not always positive. Many have disintegrated, some disastrously. The collapse of the USSR has been described by Russian Prime Minister Vladimir Putin as one of the greatest disasters of the twentieth century, while the break-up of the former Yugoslavia unleashed the bloodiest conflict in Europe since the Second World War. Even where federations have survived, some have still had to go through civil wars; Nigeria in the 1960s, the United States in the 1860s. The recent experience of Belgium, which in 2007 went for more than 150 days without a national government, also suggests that federations are not always capable of decisive national decision-making. So federations are not automatically capable of preventing violent conflict or dissolution, or of providing effective government. Yet a prime cause of the collapse of the USSR and Yugoslavia was the lack of legal support and rule of law. Without these, constitutional provisions of any kind can do little. On the positive side Stepan (2004: 441) has recently declared that "Every single long-standing democracy in a territorially based multi-lingual and multinational policy is a federal state." And Rotimi has maintained that, despite the civil war, "federalism has long been recognized as the indispensable basis for Nigeria's identity and survival" (2004: 328).

Yet in the 1970s the idea that federalism was the naturally most appropriate solution to the problems of division in deeply divided societies was challenged by the theory of **consociationalism** (introduced in Chapter 3). This was based on the experience of a few

CASE STUDY
Collapse of the Former Yugoslavia

Yugoslavia was created at the end of the First World War as a state for the South Slavic peoples. It was designed to prevent the return of imperial powers in a region formerly ruled by the Ottoman and Hapsburg empires. However, between the wars it was bedevilled by enduring enmity between the two largest ethnic communities, the Serbs and Croats. Before Yugoslavia was formed, the Serbs had their own independent kingdom. They wanted the continuation of their unitary state, in contrast to the Croats who, after centuries of colonial domination, wanted more autonomy within a federal system. In 1941 Yugoslavia was dismembered under Axis control and hundreds of thousands were killed in fratricidal conflict. Many allege that genocide was committed on Yugoslav soil during that period.

After liberation in 1945, largely by the Communist partisans under Josip Broz Tito, the Yugoslav state was restored and a new federal system was created. Even the ruling Yugoslav Communist Party was divided into separate federal units. The six federal republics (Serbia, Croatia, Slovenia, Bosnia–Herzegovina, Macedonia, and Montenegro) had equal representation in the federal government, and after 1974 the two autonomous regions of Kosovo and Vojvodina in Serbia were granted only slightly less power. Yugoslavia was by far the most genuinely federal communist state. In 1963 it created the only constitutional court in the communist world. For many decades, the memory of the blood-letting during the war, a political culture that exalted the shared heroism of the partisan resistance, the pride in a Yugoslav road to socialism based on workers' self-management, the threat of foreign intervention, as well as Tito's own robust leadership, all helped to preserve national unity. Despite occasional challenges to the leadership (in 1968 a new generation of Croat leaders tried to introduce a more liberal set of policies, the plan was rejected by Tito), Yugoslavia stayed united and prosperous until Tito's death in 1980.

Afterwards, though, the state ran into increasing difficulties. There was no cohesion in the national leadership. Tito had avoided naming a successor. He created a federal system with a collective presidency, where the leader of each of the federal republics acted as head of state for just one year in rotation. He had emphasized the need for national decision-making on the basis of "consensus," which meant unanimity. After he was gone, republic leaders put the interests of their own republics above those of the state as a whole. The national economy fragmented, as inter-republic trade declined. Inflation continued to increase throughout the 1980s. The national leaders agreed on remedies in Belgrade but then refused to implement them when they returned to their respective capitals. No one was prepared to make sacrifices for the good of the country as a whole. Popular dissatisfaction grew. All the nationalities, even the Serbs (the largest), felt that they were the losers in the Federation. Trust disintegrated across the country.

Then in 1986, the heir apparent to the Serbian leadership, Slobodan Milosevic, made a speech at an event commemorating the 600th anniversary of the defeat of the Serbs at the hands of the Ottoman Turks in Kosovo. He made an unexpected appeal for Serbs to stand up for their rights, and vowed that Belgrade would back them. Many Serbs feared that Kosovo, with its majority Albanian population, would demand autonomy or even independence. Milosevic's speech provoked an emotional response across Serbia, which he turned into a movement to restore decisive national government under his leadership. Large numbers of Serbs were mobilized to march on Montenegro and then Slovenia to bring them to heel. In turn this provoked apprehension in the other republics about resurgent Serbian chauvinism. The constitutional court proved ineffective.

Fearful of Milosevic, but also sensing the opportunity to create new, smaller states that they could control, the leaders of the Communist parties in Croatia and Slovenia called for referenda on independence for both countries. Croatia launched its own nationalist movement—which also had chauvinist features—under former Communist general and historian Franjo Tudjman. In turn this provoked Milosevic to send the federal army into Slovenia and Croatia. Within a short time a third of Croatia was occupied. When Bosnia-Herzegovina launched its referendum on independence, war spread further south. Milosevic, who died while on trial for his crimes, will be remembered for launching a civil war that became the biggest conflict in Europe since the Second World War and destroyed the state of Yugoslavia.

(For a discussion of various explanations for the collapse of the former Yugoslavia, as well as background history, see MacDonald, 2003, and Ramet, 2005.)

small states with deep multiethnic and multiconfessional cleavages, largely in Europe, that had achieved intercommunal harmony and cooperation without a formal federal system. The first example was the Netherlands. Its success was attributed not to formal constitutional arrangements or legalism, but rather to cooperation in power-sharing between elites, which generated and reinforced mutual trust. According to Arendt Lijphart (1977), there are four main characteristics of consociational democracies; see **Box 8.5**.

In fact, some of the other states that were later cited as examples of the same practice ran into serious problems. Consociationalism, like federalism, cannot guarantee social harmony. Not all the difficulties were domestic in origin. Lebanon, for instance, was destabilized by conflict between the state of Israel and Palestinian refugees living in Lebanon. Cyprus was destabilized by Turkish invasion. Nevertheless since this model was usually applied

See Chapter 3, page 73, for an introduction to consociational democracy.

KEY CONCEPT BOX 8.5
Features of Consociationalism

- Government by grand coalition: government includes deputies from the parties representing all the main communities, which usually meant that the government held far more than a bare majority of seats in parliament.
- Segmental or subcultural autonomy: each ethnic or confessional community is responsible for administering policies in specific areas affecting them.
- Proportional representation: simple majoritarian rule very unlikely, and proportional representation in the distribution of posts in government bureaucracies, the distribution of public funds, and so on.
- Agreement on minority vetoes for certain types of legislation.

to small states, it made them more vulnerable in the case of outside intervention. In fact, most consociational arrangements have proved relatively short-lived, and not just because of external intervention. Only the Netherlands has remained faithful to the model. This suggests that consociationalism may be most appropriate as a temporary solution to societies that have recently suffered from major division or conflict. It can help to stabilize the state through increased trust between communities, before the transition is made to a more permanent set of arrangements.

Nevertheless, Lijphart (1999) extended his theory to other states, focusing particularly on the first point. He claimed that democracies regularly governed by coalitions achieved better political and economic results because their policies were "owned" by much broader sections of society. This ownership was then translated into a more active commitment on the part of citizens to carry them out. He claimed that more consensual methods of government were more effective in improving living conditions for their citizens.

It is also interesting to note that in some developed states, different levels of autonomy have been offered to regions that have traditionally sought autonomy or independence, sometimes using violent means. States no longer feel that they have to make an exclusive choice between a unitary and a federal system. They sometimes devise hybrid combinations. This can be called asymmetric decentralization or asymmetric federalism. A particularly striking example is Spain, which has granted much more extensive self-governing powers to four of its regions or "autonomous communities"—Catalonia, the Basque country, Galicia, and Andalusia—than to the other 13, although the Catalan political scientist Colomer still calls the Spanish state "the clearest case of failure . . . to build a large nation-state in Europe" (2007: 80). The same principle has been applied in the UK, with varying powers granted to the Scottish, Welsh, and Northern Irish assemblies. In Canada too, the ten provinces have more power vis-à-vis the federal government than do the three territories.

Even France, where the state has traditionally been preoccupied with constitutional equality and the dominance of Paris, has granted greater autonomy to Corsica than to other *départements*, all of which are still formally unitary states. Federal states display the same tendency for hybridity. The Soviet Union for decades distinguished between federal republics, autonomous republics, autonomous regions, and autonomous districts, all of which had different sets of powers from the more "orthodox" provinces. Pakistan allows greater self-rule to the northwest frontier region and the federally administered tribal areas than to Punjab or Sindh. This means that other states that have to deal with great ethnic or religious cleavages can draw on a much wider range of possible precedents to demonstrate flexibility. In many ways the old distinction between federal and unitary states is disappearing, as similar kinds of asymmetrical relationships are introduced into both of them.

KEY POINTS

- Federalism has a dual role: as a check on centralized government, and as a way of managing profound social diversity.
- Federations may collapse without appropriate legal structures or widespread popular support.
- Consociationalism is an alternative approach to handling social diversity, relying on elite cooperation rather than legal formalism.

PHOTO 8.5 Parc Guell, in Barcelona, Spain, was designed by the renowned Catalan modernist architect Antoni Gaudi. Since 1975, the Spanish state has recognized the distinctive language and culture of Catalonia.

- Consociationalism may be understood as a more consensual form of rule than majoritarianism.
- There is increasing reliance on asymmetric arrangements to handle diversity in both federal and unitary political systems, which erodes the differences between them.

Conclusion: The Legalization of Political Life

This chapter has highlighted four points. The first is the importance of constitutions as fundamental institutions that structure political systems. By establishing the basic principles for political life, they channel political behaviour in various directions and, equally important, prevent some other forms of political behaviour; they also provide some transparency about the ways that public decisions are made.

Second, constitutions need a developed legal system to give life to their provisions. Without the rule of law, constitutions may be either flouted by government or undermined, as in Yugoslavia.

Third, different legal systems use different approaches to achieve justice. Emphases vary from one state to another, and thus interpretations of universal human rights to some extent vary from one country to another.

Fourth, federalism helps to prevent excessive concentration of powers in a nation's capital. It can also provide reassurance to some minorities that their interests will not be overridden by larger communities. It can promote harmony in heterogeneous states marked by deep cleavages. Consociationalism offers an alternative approach to the same challenge, although it has tended to succeed only in smaller states and over limited periods of time. In recent years unitary states have shown greater flexibility in devising new forms of decentralization that take regional differences into account and vary the rights that they offer to particular communities. In this way the boundaries between federal and unitary states are becoming blurred.

Finally, you may have noticed a theme underlying our discussions in this chapter: the expanding role played by law in social and political life. How central that role is varies considerably from one state to another. It is certainly most pronounced in the developed world, especially the US. Yet the trend is clearly spreading. In Pakistan, for example, President Musharraf's attempt to curtail the independence of the Supreme Court in 2007 provoked concerted resistance from lawyers, who had wide popular support.

The growing salience of law is striking in the case of China. At the beginning of its reform process, in the early 1980s, China had only 200 lawyers; today it has more than 100,000. This certainly marks a change in the direction of the rule of law, even if China's legal system is very different from Western models. The growing legalization of politics increases the checks on the power of the state and the executive branch of government; but it also makes politics more difficult for non-lawyers to understand. Dahl has remarked that the American system "is among the most opaque, confusing, and difficult to understand" of all the Western democracies (Dahl, 2001: 115).

Is politics becoming more opaque and more esoteric, increasingly confined to a limited political "class"? This is an issue to which we will return in Chapters 9 and 12.

? KEY QUESTIONS

- Go to http://confinder.richmond.edu/country.php and find the longest and shortest constitutions in the world. How do you think the political systems of these two states are likely to differ?
- Have you come across any constitutional provision that strikes you as odd or unnecessary? If so, why do you think it was included?
- Canada has a formal constitution, but Britain does not. How is this difference reflected in the political arrangements and practices of these two states?
- Have the French been right to resist the expansion of judicial review in political life and leave constitutional challenges largely to parliament?
- Assess Dahl's arguments about the weaknesses of the American Constitution. Is there any likelihood that they will be remedied?
- If federalism does indeed weaken the power of the government, does it make weaker states in the developing world too weak? What is the evidence from Nigeria, India, Brazil, and/or Pakistan?

- Do the autonomous communities of Catalonia and the Basque country in unitary Spain have greater powers for self-government than the federal Länder in Germany?
- How viable are federalism and consociationalism as solutions to the internal conflict in Iraq?
- If the rule of law is a good thing, does that mean that more laws make for a better state?

📖 FURTHER READING

Amoretti, Ugo M. and Nancy Bermeo, eds (2004). *Federalism and Territorial Cleavages.* Baltimore, MD: Johns Hopkins University Press.
An account of the ways in which federalism can manage territorial divisions within states.

Burgess, Michael (2006). *Comparative Federalism: Theory and Practice.* London: Routledge.
A recent account of the theory of federalism.

Dahl, Robert A. (2001). *How Democratic Is the American Constitution?* New Haven, CT: Yale University Press.
A study of the weaknesses of the American Constitution, including the great difficulty of changing it.

King, Anthony (2007). *The British Constitution.* Oxford: Oxford University Press.
A recent authoritative study of the British "constitution" in the broad sense.

Lane, Jan-Erik (1996). *Constitutions and Political Theory.* Manchester: Manchester University Press.
An examination of the relationship between constitutions and political theory.

Lijphart, Arend (1999). "Patterns of Democracy: Government Forms and Performance" in *Thirty-Six Countries.* New Haven, CT: Yale University Press.
Makes the case for broad coalition government and consociationalism as a more consensual and ultimately more effective form of rule.

Rocher, François, and Miriam Smith, eds (2003). *New Trends in Canadian Federalism.* 2nd edn. Toronto: University of Toronto Press.
An excellent introduction to the complexities and challenges of federalism in Canada, featuring a variety of well-known contributors.

📱 WEB LINKS

http://confinder.richmond.edu/country.php
A site offering connections to all the constitutions that are available online.

www.queensu.ca/iigr/index.html
The website of the Institute of Intergovernmental Relations at Queen's University in Kingston, ON. This is a world-class centre for research on federalism and intergovernmental relations around the world.

http://globalsolutions.org/wfi
The website of the World Federalist Institute, which is devoted to discussion and debate, as well as information-sharing on federalism in the US and around the world, and its contribution to challenges of global governance.

www.forumfed.org/en/index.php
The site of the Forum of Federations, an organization devoted to the study of federal countries.

9 Legislatures and Legislators

CHAPTER OVERVIEW

The functions of legislatures or parliaments take three basic forms: representational, governmental, and procedural. In the course of surveying them, the first section of this chapter will touch on questions such as the use of quotas to improve the representation of women in legislatures, the relative merits of parliamentary and presidential systems, and the role that legislatures can play in legitimizing dissent. A brief look at types of legislature, based on ability to stand up to the executive branch of government, is followed by an introduction to the internal structure of legislatures: the choice of single or double chambers, and the role of parliamentary committees. We will conclude by exploring trends in the backgrounds of members of parliament in various countries.

The Functions of Legislatures

At present there are 263 parliamentary chambers in 189 countries. This means that a little under one-third of the world's countries have two chambers. If we include the sub-national elected bodies that represent more restricted areas, such as provincial and state legislatures, there are thousands of elected bodies around the world. No wonder legislative studies is one of the oldest branches of political science and potentially one of the most interesting.

Legislatures are crucial institutions in any political system, but they are especially important in democracies. In fact, democracy would be inconceivable without them. They are vital elements in the structures of power within the state, serving (though to varying degrees) as checks on the executive's freedom of manoeuvre. Without legislatures, power in the modern state would be highly concentrated and potentially oppressive. Legislators can uphold constitutions by bringing public attention to attempts to subvert them; and if the executive tries to undermine or suspend the judicial system, the legislature can lend its weight to the courts. They are also open to public scrutiny, and many of their deliberations are made available to the public not only in printed form (e.g., Hansard) but on television or through the Internet.

There are two ways of presenting a comparative overview of legislatures. One way is to examine institutional arrangements such as debating chambers, standing committees, how staff members run their offices and communicate with constituents, and so on. The other way is to look at the functions they perform in their particular political systems. Here we will concentrate mainly on the latter, but we will examine one particular institutional issue: the differences between parliamentary and presidential political systems and their respective merits.

The functions of parliaments can be divided into three broad groups: representational, governmental, and procedural. It is the representational function of parliaments to represent both citizens and particular groups in society. Governmental functions include forming governments, developing policy, holding the government accountable for its actions, and enhancing government communication with citizens. Finally, the procedural functions of legislatures include ritualizing conflict and ensuring transparency.

Representation

The original function of parliaments in Europe was to provide a forum in which different classes in society could express their views to the monarch on matters of public concern. Their role was at most to consult with monarchs, often merely to rubber-stamp the decisions of the latter. There was no question of parliaments' deciding policy, let alone imposing their will on monarchs. Gradually, though, they acquired greater authority as rulers saw fit to consult them on matters such as taxation for public works or, most important, raising armies. Thus it was not only the European state that grew in response to the needs of war, as we suggested in Chapter 7; the role of parliaments also grew as they gained the authority to constrain the ability of monarchs to make war.

← See Chapter 7, page 143, for a discussion of the rise of the European state system.

Inherent in parliaments, therefore, is the notion that they are representative of the wider society. To be legitimate they have to "represent" the people. Still, over time different dimensions of possible representativeness have been proposed. In practice these are

◀ National Chief of the Assembly of First Nations Phil Fontaine speaks in the House of Commons following the government's formal apology for the residential schools in June 2008 (© Chris Wattie/Reuters/Corbis).

→ See Chapter 11, page 230, for a discussion of party systems.

difficult to reconcile, not least because the composition of parliaments is also inevitably intertwined with the electoral system on which they are based, as we will see in Chapter 11. So states with different histories and different national priorities may arrive at different institutional solutions to the same problem.

Does representation mean that deputies should be numerically representative of particular sections of society, as was originally the case with the House of Lords and House of Commons in the UK? Should the numbers of female representatives roughly correspond to the number of women in the population as a whole? What about ethnic minorities? Jacobson (1997: 207) points out that in the US Congress, African-Americans and Hispanics are both under-represented, though the disparities are not as great as in the case of women. Interestingly, Jacobson effectively excuses this situation on the grounds that "Congress is probably quite representative of the kinds of people who achieve positions of leadership in the great majority of American institutions. What it does produce is a sample of local elites from a remarkably diverse nation." Election to Congress is certainly an elite achievement, and so in Jacobson's view it is both appropriate and realistic for members of Congress to be representative of elites rather than the population as a whole.

← See Chapter 6, page 121, for Table 6.2, Political Representation of Women in Parliaments.

© ZoneCreative/istockphoto.com

PHOTO 9.1 The model for all parliaments: London's Palace of Westminster

In recent years efforts have been made to ensure that the composition of legislatures corresponds more closely to the structure of the population as a whole, particularly with respect to gender (see Table 6.2). There are now at least 40 countries that have introduced quotas for female representation in legislatures, while political parties in another 50 countries have adopted quotas for female candidates in elections (Dahlerup, 2005: 145).

KEY CONCEPT BOX 9.1
Women and Representation: But What Type?

An important contribution to the debate around women and representation was Hanna Pitkin's (1967) distinction between **descriptive** and **substantive** representation of women. "Descriptive" refers to the number of women in a particular legislature. Whether they are radical feminists, avowed neoconservatives, or anything in between, they will be represented because they are women, irrespective of their political views. By contrast, "substantive" representation refers explicitly to the representatives' politics.

Manon Tremblay and Réjean Pelletier, in their study of women's representation in the Canadian parliament, argue in favour of the "substantive conception." As they explain it, one of the standard arguments in favour of increasing women's representation is that, by virtue of "their socialization, values, and life experiences, women bring unique perspectives into the political arena" and therefore "would speak and act to support women's issues" (Tremblay and Pelletier, 2000: 381–2). But it is not enough simply to have more women in Parliament. For the authors, the key is to have more feminists: people who think about and promote policies that value women in society. In the US Congress, for example, female Democrats and Republicans both tend to be more feminist than their male counterparts in their own parties, but many male Democrats are more "feminist" in their voting behaviour than Republican women. In other words, gender and feminist viewpoints don't always correlate. In Canada, a 1982 study of Ontario politics revealed that at the provincial level, female members of the centre-right Conservative Party were far less open to the women's movement and feminist issues than male members of the more left-leaning Liberal and New Democratic parties. Tremblay and Pelletier conclude that what the Canadian Parliament needs is not just more women, but more feminists. This is one of many viewpoints that encourage us to question the belief that simply electing more women will improve women's social or economic positions in society.

There is still a long way to go before such quotas will be achieved, for reasons that Matland (2005) and Dahlerup (2005) have discussed. Nevertheless, the movement for quotas is likely to increase pressure to increase recruitment of people from other groups in society that are also regularly under-represented. In that case, at least in democracies, legislatures will undergo major changes in the coming decades.

Of course, if "representation" refers simply to expressing the views of constituents and serving as channels of communication with those in authority, the personal characteristics of the representatives are not so important. How far representatives should be obliged simply to express the views of a larger community of citizens and how far they should be free to express personal opinions is an open question. As we saw in Chapter 3, Edmund Burke argued that MPs were positively obliged to exercise their individual judgment; see **Box 9.2**.

See Chapter 3, page 63, for a discussion of representative democracy.

KEY QUOTE BOX 9.2
Burke on the Relationship between MPs and Constituents

Certainly, Gentlemen, it ought to be the happiness and glory of a Representative, to live in the strictest union, the closest correspondence, and the most unreserved communication with his constituents. . . . But, his unbiased opinion, his mature judgement, his enlightened conscience, he ought not to sacrifice to you; to any man, or to any set of men living. . . . Your Representative owes you, not his industry only, but his judgement; and he betrays, instead of serving you, if he sacrifices it to your opinion.

Parliament is not a *Congress* of Ambassadors from different and hostile interests; which interests each must maintain, as an Agent and Advocate, against other Agents and Advocates; but Parliament is a *deliberative* Assembly of *one* Nation, with one Interest, that of the whole; where, not local Purposes, not local Prejudices ought to guide, but the general Good, resulting from the general Reason of the whole. You chose a Member indeed; but when you have chosen him, he is not Member of Bristol, but he is a Member of *Parliament* (Burke, 1996: 68–9, italics in original).

While practice in the British parliament follows the Burkean model, some other parliamentary systems and have enshrined the principle of recall, whereby voters can "recall" their representatives or delegates, either to be replaced or to face re-election for failing to adequately represent the views of their constituents. This principle was instituted by the French national assembly after the revolution. It subsequently became part of the socialist tradition, so that deputies in communist and some socialist states such as China and Cuba are liable to recall if a significant number of voters conclude that the deputy has failed to carry out the mandate. Such a provision would prevent deputies elected on a one-party ticket from subsequently moving to another party without resubmitting themselves to the electorate for approval.

On the other hand, many states enshrine the principle of parliamentary immunity to protect the right of deputies to speak out without fear of prosecution or threat of libel proceedings for what they say in parliament. This also means that occasionally individuals will seek election as a way of preventing, or at least postponing, prosecution for some criminal act.

Another key question is who a particular deputy's electors are. In most parliaments there is a direct link between an elected representative and a particular district within the country. But in countries such as Israel, Peru, and the Netherlands, voters make up a single national **constituency** and choose between the lists of candidates offered by different parties, so that those elected accurately represent the preferences of the people. This ensures that members of parliament are proportionately representative—an issue to which we shall return in Chapter 11. On the other hand, critics of the Israeli system have argued that its proportional system concedes excessive power to small parties, with the result that executive policy-making is extremely constrained. According to Amotz Asa-El (2008), a former editor of the *Jerusalem Post*:

Israel maintains the most extreme model of the proportional electoral system and the results are nothing short of disastrous. This system has been depleting Israel's political energies for decades: it radicalised the territorial debate, debilitated the economy, obstructed long-term planning, derailed government action, distracted cabinets, diverted budgets, weakened prime ministers, destabilised governments, enabled anonymous and often incompetent people to achieve positions of great influence and responsibility and blurred the distinctions between the executive and legislative branches of government. Perhaps most crucially, it has led talented, accomplished, moral and charismatic people to abandon the political arena.

The relative merits of **plurality** versus **proportional representation** systems will be discussed in Chapter 11. What is important to note here is the effect of the combination of a single national constituency, proportional representation, and a low threshold for parties to be allowed to take up seats. In Israel that threshold is only 2 per cent of the popular vote—though it's important to recognize that the Netherlands has a threshold of just 0.67 per cent and yet does not seem to experience the fragmentation and polarization that Israel does. According to Asa-El, an essential element in reform will be the linking of at least some Knesset seats with specific constituencies within the country. This will increase the incentives for representatives to focus on local issues of concern to voters. At present its members are said to pay scant attention to the type of local issues that are the staple of constituency politics in other countries. At least in Israel a wide range of minority views is represented in parliament. If nothing else, this minimizes the risk that the views of minorities that are not geographically concentrated in a few places will be neglected (as can happen in plurality systems when local representatives feel little need to listen to people who did not vote for them).

In most states the connection between individual representatives and the people they represent in specific territorial constituencies is regarded as an essential contribution to the legitimacy of the legislative branch. This raises another set of questions. Is there an optimal size for constituencies? How similar in size should they be? Further, as citizens constantly move residences, who should be responsible for redrawing constituency boundaries? Most European states assign this responsibility to public officials; and in Canada, Elections Canada is responsible for drawing boundaries and monitoring elections.

In the US, however, the boundaries of districts for the House of Representatives are determined by the legislatures of each state. These state legislatures are in charge of interpreting federal census data, collected every ten years, and then redrawing the electoral districts as they see fit. In many cases, whichever political party dominates the legislature will redraw the boundaries to favour its own party, in a practice often referred to as "gerrymandering." There are two ways of manipulating boundaries, known as: "packing" and "cracking." The first refers to packing supporters of the other party into as few districts as possible (to reduce the number of seats the opposition can take) and the second to dividing opposition supporters into as many districts as possible (so that they can never gain a majority of the vote) (Schmidt, Shelley, and Bardes, 2008: 432).

The varying size of constituencies is always a highly contentious issue. In the US, for example, the Constitution grants two senators to each state of the union, irrespective of size. Thus Wyoming, the state with the smallest population, has the same number of senators as California, the state with the largest, even though California's population is 72 times larger. As a consequence, smaller states (which are often more rural) have a disproportionate impact on Senate voting. There is no prospect that this situation will change, since the smaller states will always be able to mobilize a large enough proportion of votes to prevent the required constitutional amendment.

See Chapter 11, page 221, for a discussion of proportional representation.

See Chapter 11, page 220, for a discussion of plurality versus proportional representation.

9

In Canada, tiny Prince Edward Island has far greater representation in the Senate than its population of 136,000 people would allow. Any changes to the Senate rules would not only be extremely difficult, but would probably lead to an overhaul of the entire institution. Whereas senators in the US are elected, their Canadian counterparts are appointed by the prime minister. Thus there is no direct public accountability for anything the Senate does. While the idea of an elected Senate has been discussed for decades, there has been little progress on this so far.

KEY POINTS

- Members of legislatures represent the wider society, to which they are typically connected through territorial districts.
- Legislators' legitimacy is based in part on the assumption that they are also representative of society.
- The introduction of quotas to increase recruitment of women in legislatures may lead to measures to do the same for other groups that are currently underrepresented.

Governmental

The "governmental" functions of legislatures are primarily concerned with forming governments, formulating policy and implementing it.

Presidentialism versus Parliamentarianism

In some states, one of the legislature's major functions is the formation of the government itself. In a parliamentary system, the head of the government is almost always decided by the parliament. **Parliamentarianism** is the principle that parliament is the final arbiter in the choice of the head of the government; Canada, New Zealand, Australia, and the UK all operate on this principle. By contrast, in countries that follow the principle of US-style **presidentialism**, the legislative and executive branches are separate and the legislature has no say in the choice of president (the head of the executive branch), who is elected by the whole nation and therefore has a powerful mandate.

In parliamentary systems the prime minister is normally the party leader who can command a majority in the parliament. Where a single party has a majority of the seats, as is currently the case in Canada, the choice is usually easy. Where no single party has a majority, as is currently the case in the UK, two or more parties may negotiate to form a coalition government; thus the Conservatives and the Liberal Democrats formed a coalition government headed by the Conservative leader David Cameron. Otherwise the party with the most seats will form a minority government. In such cases the government will be vulnerable to defeat if the opposition is able to unite against it, but minority governments can sometimes survive for quite a long time if they are careful about the policies they choose to pursue.

In Canada Stephen Harper managed to maintain two successive minority governments from early 2006 to early 2011. This was not an easy task, but it was facilitated by a divided opposition, which included one party whose primary goal was the separation of Quebec from the rest of Canada. In other countries like New Zealand, Australia, and Germany, coalition governments consisting of two or more parties are the norm, with parties joining in coalition until they share a workable majority of seats. New Zealand's current government is made up of the National Party in coalition with three minor parties: the indigenous Maori Party, ACT, and United Future. The previous government, a coalition between

Official White House Photo by Pete Souza

PHOTO 9.2 US President Obama and President Lee Myung-bak of the Republic of Korea greet guests on the lawn of the White House in October 2011.

the Labour Party and the single MP representing the Progressive Party, had to work out complicated agreements with United Future and New Zealand First to ensure their support. Commonly in New Zealand, the leaders of coalition or support parties hold at least one cabinet position.

Which system is better? Juan Linz (1992) has argued that parliamentarianism is more advantageous for democracy because it is more flexible and therefore more conducive to stability than presidentialism, which is quite fragile; see **Box 9.3**. He based most of his argument on the experience of Latin America. This region has experienced a high degree of political instability over decades, and almost all regimes have been presidential. Presidential rule in a democracy assumes a powerful executive based on a mandate from the whole people; yet legislators also lay claim to popular mandates. Thus president and legislature are driven by competing beliefs in their own public legitimacy. Their views naturally clash, even where they agree over basic policy goals. This makes for a "zero-sum" approach to policy-making, with each side striving for a winner-takes-all outcome.

By contrast, Linz (1992a, b) argues that parliamentary systems encourage actors holding different political positions to negotiate compromises because they have to reconcile their own individual mandates with the potential national mandate for government. They are also able to enforce tighter discipline among their members in parliament because they can offer the prospect of promotion to ministerial posts as an incentive to avoid challenging government policies. A good example of Linz's argument is the very successful transition to parliamentary democracy made by post-Franco Spain, which in 1975 changed from an authoritarian system to a democratic one. Transitions to democracy

KEY QUOTE BOX 9.3
Linz and Cheibub on Presidentialism and Parliamentarianism

Perhaps the best way to summarize the basic differences between presidential and parliamentary systems is to say that while parliamentarianism imparts flexibility to the political process, presidentialism makes it rather rigid . . . [W]hile the need for authority and predictability would seem to favour presidentialism, there are unexpected developments—ranging from the death of the incumbent to serious errors in judgement committed under the pressure of unruly circumstances—that make presidential rule less predictable and often weaker than that of a prime minister.

Presidentialism is ineluctably problematic because it operates according to the rule of "winner-take-all"—an arrangement that tends to make democratic politics a zero-sum game, with all the potential for conflict such games portend. . . . [Parliamentary elections] more often give representation to a number of parties. Power-sharing and coalition-forming are fairly common. . . . By contrast, the conviction that he possesses independent authority and a popular mandate is likely to imbue a president with a sense of power and mission, even if the plurality that elected him is a slender one. Given such assumptions about his standing and role, he will find the inevitable opposition to his policies far more irksome and demoralizing than would a prime minister, who knows himself to be but the spokesman for a temporary governing coalition rather than the voice of the nation or the tribune of the people (Linz, 1992: 122–3).

True, presidential democracies are more unstable than parliamentary ones, but this instability is not caused by the incentives generated by presidentialism itself. Presidential democracies die not because the institutions are such that they compel actors to seek extra-constitutional solutions to their conflicts. The conflicts themselves should take some of the blame, since they are probably hard to reconcile under any institutional framework. . . . One of the advantages of presidentialism is that it provides for one office with a national government (Cheibub, 2007: 165, 168).

have generally been less successful in the presidential systems of Latin America. In the early 2000s the president of the Philippines, Gloria Macapagal-Arroyo, apparently agreed that the parliamentary system was preferable; see the case study.

On the other hand, Cheibub (2007) has argued that if presidential systems appear less stable than parliamentary ones, the reason lies not in the systems themselves but in the political contexts in which they have to operate. He maintains that there has been a tendency in Latin America for authoritarian military regimes to be replaced by democratic presidential ones. If the transitions fail, therefore, the reasons have more to do with a fundamental crisis of authority than with the type of system adopted. If that is the case, the advantages of parliamentary systems over presidential ones may not be as clear-cut as they seem.

In any case, in practice there are several ways of synthesizing the two principles. One can be seen in the growing tendency of political parties to involve their wider membership in the selection of their leaders. The main British parties now invite all their members, not just members of the parliamentary caucus, to take part in the selection of their leaders, although the votes from different sections of the membership may be weighted differentially. Parties in other states, such as Canada and Germany, have generally elected their leaders at conventions of delegates chosen by party members.

CASE STUDY
Presidentialism in the Philippines

The Philippines has had a presidential system since 1935, when it was granted greater autonomy as a colony of the US. It gained independence in 1946. Since then it has for the most part been a democracy, although it spent 14 years (1972–86) as a dictatorship under President Ferdinand Marcos, who imposed martial law when the constitution barred him from standing for election for a third term. The system is closely modelled on that of the US. This means that parties remain fairly weak, and election campaigns tend to centre on individual candidates rather than on the parties they represent.

Unlike the US, however, the Philippines has been bedevilled by widespread corruption. In the Transparency International 2010 Corruption Perceptions Index, Philippines was ranked 134th out of 178 countries (Transparency International, 2010: 3). Corruption also involves elected representatives. One notable feature of Filipino politics has been the persistence of dynastic political families. Filipino **political culture** lays great stress on family values. Individual members of these dynasties are able to pass seats on local councils and the House of Representatives to their children or other relatives. In the Congress elected in 2001, 73 per cent of those elected to the House came from the second, third, or fourth generations of political families (Coronel et al., 2004: 60). The personalized nature of Filipino politics makes it easier for candidates to run expensive personal campaigns, where favours can be traded between generations of political activists. In recent years, successful candidates for the House have had to spend at least US $250,000, candidates for the Senate $375,000 (Rüland et al., 2005: 119).

Periodically in the 1990s proposals were aired for the introduction of a parliamentary system on the grounds that it would weaken the power of the president (an important consideration in the aftermath of the Marcos regime) and reduce the risk that attempts to get rid of an unpopular president would lead to impeachment and thus undermine the system as a whole (Rüland, 2003: 467–8).

In 2005 President Gloria Arroyo (herself the daughter of a former president) announced a plan to replace the presidential system with a parliamentary one. She justified this on the grounds that presidentialism favoured individuals and that a parliamentary system would strengthen the control of parties over the political system, make them more policy-oriented and reduce the scope for individuals, especially rich candidates, to escalate the costs of electoral campaigns.

While such a reform might certainly change the basic incentives for political careers, it is not clear whether it would do anything to uproot the political culture that supports and nourishes political families. When Arroyo's second term of office expired in 2010, the presidency remained in place. Her successor as president, Benigno Simeon Cojuangco Aquino III, is a fourth-generation politician. His father was a well-known senator assassinated by Marcos, and his mother, Corazon, was the country's first female president (1986–92), elected after Marcos was overthrown.

9

Another hybrid system was devised in France and has subsequently been copied in other states, including. Russia. Here the president is responsible for nominating the prime minister, but the latter must enjoy the confidence of parliament. If the parliament passes a vote of no-confidence in the prime minister, then general elections have to be called. The original reasoning behind this system was to strengthen the position of the prime minister and avoid the endless wrangling between small parties that was characteristic of the Fourth Republic until 1958. However, it can make for rivalry between president and prime minister, and this can divide the government, especially when the prime minister has ambitions to become president and uses the post to advance those ambitions. For many years the problem was further complicated by the fact that that it was not uncommon for the president and the prime minister to come from different parties because they were elected at different times. This led to uneasy periods of **cohabitation**, when the rivalry between the two often became so intense that decision-making was paralyzed.

The same effect has be observed in other states where the terms of office of directly elected heads of state and of parliaments diverge, sometimes leading to different parties controlling the two institutions; examples include Taiwan and South Korea. The US has often suffered from a similar problem since the Second World War. Although the Democrats dominated the House of Representatives for much of the time between 1954 and 1994, the Republicans controlled the presidency for longer periods, and this led to frequent "gridlock" in Washington. Gridlock continues under Obama, with a Republican-dominated House versus a Democratic Senate and presidency.

Even though elected presidents have constitutionally greater powers than the prime ministers they nominate, and therefore should to be able to overrule them, both can claim a mandate from the people and hence can appeal to public opinion to support their views; as a consequence, relations between the two offices are often quite tangled and intense. Principally for that reason, the French Constitution was amended in 2000 so that both president and prime minister now hold office for identical five-year terms. The same happened in Taiwan in 2008.

Legislation

The second governmental function performed by legislatures, especially in democracies, is to shape and pass legislation, although in most states this power is tempered by legal considerations: legislation must not only be able to stand up to judicial review, it must also respect international law. To some extent, this legal function helps to explain why so many elected representatives have been trained as lawyers. In the US, which reserves a very prominent role for the law in public affairs, roughly 40 per cent of House members in the mid-1990s were lawyers, while the equivalent figure for senators was 54 per cent (Jacobson, 1997: 207). In 2005, 68 British MPs (11.7 per cent) from the three main parties were lawyers (Cracknell, 2005).

In practice, though, the chief initiator of legislation is the executive. Generally, around the world, 90 per cent of new legislation originates in the executive rather than in parliament, and 90 per cent of that legislation is adopted (Olson, 1994: 134). This is true even in the US, where the executive cannot introduce legislative proposals to Congress but must find sympathetic members of the House or Senate to sponsor them. The picture

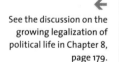

← See the discussion on the growing legalization of political life in Chapter 8, page 179.

See the discussion of legal adjudication in political life in Chapter 8, page 170.

is more complicated for members of the European Union (EU), where member states have to introduce national legislation to give force to decisions made in Brussels. The German government estimates that around 50 per cent of all regulations governing business originate in agreements in Brussels (Miller, 2007: 12, 14). In short, today national legislatures respond primarily to initiatives that originate elsewhere.

Ensuring Accountability

A third governmental function of legislatures is to hold the government to account for its actions. This is particularly important in democracies as a way of ensuring that governments honour the commitments they made to the public when seeking election. It strengthens the incentive for credible commitments and increases the likelihood that a government that fails to keep its promises will be replaced at the next election. Even in authoritarian regimes, where the government is unlikely to be defeated, the executive may not always be able to control the legislature. As examples, Olson (1994: 143–4) cites the growing activism of the Brazilian Congress under military rule in the 1970s and 1980s, and of the Sejm in Poland under martial law in the 1980s. Another example is China. There the National People's Congress meets for only two weeks per year and its function is primarily symbolic. Nevertheless, in recent years it has become an increasingly vocal critic of the policies of individual ministries, though it refrains from criticizing the government, and hence the regime, as a whole. It has cast votes condemning inadequate government action to deal with issues such as corruption and crime. Thus simply having a parliament might strengthen trends toward democracy over time.

But parliaments are not the only institutions that hold the executive to account. In most democratic states the media also perform this role. In addition there are institutions within the executive that monitor what other executive agencies do. O'Donnell (2003) calls this "horizontal accountability" and contrasts it with the "vertical accountability" performed by parliaments. Examples include the National Audit Office in the UK and the office of the Auditor General in Canada, both of which act as checks on government spending. In practice all these institutions contribute to the accountability of government, and they often cooperate with each other.

Formation of Public Attitudes

A fourth governmental function of legislatures is to contribute to the formation of public opinion and to set the agenda for public debate. This is an extension of their representative role, in which parliaments not only provide a forum but take the lead in forming public opinion. In an era of mass communications where the media do so much to inform the public about the issues of the day, the role of parliaments is less prominent than it was in the nineteenth century. Nevertheless, there are issues—abortion and genetically modified foods are two examples—on which parliamentary debates have played a key role, although the line between forming public opinion and representing it can become fuzzy. Debates in parliament and in parliamentary committees are regularly reported in the media. In North America the C-Span and CPAC cable networks offer full-time coverage of the US Congress and Canadian parliament. Some legislatures, such as the German Bundestag, the Dutch Staten-Generaal, and the Scottish parliament, have taken advantage of the Internet to stimulate public debate over current affairs. However, such efforts

See Chapter 3, page 70, for a discussion of deliberative democracy.

to develop a more reflexive approach to policy-making in society at large—the sort of **deliberative democracy** discussed in Chapter 3—seem to have had only limited success.

Another example of how legislatures can stimulate public debate can be observed in Sweden, where members of parliament regularly meet with advisory commissions to create legislative proposals. This practice constrains both the executive and the **sovereignty** of parliament, but helps to ensure that a wider variety of views are represented in the legislative process, which should lead to better legislation (Olson, 1994: 135).

KEY POINTS

- Parliaments perform a number of "governmental" functions.
- They usually play an important role in the choice of head of government in presidential systems, and in parliamentary systems their role is decisive.
- Parliamentary systems may be more stable than presidential systems.
- There are a number of hybrid systems that attempt to synthesize these two different forms of government.
- Cohabitation of an executive head of state and a prime minister from a different party can paralyze government decision-making.
- Today parliaments usually respond to policy initiatives that originate in the executive.
- Parliaments make it possible to hold governments to account for their election promises.
- Parliaments also provide a forum for national debate.

Procedural Functions

Finally, there are two procedural functions that legislatures perform.

Ritualizing Conflict

Parliamentary activities help to ritualize conflict by providing a safe forum for the expression of differing views. To that extent they legitimize diversity of views. Even in Iran, where secular parties are banned and only religious parties are allowed, the parliament provides a forum in which dissident views can be expressed and thereby gain respectability or legitimacy (Baktiari, 1996). Critics of democracy sometimes argue that parliaments exacerbate divisions in society by providing opportunities to express dissenting opinions. It is true that Westminster-type parliaments formalize the role of official opposition to the government. This theoretically forces the parties not in government into an adversarial role that is exacerbated by the seating arrangements: the government and opposition sit facing each other at a distance of a little over two swords' lengths. In some states national legislators exploit the media coverage of their debates to dramatize their differences so as to establish a partisan image that will help their chances of re-election; in Taiwan, for example, legislators have been known to throw their lunch boxes at one another.

We could respond to the critics by noting that all societies have a plurality of opinions on any issue. In fact, where dissension is particularly extreme, parliaments can help to resolve disputes that might otherwise take a more violent turn. In that sense they "routinize" conflict, and even though legislators sometimes use parliamentary debate to rouse public opinion in support of extremist goals, this does not mean that parliaments by nature manufacture conflict. Often they can tame its excesses.

AP Photo/The Canadian Press, Sean Kilpatrick

PHOTO 9.3 The ups and downs of the parliamentary system: Jack Layton, Gilles Duceppe, Stephen Harper and Michael Ignatieff shake hands before the French-language federal election debate in April 2011. Soon after the election, which gave Harper a majority government, Duceppe and Ignatieff resigned as leaders of their parties; Layton died of cancer a few months later.

Ensuring Transparency

Parliaments are generally committed to openness, to publicizing issues and policies. A parliament that kept its deliberations secret—as the Supreme Soviet did in Stalin's time—would make no sense; its value would be purely symbolic. Authoritarian regimes may publish only edited versions of parliamentary debates, but even these can help to publicize important issues and make the policy-making process more open—though full verbatim transcripts of deliberations are obviously preferable. By making the resolution of disagreements in society more open, transparency promotes social stability.

KEY POINTS

- Parliaments assume diversity of opinions and serve to ritualize political disputes.
- They also contribute to open policy-making and resolution of disputes.

Types of Legislature

Legislatures vary considerably not only in their powers but also in their relations with the surrounding political and societal structures. Mezey (1990) produced an influential typology of legislatures in an effort to identify the range of their possible operations.

He proposed a five-part classification based on the ability of a legislature to stand up to the executive:

1. An *active* legislature is at the centre of the political system and has the power to say "no" to the executive when necessary. The US Congress is the prime example.

2. A *reactive* legislature has less power to withstand the government, but it can set firm parameters within which the government has to act, and it can impose sanctions on a government that infringes those parameters. Examples include the House of Commons in Canada and the UK, the House of Representatives in Australia and New Zealand, as well as parliaments in France, Germany, India, Sweden, and Japan.

3. A *vulnerable* legislature is much more pliant, in part because of local political cultures that tolerate legislators' pursuit of their own material interests. Examples include the Philippines and Italy (the latter's legislature has been particularly vulnerable because of the difficulties of forming stable coalition governments).

4. A *marginal* legislature performs important legislative functions, but has at best tentative support from social elites. At times the executive has decided that it can do without the legislature and the latter has been unable to resist. Pakistan, Peru, Nigeria, and Russia under Putin are examples.

5. A *minimal* legislature meets rarely and serves mainly to symbolize national unity and regime legitimacy; it does not exercise any effective check on the government. This was the case in a number of communist states and is still largely true of the National People's Congress in China and the Vietnamese National Assembly.

Official White House Photo by David Lienemann

PHOTO 9.4 China's people have very little control over their government, despite the major economic changes that have taken place in the past three decades.

- Legislatures can be classified according to their capacity to impose their will on the executive.
- Some of the factors that determine this capacity are internal; others come from the broader political and social context.

The Structure of Legislatures

As we mentioned at the beginning of this chapter, roughly two-thirds of the world's legislatures are **unicameral** in structure: that is, they consist of just one chamber or house. Unicameralism is particularly common among smaller, more unitary states. **Bicameralism** (having two chambers) has generally been the choice of larger, more complex nation-states, and for that reason will be the focus of the discussion below. We will also take a look at committees—a structural feature that is central to the way parliaments work.

Bicameral Systems

There is no set formula for the powers of the two chambers, and there are many different power dynamics. As well, some bicameral systems are far more accountable to voters than others. In the late 1990s, only 19 of the world's 61 second chambers were composed exclusively of directly elected members; 15 were hybrids, with some members directly elected and some appointed; and the remaining 27 had no directly elected members at all (among them was the Senate of Canada; see **Box 9.4**). Within these three subcategories there is still room for enormous variety in the ways in which the second chambers are constituted; for details, see Patterson and Mughan (1999: 6–7). Nevertheless, it is possible to identify three general reasons for the decision to separate the legislature into an upper and a lower house.

The first is tradition. In the past, bicameralism allowed for the separate representation of different sections of society, usually the aristocrats in one and the ordinary people in the other. Most systems that were historically bicameral have remained so, even in the context of a modernizing society, although there are exceptions: New Zealand, Denmark, and Sweden all chose to abolish their second chambers and adopt unicameralism, in 1950, 1953, and 1970 respectively (Uhr, 2008: 476).

The second reason for maintaining an upper house often has to do with **federalism**. setting an upper house aside for representatives from provinces, territories, or states serves as a guarantee to those entities that their wishes will not be ignored by the national government, even if their populations are very small (e.g., Prince Edward Island, Rhode Island). In Canada, the Senate provides regional representation for each part of the country. It also ensures that the people of the smaller provinces and territories have a greater say in legislation than their numbers would warrant.

The third reason is the expectation that an upper house will lead to better legislation (Tsebelis and Money, 1997). Why should we expect this?, First, what Patterson and Mughan (1999: 12–16) call the principle of "redundancy" allows for a second opinion on the best form of a particular law. Thus in Canada the Senate was designed to be a "house of sober second thought." Its members form committees that re-examine, debate, amend, approve, or reject legislation sent up from the House of Commons (CBC, 2010). Second, the

See Chapter 8, pages 173–179, for a discussion of federalism.

9

9

KEY CONCEPT BOX 9.4
Reforming the Canadian Senate

The Senate of Canada currently has 105 members representing the ten provinces and three territories. Senators are appointed by the prime minister, often as a reward for party loyalty or for public service of some kind, and can serve until the age of 75. For decades political leaders have tried to make the Senate more accountable to voters as well as more efficient in its functioning. The latest attempt came in June 2011, when the Conservative government introduced the Senate Reform Act, a bill that would allow the provinces to hold special elections to determine a list of nominees for the Senate from which the Prime Minister would choose. All senators appointed after 14 October 2008 would be limited to one nine-year term of office, a condition that would not apply to those appointed before this date. The bill was controversial because the federal government cannot force provinces and territories to conduct elections without changing the Constitution, which would be extremely difficult. Provincial governments would have to choose to take part, and would have to decide them-selves when to hold these elections and how to fund them.

Some political leaders worry that any attempt to change the Senate could end up before the courts. Certainly the power dynamic would change if there were two elected chambers. Until now the House of Commons, as the only elected body, has always had much more power over legislation than the appointed Senate has. In the US, the power balance is the reverse: the Senate has far more power than the House of Representatives.

Some MPs would prefer that the Senate be scrapped altogether. As Dave Christopherson, the NDP's democratic reform critic, put it: "The safe move would be to get rid of the Senate because we know what we have left and how it works: the House of Commons, warts and all" (Fitzpatrick, 2011).

need to satisfy two chambers increases the likelihood that the final outcome will represent the wishes of the population at large, especially if the two chambers have been elected or selected according to different principles or at different times.

According to Tsebelis and Money (1997: 4–5), the number of chambers of parliament makes little difference to the relations between the legislature and the executive, but it does affect the legislative process. Most constitutions give more power to one chamber than to the other, especially where control of the government budget is concerned. In Canada and Britain, for instance, the House of Commons has far more control over the budget than the upper house does. The exception to the norm of imbalanced power is Italy. The fact that the Senate and the Chamber of Deputies have equal powers means that the Italian government is often paralyzed, although this system has been successful in preventing the return of a fascist dictatorship, as it was intended to do.

Even where one chamber is more powerful than the other, however, compromise is often necessary to get a bill passed into law. How compromise is achieved will also affect the legislative outcome. Must the bill be considered by a joint committee of both houses? By full sessions of each chamber? In either case, what kind of majority is needed? All these factors make a difference.

KEY QUOTE BOX 9.5
Qualifications for the Canadian Senate

Currently, the Governor General appoints senators based on recommendations made by the prime minister. To be a senator you must be a Canadian citizen, at least 30 years of age, live in the province that you plan to represent, own $4,000 of equity in land in your province, and have a personal net worth of $4,000—a requirement that does not stand in the way of ordinary Canadians being appointed to the Senate. In 1997 it was determined that the average age in the Senate was 64, while it was around 52 in the Commons. Senators are not required to retire until they reach the age of 75. The federal government estimates that there is a complete turnover in the Senate every 17 years, ensuring continuity for the sober second look at bills.

SOURCE: http://www.cbc.ca/canada/story/2010/07/09/f-senate-background.html#ixzz12kJHQPMm

Committees

In practice, legislators spend most of their time working in committees rather than in full sessions of the parliament. Most of the detailed consideration of proposed legislation is carried out in ad hoc or temporary committees created to consider particular bills. In addition, most parliaments establish permanent committees to scrutinize individual ministries. They often interrogate ministers and senior officials, and sometimes they hold enquiries into issues of policy that the members think is worthy of consideration. Committee members with long experience of parliament and government may be very knowledgeable about particular policy areas. For legislators from parties not in power, committee work offers opportunities to criticize the government's policies and propose alternatives. It also represents another way for parliament to fulfill its functions with respect to the formation of public opinion and the visibility of policy-making. Although some parliaments, such as the German and Swedish, allow parliamentary committees to propose legislation to the house as a whole, this cannot happen in the Westminster system. In France there are a few large, permanent committees that divide into ad hoc committees to consider specific bills.

KEY POINTS

- Bicameralism can improve the quality of legislation and ensure that it better reflects the preferences of the population, but it is more time-consuming than unicameralism.
- The procedures for resolving disagreements between two chambers will affect legislative outcomes.
- Most parliamentary work is done in committees of the legislature.

Legislators

Now let us turn to some common features of elected legislators. In Westminster-style democracies, members of parliament are theoretically representative of the population at large, although obviously this is true in only a broad sense. For example, legislators in general tend to be male, better educated than the average citizen, and socio-economically middle-class (even if they represent socialist parties).

In fact, it has been suggested that some Western states are now developing what Gaetano Mosca, the Italian theorist of elitism, called a "political class." By this, according to the journalist Peter Oborne (2007: 24), Mosca meant a group that is "self-interested, self-aware and dependent for its economic and moral status on the resources of the state." Oborne argues that the concept did not fit the reality of Mosca's time (the late nineteenth century) very well, because there were significant external checks on political figures and because the resources of the state were not so easily bent to serve them. Now, though, "The Political Class has won its battle to control Britain. . . . In an unannounced takeover of power, the public domain has been seized by the Political Class" (Oborne, 2007: 310). Two Italian journalists have made much the same claim about Italian politics (Rizzo and Stella, 2007).

Academics have also begun to discuss the "political class." According to Borchert (2003: 6), the term refers to a class that "lives off politics" and acts as a "class for itself." As we saw in Chapter 7, many accounts of politics in African states emphasize the widespread pursuit of politics for the purposes of making money (Bayart, 1993; Chabal and Daloz, 1999). So the term could be used as the basis for wider comparative studies. What Borchert and his colleagues highlight is a more recent phenomenon, specific to OECD democracies: the emergence of political professionals who are skilled in the art of winning elections, whether as candidates or as advisers, and who have never had another career. In the past many members of parliament were people for whom politics was a second or third career, people who brought their wider experience of life to their work as legislators. The fact that this is no longer so common is now increasingly recognized as a defect.

This trend is not uniform, of course. In Japan and Ireland, surprisingly high proportions of members of the national parliament are the children of former legislators who used to hold the same constituency. In Japan the figure had risen to 28 per cent of deputies to the Lower House of the Diet in 2003 (Usui and Colignon, 2004: 408–9), while in Ireland the figure hovered between 22 and 25 per cent from 1992 to 2002 (Gallagher et al., 2003: 114). Although this pattern certainly seems consistent with the emergence of a "political class," it does not seem to be replicated in other countries to the same extent.

If there is a trend towards professionalization of political careers and it is problematic, is there any way to reverse it? Sutherland (2004) has suggested individuals could be randomly selected for service in parliament just as they are for jury duty. This idea is similar to one adopted in the short-lived Paris Commune of 1871, which had a great influence on the world socialist movement. The Bolsheviks in Russia attempted to establish something similar in October 1917, although it came to nothing because of the rapid onset of civil war. In any case, it is not clear that such a system would make for a more effective parliament. A legislature made of people inexperienced in politics would be only too easy for an experienced executive to mislead or conceal things from.

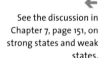

See Chapter 1, page 28, for a discussion of elitism.

9

See the discussion in Chapter 7, page 151, on strong states and weak states.

KEY POINTS

- Some countries show signs of a trend towards professionalization of political representatives.
- Some have suggested that this trend has already led to the emergence of a "political class."

Conclusion

We might expect that elected parliaments would enjoy broad popular support, especially in democracies with free and fair elections. However, the World Values Surveys suggest that people in the developing world tend to have greater confidence in their parliaments than those in the developed world. To some extent democratic citizens are becoming more suspicious of their representatives. For selected results from the round carried out in 2005–7 see Table 9.1.

The World Values Surveys also asked questions about confidence in other institutions. On average, in 1999–2002, confidence in parliament was lower than confidence in national governments (50 per cent), the press and the civil service (44 per cent each), although political parties fared worse (30 per cent). At the time of writing, this was the most recent data available.

While this does not suggest a great challenge to the existence of parliaments, it does suggest widespread scepticism about the way parliaments or politicians (or both) operate. Arora (2003: 36) remarked that the public image of the Indian parliament was "at a very low ebb," even though the World Values Survey for 1999–2002 showed a relatively high level of public confidence—55 per cent. We should also bear in mind Norton's comment (1998: 190) on legislatures in Western Europe. He observed that the fundamental relationship between the legislature and the executive has little to do with the legislature itself. Factors such as the constitution, the political culture, and the state of the economy often play crucial roles in determining how a legislature works. When people criticize their parliaments,

TABLE 9.1 Confidence in Parliament, 2005–2007

Sweden	56.3	Belgium	35.9
Finland	56.1	France	35.5
Switzerland	54.0	Australia	34.1
Denmark	48.6	Netherlands	29.7
Austria	40.7	Japan	23.2
Canada	38.2	West Germany	21.9
UK	36.2	US	20.6

Proportion of respondents in various countries answering "a great deal" "or "quite a lot" to the question: "How much confidence do you have in parliament?"

SOURCE: http://www.conferenceboard.ca/hcp/Details/society/trust-in-parliament.aspx

therefore, they are often complaining about something else. Mainwaring (2006) came to a similar conclusion in his analysis of legislatures in the Andean states of Bolivia, Colombia, Ecuador, Peru, and Venezuela. He and his collaborators chose this region because it has a particularly low levels of public confidence in parliaments by world standards as well as those of Latin America—even though all five countries had experienced a widening and deepening of representation over the previous thirty years. He concluded that the lack of confidence was caused primarily by popular perceptions of broader deficiencies in the political system as a whole. The economies had failed to develop, standards of living were low, and there were serious problems with corruption. While in principle sovereign parliaments in democracies have the power to change government, in practice they may not be able to achieve the changes that the people want. Institutions such as the judiciary or the military may resist political pressure, especially in "weak states" (the category in which almost all of the Andean states can be included). Mainwaring suggests that "Better state performance is key to promoting greater confidence in the institutions of representative democracy and greater satisfaction with democracy" (2006: 331). In short, policy implementation is just as important as policy formulation.

← See Chapter 7, page 151, for a discussion of strong states and weak states.

? KEY QUESTIONS

- How threatening for democracy is the emergence of a "class" of "professional" politicians? Can anything be done to prevent it?
- If Canada's Senate were to be reformed, what should be its powers and functions?
- Does a second chamber of parliament make it more likely that laws will reflect the preferences of the whole population? Are there any circumstances in which it might not?
- Why do you think New Zealand, Denmark, and Sweden chose to eliminate their second chambers?
- Assess the arguments in favour of presidential and parliamentary systems. Do the experiences of states that have made the transition to democracy provide any evidence that would justify one choice or the other? What difference, if any, would the replacement of presidentialism with a parliamentary system be likely to make for Filipino democracy?
- Assess the arguments in favour of special measures to increase gender equality among members of parliament. Should the same arguments be applied to other groups in society that are currently under-represented?
- Does it matter if there are great disparities in the size of constituencies electing representatives to the same legislature? Why?
- Why do you think citizens in democracies might be becoming more critical of their representatives?
- How far should parliaments seek to lead public opinion, and how far should they simply follow and represent it?
- How useful is the term "political class" in comparing the politics of different states?

📖 FURTHER READING

Tremblay, Manon, Marian Sawer, and Linda Trimble, eds (2006). *Representing Women in Parliament: A Comparative Study*. London: Routledge.

A comprehensive collection, focusing on Canada, New Zealand, Australia, and the UK, edited by three world authorities on women's representation in parliament.

Jacobson, Gary C. (1997). *The Politics of Congressional Elections*. 4th edn. New York: Longmans.

An authoritative account of the evolution of election issues in the US.

Lijphart, Arend, ed. (1992). *Parliamentary Versus Presidential Government*. Oxford: Oxford University Press.

The argument in favour of a parliamentary system.

Mehra Ajay, K. and Gert W. Kueck, eds (2003). *The Indian Parliament: A Comparative Perspective*. Delhi: Konark Publishers.

A European perspective on aspects of politics and procedure in the parliament of the world's largest democracy.

Norton, Philip, ed. (1998). *Parliaments and Governments in Western Europe*. 2 vols. London: Cass.

An authoritative compendium of material on various European legislatures.

Tsebelis, George, and Jeannette Money (1997). *Bicameralism*. Cambridge: Cambridge University Press.

An academic perspective on the two-chamber system.

📱 WEB LINKS

www.ipu.org/parline-e/parlinesearch.asp

An International Parliamentary Union database on the structure and operations of parliaments around the world.

www.ipu.org/english/parlweb.htm

Links to the websites of national parliaments around the world.

www.idea.int/gender/index.cfm

The International IDEA website on democracy and gender issues.

10 Bureaucracies, Policy-Making, and Governance

Towards a stronger European economic governance

CHAPTER OVERVIEW

This chapter will begin with a look at the history of the civil service and its contributions to the development of the state. We suggest that its relationship with the rest of society can be characterized as one of "embedded autonomy." We will then introduce theories of bureaucratic policy-making, taking the relationship between principals and agents as our starting point. A discussion of the recent proliferation of agencies created by political leaders to implement policies at arm's length from government ministries then expands the scope of study from governments to governance. Following a look at policy communities and issue networks, we conclude by considering what the emergence of a "network state" might mean.

The Civil Service

For many students, bureaucracies are among the less interesting topics covered in introductory politics courses. They cannot inspire in the way that political ideologies can. Yet if you consider the share of GDP taken by the state in modern Western societies (see **Table 10.1**), you will appreciate the immense significance of ensuring that all that money is well spent. Misguided or mismanaged projects can waste hundreds of millions of dollars. Probably no other branch of government offers the possibility of saving such large sums of money for taxpayers.

TABLE 10.1　Growth of General Government Expenditure in Selected Countries, 1870–1996 (per cent of GDP)

General government for all years	About							
	1870	1913	1920	1937	1960	1980	1990	1996
Australia	18.3	16.5	19.3	14.8	21.2	34.1	34.9	35.9
Austria	10.5	17.0	14.7	20.6	35.7	48.1	38.6	51.6
Canada	–	–	16.7	25.0	28.6	38.8	46.0	44.7
France	12.6	17.0	27.6	29.0	34.6	46.1	49.8	55.0
Germany	10	14.8	25.0	34.1	32.4	47.9	45.1	49.1
Italy	13.7	17.1	30.1	31.1	30.1	42.1	53.4	52.7
Ireland	–	–	18.8	25.5	28.0	48.9	41.2	42.0
Japan	8.8	8.3	14.8	25.4	17.5	32.0	31.3	35.9
New Zealand	–	–	24.6	25.3	26.9	38.1	41.3	34.7
Norway	5.9	9.3	16.0	11.8	29.9	43.8	54.9	49.2
Sweden	5.7	10.4	10.9	16.5	31.0	60.1	59.1	64.2
Switzerland	16.5	14.0	17.0	24.1	17.2	32.8	33.5	39.4
United Kingdom	9.4	12.7	26.2	30.0	32.2	43.0	39.9	43.0
United States	7.3	7.5	12.1	19.7	27.0	31.4	32.8	32.4
Average	**10.8**	**13.1**	**19.6**	**23.8**	**28.0**	**41.9**	**43.0**	**45.0**

SOURCE: Vito Tanzi and Ludger Schuknecht (2000), *Public Spending in the Twentieth Century*. Cambridge: Cambridge University Press: 6–7.

◀ A banner outside the headquarters of the European Commission in Brussels in 2011 (© Bosca78/Istock).

In Chapter 7 we saw how the Western state model spread across the globe in the nineteenth and twentieth centuries. One important factor in that spread was the European state's bureaucratic mode of operation. Max Weber emphasized the innovative impact of the large modern bureaucracy, which transformed government through the consistency, impartiality, and effectiveness that it brought to policy-making; see **Box 10.1**.

The foundations of the British civil service were laid in 1854, when the Northcote–Trevelyan Report recommended the establishment of a government service divided between regular staff charged with routine tasks and an administrative class responsible for policy formulation. It also called for replacement of the existing recruitment system, based on personal recommendation and prone to corruption, with one based on competitive examinations. The British civil service, which was to survive more or less unchanged for a century, would serve as a model for other states setting up their own bureaucracies.

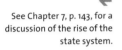

See Chapter 7, p. 143, for a discussion of the rise of the state system.

KEY QUOTE BOX 10.1

Max Weber on the Efficiency of Modern Bureaucratic Organization

The decisive reason for the advance of bureaucratic organization has always been its purely technical superiority over any other form of organization. The fully developed bureaucratic apparatus compares with other organizations exactly as does the machine with the non-mechanical modes of production. Precision, speed, unambiguity, knowledge of the files, continuity, discretion, unity, strict subordination, reduction of friction and of material and personal costs—these are raised to the optimum point in the strictly bureaucratic administration (Weber, 1968: 973).

The civil service was an important innovation in the development of the democratic state. Officials no longer served at the whim of the monarch, except in the most formal sense, and were supposed to be politically neutral. In return for abstaining from active political commitment, they were assured of protection against malicious or capricious dismissal and were guaranteed tenure as professionals. Whichever party was in power was entitled to the best impartial advice on policy and how to implement it, even if this advice was unpalatable to the political masters of the officials concerned. This objectivity reinforced the ability of democratically elected leaders to translate their ideas into the most appropriate and most effective policy.

The British civil service model puts particular emphasis on the impartiality of officials at even the highest levels. However, this principle can present a problem for leaders who wish to introduce radical changes in policy, especially after a change of government, if they feel that the officials they have to work through are still committed to earlier policies that they implemented as well as they could. Other states have been more ready to allow political appointees to hold senior administrative posts. The French system, for instance, does allow political appointees to hold posts in the offices of ministers, especially the top post of *chef de cabinet*. The US still operates a "spoils system" (as in "to the victor go the spoils"), which allows newly elected political leaders at various levels of government to fire and hire large numbers of officials. Currently, every incoming president has roughly 9,000 positions, listed in the US Government Policy and Support Positions (the "Plum Book"), to which he or she can appoint supporters. This is a tiny proportion of the total number of federal employees (close to 3 million), but it does represent all the most senior and politically sensitive posts. In continental Europe political leaders can also appoint supporters to top posts in state corporations, which in some states can include public broadcasting organizations; this practice is called *lottizzazione* ("parcelling out") in Italy.

Thus individual European states developed forms of state administration that reflected their own particular political, legal, and historical contexts. Whereas the British civil service required stringent separation of civil servants from political roles, the states of continental Europe—where the law had played a greater role in curbing the powers of autocratic regimes—have relied more on the law to establish the relationship between the state and the bureaucracy (Lynn, 2006: 58–9). According to Ginsborg (2001: 217), the concept of the law-based state or **Rechtsstaat** is most evident in the case of Italy. In 1993, a government report on administrative reform estimated that whereas France had 7,325 in force and Germany 5,587 (excluding laws passed by the *Länder*), Italy had roughly 90,000 laws or regulations with legal status. These regulations placed serious constraints on the initiative of Italian civil servants; even so, they did not necessarily make for a more impartial civil service, since officials still found ways of favouring those with clientilistic or familial connections. Over a 15-year period in the 1980s and early 1990s, 60 per cent of the hirings of state officials were initially made on the basis of "temporary" or "precarious" contracts that were not subject to the same strict regulations as permanent ones; these jobs were later converted into permanent employment (Ginsborg, 2001: 218–19).

European states also showed a greater tendency for administrative, political, and business elites to overlap. This is most evident in the case of France, where the École nationale d'administration has trained generations of public officials, some of whom have gone on to glittering careers in the state administration and some of whom have gone into politics (two of the latter, Valérie Giscard d'Estaing and Jacques Chirac, eventually served as presidents of the republic).

Colonial powers often transferred their own administrative arrangements to their colonies, and on gaining their independence, many former colonies continued to use them. A good example of how this worked in practice can be seen in India before and after independence. An examination-based appointment system was introduced in 1853—a year before the release of the Northcote–Trevelyan Report—and the Indian Civil Service (ICS) continued to attract high-quality applicants from Britain until independence, nearly a century later, though by the 1930s half of the new recruits were Indian rather than British. The service was quite small: in the early 1930s, when India had a population of approximately 353 million, the ICS employed only about 1,000 officials. Nevertheless, according to Kohli (2004: 237–40), it made long-term contributions to Indian state formation for three reasons. First, it resisted provincialism, ensured consistent all-India administration, and created a unity that nationalists would later be happy to harness. Second, its competence and efficiency facilitated good, limited government. Third, it exemplified the idea that a modern state can put public interests above private ones. All these qualities justified the praise that Weber heaped on modern bureaucratic administration.

KEY POINTS

- European states developed different variants of the civil service and national traditions of administration.
- Colonial powers transferred these forms of government organization to their colonies, with varying long-term success.

"Embedded Autonomy"

The term **embedded autonomy** is borrowed from developmental political economy. Coined by Evans (1995) in the context of the remarkable economic growth achieved by several East Asian states in the 1970s and 1980s, it describes the position of decision-makers in Asian bureaucracies, who were influenced by the society in which they were embedded and yet at the same time maintained a degree of detachment and autonomy that allowed them to determine what was in the public interest and follow that path. Today there is fairly widespread agreement that Japan's economic success can be attributed to its developmental state—specifically, the coordinating role played by the Ministry of International Trade and Industry (MITI) beginning in the 1960s (Johnson, 1982; Calder, 1993). Other states in the region—South Korea, Taiwan, Singapore—followed Japan's example and all achieved economic breakthroughs. In the course of exploring the reasons behind the success of South Korea in particular, Evans (1995) theorized that the "embedded autonomy" of state decision-makers played an important role.

See Chapter 1, p. 23, for an introduction to the developmental state.

KEY POINT

- The civil service needs a degree of autonomy if it is to pursue the public interest, but it must also be embedded in the society in order to know what that interest is.

Theories of Bureaucratic Policy-Making

Theories of bureaucratic policy-making have always revolved around **principal–agent relations**. The term comes from micro-economic game theory and refers to situations in which the actions of two or more actors need to be harmonized, but their interests are not necessarily the same; thus incentives and/or rules must be devised to ensure that those interests will converge enough for activity to be coordinated. In state bureaucracies the "principals" are the political leaders and the "agents" are the civil servants who must carry out the principals' decisions. This relationship is always hierarchical. Of course, there are further nested hierarchies within the civil service, and varying levels of principals have the authority to issue instructions for implementation by agents below them. Theories of bureaucratic policy-making always seek to do two things: (a) to clarify how bureaucracies actually implement decisions; and (b) to find ways to help principals ensure that policy outcomes conform to their policy objectives.

Theories of bureaucratic policy-making have evolved over time. Graham Allison (1971) wrote a very influential work on the Cuban missile crisis of 1962. In *The Essence of Decision*, he set out to analyze how the executive branches in both the US and the USSR formulated their policies and interacted. He identified three possible paradigms. In the first, government as a whole, and individual ministries, operated as a single rational actor and the outcomes corresponded to the original objectives. Allison's research quickly showed that this was not the case, at least not uniformly. The rational actor model left too many developments during the crisis unexplained.

In his second paradigm, which he called the "organizational process" model, Allison hypothesized that government agencies, instead of designing new structures and practices to implement new policies, adapted existing structures and practices—what Allison called "standard operating procedures" (SOPs). It seems reasonable to expect that a great deal of policy-making follows SOPs, although outsiders unfamiliar with the system are bound to have difficulty identifying them (as the Americans sometimes found when puzzling over Soviet moves that needed an urgent response). However, it clearly cannot be the case that all policy-making is the product of SOPs. Hence Allison formulated a third paradigm in which policy decisions were determined by bureaucratic politics—that is, the ways in which particular institutions interacted with each other.

In any event, the broader context of policy-making was changing. Serious economic crises in the 1970s and 1980s forced Western governments to focus on reducing spending and getting better value for money. Neoliberal ideas on economic reform, which gradually spread from the US to other parts of the world, displaced Keynesian approaches to policy-making. At the same time, the collapse of communism was opening the way for government restructuring in several countries and the EU was forcing member states to coordinate their administration more closely, especially in the area of economic policy.

In response to these circumstances a new paradigm developed that came to be known as the **New Public Management** (NPM). Proponents of this new paradigm, according to Lynn, emphasized "incentives, competition, and performance" over rule-based hierarchies and taught a new "mantra . . . : the bureaucratic paradigm is dead; long-live quasi-markets and quangos [quasi-autonomous non-governmental organizations], flattened hierarchies and continuous improvement, competitive tendering and subsidiarity" (Lynn, 2006: 2). As the terminology suggests, many of these ideas came from the fields of economics and business management.

For some critics this new approach was fundamentally mistaken, based on a confusion over the different purposes of public and private institutions. New Public Management implies that "the public sector is not distinctive from the private sector" and that its practitioners are "self-interested, utility maximizing administrators" on the model of corporate executives (Olsen, 2003: 511, 522). Even though it challenged the traditional notion of the impartial civil service, NPM has been an extremely influential approach to public sector reform. For a list of its key features, see **Box 10.2**.

As the wave has spread, international agencies such as the World Bank encouraged developing countries to adopt the NPM model (Adamolekun, 2007). But there is a problem. As Ourzik noted in an address to the second Pan-African Congress of Ministers of Civil Service, in 1998:

> The role of the State has been shaped by a trend which is today universal, that of a State as an enabler rather than a doer, a State that regulates instead of manages. Like a genuine orchestra conductor of social and economic activities, the State is required to promote private initiative without stifling or restricting it. A State that is at once modest and ambitious, since the population still expects much of it: it must, while ensuring that overall balances are maintained, protect the environment, ensure proper land-use management, put in place new infrastructures, provide health and education services, etc. (Ourzik, 2000: 44).

See the discussion of the modern state in Chapter 7, p. 150.

10

KEY CONCEPT BOX 10.2
Key Features of New Public Management

Toonen (2001) identifies six key features of NPM:

- [A] business-oriented approach to government;
- a quality- and performance-oriented approach to public management;
- an emphasis on improved public service delivery and functional responsiveness;
- an institutional separation of public demand functions (councils, citizens' charters), public provision (public management boards) and public service production functions (back offices, outsourcing, agencification, privatization);
- a linkage of public demand, provision, and supply units by transactional devices (performance management, internal contract management, corporatization, intergovernmental covenanting and contracting, contracting out), and quality management; and
- wherever possible, the retreat of (bureaucratic) government institutions in favour of an intelligent use of markets and commercial market enterprises (deregulation, privatization, commercialization, and marketization) or virtual markets (internal competition, benchmarking, competitive tendering) (Toonen, 2001: 185).

10

The problem is one of context. The countries in which NPM was developed already had relatively well established civil services, with traditions of impartiality and incorruptibility, but this is not necessarily the case in the developing world. In Africa, for example, many states suffer from widespread official corruption, but the NPM model does not take this into account.

In the case of Nigeria, Salisu (2003: 171–2) reports serious problems with the internal organization of the civil service: overstaffing and poor remuneration of employees, poor assessment of labour needs, inadequate training, and lack of qualified technical support. Meanwhile, political interference in personnel administration has bred apathy, idleness, and corruption. Although efforts have been made to reorganize the structure and operation of the service so that incentives and performance are better aligned, corruption remains a huge problem. Thus there is a real danger that following the NPM model and treating civil servants as if they were business executives will undermine efforts to establish an ethic of incorruptibility.

KEY POINTS

- Theories of public administration have always revolved around principal–agent relations.
- New Public Management borrowed its basic principles from business studies and economics.
- Introduction of NPM principles in developing countries may undermine efforts to eradicate corruption in public administration.

"Agencification"

One key NPM reform involves splitting government departments and dividing functions to create new agencies—a process known as "agencification." In the UK the creation of institutions such as the Child Support Agency (1993) and the Driver and Vehicle Licensing Agency (2007) was justified on the grounds that they would simplify government administration. In a sense agencification extended the well-established principle of public administration according to which "policy" is separated from "implementation." In this case, however, the result was a proliferation of external agencies that were not directly under the control of the policy-makers. Most were created from portions of existing administrative structures. Implementation was to be the responsibility of different principals, who would establish distinct rules and procedures for their own agents. This undermined the homogeneity of a civil service with common standards and operating procedures. Control of the agencies' performance was in many cases to be exercised by setting targets and judging the agencies on their success in reaching them. Thus target-setting became an increasingly important feature of administrative leadership.

Talbot (2004: 6) has concluded that there are really three dimensions to the idea of "agency":

- "structural disaggregation and/or the creation of 'task-specific' organizations;
- performance "contracting"—some form of performance target-setting, monitoring, and reporting;
- deregulation (or more properly reregulation) of controls over personnel, finance, and other management matters."

Agencification represented a move towards what Rhodes (1997: 87–111) has called the "hollowing out" of the state. In a period when decision-making authority was being devolved to Scotland, Wales, and Northern Ireland, the devolution of implementation authority to agencies outside the British civil service was part of a larger trend. Now actors outside the government would play a larger role in policy-making.

On the other hand, this trend was to some extent contradicted by another aspect of the NPM model, which called for a new focus on the delivery of services as an activity in its own right. Making service delivery more consumer-friendly became an increasingly high priority in the later years of Tony Blair's Labour government. Michael Barber, a former key official in that government who has written an insider's account of NPM reforms in Britain, argues that better implementation is essential if the huge sums of money spent on public services are to be politically sustainable (Barber, 2007: 294). For the reforms to become permanent, though, civil servants would have to internalize them and make them the basis of their official behaviour. Blair believed this could be achieved only if the prime minister's office acquired greater power to supervise the implementation processes.

In addition, the separation of policy-making from implementation added to problems of accountability. Though elaborate means were developed to make implementation agencies accountable to the policy principals (Lynn, 2006: 139–40), enforcing policy-makers' accountability to parliament was more difficult. If particular targets were not met, was it the fault of the principals for setting them unrealistically high? Was it the fault

See Chapter 1, p. 41, for a discussion of the "hollowing out" thesis.

of the "agents" (i.e., the officials) for lacking sufficient commitment? Were the targets contradictory or incompatible? If so, whose fault would that be—and who would decide? The greater the incentives for meeting targets (and the penalties for failing to do so) the greater the danger that other important work for which targets were more difficult to specify might be neglected. The overall effect was to reduce the salience of politics in policy-making, make the policy process more technocratic, and attenuate the principle of ministerial responsibility.

KEY POINTS

- The creation of agencies charged with implementation of policies formulated elsewhere facilitated concentration on delivery.
- In Britain the Prime Minister's Office became directly involved in pushing through the reforms.
- There was a heavy reliance on targets as performance indicators.
- Agencification weakened ministerial accountability.

Governance

"Governance" is an old word that has undergone something of a revival in recent years. Its root is a Greek word meaning "to steer," and in its simplest sense it refers to the function of governments. Thus Pierre and Peters (2000: 1) use "governance" to mean "the capacity of government to make and implement policy—in other words, to steer society," and the UN Economic and Social Commission for Asia and the Pacific defines it as "the process of decision-making and the process by which decisions are implemented (or not implemented)" (UNESCAP, "What Is Good Governance?"). But governance is not restricted to governments: "corporate governance," for example, refers to the processes by which corporations make decisions. Non-state actors working on behalf of the state may also be said to practise governance when they take the lead in formulating or implementing policies in their areas of expertise. Thus private security organizations hired to protect government offices or provide protection for a country's nationals abroad (in Iraq, for example) can have considerable input into policy because they are crucial to its implementation.

A related concept that is now widely used in international politics is "good governance." Governments in the developing world are encouraged to practise good governance, sometimes as a condition for foreign aid. UNESCAP's discussion of the term emphasizes that government is only one of many actors with a role to play in good governance; see **Box 10.3**.

Kayizzi-Mugerwa (2003: 17) presents the concept of good governance in more concrete terms, focusing on institutions. In his view it includes:

- an effective state that enables economic growth and equitable distribution;
- civil societies and communities that are represented in the policy-making process, with the state facilitating political and social interaction and promoting societal cohesion and stability;
- a private sector that plays an independent and productive role in the economy.

KEY CONCEPT BOX 10.3
The Elements of Good Governance

UNESCAP has identified eight features of good governance. It accepts that few states meet all these criteria, but emphasizes that without progress in most of them, real **sustainable development** is not possible:

- Participation: encouraging the involvement of a wide range of actors in making and implementing decisions; implies freedom of expression and association, as well as an organized civil society.
- Rule of law: clear legal frameworks and impartial enforcement; implies respect for human rights, an independent judiciary, and an incorruptible police force.
- Transparency: decisions are made and implemented openly, in accordance with rules; information is readily available to all those affected by decisions.
- Responsiveness: policies are formulated and implemented in ways that respond to social needs.
- Consensus-oriented: the decision-making process mediates among different interests.
- Equity and inclusiveness: all members of society, especially the most vulnerable, have opportunities to maintain or improve the conditions under which they live.
- Effectiveness and efficiency: policies are designed to make the best use of available resources and protect the environment.
- Accountability: procedures must be in place to ensure that decision-makers, both public and private, are held responsible to society as a whole.

SOURCE: http://www.unescap.org/pdd/prs/ProjectActivities/Ongoing/gg/governance.asp

As this summary suggests, the steering of society implicit in the term "governance," and even more so in "*good* governance," cannot be accomplished successfully without the active involvement of **civil society** and the private sector.

KEY POINTS

- "Governance" reflects a broader perspective than "government" alone.
- Developing states are encouraged to practise good governance, which also downplays the state–society distinction.
- Good governance requires wide societal involvement in the formulation and implementation of policy, as well as accountability to the people for policy outcomes.

Policy Communities, "Iron Triangles," and Issue Networks

We have gradually expanded the focus of this chapter from the civil service to the totality of the policy-making and steering processes. A link between the two is provided by the concept of **policy communities**: closed, stable "subgovernments" consisting of the civil servants responsible for policy-making in particular areas and external groups with a special interest in those areas (Thatcher, 2001: 7940). Early proponents of the policy community theory argue that, through long-term exchange and interaction, the views of those officials and interest groups gradually converge, and they come to see issues in similar ways. Even if the policies are ultimately formulated by the civil servants, the fact that some of the ideas informing them have come from outside the government may give them additional legitimacy.

In the US, a particular type of policy community has been called an **iron triangle:** a group of officials, politicians, and interest groups who work together to formulate policy in a particular issue area. What differentiates iron triangles from other policy communities is their explicit inclusion of politicians. Thus it is a long-established feature of politics on Capitol Hill that members of the US Congress are subject to lobbying both by various interest groups (often business organizations) and by other members of Congress.

A variation on the theme of lobbying can be found in Japan, where the Liberal Democratic Party (LDP) held power almost continuously from 1955 to 2009. Over the years the LDP established powerful committees for specific areas of public policy (welfare, construction, agriculture, etc.) that met regularly with both ministry officials and representatives from the sector to discuss the operation of existing policies and the formulation of new ones. For many years these policy "tribes" (*zoku*) were able not only to set the parameters for policy-making but also to resist changes proposed from outside, even by the prime minister. As a consequence they had a significant impact on Japanese policies (Kim, 2006).

AFP/Getty Images

PHOTO 10.1 Newly appointed Prime Minister Yoshihiko Noda (left) and senior officials of Japan's Democratic party lead caucus members in a chant in August 2011. Many Japanese organizations have their own themed chants to encourage pride and solidarity.

Other theorists have argued that the policy community concept is too restrictive to take into account such "key aspects of policy making . . . as ideas, the distribution of power among actors, and change" (Thatcher 2001: 7940). In its place they have proposed the looser concept of the **issue network**. As Thatcher (2001: 7940) describes it:

> An issue network consists of a large number of issue-skilled "policy activists" drawn from conventional interest groups and sections of the government, together with academia and certain professions but also comprising expert individuals regardless of formal training. Participants are constantly changing, and their degree of mutual commitment and interdependence varies, although any direct material interest is often secondary to emotional or intellectual commitment.

Building on this insight, some theorists have attempted to identify different types of network and to show how they interact in the overall policy process.

One of the best-known network typologies was proposed by Rhodes (1997: 38). It has five elements that represent a continuum of organizational strength, running from weak (issue networks, which share only common ideas) to strong (policy communities, which share both ideas and organization). In general, issue networks are large, encompassing a wide range of interests; contact between members is irregular and disagreement common; group resources are limited; and powers, resources, and access vary. By contrast, policy communities are relatively small and clearly focused; interaction between members is both frequent and of high quality; and their hierarchical leadership is able to deliver support from members to government (Rhodes, 1997: 44).

KEY POINT

- Where officials and non-governmental actors are jointly involved in policy formulation and implementation, their relations can be located somewhere along a continuum that stretches from issue networks to policy communities.

Conclusion: Towards a Network State?

In previous decades civil services brought efficiency and effectiveness to government policy-making, especially in North America and Western Europe. More recently, however, their role has been questioned by policy makers as well as the public, as governments seek to reduce their own size and increase efficiency. This is especially true in light of the economic crises that have hit the US and Western Europe since 2008. The result has been a widening of the focus in studies of policy-making, which now devote much more attention to non-governmental actors, both individuals and groups, than to the state in many policy areas. Whether this shift in attention can be reconciled with the need in many developing countries to establish effective and clean administration remains to be seen.

As we noted in Chapter 1, there is a growing literature that envisages a hollowing out of the nation state in response to globalization. The literature on governance suggests a rebalancing of relationships between state and society, in favour of society. Various commentators have predicted a future in which the state will look more like a network than a traditional Weberian bureaucratic hierarchy (Bobbitt, 2003; Castells, 1998).

See Chapter 1, p. 41, for a discussion of the "hollowing out" thesis.

Kamarck has gone so far as to claim that we are witnessing the end of government as we know it, at least in the US, and the emergence of a new kind of state. She looks forward to two things, which she calls "government by network," and "government by market." In the case of the first, the state would decide to create "a network of nongovernmental organizations . . . for the purpose of implementing a policy" (Kamarck, 2007: 100–1). In the case of the second, the government would "create a market that fulfils a public purpose" (2007: 127). As an example she points to the market in carbon emissions, which was designed to reduce overall emissions by offering governments and businesses the opportunity to buy and sell emission credits. In the same way, Kamarck suggests, markets could be created in education or the provision of welfare services. This approach to service delivery would require "few, if any, public employees and no public money."

Such a state would be very far removed from the traditional model. But how much power could networks and markets wield, compared with organized state institutions? Clearly, non-governmental entities would not have the capacity to impose or implement policies. Nor would the legal basis of state administration in continental Europe be easily eroded. Nevertheless, it's clear that groups and organizations outside the state and civil service are playing a much bigger role in governance today than they did in the past. The next few chapters will deal with the roles of three of those external actors: political parties, interest groups, and the media.

? KEY QUESTIONS

- Can we draw a valid distinction between the values and motivations of public administration and business management?
- How far do the groups involved in British transport policy correspond to the different categories of issue networks and policy communities proposed by Rhodes? (See Glaister et al., 2006: ch. 2, 3, 6.)
- Compare the ways in which the Thatcher and Major governments attempted to reform transport policy with those of Presidents Chirac and Sarkozy.
- Is it unrealistic to expect civil servants to be politically impartial?
- How can civil services be made incorruptible? Will New Public Management help?
- Is good governance a Western imposition on the developing world? Did the West have it at similar levels of development? Did it matter then?
- What are the advantages and disadvantages of the "spoils" system in the US?
- How can agencies and officials be made accountable under the New Public Management?
- What would a network state look like? In what ways would it differ from more traditional states?

📖 FURTHER READING

Kamarck, Elaine C. (2007). *The End of Government . . . As We Know It: Making Public Policy Work*. Boulder, CO: Lynne Reinner.
    Details the prospects for state administration transformed by new technology.

Lynn, Laurence E., Jr (2006). *Public Management: Old and New*. London: Routledge.
    An account of changing approaches to public management.

Miljan, Lydia (2008). *Public Policy in Canada: An Introduction*. Toronto, Oxford University Press.

> An excellent introduction to public policy in Canada; takes a hands-on approach to the subject, integrating theory and practice.

Pierre, Jon, and B. Guy Peters (2000). *Governance, Politics and the State*. Basingstoke: Palgrave.

> A good introduction to the concept of governance and its implications.

WEB LINKS

www.civilservant.org.uk/index.html

> How to be a civil servant: a master site of information about the civil service in the UK.

www.gpo.gov/fdsys/pkg/GPO-PLUMBOOK-2008/pdf/GPO-PLUMBOOK-2008-6-3.pdf

> The "Plum Book": the list of US government positions that an incoming administration is entitled to fill with political appointees.

http://jobs-emplois.gc.ca/index-eng.htm

> The website of the Canadian public service commission; provides information about federal government departments and careers.

10

11 Votes, Elections, Parties

CHAPTER OVERVIEW

Elections and political parties are core institutions of democracies: it is through them that citizens are represented in government. They are also important, if largely powerless, in most authoritarian regimes, which use them to legitimate the rulers. In this chapter we will first explain some of the basic issues involved in assessing voting and electoral systems. Then we will look at political parties: why they emerged, how they can be classified, what functions they perform, how they interact, and, finally, the challenges they face today.

The Voting Paradox

Voting is a mechanism for making collective decisions, and as such it is a key ingredient in the concept of representation. It is also widely assumed to ensure that the majority preference is reflected in the ultimate decision. While this is the case when there are only two options, as soon as there are more than two it becomes extremely difficult to determine which one is "most preferred." A mathematical proposition known as **Arrow's impossibility theorem** explains why: when a group of people are asked to choose one preference from three or more alternatives, it is impossible to conclude that any option is the one "most preferred" unless more than 50 per cent vote for it. **Table 11.1** illustrates the problem.

See the discussion of the role of the state in Chapter 1, p. 34.

TABLE 11.1 Hypothetical Distribution of Votes

No. of voters	1st choice	2nd choice	3rd choice
8	A	B	C
4	B	A	C
6	C	B	A
4	C	A	B

None of the three alternatives wins a majority of first choices, but if we count only first choices, then C wins with 10 votes out of 22. If the first two choices are counted equally, then B wins, with 18 votes out of 44. However, it might be fairer to give extra weight to first choices over second ones, since that would reflect more genuine strength of preference. Suppose first choices are given two points, and second choices are given one. In that case, A wins with 24 points out of a possible 66.

In fact, any of the three options could win, depending on the counting system used. But since none of them achieves a majority of the total votes or points available, whichever system is used, it would be impossible to conclude that the general preference is "clearly" in favour of one particular option. As you can imagine, this problem gets worse as the number of alternatives increases, whether we are talking about candidates for election or policy options. In practice, then, how we determine preferences depends on the procedure we use for counting votes. Any procedure we choose will have to be a compromise between theory and practicality. This also explains why referenda rarely offer more than two options: forcing an either/or choice is the only way to ensure an unambiguous outcome.

See the discussion of policy communities in Chapter 10, p. 213.

As you can see, the method we choose for assessing votes is crucial, and really can alter the outcome. To give one famous example, when Abraham Lincoln won the US presidential election in 1860, he was one of four candidates in the race, and different methods of counting the votes (used in various parts of the world today) could easily have given the presidency to either John C. Breckinridge or John Bell (Riker, 1982: 227–32). If that had happened, history might have developed along quite different lines: the US Civil War might never have taken place; the South might have become a separate country; slavery might have continued for decades, if not longer; and so on. In turn, any of these scenarios would have had implications for the world.

◄ A woman in Teheran walks past posters of candidates for the parliamentary elections of February 2012 (Majid Saeedi/ Getty Images).

KEY POINT

•   **The method used to assess votes plays a crucial part in determining the outcome.**

Elections

Election can be defined most simply as a method of assessing preferences through votes. Elections are vital to democracy. According to Article 12 of the Universal Declaration on Democracy, "The key element in the exercise of democracy is the holding of free and fair elections at regular intervals enabling the people's will to be expressed" (Inter-Parliamentary Union, 1997).

There are two basic types of electoral system, with several subvariants; see **Box 11.1**. The first basic type is the simple **plurality**, first-past-the-post majority system. This has the advantage of simplicity. In theory, it allows voters to choose individual candidates based on their own merits, rather than simply on their ties with a party. Although it can produce minority governments, it often gives the winning party a clear majority of the seats, which can make for a more decisive style of governance than is possible when rival parties are in a position to water down the governing party's policies. The first-past-the-post system can also facilitate a strong opposition and broadly based parties. It disadvantages extremist parties of either the right or the left. On the other hand, it can lead to large numbers of "wasted" votes for candidates who have no realistic chance of being elected, which may discourage their supporters from voting in future elections (International IDEA, 2007: 36–7).

KEY CONCEPT BOX 11.1
Types of Electoral System

1. Majoritarian systems (first-past-the-post)
    •   single-member plurality systems (Canada, UK, US, India)
    •   two-round system (France)
    •   alternative vote (Australia)
    •   block vote (Singapore, Syria)
2. Proportional representation
    •   party list (Netherlands, Israel, Brazil)
    •   single transferable vote (Ireland)
3. Hybrids (New Zealand, Germany, Russia, Japan, Scottish Parliament, Welsh Assembly)

Most majoritarian systems today allow for only one member to be elected from each district. However, in the past both the US and UK had some multimember constituencies, and "at-large" or "block" voting still occurs at the municipal level. In such cases, the entire city constitutes a single district and all voters choose from the same list of candidates for, say, the city council or school board. In some systems they will have as many votes as there are seats to be filled; this can produce very strong majorities if people vote consistently for the same group or party. In others they will have only one vote; this means that candidates can be elected with as little as 20 per cent of the vote, which may undermine their legitimacy. (An up-to-date list of countries practising these and the other alternative systems mentioned can be found at www.idea.int/esd/world.cfm.)

The alternative principle is **proportional representation** (PR). Here the priority is to ensure adequate representation of the range of public opinion; whether the resulting government is strong or weak is less important. This system has the advantage of reducing the number of "wasted" votes. It also favours minorities, and can encourage parties to try harder to appeal to voters outside their core districts. It may contribute to greater stability of policy and make coalition agreements more visible. On the other hand, it is more likely to lead to coalition government and fragmentation of the party system. In such an environment, small parties will be able to negotiate a disproportionate say in policy-making: recall Amotz Asa-El's scathing condemnation of the effects of proportional representation in Israel in Chapter 9. As well, holding coalition governments to account for individual decisions is more difficult under proportional representation (International IDEA, 2007: 58–9).

See Chapter 9, pp. 210–11, for Asa-El's criticism of proportional representation.

Since first-past-the-post and proportional representation systems tend to produce different kinds of outcomes, both of which have much to commend them, a number of hybrids have been developed. In the **alternative member model**, for instance, some seats are elected on the basis of a simple majority and some on the basis of proportional representation. Germany, Japan, New Zealand, and Russia have all gone down this route. In New Zealand, Helen Clark of the Labour Party was able to win three successive terms of office (using a hybrid voting model; she led a series of minority coalition governments from 1999 to 2008.

PHOTO 11.1 New Zealand's Labour Prime Minister Helen Clark concedes defeat in the election of November 2008, after three consecutive terms in office.

In one alternative system, which falls somewhere in the middle, a second round of elections is held in constituencies where the first round does not produce an absolute majority. In the second round, only the two most successful candidates remain on the ballot; this prevents strategic voting and ensures that there is no doubt about the preference of the majority. This is the system used in France and many of its former African colonies, as well as Iran and several former republics of the Soviet Union.

Altogether, 70 countries use a list proportional representation system, 47 use first-past-the-post (plus 22 with two-round elections), and 21 use a hybrid of some kind (International IDEA, 2007: 32).

Around the world, according to Colomer (2004), the direction of electoral reform has been towards increasingly inclusive formulas, which involve fewer risks for the parties involved. Thus the tendency has been to move from a majoritarian to a mixed or proportional system. Colomer's explanation is party self-interest: when threatened by challenges from newcomers, parties generally prefer to minimize the risk of complete extinction, which is far greater under majoritarianism. The chances of survival are better under PR, even though the numbers of representatives elected are likely to be reduced (Colomer, 2004: 4, 58; Farrell, 2001: chs 7, 8).

KEY POINTS

- The two most widely used voting systems are and proportional representation.
- Each has its own virtue: first-past-the-post produces stronger government, while PR produces more representative government.
- Hybrid or intermediate alternatives attempt to mitigate the disadvantages of theoretically purer systems.
- Voting systems have a big impact on party systems.

Political Parties

There is a paradox about political parties. On one hand, even **authoritarian** regimes generally agree on their importance. The Universal Declaration on Democracy includes in Article 12 "the right to organize political parties and carry out political activities" as one of the "essential civil and political rights" (Inter-Parliamentary Union, 1997). On the other hand, some theorists question the logic of parties on the grounds that rational individuals will form groups to pursue their interests only when they can be sure that the benefits of membership will be greater than the costs. This is likely to be the case only for small groups in which the share of benefits that any individual member can expect will be relatively large. For big organizations such as political parties, especially at the national level, the benefits that any individual member is likely to gain are bound to be very small, while the costs of membership are significant. Thus it is irrational for people to join anything larger than a (small) **interest group**.

Parties have also been criticized for promoting divisions in society rather than helping to mitigate them; for example, see the quotation from the former Tanzanian president Julius Nyerere, below. This risk is particularly serious when political parties represent specific ethnic communities (as was the case in Uganda; see the case study on p. 227). The leaders of the People's Republic of China use the same argument to justify the leading role of the Communist Party.

> **KEY QUOTE BOX 11.2**
> Nyerere on Party Politics
>
> Julius Nyerere of Tanzania considered the British-style party system intentionally divisive and fundamentally un-African. In 1963, he argued that
>
> > To try and import the idea of a parliamentary opposition into Africa may very likely lead to violence—because the opposition parties will tend to be regarded as traitors by the majority of our people, or at best, it will lead to the trivial manoeuvrings of "opposing" groups whose time is spent in the inflation of artificial differences into some semblance of reality (quoted in Meredith, 2005: 168).

Carothers (2006: 4) expands on what he terms the "standard lament" about political parties in various countries where he has done research:

1. Parties are corrupt, self-interested organizations dominated by power-hungry elites who pursue their own interests, or those of their rich financial backers, rather than those of ordinary citizens.
2. Parties do not stand for anything: there are no real differences among them. Their ideologies are symbolic at best and their platforms vague or insubstantial.
3. Parties waste time and energy squabbling with one another over petty issues for the sake of political advantage, rather than trying to solve the country's problems in a constructive, cooperative way.
4. Parties become active only at election time, when they come looking for your vote; the rest of the time you never hear from them.
5. Parties are ill-prepared to govern and typically do a bad job, whether in government or in opposition.

KEY POINTS

- Parties are a vital element in modern political systems, especially in democracies.
- Yet the benefits of party membership are questionable, given the costs.
- Parties generally suffer from low public esteem and are often associated with corruption.

Emergence of Parties

Historically, there were two phases in the development of political parties. Originally they emerged within the parliaments of the first democracies. Factions developed as groups of independently elected representatives formed groups to create and pass legislation. These were caucus parties, loose organizations of like-minded representatives, which in the American case were at first loosely split between Federalists and anti-Federalists. Later, as the voting franchise expanded to include non-property-owning white males, parties became involved in efforts to structure the vote in popular elections. In most countries these two stages were combined, because the multiparty model was imported from abroad at the same time as parliamentary model, but in the case of party pioneers, such as Britain and the US, it is possible to separate the two stages.

Another way of thinking about the birth of parties is to think about the roles or functions they perform—in other words, the systemic needs that parties meet. Thus in the US it is often suggested that parties first developed in Congress because the task of finding a new coalition each time a proposed bill was being considered for legislation was extremely time-consuming. Forming blocs of relatively like-minded representatives simplified the negotiating process, and at the same time increased the influence of individual members over legislation.

It was easier for a group to have an impact because together its members were more likely to have the deciding vote over a particular bill together than as individuals. Voting as a group also enabled them to demand greater concessions in the bill itself, or to trade concessions in one bill for advantages in another—a practice that American politicians call "log-rolling." In addition, since legislation is an ongoing activity, group commitments encouraged greater confidence than those of individuals: a group of legislators could be held to their word (or punished) more easily than an individual could. Thus a relatively coherent group of legislators provided greater predictability for other legislators.

Curiously, the American Founding Fathers had a distinct antipathy for any kind of party or faction, which they regarded as incompatible with real democracy. In *Federalist Paper No. 10*, James Madison attacked "factions" on the grounds that they could oppress or exploit the people as a whole. He defined "faction" as follows:

> a number of citizens, whether amounting to a majority or a minority of the whole, who are united and actuated by some common impulse of passion, or of interest, adverse to the rights of other citizens, or to the permanent and aggregate interests of the community.

Nevertheless, by the Third Congress (1793–4) like-minded legislators had begun to form groups to smooth the passage of bills. Even in a period when Congress met for only one or two months per year, and had a tiny legislative load compared with today, this predictability was an important benefit (Aldrich, 1995: 68–96).

Later, parties began to form outside Congress to mobilize support for candidates first in presidential and then in local elections. This happened for the first time in 1828, when supporters of General Andrew Jackson's presidential candidacy formed what they called the Democratic Party. The effectiveness of the party was indicated not only by the fact that he won this election, having lost the previous one in 1824, but by a significant increase in the voter turnout (from 30 per cent of the electorate to more than 50 per cent). The lesson was clear: party organization motivated supporters to vote. In 1840, after opponents followed suit by organizing the Whig Party (which lasted for about 25 years), the turnout rate rose to more than 78 per cent. The emergence of **mass parties** changed the course of elections and stimulated greater interest in politics in general, at least as measured by turnout. Thus, as Aldrich (1995: 97–125) points out, they strengthened democracy.

The effectiveness of the American parties, together with Britain's growing party democracy, made political parties a vital element in the extension of democracy elsewhere in Europe and around the world. Meanwhile, industrialization was overturning traditional patterns of authority and driving increasing numbers of people into urban areas, where parties could more easily mobilize support. Political issues associated with industrialization provided the subject matter for a new, more popular democracy in which mass parties became the norm and the franchise was extended to include first all male citizens and eventually all female citizens as well. This was the era when party membership was highest. This period also entrenched a social divide that is still extremely important: the division between capital and labour. Though not all party systems revolved around this division, many did, among them the Canadian and British systems (Conservatives versus Liberals in Canada, Labour versus Conservative in Britain).

To cope with the increase in party membership and to ensure greater coordination both in their activities and also those of party elected representatives, the numbers of full-time party officials also increased. While this brought greater professionalism to political parties, it also complicated the practice of democracy in internal party decision-making. How much weight should be given to the views of ordinary party members as opposed to those of party officials? Should they all be treated as equal? Could they be?

Since the Second World War, parties in Europe have evolved further towards what have been termed "catch-all" parties. These are parties that devote less attention to ideology and more to strategies to win over the median (or middle-of-the-road) voters who make the crucial difference in general elections, even if that means appealing to voters who would instinctively support a different party. In practice this trend has had the effect of increasing power the party leadership's power to make strategic decisions. An early indication of the change came in West Germany in 1959, when the Social Democratic Party renounced Marxist ideology and committed itself to a market economy and liberal pluralism.

More recently European and American parties have undergone a further mutation as they have turned into **cartel parties**. As party membership has declined, this has strengthened the authority of the party machine, which has become increasingly professional in its handling of all the media alternatives for putting out its message. We can see this evolution in the dominant American parties since the 1960s. Previously parties were dominated by local machines such as that of Chicago's Democratic Mayor Richard M. Daley. The party machine made the careers of elected office holders. Now, parties have turned into organizations of media-savvy professionals ready to serve whichever candidates emerge to prominence. Thus parties have become candidate-centred rather than machine-centred (Aldrich, 1995).

This historical outline suggests that analysis of any modern party can usefully be divided between its activities in three arenas: (a) the party-in-government (including parliament); (b) the party-in-the-electorate (i.e., its strategies for winning popular support and votes); and (c) the party's internal organization (Aldrich, 1995). All parties that seek election have to establish their own balance of these three roles, which will depend in part on the political system in which they operate, the policy goals they set for themselves, and the attitudes of ordinary citizens towards them.

- The first parties emerged to structure the work of legislatures.
- Later variations included mass parties (designed to structure the votes of electors), catch-all parties (which make it their priority to win votes irrespective of ideological appeal), and cartel parties (dominated by party professionals).
- All parties seeking electoral success have to balance three sets of roles: vis-à-vis government, the electorate, and their own internal professionals.

Functions of Parties

The modern **political party** performs an extremely wide range of functions in the pursuit of political power. As Ware defines it, "A political party is an institution that (a) seeks influence in a state, often by attempting to occupy positions in government, and (b) usually consists of more than a single interest in the society and so to some degree attempts to "aggregate interests"" (Ware, 1996: 5).

In general there are seven functions that a party may perform, though not all parties perform all seven. The balance between them varies depending on the type of state the party operates in (democracy or authoritarian regime); see **Box 11.3**. In democracies the most important roles that parties perform involve choice, whether between individual political actors or between policies (points 6 and 7 in the box). In authoritarian regimes the second function, "integration and mobilization of citizens," tends to be the most important—though the interpretation of those activities is generally more top-down than bottom-up. While it may be almost unthinkable for a democracy to exist without political parties, it is not impossible; see the case study of Uganda on the facing page. The majority of states without party systems are Islamic. Even communist regimes, which never tolerated challenges to the leading role of the Communist Party, organized regular elections at all levels of the state as a way of re-engaging citizens' commitment to the goals of the regime, and also of demonstrating their popular legitimacy to the rest of the world. Authoritarian regimes too have devoted considerable resources to holding regular elections and mobilizing support for the ruling parties, even though there was never a realistic possibility of political alternatives winning power; an example was South Korea between the 1960s and the end of the 1980s. Thus legitimation of the political system, whatever its basic structure, remains the single most common function of political parties.

> **KEY CONCEPT BOX 11.3**
> Functions of Political Parties
>
> 1. Legitimation of the political system;
> 2. Integration and mobilization of citizens;
> 3. Representation;
> 4. Structuring of the popular vote;
> 5. Aggregation of diverse interests;
> 6. Recruitment of leaders for public office, which (normally) facilitates non-violent choice between individuals; and
> 7. Formulation of public policy, facilitating choice between policy options.

CASE STUDY
Uganda as a No-Party State

Uganda is a rare example of a state that has attempted to practise democracy without political parties. Since gaining its independence from Britain in 1962, Uganda has gone through civil war, genocide, and revolution. Put together as a colony from a variety of former tribal kingdoms and principalities, it had no tradition of democracy, even after some 70 years of British rule. This was not unusual: colonial regimes in general discouraged democratic accountability among the people they ruled. Although parties were formed and a number of elections held in preparation for independence, democratic values did not take root. Within two years of Milton Obote's election as the country's first prime minister Uganda was effectively a one-party state. In 1971 Obote was overthrown by General Idi Amin, who declared himself president for life. Gradually the country slid into tyranny, chaos, violence, and economic collapse. In 1979 Amin was overthrown and Obote was reinstalled as president. This time he attempted to restore a multiparty system, but the party leaders refused to cooperate with each other and violence returned. It is estimated that one million Ugandans were killed between 1971 and 1986, when Yoweri Museveni of the National Resistance Movement was sworn in as president. In an effort to prevent further sectarian violence, he announced that political parties would not be permitted to contest elections. In the place of the ethnic division and antagonism exacerbated by party politics, the new regime would promote unity, mutual tolerance, and democracy through a system of local councils in keeping with local traditions of tribal consultation. Although parties were not banned outright, from 1986 onwards their representatives were permitted to stand for election to parliament only as individuals.

A new constitution, adopted in 1995 after nearly a decade of military and transitional rule, set a limit of two five-year terms for any president. As Museveni's second term drew to a close, however, the regime floated the idea of a third term. This provoked unease at home and abroad, among foreign governments that gave aid to Uganda. In the end a referendum approved adoption of multiparty democracy. Thus the reintroduction of open political parties was a response to both domestic and external pressure.

When a general election was held in early 2006, Museveni won a majority amid allegations of electoral irregularities, but the Supreme Court upheld his victory by a vote of four to three. Critics have alleged that little has changed in the way the country is ruled. Whether the era of non-party politics did indeed lay the foundation for a more enduring democracy in Uganda remains to be seen.

SOURCE: Mugaju and Oloka–Onyango (2000).

How parties perform these functions depends on three things:

1. The constitutional framework within which they operate: As we saw in Chapter 8's discussion of the constitutional distinction between federal and non-federal regimes, the degree of central authority in a state has a major impact on the organization of political parties. The relative powers of a party's central apparatus and local organizations reflect the relative powers of the corresponding government authorities.

← See Chapter 8, p. 173, for a discussion of federalism.

2. The way the nation organizes elections: Countries that use primaries (preliminary election) to select candidates for election have to organize their activities to a different timetable from that of other countries.

3. The communication technologies available to them: As television and advertising have become more powerful, parties have increasingly come to rely on them (rather than door-to-door canvassing by party activists) to get their messages to the public, even though this has greatly inflated election costs. Now the Internet is beginning to offer new possibilities for more personalized campaigning, with candidates contacting voters individually to respond to their particular concerns.

→
For a discussion of the impact of the media on politics see Chapter 12, p. 249.

KEY POINTS

- Political parties perform an extremely wide range of functions.
- These are structured by the constitutional framework of the political system, the national system of elections, and the technologies available for communicating with voters.

Typologies of Political Parties

Developing a typology of political parties allows a political scientist to think more systematically about their activities to make more meaningful comparisons. **Box 11.4** presents a recent typology of political parties in various regions of the world by Gunther and Diamond (2003), based primarily on the ways in which and the extent to which parties organize themselves; in this case, the least organized types are at the top of the table and the most organized at the bottom.

Below is a different typology based on nine general types of political program. It is an extension of one developed for Western Europe by Beyme (1985: 29–158), adapted for a larger context:

1. Liberal or radical parties stand for equal legal and political rights, as well as free trade.

2. Conservative parties tend to support traditional forms of social relations, including hierarchy. They often appeal to nationalism as well. Recently, however, some conservative parties have veered towards more radical, neo-liberal, free-market economic policies.

3. Christian democratic parties were established after the Second World War as a third, Catholic-influenced, way between liberalism and socialism. While such parties endorse more traditional authority relations, preferring women to stay at home and raise children, they have accepted a significant role for state-provided welfare.

4. Socialist or social democratic parties advocate workers' control of the means of production. Usually they have had close connections with trade unions. They also advocate state welfare systems. Unlike Communist parties, they accept the need for market capitalism but call for state regulation and planning as well.

5. Communist parties were inspired by the Russian Revolution of 1917 and sought to spread the communist alternative to socialism based on the teachings of Marx and Lenin. Such parties were distinguished by their doctrine of unconditional loyalty to the party ("democratic centralism") and strict party discipline.

KEY CONCEPT BOX 11.4
Typology of Political Parties

Basic category	Variants	Sub-variants
Elite-based	Traditional local notables (esp. 19th century)	
	Clientelistic	
Electoralist	Personalistic	
	Catch-all	
	Programmatic	
Movement	Left-libertarian	
	Post-industrial extreme right	
Ethnicity-based	Exclusive ethnic	
	Congress/coalition movement	
Mass-based	Religious	Denominational
		Fundamentalist
	Nationalist	Pluralist
		Ultranationalist
	Socialist	Class/mass based
		Leninist

SOURCE: Gunther and Diamond (2003: 173)

6. Regional parties stand for the interests of particular regions of countries and often seek, whether overtly or covertly, to establish their own states. They have experienced a surge in popularity in Europe over the last twenty years. Perhaps the most successful has been the northern Italian separatist party Lega Nord, which has occasionally participated in national coalition governments.

7. Environmental parties are a relatively recent phenomenon, initially developing out of interest groups such as Friends of the Earth. Typically, they win support from younger and middle-class voters and tend to be skeptical of free market economic policies. They advocate consensus-based decision-making and social justice. Green Parties have recently formed part of coalition governments in both Germany and New Zealand.

8. Nationalist parties flourished in former colonies, as the new regimes sought to establish their national values. The end of the Cold War removed some alternative poles of political organization, allowing freer rein for nationalists in Eastern Europe and the former Soviet Union. Because such parties' ideology is based on a concept of

the whole nation, as opposed to the interests of a part of it (e.g., a particular class or region), they seek to dominate the political system, which can make cooperation with other parties difficult.

9. Islamic parties are relatively recent, since many secular regimes in the Middle East did not tolerate them. In Iran, all the parties represented in the Majles (parliament) today are Islamic, but they represent a fairly wide spread of opinions. Like nationalist parties, Islamic parties seek to speak for the whole of society rather than a specific part of it, and therefore they too aim for a dominant position in the political system. Since the Arab Spring, Islamic parties in a number of countries now have a chance to compete in multi-party elections, and are gaining popularity.

KEY POINTS

- Typologies facilitate more systematic comparison between party activities.
- They vary depending on the nature of the features they highlight.

Party Systems

Any state with more than one political party also has a party system, defined by Giovanni Sartori as "the system of interactions resulting from interparty competition" (1976: 44). These interactions are affected by three factors:

1. The nature of the political system as a whole. Clearly, a state's constitution will have a major impact on the competition between parties, as parties have to operate according to its rules. Parties operate differently in liberal democratic regimes, where electoral success does lead to changes of government, than they do in more authoritarian regimes where rulers will not contemplate electoral overthrow and where opposition parties, if tolerated, have to be much more careful in their criticisms. It also matters whether a regime is presidential or parliamentarian.

2. The pattern of basic social cleavages that underlie the differentiation between parties. The pattern of relations between political parties is partly determined by the fundamental cleavages in society. As originally theorized by Lipset and Rokkan, there were four fundamental cleavages that structured the rise of the new mass parties in Europe in the late nineteenth century and the first quarter of the twentieth. Since then these "frozen" cleavages have remained the basis of West European party systems: (a) centre versus periphery: different communities within the same state vied for power both at the centre and in regional authorities (sometimes these were also based on different linguistic communities, but not necessarily); (b) state versus church: this cleavage was particularly important in Catholic states, where a significant part of the challenge to the Church's temporal powers was mounted by anti-clerical liberals and radicals; (c) land versus industry: the growth of industrialization and of industrial capitalists posed a challenge to more traditional rural elites; and (d) owner versus worker: the rise of capitalism pitted the interests of the new industrial workers against those of their employers (Lipset and Rokkan, 1967). All West European states were

affected to varying degrees by these divisions, and similar cleavages can be seen in North America and other parts of the world.

3. The channels open for competition between the parties, primarily the electoral system.

See Chapter 9, p. 188, for a discussion of presidentialism versus parliamentarianism.

In his classic *Political Parties*, Maurice Duverger argued that first-past-the-post electoral systems tend to produce two-party systems; this later became known as **Duverger's Law**. By contrast, he argued, proportional representation tends to produce multiparty systems (Duverger, 1964). While these are more generalizations than uniform "laws" (in the past, for example, Venezuela had both proportional representation and a two-party system), there is no doubt about the logic of the argument.

Given these factors, most typologies of party systems focus on the numbers of parties they contain. One version gives the following classification (Ware, 1996: 159):

1. Predominant party systems, where one party dominates the national legislature. Among developed democracies, Japan offers the only example, but single-party dominance can also be seen in Russia and is very common in sub-Saharan Africa, where non-ruling parties are short of resources (Doorenspleet, 2003: 205). Some authoritarian regimes, such as Indonesia under Suharto (1968–98), have explicitly favoured this system on the grounds that representation of different interests and groups within a single party promotes social cohesion, whereas unrestricted party competition would jeopardize it (Reeve, 1985).
2. Two-party systems, as in the US.
3. Systems with three to five parties, as in Canada, France, Germany, and the UK.
4. Systems with more than five parties, as in Belgium, Denmark, and New Zealand.

The nature of the party system in place can play a big part in determining how well a democracy operates; the two-party model has generally performed very well, whereas highly fragmented systems such as Italy's since the Second World War have not. Yet it is almost impossible for a democracy to change a dysfunctional party system once it has become established, even when voters are well aware of its flaws.

Take the case of Japan. The Liberal Democratic Party (LDP) held power almost continuously from 1955 to 2009. The brief exception came in 1993, when a series of scandals involving the LDP's connections with big business led to election of a reformist coalition. The reformers attributed much of the LDP's reputation for corruption to Japan's multimember-constituency system, in which candidates from the same party had to compete against one another as well as against other parties. In an effort to break this pattern and establish a genuine two-party system, more than half the country's constituencies were converted from multi- to single-member and plurality (first-past-the-post) voting. It was thought that reducing the competitive pressure would reduce campaign expenses and strengthen opposition to the LDP (Rosenbluth and Ramseyer, 1993). Yet the LDP managed to upset those calculations, regaining power in 1994, adapting to the new circumstances, and continuing to win the majority of seats in the lower house of the Diet (parliament) until 2009. Nor has campaign spending been noticeably reduced.

AP Photo/Christian Lutz

11

PHOTO 11.2 The European Parliament in session (2011): EuroMPs are grouped by the ideology of their political party, not (as in the case of the United Nations) by the countries they represent. This system is unique to the European Union.

KEY POINTS

- In genuine democracies, party systems are not designed and imposed: rather, they develop as the product of sociological and institutional interactions.
- This means that, once formed, they are very difficult to reform.

Problems Facing Parties

Political parties today face serious problems. In Western Europe the traditional parties and party systems survive, but party membership is declining. In general, the mass parties that were typical of the inter- and post-war eras are a thing of the past. Although parties do not always maintain close records of members, in part because of the need to appear strong to outside observers, the trend seems clear throughout Europe (see **Table 11.2**). In Spain, one of the two exceptions to this general trend, we should note that the base year of 1980 was only five years after the death of the dictator Francisco Franco and only two years after the adoption of a new constitution.

This means that by the end of the 1990s party membership across Europe averaged only 5.7 per cent of the population—approximately one-third of the percentage three decades earlier (Mair, 2005: 15). By coincidence, this figure is almost exactly the same as the percentage of China's population who were members of the Chinese Communist Party (CCP) in 2007. The fact that CCP membership appears to be increasing while party membership in the West is declining may be explained by the access to power and economic prosperity that CCP members can expect; in the West, party membership generally does not offer such benefits.

Many political leaders have devoted time and effort to uncovering the reasons behind Europeans' lack of enthusiasm for party activism. In Britain, the Power Inquiry (held between 2004 and 2006) recommended a number of measures, including adoption of a more "responsive electoral system—which offers voters a greater choice and diversity of parties and candidates—to replace the first-past-the-post system," a minimum voting age of 16, and state funding for parties through a voucher system that would allow each voter in a general election to assign £3 to his or her preferred party (Power Inquiry, 2006).

TABLE 11.2 Membership Trends in European Parties, 1980–2000

Country	Period	Change in numbers	Per cent change in original membership
France	1978–99	–1,122,128	–64.59
Italy	1980–98	–2,091,887	–51.54
UK	1980–98	–853,156	–50.39
Norway	1980–97	–281,891	–47.49
Austria	1980–99	–446,209	–30.21
Sweden	1980–98	–142,533	–28.05
Germany	1980–99	–174,967	–8.95
Greece	1980–98	+375,000	+166.67
Spain	1980–2000	+808,705	+250.73

SOURCE: Peter Mair and Ingrid van Biezen (2001), "Party Membership in Twenty European Democracies, 1980–2000," *Party Politics* 7, 1: 5–21.

The latter principle—state funding for political parties—has become increasingly common around the world in recent years, as a way of supporting the vital functions that parties perform in democracies while reducing their dependence on contributions from big business. Critics warn that it's important to ensure that such support does not serve to protect established parties from new challengers and prevent newcomers from winning seats in parliament, as happened in Venezuela (International IDEA, 2003); see the case study on page 234. State funding can also encourage party fragmentation rather than consolidation, by giving dissident factions the funds they need to set themselves up as new parties, as happened in Japan in the 1990s and more recently in New Zealand. Other critics argue that public indifference reflects a general feeling that individuals can make no impact on government or party decisions. From this perspective, the only solution is to change the process of political decision-making to make it more "relevant." Once this has happened, they say, people would flock back to parties.

CASE STUDY
Venezuela and the Downfall of Liberal Democracy

For half a century Venezuela had the reputation of the most stable and most liberal democracy in South America. Yet recent years have seen this tradition pushed aside in favour of a more populist democracy. It is a reminder that while liberal democracy may seem to be the most desirable form of political system, it is not invulnerable. What happened in Venezuela?

In 1958, dictator Pérez Jiménez was overthrown in a military coup and democracy was re-established. The leaders of the three main parties signed a pact that committed them to observing the same basic rules of the political game for the sake of preserving democracy. Subsequently, Venezuela evolved into a state with two effective parties: Acción Democrática (AD) and Comitida de Organización Política Electoral (COPEI). The concept of "pacted democracy" became a model for the establishment of a successful democracy, especially in Latin America, and for many years it underpinned US policy for promoting transitions to democracy there.

The two parties extended their reach into a wide range of other organizations (professional associations, peasant federations, state enterprises), which helped both to strengthen their control and also to increase their membership. Although both parties exercised very strict control over their members, they sought consensus between themselves wherever possible, though this did not prevent energetic competition for power; the presidency changed hands regularly.

This system worked well for nearly two decades, reinforced by prosperity based on oil wealth. In the mid-1970s, however, the economy began to stagnate and decline, partly because of falls in the international price of oil, but partly also because of corruption and waste. Popular dissatisfaction grew, and the parties responded not reforming but by becoming more isolated from the public.

In 1998 former Lt. Colonel Hugo Chávez, an outsider to both parties, was elected president. He promised what he called a "Bolivarian" revolution, associating his own socialist program with Simon Bolívar, the nineteenth-century liberator from Spanish rule, even though Bolivar has traditionally been seen as a liberal admirer of the American Revolution. Chávez aimed at sweeping away corruption and redistributing wealth to ordinary people. He attacked the "partocracy" (*partidocratia*) that kept all power in the hands of the two parties; their state funding was abolished. What emerged was a populist regime that promoted social polarization rather than consensus. Chávez introduced a new constitution that removed many of the checks on the powers of the president. Attempts to overthrow him, first through a coup and then by holding an election to recall him from office, both failed. The old party system fragmented, to be replaced by a multiparty system with numerous small parties overshadowed by Chávez's Fifth Republic Movement (now the United Socialist Party of Venezuela).

Aided by the additional wealth that came from increasing world oil prices, Chávez won a second term of office in January 2007.

SOURCES: Coppedge (2002); McCoy and Myers (eds) (2004); Gott (2005); Corrales and Penfold (2007)

The US has a similar problem, though it is not one of resources. In the 2004 presidential election the two parties declared combined expenditure of US$880 million—an increase of two-thirds since 2000. Even more was spent (much of it on media campaigning) in the 2008 election that finally saw John McCain and Barack Obama battle it out. The US Federal Election Commission (2009) reported that more than $1.6 billion was spent by all candidates. At least the same amount is spent every two years on elections to Congress and state legislatures. Although there is no shortage of volunteers willing to help on campaigns without pay, the trend towards declining party membership is evident in the US as well. Meanwhile, party professionals are playing bigger roles in shaping party image and designing campaign strategy.

New democracies have no trouble forming new political parties, but many of these parties are not particularly viable. New parties often find it difficult to establish a clear image, raise funds, bring in large numbers of members, and compete in elections. An added complication is the absence of the obvious social cleavages that can help to create a party system. With the Cold War over, socialist parties on the defensive, and the emergence of post-industrial economies in which social identities are more fluid, the old divisions between capital and labour are no longer central to political systems (Biezen, 2003: 37–8).

Taiwan is an exception that proves the rule. Since 1987 Taiwan has become one of the most successful new democracies. It has a stable party system, with two major parties and one or two minor ones. The two main parties—the Nationalist Party (KMT) and the Democratic Progressive Party (DPP)—confront each other over a vital political issue, but it is not one of the four issues that, as we saw earlier in this chapter, Lipset and Rokkan identified as traditional dividing lines. It is unique to Taiwan: the issue of independence from mainland China. The DPP calls for formal independence and the KMT opposes it, although there is not complete unanimity within either party on the issue of reunification. Although both parties have a variety of other policies to appeal to voters, some of which overlap and cut across the basic cleavage, preventing the antagonism from becoming irreconcilable, the fundamental difference with respect to independence serves to stabilize Taiwan's party system. Because other new democracies lack an analogous cleavage, their party systems are more volatile.

Despite the many differences between parties in the established Western democracies and the newer democracies in other parts of the world, there does seem to be one area in which they converge. In all cases, the jobs of establishing the party's "brand" and designing its platform are increasingly handled by party professionals. This trend reflects a combination of factors, among them declining party membership and growing dependence on the state for party funding. Since the 1960s the Democratic and Republican parties have both changed from mass parties to candidate-centred cartel parties in which party professionals play a dominant role (Aldrich, 1995: 254).

There is a growing divide between party professionals and party rank-and-file. According to Mair, in Europe parties "have reduced their presence in the wider society, and have become part of the state." They are less concerned with playing the function of opposition and more concerned with preparing for government. "Within politics . . . the parties are either all governing or waiting to govern" (Mair, 2005: 20).

11

KEY POINTS

- Political parties are facing a range of new challenges.
- In various parts of the world the balance between rank-and-file party members and party professionals is tipping towards the latter.
- Despite the generally negative public attitudes towards them, parties continue to play a vital role in the formulation and legitimation of public policies.

Conclusion

Today, as ever, parties and party systems are in transition, though their future shape is not clear. There seems little chance that the old mass parties will return. Yet parties will continue to play an important role in determining how policy choices are presented to the public. Indeed, parties with access to the necessary resources will have an increasing impact on the presentation of policies, managing a widening variety of media strategies. They will also continue to play important roles in structuring the work of parliaments. They will act as recruitment channels for ministerial positions, and they will certainly continue to legitimize—or be used for the purpose of legitimizing—political regimes. Although they often receive bad press, and are sometimes accused of intensifying social divisions, efforts to replace them with alternative organizational forms (such as "movements") have generally failed. Political parties structure the formulation of public policies, but their leaders still have to make choices about priorities and they can change them. They make mistakes, antagonize people, seem self-interested; but without them a politics dominated by narrower interest groups would be even less attractive (Fiorina, 2002: 541). It's hard to imagine how states would function without parties.

? KEY QUESTIONS

- Why did New Zealand change from majoritarian voting to a mixed-member proportional representation system? (See Nagel in Colomer, 2004.)
- How stable is the party system in your country? What might upset it?
- Do you take an active part in the life of a political party? How do you justify this activity (or lack of it)? How rational is it?
- How appropriate is state funding of political parties? How valid are the objections?
- Are parties' programs becoming more difficult to distinguish from each other? Are they becoming less "ideological"?
- Are parties in other parts of the world becoming more "American"? If so, in what ways? Does it matter?
- How well do the typologies presented in this chapter fit the party system in your country?

📖 FURTHER READING

Aldrich, John H. (1995). *Why Parties? The Origin and Transformation of Political Parties in America*. Chicago: Chicago University Press.
   A theoretically informed history of the rise of parties in the USA.

LeDuc, Lawrence, Jon H. Pammett, Judith I. McKenzie, and André Turcotte (2010). *Dynasties and Interludes: Past and Present in Canadian Electoral Politics*. Toronto, Dundurn Press.

An excellent recent overview of Canada's electoral system, which devotes special attention to the rise and fall of major parties.

Cross, William (2002). *Political Parties, Representation, and Electoral Democracy in Canada.* Toronto: Oxford University Press.
A fascinating collection of essays on political parties and electoral democracy in Canada by a well-known political scientist.

Farrell, David M. (2001). *Electoral Systems: A Comparative Introduction.* Basingstoke: Palgrave.
A very approachable introduction to the various types of electoral system.

Gallagher, Michael, Michael Laver, and Peter Mair (2001). *Representative Government in Modern Europe: Institutions, Parties and Governments.* 3rd edn. Boston: McGraw Hill.
Chapters 7–10 offer a survey of parties in various European states.

Held, David (2006). *Models of Democracy.* 3rd edn. Stanford: Stanford University Press.
A wonderful history of democracy and political systems, with some very innovative conclusions for future world government.

International IDEA (2007). *Electoral System Design.* Stockholm.
Details the considerations that should underlie the choice of electoral system, especially for regimes in transition to democracy.

Katz, Richard S., and William Crotty (eds) (2006). *Handbook of Party Politics.* London: Sage.
A compendium of information on many features of political parties.

Lewis, Paul G. (2000). *Political Parties in Post-Communist Eastern Europe.* London: Routledge.
A study of parties in the transitional states of Eastern Europe.

Mair, Peter (1997). *Party System Change.* Oxford: Oxford University Press.
A theoretical discussion of how modern parties change.

Mainwaring, Scott, and Timothy Scully, eds (1995). *Building Democratic Institutions: Party Systems in Latin America.* Stanford: Stanford University Press.
A study of party systems in Latin America.

Mohamed Salih, M.A., ed. (2003). *African Political Parties.* London: Pluto.
An introduction to African political parties.

WEB LINKS

www.idea.int/vt
A comprehensive source of information on voter turnout around the world.

www.psr.keele.ac.uk/parties.htm
Links to websites of political parties, social movements, and interest groups around the world.

www.opendemocracy.net/democracy-open_politics/article_2312.jsp
Paul Hilder discusses possible future organizational forms in an essay entitled "Open Parties? A Map of 21st Century Democracy."

http://repositories.cdlib.org/csd/05-06
Peter Mair (2005) discusses the changing politics of the party in "Democracy Beyond Parties." Center for the Study of Democracy, University of California, Irvine.

www.bepress.com/wpsr/vol3/iss3/art1/
Giovanni M. Carbone(2007), "Political Parties and Party Systems in Africa: Themes and Research," *World Political Science Review* 3(3). A recent attempt to systematize African political parties.

12 Civil Society, Interest Groups, and the Media

CHAPTER OVERVIEW

In this chapter we will explore several dimensions of political life outside the state and political parties. We begin with a look at "civil society": a broad concept that encompasses the political activities of apparently non-political (certainly not "politically organized") actors. After considering interest groups and corporatism we turn to what political anthropologists call "infrapolitics" or "politics from below," with a particular focus on the developing world. Then we examine the role of media in political life. We conclude by considering the impact of new communications technologies and the extent to which they are transforming political practices.

Civil Society

The term "**civil society**" was coined in the eighteenth century. Robertson (1993: 69) defined it as follows:

> Civil society is the framework within which those without political authority live their lives—economic relationships, family and kinship structures, religious institutions and so on. It is a purely analytic concept because civil society does not exist independently of political authority, nor vice versa, and, it is generally believed, neither could long continue without the other; therefore, no very clear boundary can be drawn between the two.

The concept of civil society came into wider use in the late 1980s, when a number of regimes were overturned by apparently unorganized, previously non-political forces. In 1986 the **authoritarian** President Ferdinand Marcos of the Philippines was overthrown by waves of "people power" demonstrations in the capital city, Manila, supporting Corazon Aquino, the widow of one of his most famous victims, Senator Benigno Aquino. In 1987, demonstrations in Seoul, South Korea, destabilized plans for an orderly handover of power by President Chun Doo Hwan to his chosen successor, General Roh Tae Woo. This set in motion a sequence of events that led to the reintroduction of democracy. In the spring of 1989 a demonstration in Beijing by thousands of students mourning the death of the Chinese Communist Party's former General Secretary, Hu Yaobang, turned into a massive challenge to the nation's leaders. Mass protests in Beijing's Tiananmen Square, and many other cities, were put down on 4 June with the loss of thousands of lives.

The biggest demonstration of the potential power of civil society, however, came in the autumn of 1989 in Eastern Europe. Civil society brought down the communist regimes there and hastened the end of the Soviet Union in 1991. After decades of organized repression of opponents, these regimes had very powerful secret police forces. Their brutal suppression of protests in Hungary in 1956 and Czechoslovakia in 1968 served as enduring warnings for anyone considering rising up against the government or rebelling against Soviet domination. Amazingly, the victory of the demonstrators in Eastern Europe was achieved with minimal casualties. It was a striking affirmation of the political power of civil society, if roused.

The victory of civil society was achieved despite—or more likely because of—the relentless repression of more "regular" political groupings such as parties. Communist regimes had devoted enormous resources to identifying, dispersing, and punishing organized opposition; yet their efforts proved to have been in vain. The more amorphous groupings that made up civil society had overthrown them; for a more detailed discussion, see the case study below. As a result, civil society became the focus of intense attention, as it seemed to offer the promise of an alternative, more consensual, non-coercive democratic politics. For some it became a metaphor for the good society; see **Box 12.1**.

Would-be reformers in Western countries started looking at other authoritarian regimes to try to identify groupings similar to the ones that had triumphed in Eastern Europe in the hope that they might achieve similar results. It did not matter whether these groups were well-organized or agreed on their long-term goals. Policy-makers in Western governments and international charities had become disenchanted with giving aid to governments in the developing world that failed to reduce poverty. In particular, they were exasperated by official corruption, and saw civil society and the voluntary sector as vehicles of **good governance** and democracy. Aid money was widely dispensed to

◀ Supporters of Italian Democratic Party leader Walter Veltroni attend a public meeting in 2008. Veltroni wrote the preface to the Italian translation of Barack Obama's memoirs (© Alessandra Benedetti/Corbis).

CASE STUDY
Civil Society and the Collapse of Communism

By 1989 the communist regimes in Eastern Europe faced mounting difficulties. Imposed by the USSR after 1945, they lacked popular legitimacy, their leaders were aging, and their economies were stagnating. Yet attempts to pull away from Soviet dominance had provoked brutal repression in Hungary in 1956 and Czechoslovakia in 1968, and the regimes continued to crush all attempts at organized political opposition.

Meanwhile, the Soviet Union itself was descending into turmoil. After four years of **perestroika** (restructuring), the economic revival promised by Gorbachev still had not arrived. Yet instead of offering the Eastern European leaders unconditional support in return for their political loyalty, as his predecessors had done, Gorbachev was pressuring them to undertake the same kinds of reform that he was attempting to achieve in the USSR.

The crisis first broke out in Poland, where the regime faced severe economic and political problems. There the independent trade union, Solidarity, which had been challenging the regime throughout the 1980s despite martial law, forced the government into negotiations over reforms. As the price for agreeing to participate in what were expected to be rigged elections, Solidarity extracted an agreement for its own legalization. Then—contrary to all expectations, including its own—it won all but one of the seats it contested in the elections in June. This fatally undermined the legitimacy of the communist rulers, and by September Solidarity had become the dominant actor in a new government.

The excitement of change spread to other states. In September 1989 Hungarian authorities announced that they would not seek to prevent East German refugees from crossing to the West via Hungary when Moscow would not commit itself to support such action. Their decision to open the border was noted in other capitals, where it encouraged new hopes of change. The aging East German leader, Erich Honecker, was deposed, and his successors began to make conciliatory noises. Demonstrations were held and, when they were not repressed, attracted growing numbers of people. By November the demonstrations had spread to Prague, and the authorities there capitulated with virtually no loss of life in what came to be known as the "Velvet Revolution." Change was remarkably peaceful and amicable. Also in November, the new East German leadership abandoned its increasingly feeble efforts to keep the Berlin Wall closed. With the Wall open, it was no longer possible to prevent people from crossing to the West. After that, resistance in most East European regimes crumbled. The last hold-out was Romania, but in mid-December the dictator Nicolai Ceausescu was overthrown. Within a few days he and his wife had been condemned to death and summarily executed.

The regimes collapsed remarkably easily. Through a combination of circumstances, they had become inefficient and weak, with very little support. Nevertheless, it had taken the courage and heroism of tens of thousands of demonstrators to reveal the authorities' weakness. Although largely not organized beforehand, they quickly found ways of cooperating. It was a movement of joyous good humour—as one account put it, "a carnival of revolution" (Kenney, 2002). The legend of the power of civil society was born.

12

non-governmental organizations (NGOs) in the developing world in the hope that their activities would serve to spread their enthusiasm and experience among the citizenry. They had the advantage of large numbers and, unlike political parties in dictatorships, they operated at the grassroots level. Even democracies such as Japan began to pay more attention to their NGOs. The 1990s was a heroic decade for civil society, which seemed to symbolize the ability of the downtrodden to rise up and overthrow their oppressors.

KEY QUOTE BOX 12.1
Michael Edwards on Civil Society

It is a truism that civil society is what we as active citizens make it, but it is also true that "social energy," or "willed action," is the spark that ignites civil society as a force for positive social change. The determination to do something because it is the right thing to do, not because we are told to do it by governments or enticed to do it by the market, is what makes associational life a force for good, provides fuel for change in the practices of states and business, and motivates people to raise their voices in the public sphere. . . . Against the background of weak democracies, strong bureaucracies, corporate power, legalism and nationalism resurgent, civil society, as both concept and reality, is essential to the prospects for a peaceful and prosperous world order in the twenty-first century. . . . Warts and all, the idea of civil society remains compelling, not because it provides the tidiest of explanations but because it speaks to the best in us, and calls on the best in us to respond in kind (Edwards, 2004: 111–12).

At the same time, NGOs offered a way of channelling aid to developing countries that could not afford to support a Western-style welfare state. NGOs were attractive for donors because they offered some assurance that the aid they sent would actually reach the grassroots; in addition, NGO activity often involved women, who in the past had had no direct access to aid. It was attractive for governments in the developing world because it helped to reduce the pressure on them to provide welfare. Finally, it was attractive to the recipients not only because of the aid itself but because NGOs offered them opportunities to organize and stand up for their rights. Left-leaning municipal authorities in developing countries such as Brazil (Bruce, 2004) and India occasionally experimented with ways of drawing groups of citizens into active participation in the compiling of budgets. In this way the line between civil society and elected representatives began to blur.

Problems quickly emerged, however. On the one hand, the NGO-centred approach to aid became a victim of its own success. Many NGOs in the developing world became dependent on foreign funding to support their activities. This meant their leaders had to spend as much time, if not more, on devising projects that would attract foreign funding as they did on projects that their communities needed most urgently. On the other hand, as dictatorships became aware of the political threat that civil society represented, they moved to reduce that threat. Authoritarian regimes also tried to restrict flows of foreign aid that might undermine their authority. Sometimes a state such as Russia would play the nationalist card and complain about unjust foreign interference from organizations like the Carnegie Foundation for International Peace. Many regimes started creating alternative civil-society organizations that they could control. In Indonesia, for instance, when one of President Suharto's ministers (later his successor as president), B.J. Habibie, created an organization of Muslim intellectuals (ICMI), ostensibly to serve as a think-tank for new ideas on furthering Islam and promoting education, many believed its real purpose was to serve as "an instrument of political management" and bolster Muslim support for the regime (Leifer, 1995: 133). Established in 1990, by 1994 it claimed to have 20,000 members.

Among the benefits of the concept of civil society for comparative politics was the fact that it directed scholars' attention to informal social politics, as well as political activity at the margins of institutions. In India, for example, Jenkins (2005: 280–1) explored the long-standing relationship between political parties, especially the Congress Party, and informal organizations associated with the independence movement—a relationship that continues to be an important element in Indian politics. The concept also attracted a great deal of interest among students of Middle Eastern politics. Social institutions such as the *diwaniyya* (a kind of salon) in Kuwait, where all sorts of subjects could be discussed, including politics, or the informal *dawra* ("circle") in Iran were known to play a significant part in political life (Eickelman, 1996: x–xi). Traditionally the state had played a more limited role in the lives of Muslims, and non-state actors, such as charitable foundations, had provided many public services, including education and water supplies. Although their roles have become more limited, they are still important. So too are professional organizations of doctors, engineers, teachers, and such (Ibrahim, 1995). They embody the principle of a self-organizing society separate from the state.

The concept of civil society has been subject to many contradictory interpretations. There has been disagreement over whether it is primarily an analytical term or a normative one. Does civil society mean that all the groups involved share some kind of common perspective when they pursue political goals? Does it signify commitment to altruistic advocacy of policies that are judged to be in the public interest? Or commitment to some kind of "civility," which would mean excluding groups that pursue non-civil goals and advocate violence or exclusion? Could it include **interest groups**? Could it include mafia organizations, fundamentalist religious sects, extreme right-wing nationalist groups? Does it provide some protection against the **anarchy** of weak or failed states? (Chabal and Daloz, 1999: 17–18). Is it some form of civil society that has kept Somalia together after the collapse of the state, as we outlined in Chapter 7? Or is "civil society" simply a collective term covering all groups and organizations that are not part of the state or political society? Is civil society vulnerable to existing inequalities in society, which may privilege some groups and disadvantage or even silence others?

At the same time, the connotations attached to the English term "civil society" have made it difficult to translate into other languages. In Chinese the most commonly used equivalent is *gongmin*, which really means citizens. The same is true of *shimin*, in both Japanese and Korean. Right-wing critics of Japanese democracy such as Saeki (1997) stigmatize civil society as a (harmful) Western import, and for a time, Islamic societies were

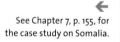

← See Chapter 7, p. 155, for the case study on Somalia.

also suspicious of the concept because they associated it with secular Western thought. But the idea of civil society has become much more appealing since the Arab Spring of 2011.

Finally, the evolution of the groups that brought about the fall of communism in Eastern Europe weakened enthusiasm for civil society as a model for the future. The euphoria that greeted the remarkable success of groups such as Solidarity evaporated, and hopes that such groups might lead the way towards a new kind of consensual rule were quickly dashed, despite considerable encouragement and approval from outside. The need to make radical changes and take drastic decisions in the face of mounting economic crises revealed the difficulty of maintaining cohesion in the absence of formal organization and shared ideologies. Instead of unifying the groups' members, the crises polarized them. Solidarity—the largest such organization and the one with the longest and most distinguished history of struggle against the communist authorities—fragmented and new political parties began to appear like mushrooms. By 1992, only three years after the collapse of the communist regime, 222 parties had been registered in Poland, although not all of them had candidates standing at elections.

All these uncertainties have made the concept of civil society problematic. Comaroff and Comaroff (1999: 33) suggest that it is "deeply flawed as an analytic construct." Even so, they argue that "it still serves, almost alone in the age of neoliberal capital, to give shape to reformist even utopian visions."

KEY POINTS

- "Civil society" is an ambiguous term subject to a wide variety of interpretations.
- It acquired a heroic aura because of its association with the protests that brought down the communist regimes of Eastern Europe.

Interest Groups

Interest groups are a big component of civil society. They are also an essential element of democracy: it's impossible to think of a democracy without interest groups. From a normative perspective they have attracted a variety of responses. Some writers see them as a negative influence on democracy, because they privilege some interests at the expense either of others or of the public interest as a whole. This was the reasoning behind James Madison's rejection of "factions," which we mentioned in Chapter 11. For others, however, interest groups are entirely positive because they facilitate the input of new ideas into the political process. According to this view, they are a key element in the pluralism that is an essential feature of (liberal) democracy. For rational choice theorists such as Mancur Olson, interest groups are the most rational form of political activity for ordinary citizens because they are smaller than parties and offer a greater likelihood of return on effort. On the other hand, group interests are not confined to democracies. They are present in all societies, including dictatorships, even if the opportunities to express them may be limited in the latter.

Interest groups have attracted an enormous amount of comment and analysis, both in general and with respect to particular political systems. There is also a long-standing

See the discussion on the emergence of parties in Chapter 11, p. 223.

See Chapter 1, p. 25, for a discussion of pluralism.

12

argument about the term itself. What counts as a "group"? Does it have to be a self-consciously cohesive organization, like Friends of the Earth? Or could it be a disparate group of people who share common interests but do not act in a cohesive manner, as in the case of a corporation or a social class? There is no definitive answer.

According to Robertson (1993: 240), interest groups are "associations formed to pro-mote a sectional interest in the political system." Unlike political parties, they do not seek to form governments, mainly because they focus on a relatively narrow range of issues, although it is possible for interest groups to evolve into political parties, as environmental groups have done. A distinction is often made between **insider** and **outsider groups**. Insiders concentrate on winning support through lobbying and personal contacts, while outsiders rely mainly on winning over public opinion through campaigning, the media, and so on. Although some interest groups may be permanently oriented towards a particular role because of their ideological stance (greens and radical environmentalists, for example, are unlikely to become insiders in the US), the role that a given group plays at a particular time will often depend on its relationship with the government in power. For example, conservative governments are typically inclined to treat employers' associations as insiders, giving greater attention to their views in formulating policy, while labour or socialist governments typically treat trade unions as insiders.

Puhle (2001: 7703–4) has usefully sorted interest groups into eight types:

1. professional associations;
2. groups of business, commerce and industry;
3. trade unions;
4. agricultural organizations;
5. single-interest groups, such as the National Rifle Association in the US;
6. ideological interest groups, such as the Fraser Institute (see **Box 12.2**) or religious groups;
7. public interest groups, such as Amnesty International; and
8. welfare associations, such as the Canadian National Institute for the Blind.

Interest groups operate in many different ways, but when they pursue political goals they adapt themselves to the structure of the institutions they wish to influence. If they want to influence the national government, they will turn most of their attention to the national capital, appealing to public opinion and lobbying ministers, officials, and members of parliament. In federal systems they will also try to win support in individual provinces or states. In more centralized unitary systems such as France or the UK, interest groups will concentrate on lobbying officials. The enormous range of interest group activities around the world makes it is very difficult to generalize about them. What any particular interest group does, and how it operates, depends on the nature of the political system within which it exists.

KEY POINTS

- "Interest group" is an ambiguous term.
- It can refer to a consciously organized group promoting a particular interest or concern, in which case it is an essential element in any democracy.

KEY QUOTES BOX 12 .2

On the Fraser Institute

A right-wing interest group based in Calgary, Alberta, the Fraser Institute took a leading role in shaping some of the policies of the Conservative Party of Canada as it exists today. The Institute's website claims a high level of impartiality:

> The Fraser Institute measures and studies the impact of competitive markets and government interventions on individuals and society. Our peer-reviewed research is distributed around the world and has contributed to increased understanding of how economic policy affects people. The Institute is an independent non-profit research and educational organization. We do not accept government grants or contracts for research. We depend on contributions from thousands of individuals, organizations, and foundations.

The Canadian Labour Congress takes a different view of the Institute's "independence" from big business and government. Ken Georgetti, the CLC's president argued in 2011:

> The Fraser Institute attacks trade unions for an alleged lack of transparency in how we disclose financial information. . . . We will gladly compare our transparency with theirs any day of the week. . . . I have read the Fraser Institute's annual report for 2010. It does not provide a financial report, but rather selective "financial highlights." We know that they took in $10.8 million dollars but they don't tell us who gave them that money. The Fraser Institute is registered as a charitable organization with many of its donors receiving tax receipts with their thank you letters but the actual list of donors and financial statements are nowhere to be seen. The board of directors, however, is comprised mainly of big business bosses. Might they just have an agenda when it comes to trying to discredit unions? I challenge the Fraser Institute to come clean on who finances their anti-union agenda.

SOURCES: www.fraserinstitute.org/ and "Georgetti challenges the Fraser Institute to come clean on who finances their anti-union agenda," 11 Sept. 2011; accessed 9 Feb. 2011 at www.canadianlabour.ca/news-room/editorials/ken-georgetti-challenges-fraser-institute-come-clean-who-finances-their-anti-unionagenda

- Or it can refer to a group in society with some interests in common, in which case it can be found in any state.
- In either case, interest groups adapt to the institutional framework in place to maximize their effect.

Modern Corporatism

As we noted above, governments do not treat all interest groups equally: they will naturally be more inclined to listen to "insiders" than "outsiders." The term **modern corporatism** refers to a model in which the state formalizes its relations with the "insider" groups that it

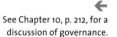
See Chapter 1, p. 29,
for earlier forms of
corporatism.

See Chapter 10, p. 212, for a
discussion of governance.

considers most important: namely, those representing sections of society that are politically or economically strategic. These groups are termed "peak" associations. Thus in Britain the government holds regular consultations with the Confederation of British Industry and the Trades Union Congress in an effort to improve policy-making. This practice is consistent with the recent emphasis on "governance" as opposed to "government" as the most appropriate framework for national decision-making. In the more conventional interest-group model, the groups in question have a particular view that they want to express to the government. Here, however, select organizations act as channels for the exchange of views between their members and the government, and do not necessarily promote a set view. Philippe Schmitter (1980) coined the term "interest intermediation" to refer to this process.

Schmitter also identified two distinct types of modern corporatism. In what he termed "societal" corporatism, the relationship is formed in response to social or economic pressures originating outside government; in this case, the nature of the pressures will help to determine which actors the state will work with. In the alternative variant, which he termed "state" corporatism, the state takes the lead and chooses the partners it prefers.

Lehmbruch (2001) suggests that corporatism has been more prominent at certain periods of history and in certain groups of countries than others. It was particularly important in the era of Keynesian economic management in the 1960s and 1970s, when government, employers, and trade unions regularly consulted over trade-offs between levels of unemployment, wages, and inflation rates. Although several European countries later turned away from corporatism, Germany, France, and the Nordic countries all continue to practise variants of "organized" or "concerted" capitalism, in which socio-economic policies are determined, at least in part, by negotiations between national partners, as opposed to impersonal market forces.

While corporatism has been tried extensively in Europe, the same is not true of all Western countries. In Canada, for instance, it has been relatively rare. Hale (2006: 337) attributes this partly to the decentralized nature of the federal system and the "fragmented, highly individualistic character of many Canadian business associations," and partly to an "adversarial parliamentary political culture does not lend itself to corporatist policy-making." Although corporatist negotiations have taken place among federal and provincial governments, alongside unions and business, they are not as common in Canada as in Europe.

KEY POINTS

- Corporatism privileges certain national "peak" organizations as negotiating partners for the state in determining socio-economic policies.
- There are two variants: society-led and state-led.
- Corporatism is still a common approach to governance in countries in continental Europe but is rare in Canada.

Infrapolitics and Subaltern Studies: The State Viewed From Below

Looking at politics from the perspective of civil society and interest groups offers us a view "from below" that is no less important than the view "from above" offered by studies that focus on national governments and state leaders. Another useful view from below is offered by political anthropology, which examines the connections between political behaviour and cultural contexts, especially at the grassroots level. Among the key concerns of political anthropologists is what Gledhill (1994) called "power and its disguises." How do ordinary people relate to political systems? How do they defer to rulers? How do they manipulate the system for their own ends? A very influential work in this field was James Scott's *Domination and the Arts of Resistance* (1990). Doing fieldwork among peasants in Malaysia, Scott noticed that they spoke differently among themselves than they did with their social superiors. This alerted him to the existence of what he called "infrapolitics"—the subtle ways in which the powerless subvert or undermine the authority of the powerful. Most often, infrapolitics relies on ambiguity rather than direct expression of opinions, which could attract retribution. "Infrapolitics is the realm of informal leadership and nonelites, of conversation and oral discourse, and of surreptitious resistance" (Scott, 1990: 200). Common forms of covert resistance—elsewhere Scott has called them "weapons of the weak"—include poaching, land-squatting, desertion (by slaves), evasion, and foot-dragging. It can also express itself in dissident subcultures of resistance: millenarian religions, folk myths of social banditry, and class heroes such as Robin Hood (1990: 198).

One recent approach in political anthropology is to study non-Western politics and societies in their own right and on their own terms, without reference to Europe (Chatterjee, 2001: 15, 240. An example is the school of "subaltern" studies that has become established among academics specializing in South Asia in particular. The concern is with the subordinated groups in society. For example, as Gupta (2006) explains, there is relatively little ethnographic evidence of what lower-level officials do in the name of the state and how this affects the lives of ordinary people. These officials are "differentially positioned" in hierarchical networks of power, which means that their behaviour varies depending on whether they are dealing with their administrative superiors or with ordinary people (a classic example of the "kiss up, kick down" pattern). Gupta argues that this means there is no such thing as a single state. Instead there are multiple variants of the state within the same nation, and different groups have different experiences of it, depending on how powerful they are.

The subaltern school also seeks to "decentre" or "provincialize" Europe. In addition to trying to give a voice to the underprivileged in society, its proponents seek equality of respect with and from the West. They want to find an alternative path to modernity, one that is more in tune with local circumstances.

Indigenous studies reveal that the same sorts of hierarchical networks of power operate in the Western world. Life in countries such as Canada, the US, Australia, and New Zealand is often very different for Aboriginal people than for their non-Aboriginal counterparts. Indeed, while many Western countries claim to be tolerant, multicultural societies, relatively free of racism, indigenous scholars often assert that the countries they live in are hardly post-colonial. In their classic text *Unequal Relations*, Fleras and Elliott (1999) point out that for many people in Canada the present-day reality still depends on race and class. "People of colour continue to experience all manner of discrimination at personal and institutional levels" (Fleras and Elliot, 1999: 6). They also note that the situation has been particularly difficult for indigenous people:

> Decades of colonialist subjugation and demeaning clientelism have diminished Canada's luster as a pacesetter in aboriginal affairs. Annual reports of Canada's Human Rights Commission routinely castigate the government's treatment of aboriginal

See Chapter 7, p. 146, for a discussion of the spread of the Western state.

See Chapter 14 for a more detailed discussion of the rise and spread of the state system.

12

The Canadian Press/ Patrick Doyle

PHOTO 12.1 Politicians like to demonstrate their multicultural credentials; here Prime Minister Stephen Harper celebrates Diwali, the Hindu festival of light (2011).

peoples as the country's most egregious human rights violation. But aboriginal peoples are challenging the status quo by engaging central authorities in a power struggle over who controls what and why" (Fleras and Elliot, 1999: 7).

The Mohawk academic Taiaiake Alfred acknowledges that "There have been some improvements." Yet

> our people still suffer. . . . The state has shown great skill in shedding the most onerous responsibilities of its rule while holding fast to the lands and authorities that are the foundations of its power. Redefining without reforming, it is letting go of the costly and cumbersome minor features of the colonial relationship and further entrenching in law and practice the real bases of its control. It is ensuring continued access to indigenous lands and resources by insidiously promoting a form of neo-colonial self-government in our communities and forcing our integration into the legal mainstream (Alfred, 2009: 10)

KEY POINTS

- Political anthropology examines the connections between political behaviour and cultural contexts, especially at the grassroots level.
- Subaltern studies focus on subordinated groups in society.

AP Photo/Andrew Vaughan, The Canadian Press

PHOTO 12.2 RCMP Deputy Commissioner Steve Graham, left, presents a copy of a report documenting the force's involvement in Canada's infamous Indian Residential School system during the national event of the Truth and Reconciliation Commission in Halifax in 2011.

- Subaltern studies also demand consideration for development strategies that are not borrowed from the West and are better adapted to local (non-Western) circumstances.
- Studies of indigenous peoples' experience of the state in Canada, the US, Australia, and New Zealand suggest some parallels with the findings of subaltern studies.

The Impact of the Media

At the time of American Revolution, newspapers such as Benjamin Franklin's *Pennsylvania Gazette* played a key role in explaining the issues at stake to people of the thirteen colonies. Today the media still play a crucial role in determining how citizens in a particular country perceive politics and the state. Democracies certainly recognize the importance of the media in maintaining an informed democratic citizenry. The First Amendment to the US Constitution established freedom of speech as an essential principle of democracy, and since then many other states have incorporated this principle as a central feature of their constitutions.

12

← See Chapter 9, p. 193, for a discussion of accountability.

Traditionally, the press was seen as serving a "watchdog" function similar to that of the opposition in parliament, holding the established authorities to account on behalf of ordinary people. Journalists had both the skills and the resources to investigate matters of public interest in ways that ordinary people, even politicians, could not, and in some cases they were granted special legal immunities, such as the right to keep their sources of information confidential. In its capacity as a check on the power of the executive, the press became an important branch of civil society.

The press can bring about dramatic changes in national politics. Probably the best-known example is the *Washington Post's* dogged investigation of the Watergate affair—a political scandal that began with a bungled attempt, financed by the committee to re-elect Richard Nixon, to install a wiretap at the headquarters of the Democratic Party and ended with Nixon's resignation in 1974. Internationally, brave journalists operating in conflict zones regularly put their lives at risk; around the world, 81 journalists and 32 media assistants were killed in 2006 alone (Reporters Without Borders, 2006).

At the same time, the owners of media outlets—above all, newspaper proprietors—have often seen it as their role to advocate for particular political standpoints. Thus the Fox News network in the US has been accused of favouring the Republican Party, and spends much of its time criticizing Democratic leaders, while in Canada the *Toronto Star* for many years supported the Liberal Party. But the extent to which the media is biased can often be exaggerated. Some media owners have become politicians in their own right; Silvio Berlusconi and Thaksin Shinawatra, the former prime ministers of Italy and Thailand respectively, were both media tycoons. Instead of acting as tribunes for particular views, these men have used their media outlets to cultivate public attention and support for their political ambitions. At a more local level, billionaire media tycoon Michael Bloomberg has been mayor of New York for three successive terms. Although he has spent millions of his own dollars on his campaigns, he has not used his media empire (which specializes in financial news) to advance his political career.

Regardless of who owns or influences them, media companies must attract readers and viewers in order to sell the advertising that keeps most of them in business: therefore they must present the news in ways that will appeal to the public. Even public broadcasters such as the CBC and BBC, which depend on the state for their existence and are administered by government appointees, generally try to appear even-handed in their political reporting, although the BBC tends to be more critical of Westminster than the CBC is of Canada's federal Parliament. (In the UK, viewers pay an annual fee that help to support the BBC, and it has been suggested that this fee creates a form of "social contract" whereby BBC news reporters feel a special responsibility to represent the interests of the public that ultimately pays their salaries; see Hill, 2005: 112.) Even in China, newspapers can no longer rely on state subsidies: they are becoming commercial enterprises, and as such must find ways to attract readers. One consequence of the media's dependence on audiences for survival, at least in the West, has been a growing preference for human-interest political stories—what is sometimes called "infotainment"— rather than dry dissections of policy, even if this leads to accusations of "dumbing down" politics.

On the other hand, both governments and individual politicians need the media to help sell policies and win election campaigns. As Matthew Parris (a political columnist and former British MP) once put it: "Politicians run on publicity like horses run on oats" (quoted in Franklin, 2004: 5). So they also need to court the media and "spin" policies. The ability to come up with memorable sound bites is an invaluable asset for any politician.

In short, as Franklin (2004: 14) points out, politicians and the media are sometimes adversaries and sometimes accomplices. This is a complex relationship, and explaining how it works is not easy. Franklin outlines four theories that have tried to do so (208–28):

1. The "magic bullet" or "hypodermic needle" model: Powerful media either "inject" their audiences with messages or batter them into acceptance. Identifying where and how this happens, however, has presented a methodological challenge
2. The "two-step" flow of influence model: The media are influential only in so far as their messages are reinforced by personal interaction of readers or viewers with local opinion-formers.
3. The theory that people "use" the media to gratify certain needs. Here the standard assumption that audiences are passive consumers is reversed and the goal is to understand what causes them to respond to media messages. How can we reliably identify the "needs" that the media fill, let alone explain how they may structure viewing and reading habits?
4. The theory that broadcasters "encode" political messages and audiences "decode" them, though not necessarily in the way intended. A journalist may "construct" a message to convey certain political information, but the audience may interpret it to mean something quite different. This account of the relationship is more realistic than the others, since it focuses equally on both sides. Even so, identifying regular social patterns in this process is difficult.

There is still no consensus on the superiority of one theory over the others. "The power of the press" is a truism, and yet how it works is extremely difficult to pin down. To complicate matters further, audience views of politics may be influenced by entertainment programs as well as "straight" news reports. Audiences do not neatly separate political entertainment from factual news. The television series called *The West Wing*, which aired for seven years, was built around a character that some people considered to be the best Democratic president that the US never had. That character, Josiah Bartlet (played by Martin Sheen), created a more positive impression of American politics than any current affairs program could. Factoring this kind of fictional influence into an analysis of the relationship between politics and the media adds further layers of complexity to an ever-fascinating subject (Street, 2001).

Now there is an additional complication. New forms of communication are appearing that promise to change the traditional relationships between politics and the media. This will be the subject of the next section.

KEY POINTS

- Traditionally the media, especially the press, have been seen as an essential element of liberal democracy and a check on the power of the executive.
- Politicians and the media are by turns adversaries and accomplices.
- In recent years the media have been criticized for "dumbing down" politics, while politicians have been criticized for "spinning" their activities.
- Analyses of the political influence of the media need to take into account the way politics is presented not just in news and current affairs but in all contexts, including entertainment.
- Exactly how "the power of the press" operates is extremely difficult to pin down.

The Challenge of New Technologies

In recent years new communications technologies have revolutionized the role of the media in politics. Indeed, they may have a greater impact than newspapers and TV did in the past, not least because they provide civil society with new arenas for activity and offer ordinary citizens a new **public space** in which they can make an impact on politics. There are three reasons for this. First, the Internet and mobile phones have transformed the ability of ordinary citizens to organize themselves in groups even in repressive regimes. Second, they have widened the opportunities for people outside the media world to report news and offer influential commentary. In that sense they have democratized access to the media. Third, they have the potential to transform decision-making institutions as well, through direct voting and referendums. We will consider each of these three dimensions in turn.

Promoting Horizontal Communication

In the past, communication channels within states were mainly vertical. The most influential media outlets tended to congregate in national capitals; this was especially true of broadcasters. Political parties and interest groups achieved results by concentrating their efforts there. The opportunities for other groups to have significant impact were constrained by the difficulty of contacting people via landline telephones and the mail. Now there are much greater opportunities for would-be political actors to mobilize support using horizontal communications technology—notably mobile phones (including SMS texting) and the Internet.

In the early years of the Internet there was optimism about the possibilities that new media offered for organizing political parties. In the US, the enormous cost of standing for office made it very difficult for outsiders to be elected. Much was made of the success of the former wrestler and actor Jesse Ventura when—against all expectations—he was elected governor of Minnesota in 1998 as a third-party candidate. Ventura used the Internet as a cheap means to get his message across. His example seemed to open the way for other outsiders to get into politics. However, the established parties recognized the threat and started developing their own Internet strategies. They have refined the techniques of using the Internet for candidates to communicate directly with individual voters and target specific messages to their various concerns. Once again they have outflanked the challengers.

On the other hand, the new technologies have also empowered dissident groups, allowing them to mobilize supporters and organize protests with minimal advance notice to authorities. This can be very effective, as the rapid fall of the Mubarak regime in Egypt in 2011 showed. Young Egyptians used social media to document abuses by the government as well as to organize protests. Sam Gustin of *Wired* magazine observed:

> Did social media like Facebook and Twitter cause the revolution? No. But these tools did speed up the process by helping to organize the revolutionaries, transmit their message to the world and galvanize international support (Gustin, 2011).

The Philippines had seen an earlier version of the same phenomenon in 2000, when an explosion of SMS texting made a decisive contribution to the overthrow of President Joseph Estrada; see **Box 12.3**. Now social networking sites such as Facebook and Twitter can be used for similar purposes. The Internet also played a major role in the 2008

US presidential election, when both the McCain and Obama campaigns used it to raise funds and generate support for their candidates.

These new possibilities for self-organization will have an impact on both democratic and authoritarian states, though in different ways. More open systems are vulnerable to unexpected demonstrations by what Rheingold (2002) termed "smart mobs." Such protests can amount to a kind of political blackmail; and if the state does satisfy the demonstrators' demands, it runs the risk of alienating those segments of the society that did not take part. The demonstrators in the Philippines were a much larger manifestation of the same phenomenon. As for authoritarian states such as Egypt, Tunisia, and Libya, it's clear that social media can play a crucial role in accelerating the pace of change while offering new avenues for everyday people to gain information and organize protests. Obviously, authoritarian regimes place more emphasis on controlling the freedom to organize in this way because any such protest is fundamentally more threatening; see **Box 12.3**.

CASE STUDY
The Fall of Joseph Estrada

In 1998 Joseph Estrada was elected president of the Philippines. A former actor and producer who had played the lead in more than a hundred movies, he entered politics in the late 1960s as mayor of a town in Metro Manila. Gradually his political career took off as he was elected first a senator and then, in 1992, vice-president. Coming from a poor background in a country whose politics are dominated by traditional elite families, he won the support of the poorer strata of society.

By 2000, however, his administration was in trouble and his popularity in opinion polls was sliding. He launched a costly military campaign against the Moro Islamic Liberation Front on the island of Mindanao. Then it was alleged that he had taken several million dollars in bribes from gambling, and the Senate moved to impeach him. In January 2001 pro-Estrada senators prevented a key piece of evidence from being presented in court. This plunged the country into crisis (Doronila, 2001).

In Manila, outraged citizens began to organize public demonstrations using mobile phones. In a normal week Filipinos had been exchanging 50 million text messages per day, but as the crisis deepened this figure rose to 80 million. On very short notice, people intending to demonstrate passed on information about the location to all their contacts, who then passed it on to others. The organizers of the demonstrations quickly realized that the short timescale made it extremely difficult for the authorities to respond. Hundreds of thousands of people kept gathering on or around the site where demonstrations of "people power" had toppled President Ferdinand Marcos in 1986.

After five days of demonstrations that paralyzed the capital, Estrada was forced to step down in favour of Vice-President Gloria Macapagal-Arroyo. He was the first political casualty of SMS texting. Three months later he was arrested and put on trial. After proceedings lasting six years he was found guilty in 2007 and sentenced to life imprisonment. Almost immediately afterwards President Arroyo pardoned him on the grounds that he had reached the age of 70 (the age at which prisoners in the Philippines are released), and in return for a commitment that he would retire from politics.

China in particular has devoted enormous efforts to surveillance of the Internet. Authorities have erected a firewall to limit access to politically sensitive material posted in other parts of the world. They also have a large number of censors (nicknamed "Internet mamas") who supervise electronic message boards and demand the deletion of politically or socially undesirable materials. Meanwhile, technologically sophisticated netizens use mirror servers to obtain sensitive information from abroad and outwit the censors. The danger for these sorts of regime is that even if they are able to control the Internet in normal times, it is unlikely that they will be able to do so at a time of serious crisis. In the absence of legitimate democratic institutions to channel protests in a constructive direction, citizens may feel justified in taking advantage of new technologies to organize against the regime.

KEY QUOTE BOX 12.3
Rolling Stone on the Internet and Authoritarian States

The Internet is the censor's biggest challenge and the tyrant's worst nightmare. . . . Unbeknown to their governments, people in China, Iraq and Iran, among other countries, are freely communicating with people all over the world.

SOURCE: *Rolling Stone* magazine, 1995; accessed 9 Feb. 2012 at http://www.fas.org/cp/swett.html.

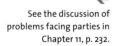

Of course, not all groups that use the new technologies are benign. The Internet can be extremely useful to small extremist groups, which in the past had to rely on personal contacts, public meetings, pamphlets, and posters to attract new adherents. This includes terrorist organizations like al-Qaeda. New communications technologies make it more difficult for all governments, whether democratic or authoritarian, to combat groups bent on violence or terrorism.

Everyone a Blogger, Everyone a Journalist

The new media have also made it much easier for non-journalists to publish their own reports and commentaries. Some bloggers have become more influential than established commentators and are quoted by journalists, especially around elections. Equally, more and more political figures, including British Prime Minister Cameron or US President Obama, now use blogs to connect with voters. Michael Ignatieff, the former leader of the Liberal Party of Canada, tried to do the same thing, hoping to use his personal story as the son of a Russian immigrant to present himself as a feeling, approachable "people person," as opposed to the out-of-touch elitist portrayed in Conservative Party attack ads. These are all examples of the shift in emphasis we mentioned in Chapter 11, from the party program to the personal image of the candidate.

Equally, individuals can now report breaking news as quickly as news agencies if they happen to be in the right place at the right time. They can also publish alternative

←
See the discussion of problems facing parties in Chapter 11, p. 232.

Official White House Photo by Samantha Appleton

PHOTO 12.3 White House aides monitor Obama's live YouTube interview in February 2010. Social media are becoming indispensable to politicians seeking to reach out to the public, especially younger voters.

versions of events if official government sources are perceived to be putting their own (inaccurate) spin on what happened. This has already begun to happen in China, despite government-imposed controls; increasingly, officials have been forced to apologize after on-the-ground reports by ordinary citizens have revealed that state accounts of various events were inaccurate. In both these ways, the new media have begun to change the traditional media landscape and potentially also the structure of authority in society. Gradually they are giving substance to Scott's "infrapolitics."

Electronic Decision-Making

Advocates for the new media have also suggested that they can be used to bring public decision-making much closer to the people than ever before. Barber (1998, 1984), for instance, has predicted that new technology will facilitate "strong" democracy—a modern equivalent of ancient Athenian democracy, in which citizens will have a direct say in how decisions are made. For the moment, however, actual proposals have focused on two strategies: one based on local government and the other on greater use of referendums.

The local government option is based on the American model of the town meeting, in which members of the local community meet to debate and decide policy. In the electronic version, citizens connected through cable would propose, debate, and decide on policies online (Becker and Slaton, 2000). The expectation is that this approach would enable a richer form of democracy to take root locally and then gradually spread throughout the nation.

An alternative would be to organize regular electronic consultations with citizens about proposals put forward either by political representatives or by administrators. This model would be based on the referendums regularly organized in Switzerland (Budge, 1996). It represents a "weaker" form of democracy than the American town-meeting model does, though the one might lead to the other. Neither variant has yet made a great deal of progress. The same is true of research on electronic voting in Europe.

There is an important issue hanging over all such proposals. How reliable is the technology, especially for voting? A recent American report reminds us that there are many potential dangers, including identity theft and hacking (*Asking the Right Questions About Electronic Voting*, 2005). The risk of such problems is likely to be relatively low when voting is confined to localities, but when voting is aggregated at higher levels, there is a serious danger that the process will be compromised. Votes could be stolen or redirected or simply dumped without the voters ever knowing. In addition, the whole process could be disrupted by computer viruses. Even though the voting system used today in many US states ran into serious criticism after the shambles of the 2000 presidential election recount in Florida, there are still good reasons not to replace it with electronic voting until a more secure system can be devised.

KEY POINTS

- New communications technologies have the potential to transform politics by deepening citizen involvement and allowing outsiders and new ideas to penetrate established political systems.
- They can also enable "smart mobs" to disrupt government and hold the public to ransom.
- Their effect is likely to be greatest in states where democratic institutions for the expression of citizens' views are lacking, especially in times of crisis.
- They also allow non-journalists to publish news stories and influential blogs.
- They may enable greater participation in local decision-making.
- Electronic voting is still subject to serious risks.

Conclusion

In this chapter we have concentrated on substate actors and their ability to influence the state from below. We have discussed the concept of civil society and some aspects of its impact since the 1980s, as well as some of its ambiguities. The final section focused on the impact of new communications technologies on political life. The e-revolution in political behaviour is only just beginning, but already it's clear that new communications technologies allow citizens to organize for political goals more easily than ever before.

It's also clear that new technologies are not great respecters of national frontiers. The new ability of like-minded groups to organize across borders could already be seen in the demonstrations that disrupted the 1999 WTO summit in Seattle, which brought together protest groups from around the world. Since then, meetings of the WTO and G8 have attracted swarms of protesters, although not always with the same degree of violence. The new possibilities for group self-organization are not only transforming civil society within individual states: they are also contributing to the development of an **international civil society**, a global community of political activists and organizations that demand a greater say in the running of international politics. New technologies are not merely promoting alternative views of the state from below; they are also promoting alternative views of the international order from below. Castells (1996) referred to the emergence of the "network society." What we are witnessing now may be the beginning of the "network world."

? KEY QUESTIONS

- If you go to Technorati.com you can find an interesting collection of political blogs. Is there anything about such blogs that differentiates them from the kinds of commentary you have seen in newspapers or on TV? Do they have more credibility?
- What makes a politician's blog good?
- Do you think TV series such as *The West Wing* or *Yes Minister* do more to shape political opinions than "straight" political reporting? How would you measure their impact?
- Is there any point in trying to preserve public broadcasting as something distinct in an era when broadcasting possibilities are expanding almost exponentially on the Internet?
- What needs to be done to make electronic democracy work?
- How do the various media make their coverage of politics credible? Are the same techniques used for fictionalized accounts of politics as for straight political reports?
- Is the rise of single-issue interest groups good for democracy?
- Why is there not a single model of a successful interest group that others could follow?
- Identify some "weapons of the weak" with which you are familiar. How are they used by marginalized peoples?

📖 FURTHER READING

Chadwick, Andrew (2006). *Internet Politics: States, Citizens and New Communications Technologies*. Oxford: Oxford University Press.
> A wide-ranging account of the impact of the new technologies on politics.

Coleman, Stephen (2003). *The e-Connected World: Risks and Opportunities*. Montreal: McGill–Queen's University Press.
> An excellent review of new technologies, covering topics such as crime, education, social exclusion, and democracy. It weaves a balance between views of the internet as either a great liberator or dystopia.

Edwards, Michael (2004). *Civil Society*. Cambridge: Polity Press.
> A committed discussion of civil society's potential to transform politics by the Director of the Ford Foundation's Governance and Civil Society Program.

Kroker, Arthur, and Marilouise Kroker (2008). *Critical Digital Studies: A Reader*. Toronto: University of Toronto Press.
> A fascinating overview of new media innovations and their impact on contemporary society, culture, and politics. The editors are internationally renowned theorists of digital culture.

Scott, James C. (1990). *Domination and the Arts of Resistance: Hidden Transcripts*. New Haven, CT: Yale University Press.
> An influential examination of the ways in which ordinary people get around authoritarian rulers.

Wilson, Graham K. (1990). *Interest Groups*. Oxford: Blackwell.
> A well-regarded analysis of interest groups.

12

📱 WEB LINKS

http://cwf.ca/_webapp_3846382/Electronically_Enhanced_Democracy_in_Canada?A=Searc hResult&SearchID=738881&ObjectID=3846382&ObjectType=35
> Calvin Hanselmann (2001), "Electronically Enhanced Democracy in Canada": a report on e-democracy and cybercitizenship prepared for the Canada West Foundation.

https://fp.auburn.edu/tann
> For the TAN+N (Teledemocracy Action News + Network).

www.publicus.net
> An e-democracy network.

http://edc.unige.ch
> For the European E-Democracy Centre.
> A still-topical list of publications on e-voting up to 2006.

www.socialcapitalgateway.org/eng-index.htm
> Links to large number of sites devoted to social capital and interest group activity.

Political Culture

CHAPTER OVERVIEW

We begin this chapter by presenting some of the ideas and objectives behind the concept of political culture. Then we look at some of the problems that have arisen in applying it. A case study of Russia illustrates the difficulty of establishing exactly how political culture influences political change. We then argue that despite these problems, political culture remains an important field of study in political science. We conclude by suggesting a more realistic approach to political culture that takes into account the centrality of institutions in political life and the multiplicity of political cultures that may influence the political climate in any particular nation.

Civic Culture and Political Culture

← See Chapter 7, p. 153, for a discussion of the domestic factors affecting the strength of states.

As we noted in Chapter 7, all normally functioning states require legitimacy: the people must accept both the state's policy goals and the processes by which its leaders gain power and govern. In earlier chapters we emphasized the importance of the system used to select political leaders, but it is equally important that the state's policies and processes are deemed appropriate by the particular national community in question. In other words, legitimacy also depends on the "political culture" of the people concerned.

Political culture may be defined as "the totality of ideas and attitudes towards authority, discipline, governmental responsibilities and entitlements, and associated patterns of cultural transmission such as the education system and family life" (Robertson, 1993: 382). One of the pioneering works in the field of political culture was Gabriel Almond and Sidney Verba's *The Civic Culture*, published in 1963. The authors began with the hypothesis that for a state to be stable, there must be substantial congruence between the values of the society and the behaviour of the government.

The notion that democracy rests on a broad set of social values was not new; Alexis de Tocqueville had examined it more than a century earlier in his classic *Democracy in America* (1835–40), drawing attention to differences between democratic America and aristocratic France with respect to family relations and social life; see **Box 13.1**. Almond and Verba expanded the scope of the comparison and quantified it, using public opinion surveys to compare political attitudes in five countries: the US, the UK, Germany, Italy, and Mexico. Their fundamental objective was not just to show how attitudes differed from one country to another: they also wanted to test the hypothesis that popular attitudes towards politics and the state in established democracies differed from those in other political systems. For this purpose they assumed the UK and US to be mature democracies.

13

KEY QUOTE BOX 13.1

Alexis de Tocqueville on "Mores" and Democracy

It is therefore particularly mores [habits and opinions] that render the Americans of the United States . . . capable of supporting the empire of democracy, and it is again [mores] that make the various Anglo-American democracies more or less regulated and prosperous. . . . I am convinced that the happiest situation and the best laws cannot maintain a constitution despite mores, whereas the latter turn even the most unfavourable positions and the worst laws to good account. The importance of mores is a common truth to which study and experience constantly lead back. It seems to me that I have it placed in my mind as a central point; I perceive it as the end of all my ideas (de Tocqueville, 2000: 295).

Almond and Verba were part of the behavioural movement that was gathering momentum in American political science during the 1960s and '70s. Inspired in part by Dahl's (1961) rethinking of the nature of modern democracy as **polyarchy**, this

◀ Schoolchildren watch President Barack Obama greet President Lee Myung-bak of the Republic of Korea at the White House in October 2011 (© Alex Wong/Getty Images).

movement sought to expand the boundaries of analysis to include the impact of social forces on the institutions that until then had been the main focus of attention. A key area of study was the political culture of individual states and how it helped to determine both the types of institutions chosen and their effectiveness. In *The Civic Culture* Almond and Verba hypothesized that there were three possible collective attitudes towards politics: "parochial," "subject," and "participant." "Parochial" groups would take little interest in politics, certainly at the national level. If they were interested in politics at all, it was only in the context of issues and events directly affecting their personal interests. "Subjects" had a wider perspective. They would be interested in national politics, but only as observers. They might cast votes in elections but would not feel capable of making any greater contribution to political life: thus they would leave it to established elites to make the decisions. Finally, "participants" would feel that they could and should contribute to national decision-making, and not just by casting the occasional vote. They would feel they were entitled to ensure that their views were taken into account when decisions were made; to that end, they would join interest groups, make contact with the media, and so on.

Almond and Verba assumed that all three types of political attitude would be present in almost all societies, but in differing proportions, and that those proportions would determine the degree to which a given system was democratic. They assumed that the proportion of participant attitudes would be greatest in a mature democracy, but that no democracy could be viable if everyone wanted to participate. It was essential, therefore, that a significant proportion of the population in a modern democracy accept the more passive "subject" orientation. In other words, most people would have to be deferential towards authority if the system was to be stable.

A companion work by Verba and Lucian Pye (1965) introduced a theme that was also widely taken up later: political culture and "modernization." Do political attitudes change with socio-economic development? If so, what is the best way to achieve a democratic political culture? What role can new institutions play? And which sort of institutions are desirable? Pye and Verba hypothesized that questions like these could be answered by focusing on four themes or pairs of values; see **Box 13.2**.

13

KEY CONCEPT BOX 13.2
The Four Pairs of Values of the Civic Culture

1. Trust versus suspicion: to what extent do individuals in a given society trust strangers, or even people with whom they are familiar?
2. Hierarchy versus equality: how far do individuals respond to traditional social hierarchies and hierarchies of power?
3. Liberty versus coercion: how far do individuals and groups insist on their freedom to act?
4. Levels of loyalty and commitment: how far do individuals and groups focus their loyalty on family or parochial grouping and how far on the nation as a whole?

SOURCE: Pye and Verba (1965: 22–3)

These studies of political culture offered a whole new way of conceptualizing political life, one that could incorporate findings from other disciplines such as psychology. They inspired a large number of studies that applied similar approaches to other political systems, including studies by people who did not share all of the original researchers' assumptions or objectives.

Sodaro has classified the findings of this research in three categories, each of which covers a spectrum of alternatives:

1. Attitudes towards authority run from submissive at one end, through deferential and then alienated, to rebellious at the other end.
2. Attitudes towards society express themselves along two dimensions. The first runs from highly consensual to highly conflictual, with various combinations of the two in between. The second runs from extreme individualism to extreme collectivism.
3. Attitudes towards the state run from approval for a very permissive state at one end to approval for a very interventionist state at the other (Sodaro, 2008: 300–4).

Thus the field opened up and it became common for studies of individual political systems to include political culture as a variable. Nevertheless, this is among the areas of political science where challenges have been most frequent. The original works by Almond, Pye, and Verba were theoretically more nuanced than many of their detractors later claimed, and they did not make unqualified assertions about the explanatory power of their approaches. Yet there are several reasons why using political culture to explain political outcomes is problematic. We will look at some of those problems in the next section.

KEY POINTS

- The intellectual origins of the concept of political culture lie in efforts to identify the civic culture—that is, the particular set of attitudes—that makes democracy work.
- Enquiries focused on attitudes towards authority, society, and the state that could be combined to identify the political culture of a particular state.

Challenges to the Concept of Political Culture

In this section we will look at five points on which to the concept of political culture has been challenged. The first four relate to operational difficulties, while the fifth involves one of the ways in which it has been used.

1. Identifying a Homogeneous National Political Culture

The first challenge has to do with the assumption that any nation will have a single political culture. Italy offers a useful example. In fact, there are several ways in which Italy does not fit the standard picture of Western European politics. For example, the Italian state enjoys much less respect from citizens than other European states do. Almond and Verba concluded that Italy had an "alienated political culture," characterized by social isolation and distrust (Almond and Verba, 1965: 308). In some parts of Italy, especially in the south, alternative social institutions, even organized crime, may perform functions on behalf of local communities that in other countries are carried out by the state. Even before *The Civic Culture* was published, the sociologist Edward Banfield (1958) had examined this phenomenon in poor parts of Sicily. He concluded that the lack of community spirit he saw could be explained by what he termed **amoral familism**: a tendency to put the needs and interests of one's own families above those of the rest of society. The entire focus was on the advancement of the family; the only morality worth mentioning consisted in promoting the family's interests by any means possible. Indeed, there were few if any moral checks on the pursuit of those family interests. The result was a highly divided society where people were unwilling to contribute to the public good and where politics was dominated by the interests of particular families (Banfield, 1958).

In 1993, Robert Putnam and two co-authors (Robert Leonardi and Raffaella Y. Nanetti) produced another influential work on Italian political culture. *Making Democracy Work* was a comparative study that found civic engagement to be much stronger in the north of Italy than in the south, where Putnam observed the same type of amoral familism that Banfield had identified. After surveying the historical traditions of particular regions in the north, Putnam concluded that

> The regions characterized by civic involvement in the late twentieth century are almost precisely the same regions where cooperatives and cultural associations and mutual aid societies were most abundant in the nineteenth century, and where neighbourhood associations and religious confraternities and guilds had contributed to the flourishing communal republics of the twelfth century (Putnam, 1993: 162).

In other words, the north had **social capital**, which translated into democratic practice. Putnam's study was a striking reaffirmation of the importance of political culture in democracy.

Putnam's study has been extremely influential, and his conclusions have been turned into hypotheses for the analysis of other states, although it has also provoked controversy (Jackman and Miller, 2004). For our purposes, however, the important point is that *Making Democracy Work* describes two very different political cultures within a single country. Almond and Verba, by contrast, tried to identify a single national political culture in Italy. Even though they did not assume complete homogeneity—they did examine the impact of different levels of education on political views, for example—they did not take into account regional variations. The Putnam study demonstrates why that is a problem.

The same point could be made about Almond and Verba's analysis of politics in the UK. Again they assumed a territorially homogeneous political culture; yet within a few years Northern Ireland was swept up in a surge of protest and violence that was to last for more than three decades. The problem of identifying a single national political culture is especially acute in religiously or ethnically divided states. The Irish "troubles" showed that Britain did not in fact have a single deferential political culture, and the more recent rise of Scottish and Welsh **nationalisms** is further evidence that "British" political culture is anything but homogeneous.

Size and regional diversity also matter. The American Civil War ended almost a century and a half ago, and yet political attitudes are still divided between the North and the South. Before 1861 the South had produced most of the country's presidents, but it took 115 years for the next southerner to be elected in his own right—Jimmy Carter in 1976 (Woodrow Wilson had moved to the North first, while Truman and Johnson were vice-presidents who took over the presidency after the deaths of the incumbents). David Hackett Fischer, in *Albion's Seed* (1989), argues that four main groups from different parts of Britain carried their "hearth cultures" to the American colonies in four waves: Puritans from eastern England to New England (1629–40); royalist Cavaliers from southern England to Virginia (1642–75); Quakers from the north Midlands to Pennsylvania and Delaware (1675–1715) and Scots–Irish from lowland Scotland, northern Ireland, and northern England to the backcountry (1717–75). Each group brought with it a different idea of freedom: a moralistic "ordered freedom" for the Puritans; "hegemonic freedom" for the aristocratic Cavaliers; "reciprocal freedom" for the Quakers; and "natural freedom" for the Scots–Irish. These differing conceptions were reflected in the societies that the four groups built: thus the South was characterized by ideals of tradition and hierarchy and a tendency to seek "violent retaliation over insults" (see also Lind, 2002: 122–4), while the North was associated with individualism and moralism. Such differences would become manifest during the Civil War and, as Fischer notes, they are still reflected today in regional attitudes and voting patterns.

Canada is even more divided, by language and ethnicity as well as region. Four regional power centres (Ontario, Quebec, Alberta, and British Columbia) all have their own distinct cultures, as do smaller regions such as Atlantic Canada and the North. Under such circumstances any attempt to identify a common national political culture is problematic—as the authors themselves later acknowledged (Almond and Verba, 1989: 406).

2. Identifying Causal Linkages between Attitudes and Political Outcomes

A second challenge in operationalizing the concept of political culture is to identify the chain of causation between the sources of the political attitudes held by a particular group of people, or even a whole society—attitudes formed largely in youth—and political outcomes years or even decades later. How do we know which cultural attitudes and values lead to which sorts of policies or institutions? By focusing on the sources of national values, behaviouralists such as Almond, Verba, and Pye tended to imply that political outlooks were largely set by the time of adulthood, or at any rate soon afterwards. In so doing, they discounted the human potential for learning and changing in response to events. Even if a great many decisions are made in conformity with values absorbed in youth, it's clear that not all of them are: every revolution, for example, represents a break with previous trends and traditions.

3. The State May Shape Political Culture to Its Own Ends

An underlying assumption of *The Civic Culture* was that the legitimacy of a political system depended on its fit with pre-existing social and political values. For countries with a well-defined, historical national identity, such as Canada, the US, and many Western European nations, it seemed plausible to assume that the state reflected a particular set of pre-existing social values. In fact, though, most if not all states actively work to instill national values as part of the school curriculum and to socialize young people into approved political values and national identity. In so doing, a state effectively shapes the expectations by which it will be judged, and the greater its success in this effort, the greater its legitimacy will be. In other words, the state does not simply accept national identity and national political culture as givens: it actively works to shape them. This was a possibility that theories of political culture did not really take into account.

For example, consider China. The Chinese state has more than 5,000 years of recorded history, although it is only for the last 2,000 that the recording has taken place roughly contemporaneously with the events being recorded. Not surprisingly, history plays a very important role in Chinese political culture. Mao Zedong repeatedly drew parallels between his own actions and those of past emperors. As Jenner remarked,

> Chinese governments have, for at least 2000 years, taken history much too seriously to allow the future to make its own unguided judgements about them. . . . Historical myth-making has so far been remarkably effective not just in inventing a single Han Chinese ethnicity but also—and this is a far bigger triumph—in winning acceptance of it. . . . The religion of the Chinese ruling classes is the Chinese state, and it is through history that the object of devotion is to be understood (Jenner, 1992: 3–4).

Officially sanctioned Chinese history has left a long shadow over Chinese political identity and political culture.

Russia is another example of the same phenomenon. Across the Eurasian landmass there are few geographical features to serve as natural boundaries. The whole area has been subject to periodic invasion from east and west. Thus Russians identify their territory with the state that established secure borders, and a concern with "state-ness" (*gosudarstvennost*), or the ability of the state to operate effectively, is an enduring feature of Russian political culture. Russian leaders have traditionally played on this concern, reminding the people that a strong, effective state is a precondition for "normal" social life. Russian attitudes towards democracy are coloured accordingly: even today, many Russians believe it's more important for the country to be strong than to be democratic.

The state's role in the creation of the nation's political culture is even more important in states with a very short history of independence, notably the former colonies in Africa and Asia. In many cases the borders of these states were drawn by the colonial regimes and did not take into account the connections and divisions between communities, clans, tribes, and so on. Thus, as we argued in Chapter 7, post-colonial states often had to create the nation by selecting the cultural attributes, languages, and religions they would promote, and establishing both national identity and national values. Some have been more successful at this task than others.

According to the 2005 World Values Survey, 54 per cent of Tanzanians described their political system as "very good"; this score was the highest for any African state and meant that the Tanzanian system had the greatest legitimacy. Although Tanzania's founding president, Julius Nyerere, was committed to a socialist economic program that proved to be unsustainable, politically he succeeded in establishing national unity through the creation of a one-party state. He was able to do so because colonial rule had undermined traditional political structures and suppressed attempts at "native rebellion." Thus the Tanzanian African National Union imposed itself as the sole political force after independence, and it has preserved its dominance as the Revolutionary Party despite the introduction of multiparty elections in 1995 (Baregu, 1997). It has avoided exploiting tribal divisions, and has achieved diffuse but broad popular support. There is widespread participation in political rallies and campaigns, but little individual political activism, despite intense dissatisfaction with poor economic development and corruption. All in all, it would seem that the dominant orientation is that of what Almond and Verba called "subjects." Political change has been top-down but fairly flexible (Martin, 1988). In short, Nigeria has been relatively effective in establishing political values and support for them, and in this respect, according to Afrobarometer, it stands out among African states (Chaligha et al., 2002).

See Chapter 7, p. 147, for a discussion of the spread of the Western state.

13

By contrast, only 8 per cent of Pakistani respondents to the World Values Survey regarded their political system as very good—the lowest figure for any state in Asia or sub-Saharan Africa. This is not surprising, given the shocks that Pakistan has endured since its creation as an independent state in 1947. First, the partition of India was carried out on very short notice, with the result that the boundaries were not well thought out and the people did not have time to prepare. More than ten million Muslim refugees were forced to flee from India, while millions of Hindus were similarly uprooted from Pakistan. Furthermore, Pakistan was divided into two parts on either side of India, with quite different historical traditions and attitudes towards the place of religion in public life (Humayun, 1995).

West Pakistan maintained control over East Pakistan, until 1971 when the latter seceded to form the new country of Bangladesh. The Pakistani regime was forced to recreate the country's national identity after losing half of its population and territory. Meanwhile, the task of maintaining popular support in a military-dominated regime was exacerbated by two wars that Pakistan initiated with India, in 1965 and 1971, both of which it lost. Today significant numbers of Pakistanis reject state attempts to impose laws that they believe to be inconsistent with Islam—a major problem for a state whose Islamic identity is fundamental (Yilmaz, 2005: 126–7). In addition the state has had to deal with alternating military rule and attempts at democracy, a great deal of corruption, and widespread tendencies towards the kind of "amoral familism" that Banfield identified in southern Italy. Under those circumstances it is not surprising that the Pakistani regime has found it difficult to establish a durable political culture.

4. The Impact of Globalization

Globalization makes it all the more challenging to clearly identify a national political culture. Borders separating inside from outside become more porous. At the elite level, ambitious politicians eagerly search for new ideas to win elections, manipulate the media, and mould public support. Presidents Sarkozy of France and Berlusconi of Italy are among the most recent examples of national leaders who have used American campaign techniques to outwit their opponents and win large majorities. At the popular level, increasing cross-border migration by workers means that appeals for political support can no longer rely on traditional themes and approaches. We can see this clearly in the strenuous efforts that both American parties now put into winning the Hispanic vote.

5. Political Culture Is Used to Explain Why Change Cannot Happen

Finally, the notion of national political cultures is often used to justify failures in developing democracy, or even to argue that democracy is inappropriate for certain states. Such arguments usually begin with the assertion that democracy is a Western concept, implying that states in other parts of the world have different cultural traditions. This was the argument used in Singapore to explain why the regime had been so slow to move towards more open democracy, although its standard of living has matched or even exceeded that of many European countries. "Asians" were said to value order and stability more highly than freedom (Emmerson, 1995), and for this

13

reason confrontational party democracy was inappropriate and undesirable for them. Famously, former Prime Minister Lee Kuan Yew argued that "Asian values" were very different from those of the West. His remarks and the responses they provoked led to some very interesting debates about the role of culture in human rights and democracy. As Fareed Zakaria has observed, "Many Asian dictators used arguments about their region's unique culture to stop Western politicians from pushing them to democratize. The standard rebuttal was that Asians prefer order to the messy chaos of democracy" (Zakaria 2002).

There is certainly some truth in the claim that "Asians" value order and stability more highly than freedom, but the supposed incompatibility of democracy with non-Western political traditions is often exaggerated by elites seeking to maintain the status quo, especially when it favours them. Until the late 1980s, it was regularly assumed that Confucianism was incompatible with democracy because it advocated obedience to authority, whether the head of the household or the head of the state. There was no requirement for consultation with other family members or members of society, let alone any right to joint decision-making. Until the 1980s the evidence from East Asia supported the assumption: no Confucian society practised democracy.

In 1987–8, however, two states still heavily influenced by Confucianism—Taiwan and South Korea—went democratic, and they have not looked back. Even though their democratic regimes still have problems, such as corruption, no attempts have been made to overthrow them. So now Confucianism is increasingly seen as compatible with democracy (Fukuyama, 1995). And in 1999–2001, in a World Values Survey in which an overall average of 91 per cent of respondents in 80 countries answered that that democracy was a "very good" or "fairly good" way of running a country, only one of the main "Confucian" states (South Korea) returned a score lower than that of the US— which at 89 per cent was below the average. All the others (China, Singapore, Taiwan) ranked higher than the US (Inglehart et al., 2004: E117). Of course, we should not assume that all the respondents understood the term "democracy" in the same way. Nevertheless, these findings certainly do not suggest that "Confucian" states have a culturally based hostility to the principle of democracy.

KEY POINTS

- There are several fundamental objections to the concept of political culture.
- It assumes homogeneous national values.
- It remains extremely difficult to operationalize.
- It is difficult to link values and political outcomes, especially at the systemic level.
- The fact that many states educate their peoples in political values makes it difficult to analyze the effect of those values on policies and institutions.
- Globalization multiplies the factors affecting political values.
- Political culture is commonly used to justify failure to move towards democracy.

The Significance of Political Culture: A Case Study

To illustrate the difficulty of relying on political culture to explain political outcomes, consider the following case study of post-Soviet Russia.

CASE STUDY
Political Culture and the Collapse of Soviet Communism

Certainly, Russia has enjoyed less success than most states in Eastern and Central Europe in managing the transition to democracy. There was much optimism at first. The collapse of Soviet Union was surprisingly peaceful, given the size of the KGB and armed forces; only three people died in the aftermath of the short-lived attempt to depose Mikhail Gorbachev in August 1991. This led to euphoria about the possibilities for a smooth and relatively painless political transition. Yet by the time the World Values Survey was carried out in Russia in 2000, only 3 per cent of respondents rated the current political system as "good" or "very good"—the lowest figure for any country in the world (Inglehart et al., 2004: E111A). What accounts for this disillusionment? To what extent can Russia's political culture be blamed?

In favour of the political culture argument is the fact that Russia had never had a fully functioning democracy. Seventy-four years of communist rule had been preceded by a dozen years of limited parliamentary democracy under the last Tsar and, before that, centuries of autocracy during which millions of people had been regarded as the property of their aristocratic landlords; in some cases the lives of serfs were little better than those of slaves. Although there was no national democratic tradition on which reformers could draw, Russia did have a tradition of collectivism stretching back long before the advent of communism. As various foreign commentators have noted, this tradition stood in strong contrast to Western individualism.

It is also true that the collapse of the Soviet Union took the new leaders, including President Boris Yeltsin, almost by surprise. They had no plans for a democratic transition and had to improvise as they went along. Few newly created political parties turned into viable national institutions. The strongest remained the Russian Communist Party, which retained significant amounts of its Soviet-era assets and support. Most of the politicians and new parties were active only in Moscow. The lack of a democratic political culture of give-and-take was exemplified by the events of 1993, when the parliament defied the president and in the end the army was authorized to intervene and shell the parliament building. President Yeltsin himself was not preoccupied with establishing robust political institutions—apart from the presidency. He was suspicious of potential rivals and often went out of his way to undermine them.

On the other hand, many other things also went wrong in the transition. The program of economic reforms initially led to a dramatic fall in economic output—greater than the fall that Canada and the US experienced during the Great Depression of the 1930s. Massive inflation in 1992–3 wiped out the savings of millions of people. Then, just as the economy was beginning to recover, another financial crisis wiped out savings in 1998. Russia was also hit by a mounting security crisis after the mid-1990s, centered on Chechnya and other break-away republics seeking independence. Many people felt that, without the former republics, the very survival of Russia was in doubt. While there was significant financial help available through institutions such as the World Bank and the IMF, the EU did not try to encourage reform by offering Russia the carrot of possible EU membership, as it did for Eastern and Central Europe.

Under those circumstances, it is easy to understand why Russia had difficulty making the transition to democracy. Clearly, political values played a part in terms of the persisting effects of earlier political socialization, as well as the lack of preparation for the post-communist era. We could also argue that the financial crashes and internal terrorism both had the effect of undermining the regime's legitimacy. Earlier political traditions might have contributed to the weakness of the legislature, but even here it would be wrong to attribute great significance to culture. The problem is compounded on the level of individual political leaders. Yeltsin was a product of the communist system and its ideological indoctrination; his authoritarian tendencies made it difficult for him to conceptualize a post-communist regime. Yet he, more than any other political figure, brought down communism in the USSR. Though he was a product of communist political culture, even in late middle age he moved decisively against it.

The Persisting Significance of Political Culture

Despite all the problems of operationalizing the concept, it would be wrong to reject political culture entirely. There are a number of points to make in its favour:

1. Citizens of different states do have different attitudes towards similar institutions and issues. As we noted in Chapter 7, residents of North America and the Islamic world not only have different perspectives on their states; they also live in very different kinds of state.

See the discussion of illiberal democracy in Chapter 7, p. 157.

Even attitudes towards politics in general vary considerably from one state to another. According to the World Values Survey conducted in 1999–2002, only 45 per cent of roughly 2,000 respondents across all countries reported that they were "very" or "somewhat" interested in politics, but the figures for individual countries showed wide variation. Table 13.1 makes it clear that interest in politics in general varies considerably from country to country, irrespective of geographical region, level of economic development, and whether or not the state is democratic. Level of interest has an impact on the political culture (or political cultures) of individual states.

2. Political actors believe that there differences in political culture. President Charles De Gaulle of France more than once remarked, only partly in jest, that it was extremely difficult to govern a country so individualistic that it had 246 varieties of cheese (and now there are over 400). Here are four more examples.

The first relates to American foreign policy-making in the 1990s. The Yugoslav civil war was marked by widespread brutality against civilians and many massacres. Western states debated whether to intervene, but although the UN did agree to send peacekeepers, the US for a long time refused to get involved. There were many reasons for this—the legacy of the Vietnam experience, the feeling that European states should take the lead—but another was reportedly that President Clinton had read journalist Robert Kaplan's book *Balkan Ghosts* to gain background information on the region. Kaplan's depiction of the Balkans as a region of ancient hatreds and blood feuds made Clinton reluctant to risk American troops there.

The second example concerns Samuel Huntington's widely cited 1996 book *The Clash of Civilizations and the Remaking of World Order*. A well-known political scientist at Harvard University, Huntington argued that with the end of the Cold War the major

13

TABLE 13.1 Percentage of Respondents in Selected Countries Agreeing that they were "Very" or "Somewhat" Interested in Politics, 1999–2002

Country	Percentage	Ranking
Vietnam	80	1
Tanzania	72	2
China	71	3
Israel	70	4
Czech Republic	70	4
Norway	69	6
Austria	67	7
Netherlands	67	7
US	66	9
Japan	64	10
Germany	61	11
Canada	49	25
India	45	34
Turkey	40	48
Russia	39	50
France	37	54
UK	37	54
Italy	32	60
Pakistan	30	63
Venezuela	24	69
Algeria	24	69
Morocco	20	71
Argentina	18	72
El Salvador	15	73

SOURCE: Inglehart et al., eds, *Human Beliefs and Values: A Cross-Cultural Sourcebook Based on the 1999–2002 Values Surveys* (Mexico: Siglo XXI Editores): E023.

sources of international conflict would be the differences between the major world civilizations—principally Christianity and Islam. Clashes would arise because of conflicting values and the desire on the part of each to increase its sway in the world, the West to spread democracy and the Muslim world to resist it. In Huntington's view, the fault was primarily attributable to the political culture of Islam. "Muslims," he argued, "have problems living peaceably with their neighbors," and were thus responsible for the majority of inter- and intra-civilization conflicts in modern history. Based on a "casual survey of intercivilizational conflicts," he declared that "Islam's borders *are* bloody, and so are its innards" (Huntington, 1997: 256-8). Even though it was not based on any survey research, and its conclusions have been challenged by numerous commentators, including Inglehart and Norris (2003) on the basis of World Values Survey findings, Huntington's thesis attracted a great deal of attention around the world, and it gained additional legitimacy after the terrorist attacks of September 2001, as an explanation for the apparent "anti-Americanism" of so many people in Islamic countries (MacDonald, 2009: 101).

The third example comes from India. Since independence India has prided itself on being a secular state that treats believers from all religious backgrounds equally. This was a principle laid down by the Congress Party, which ruled India from independence in 1947 until 1989. In more recent years, however, the Bharatiya Janata Party (BJP) has asserted an alternative principle of *Hindutva* ("Hindu-ness"), which would give political recognition to the dominant position in Indian society occupied by Hindus. This is based on a quite different conception of Indian political identity and would transform Indian political life (Malik and Singh, 1995).

The fourth example concerns the European Union. Gradually the EU has expanded from six to 27 member countries, and further expansion is still possible, in particular for Turkey, Serbia, Bosnia, and Albania. Farther east, countries such as Russia and Ukraine may also apply at some point in the future. All candidate countries must comply with the so-called Copenhagen criteria laid down in 1993; see **Box 13.3**.

With respect to Turkey, the former French President Valéry Giscard d'Estaing added a further set of conditions relating to what he called "the foundations" of European iden- tity: things such as "the cultural contributions of ancient Greece and Rome, the reli- gious heritage pervading European life, the creative enthusiasm of the Renaissance, the philosophy of the **Enlightenment** and the contributions of rational and scientific thought" (Giscard d'Estaing, 2004). Earlier, he had highlighted as problems Turkey's geographical location, mostly in Asia, as well as the size of its population and its potential impact on future European decision-making. He did emphasize that Turkey has its own distinguished history and culture and that its Muslim society was not a problem. But he implied that Turkey had not shared European history, and that this presented a serious obstacle. Whether this judgement was really intended to rationalize objections based on

13

KEY CONCEPT BOX 13.3
The EU's Copenhagen Criteria for New Members

A candidate country must have achieved:

- stable institutions guaranteeing democracy, the rule of law, human rights and respect for and protection of minority rights;
- a functioning market economy as well as the capacity to cope with competitive pressure and market forces within the Union;
- the ability to take on the obligations of membership including adherence to the aims of political, economic, and monetary union.

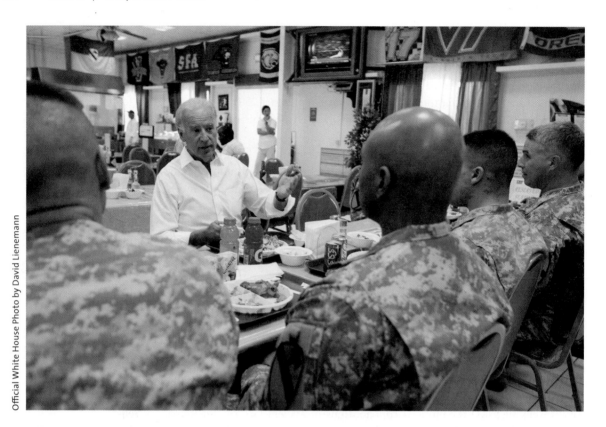

PHOTO 13.1 US Vice President Joe Biden joined troops in Iraq for lunch in 2009. The last US troops left the country in December 2011.

racism or xenophobia is impossible to know. In any event, debates about what it means to be European will become more pronounced as the borders of the EU continue to expand eastwards.

3. Political culture can be extremely important when we look at the imposition of democracy in other countries. The experience of the Confucian world shows that democracy can take root even when preconditions favouring it are absent. And the successful establishment of democracy in Germany and Japan after the Second World War shows that it can be transplanted. Even so, the more recent experience in Iraq shows that foreign models of democracy cannot simply be grafted onto indigenous social structures. Unless occupying forces are prepared to impose their will and suppress resistance for as long as it takes to change hearts and minds, they must take local attitudes into account. This is unavoidable.

4. Political culture may indeed help to explain different policy outcomes. Attitudes towards the **welfare state** differ considerably between Europeans and Americans. Alesina and Glaeser (2004) suggest that Americans tend to have different attitudes from Europeans towards income inequality and income redistribution. Based on several rounds of the World Values Survey, they estimated that that some 60 per cent of

Americans believe that the poor are lazy, as against 26 per cent of people in the EU. On the other hand, 60 per cent of those in the EU believe that the poor are trapped in poverty, while only 29 per cent in the US believe this.

Curiously, it was not always the case that Europeans believed in state redistribution to help the poor. In the nineteenth century there was no welfare state on either side of the Atlantic. Alesina and Glaeser conclude that Europeans' ideas about the poor were shaped by political institutions. Beginning in the late nineteenth century, European labour and socialist parties promoted the view that the poor were trapped and deserving of government help. The success of those parties helped to spread the ideas behind the welfare state, so that even their opponents accepted the validity of the concept and sought only to limit the size of the state based on it. Welfare came to be seen as a right, an entitlement of every citizen who needed it, however much it cost. In the US, by contrast, organized labour never achieved the same political success during industrialization. One reason was the enduring power of the founding myth of the US as a land of opportunity for all. Another was the fact that the vast geographical size of the US made it difficult for workers scattered across the country to take concerted political action. At the same time, for many middle-class Americans the real poor were African Americans, who in their view made no effort to overcome their situation. The US constitution also played a role to the extent that it enshrined the property rights of recent colonizers and was not subject to strong challenges from social groups with different attitudes and interests. Hence welfare issues were always presented in terms of costs and benefits for the whole of society, with the emphasis on the costs (Alesina and Glaeser, 2004).

Alesina and Glaeser highlight the value of political culture as an explanatory tool that can help to shed light on the factors behind different political outcomes. However, instead of relying on political culture as their only explanation (as we did in our case study of Russia, above) they treat it as one factor among several that together can offer a more complete explanation of policy outcomes. They also suggest that the political culture in question was itself an amalgam of original values and more recent ones, and that it was in part created by political institutions. The result is a much more dynamic understanding of the way political culture both evolves and affects policy.

5. A nation's political culture is part of the national identity without which nationalism could not exist, so ways of analyzing it have paralleled those applied to the study of nationalism. Primordialist and Perennialist theorists of nationalism stress the enduring elements of a nation's political culture. They argue that the nation pre-dates the industrial revolution, and they take religious and other forms of group identity into account in tracing the origins of a particular nation (Greenfeld, 1992). Newer theoretical approaches to nationalism, such as **ethno-symbolism**, seek to identify core symbols of a nation's identity that can be used to bolster national pride. The most potent symbols have a long history. They may be subject to various interpretations by different groups over time, but this is less important than the fact that they always reinforce identity, even when their connotations are negative (Leoussi and Grosby, 2006).

Aronoff (2001) suggests that students of political culture are now taking a similar approach: instead of searching for some permanent core of a nation's political culture, they are focusing on common symbols of that culture (Aronoff, 2001: 11, 640). Even if those symbols give rise to radically different evaluations, positive or negative, they still serve to reinforce the sense of national identity. The potential range of symbols with special significance for members of a given nation is enormous, and may include not only people (individuals and groups), events, and achievements, but even failures.

Because of the radical changes in domestic policies that followed the death of Mao Zedong in 1976, the People's Republic of China has changed its official assessments of many elements of Chinese political culture. Let us give two examples, first of a famous individual, and then of a symbol of national achievement. The individual is Confucius. While Mao was ruling China, he wanted to radicalize popular ways of thinking, so he used Confucius as a symbol of the old "feudal" ways, especially during the Cultural Revolution. Major campaigns were waged against Confucius and "Confucianists." Yet since Mao's death Confucius has regained official approval as a symbol of the greatness of Chinese civilization. And in 2004 the state established the first in what are now more than a hundred government-run Confucius Institutes outside China, designed to spread knowledge of Chinese culture, language, and civilization around the world.

A key symbol today for the greatness of Chinese national achievement is the Great Wall. Again, in Mao's time the Great Wall was treated as a symbol of China's "feudal" past—in particular, of the sufferings imposed on the subservient masses by a cruel imperial system—and used to inspire popular support or socialism. Since Mao's death, however, the Great Wall has become a symbol of China's past greatness. (It was even alleged, though wrongly, that the Wall is the only man-made structure that can be seen from space.) Today the Wall is presented as a symbol of the future achievements of the Chinese people (Waldron, 1993).

Most nations have historical achievements that they point to as sources of national pride. The civilizations of ancient Greece and Rome, the French Revolution, and the British Empire are just a few examples. Even if some of these achievements are subject to radically different interpretations, positive and negative, they still serve to highlight enduring features of a particular political culture. As we noted in Chapter 11, the liberator Simon Bolívar was until recently a unifying symbol for Venezuela, and today President Chávez uses Bolívar as inspiration for standing up to the forces of globalization, especially the US.

Social values can also become symbols of national identity and pride. The British sense of "fair play," Americans' "can-do" attitude, the "broad," generous nature of Russians (as opposed to the supposedly narrow, mean attitude of Western Europeans) have all served this purpose. In Britain, interviews carried out for the Commission for Racial Equality identified a number of values, attitudes, and behaviours associated with "Britishness," ranging from the **rule of law**, fairness, tolerance, mutual help, stoicism, and compassion to drunkenness and hooliganism. Interestingly, some characteristics that white English interviewees treated as positive (e.g., pride) were seen as negative by those of Scots, Welsh, and immigrant backgrounds (Commission for Racial Equality, 2005: 25–9).

Symbols of failure are less often called on to represent national identity, but Serbia provides one example. In 1389 the young Serbian empire was destroyed by Ottoman Turkish forces at Kosovo Polje. What followed was 500 years of Ottoman domination. Exemplifying Serbian heroism and refusal to surrender even in the face of overwhelming odds, the battle of Kosovo Polje has been cited by Serbs in military and political struggles down the centuries. It also came to be seen as a sacrifice that Serbs made for the sake of "Europe," since their ongoing resistance to Turkish rule helped to prevent the Ottomans from pressing farther west; thus it is also used to assert Serbs' European-ness, even though

←
See Chapter 11, p. 235, for the case study on Venezuela.

13

most of the EU has sanctioned Kosovo's independence. Similarly, Quebec nationalism is based in part on symbols of defeat, such as the battle of the Plains of Abraham and Quebec's exclusion from the 1982 constitution, sometimes recalled as "night of the long knives" (Mock, 2011: 4).

These examples illustrate an important point: political culture is not a national consensus on the appropriate goals and processes of politics, but a set of narratives and symbols of national identity that different groups try to manipulate for their own political advantage.

KEY POINTS

- Obvious differences in political attitudes between citizens of different states are reflected in significantly different policy outcomes. This is one reason it is so difficult to transplant democracy from one state to another.
- Political actors accept this reality, and governments sometimes base policies on it.
- Political culture is closely linked to nationalism.

Conclusion

In this chapter we have argued that even though the concept of political culture is open to challenge, it will continue to inform political analysis both within states and between them. Political culture is important for several reasons. First, it can help to clarify genuinely different attitudes towards politics between peoples in different parts of the world; for a political science that seeks to be genuinely international, this is crucial. Second, politicians and decision-makers do sometimes base their policies on their perceptions of different political values in various states. Third, because it involves notions of national identity, any analysis of nationalism must take it into account. Fourth, it has a broader disciplinary relevance.

In Chapter 7 we emphasized the crucial importance of institutions in the study of politics. Any plausible theory of political culture must recognize that the institutions it shapes play a role not only in spreading political values but also in shaping them. In other words, arguments based on political culture should reflect the fact that influence is a two-way street. And instead of searching for an unrealistic national consensus over values, they should explore the multiple political *cultures* of a nation.

Finally, political culture can be linked to **constructivism** in international relations theory, which we will discuss in Chapter 16. Constructivism focuses on national identity. It assumes that the identity of nations determines the pattern of interactions between them; but this interaction is complicated to pin down, because it involves not only the evolving identity of a particular state but also how that state is perceived by other states.

13

→
See Chapter 16, p. 322, for a discussion of constructivism.

? KEY QUESTIONS

- Why is socialized health care so central to national identity and public policy in Canada, yet so controversial in the United States?
- Identify some basic symbols associated with the political culture of one or more states with which you are familiar. Have various groups attempted to manipulate those symbols to achieve political success? How?

- How much weight would you put on political cultural factors in explaining the failures of democracy in Russia?
- What are the European values of the EU? Do Russia and Turkey share enough of those values to allow them to join the union?
- How effective are state educational systems in instilling national political values?
- Is success in this effort a function of economic development? Are states in the developing world as successful as those in the developed one?
- How far does religion structure national political culture?
- Does globalization erode a nation's political culture or help to shape it?
- How objectively can any of us analyze the political culture of our own country?

📖 FURTHER READING

Adams, Michael (2004). *Fire and Ice: The United States, Canada, and the Myth of Converging Values*. Toronto: Penguin.

> Using a wealth of statistics and polling data, Adams critically examines important differences in political culture between Canada and the US and argues that these differences help to explain various social attitudes and public policies.

Almond, Gabriel A. and Sidney Verba (1963). *The Civic Culture*. Boston: Little Brown.

> The classic original study of the subject.

Bell, Daniel A. (2006). Beyond Liberal Democracy: Political Thinking for an East Asian Context. Princeton: Princeton University Press.

> A recent attempt to identify ways in which liberal democracy is questioned in East Asia.

Fish, M. Steven (2005). *Democracy Derailed in Russia: The Failure of Open Politics*. Cambridge: Cambridge University Press.

> A readable analysis of the reasons why democracy has not taken firm root in Russia since 1991.

Fukuyama, Francis (1995). "Confucianism and Democracy." *Journal of Democracy 6* (2) (April): 20–33.

> An alternative view to that of Pye and Bell on the compatibility of democracy and cultural traditions in Asia.

Halman, Loek, Ruud Luijkx, and Marga van Zundert (eds) (2005). *Atlas of European Values*. Leiden: Tilburg University.

> An examination of European identity along various attitudinal dimensions, with variations by country.

Putnam, Robert (2001). *Bowling Alone: The Collapse and Revival of American Community*. New York: Simon & Schuster.

> A very influential study of social capital and its significance for democracy.

📱 WEB LINKS

www.pollingreport.ca
> Comprehensive information on current public opinion polls (Angus Reid, Ekos, etc.) in Canada.

www.worldvaluessurvey.org
> The website of the World Values Project at the University of Michigan.

www.europeanvalues.com
> Links to various studies of European values.

PART III

International Relations

Nuclear war, terrorism, diplomacy, international trade, multinational corporations, global inequality, international institutions, UN peacekeeping, weapons of mass destruction: these are a few of the terms that come to mind when we think of the discipline known as International Relations (often abbreviated as IR). As the name suggests, IR has traditionally focused on relations *between* nation-states operating within an international system, disregarding the political environment *within* individual states. Some scholars insist that this separation is necessary, in order to keep the focus squarely on the dynamics of the international system and prevent domestic considerations from clouding the issues. Today, however, increasing numbers of theorists argue that to fence off activities within the state from those in the international sphere is no longer plausible.

You may recall that the introduction to Part 1 of this book noted a similar trend in political theory, which in the past focused almost exclusively on the sovereign state. In both cases, **globalization** is blurring the traditional boundaries between the domestic and international spheres. At the same time, non-state actors and forces are becoming increasingly important.

The chapters that follow provide broad overviews of the main fields of study within IR, introducing you to a range of theoretical, methodological, and empirical issues and themes that you may choose to explore in greater depth at some later stage in your studies. They will also illustrate the close links between theory, method, and practice, since the way people—whether private citizens or military leaders, businesspeople or statesmen and women—acquire knowledge, interpret facts and events, and generally *think* about IR has a crucial impact on the way they act in the world. This should become obvious when we consider matters such as sovereignty, the state, and international order in Chapter 14. Sovereignty, for example, is not a material "fact" in the sense that the boundary between land and sea is a fact. Rather, it is an idea that has a particular history, and it was that particular history that contributed to the development of the political institutions and practices we know today.

In Chapters 15 and 16 we will compare and contrast the dominant theories of IR, while emphasizing that most of those approaches have a distinctive *normative* basis, explicit or implicit. That is, they make claims about how we *ought* to act in the world; this is true even of theories (such as neorealism) that claim to be scientific and impartial. This distinguishes them from theories that simply purport to *describe* the world. Chapter 17 deals with the central concern of traditional IR: security (and insecurity), looking at both conventional and newer approaches. Chapter 18 presents an account of the closely related areas of diplomacy and foreign policy. These key activities in the everyday world of IR are also based on ideas about how the world works, or *ought* to work. In Chapter 19 we examine international organizations, which have proliferated in the world, and have an impact on almost every aspect of IR. Finally, in Chapter 20 we offer an overview of the field of international political economy (IPE), from the modern origins of international trade and commerce to the present period of deepening globalization and regionalization. As before, we will show how practice is related to ideas. Chapter 20 provides further insight into issues of wealth and poverty, how these relate to the dynamics of contemporary IR.

14

Sovereignty, the State, and International Order 14

CHAPTER OVERVIEW

In this chapter we begin by introducing some basic terms and concepts. We also explore the emergence of the discipline. We then consider the central institution of traditional IR—the state—with special reference to the diversity of state models throughout history. We also look at empire as a form of international order. Next, we consider the rise of the modern state and state system in Europe, along with the theory of sovereignty and its implications for the conduct of relations between states; here we will see why the concept of anarchy has a special place in IR theory. Finally, we consider how the globalization of the European state system through imperialism and colonialism produced the present international state system, concluding with an examination of weak states, quasi states, and state failure in various parts of the world.

Discipline, Definitions, and Subject Matter

You may have noticed that IR is often referred to by other names, including "international politics," "world politics," and "global politics." Each term has its own nuances and denotes a somewhat different approach to the subject. When IR emerged as a formal field of academic study, after the First World War, its practitioners were (not surprisingly) concerned primarily with the causes of war and the conditions for peace in the international system. Early practitioners believed that relations between states and the maintenance of international order should be the subjects of specialized study in their own right, without reference to political institutions within states or to disciplines such as law and history. In the US, especially in the aftermath of the Second World War and the dangerous climate of the Cold War, there were renewed calls to promote the specialized study of politics in the international sphere. A quotation from Frederick Dunn, a pioneer of IR in the US and the long-time director of Princeton University's Center of International Studies, gives us a fairly conventional understanding of IR's standing and importance as a distinct field of study in the mid-twentieth century; it also highlights the fact that a world of sovereign states constitutes a special kind of community in which there is no centre of authority to enforce order; see **Box 14.1**.

Since that time, however, many IR scholars have come to a broader, more multifaceted understanding of their field. In their view, the international and domestic spheres are in constant interaction—politically, socially, economically. Furthermore, sovereign states

KEY QUOTE BOX 14.1
The Case for a Specialized Discipline of International Relations

The questions which arise out of the relations among nations are certainly important and difficult. They likewise possess their own coherence and uniqueness since they arise out of the relations in a special kind of community, namely, one made up of autonomous units without a central authority having a monopoly of power. Pulling together the scattered fragments of knowledge about them obviously serves to focus attention on them and encourage the development of more intelligent ways of handling them. Recent events have reinforced the growing conviction that the questions of international relations are too complex and dangerous to be dealt with any longer as sidelines of existing disciplines. . . . (Dunn, 1948: 142–3)

◄ Women in Pristina, Kosovo, march in protest against the killings of ethnic Albanians in the Drenica region carried out by Serbian police in March 1998 (© Anja Nierdringhaus/epa/Corbis).

are no longer the only important actors on the world stage: a multiplicity of non-state actors—from multi- or transnational corporations and **non-governmental organizations (NGOs)** to international organized crime groups and international terrorism organizations—must also be taken into account. In this broader context, the traditional term "international relations" is increasingly replaced by a broader term such as "world (or global) politics."

This is not to say that the concept of "international relations" is no longer useful. There are many contexts in which "world politics" or "global politics" will not do: for example, we can talk about the international relations or international politics of the Asia–Pacific region, but not the "world" or "global" politics of the region. We must also be careful not to imply that states don't matter anymore: clearly, states are still major players. In a world of nuclear weapons and weapons of mass destruction (WMD) only states can really ensure the survival of their citizens. State governments control national militaries, economies, and bureaucracies, and they are responsible for the security of the people living within their country's borders. No other actors possess the same level of legitimacy or the same capacity for action.

The term "global" is almost always used to refer to the entire world, regardless of state boundaries. Indeed, thinking in global terms tends to have the effect of erasing these boundaries. The idea of a "global environment" helps us to understand that in the context of issues such as global warming and climate change, borders are largely irrelevant. The idea of the global citizen, which is linked to the concept of **cosmopolitanism**, also emphasizes that we all belong to "one world," not just to one country. Human beings share common problems, common interests, and a common fate, all of which go beyond particular political communities. Cosmopolitanism also represents a different *ethical* vision of international order, implying a moral concern for the world and its people as a whole; see **Box 14.2**. Similarly, the concept of **globalization** emphasizes a global interconnectedness that transcends state boundaries and controls.

We should also give the terms **state** and **nation** some scrutiny. Although they are often used synonymously (or joined together to produce "nation-state"), they actually refer to two quite distinct entities. For our purposes—and those of politics more generally—we

See also Chapter 4, page 88, for a discussion of the cosmopolitan approach.

Also see the Introduction, page 3, and Chapter 1, page 41, for discussions of globalization.

14

KEY QUOTE BOX 14.2
Peter Singer's One World

We have lived with the idea of sovereign states for so long that they have come to be part of the background not only of diplomacy and public policy but also of ethics. Implicit in the term 'globalization' rather than the older 'internationalization' is the idea that we are moving beyond the era of growing ties between nations and are beginning to contemplate something beyond the existing conception of the nation-state. But this change needs to be reflected in all our levels of thought, and especially our thinking about ethics (Singer, 2002: 9).

might define the "state" as a distinctive political community with its own set of rules and practices, more or less separate from other such communities. For the specific purposes of IR, "the state" refers to the modern sovereign state, which possesses a "legal personality" and is recognized as possessing certain rights and duties. (Of course, this kind of state is distinct from the states that make up a federation, as in the US, Australia, or India.)

As we saw in Chapter 7, the sovereign state was legally defined by the 1933 Montevideo Convention on the Rights and Duties of States. Of the 16 Articles adopted, the most important are the first 11. Article 1 summarizes the criteria for a modern sovereign state: *a permanent population; a defined territory and a government capable of maintaining effective control over its territory and of conducting international relations with other states.*

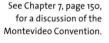

See Chapter 7, page 150, for a discussion of the Montevideo Convention.

A particularly important provision highlighting the sovereign aspect of international statehood is Article 8, which asserts the right of states not to suffer **intervention** by any other state. Article 10 identifies the conservation of peace as the primary interest of all states. And Article 11 reinforces both these messages in no uncertain terms (see **Box 14.3**). In summary, IR understands the state to be a *formally constituted, sovereign political structure encompassing people, territory and institutions.* As such, the state interacts with similarly constituted structures in an international system that is ideally characterized by peaceful, non-coercive relations, establishing a similarly peaceful international order conducive to the prosperity of all. Sadly, the reality often falls far short of this ideal.

KEY CONCEPT BOX 14.3
Article 11, Montevideo Convention on the Rights and Duties of States, 1933

The contracting states definitely establish as the rule of their conduct the precise obligation not to recognize territorial acquisitions or special advantages which have been obtained by force whether this consists in the employment of arms, in threatening diplomatic representations, or in any other effective coercive measure. The territory of a state is inviolable and may not be the object of military occupation nor of other measures of force imposed by another state directly or indirectly or for any motive whatever even temporarily.

SOURCE: www.molossia.org/montevideo.html (accessed 17/10 /2007)

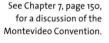

See Chapter 13, page 262, for a discussion of homogeneous national political culture.

We now turn to the idea of the nation, a term that refers specifically to "a people" as opposed to a formal territorial entity. There is no widely agreed definition of what constitutes "a people"; in general, though, the term generally denote a kind of collective identity that is grounded in a shared history and culture and may or may not lay claim to some kind of political recognition as well as a specific territory. We have already discussed (in Chapter 13). the difficulty, if not impossibility, of identifying a single **political culture** in any nation. We have also seen (in Chapter 5) that **nationalism**, as an ideology, calls for political organization to be based on "national identity." Thus nationalism supports the claim of each nation to a state of its own—a claim that, since the early twentieth century, has generally been based on the apparently democratic principle of national **self-determination**. Nationalism, at least in its more extreme xenophobic versions, may also seek the exclusion of "alien" elements from an existing state to safeguard the "authenticity" of its national character.

However they are defined, "nations" are often assumed to populate sovereign states and are very often thought of in singular terms: that is, one state may be assumed to contain one nation. Thus the state of France is occupied by the "French nation," Japan by the Japanese and so on. These examples reflect the commonly accepted conflation of state and people that produces the familiar term "nation-state," which, again, reflects the principle of national self-determination. In practice, though, the matching of state and nation has rarely, if ever, been so neat and unproblematic. There is virtually no state in the world that contains a single, homogeneous nation. Many states are made up of two or more "nations" and even these are not always distinct. The contemporary British state is composed of recognized sub-state national entities—Welsh, Scots, English, and Northern Irish—but these entities themselves are multilayered, especially since immigration over the centuries has brought dozens of different "nationalities" to the British Isles. Contemporary Britain is far more "multicultural" and indeed "multinational" than it has been at any other time in history. The same can be said for France, which contains a plethora of ethnic, linguistic, and religious groups. Japan, by contrast, has maintained a high level of ethnic homogeneity by keeping its immigration rates low; as a consequence, its population is rapidly aging.

 See Chapter 5, page 105, for an exploration of nationalism.

© Melanie Lowe/istockphoto.com

PHOTO 14.1 A dancer from Toronto's annual Caribbean parade—founded by immigrants from Trinidad and Tobago—wears a peacock-inspired costume.

Close inspection of other national entities will reveal similar stories. What started out as British settler colonies (a legacy of modern empire and mass migration) are now among the most "multinational" nations in the world today. We need look no further than Canada, which has one of the highest levels of immigration in the Western world and a rapidly evolving multicultural identity. The *Encyclopedia of Canada's Peoples* identifies 118 different settler populations, as well 12 distinct groups of Aboriginal peoples (Multicultural Canada, 1998). Even relatively small states can be amazingly diverse. Papua New Guinea, for example, has a population of just under six million but more than 850 different languages, and each language group could theoretically consider itself to be "a nation." Such diversity is often associated with "weak states" (a topic we will explore further below). Nonetheless, states are still widely assumed to contain singular nations, and although most states are recognized to contain many more, their identities are still to some extent equated with a dominant majority. Thus in Canada, the US, and Australia, a dominant white English-speaking majority constitutes the mainstream population. Multiculturalism may be important, but the institutions and values of these countries are based on European-centred ways of perceiving and acting in the world.

Although this explanation of the basic distinctions between "state" and "nation" does not exhaust all the nuances of those terms, it does demonstrate how simple terms can fail to capture complex realities. It also suggests that the name of the paramount organization in international affairs, the United Nations (UN), is not completely accurate. After all, its members are states, not nations. This brings us to the last of our complex key terms: "international." The entities that interact formally in the "international" sphere are not nations in the sense of "peoples": they are sovereign states. Thus a more appropriate term might be "interstate" or "interstatal" relations. Of course, if we used either of those terms we would run the risk of confusion with states in a federal system.

KEY POINTS

- Although the distinctions between IR and other fields of political science are often difficult to maintain, IR is generally treated as a specialized area of study, if not a separate discipline.
- IR terminology is a complex of overlapping terms. However, "international relations," "world politics," and "global politics" all have different nuances.

States and International Systems in World History

The fact that empires have risen and fallen throughout history suggests that the sovereign state system as we understand it may sooner or later be replaced by another system made up of quite different units. Indeed, proponents of "globalism" believe that a transformation is under way now, and that boundaries and controls will become increasingly meaningless in the future. Others believe that we are entering a new era of **empire**, although there is no consensus on where its centre of power might lie.

States in the simple sense of political communities date more or less from the time when human groups first developed settled agricultural or animal husbandry practices. These activities required three basic things: an ongoing association with a particular part of the earth's surface, a way of organizing people and resources, and some form of protection for them. As we have seen, a fundamental part of the definition of the modern state is a relationship between a permanent population and a defined territory. This characteristic covers numerous historic cases, although there have been "stateless communities" throughout history—typically groups with a nomadic lifestyle and no fixed attachment to, or control over, a particular territory. The formation of states has also given rise to "state systems" or "international orders": ways of organizing relations between and among political communities either in the same geographical area or further afield.

Since IR is, by and large, a discipline that developed in "the West," it is scarcely surprising that it has looked for historical antecedents of statehood and international orders in the "cradle of Western civilization": the eastern Mediterranean region where the ancient Greek and Roman civilizations flourished. These civilizations were not isolated, however: they had close connections with the civilizations of northern Africa and the Near East, and both Greece and Rome drew on the rich sources of knowledge and cultural practices of those regions. In turn, the communities of northern Africa and the Near East were connected to other communities. Through cross-cultural exchange, knowledge of all kinds, including political knowledge, was transmitted from much farther afield as well.

The "state" of the ancient Greeks was the *polis* or "city-state." The largest and best known was the Athenian *polis*—often seen as the archetypal model of classical democracy. The political philosophy of certain thinkers who gathered in Athens has been the foundation of much subsequent political theory concerning the nature and purposes of the state. Aristotle, for example, saw the state not as an artificial construct separating the human from nature, but as the *natural* habitat for humans. When he described "man" as a *zōon politikon* (political animal) he did not mean that humans were naturally scheming, devious creatures. What he actually said was that since the *polis* "belongs to the class of objects

UN Photo/Evan Schneider

PHOTO 14.2 Running the world: A G20 meeting in 2011 brought together the leaders of the world's 20 most influential countries. While all countries are legally equal in sovereignty (at least those recognized by the UN), there is no equality in terms of economic, military, and political influence.

See Chapter 3, page 63, for
a discussion of the history
of democracy.

which exist by nature," it follows that the human is "by *nature* a political animal"—a creature designed by nature to live in a *polis* (Aristotle, Iii). In IR, Athens stands out as a historic example of a state driven by the imperatives of political **realism**, especially when it fought for supremacy against the Spartans. The historian and general Thucydides, eyewitness to some of the events of that war and author of *The Peloponnesian War*, stands at the forefront of a long tradition of realist thought for his interpretation of the war and his observations on human nature (these ideas will be discussed in the next chapter.)

Although Athens for a time headed its own empire, the best-known empire of the ancient world was that of Rome. Roman thought played a major role in the historical growth of "the West," especially with respect to republicanism and the development of the legal systems of significant parts of Europe. It was also partly because of the Roman Empire that Christianity became firmly established in Europe, a development that had very significant consequences for subsequent political ideas and practices.

In considering empire as a form of international system, it is important to note that empires, like states, have existed at various times throughout most of the world and have taken different forms. In general, though, they have been relatively large-scale political entities made up of a number of smaller political communities (generally states) under the control of a central power. In most cases they have been held together by force. Although empire can constitute a kind of international order, this order is quite different from the current international state system, which is underpinned by a theory of sovereign equality among its constituent members. Empires are characterized explicitly by relations of domination and subordination, although (as contemporary critics would point out) this can occur in the present system as well. The brief outline of historical empires in Table 14.1 reminds us that not everything of historical significance happened in Europe.

TABLE 14.1 A Brief Guide to Historical Empires

Pre-Modern Empires

African empires: Ethiopian Empire (ca. 50–1974), Mali Empire (ca. 1210–1490), Songhai Empire (1468–1590), Fulani Empire (ca. 1800–1903)

Mesoamerican empires: esp. Maya Empire (ca. 300–900), Teotihuacan Empire (ca. 500–750), Aztec Empire (1325–ca. 1500)

Byzantine Empire (330–1453)

Andean empires: Huari Empire (600–800), Inca Empire (1438–1525)

Chinese pre-modern empires: including T'ang Dynasty (618–906), Sung Dynasty (906–1278)

Islamic empires: esp. Umayyid/Abbasid (661–1258), Almohad (1140–1250), Almoravid (1050–1140)

Carolingian Empire (ca. 700–810)

Bulgarian Empire (802–827, 1197–1241)

Southeast Asian empires: Khmer Empire (877–1431), Burmese Empire (1057–1287)

Novgorod Empire (882–1054)

Medieval German Empire (962–1250)

Danish Empire (1014–1035)

Indian empires: including Chola Empire (11ᵗʰ century), Empire of Mahmud of Ghazni (998–1039), Mughal Empire (1526–1805)

Mongol Empire (1206–1405)

Mamluk Empire (1250–1517)

Holy Roman Empire (1254–1835)

Modern Empires

Portuguese Empire (ca. 1450–1975)

Spanish Empire (1492–1898)

Russian Empire/USSR (1552–1991)

Swedish Empire (1560–1660)

Dutch Empire (1660–1962)

British Empire (1607–ca. 1980)

French Empire (ca. 1611–ca. 1980)

Modern Chinese Empire: esp. Ch'ing Dynasty (1644–1911)

Austrian/Austro-Hungarian Empire (ca. 1700–1918) [See also Habsburg Empire]

US Empire (1776–present)

Brazilian Empire (1822–1889)

German Empire (1871–1918, 1939–1945)

Japanese Empire (1871–1945)

Italian Empire (1889–1942)

Habsburg Empire (1452–1806)

Ottoman Empire (1453–1923)

SOURCE: Global Policy Forum: http://globalpolicy.org/empire/history/2005/empireslist.htm.

The fact that the earliest known empires were situated around the river systems of the Tigris, Euphrates, and Nile suggests a certain correlation between the conditions required for successful agriculture and the establishment of settled political communities connected by extensive networks of relations. The same broad region saw the rise of the Sumerian, Egyptian, Babylonian, Assyrian, and Persian empires between roughly 4,000 and 400 BCE. The domination exercised by the controlling powers of these empires varied in form, from direct control of smaller subject communities to more indirect methods that allowed local groups some autonomy, provided they paid the expected tributes (Stern, 2000: 57; Lawson, 2003: 24–5). Africa also produced a number of empires, both ancient and modern. Among the latter was the Malian empire, which thrived between the thirteenth and seventeenth centuries and made Timbuktu a significant centre of learning as well as trade and commerce. The Ottoman Empire, with its capital in Istanbul, emerged at around the same time, and lasted until the early 1920s.

Farther east, the ancient kingdoms of the Indus Valley formed a broad civilizational entity. Although Hindu religious traditions and Sanskrit writing provided some basic cultural cohesion over much of the region, political communities within it varied widely, ranging from oligarchies to republics. The region's best-known empire was established in the north in 300 BCE. Although it lasted less than a century, its reputation was assured largely because one of its leading figures, Kautilya, produced a highly sophisticated text on **statecraft** known as the Arthasastra, which set out the ways and means of acquiring territory, keeping it, and reaping prosperity from it. It is comparable to Niccolò Machiavelli's writings on statecraft, although some see it as presenting a far harsher picture of the struggle for domination (Boesche, 2002: 253–76; Lawson, 2003: 24–5).

One of the most extensive and durable empires of all was the Chinese, which lasted from the time of the Shang dynasty in the eighteenth century BCE until the early twentieth century, although there was a substantial interlude during which it disintegrated into a number of warring states. It was during a period of chaos and violence that the ancient philosophy of Confucius, which is largely concerned with political and social arrangements conducive to good order under strong leadership and **authority**, is thought to have developed (see Lawson, 2006: 155). European theorists of **sovereignty**, which is ultimately concerned with the same problems, were to develop their ideas under similar conditions.

In the early modern period, the Ottoman Turks ruled over some 14 million subjects from the Crimea to Hungary, while the Moghuls pushed farther towards the south and east. By the end of the sixteenth century, Islamic forces—cultural, political, and military—controlled not only the Middle East but significant parts of Africa, Central Asia, South Asia, Southeast Asia (especially present-day Malaysia, Indonesia, and parts of the Philippines) as well as sizeable parts of Eastern Europe. The list in Table 14.1 shows just how common the empire has been as a form of international system. The list is by no means exhaustive.

© The Print Collector/Alamy

PHOTO 14.3 Countless indigenous people in the Americas were killed or forced into slavery in the process of colonization. Spanish conquistadors such as Hernando de Soto, shown here in Florida, c. 1540, were reputed to be particularly cruel.

Virtually all empires have left important legacies of one kind or another, but the ones that have had the most profound impact on the structure of the present international system are the modern European empires, the largest and most powerful of which was the British Empire. France, Spain, Portugal, Holland, Denmark, Belgium, Italy, Russia, and Germany were all colonial powers at one time or another, but none of them equalled Britain in influence.

The transmission of culture is greatly facilitated by **imperialism**, so it's not surprising that British—or, more specifically, English and Scottish—culture established itself around much of the world; even today, English prevails as the most important international language. At its height in the late nineteenth century, the British empire ruled over hundreds of millions of people and encompassed nearly one quarter of the world's land area. To a certain extent, the mantle of power passed to the US after the Second World War.

KEY QUOTE BOX 14.4
A "Band of Brothers": New Zealand's Prime Minister Declares Support for Britain (1939)

Prime Minister Michael Savage's declaration of support for Britain at the beginning of the Second World War reflected the feelings of many people in the "dominions": when the "mother country" came under threat, they rushed to its defence. The ties that held the Empire together were emotional and moral as well as financial and military.

> I am satisfied that nowhere will the issue be more clearly understood than in New Zealand—where, for almost a century, behind the sure shield of Britain, we have enjoyed and cherished freedom and self-government. Both with gratitude for the past and confidence in the future, we range ourselves without fear beside Britain. Where she goes, we go. Where she stands, we stand. We are only a small and young nation, but we are one and all a band of brothers and we march forward with union of hearts and wills to a common destiny.

SOURCE: http://www.nzhistory.net.nz/timeline/05/09; accessed 31 July 2010.

But cultural spread travels both ways. Contemporary European states have absorbed many cultural influences from the places they once colonized, and many people from those places immigrated to the former "mother countries." Thus the UK is home to large Indian, Sri Lankan, Bangladeshi, and Pakistani communities, France to many North Africans, and Holland to many people from Indonesia and other former Asian colonies. The influence of former colonies may be most obvious in the case of food—Indonesian rijstaffel and Surinamese curry in Amsterdam, couscous in Paris, chicken vindaloo in London—but it makes itself felt in areas of life, including language. The history of empire, which encompasses exploration, trade, proselytization, and migration as well as other more explicitly political aspects, is also part of the history of globalization. The beginnings of contemporary global **interdependence** can largely be traced to the global reach of the modern European empires and the networks and movements of people, technological innovations, and financial and economic systems they gave rise to.

Arthur Edwards/The Sun/PA Wire URN:877010 8 (Press Association via AP Images)

PHOTO 14.4 Prince Charles meets with soldiers at the mayor of London's "Big Curry Lunch" (2010).

Globalization has recently been linked to a new form of empire which, some argue, is replacing traditional state sovereignty with a new kind of sovereignty that involves neither a territorial centre of power nor fixed boundaries. This new imperial order is based on the power of transnational corporations and forms of production that owe no allegiance to territorial entities and in fact seek to supplant their sovereignty (see Hardt and Negri, 2000: xi–xiv). Some may see this scenario as grossly exaggerated, but at the very least it offers a basis for critical reflection on key aspects of the phenomenon of globalization and the growing power of deterritorialized corporations.

Is the old concept of empire obsolete today? A contemporary definition formulated by John Perkins, together with various groups of students, in 2005–6 may be useful here: an empire is a

> nation-state that dominates other nation-states and exhibits one or more of the following characteristics: (1) exploits resources from the lands it dominates, (2) consumes large quantities of resources—amounts which are disproportionate to the size of its population relative to those of other nations, (3) maintains a large military that enforces its policies when more subtle measures fail, (4) spreads its language, literature, art, and various aspects of its culture through its sphere of influence, (5) taxes not just its own citizens, but also people in other countries, and (6) imposes its own currency on the lands under its control (Perkins, 2007: 4-5).

According to Perkins, virtually all the students he consulted believed that the US fits this definition. He goes on to argue that the US has used the above strategies to maintain a "secret empire" around the world. Certainly resource use and the spread of economic and other forms of influence are crucial to an understanding of empire in today's world.

Yet many Americans, including political leaders, are uncomfortable with the idea that their country exercises imperial control. For example, President George W. Bush claimed in 2000 that "America has never been an empire. . . . We may be the only great power in history that had the chance, and refused"—a theme he repeated when declaring a victory in Iraq in May 2003 over the forces of Saddam Hussein; while other nations had "fought in foreign lands and remained to occupy and exploit," Americans "wanted nothing more than to return home" (Ferguson, 2003a). Conservative historian Niall Ferguson has concluded that the US has taken on the global role formerly played by Britain, without facing the reality that an empire comes with it. In short, it is "an empire in denial" (Ferguson, 2003b: 370).

Whether or not the US itself is an imperial power, it clearly exists in a world of powerful states that exert at least regional hegemony. Russia and Japan, the larger member states of the European Union (France, Britain, Germany), and the rising states of China and India all display at least some of the characteristics that Perkins attributes to an empire. This means that if the US is an empire, it must jockey for power with empires or "semi-empires" in the international system. The interaction of imperial states today, as in previous centuries, helps create the texture of world politics.

KEY POINTS

- States as political communities have existed for thousands of years and have varied widely in size and institutional features. Although the sovereign state remains the dominant form and the foundation of the international system, many commentators today believe that the forces of globalization are undermining it.
- Empires have existed in different parts of the world from ancient times through the modern period. Some argue that the US now plays an imperial role in everything but name, while others argue that the power of transnational corporations trumps that of any state. Still others emphasize competition among a number of hegemonic powers, including the US, China, India, Japan, the EU, and Russia.

The Rise of Modernity and the State System in Europe

Modernity is a complex phenomenon associated with the rise of European science and technology, which began around 1500 and led to industrialization and increased military power as well as enormous political and social changes, including a gradual decline in the authority of religion. But these changes did not occur in isolation from other influences. Stern (2000: 72) notes that many important ideas and inventions were transmitted to Europe from China and Arabia, and that significant aspects of the Greek and Roman learning central to the Renaissance had been preserved by Islamic scholars. The "discovery" of new worlds in the Americas and the Pacific also served to acquaint Europeans with a vast array of unfamiliar social and political models, all of which prompted new comparisons and questions (Lawson, 2006: 60). (As we noted in Chapter 3, indigenous traditions, notably those of the Six Nations or Iroquois Confederacy, may have contributed far more to the shaping of American democracy than many theorists have cared to admit.)

14

Few people in the year 1500 would have suspected that a cluster of rather insignificant states in Western Europe would eventually control most of the world's surface (Kennedy, 1989: 3). Chinese civilization at the time seemed vastly superior to any other. Technological innovations such as moveable type, gunpowder, and paper money, together with advances in ironwork, contributed to an expansion of trade and industry that was further stimulated by an extensive program of canal-building. With an army of more than over a million troops, and an efficient hierarchical administration run by an educated Confucian bureaucracy, China was "the envy of foreign visitors" (Kennedy, 1989: 5). Islamic civilization was also thriving, and there were many important centres of power outside Europe. In terms of political organization, Europe in 1500 was a chaotic patchwork of overlapping jurisdictions and fragmented authorities. The only institution providing any sort of unity was the Catholic Church centred in Rome, the seat of religious authority throughout the continent. From 1519, however, the Protestant Reformation challenged the supremacy of the established Church, triggering massive theological and political fallout.

The devastating struggle between Catholic and Protestant forces continued for more than century. The treaty that ended it, the Peace of Westphalia (1648), is conventionally credited with consolidating several key characteristics of the modern state (see the case study on the facing page). These included not only the principle of religious co-existence, but also the state's claim to sole authority in matters such as the declaration of war and the negotiation of peace, diplomatic representation, and the authority to make treaties with foreign powers (Boucher, 1998: 224). For these reasons, Westphalia has long been regarded as the founding moment of the modern *sovereign* state, although some contemporary scholars (for example, Clark, 2005) dispute that assessment.

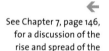

← See Chapter 7, page 146, for a discussion of the rise and spread of the Western state.

KEY POINTS

- "Modernity" is associated with social, political, intellectual, and technological developments in Europe that brought significant changes to the political landscape, although there were influences from other parts of the world as well.
- The Peace of Westphalia is conventionally regarded as the founding moment of the doctrine of state sovereignty and therefore of the modern state.

14

The Emergence of Sovereignty

The principle of sovereignty is seen as effectively *enclosing* each state within the "hard shell" of its territorial borders. It was meant to guarantee the state against any external intervention in its domestic affairs, including internal governmental arrangements. The theory possessed an attractive simplicity. Rulers could not only follow the religious and moral principles of their choice (and demand that their subjects conform), but could govern according to whichever form of rule they preferred. The protective shell of sovereignty guaranteed the freedom of all states—or rather the ruling elements within each state—to arrange their domestic affairs as they liked, regardless of either what external actors might think or the state's relative standing in terms of size, power, and capacity. As we pointed out in the introduction to this book, the state is sovereign in the sense that it is the supreme law-making body within a particular territory, with the ultimate power of life and death over individuals. The juridical sovereignty possessed by individual states remains a basic principle of international law today.

CASE STUDY
The Peace of Westphalia

The Thirty Years War ended in 1648 with the Peace of Westphalia. The treaty was the product of five years of complex diplomatic negotiations, which ended when the Treaties of Osnabruck and Munster were signed to form a comprehensive agreement containing 128 clauses covering matters of law, religion, and ethics as well as numerous practical issues.

Some of the principles enshrined in the Peace, such as the authority of rulers to determine the religious affiliations of their subject, were very similar to provisions included in an earlier agreement, the Peace of Augsburg of 1555. However, Westphalia was infused with emergent ideas about a kind of international law that could transcend religious differences and therefore be applied to Catholic and Protestant states alike. The foremost thinker along these lines was the Dutch jurist Hugo Grotius (1583–1645), whose influential work *Laws of War and Peace* confronted the problem of conflicting moralities and the need for toleration and set out minimum standards for conduct. Importantly for the development of the state system and international order, it granted co-equal juridical status to states.

Westphalia has been described as the first, and perhaps the greatest, of the modern European peace treaties: a benchmark for both critics and supporters of the sovereign state system, as well as for those who predict its eventual demise in the face of the state-transcending forces of globalization.

The principle of state sovereignty is admirable in its simplicity, but putting it into practice has been difficult. Indeed, for much of the 300 years following Westphalia, Europe was no less prone to warfare among its constituent states than it had been before. Whatever the historical reasons for war may have been, it is really only since the Second World War that Europeans seem finally to have struck on a formula for peaceful relations. That this was achieved via a regional supra-state framework in the form of the European Union is somewhat ironic. Although the principle of state sovereignty was initially formulated to prevent warfare, it seems that a lasting peace was possible only when the European states overcame their obsession with safeguarding their sovereignty. The degree to which the EU—and other regional experiments elsewhere in the world—will undermine the principle of state sovereignty remains to be seen.

Another factor to be considered here is the moral conundrum raised when states mistreat people—whether their own citizens or others—within their borders. A strict interpretation of the theory of state sovereignty prohibits any intervention by actors outside the state, even in cases of civil war, genocide, or other human rights abuses. Today, though, there is a widely assumed right of **humanitarian intervention** that trumps the sovereign right of states—or their rulers—to do as they please within their own borders. This assumed right is a complement to the recent idea that sovereignty entails the *responsibility to protect* the state's inhabitants.

The theory of state sovereignty is often seen to have two dimensions: external and internal. As Evans and Newnham (1998: 504) put it, the doctrine makes a double claim: "autonomy in foreign policy and exclusive competence in internal affairs." This claim

14

depends on there being an ultimate authority within the state that is entitled to make decisions and settle disputes. This authority is "the sovereign," and may be either a person (such as a monarch) or a collective (such as a parliament representing the sovereignty of the people). As the highest power in the state's political system, the sovereign cannot be subject to any other agent, domestic or foreign (Miller, 1991: 492–3). In other words, the traditional doctrine of sovereignty holds that the finality of sovereign power applies not only within the domestic arena but in the external realm as well.

Yet in an international system in which all states are sovereign, there can be no higher authority to function as a ruler (see Evans and Newnham, 1998: 504). Externally, therefore, the doctrine of state sovereignty has the paradoxical effect of creating **anarchy**—literally, "absence of a ruler." And in that case there is nothing to stop a large, powerful state from taking over lesser states by sheer force. This is what many see as the prime danger posed by the anarchic nature of the international sphere. The disorder produced by unchecked power is likened to a dangerous **state of nature** in which there is no law and order.

The theory of sovereignty was first worked out in relation to the sphere of domestic rather than international politics, and various well-known figures contributed to its development through the centuries. Among the earliest was Jean Bodin (ca. 1530–96), who, like many others concerned with political order, lived in disordered times, experiencing civil and religious conflict through much of his life. He contributed to the development of sovereignty not just as a doctrine but as an "ideology of order" (see King, 1999). However, the best-known theorist of sovereignty is Thomas Hobbes (1588–1679), the author of *Leviathan*, who is generally regarded as standing in the same tradition of political realism as Thucydides and Machiavelli. He, too, lived during a period of civil war and (as we saw in Chapter 1) believed that only an all-powerful sovereign could establish order. (We will consider his ideas and their contribution to IR theory in the next chapter.)

Another important development that must be considered along with the rise of the modern European state system is nationalism. The assumption implicit in the principle of self-determination is that each "nation" is entitled to have a state of its own. This can be problematic, given that there are probably thousands of groups around the world that could make some credible claim to constituting a nation. Practical difficulties aside, the idea that nations and states go together seems very persuasive; but like the sovereign state itself, it is a relatively recent idea. Indeed, its origins lie in the period of state-building dynamics that followed the Peace of Westphalia.

At the time of Westphalia, the link between nation and state was practically non-existent. Sovereignty resided in the person who occupied the top position in the state's political hierarchy, in most cases the king, though occasionally the queen. Monarchs did not regard the masses over whom they ruled as constituting "nations." Indeed, the people within these states did not begin to acquire a common political identity until the late eighteenth century, when the emerging idea of democracy required a distinct body of people—citizens—to constitute a *sovereign people* and the most likely candidate for this position was "the nation." Although the record of democratic development in Europe remained patchy until quite recent times (women in Switzerland did not gain the right to vote until 1971), the idea of the nation caught on rapidly. The later development of the modern state and state system brought together the three prime characteristics of the modern state: *sovereignty, territoriality, and nationality.* These characteristics also support an international order based on the state system.

See Chapter 1, page 35, for the discussion of the "state of nature" in the liberal social contract tradition.

14

The French Revolution, as we noted earlier, marked a turning point in the rise of the modern European state system. It converted the mass of people, who until then had been merely "subjects" of the monarch, into citizens of the French state. Nevertheless, the entity that emerged as the "French nation" was far from unified, since the territory covered by France was occupied by a variety of groups with their own distinct languages and customs. Whatever legal and administrative unity existed had to be imposed from above. The same was true in most other parts of Europe.

Another significant development came in the wake of the Napoleonic wars. This was the **Concert of Europe**: an agreement among various European powers to meet regularly to resolve diplomatic crises between states. Beginning with the Congress of Vienna in 1815, this arrangement lasted until the mid-1850s and although the meetings were eventually discontinued, the art of diplomacy became an important instrument of the European state system. At the beginning of the nineteenth century, the modern European state system was still more a matter of theory than practice, and the concept of the "nation-state" did not exist. But the idea of the nation was a powerful driving force, and it became more prominent as the century progressed, leading to the emergence of new "national" states in Greece (1830), Belgium (1831), Italy (1861), Germany (1871), and Romania, Serbia, and Montenegro (1878). By the beginning of the twentieth century, the sovereign state system was reasonably well entrenched in Europe, as well as in Western settler societies such as Canada, the US, Australia, and New Zealand, but it scarcely existed in other parts of the world.

KEY POINTS

- Theories of sovereignty developed in response to events, including both civil and inter-state wars in Europe.
- In political philosophy the "state of nature" was associated with anarchy, violence, and the drive for power. It was in order to safeguard the people and give them with some protection from those conditions that centralized sovereign government was seen as necessary.
- Nationalism in the sense of political/cultural identity is closely associated with the rise of the modern sovereign state and state system.

The Globalization of the Sovereign State System

As we have seen, numerous empires have existed since ancient times, and in many different parts of the world. Imperialism and colonialism only increased with the rise of the sovereign state, and European empires (sometimes unwittingly) exported the sovereign state system to the rest of the world, where it has met with varying success. Early Spanish, Portuguese, and Dutch explorers and traders were followed by the British, French, Belgians, and Germans. Shipping routes and trading posts encircled the world, facilitating further colonization. With the end of the Second World War, however, the future of colonialism was soon called into question. The devastating cost of the war was one factor; many European countries were near bankruptcy and

See Chapter 7, page 146, for a discussion of the European concepts of borders and sovereignty on colonial territory.

simply too weak to maintain their hold on their overseas possessions. Another was the principle of self-determination. Originally developed with Europeans in mind, this principle was now invoked as a right of colonized people, calling the legitimacy of colonialism into question. This normative change drove a decolonization movement that saw almost all former European colonies achieve independence by the end of the twentieth century.

Among the legacies of European colonization were more or less clear borders dividing one colonial state from another. The imposition of such boundaries on territories traditionally used by a variety of indigenous peoples in a fluid system of occupation frequently resulted in arbitrary divisions of tribes or ethnic groups between two or more different colonies. This problem was especially common in Africa, but also occurred in settler societies such as Canada, the US, and Australia. In these countries, the boundaries of provinces and states had little if anything to do with traditional Aboriginal territories. The lack of regard for pre-existing groupings and boundaries is especially clear in the case of borders represented on maps as straight lines. The arbitrary divisions created in this way have made the task of **nation-building**—the effort to develop a coherent sense of national identity among disparate groups of people—particularly difficult.

The relatively clear boundaries, established administrative centres, and more or less permanent settled populations of many colonial states mimicked the structure of European states. When decolonization came on the agenda, in many cases the colonial borders were retained and sovereignty was simply transferred from the colonizing power to members of an indigenous elite who had been educated in the colonizing country, with structures of governance—parliaments, bureaucracies, and so on—that reflected European practices. A partial exception was colonial India, which was partitioned at the last minute to form the Republic of India (officially multiconfessional, but primarily Hindu) and the Islamic Republic of Pakistan. No doubt the lack of time to adjust to the division was largely responsible for the violence that ensued: at least a million people are estimated to have lost their lives in the partition period.

The fact that virtually all former colonies became part of an international system of states based largely on the European state system effectively ensured the globalization of that system. Even states that had not been colonized, from Japan and Turkey to Thailand and Tonga, adopted the European state format.

For a number of former colonies, though, independent sovereign statehood has proved extremely difficult. Few postcolonial states have collapsed completely, but a number have been unable to exercise effective statehood. These states have been variously characterized as weak, quasi, and failing or failed states.

States that lack the capacity to organize and regulate their societies and therefore cannot deliver an adequate range of political, social and economic goods to their citizens are usually described as *weak states*. *Quasi state* is a label that has been used in various ways, and sometimes overlaps with *weak state*; however, Robert Jackson (1990) uses it to refer specifically to developing states that are dependent on the support of the international community and therefore possess what he calls "negative sovereignty." The idea of *state failure* comes into play when a state that is already weak reaches a point where factors such as corruption, incompetence, unfair distribution of resources, human rights abuses, favouritism on the basis of ethnicity, and the direct involvement of the military in politics, feed into social unrest, persistent violence, economic breakdown, and political turmoil

See Chapter 7, page 147, for a discussion of Japan and Turkey's adoption of the European state format.

(Rotberg, 2003: 1–2). Among the states that have been described as weak, quasi, or failing are Congo, Sudan, Sierra Leone, Afghanistan, Columbia, Tajikistan, Haiti, Lebanon, Fiji, the Solomon Islands, and Papua New Guinea. Somalia is more or less a failed or collapsed state, since it has no functioning centralized institutions.

Even though many of the problems leading to state weakness or failure may be internal, there are almost always external factors—colonial legacies, the activities of transnational organizations, inequitable trading regimes—that have played a contributing role. The forces of economic globalization have been especially problematic for fragile developing states with underdeveloped capacity; the fact that such states lack negotiating power in the international arena ensures that they remain vulnerable to failure at one level or another.

All these problems bring into question both the assumed benefits of the globalization of the European state system and its long-term prospects as an effective system of international order. Although it is true that many other postcolonial states, especially in Asia, have been relatively successful, it is also true that Europe has had its share of failed states. The most recent is the former Yugoslavia, which is now divided into nine separate entities (including Slovenia, Croatia, Bosnia–Herzegovina, Montenegro, Serbia, Kosovo, and the Former Yugoslav Republic of Macedonia). At the same time, the deepening and widening of the EU is a project in **regionalization** that raises questions about the future of the traditional sovereign state in its original heartland.

See Chapter 7, p. 151, for discussion of strong and weak states.

KEY POINTS

- Largely because of the global reach of the European empires and their political legacies, the European state system became the basis for the current international state system and international order.
- Formal sovereign statehood has not always delivered significant benefits, especially in the Third World, where weak or failing states are unable to meet the needs of their citizens.
- Jackson's concept of the "quasi state" highlights the fact that some Third World states depend so much on the international community for their continuing existence that their sovereignty is essentially "negative."

Conclusion

In this chapter we have provided a broad overview of key aspects of the study of International Relations, from its foundations as a discipline and its basic terminology to the main concepts on which it has traditionally been based: sovereignty, the state, and international order. We have also sketched how states and international systems, including empires, have developed from the earliest times to the present era of globalization. Setting the rise of the contemporary international order against this world historical background has helped us to illustrate the variety of state forms and international systems in history. It has also allowed us to demonstrate that while some systems have achieved impressive longevity, no system has ever achieved permanence. It would therefore be a mistake to assume that the present state system will necessarily remain as it is over the longer term, especially given the challenges of globalization and the various pressures it exerts on all aspects of sovereign statehood.

? KEY QUESTIONS

- What does "International Relations" signify and how does it differ from terms such as "world politics" or "global politics"?
- How do empires form an international system?
- Under what circumstances did the idea of sovereign statehood arise in Europe?
- What are the distinguishing features of the modern state?
- What is the relationship between states and nations?
- What do you understand by the terms "anarchy" and "international order"?
- How did the European state system become globalized?
- What are the implications of weak and failing states for the state system as a whole?
- What is "negative" sovereignty?
- What are the alternatives to the current international order?

📖 FURTHER READING

Scott Burchill and Andrew Linklater, eds (2009). *Theories of International Relations Fourth Edition*. London: Macmillan.

   A good basic guide to some of the main concepts, themes, and institutions in the study of International Relations.

Hall, Anthony J. (2005). *The American Empire and the Fourth World: The Bowl With One Spoon, Part One*. Kingston, ON: McGill-Queen's University Press.

   An examination of encounters between the European–American empires and indigenous peoples from the fifteenth century to the twenty-first, Hall concluding with an analysis of what the rise of multinational corporations and the advent of globalization mean for the "fourth world."

Greenfeld, Liah (1992). *Nationalism: Five Roads to Modernity*. Cambridge, MA: Harvard University Press.

   A classic of political history, exploring the roots of five distinct nationalisms (British, French, Russian, German, and American) and arguing (contrary to the standard view) that nationalism preceded industrialization and urbanization.

Hobson, John M. (2004). *The Eastern Origins of Western Civilization*. Cambridge: Cambridge University Press.

   An interesting attempt to counter the ethnocentricity of mainstream accounts of the rise of "the West," in which other regions, especially "the East," are portrayed as passive bystanders.

Treasure, Geoffrey (2003). *The Making of Modern Europe 1648–1780*. London: Routledge.

   A comprehensive account of the growth of the European state, including events such as the Thirty Years War and the French Revolution.

📱 WEB LINKS

www.history-world.org

   A very extensive site offering essays, documents, and maps as well as music and videos relating to the history of the ancient world, Africa, Europe, Asia, India, the Middle East, Australia, and the Americas.

www.history.ac.uk/ihr/Focus/Empire/index.html

   Links to information on a range of historical empires, with a particular focus on the British.

14

Traditional Theories of International Relations

15

CHAPTER OVERVIEW

Theory is a way of organizing the basic elements of our thinking about the world around us. We can neither explain nor understand that world without some kind of theoretical framework in which the "facts" of international politics can be arranged and made meaningful. In this chapter we will examine the two major bodies of theory that form the core of traditional IR: liberalism and realism. Each has offered different explanations of the causes of war and the conditions for peace in the international sphere. A look at the tension between behaviouralism and normative analysis, especially in the US, sheds light on some important issues of methodology. We then turn our attention to the "English School" of IR. This school focuses on the idea of international society, advocating an alternative methodological pathway to that of the "scientism" of American political science. Finally, we consider neoliberalism and neorealism, updated versions of the more traditional theories. From the start we should note that traditional theories, although they attempt to provide universally valid explanations of political behaviour, have been developed largely in "the West" and therefore draw largely on European and North American experiences.

Liberalism and the Rise of IR

Arguably, the main impetus for the emergence of IR as a formal academic discipline was the First World War. The unprecedented scale of this conflict brought into our vocabulary the term "total war": the militarization of a state's entire resources for the purpose of annihilating the enemy. The rise of total war as a military strategy prompted an urgent search for a new international order that would make lasting peace and security possible. Under the influence of US president Woodrow Wilson, this order was to be essentially liberal. See **Box 15.1**.

> ## BIOGRAPHY BOX 15.1
> ### Woodrow Wilson (1856–1924)
>
> Woodrow Wilson served as US president from 1913 to 1921. A Democrat, he took the US into the First World War in 1917 to help "make the world safe for democracy," an idealist notion that has resonated in American foreign policy ever since. Wilsonian idealism was also reflected in efforts to establish a new international order at the end of the war along essentially liberal lines. A chief architect of the League of Nations, Wilson was unable to persuade a Republican-dominated Congress to join (see Chapter 5). However, he was recognized for his efforts when he received the Nobel Peace Prize in 1919. The first Chair in the emergent discipline of IR—the Woodrow Wilson Chair of International Politics at University College Wales, Aberystwyth—was established in the same year, honouring his commitment to the establishment of a peaceful international order.

15

← See the case study on the Peace of Westphalia in Chapter 14, page 293.

Liberal international theorists drew on a pre-existing body of philosophy in constructing their notion of international order. Ancient philosophers had emphasized the capacity of individual human reason to determine the "good life," although modern liberal thinkers advocated concrete political action to achieve reform when the existing order was found wanting. Among the most important contributors to liberal ideas in international politics were Hugo Grotius (1583–1645) and Samuel Pufendorf (1632–94), both of whom experienced the Thirty Years War discussed in Chapter 14.

Grotius promoted the view that the natural condition of humanity was peace, not conflict; this assumption has been a foundation of liberal international thought ever since. He also formulated some of the earliest ideas in the modern period about the "sociability" of the international sphere; these ideas were highly influential in later thinking about international society (Dunne, 1998: 138–9). Pufendorf, for his part, incorporated a basic **natural law** of self-preservation in his work on universal jurisprudence and the law of nations.

◀ Palestinian President Mahmud Abbas and United Nations Secretary-General Ban Ki-moon at the UN headquarters in 2011. Abbas visited the UN to request recognition of Palestine as a full member state (© Xinhua/Shen Hong/Corbis).

He too argued (against Hobbes, primarily) that humans are essentially sociable and not excessively self-interested (see, generally, Hochstrasser, 2000). Another major figure is Immanuel Kant (ch. 4), whose seminal work *Perpetual Peace* was published in 1795. In order to secure lasting peace among states, Kant proposed a set of principles for a law of nations founded on a federation of free states; these ideas have remained highly influential in peace theory (see Kant in Brown, Nardin, and Rengger, 2002: 432–4).

Kant further proposed that under republican forms of government, the rational concern of the individual for self-preservation would ensure that citizens effectively vetoed warmongering. Wilson also endorsed the idea that democracies are inherently peaceful, both within themselves and in their relations with each other, and believed that if all countries were governed democratically, then warfare would be virtually eliminated. He thought that war could have been avoided if all European countries had been democracies in 1914 (Lawson, 2003: 42–3).

A major theme uniting liberal thinkers from Grotius onwards, one that helps to distinguish liberal from realist thought, is their optimistic view of the potential for peaceful relations. This optimism reflects a positive view of **human nature**, at least to the extent that people can learn from their mistakes. Beyond this, liberals believe that the rationally chosen, self-regarding action of individuals tends to lead to better outcomes for all, or at least for the majority. Thus humans can *progress* over time towards a better state of existence as individuals within their political communities and in their relations between communities. None of this comes about by itself. People (agents) need to make it happen. Just as human rationality *and* **agency** are required to build a satisfactory social and political order within a state, so rationality is required in the construction of international institutions designed to overcome the negative effects of **anarchy**. This kind of thinking was a crucial underpinning of the peace-making efforts that were undertaken in the immediate aftermath of the First World War.

President Wilson had led his country into war in the belief that once the forces responsible for the conflict were defeated, a strong international organization dedicated to preserving international peace and security could flourish. He proposed a general association of nation-states whose members would promise to respect one another's economic and political independence and territorial integrity.

This proposal was operationalized through the 1919 Treaty of Versailles. Although the treaty was progressive in that it created the Covenant of the League of Nations, by imposing harsh reparations on Germany for loss and damage caused by the war it "creat[ed] the pre-conditions of a future war" (Evans and Newnham, 1998: 559); many of the treaty's authors lived to regret the harshness of those provisions. The League, which we will discuss again in Chapter 19, provides a useful case study of how theory and practice are interwoven (see below).

Another important aspect of liberal theory pushed by Wilson and others was the principle of **self-determination**—a term that has several nuances. First, it can refer to the right of states to freely determine their own policies and practices. Second, it can refer to the right of citizens to determine their own government and therefore a preferred set of policy options—a defining characteristic of **liberal democracy**. Third, it can refer to the quest of a nationalist movement to secure political autonomy by, for example, seceding to form a new sovereign state. This right to *national* self-determination further strengthens the legitimacy of the nation-state idea. Historically, the principle of the self-determination of "peoples" (understood as "nations") originally applied within Europe only, and although

See Chapter 19, page 388, for a discussion of intergovernmental organizations.

15

CASE STUDY
Liberal Theory and the League of Nations

It is often said that the League of Nations was a failure because it did not prevent the outbreak of the Second World War. The liberal **internationalism** that underpinned the League was criticized, at least by realists, as a form of wishful thinking, bound to fail when faced with the realities of power politics in an anarchic international sphere. The institutional design of the League was workable enough, and the UN is based in part on the League's structure. As the first major attempt to set up a mechanism for collective security on such an extensive international scale it was a considerable achievement, despite its shortcomings. External factors were far more important in undermining its chances for success. When the liberal internationalist League is accused of failing to stop Germany, Italy, and Japan, we must remember, first, that the US refused to join and that the League itself refused to extend membership to communist Russia. A second crucial factor was the aggression shown by France and Belgium when they invaded a German industrial area in an attempt to exact reparation dues (Kerr, 2003: 27). The fact that Britain failed to condemn this violation of League rules further demonstrated the potentially vengeful nature of the treaty's reparations provisions (Michelak, 2001: 61). A humiliated Germany was ripe for the rabid nationalism that Hitler promoted. The question then is: did the League of Nations fail, or did state leaders fail the League of Nations?

it was taken up in South America in the nineteenth century, it was not extended to the rest of the colonized world until after 1945.

Liberal IR theory reached a high point in the interwar years. Among the prominent liberal scholars of the time was the British academic and MP Sir Norman Angell, who was awarded the 1933 Nobel Peace Prize for his extensive writings on the futility of war. Although liberal ideas were soon to be overshadowed by **realism** when the League collapsed and Germany, Italy, and Japan surged ahead in their quests for imperial expansion, early twentieth-century liberals have been recognized as the founders of IR as an academic discipline. As we shall see, liberalism made a comeback in the latter part of the twentieth century, and it remains a highly influential stream of IR theory. In practical terms, it now underpins an extensive system of international law as well as the principal political institutions of contemporary **global governance**, which we find in the UN system. It is also a central part of international political economy (the subject of Chapter 20).

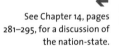
See Chapter 14, pages 281–295, for a discussion of the nation-state.

15

KEY POINTS

- A key motivation for the rise of liberal internationalism in the early twentieth century, and for the establishment of IR as a distinctive academic subject, was the devastation wrought by the First World War, which drove theorists and political leaders to try to identify the causes of war and the conditions for peace.
- Liberal international theory promotes optimism about the prospects for a peaceful international order, established through strong international institutions underpinned

by international law. It accepts that sovereign states are the key actors in international affairs but maintains that their behaviour, even under conditions of anarchy, can be bettered through such institutions. Briefly, it sees human nature as amenable to positive change and learning.

The Realist Turn

The Treaty of Versailles not only failed to resolve a number of Europe's political problems: it also made others worse, particularly by imposing onerous reparations requirements on an economically weak Germany. Following the principle of national self-determination, new states were created in Eastern Europe, among them Poland and Czechoslovakia. These states also had a strategic purpose, however: to serve as "buffers" between Western Europe and the USSR, which had its own brand of internationalism in the form of its commitment to the overthrow of the liberal, capitalist economic order by means of world-wide revolution. Although relative peace was the order of the day throughout the 1920s, and even Germany joined the League of Nations, none of this prevented the rise of Hitler, who set about building the Third Reich on an ultranationalist basis.

Developments in other parts of the world were significant too, especially in Asia. Japan had achieved extraordinary industrial growth over the previous half-century. It had also begun to carve out its own empire, winning a war with Russia in 1905 and annexing Korea in 1910. Japan had been a member of the League of Nations, and some Japanese leaders remained committed to internationalism. But aggressive militarism and **imperialism** prevailed in the 1930s when the military elite effectively took control of the country. Having occupied the Chinese province of Manchuria since 1931, Japan mounted a full-scale invasion of China in 1937—two years before Nazi Germany's invasion of Poland drew the world into its second large-scale war. But it was not until 1940 that Japan joined Italy and Germany in the "Axis Alliance" against Britain and its allies. Canada, Australia, and New Zealand had all entered the war in 1939; the US did not enter until 1941, when the Japanese attacked Pearl Harbor.

Over 50 million people were killed as a direct result of the Second World War (1939–45): more than five times the number killed in the previous world war. Among them were at least six million Jews murdered in what came to be known as the Holocaust—the most notorious act of genocide in human history. The death camps in which, along with the Jews, large numbers of Europe's Roma and Sinti (Gypsy) people were killed testified to the consequences of racialist nationalism gone mad. For the discipline of IR, which had been founded by people dedicated to the prevention of war, such horrors represented a devastating setback. It was at this point that realism came to the fore, offering to explain how the world *really* is rather than how it *ought* to be.

There is no single theory that goes under the name of "realism." However, virtually all realist approaches in IR emphasize the struggle for power and security by sovereign states in the anarchic world of international politics. Although realism emerged as a distinct school of thought within IR only in the twentieth century (beginning in the 1930s), many realists claim that they are part of an ancient tradition. As evidence they point to a passage in Thucydides' history of the Peloponnesian war that they claim illustrates two central

15

See the discussion of the history of states and the international system in Chapter 14, page 284.

principles of political realism: that power politics is the name of the game in relations between states, and that issues of morality are irrelevant in that sphere. In other words, the international sphere is *amoral* (without morality, in the sense that moral rules can't be applied to it), as opposed to *im*moral (contrary to existing moral rules). This passage is known as the "Melian Dialogue"; see **Box 15.2**.

15

KEY QUOTE BOX 15.2
The Melian Dialogue

The inhabitants of the island of Melos were neutral in the war between Athens and Sparta. When pressured by the Athenians to surrender, the Melians tried to negotiate. Thucydides presents the dialogue between the Athenian envoys and the Melian leaders as follows:

Athenians: [We will] not go out of our way to prove at length that we have a right to rule. . . . But you and we should say what we really think, and aim only at what is possible, for we both alike know that in the discussion of human affairs the question of justice only enters where the pressure of necessity is equal, and that the powerful exact what they can, and the weak grant what they must.

Melians: But must we be your enemies? Will you not receive us as friends if we are neutral and remain at peace with you?

Athenians: No, your enmity is not half so mischievous to us as your friendship; for the one is in the eyes of our subjects an argument of our power, the other of our weakness. . . .

Melians: But do you not recognize another danger? For . . . since you drive us from the plea of justice and press upon us your doctrine of expediency, we must show you what is for our interest, and, if it be for yours also, may hope to convince you: Will you not be making enemies of all who are now neutrals? . . .

Athenians: . . . you are not fighting against equals to whom you cannot yield without disgrace, but you are taking counsel whether or no you shall resist an overwhelming force. The question is not one of honour but of prudence. . . .

Melians: We know only too well how hard the struggle must be against your power, and against fortune. . . . Nevertheless we do not despair of fortune; . . . because we are righteous, and you against whom we contend are unrighteous.

Athenians: . . . of men we know, that by a law of their nature wherever they can rule they will. This law was not made by us, and we are not the first who have acted upon it; we did but inherit it, and shall bequeath it to all time, and we know that you and all mankind, if you were as strong as we are, would do as we do. . . . the path of expediency is safe, whereas justice and honour involve danger in practice . . . [and] . . . what encourages men who are invited to join in a conflict is clearly not the goodwill of those who summon them to their side, but a decided superiority in real power . . . " (Thucydides, V, 84–109).

Thucydides records that the Melians refused to surrender. The Athenians laid siege to the city and eventually forced a surrender, after which they put to death all males of military age and enslaved the women and children.

Another significant figure is Niccolò Machiavelli (1467–1527), who developed a pragmatic approach to politics, dismissing idealism and moralizing as harmful in the practice of politics. As we mentioned in Chapter 14, the ancient Indian text called the *Arthasastra*, by Kautilya, has been compared to Machiavelli's writings on **statecraft**. A particularly important idea, often traced to Machiavelli, is that of *raison d'état* (**reason of state**); a more common contemporary equivalent would be the phrase **national interest**. Although Machiavelli did not use the term "reason of state," he urged that where the safety of the country is at stake, a ruler should not consider what he or she personally feels is just or unjust, merciful or cruel, but rather what will secure "the life of the country and maintain its liberty" (Machiavelli, Bk 3, Ch. XLI).

See the discussion on the history of states and the international system in Chapter 14, page 284.

Perhaps the most important figure claimed for the realist tradition is Thomas Hobbes (1588–1679). As we saw in Chapters 1 and 7, Hobbes starts by positing a **state of nature** and a certain human nature, both of which are assumed to be universal, that is, *constant for all times and all places*. Hobbes' state of nature lacks all that is necessary for the good life, including security, justice, and any sort of morality. And it lacks these elements precisely because there is no sovereign power to enforce them. In this condition of **anarchy**, fear and insecurity drive individual humans to protect their lives above all else. Since domination is the only viable means of self-preservation, the inevitable result is a war of each against all. It was in this context that Hobbes wrote what was to become his most famous line: the "life of man" in the anarchic state of nature is "solitary, poor, nasty, brutish, and short."

To escape this terrible scenario and enter a realm of peace and security, Hobbes argued that individuals must contract together to live under a single, indisputable political authority—a sovereign power—that can enforce order and obedience to a set of laws. People keep only the fundamental right to self-preservation that led them to submit to the sovereign authority in the first place. Political communities for Hobbes are therefore artificial constructs created to allow humans to escape the miserable, insecure conditions of the state of nature. In the realm of relations between states, exactly the same conditions apply as for individuals in the state of nature. Since no overarching sovereign authority controls the international sphere, states are condemned to operate under conditions of perpetual anarchy in which the name of the game is survival, and survival can be achieved only through domination and the rational pursuit of pure self-interest. Justice and morality have no place in such an environment (Lawson, 2003: 34–5).

These are some of the basic ideas on which theories of *classical* realism in IR developed from the 1930s until roughly the late 1960s. Another central element of classical realism was its critique of liberalism. Indeed, classical realism is basically a conservative response to liberal international thought. One of the most prominent critics, E.H. Carr (1892–1982), is often described as a disillusioned liberal who considered the peace settlement that followed the First World War to have been a fiasco. As he saw it, the principal defect of liberalism was its almost complete blindness to the power factor in politics, which he likened to a law of nature. Carr argued that no political society, whether national or international, can exist unless people submit to certain rules of conduct. He also asserted the primacy of politics over ethics, arguing that as a matter of logic, rulers rule because of their superior strength, and the ruled submit because they are weaker. **Political obligation** comes from the recognition that "might is right." In preparing the ground for a theory of realism, Carr described his position as a reaction to utopianism and cited Machiavelli as initiating a revolt against utopianism in political thought in his own time (Carr, 1948: ch. 4). See **Box 15.3**.

15

KEY QUOTE BOX 15.3
Machiavelli on the "Real" versus the "Ideal"

. . . it appears to me more appropriate to follow up the real truth of a matter than the imagination of it; for many have pictured republics and principalities which in fact have never been seen and known, because how one lives is so far distant from how one ought to live that he who neglects what is done for what ought to be done sooner effects his ruin than his preservation (Machiavelli quoted in Carr, 1948: 63).

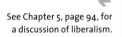
See Chapter 5, page 94, for a discussion of liberalism.

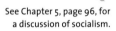
See Chapter 5, page 96, for a discussion of socialism.

15

Even so, Carr sought a balance between what he saw as two extremes. He concluded that sound political thinking must be based on elements of both **utopia** and reality, for when utopianism "has become a hollow and intolerable sham, which serves merely as a disguise for the interests of the privileged, the realist performs an indispensable service in unmasking it." Pure realism, on the other hand, offers "nothing but a naked struggle for power which makes any kind of international society impossible" (ibid.: 93). As we shall see, the idea of **international society** was to become a central theme in the English School's contribution to IR theory.

After the Second World War, as the Cold War began, IR developed rapidly in the US and acquired a distinctive realist tone. The principle figure in post-war American IR was the German-Jewish theorist Hans Morgenthau (1904–80). His 1948 book *Politics Among Nations* became a key text for political scientists and diplomats for a generation, going through multiple editions. Forced to flee Frankfurt, where he had taught law, Morgenthau eventually settled in the US in 1937, first in Chicago and then in New York. The Nazi regime had a formative impact on Morgenthau, who was dismayed by the collapse of the rule of law under Hitler, and the brutality of the Third Reich. His dismay reflected not only a general pessimism about human nature but the belief that, in the international system, power trumps morality most, if not all, of the time. This perception of the world coloured the advice he gave to the US government while serving as a long-term consultant at the State Department. Other influential thinkers of the era, including Hannah Arendt and George Kennan, held similar views (Brown, 2001: 31–4). Contemporary authors have compared Morgenthau's ideas to those of Thucydides. Richard Ned Lebow (2007: 52–70), for example, observes that both Thucydides and Morgenthau see politics, in any time and any place, as subject to a basic human instinct revolving around power.

Realism sees politics in the domestic sphere in much the same terms as it does politics in the international sphere, with one crucial difference: the state has a sovereign authority to enforce domestic order through police forces, courts, legislatures, and so on. Although the anarchic international sphere does have some mechanisms to establish order, they are comparatively fragile. These mechanisms include, first and foremost, a **balance of power** among the states that make up an international system. In realist thought, this balance of power has a **deterrent** effect: states rationally weigh the pros and cons of declaring war, and usually find it in their interest to maintain peace, in order to preserve themselves.

More sophisticated versions of realism also recognize the potential for a deterrent effect to arise from *sociability* in an international system. If a group of states acknowledges a "community of interests" or are otherwise bound by some common elements of culture, personal ties, and so on, then competition for power is greatly moderated and less likely to generate warfare. For example, no English-speaking countries have gone to war against each other since the War of 1812.

Nevertheless, some states and rulers will aggressively pursue what they perceive to be their own interests regardless of the costs. A state such as Athens during the Peloponnesian War, or a ruler such as Napoleon or Hitler, cannot be deterred. Thus even though everyday diplomacy may be peaceful, prudent leaders must always prepare for the worst-case scenario, since it takes only one international "bully" to destroy the system. Lebow quotes Morgenthau's wry observation that a balance of power "works best when needed least" (Lebow, 2007: 58); see **Box 15.4**.

KEY QUOTE BOX 15.4
Hans J. Morgenthau on Power Politics

International politics, like all politics, is a struggle for power. Whatever the ultimate aims of international politics, power is always the immediate aim. Statesmen and peoples may ultimately seek freedom, security, prosperity, or power itself. They may define their goals in terms of a religious, philosophic, economic, or social ideal. They may hope that this ideal will materialize through its own inner force, through divine intervention, or through the natural development of human affairs. But whenever they strive to realize their goal by means of international politics, they do so by striving for power (Morgenthau, 1948: 13).

Interestingly, Morgenthau was not always a proponent of war. In the 1960s, he protested against the Vietnam War and attended "teach-ins," arguing that military involvement in Indochina was not in America's national interest (see Brown, 2001: 33–4).

KEY POINTS

- "Realism" purports to analyze things as they really are, rather than as they ought to be. In this way it marks itself off from the idealism of liberal thought, which in the interwar years was often criticized as "utopianism." In developing their ideas, classical realist scholars of the mid-twentieth century claimed to belong to a tradition they traced to thinkers such as Thucydides, Machiavelli, and Hobbes.
- Realism comes in different forms, but virtually all realist international theory takes as its central focus the struggle for power and security of sovereign states in conditions of international anarchy. Under such conditions, the key to maintaining international order is deterrence, achieved through mechanisms such as the balance of power.

Behaviouralism versus Normative Analysis

We noted in the introduction to this book that the study of politics involves different kinds of analysis and **methodology**. Among the important influences on IR following the Second World War, especially in the US, was **behaviouralism**—an approach that rejects legal, historical, and comparative studies in favour of quantifiable data and relies on the scientific method to produce objective, *positive* knowledge. The closely related concept of **positivism** is grounded in the belief that there is a neutral, universally valid, body of knowledge about subjects such as politics and IR. Positivists argue that the social sciences can use the same methodology as the natural sciences—formulating and testing hypotheses, collecting empirical facts, identifying relevant variables, determining cause and effect—to make predictions in international politics. Because normative considerations are "unscientific," positivist approaches are by definition concerned with what is, rather than what *ought* to be.

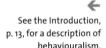

See the Introduction, p. 13, for a description of behaviouralism.

Normative analysis, by contrast, is very much concerned with norms, values and ethics. It asks questions about right and wrong, justice and injustice. For this reason, *normative international theory* does not attempt to sell itself as "scientific" in the sense that neutral or "objective" knowledge gained through experiments or statistical correlations is scientific. It is impossible to empirically "test" the truth or falsity of moral claims, and "cause and effect" in political science is very different from "cause and effect" in a field such as physics or chemistry. On the other hand, even though normative theory does not involve testing hypotheses or accumulating "facts," normative theorists still conduct systematic investigations and construct theory on the basis of reasoning as well as intuition.

In countering positivist critiques, most normative theorists would argue that knowledge produced by positivist methodologies is never completely objective, and that it often reflects the biases of the scientists concerned, even in the natural sciences. There have been many cases where bias is fairly obvious: for instance, when scientific studies commissioned by major coal or oil producers show that fossil fuels are not to blame for global warming, or that climate change is not occurring at all. Even where no interest appears to be served, it is difficult to maintain that any study in any field is entirely free of biases. Some go so far as to claim that all knowledge is a matter of interpretation. (We will consider some related issues in the next chapter.)

The positivist emphasis on what *is*, rather than what *ought* to be, may help us to understand some of the tenets of classical realism. As we have seen, key figures from Thucydides onwards have stressed that in the world of politics we need to accept what is "real" rather than striving for unattainable ideals. Thus even though realism (as a theory of politics) and positivism (as a methodology) are not the same thing, they share certain important assumptions. Morgenthau's classical realism was not very scientific, however, and many of his lists of lessons and observations could not be tested scientifically. Realist theory would take a more scientistic direction in the late 1970s, when it would be rebranded as **neorealism**.

KEY POINTS

* Positivists believe that the same basic scientific method employed in the natural sciences can be used to produce a universally valid and normatively neutral (that is, value-free) body of knowledge about subjects such as politics and IR.

- To the extent that realist IR is concerned with what *is*, rather than what *ought* to be, it shares something with positivism, even though classical realism is not particularly scientific and is largely incompatible with positivist methodology. Nevertheless, realism, liberalism, and positivism all subscribe, in one way or another, to notions of universally valid propositions.

The English School and the Idea of International Society

While social scientists in the US were absorbing the influence of behaviouralism, scholars on the other side of the Atlantic were developing very different approaches to IR. Gathering for the first time in London in 1959 to address core questions of international theory, they eventually came to be known as the English School (Dunne, 1998: xi). One member, Martin Wight, thought the entire field of IR was theoretically underdeveloped compared to the field of domestic politics. He proposed that just as political theory asks fundamental questions about the state, so international theory must ask fundamental questions about the international sphere as a "society of states." The fact that it had not done so meant that the entire field suffered from a profound intellectual poverty (Wight, 1966: 18). While individual members of the group adopted varying positions, some emphasizing realist perspectives and others subscribing to more liberal ideas, they shared a common interest in historical and normative approaches, rejecting the scientism of much academic work in the US.

As Wight's argument suggests, English School theorizing revolved around the concept of international society, understood as a society of sovereign states formed under conditions of anarchy. While English School theorists agreed that conditions in the international realm are less stable than domestic conditions, they were interested in the extent to which a stable order was still possible. A prominent member of the school, the Australian theorist Hedley Bull, accepted the basic tenets of realism, but proposed that state behaviour could be significantly changed through the creation of rules and institutions that would "socialize" the international environment and allow norms, values, and common interests to play more important roles. Basically, the experience of cooperating in international institutions would encourage states to develop *relationships* with one another. See **Box 15.5**.

15

KEY QUOTE BOX 15.5
Hedley Bull on the Society of States

[A] society of states (or international society) exists when a group of states, conscious of certain common interests and common values, form a society in the sense that they conceive themselves to be bound by a common set of rules in their relations with one another and share in the working of common institutions (Bull, 1997: 13).

Although the English School theorists agreed on the basic principles of international society, there were diverging views on the feasibility of establishing a common core of norms that all states could accept. The English-speaking states enjoyed warm relationships with one another, and the fact that they had fought together in two world wars demonstrated that close cooperation was possible between states, even if they were located in very different parts of the world and seemed on the surface to have diverse national interests. But would states that did not share a common language, culture, religion, or body of traditions find it so easy to get along?

Bull, Wight, and others were living in an era of decolonization; states very different from those of Europe were emerging around the world. Could a theory as Eurocentric as theirs apply universally? Could the norms of their society really be exported to the rest of the world? These questions about cultural difference drew attention to the fact that much theorizing in the discipline was characterized by **ethnocentric** assumptions.

Should norms be exported? Opinion was divided. Some, including Bull, adopted the **pluralist** position, recognizing that different "cultures" invariably have different norms and values and therefore different standards of justice. Some states might choose democracy, but others would prefer a hereditary chief. If each state has different standards of justice, there can be no universal yardstick against which behaviour can be evaluated. This argument seemed to promote a sort of ethical relativism, suggesting that the international system lacks not only a legitimate sovereign power but an overarching moral authority. The absence of a universal standard for "right conduct" does not necessarily prevent the formation of an international society, but it does mean that such a society will be fairly minimalist. International society would be held together simply by agreement on the importance of international order itself and a normative commitment to supporting the goal of peaceful *coexistence* (Dunne, 1998: 100). This position is close to **communitarianism**, according to which (as we saw in Chapters 1 and 4) morality develops within particular communities and basically holds good only for those communities. For the purposes of international relations, such moral communities are, in effect, states.

Others, however, adopted a "solidarist" approach, recognizing the plurality of values among states in the international sphere, but still seeking a more robust commitment to shared norms of both domestic and international behaviour, especially in the context of serious human rights abuses. **Solidarism** is not just about respecting state sovereignty; it implies a broader commitment to the solidarity of human beings around the world. While non-intervention may be taken as a norm of the society of states in the ordinary course of events, a solidarist position allows, in principle, for this norm to be overridden by an *extra*ordinary turn of events: for example, when a population group within a state becomes a target for genocide.

Solidarism thus shares some common ground with **cosmopolitanism**, which contemplates the transcendence of state boundaries. And for pluralists this means that it moves too far away from an international society, understood as a society *of* states, in the direction of a "world society" that de-emphasizes state boundaries and the notion of a state system as such (Buzan, 2004: esp. 139–60), stressing instead a sense of connectedness and shared humanity.

English School theory has experienced a significant revival in recent years. As two prominent authors have remarked, the English School's concern with the relationship

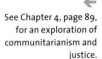

← See Chapter 1, page 39, for a discussion of communitarianism.

15

← See Chapter 4, page 89, for an exploration of communitarianism and justice.

between international order and human justice is at the heart of current debates about state sovereignty, global human rights culture, and **humanitarian intervention**. Nick Wheeler (2002), in reviewing cases of gross human rights abuses and genocide, has argued against the idea (increasingly common today) that Western countries intervene in humanitarian trouble spots solely for reasons of naked self-interest. Rather, he writes, political leaders are often forced by domestic public opinion to intervene:

> [T]he view that US and Western policy-makers manipulate the legitimating ideology of humanitarianism to serve selfish interests ignores the extent to which the solidarist claims advanced by Western states are a result of normative change at the domestic level: the pressure for humanitarian intervention in the cases of northern Iraq and Somalia came from domestic publics, shocked by television pictures of slaughter and suffering, demanding that something be done. (Wheeler, 2002: 288)

English School theory is also very concerned with legitimacy: under what conditions one state or a collection of states can rightfully intervene in another country to stop human rights abuses. Bodies such as the United Nations are seen crucial to IR since they can legitimately **intervene**, for humanitarian or other reasons (see Clark, 2005). In addition, important aspects of English School theorizing resonate with theories of social **constructivism**, which we will examine in the next chapter.

UN Photo/Paulo Filgueiras

PHOTO 15.1 The tension between sovereignty and intervention is never easily resolved. In April 2011, UN Secretary General Ban Ki-moon met with other world leaders in Doha, Qatar, to discuss the deteriorating situation in Libya. Ultimately, NATO took action.

KEY POINTS

- The English School, while accommodating both realist and liberal perspectives, pro-motes the idea of a society of states underpinned by a set of common norms. Its early members also embraced historical and normative enquiry, seeking a basis in political philosophy that distinguished its thinking from the positivism of much American IR.

- Two main approaches developed: "pluralists" sought to accommodate the varying norms, values, and standards of justice of different states within a framework of coexistence based on respect for sovereignty. "Solidarists," by contrast, promoted a set of common norms and standards, including respect for human rights and, in exceptional circumstances, a right of humanitarian intervention.

Neoliberalism and Neorealism

The creation of the United Nations in 1945 reflected the classic liberal desire to make the world a better place. The UN's founders did not consider the old League to have been such a failure that its institutions could not serve as models for the new organization. Among the features of the League that the UN incorporated were the General Assembly and Secretariat presided over by a Secretary-General, the Court of Justice, and the executive Council. In addition, specialized agencies were formed to assist in building an international system with a strong economic and social framework. As decolonization progressed in Africa, the Middle East, Asia, and the Pacific—"globalizing" the liberal principle of self-determination—the UN's membership grew, and by the mid-1950s it was becoming global in scope.

Both liberal and realist thought continued to develop, however, and in the 1970s, each gave rise to a "neo" form that replaced the somewhat impressionistic approaches of the past with more scientific methods. Neorealism and neoliberalism both reflected the belief that theory should be parsimonious, falsifiable, and amenable to testing.

Neorealism, also known as "structural" realism, concentrates on the structure of the international system, largely ignoring domestic politics. It argues that the logic of the system sends cues that determine the actions of state-based decision-makers, rather than the other way around. Thus neorealism maintains that leaders should not bow to domestic pressure; nor should they act according to their own private morality. They must look only to the international system and make rational calculations based on what is happening there. The seminal theorist in this area, as we shall see, was Kenneth Waltz, whose 1979 work *Theory of International Politics* reflected a more scientifically robust approach to understanding world politics.

Since the Second World War, liberal IR theorists had come to accept the realist position that the international sphere was essentially anarchic. Nevertheless, neoliberals such as Robert Keohane (1984) challenged what they saw as neorealism's simplistic approach to this reality, arguing that international institutions such as the UN had a crucial role to play in reducing the negative effects of anarchy and power politics. They also argued for recognition of non-state actors—from transnational corporations to NGOs such as the Red Cross/Red Crescent or the International Chamber of Commerce—as significant factors in IR (Keohane and Nye 1977: 23). Today these bodies are seen as constituting an **international civil society** that operates alongside the state system and the regional and international institutions based on that system, even if states remain the primary actors. Another neoliberal innovation was a finer-grained analysis of sovereign states. Whereas neorealists tended to regard states as unitary actors in the international sphere, neoliberals acknowledged that many state characteristics and modes of behaviour were influenced by domestic political constraints.

This model had important implications for international political economy, since the neoliberals expanded the understanding of security (and potential threats to it) to include not only military factors but a variety of economic and other resources deployed by the state and other actors such as multinational corporations. As Keohane and Nye (1977) argued, relations of interdependence are generally much more complicated than the relations generated by strictly military alliances, especially since the processes of industrialization, modernization, and globalization have given rise to many more dynamics than can be accommodated in realist theory. Thus neoliberals began to describe the modern international system, with its multiple actors, agencies, and forces, as a system of **complex interdependence**. Nye posited a different kind of world from the one depicted by realists, one in which states are not the only significant actors, economic manipulation can take the place of military force, and the dominant goal is no longer security but welfare (Nye, 2005: 207).

As we have seen, liberalism has always been deeply concerned with creating positive conditions for peace. The link between theory and practice here can be seen not just in the construction of international institutions but in the work of the peace movement more generally. Specialist peace studies programs in universities and other institutions around the world have supported the work of international institutions, from Sweden, the home of the Nobel Peace Prize, to Japan, where peace activism has had a high profile ever since the end of the Second World War (no doubt because of the devastation wreaked by the atomic bombs dropped on Hiroshima and Nagasaki). From the end of the Second World War until 1952, Japan was occupied by American forces, and during that time it adopted a new constitution that forbade the creation of any conventional military force. Although it does maintain a basic defensive force, it has been reluctant even to deploy peacekeepers (MacDonald, 2005: 18–20).

With neoliberalism providing a plausible alternative account of the international system, neorealism has restated the prime importance of power in an anarchic international sphere. Adopting a more scientific approach, neorealists have sought a stripped-down, "parsimonious" theory of IR that can be used to generate testable hypotheses. Waltz, in his pioneering *Theory of International Politics* (1979), proposed that the determining factor in the behaviour of individual states is the *structure* of the international state system as a whole. Although states remain the principal actors, Waltz argues that there is no need for IR theorists to understand the details of their domestic politics, since these have little, if any, effect on the larger constraints and opportunities that exist in the international system.

Waltz had laid some of the groundwork for neorealism/structuralism in an earlier work entitled *Man, the State and War* (1959). Here he identified what he called three "images" of international relations, according to which the causes of war might be found in (1) the individual, (2) the state, and (3) the international system of states. The first image focused on human failings—greed, stupidity, misdirected aggression (recall the early realist Morgenthau's pessimism regarding human nature). The second focused on the internal (domestic) organization of states; and the third focused on the anarchic structure of the international system—specifically, the absence of restraints. Waltz argued that the third "image" was the one that IR should direct its attention to. In effect, Waltz eliminated both human nature and domestic politics as factors in international politics, arguing that the struggle for power is determined by the structure of the system, which imposes its own logic on the actors involved.

Later neorealists have continued to see the international system as a dangerous place. John Mearsheimer, for example, argues that the anarchic nature of that system, in which there is no guarantee that one state will not attack another, means that each state must acquire sufficient power to protect itself in the event of attack: "In essence, great powers are trapped in an iron cage where they have little choice but to compete with each other for power if they hope to survive" (Mearsheimer, 2007: 72). However, this competition creates other problems, because the action taken by one state to enhance its security relative to other states (by building up its military forces) will invariably provoke other states to enhance their military capabilities, making all of them more dangerous than they were before. The result is a **security dilemma**, in which the more each state arms itself against a rival, the more insecure it feels (see Herz, 1950). This situation illustrates the key realist concept of the balance of power in so far as each state strives to increase its capabilities in order to balance any increase in the capabilities of other states, or at least those states that are considered relevant to the equation.

Waltz and Mearsheimer are certainly not the only neorealists. Another influential writer is Joseph Grieco (1988), who has elaborated on the idea of relative and absolute gains among states in terms of power and influence. Whereas liberals believe that states are content to make an absolute gain (measured against their own existing capacities rather than relative to other states), realists hold that states always seek both absolute and relative gains. Furthermore, states may cooperate to enhance their overall position within the state system, but realists believe that states will cheat if they think this will give them greater power, or if continued cooperation appears likely to weaken their position. Overall, though, relative gains matter more to realists, because international politics is about competition. For example, it doesn't matter if both the US and China profit from their trading relationship: if China gains more from it and thus has *relatively* more money to buy weapons to impose its will on the international system, then the US becomes the loser in the relationship. Because economic power can be converted into military power, it represents "latent" power.

Another branch of the structural school distinguishes between defensive and offensive realism and relates these concepts to **hegemony**—a situation in which there is a dominant centre of power. Offensive realists such as Mearsheimer (who is critical of the rise of China) hold that states constantly seek to maximize their power relative to others in the system, which is a perfectly rational means of guaranteeing survival. A state that acquires hegemonic status enjoys the greatest measure of security precisely because of its superior power. If a state does not seek to maximize its power, it will appear weak to its rivals, and therefore risk being dominated by them. A lack of willingness to arm signals to competitors that a strategic vacuum exists, which will be filled by others. Defensive realists like Waltz, on the other hand, argue that seeking too much power will provoke a reaction in other states, creating a security dilemma. Waltz argues that states should strive to have *enough* power, but not so much that they will worry or anger their rivals (he never specifies how much is enough). Although the combined power of other states may well be greater than that of the aspiring hegemon, leading ultimately to its defeat, realists of all varieties see the dangers of expansionism and other ill-advised adventures abroad. According to Mearsheimer, almost all realists opposed the 2003 Iraq War, which in fact proved to be a strategic mistake for the US and its allies (2007: 86).

Ideas about absolute and relative gains, offensive realism and defensive realism, are variations on the neorealist theme. Some of these ideas have been criticized for over-simplifying IR theory, limiting its ability to ask deeper questions about the state of the political world and what the future might hold. The feminist critique of neorealism is particularly poignant, as we will see in the next chapter. Overall, critics point out that neorealists have little to say about pressing problems that go beyond military security, from global environmental problems to imbalances in resource allocation and consumption around the world. In their defence, neorealists argue that these concerns are less pressing than the problem of weapons of mass destruction in the wrong hands. Once the threat of total annihilation disappears, the neorealist argument runs, we can turn to other issues; until then, international politics must focus on existential security threats. Liberals, of course, point out that neorealism says nothing about questions of justice either for present or for future generations. Today a school of *neo*classical realism is emerging that seeks to broaden the scope of realist theory and return to some of the issues that Morgenthau and others addressed in the 1940s (see Rose, 1998: 144–72). We may well see a new school of realist thought develop along these lines in the future.

KEY POINTS

- Central to neoliberalism is the idea of "complex interdependence," according to which there are multiple actors, agencies, and forces at work in the international system, and the boundaries between the domestic and international spheres are porous. States are seen as operating alongside many other significant actors, and economic power can be just as effective a tool as military force. For some neoliberal thinkers, welfare is at least as important a goal as security (traditionally the primary concern).

- Neorealism takes structure to be the primary determinant of behaviour in the international sphere and argues that it must be studied on its own terms, without reference to the domestic politics of the states concerned. By eliminating human nature and individual agency as relevant factors, Waltz narrowed the scope of IR and produced a more parsimonious theory, which its proponents say can generate testable hypotheses.

Conclusion

This chapter has shown how, and under what circumstances, two competing bodies of IR theory came to form a framework for the discipline. Although explicit theorizing about IR did not begin until the twentieth century, both liberalism and realism drew on existing bodies of political thought to address basic problems of international order. Neither school of thought represents a single body of theory: both contain several different strands, and both have been modified over the years. At the same time, both liberalism and realism assume that certain propositions are universally valid—the "fact" of international anarchy is a prime example. In the next chapter we will consider some more recent bodies of theory that have challenged these propositions.

15

? KEY QUESTIONS

- What were the major factors behind the rise of liberal international theory in the early twentieth century? What did the early theorists hope to achieve?
- In what way does the right to national self-determination strengthen the legitimacy of the nation-state idea?
- Why did E.H. Carr describe early liberals as utopians? Was this description fair?
- What are the distinguishing features of classical realist thought?
- What is "positivism"? In what sense does it critique normative theory?
- How does the idea of "international society" contribute to our understanding of international relations?
- How could the English School accommodate both realism and liberalism and remain coherent?
- In what ways does neorealism differ from classical realism? How do offensive and defensive realism differ from one another?
- Is neorealism's parsimony a strength or a weakness?

📖 FURTHER READING

Angell, Norman (1934). *The Great Illusion*. London: W. Heinemann.
A critique of nationalist expansionism and arms-racing in early twentieth century Europe. Originally published in 1910, it is an early and influential statement of idealism, arguing against the notion that national prosperity depends on a preponderance of military power. A sample of the text is available at http://net.lib.byu.edu/rdh7/wwi/1914m/illusion.html.

Mearsheimer, John J. (2001). *The Tragedy of Great Power Politics*. New York: Norton.
Mearsheimer practically invented offensive realism as a focus of academic inquiry. In this work, he argues for a hard-headed approach to international politics, where power and self-interest take centre-stage. Goodwill, altruism, and alliance-building are far less important, in his view, than the need to protect one's own national security. Mearsheimer is particularly critical of the US for what he sees as its soft approach to engagement with China.

Bellamy, Alex (ed.) (2005). *International Society and its Critics*. Oxford: Oxford University Press.
An edited book in which leading scholars consider "international society" and the ways it is theorized. There is a particular focus on the English School and its relevance to the analysis of contemporary issues such as global governance, international law, and terrorism.

Nye, Joseph Jr, and David A. Welch (2010). *Understanding Global Conflict and Cooperation: An Introduction to Theory and History*. 8th edn. London: Pearson Higher Education.
Substantially updated by Canadian IR theorist David Welch, this 8th edition of Nye's classic work combines theory and history to explain cooperation and conflict between global actors. Nye is well known for his promotion of neoliberalism in the 1970s, as well as his work on "soft" and "smart" power during the George W. Bush era.

📱 WEB LINKS

www.irtheory.com
The International Relations (IR) Theory website describes itself as an online resource for students, scholars, and other professionals interested in International Relations theory.

http://isacanada.igloogroups.org/
The Canadian Homepage of the International Studies Association, with links to articles by Canadian IR scholars, as well as ISA Canada's Distinguished Scholars profiles. It also features funding and other opportunities for graduate students.

15

Alternative Approaches to International Relations

16

CHAPTER OVERVIEW

Liberal and realist theorists of IR probe each other's ideas for faults and weaknesses, but both operate within the same paradigm: an international order of sovereign states interacting under conditions of anarchy. Neither theory has challenged capitalism and its implications for the global economy. With the exception of Marxism, major challenges to traditional approaches did not emerge until roughly the 1970s.

These challenges gained impetus with the end of the Cold War, which prompted many scholars to start asking new questions about the world of IR and its assumptions. In addition to the place of Marxism in IR and some important critiques of capitalism and modernization inspired by it, this chapter considers five broad schools of thought: Critical Theory, constructivism, feminism, postmodernism, and postcolonial theory. Some of these approaches have been discussed in previous chapters (Marxism and power in Chapter 2, feminism and postmodernism in Chapter 6). Here the focus is on their implications for the study of IR.

Marxism

Neither Karl Marx nor his close collaborator Friedrich Engels wrote extensively on international matters. Nevertheless, their ideas have had a very significant influence on critical approaches to the field. Here we examine several major strands of Marxist-influenced theory that are directly relevant to international politics, including dependency theory, world-system theory, and contemporary critical theory (CT). Virtually all the strands discussed here are variants of "Western Marxism"; the legacy of Marx and Engels has been theorized differently in **authoritarian** communist regimes, especially in China and the former USSR. However, some early communists, including Lenin, Stalin, and Mao, did contribute to the development of Marxist ideas in international politics. The models of "scientific socialism" exported from China and the USSR to the developing world, for example, were based on Maoist and Stalinist principles.

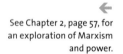

See Chapter 2, page 57, for an exploration of Marxism and power.

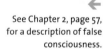

See Chapter 2, page 57, for a description of false consciousness.

We introduced the theme of power in Marxist theory in Chapter 2, where we discussed ideology, **hegemony**, and the ways in which ruling classes maintain control and promote the legitimacy of the capitalist enterprise. The Marxian notion of ideology as "false consciousness" is especially important, explaining how the interests of any ruling class are presented as natural, inevitable, and desirable and therefore compatible with the interests of subject classes. This ideology is "false" in the sense that it masks the deeper "truth" about domination and subordination, and who benefits from them. Here we should also note the Marxist emphasis on the role of the **bourgeoisie**, which is generally defined as a merchant and/or propertied class wielding essential economic power and control. In their classic statement of the principles and purposes of communism, Marx and Engels describe the crucial role that the bourgeoisie played in the spread of capitalism around the world through **imperialism** (the forerunner to the contemporary phenomenon of **globalization**). The opening passages of the *Communist Manifesto* (1848) describe how the "need of a constantly expanding market for its products chases the bourgeoisie over the entire surface of the globe," settling and establishing connections everywhere. The first Russian communist leader, V.I. Lenin (1870–1924), developed a more elaborate critique of imperialism as the final stage of capitalism, explaining how its parasitic exploitation of peripheral countries increases the gap between rich and poor nations and leads to wars for control of territory and resources (Lenin, 1986).

Since the Second World War, the most prominent figures working in this area have been André Gunder Frank and Immanuel Wallerstein. Frank's dependency theory and world system analysis use a deep historical perspective, reaching back over several thousand years to de-centre Europe as the principal agent of historical change. This distinguishes Frank's view from most versions of globalization, which put Europe and

◀ A detail of a mural depicting the Italian political theorist Antonio Gramsci in the town of Orgosolo, Sardinia (© Marina Spironetti/Getstock).

the West in general at the centre of virtually all world-transforming dynamics. Frank's theories resonate with some of the ideas we introduced in Chapter 12, notably the need to "de-centre" and "provincialize" Europe, and to challenge the appropriateness of the Western path to **modernity**.

See the discussion of infrapolitics and subaltern studies in Chapter 12, page 246.

Frank's dependency theory is part of a larger critique of modernization and development theories that was initially applied to Latin America and then to the Developing world in general. It explains underdevelopment in poor countries in terms of the exploitative legacy of Western imperialism and **colonialism** rather than local cultural factors. Independence has scarcely improved matters for many Third World countries because the underlying structures of exploitation remain. Many postcolonial indigenous elites have simply colluded with the "core" states (generally those of the industrialized North) in continuing relations of exploitation. A major concern of dependency theory is core–periphery relations and their role in the world system (Frank, 1967; Frank and Gills, 1996).

Wallerstein's world system approach critiques the totality of exploitative economic and political relations from a sociological as well as a historical perspective. He broadens the basic assumptions of dependency theory by questioning whether the international system really is based on a nation-state model. Wallerstein's choice of the term *world* as opposed to *international* was deliberate, since the capitalist world economy transcends the nation-state model of separate political and economic units. Further, his world system "is a *social* system, one that has boundaries, structures, member groups, rules of legitimation, and coherence" (Wallerstein, 1976: 229; emphasis added). In addition, Wallerstein offers a thought-provoking critique of the way social science is constructed as a discipline, arguing that it forces thinking processes, especially in terms of "development," along very restricted pathways (Wallerstein, 2001).

KEY POINTS

- Marx and Engels' critique of capitalism provided a basis for later critiques of traditional IR theories. Marx and Engels were also the first to observe how capitalism is implicated in the development of a global system.
- Dependency theory and world systems analysis draw on Marxist thought in critiquing theories of modernization and development, especially in relation to the Third World and the exploitative structure of the international economic and political systems.

Critical Theory

The term "Critical Theory" (usually abbreviated as CT) refers to a range of social science theorizing that critiques traditional theories of society and politics such as liberalism, realism, and conservatism. It includes, but is not limited to, Marxist theory, although most versions of CT address the negative impact of capitalism on social life in one way or another. However, both the problems identified and the remedies proposed can differ widely. Many proponents of CT have moved away from the main premises of Marxist theory, and its focus on economics and class struggle, while retaining its emphasis on the ethical notion of **emancipation** from oppressive social and material conditions. In part, this move has been prompted by the collapse of the Soviet system and the marketization of China—the only other viable communist model.

16

A formative influence on CT was the thought of the Italian intellectual Antonio Gramsci (1891–1937). Focusing on the *naturalization* of power in the creation of hegemony by elites, Gramsci argued that ruling classes maintain power and control, even in the absence of constant coercive force, because they make inequalities seem natural, inevitable, and even right. Although the idea that *cultural power* can be used to control "hearts and minds" resonates with the Marxist idea of ideology as false consciousness, Gramsci emphasized the consensual nature of the masses' support for hegemony; see **Box 16.1**.

BIOGRAPHY BOX 16.1
Antonio Gramsci (1891–1937)

Antonio Gramsci was a political theorist and activist who at one time served as the leader of the Italian Communist Party. Deeply opposed to fascism, he was imprisoned under Mussolini's regime. His notes and essays were collected and published posthumously as *Prison Notebooks*. Gramsci accepted Marx's analysis of capitalism and the idea that struggle between the ruling and working classes was the driving force of society. But he rejected the materialist basis of Marxist theory, including the notion of an "objective reality" that could be described "scientifically," arguing that "reality" does not exist independently of human interest, purpose, or interpretation. Similarly, he drew attention to the danger of believing that society as we know it is the way it should be, of assuming "that it is 'natural' that [what exists] should exist, that it could not do otherwise than exist. . . ." (Gramsci, 1967). The Gramscian theory of cultural hegemony combines coercion and consent to explain how the dominated (the masses) come to accept their subordination by an elite, as well as the values of that elite, as part of the natural order of things.

Later theorists, such as Robert W. Cox, have found Gramsci's insights highly pertinent. Earlier conceptions of hegemony focused on material (mainly economic and military) capabilities, but Gramsci's cultural hegemony opened the way for Cox to explore the *hegemony of theories and ideas* in the international sphere. Cox is well-known for declaring that "theory is always *for* someone, and *for* some purpose" (Cox 1981: 128). In other words, theorists are never neutral in their selection and interpretation of facts around us, and since their theories reflect subjective values and interests, they tend to support those values and interests. If facts and values do not exist independently of each other, it follows that no theory can be "value-free" and no knowledge can be totally objective.

Realism, Cox suggests, is an *ideology of the status quo*. It supports the existing international order and therefore the interests of those who prosper under it. Furthermore, because it perceives the existing order as *natural*, inevitable and unchanging, it sees any difficulties that arise within the order as problems to be solved within the parameters *of* that order. The order itself does not come under challenge. By contrast, Cox and other Critical Theorists insist that no order is "natural" or immune to change. All political orders, whatever their size—from the smallest community to the world at large—are constructed by humans and can in principle be reconstructed in a more just and equitable way. CT aims to provide the intellectual framework for emancipation from unfair and unjust social, political, and economic arrangements that benefit the few at the expense of the many. To the extent that **liberalism** participates in the perpetuation of injustices and effectively justifies inequalities, especially through capitalism, it is subject to a similar critique.

The most creative Critical Theories do not simply critique existing theories and practices; they put forward alternative visions of how the world *could* (and *should*) be. Andrew Linklater sets out such a vision in his book *The Transformation of Political Community: Ethical Foundations of the Post-Westphalian Era* (1998). Although modernity has a dark side, Linklater argues that it still carries within it the seeds of the **Enlightenment**'s emancipatory aims. While modernity gave us the Westphalian state system, its "unfinished project" is a post-Westphalian world in which states, as political communities, no longer operate in the service of inclusion and exclusion. This transformation, he suggests, seems most likely to occur in the very region that gave rise to the state system in the first place and that has since produced the European Union—a project with considerable normative potential. The German theorist Jürgen Habermas sees similar possibilities in the European project.

Perhaps the most detailed study of what emancipation means and should mean has been done by Ken Booth. He defines emancipation as

> the freeing of people (as individuals and groups) from those physical and human constraints which stop them from carrying out what they would freely wish to do. War and threat of war is one of those constraints, together with poverty, poor education, political oppression, and so on (Booth, 1991: 319).

For Booth, emancipation is closely tied to security, because it is emancipation "rather than power or order" than brings about real security (Booth, 2005: 191). He and Hayward Alker have done ground-breaking work in promoting the concept of emancipation in world politics.

Overall, CT poses a strong challenge to neorealism, with its focus on hard power and "facts" about the world. It also emphasizes the "constructed" character of the social/political world. But it is not the only school of thought in IR to have taken up the idea of the constructed nature of social reality. There is now a more general school of constructivist thought in IR that has become increasingly influential in recent years. We will consider that school next.

KEY POINTS

- CT provides an intellectual and normative framework promoting a project of emancipation from social, political, and economic arrangements that benefit the few at the expense of the many through hegemonic control in a system of coercion and consent.
- CT emphasizes that all political, economic, and cultural orders are humanly constructed, not dictated by nature. Once recognized, relations of domination and subordination can be challenged at their foundations rather than simply taken for granted.
- Cosmopolitan elements of CT transcend nation-state barriers to produce broader, more inclusive notions of political community.

16

Constructivism

Constructivism draws on a significant tradition of European social theory developed by classical sociologists such as Émile Durkheim, Max Weber, and Karl Mannheim. Berger and Luckman, in their influential work *The Social Construction of Reality* (1966), argued that social order (beliefs, norms, values, interests, rules, institutions, and so on) is an ongoing human production. Like CT, constructivism argues that the *ontological status* of that order—its very being or existence—is the product not of nature but of human activity alone. To understand how social orders are produced, a theory of institutionalization is required that incorporates a process of habitualization in which social actions that are practised routinely solidify over time into taken-for-granted constructs that we call **institutions** (59–61). If we consider the world of international relations through the lens of social constructivist theory, we can see the extent to which it is a "world of our making."

Social constructivism challenges the way both neorealism and neoliberalism take the primacy of states and the anarchic character of the international system as givens. Some constructivists are especially critical of the tendency in traditional theories to focus largely on *material* forces such as guns and bombs, ignoring the *ideational* forces—norms, values, rules, symbols—that influence how people act in the world. They argue that it is in the realm of ideas that *meaning* is created, including the meaning of material objects. As one of the best-known constructivist theorists, Alexander Wendt, points out, a gun is perceived differently in the hands of an enemy than in the hands of an ally. In other words, "enmity is a social, not material, relation" (Wendt, 1996: 50).

This is not to deny the importance of material force: it is simply to argue that recognizing the connection between material and ideational forces provides a better understanding of how "social facts" are produced. Thus fundamental institutions, such as states and their sovereign properties, are social rather than material facts constructed at an *inter-subjective* level by agents (us!). **Anarchy** and **sovereignty**—or any other concept invented by humans—have no existence or meaning except in the minds of the humans who believe in them. Thus anarchy is simply "what states make of it" (Wendt, 1992: 391–425). The institutions we take for granted as "realities" of the world around us—the market, the government, the UN, the stock exchange—are invented by humans. It is precisely because these "things" are ideational, not material, that we cannot see, feel, hear, smell, or taste them. When we treat these ideational constructs as if they were actual "things," we *reify* them.

All this casts a different light on the relationship between *agents* and *structures* (people and institutions). Here many constructivists emphasize that agents and structures are *mutually constituted*. In other words, humans are born into an existing world—one that has both material and ideational aspects—and are shaped by that world as they mature and develop their own ideational perspectives. The existing structures, including norms and values, that shape each emerging generation of agents are not natural but were put in place by previous generations of agents. Thus it is theoretically possible for each new generation to change them. However, such change requires significant *norm change* among the relevant actors.

A close study of post-war Japan led Peter Katzenstein (1996) to observe that institutional change is often slowed by the deep entrenchment of certain norms. Although "[n]orms

← See Chapter 7, page 140, for a description of structuration.

16

AP Photo/Ira Schwartz

PHOTO 16.1 Mikhail Gorbachev and Ronald Reagan in Red Square in May 1988. Wendt argued that the warm relations between the two leaders helped to ease the tensions of the Cold War, facilitating mutual concessions, and, eventually, an end to the conflict.

are not static; they are contested and contingent," Katzenstein argues that they do not change in response to "the push-and-pull of daily politics" (1996: 3), for two reasons. First, "actors attribute far deeper meanings to the historical battles that define collective identities than to the transient conflicts" that characterize everyday politics. Second, "the taken-for-grantedness of *institutionalized* norms [such as the law] limits the range of choice at any particular time. . . . History and institutions thus give norms both importance and endurance" (1996: 3).

Constructivism, like other bodies of theory, comes in different forms. Some versions, such as Wendt's, tend towards *rationalism* and do not move too far away from the dominant realist and liberal approaches. "Rationalist" theories subscribe to the idea that there is an underlying rationality that directs human behaviour towards particular ends. They also assume that knowledge can be obtained through empirical investigation. Wendt is

16

seen as the most realist of the constructivists because he accepts the standard assumption that states are the central actors in a system that is essentially anarchic. By contrast, *reflectivist* scholarship, sometimes called post-positivist or interpretive, rejects the positivist scientism of rationalist approaches, challenging the knowledge they claim to produce (Smith, 2000: 374–402). However it may be defined or located, constructivism has become an increasingly popular mode of IR scholarship for those seeking more complex, socially oriented accounts of the contemporary world.

KEY POINTS

- Constructivism draws on a body of European social theory developed by earlier thinkers such as Durkheim, Weber, and Mannheim. Constructivists argue that the components of social order, including beliefs, norms, values, interests, rules, and institutions, are socially constructed by humans.
- Constructivism criticizes neo-realism and neoliberalism for focusing on *material* forces at the expense of *ideational* forces, formed through social interaction, that are equally important. These forces are the norms, values, rules, and symbols that influence how people act in the world.
- Theoretically, agents can change existing structures, but change is often slow and difficult because people have become habitualized to a certain way of thinking.

Feminism and Gender Theory

In her book *Bananas, Beaches and Bases* (2001), Cynthia Enloe asks a question often posed by feminists in the field of IR: "Where are the women?" In fact, mainstream accounts of world politics often do not take into account the roles that women play as leaders, followers, supporters, victims, collaborators, innovators, and authors of resistance (Enloe and Zalweski, 1999: 138–9).

Feminism in IR is not a single body of theory. It incorporates a range of approaches to the problems of **patriarchy**: liberal, socialist, critical, constructivist, postcolonial, and postmodern. Therefore it draws from, interacts with, contributes to, and often critiques other schools of theory. Thus "liberal feminists" will draw on certain insights of liberal theory—for example, the essential equality of all individuals—to critique the ways in which conventional liberal theory has ignored or even supported patriarchal structures of authority. Feminism is a principal strand of the broader field of gender theory, which is concerned with both femininities and masculinities.

The study of gender issues in IR has been carried out largely by feminist scholars concerned with how women have been depicted in or (more often) written out of the script of international politics. In other words, the sphere of the international—characterized largely by the struggle for power in an anarchical world—has often been depicted in such masculine terms that women seem to disappear as active agents. They are painted as essentially passive, simply supporting men in their various roles as soldiers and statesmen. The same applies to studies of the global economy, where trade and commerce tend to be depicted as the preserve of men. Any woman who becomes prominent in these spheres is always an exception to the rule.

Yet the contributions of feminist IR theorists can be enormous. They can help us challenge many assumptions about politics, the military, and what we consider to be normal. In her book *Does Khaki Become You?* (1983) Enloe examined how our understandings of the state and war change when we uncover the real roles played by women, which state leaders make an active effort to hide. She later explained the rationale behind her research:

> If I could show that the state is so dependent on these people called military wives who are never thought of as serious political actors, I could show two things: one, that states were more fragile than was presumed because look, they were dependent upon a whole group of actors that people didn't give the time of day to; and two, the state is conscious of that dependence and expends scarce resources to try to control those women" (Enloe and Zalewski, 1999: 141–2).

Historically, feminist scholars began to make an impact in political science in the 1960s and 1970s, but it was not until the late 1980s that they came to question the apparent absence of women in *international* politics and economics and to examine how traditional IR discourse, because it was founded on masculine assumptions, excluded women as participants. That this has been made to appear "normal" or "natural"—even to many women—is a major epistemological and ontological problem. Like other groups that have found themselves marginalized by a dominant mainstream, many feminists have questioned the extent to which "knowledge" itself is constructed to suit the interests of that mainstream.

Traditional IR "knowledge" has often implied the creation of socially constructed boundaries that reflect distinctly male views of how the world operates. As theorist Jill Steans explains questioning masculine assumptions about politics means looking at the many artificial divisions that IR scholars have created: "rigid boundaries between the international (outside) and domestic (inside) and between private and public realms [that] removed gender relations from the field of inquiry." Since gender has played a central role in the "carving out of political spaces, the construction of identities and demarcating the boundaries of community in practices of 'state-making'," we have to be careful not to see such borders and arrangements as the product of nature, but of war and other instruments of **statecraft** that exclude as well as include (Steans, 2003: 43–4). Debates over human rights are of particular concern to feminists, who see issues of gender and identity as transcending state borders and requiring action at the international level.

Certainly, feminism comes in various forms and there are different strands even within feminist IR. Here we consider two general typologies. The first sets out three broad overlapping forms of feminism that reflect particular theoretical/methodological orientations:

1. *Empirical feminism* focuses on correcting the denial or misrepresentation of women as active agents in the international sphere based on mistaken assumptions: for example, that women are either absent from or irrelevant to international processes and activities; or that male experiences count for both sexes.
2. *Analytical feminism* addresses gender biases more directly by highlighting the asymmetrical and socially constructed concepts of masculinity and femininity evident in traditional theoretical frameworks in IR that favour masculine interpretative practices.

16

See the discussion of feminism in Chapter 6, page 119.

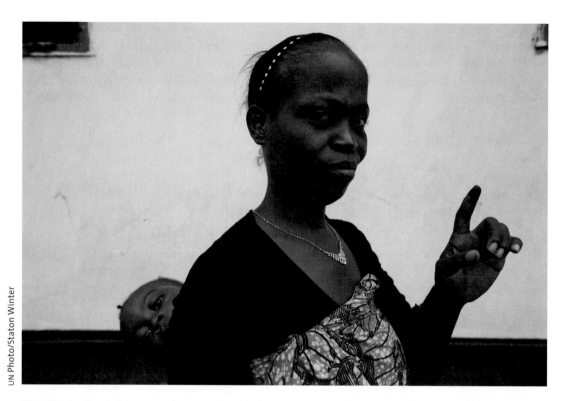

UN Photo/Staton Winter

PHOTO 16.2 Feminists argue that women and children are often taken for granted in situations of war. Here, a woman in Monrovia, Liberia, shows her inked finger, indicating that she has voted in the election of October 2011. Of the nearly 2 million voters in that election, half were women.

3. *Normative feminism* incorporates reflection on IR theorizing and feminist concerns within a broader, explicitly normative agenda for global change. For example, normative feminism questions not only how gender hierarchies are reproduced in IR but also how they serve to naturalize other forms of power (True, 2005: 216–29).

A second typology, devised by two other feminist scholars, uses more traditional IR labels:

1. *Liberal feminism* highlights the subordination of women in world politics but does not challenge the premises of traditional IR. It is similar to empirical feminism in that it investigates particular problems—say, of refugee women, gendered income inequalities, trafficking of women, rape in war, and so on—usually within a positivist framework. Liberal feminism seeks equality of women in a man's world without questioning the foundations of that world.
2. *Critical feminism* builds on Critical Theory, examining relations of domination and subordination, the play of power in world politics, and the relationship between material and ideational factors through a gender-sensitive lens. As a theory seeking action and not just interpretation, it promotes a project of emancipation that takes explicit account of women's subordination.
3. *Feminist constructivism* criss-crosses the terrain of constructivist IR. Some practitioners concede much methodological ground to **positivism** (as do American constructivists

such as Wendt). Others lean towards a postpositivist questioning of the foundations of knowledge. Feminist constructivism often focuses attention on ideational forces and the essentially social nature of the international sphere.

4. *Feminist poststructuralism*, like poststructuralism (or postmodernism), highlights the construction of meaning through language and, in particular, the relationship between knowledge and power and the extent to which these are reflected in dichotomies or oppositions. Feminist poststructuralism critiques the way dichotomies such as strong/weak, rational/emotional, and public/private, not to mention masculinity/femininity, have served to empower men at the expense of women.

5. *Postcolonial feminism* often goes hand in hand with feminist poststructuralism in exposing certain relations of domination and subordination, but focuses its critique on how these relations were established through imperialism and colonialism and persist through to the present period. In addition, postcolonial feminists are often critical of the way Western feminists construct knowledge about non-Western women, as well their tendency to treat "women" as a universal and homogeneous category regardless of differences in culture, social class, race, and geographical location. (Tickner and Sjoberg, 2007: 188–92.)

We next consider feminism and gender in relation to traditional IR's central concern—war—which is one of the most conspicuously gendered activities of all. Not only have great matters of state such as war been almost exclusively the preserve of males, but active participation has been historically confined largely to male warriors. Feminists have made several important contributions to security studies. By questioning the supposed irrelevance of women in international security and exposing the workings of gender and power in international relations, they have ensured that women's experiences are now taken more seriously, and gender-based exclusion from decision-making roles is at least recognized. Feminist security theory has also questioned the extent to which women are actually "secured" by the protective mantle of the state in both war and peace. At the same time, the unreflective tendency to link women with peace is now more likely to be balanced by recognition of the fact that women have long participated in wars, if not as warriors then at least in vital supporting roles.

The attention to gender issues forced by feminists has also helped to unpack the concept of masculinity itself (Blanchard, 2003: 1290). Connell has pointed out that the "rugged male warrior" type, often constructed as an ideal, is a stereotype which many "real" men do not actually fit (Connell cited in Tickner, 1992: 6). More recently, Connell has argued that "There is a gender politics within masculinity" and we need also to recognize the power relations between different kinds of masculinity "constructed through practices that exclude and include, that intimidate, exploit, and so on" (Connell, 2005: 37). Another scholar has investigated the male soldier's gendered construction of his own identity as masculine in relation to his ability to function as a combatant. Such constructions might explain not only the almost complete exclusion of women from warrior ranks (until recently, and then only in some armies) but also how masculinity frequently depends on an "other" constructed as feminine (and therefore opposite). It has also been argued that war does not come "naturally" to men, and that warriors need to be socialized and trained to make them fight effectively. Gender identity thereby "becomes a tool with which societies induce men to fight" (Goldstein, 2001: 251–2). This tactic is also evident in the modern construction of masculinity in relation to nationalism, which is linked very closely with war as well as with the manipulation of gender roles (see Mosse, 1996).

16

KEY QUOTE BOX 16.2
Radical Feminism and the "Heterosexist" Nation-State

More "radical" feminists such as V. Spike Peterson have argued for a feminist questioning of both masculinity and "heteronormativity" as the basis of the modern state. She argues that the nation-state reflects the fact that heterosexual males have historically dominated the private family unit, while banning women and children, as well as less "manly" men, from the public arena, As she puts it: "the conjuncture of heterosexist ideology and practice is inextricable from the centralization of political authority/coercive power that we refer to as state-making" (Peterson, 1999: 39). She explains:

I argue that the conjuncture of heterosexist ideology and practice is inextricable from the centralization of political authority/coercive power that we refer to as state-making. Heterosexist ideology involves a symbolic order/intersubjective meaning system of hierarchical dichotomies that codify sex as male–female biological difference, gender as masculine–feminine subjectivity, and sexuality as heterosexual–homosexual identification. Heterosexism is "naturalized" through multiple discourses, especially western political theory and religious dogma, and by reification of the (patriarchal) "family" as "pre-political"—as "natural" and non-contractual. The binary of male–female difference is exemplified and well documented in western metaphysics (hence, political theory/practice) but evident in all collective meaning systems where the hierarchical dichotomy of gender is foundational to symbolic ordering and discursive practice. . . .

Heterosexism as sex/affect involves the normalization of exclusively heterosexual desire, intimacy, and family life. Historically, this normalization is inextricable from the state's interest in regulating sexual reproduction, undertaken primarily through controlling women's bodies, policing sexual activities, and instituting the heteropatriarchal family/household as the basic socio-economic unit. . . .

Heterosexism as social institution is inexplicable without reference to state-making in two senses: early state-making (as the pre-modern transition from kin-based to centralized political orders) and subsequent state-based orders (modern states and state-centric nationalisms). Early state-making (the urban revolution, the emergence of civilization) marks the convergence of centralized power/authority, the exploitation of re/productive labor, and the technology of writing such that, once established, centralized authority was able to turn coercive power to historically novel effect through enhanced systemic control. . . . In the western tradition, this involved "normalizing" definitive dichotomies (public–private, reason–affect, mind–body, culture–nature, civilized–barbarian, masculine–feminine) both materially, in divisions of authority, power, labor, and resources, as well as conceptually, in western metaphysics, language, philosophy, political theory. . . . (Peterson 1999: 39–41).

State Dept Image/Oct 22, 2011

PHOTO 16.3 Promoting a new form of US "smart power," Hillary Clinton is one of the most high-profile diplomats in the world. Here she meets with the president of Tajikistan, Emomali Rahmon, in 2011.

A particular aspect of war that is often highly gendered is the treatment of "enemy" civilians. Nowhere was this illustrated more clearly than in Bosnia during the war of 1992–5; see the case study on the next page.

At the same time, more women are entering politics than ever before. In the US Madeleine Albright, Condoleezza Rice, and Hillary Clinton have all served as Secretaries of State. In New Zealand Jenny Shipley and Helen Clark both served as Prime Minister, Clark for three successive terms of office. Angela Merkel, as Chancellor of Germany—the EU's largest economy—has played a key role in the efforts to solve the EU's financial problems. So too has Christine Lagarde, head of the International Monetary Fund and former French Minister of Economic Affairs, Finances and Industry as well as Minister of Trade.

KEY POINTS

- Feminism and gender theory offer very different perspectives on the world of IR than do traditional theories, pushing the boundaries of what is relevant to IR ever wider to incorporate more critical perspectives in every aspect of the field.

- Although gender theory is sometimes assumed to focus solely on "women's issues," in IR it is very much concerned with various forms of masculinity as well as femininity and the ways in which they are deployed in both war and peace.

16

CASE STUDY
Gender and Genocide in the Bosnian War, 1992–5

With the end of the Cold War, the Socialist Federative Republic of Yugoslavia (created in 1945) began to disintegrate, generating bitter conflict. First, in 1991, the republics of Slovenia and Croatia held referenda on their future status within the SFRY. Slovenia managed to leave the federation relatively peacefully, but Serbia, ruled by the nationalist leader Slobodan Milosevic (former president of both Yugoslavia and Serbia at various times), refused to recognize Croatian independence, since more than 10 per cent of Croatia's population was ethnically Serbian. The next Yugoslav republic to hold a referendum on independence, in 1992, was Bosnia–Herzegovina. With a multiethnic population of Catholic Croats, Orthodox Serbs, and Bosnian Muslims who had lived in relative harmony for years, Bosnia became the scene of gruesome bloodshed. Many Bosnian Serbs (a minority in the republic) refused to support the separation plan and held their own counter-referendum. They were supported by nationalists in Serbia, including Milosevic, who backed the Bosnian Serb separatist political party, and various Serbian militia groups (MacDonald, 2002: 78–82; 98–106; 220–4).

The war that ensued saw several notorious episodes of "ethnic cleansing," among them the slaughter of an estimated 8,000 Bosnian Muslim men and boys in Srebrenica in July 1995, carried out by units of the Army of Republika Srpska (VRS). At the subsequent trial of one Serbian leader, Radislav Krstic, a statement before the International Criminal Tribunal for the former Yugoslavia (ICTY), summed up the character of the Srebrenica massacre:

AP Photo/str

PHOTO 16.4 In July 1995, some 30,000 Muslim refugees fled the city of Srebrenica as the Bosnian Serb army overran the area.

By seeking to eliminate a part of the Bosnian Muslims, the Bosnian Serb forces committed genocide. They targeted for extinction the forty thousand Bosnian Muslims living in Srebrenica, a group which was emblematic of the Bosnian Muslims in general. They stripped all the male Muslim prisoners, military and civilian, elderly and young, of their personal belongings and identification, and deliberately and methodically killed them solely on the basis of their identity. The Bosnian Serb forces were aware, when they embarked on this genocidal venture, that the harm they caused would continue to plague the Bosnian Muslims. The Appeals Chamber states unequivocally that the law condemns, in appropriate terms, the deep and lasting injury inflicted, and calls the massacre at Srebrenica by its proper name: genocide. . . . (ICTY, 2004)

Female civilians among the Bosnian Muslim population, and some other groups, were subjected to a different kind of treatment. From an early stage, accounts emerged of women being raped as part of a systematic strategy that included *rape camps* where women were subjected to multiple assaults, often with the intention of impregnating them with "Serbian" babies. This came to be seen as part of the wider pattern of genocide. In 1995, a charge of rape was brought before the ICTY; this was the first time that a sexual assault case had been prosecuted as a war crime by itself, and not as part of a larger case. Estimates of the numbers of women raped during the war run as high as 50,000.

The slaughter of men and boys on the one hand, and the systematic rape of women on the other, during this war, illustrate gendered warfare in its most extreme form. In recent years, rape in war (which can also be perpetrated against men as an attack on their masculinity, although it is much less common) has achieved much greater prominence.

Postmodernism/Poststructuralism

Postmodernism is manifest in an array of ideas that, in one way or another, challenge the assumptions of modernity. Some IR scholars who might be classified as postmodern prefer to describe their approach as poststructuralist, emphasizing the linguistic aspects of meaning and interpretation that produce knowledges (note the plural). Typically, poststructuralists reject the tendencies to *essentialize* things—such as "masculinity" and "femininity"—in opposition to each other and to present *totalized* forms of knowledge (schemes of thought that bring complex phenomena under a single explanation such as "the natural order of things"). Nevertheless, at the risk of oversimplification, we will use the term "postmodernism" here.

See Chapter 6, page 117, for a discussion of postmodernism.

Although it shares some important basic assumptions with CT and constructivism, postmodernism in IR is more radical in its epistemology, rejecting the essentially *modernist* assumption that that we can ever have certain grounds for knowledge. In the absence of any final, incontestable Truth, the best we can hope for are fleeting "moments of clarity" that might allow us to grasp partial truths.

Postmodernism's greatest strength lies in its insights into the relationship between power and knowledge and its capacity to critique existing institutions, practices, and ideas. Its weakness lies in its inability to move beyond critique and map out a program for positive social and political change. Some would say that, taken to its logical conclusion,

16

postmodernism ends in absolute relativism, nihilism, and, ultimately, incoherence. For example, if "there is no truth," this claim itself cannot be true. As a further consequence of its relativism—that is, its insistence that no "standard" can be regarded as superior to any other, because there is no objective way of adjudicating between them—it also stands accused of creating a moral vacuum in which good and evil may be regarded as nothing more than competing narratives.

Armed with the insight that knowledge is very often a product of power, postmodernists argue that power is often used to construct **metanarratives**: comprehensive accounts of history, experience, and knowledge produced and transmitted by those in positions of power to further their own ends, even if they are unaware of how self-serving such accounts might be.

For example, in the nineteenth century, when indigenous peoples in Canada, the US, Australia, and New Zealand began to die out in massive numbers, historians and social commentators often expressed a kind of romantic regret at their "vanishing" or "melting away," but made no reference to the actual causes: disease, massacre, the loss of traditional lands and food supplies. Instead they constructed a metanarrative according to which the "disappearance" of indigenous people, though sad, was no one's fault: it was simply a natural consequence of social evolution and western "progress." It was only much later that historians were able to look at the root causes behind these demographic losses and understand that the practices of settlers, police forces, military, and governments were in many cases directly responsible for the destruction of indigenous populations. Many of these practices could have been prevented (MacDonald, 2008, 61). For another example of a metanarrative, see the case study below.

A leading figure in the rise of postmodern thought was the French philosopher Michel Foucault (1926–84), who pioneered a "genealogical" form of analysis. This style of analysis interrogates claims about what we believe to be true. Truth claims are put forward as if they constituted objective knowledge about the world, when in reality they often conceal the machinations of power. For example, many people believe that children should go to school from the age of five, that those who break laws should be put in prison, and that the insane should be hospitalized. Foucault argued that these beliefs have no basis in objective truth, but are instilled by the state through "discourses" designed to gain public consent for the use of bureaucratic power to control the individual. He also suggested that the human sciences have helped the state to conceal its real goals, lending a mask of authority to all kinds of knowledge claims that, in the end, can be exposed as operating in the service of power (Foucault, 1980: 13).

Postmodernism does raise awareness of the extent to which knowledge serves power and interests and how deeply the human sciences, which themselves exist as a set of interlocking discourses, tend to be implicated in the production of power/knowledge. We must keep in mind, however, that power as such is not necessarily a "bad" thing. As we pointed out near the beginning of this book, it can also be used for "good."

To summarize this section, postmodern or poststructuralist analyses interrogate the connections between power and knowledge, generally in a negative sense, as well as the grand narratives and discourses that purport to explain the nature and dynamics of the international system. Sovereignty, **statecraft**, anarchy, warfare, borders, identities and interests, the interpretation of history, the idea of history itself—all are subject to the

16

← See Chapter 2, page 49, for a discussion of whether power is "a good thing."

CASE STUDY
Positioning Iraq in the Metanarrative of the War on Terror

The "war on terror" was launched by US President George W. Bush in response to the attacks of 11 September 2001. Two countries were invaded as part of that "war": Afghanistan and Iraq. As the base used by the leader of the group responsible for planning and carrying out the 9/11 attacks, Afghanistan was a logical target. The reasons for invading Iraq, however, were not clear.

The following are well established:

1. Most of the al-Qaeda operatives responsible for the 9/11 attacks were Saudi nationals; none were Iraqi. Their leader, Osama bin Laden (also a Saudi national) was based in Afghanistan, which was governed by a religious fundamentalist government known as the Taliban.

2. Saddam Hussein, the president of Iraq from 1979 to 2003, had no demonstrable connection with Afghanistan, al-Qaeda, or the Taliban. Although he was hostile to the US (having been an ally during the 1980s), he was a secular leader and actually repressed religious fundamentalism in Iraq. Furthermore, bin Laden on several occasions described Saddam as a "socialist," an "infidel," a "thief and an apostate."

3. No weapons of mass destruction were found in Iraq, contrary to the claims of the Bush administration.

4. The presence of terrorists in Iraq following the US-led invasion (as evidenced by a relentless campaign of suicide bombing by various factions) can be attributed almost entirely to the war on terror itself and the heavy-handed way the occupation was carried out.

Despite the lack of any evidence linking Iraq to the 9/11 attacks, a *Washington Post* poll taken roughly six months after the invasion found that some 70 per cent of Americans still believed that such a link did exist. How did that link become established in the public mind? One answer was suggested by the *Post* in the article that reported the poll findings. Milbank and Deane (2003: A1) drew attention to a series of comments by senior members of the Bush administration in which they created the impression of a link without explicitly telling falsehoods. For example:

President Bush: March 8, 2003 — Weekly Radio Address:
If the world fails to confront the threat posed by the Iraqi regime, refusing to use force, even as a last resort, free nations would assume immense and unacceptable risks. The attacks of September the 11th, 2001, showed what the enemies of America did with four airplanes. We will not wait to see what terrorists or terrorist states could do with weapons of mass destruction

President Bush: May 1, 2003 — Speech on the USS Abraham Lincoln Declaring the End of Major Combat in Iraq:
The battle of Iraq is one victory in a war on terror that began on September the 11, 2001. . . .

16

The liberation of Iraq is a crucial advance in the campaign against terror. We've removed an ally of al Qaeda, and cut off a source of terrorist funding. . . . No terrorist network will gain weapons of mass destruction from the Iraqi regime, because the regime is no more. . . . We have not forgotten the victims of September the 11th. . . . (Milbank and Deane, 2003: A1)

In short, it seems that the power of the presidential office was used to promote a metanarrative about terrorism that served to justify the invasion of Iraq despite the lack of evidence. This effort was facilitated by the fact that the media largely avoided asking hard questions, perhaps because reporters feared losing access, especially in a tense environment, with a president who was heavily controlled by his advisors. In a study of network television news stories about Iraq over a two-week period in 2003, more than half of the nearly 400 sources cited were US officials. Only 17 per cent of sources were critical of the administration's plans for war (Kaufman, 2004: 44). Former White House press secretary Scott McClellan later observed that the media became too focused on the administration's effort to sell the war, whether Bush was winning or losing the argument, and what the polls were saying. Lost in the reportage was the media's watchdog role, "aggressively questioning the rationale for war or pursuing the truth behind it" (McClellan, 2008: 125–6).

PHOTO 16.5 "OK poodles, time for walkies": George Bush heads for Iraq, taking prime ministers Tony Blair (Britain) and John Howard (Australia) along with him; by Chris Grosz.

Grosz, Chris, courtesy www.cartoonstock.com

16

In the UK, by contrast, although former Prime Minister Tony Blair used similar rhetoric on many occasions, support for the war was always relatively weak. This may be attributed to greater skepticism about the link with 9/11, a more critical press, a more critical attitude towards political leaders nurtured by a stronger system of government and opposition, and a less nationalistic world view among the public at large. The Canadian response to the targeting of Iraq was even more critical: the Liberal government of Jean Chrétien refused to participate in the Iraq war, which led to a partial freeze in relations with the US. From a postmodern perspective, we might conclude that the power/knowledge nexus that supports successful metanarratives was not as strong in the UK as it was in the US, and was even weaker in Canada, where the Liberal government paid lip service to the war on terror but strongly resisted US pressure to go into Iraq.

Mainstream Canadians rejected the Bush administration along with the war and articulated their own narrative about the US president. Environics Research described Bush as "the personification of every negative stereotype Canadians have of America," observing that he gave Canadians "a smug sense of superiority, because he lends himself to obvious forms of ridicule. He has been the best thing to happen to Canadian nationalism in a long time" (cited in Lachner, 2004). Polls by Environics and Pollara indicated that only 15 per cent of Canadians would have voted for Bush in the 2004 elections (Lachner, 2004). A further poll in 2005 revealed that 38 per cent of Canadian respondents agreed that Bush was "more dangerous to world security than Osama bin Laden." At the same time, 68 per cent reported having favourable impressions of Americans (Humphreys, 2005).

critical gaze. Despite frequent complaints about the difficult language used in much postmodern writing, postmodernism has gained a foothold in the study of IR, highlighting the idea that "reality" is not a concrete, unalterable state of affairs that exists somewhere "out there," but is something that ultimately exists only in our ways of viewing the world.

KEY POINTS

- Postmodernism/poststructuralism in IR shares some common ground with CT and constructivism in IR but has a much more radical epistemology derived from its rejection of modernist assumptions about knowledge.
- A common criticism is that its radical relativism means that postmodernists cannot make moral arguments in politics, or any other sphere, and does not allow for any objective way of judging between different standards.
- Despite these criticisms, postmodernism/poststructuralism in IR is valuable in showing just how tenuous truths are, including those embedded in metanarratives.

Postcolonial Theory

"Postcolonialism" is an interdisciplinary enterprise that uses a set of critical theoretical approaches to study the direct and indirect effects of colonization on subject peoples. Although it is not identical with the "subaltern studies" discussed in Chapter 12, the latter is certainly an aspect of postcolonial theory. An important figure in the development of postcolonial thought was Edward Said (1935–2003), a professor of comparative literature at Columbia University. His critical work on "Orientalism" argued that Europeans—especially the English and French but also the Germans, Russians, Spanish, Portuguese, Italians, and Swiss—had for centuries treated the Middle East (or "Orient") as its major "cultural contestant." Thus Europeans defined *themselves* against, or in contrast with, the people of the Orient. But for Said, Orientalism is more than just a style of thought; it is an *activity* dedicated to the production and dissemination of knowledge *about* the Orient and a means of exercising authority over it. In developing his ideas, Said drew on Gramsci's ideas about hegemony as well as Foucault's insights into the power/knowledge nexus. He argued that Orientalism was a hegemonic discourse: a narrative used by European elites to dominate the Middle East, while promoting a very partial view of history. Although Said focused on the Middle East, his ideas have been generalized so that the concept of "Orientalism" is now applied to almost any construction of non-European "Others" by Europeans—or any members of "the West" for that matter.

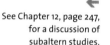

Within IR, postcolonial theorists often emphasize the Eurocentrism of traditional IR theory. The implication is that realism and liberalism not only provide a very partial view of the wider reality of the world, but play a role in determining how we think of world politics. The feminist IR theorist J. Ann Tickner suggests that "As a social practice, IR constitutes a space in which certain understandings of the world dominate others, specific interests are privileged over others, and practices of power and domination acquire a normalized form" (Tickner, 2003: 300).

Conclusion

This overview of IR theory shows that whenever we think about the world around us, we do so on the basis of a certain set of assumptions about the reality of that world. Different theorists see the world in different ways and will interpret facts accordingly. In other words, facts do not speak for themselves. The study of international politics requires something more than the unquestioning accumulation and arrangements of the facts that we know (or think we know). A constructivist would be quick to point out that different theorists see the world in different ways because each has arranged and interpreted the facts about the world in a different way. Similarly, theory is not an "abstraction" from reality: it frames the way we see reality and how we create it. The important thing is to give theory serious attention and to allow our existing beliefs to be challenged.

If theory "creates" the world, do the "Western" theories reviewed here create it from a "Western" perspective? Certainly, the phenomena that IR theories describe (and criticize) were created in Europe and effectively globalized via colonization and decolonization. Indeed, those theories themselves are products of the same system (a fact that the development of postcolonial theory within IR is beginning to draw attention to). On the other hand, if we examine "Western civilization" (if there really is such a "thing") closely, we find that it is the product of so many historical and cultural influences, many of which travelled from East Asia and the Pacific, India, the Middle East and Africa as well as the Americas, that to describe it as an entirely European project would clearly be inaccurate. What is certain is that, as IR theory continues to develop, and as the centres of power around the world themselves continue to shift, the discipline will inevitably be enriched by insights from an ever-wider academic community and an ever-broadening set of perspectives.

? KEY QUESTIONS

- How has Marxism influenced theoretical development in IR?
- What are the main elements of Gramsci's notion of hegemony?
- How does the idea of "emancipation" contribute to the critical theorization of IR?
- What is "normative theory"?
- What do constructivists mean when they refer to IR as "social theory"?
- How do "agents" and "structures," and "material" and "ideational" factors, interact in constructivist theory?
- In what ways do the various feminist perspectives broaden the field of IR theory?
- What does a "gender lens" expose about the construction of masculinity and femininity in IR?
- What is the relationship between power and knowledge in postmodern approaches to IR?
- Is IR theory thoroughly ethnocentric?

📖 FURTHER READING

Turenne Sjolander, Claire, and Wayne Cox, eds (1994). *Beyond Positivism: Critical Reflections on International Relations*. Boulder, CO: Lynne Rienner.
> A collection that provides a strong grounding in post-positivist theory, featuring a wide range of critical theorists and their work.

Acharya, Amitav, and Barry Buzan, eds (2007). *Why Is There No Non-Western IR Theory?*, *Special issue of International Relations of the Asia-Pacific* 11, 3: 287–312.
> The title of this collection of articles suggests that part of the problem with the ethnocentricity of IR theory is the lack of alternative approaches from outside "the West." It explores various reasons for this and speculates about future developments, using material mainly from the Asia–Pacific region.

Jarvis, D.S.L. (2000). *International Relations and the Challenge of Postmodernism: Defending the Discipline*. Columbia: University of South Carolina Press.
> A readable, detailed account of the rise of postmodernism in IR, its critique of modernity, and its impact on the discipline. Jarvis makes a concerted effort to provide a "manual" for understanding and making transparent just what the epistemological and ontological positions adopted by postmodernists are.

Jones, Branwen Gruffydd, ed. (2006). *Decolonizing International Relations*. Lanham, MD: Rowman & Littlefield.
> The introduction argues that IR must develop greater self-awareness: of its origins, how it has been implicated in imperialism, and the problems that Eurocentrism poses for understanding the power/knowledge nexus.

Fierke, Karin M., and Knud Erik Jørgensen (eds) (2001). *Constructing International Relations: The Next Generation*. New York: M.E. Sharpe.
> The contributors to this book place the constructivist approach to IR in the wider context of social sciences around the world, introducing interdisciplinary perspectives and extending the analysis beyond the world of European scholarship.

Sylvester, Christine (2002). *Feminist International Relations: An Unfinished Journey*, Cambridge: Cambridge University Press.

A personal and historical account of feminism's "journey" in IR and the difficulties encountered in the effort to give gender relations a proper profile in the field. It also touches on a range of related issues, including elements of postcolonial theory not found in conventional scholarship.

WEB LINKS

http://ftgss.blogspot.com/

The blog of the Feminist Theory and Gender Studies (FTGS) section of the International Studies Association, the largest network of IR scholars in the world; contains details on new research, conferences, and other activities in North America and around the world.

www.marxists.org/archive/marx/

www.marxists.org/archive/gramsci/

www.marxists.org/subject/frankfurt-school/index.htm

Related sites providing useful summaries as well as archives of key works for Marx and Gramsci.

http://plato.stanford.edu/entries/critical-theory/

The online Stanford Encyclopaedia of Philosophy; contains a wide-ranging account of critical theory.

www.cddc.vt.edu/feminism/enin.html

A very comprehensive site covering all aspects of feminist theory.

http://plato.stanford.edu/entries/postmodernism/

The Stanford Encyclopaedia of Philosophy's useful entry on postmodernism.

16

Security and Insecurity

17

CHAPTER OVERVIEW

Traditionally, IR's focus has been on the security of the sovereign state in a system of states existing under conditions of anarchy. Thus IR has been largely concerned with the threats that states pose to each other. This chapter begins with a look at traditional concepts of security and insecurity, revisiting the Hobbesian state of nature and tracing security thinking through to the end of the Cold War. It then explores specific ideas about collective security as embodied in the United Nations and the UN Security Council, as well as the rise of security cooperation in organizations such as NATO. We then consider some pressing security challenges in the post-Cold War period and the broadening of the security agenda to encompass a host of more recent concerns such as environmental security, energy security, and the diffuse concept of "human security." We conclude with an overview of the war on terror that raises further questions about how best to deal with non-conventional threats.

Security, Insecurity, and Power Politics

Traditional realist approaches to IR, taking their cue from classic English social-contract theorists such as Thomas Hobbes, have associated the **state of nature** with a permanent state of **anarchy**. The anarchic state of nature represents the most insecure existence imaginable. With the formation of states in the form of bounded political communities headed by a sovereign power, however, anarchy was banished from within the state, enabling a measure of security domestically.

For realists, the study of life *within* the state has nothing to do with IR: it is the business of traditional political science, in particular of comparative politics. The proper concern of IR is to secure the survival of the sovereign state in the anarchic environment of the international system, for it is only when the state is secure that people can effectively work to achieve "the good life" within it. As Mearsheimer argues:

> States seek to maintain their territorial integrity and the autonomy of their domestic political order. They can pursue other goals like prosperity and protecting human rights, but those aims must always take a back seat to survival, because if a state does not survive, it cannot pursue those other goals (Mearsheimer, 2007: 74).

This is not to say that the international sphere is a place of perpetual chaos or warfare; some order can exist in anarchy. Still, at any given time peace and security are tenuous. Perpetual anarchy means perpetual underlying insecurity because even in times of apparent peace, the destructive forces of anarchy are always there, waiting to be unleashed when the fragile order characterizing international relations weakens or breaks down. As we have seen, this kind of thinking crystallized in realist theory following the breakdown of international order that led to the Second World War, culminating in the turn to **power politics** that characterized the post-war period.

The "power politics" approach to security as worked out by Morgenthau and his successors takes as given the notion of "peace through strength." Here "strength" is equated with military capacity and a robust approach to "national security" (Shimko, 2005: 121). The power politics approach also involves consideration of both **balance of power** mechanisms and the **security dilemma**, which ensures a perpetual competitive struggle for security. In the final analysis, states can depend only on their own resources. *Self-reliance* is therefore the ultimate key to survival in the international sphere. This does not mean that diplomacy should not be pursued, or that the UN doesn't matter. It does mean that for any practical decision-maker, state survival must be the bottom line.

During the Cold War period, the use of the term "security" by both sides came to denote much more than simple protection against invasion. On the Soviet side, "security" and imperial expansion in Eastern and Central Europe went hand in hand, while on the other side "any state controlling large geographical areas containing significant quantities of natural resources in a way unacceptable to the USA [presented] a threat to the 'national security' of the United States" (Young and Kent, 2004: 10).

Another factor prominent in neorealism is the distribution of power in the international system and its effects on the security environment. Reflecting on the history of the state system in Europe from 1648 to 1945, observers of international politics have generally agreed that the system during that period was "multipolar" (Mearsheimer, 2007: 78–80). In other words, significant power was distributed among three or more states within the system. The Cold War period, by contrast, is generally described as "bipolar," since power was essentially

◀ US President Barack Obama greets New Zealand Prime Minister John Key (© Brooks Kraft/Corbis).

divided between the US and its allies on one hand and the USSR and its allies on the other. The structure of **bipolarity**, together with the deterrent effect of the nuclear weapons possessed by both sides, is often said to have produced the "long peace" of the Cold War period in which major warfare between the superpowers never took place. With the Cold War long over and the US in a position of global **hegemony** (notwithstanding the rise of China), the system is generally described as unipolar. Whether unipolarity will prove to be more or less conducive to peace than bipolarity is hard to predict. Waltz has argued that is inherently unstable and dangerous (2000: 4–15). As of 2012, the war on terror continues in Afghanistan, although President Obama is clearly interested in winding it down in order to focus on economic problems closer to home. Traditional realist theory has little to say about conflicts that are not essentially state-based and therefore do not lend themselves to balance-of-power analysis.

Liberal approaches to security challenge the premises of **realism** with regard to state security, often with considerable success. Despite the apparent failures of the League of Nations in the interwar period, **liberal institutionalism** prevailed after 1945, when the UN was created in the hope of reducing the negative effects of anarchy by ensuring the cooperation of the great powers (the US, USSR, China, Britain, and France) and various collective security mechanisms were put in place by international treaty; see **Box 17.1**.

KEY CONCEPT BOX 17.1
Treaties and Alliances

A treaty in international relations is defined simply as "a written contract or agreement between two or more parties which is considered binding in international law" (Evans and Newnham, 1998: 542–3). A treaty may take the form of an alliance, which is usually defined primarily in security terms as "a formal agreement between two or more actors—usually states—to collaborate together on perceived mutual security issues" (Evans and Newnham: 1998: 15). The anticipated security benefits of such collaboration generally include one or more of the following:

* a system of deterrence will be established or strengthened;
* a defence pact will operate in the event of a war;
* some or all of the actors will be precluded from joining other alliances (ibid.).

As tools for securing some kind of international order, treaties and alliances have a very long history. Thucydides refers to a number of treaties between rival forces, while many other political communities around the world have also used treaties to maintain workable arrangements. Not all treaties take the form of security alliances, but historically this was probably the most common form. A treaty may be negotiated between formerly hostile parties that see a mutual advantage in establishing more peaceful relations. This does not mean that each party will cease to regard potential rivals with suspicion, nor will it guarantee that aggression will not occur in the future. The non-aggression pact negotiated between Hitler and Stalin in 1939, for example, did not prevent Hitler from launching an invasion of Soviet territory just two years later. A treaty may also be forced on one or more of the parties at the conclusion of hostilities, to the benefit of the victorious side and/or as a punitive mechanism. The Treaty of Versailles was an example of the latter, and, as we have seen, it is often regarded as a major factor in Hitler's rise to power and support within Germany for his ultra-aggressive militarism.

17

The United Nations and Collective Security

As the Second World War drew to a close, delegates from 50 countries, all opponents of the Axis powers, met in San Francisco to approve a charter for a new body capable of establishing a framework for maintaining international peace and security. Work on a successor organization to the old League of Nations had been underway at least since 1941, when representatives of countries committed to establishing a more secure world order met in London. Soon after, British Prime Minister Winston Churchill and US President Franklin D. Roosevelt signed the Atlantic Charter. This document had no legal standing, but it denounced the use of force while affirming hopes for a stable new world order when hostilities eventually ceased. This new order would uphold the rights of people to live in peace and freedom within the boundaries of their own states and to travel abroad in safety. At a further meeting in London, representatives of most European governments-in-exile and the USSR pledged support. By 1943 the process of securing broad agreement on a new organization took another step forward with a meeting in Moscow of the major powers, now including China, and another in Teheran a few months later attended by the UK, the US, the USSR, and China.

In August 1944 a proposal for a Charter was drawn up by the four major powers at the "Dumbarton Oaks" meeting in Washington DC. By this stage, agreement had been reached on the main elements of a new United Nations Organization, including a General Assembly, a Security Council, an International Court of Justice, and a Secretariat. A subsequent meeting produced the procedures for voting in the Security Council. A UN Charter was formally signed in San Francisco by representatives of 51 countries on 26 June 1945. The organization came into official existence on 24 October 1945. Canada was a founding member of the UN and took an active role in creating the Charter, which laid out the basic duties and principles of membership. UN membership grew steadily during the era of decolonization in Africa, the Middle East, South Asia, East Asia, the Pacific, and the Caribbean. This process led to the formation of many new independent states. The UN saw a further boost in membership after the end of the Cold War, when some former federal republics of the Soviet Union became sovereign states. Membership now stands at 193.

The UN Charter establishes basic principles of order in support of international peace and security which every new member must agree to. It is thus an international treaty setting out the rights and obligations of its member states in terms of the Charter's main purposes. These purposes are set out in the Preamble to the Charter, which reaffirms member states' "faith in fundamental human rights, in the dignity and worth of the human person, in the equal rights of men and women and of nations large and small," and declares their intention "to establish conditions under which justice and respect for the obligations arising from treaties and other sources of international law can be maintained" and "to promote social progress and better standards of life in larger freedom." Members commit themselves to practise tolerance and live together in peace with one another as good neighbours; to unite in maintaining international peace and security; to ensure that armed force will not be used, except in the common interest; and to use international machinery for the promotion of the economic and social advancement of all peoples (Charter of the United Nations, Preamble, as adopted 26 June 1945). There follow 19 chapters containing a total of 111 Articles spelling out the more detailed structure of the UN and the various powers and responsibilities of its principle organs.

17

The UN Security Council

The Security Council was established under Chapter V of the Charter. It was originally composed of five permanent members (the UK, US, USSR, France, and China) and six non-permanent members. There are now ten non-permanent members, each of which serves a two-year term. The five permanent members—or "P5"—each retain veto power over any Security Council decision. This extraordinary power reflects the founding members' belief that the new UN could not function if it did not give a special place to the most prominent states, thereby rectifying a perceived weakness of the old League. More generally, the Security Council embodies the UN's mission to provide for "collective security"; the term underlines the founders' conviction that true security can never be achieved unless the great powers abandon the principle of "every state for itself" and work cooperatively.

The composition and functioning of the Security Council has been subject to much criticism over the years. One is that the extraordinary power given to the P5 more than sixty years ago, in a world where decolonization had scarcely begun, no longer reflects the current balance of power, nor the way global population is distributed. The UN's membership has almost quadrupled since then, and many leaders in the developing world see the permanent membership as unfairly skewed in favour of the developed world. Certainly, the geographic distribution of the P5 is relatively narrow, with no representation whatever from Africa, the Middle East, South Asia, or South America—regions that are home to many of the world's largest states.

UN Photo/Paulo Filgueiras

PHOTO 17.1 In October 2011 China and Russia vetoed a draft UN resolution that strongly condemned the violence perpetrated by Syrian authorities against civilian protesters.

Reform of the P5 seems unlikely, at least in the near future. If reform entailed an expanded permanent membership, the veto power would be extended, which would make decision-making even more difficult than it is now. On the other hand, if the number of permanent members were to stay at five, which of the current P5 should, or would, vacate their seats to make way for new members? One solution would be to remove the UK and France and give the European Union a single seat: this would give Germany (and all other European states) some representation and free up one seat for a new member. But the UK and France are unlikely to agree, and for many people such an arrangement would take pan-European institution-building too far. Furthermore, if one new member were to be admitted, which would it be? Brazil, Japan, India, Nigeria, and Egypt are possible claimants, but none would be uncontroversial.

The remaining option would be to eliminate the permanent members altogether. However, this would almost certainly change the dynamics of the Security Council, and there is no guarantee that the change would be for the better. In any case, reform of the Security Council is unlikely to occur any time soon, since any one of the P5 can easily veto any proposal that is not in its national interest. It's hard to imagine the US or China agreeing to have its power diluted. Beyond this, some argue that the more pressing issue now is not whether the permanent membership can be reformed but whether its most powerful members can be restrained (Weiss, 2003: 146–61). The Iraq War raised many concerns about unchecked US power, as did Russia's conflict with Georgia in 2008. China has been sparring with Taiwan since the communist revolution in 1949 and the tension shows little sign of easing, although their trade relationship is very strong and suggests a high level of economic interdependence.

The UN was arguably founded on some fairly liberal ideals. First, it was designed to minimize conflict in the international sphere through cooperation and institution-building. Second, the language of the various declarations was full of idealist visions of a better world in which security for all states would be the norm rather than the exception. Third, with membership open to all on equal terms and a normative commitment to decolonization, the UN reflected a strong spirit of egalitarianism. Its provisions for the social and economic advancement of all nations ensured that it would take a proactive role in areas outside mainstream security concerns.

This tendency was strengthened with the Universal Declaration of Human Rights and the UN Genocide Convention in 1948 and an expanded humanitarian role in various areas in later years. Also introduced were provisions for the participation of NGOs. In short, the UN system may be founded squarely on the sovereign state system and its preservation, but the organization's basic principles and vision for world order extend further to embrace a range of liberal ideals and a broader interpretation of the international security agenda. Thus its wide-ranging charter has seen it respond to significant non-military international security concerns such as the environment, health, food, global inequality, and so on.

On the other hand, the structure of the Security Council and the dominance of the P5 reflect a realist concern for the accommodation of power politics, even within an "idealist institution." In addition, the broader liberal vision for collective international security is still tied to a traditional state-based vision of world order focused primarily on military issues. The same is true of other forms of collective security, such the North Atlantic Treaty Organization (NATO).

KEY CONCEPT BOX 17.2
UN Peacemaking, Peacekeeping, and Peacebuilding

The UN has been engaged in **peacekeeping** since 1956. The idea of using forces from UN member states to defuse conflict was introduced by Canadian diplomat (and later Prime Minister) Lester B. Pearson, who proposed that an international police force supervise the ceasefire between the combatants in the Suez Crisis (a conflict pitting the UK, France, and Israel against Egypt over control of the Suez Canal). For his efforts Pearson was awarded the Nobel Peace Prize in 1957. Former UN Secretary-General Boutros Boutros-Ghali, in his 1992 report to the Security Council, described peacekeeping as

> the deployment of a United Nations presence in the field, hitherto with the consent of all the parties concerned, normally involving United Nations military and/or police personnel and frequently civilians as well. Peacekeeping is a technique that expands the possibilities for both the prevention of conflict and the making of peace.

These forces are coordinated by the UN Department of Peacekeeping Operations.

Early peacekeeping missions were military, but over time peacekeepers' activities have become more complex, partly because many conflicts are now internal, and therefore the parties to conflict are often non-state actors (e.g., militia groups). The UN mission in Cambodia from 1991 to 1993 was one example of non-traditional peacekeeping. Other examples include the missions in Somalia (1992–3) and the former Yugoslavia (1992–5), in which the role of peacekeepers was to distribute relief supplies and promote stability. Other missions in Haiti, Kosovo, and East Timor have focused more on monitoring peace agreements and training police forces.

© Niko Guido/istockphoto.com

PHOTO 17.2 UN soldiers in Haiti provide crowd control as relief workers distribute rice following the earthquake of 2010.

17

Peacekeeping is now seen as part of a larger strategy of **conflict prevention**, based on the idea that it's better to intervene early, to prevent political disputes from escalating, than to wait until they have reached the stage of physical violence. When the Canadian government sent troops to Afghanistan, for example, the goal was to resolve conflicts before they become violent. The emphasis is on promoting dialogue between hostile parties and trying to address the root causes of conflict, which may include poverty, inadequate development, lack of democracy and good governance, problems of public health, sanitation, and education, as well as poorly trained armed forces and police. Corruption, weapons and drugs smuggling, human trafficking, and mercenary activity are also serious issues. If peace does break down, the next step is **peacemaking**. In addition to using formal techniques such as mediation and arbitration, UN peacemakers try to promote a general willingness to seek peace. Of central importance is the protection of women and children; civilians constitute 85 per cent of casualties in civil conflicts today. The UN also privileges the protection of refugees and internally displaced people.

Peacebuilding efforts are directed at preventing the re-emergence of conflict and promoting a return to normal life in conflict zones. In many cases today, this means that the UN has to establish basic institutions of government—a job that state governments are normally expected to do. Peacebuilding involves cooperating closely with local experts to help rebuild infrastructure, design electoral systems, and perform a multitude of similarly complex tasks that would have been beyond the scope of UN operations during the Cold War.

Peacekeeping activity greatly increased after the end of the Cold War. By 1996 there were 24 new peacekeeping missions; from 1953 to 1989, there had only been 18 such missions in total. By the end of 2008, there were over 88,000 peacekeepers, deployed from 118 countries. The largest contributors at that time were India, Pakistan, and Bangladesh, each of which contributed between nine and ten thousand peacekeepers. In 2008, Canada committed 169 troops and the US 297, alongside observers and police. In mid-2010, more than 101,000 uniformed personnel from 115 countries were involved in 15 separate UN missions.

In the past the UN performed the lion's share of peacekeeping duties. Today, however, regional organizations such as the Organization for Security and Co-operation in Europe, the African Union, and NATO are taking on more of this work. It has been under NATO rather than UN auspices that Canada and the US have made their peacekeeping contributions in recent years. Various NGOs are also playing a greater role in peacekeeping and peacebuilding.

SOURCE: www.international.gc.ca/peace-paix/; accessed 23 July 2010.

The Role of NATO

The North Atlantic Treaty Organization was created in 1948 and has played a major role in shaping world order ever since. The Cold War had begun almost immediately after the end of the Second World War. In the absence of the common enemy that had held the "Grand Alliance" together, the USSR and its wartime Western allies soon began jockeying for territory, giving rise to mutual suspicions and intense disputes over the systems of government to be imposed on newly liberated countries such as Poland, Hungary, and Czechoslovakia. At the same time, in response to the dire economic conditions in

Western Europe, was developing following the war were dire and rebuilding programs were sluggish. This led to the European Recovery Program, informally known as the "Marshall Plan." The Plan was named for US Secretary of State George Marshall, who announced a large-scale plan to deliver economic aid to Europe in June 1947. European recovery was seen as vital to US interests for a number of reasons. These included the restoration of its own lucrative markets, the strengthening of Europe economically and militarily vis-à-vis the Soviet Union, while also containing "Euro-communism" which was popular in France, Italy and other countries. The Soviet communist ideology was seen as a major threat to the "American way" and there were widespread fears that Stalin was bent on world domination, or at the very least on spreading communism as far as he could.

In 1947, US president Harry Truman laid out a doctrine of "containment" that claimed a leading role for the US in opposing the spread of communism. Together with the Marshall Plan, the broad doctrine became known as "containment" (of communism). Although designed to play to his domestic audience, the Truman Doctrine had long-term international effects, legitimizing US intervention in civil wars abroad where communist interests were involved.

It was in this general atmosphere that NATO was established, with all its founding members committing to a basic principle of indivisible collective security. Thus an attack on one member was to be regarded as an attack on all. Although NATO is a military alliance, the initial reasons for its creation had as much to do with the perceived need to strengthen political will and confidence against communism as with the need to protect Western Europe against military attack (Young and Kent, 2004: 128–9). Canada and the US were key members from the beginning, along with ten Western European states: the UK, France, Denmark, Iceland, Italy, Norway, Portugal, Belgium, the Netherlands, and Luxembourg. Seven years later, in 1955, the USSR established a rival organization with its communist allies in Eastern and Central Europe. This "Treaty of Friendship, Co-operation and Mutual Assistance," better known as the Warsaw Pact, was in part a response to West Germany's entry into NATO in the same year. Curiously, the USSR itself had attempted to join NATO a year earlier, in order (it claimed) to safeguard peace in Europe. The overture was rejected (CBC News, 2009).

In the course of the Cold War NATO membership expanded to include Greece, Turkey, and Spain. NATO allies sometimes had serious policy disagreements, however. In 1966, tensions with the US over a variety of issues (among them the war in the former French colony of Vietnam) led France to withdraw from NATO's integrated military structure. France remained a signatory to the "paper treaty," but remained outside the military structure until 1993.

Although clearly a Cold War institution, NATO has renewed its *râison d'être* in the post-Cold War period as the primary security organization for Europe and the North Atlantic. In recent years its membership has expanded yet again to incorporate a number of former Soviet-dominated countries. The Czech Republic, Hungary, and Poland joined in 1999. Bulgaria, Estonia, Latvia, Lithuania, Romania, Slovakia, and Slovenia followed suit in 2004, and Croatia and Albania in 2009, bringing the organization's current membership to 28. As it welcomed the first three of its former communist members, a new "strategic concept" was announced and a 65-point document was released, spelling out NATO's vision of its past, present, and future roles as a pre-eminent international treaty-based security organization; see **Box 17.3**. Apparently its members believe that NATO has a long-term future.

KEY CONCEPT BOX 17.3
History: Reformulating NATO's Strategic Concept

The end of the Cold War and the collapse of communism in Eastern Europe and the former USSR required a rethinking of NATO's essential mission. The results of that exercise were formally introduced as follows:

1. At their Summit meeting in Washington in April 1999, NATO heads of state and Government approved the Alliance's new Strategic Concept.

2. NATO has successfully ensured the freedom of its members and prevented war in Europe during the forty years of the Cold War. By combining defence with dialogue, it played an indispensable role in bringing East–West confrontation to a peaceful end. The dramatic changes in the Euro–Atlantic strategic landscape brought by the end of the Cold War were reflected in the Alliance's 1991 Strategic Concept. There have, however, been further profound political and security developments since then.

3. The dangers of the Cold War have given way to more promising, but also challenging prospects, to new opportunities and risks. A new Europe of greater integration is emerging, and a Euro–Atlantic security structure is evolving in which NATO plays a central part. The Alliance has been at the heart of efforts to establish new patterns of cooperation and mutual understanding across the Euro–Atlantic region and has committed itself to essential new activities in the interest of a wider stability. It has shown the depth of that commitment in its efforts to put an end to the immense human suffering created by conflict in the Balkans. The years since the end of the Cold War have also witnessed important developments in arms control, a process to which the Alliance is fully committed. The Alliance's role in these positive developments has been underpinned by the comprehensive adaptation of its approach to security and of its procedures and structures. The last ten years have also seen, however, the appearance of complex new risks to Euro–Atlantic peace and stability, including oppression, ethnic conflict, economic distress, the collapse of political order, and the proliferation of weapons of mass destruction.

4. The Alliance has an indispensable role to play in consolidating and preserving the positive changes of the recent past, and in meeting current and future security challenges. It has, therefore, a demanding agenda. It must safeguard common security interests in an environment of further, often unpredictable change. It must maintain collective defence and reinforce the transatlantic link and ensure a balance that allows the European Allies to assume greater responsibility. It must deepen its relations with its partners and prepare for the accession of new members. It must, above all, maintain the political will and the military means required by the entire range of its missions.

5. This new Strategic Concept will guide the Alliance as it pursues this agenda. It expresses NATO's enduring purpose and nature and its fundamental security tasks, identifies the central features of the new security environment, specifies the elements of the Alliance's broad approach to security, and provides guidelines for the further adaptation of its military forces.

SOURCE: www.nato.int/docu/pr/1999/p99-065e.htm; accessed 2 March 2012.

Alternative Approaches to Security

Since at least the 1960s, peace activists have promoted the idea that no state can achieve genuine security simply by defeating its enemies in war: adversaries must work together to resolve conflicts. They have also argued that security must be rethought in terms of a concept that has come to be known as "positive peace," according to which peace means something more than simply the absence of violent conflict. Theorists such as the Norwegian sociologist Johan Galtung have focused attention on the causes of conflict and the use of cooperative social mechanisms to resolve them (see Galtung, 1969: 167–91).

The peace movement itself was (and remains) multifaceted, taking on different causes and promoting different issues according to time, place, and circumstance. During the Cold War, for example, peace activists campaigned variously against "hot" warfare in Vietnam, Korea, and other parts of the developing world; against the advancement of nuclear technology for any purpose, military or non-military (see **Box 17.4**); against poverty, underdevelopment, and neocolonialism in the developing world; and for the promotion of grass-roots democracy and **social justice** in industrialized nations. There were also cross-cutting links with other **social movements**: for example, both the women's movement and the environmental movement advanced their own conceptions of security and alternative agendas for policy-makers well before the end of the Cold War. These developments took place alongside intellectual challenges to traditional security studies coming from **postmodernism**, feminism, and critical theory throughout the 1970s and 1980s.

KEY CONCEPT BOX 17.4
New Zealand and the Anti-Nuclear Movement

The Pacific anti-nuclear movement began in New Zealand in the early 1960s and became more vocal after Algeria gained its independence from France in 1962. Forced to abandon its nuclear testing grounds in the Sahara, France chose to relocate its testing operations to the French island colonies of Mururoa and Fangataufa in the South Pacific, to the east of New Zealand. Anti-nuclear protests in New Zealand intensified when testing began in 1966. The government of New Zealand was solidly behind the anti-nuclear campaign, even sending the frigate HMNZS *Otago* to the test zone in 1973 (Bennett, 1988: 92). The following year, New Zealand joined Australia and its Pacific Island neighbours in taking France to the International Court of Justice to halt further atmospheric testing. They scored a notable victory when the ICJ ruled against France, which eventually moved its testing underground (Henderson, 1999: 281–2).

Anti-nuclear sentiment took centre stage in 1985, when New Zealand's Prime Minister David Lange refused port access to the navy destroyer USS *Buchanan* on the grounds that the US would neither confirm nor deny the presence of nuclear materials on board the ship. The US annulled its ANZUS pact with New Zealand the following year, and to this day the two countries still do not have any formal security alliance. Finally, in 1987 New Zealand became the first state to pass legislation declaring itself a nuclear-free zone (MacDonald, 2005: 178-9). Since that time, New Zealand has been instrumental in promoting anti-nuclear policies.

17

← See Chapter 16, page 330, for the case study of the Bosnian War, 1992–5.

Feminism has provided some interesting and challenging critiques of conventional approaches to security. Although there are many schools of feminist thought, a common theme is that thinking about international relations in general, and security in particular, has been dominated by masculine perspectives, with the result that issues of particular concern to women have tended to be marginalized. A prime example is the issue of rape in war, which came to international attention during the war in Bosnia–Herzegovina. Just as domestic violence against women in the home has often been concealed or downplayed, so too has violence against women in times of war.

As a result of the publicity surrounding the strategic raping of women in the former Yugoslavia, scholars began to explore the incidence of rape in earlier conflicts. Thus long overdue attention was directed to the rape of German women, mainly by the victorious Red Army, at the end of the Second World War, and the Japanese army's use of rape during the war in the Pacific: an estimated 20,000 Chinese women (and possibly more) were raped during the siege of Nanjing in 1937, and women throughout the Japanese-occupied territories were forced into prostitution as sex slaves ("comfort women"). These are clearly not the only historic cases: soldiers from many other countries have engaged in rape either en masse or individually, and almost always with impunity. As we have seen, the first time that sexual assault was treated separately as a war crime was in 1996, when eight Bosnian Serb military and police officers were indicted in connection with the rape of Bosnian Muslim women. This has scarcely prevented the continuation of the practice in other war zones, as reports about the plight of women refugees from the Darfur region of western Sudan indicate (see www.amnesty.org/en/library/info/AFR54/076/2004; accessed 2 March 2012). Nevertheless, it does indicate that the practice of rape in war is now being treated as an important security issue.

AP Photo/Ahn Young-joon

PHOTO 17.3 Many South Korean women were forced to serve as sexual slaves for the Japanese Army during the Second World War. In 2011, former "comfort women" gathered in front of the Japanese Embassy in Seoul to demand an official apology and compensation from the Japanese government.

Another important item on the agenda for security in the post-Cold War period has been the increasing gap between the "haves" and "have nots." The former live mainly in the prosperous, industrialized countries of the northern hemisphere; the latter, in under-developed countries, most of which lie in the **global South**. We will consider the issue of globalization and some of its consequences in the context of international political economy in a later chapter; for now we will simply note that the "North–South" economic/developmental divide is widely recognized as having significant security dimensions, and that concerns in this regard pre-date the end of the Cold War.

In 1980, a UN-sponsored commission headed by the former West German Chancellor and Nobel Peace Laureate Willy Brandt, published an influential report entitled *North–South: A Programme for Survival*. It examined in depth the range of problems arising from the significant socioeconomic disparities between countries. The report emphasized that both North and South have a strong interest in putting an end to dependence, oppression, hunger, and general human distress. Its main recommendations related to the operation of transnational corporations, agricultural production and distribution, terms of trade, **protectionism**, energy costs, international financial institutions, foreign debt loads, levels of development assistance, population growth, and the cost of the arms race. It proposed vastly increased aid flows, arguing that the transformation of the international economy would be in the long-term interests of all counties, and that the implementation of its recommendations was not a matter of charity on the part of the North but a condition of survival for all.

Even so, some developed countries were lukewarm to the report. In the US, President Ronald Reagan had little interest in development-oriented issues except where aid might serve to counter Soviet influence. Overall, though, aid flows did increase. Just as important, the commission opened up new public debate on the relationship between global development and security by emphasizing that a narrow focus on military concerns was insufficient in an era of increasing global **interdependence**. Certainly, by 1989 it was clear that the Cold War had virtually ended and that the time had arrived for new thinking on security in an increasingly globalized world.

Attention turned not only to the plight of billions of people in the developing world and the multifaceted security threats they faced, but also towards the environment. Concerns with regard to latter had also been raised well before the end of the Cold War; for example, the UN had held an environmental summit in 1972. However, the post-Cold War world seemed much more conducive to consideration of environmental issues expressly in terms of *security*. The UN again took a lead, organizing a world summit in Rio de Janeiro in June 1992 (see www.un.org/geninfo/bp/enviro.html). Although the summit was wide-ranging, three major concerns were given particular attention: the world's forests, biodiversity, and climate change.

The summit produced the UN Convention on Climate Change, which entered into force in 1994. The Convention recognized that the climate system is a shared resource affected by the emission of "greenhouse gases" and set up a framework for intergovernmental efforts to address the problem of global warming. Three years later, the Kyoto Protocol of 1997 strengthened the Convention by committing its signatories to binding targets for the reduction of greenhouse gases (http://unfccc.int/kyoto_protocol/items/2830.php). But the US under the Bush administration and Australia under the Howard government refused to ratify the Accord on the grounds that (a) the emissions reduction targets would damage their respective economies and (b) rising industrial powers such as China and India, which as developing countries were never bound by the Accord, should not be given special treatment. Australia under a new Labor government elected in 2007, changed

17

tack but the US has maintained its position, and in 2011 it was joined by Canada, whose Conservative government withdrew from the Accord on the grounds that it discriminated in favour of the rapidly developing countries.

The economic costs of reducing greenhouse emissions are undoubtedly high, but the costs of inaction seem likely to be even greater. The consequences of global warming for security alone are enormous. Rising sea levels—just one consequence—threaten not just small island states and low-lying countries such as Holland, but extensive coastal regions of countries such as the US, Australia, Bangladesh, China, and many more. New forms of fossil fuel pose additional problems. Canada, home of the world's largest oil sands, is creating a very dirty form of energy. Extracting and refining the oil held in oil sands requires vast amounts of water (four and a half cubic metres to produce one cubic metre of oil) as well as energy, usually in the form of natural gas, and large amounts of toxic chemicals are left in the tailings (CTV News, 2008; Simpson, 2006). Furthermore, the methane released as the Arctic tundra thaws could significantly increase the levels of greenhouse gases in the atmosphere (Spotts, 2010).

Climate change will also have an impact on food and water security, especially as "environmental refugees" migrate en masse from low-lying areas such as Bangladesh. The views of skeptics notwithstanding, the scientific evidence regarding the changes now under way as a result of greenhouse gas emissions, and the devastating effects these changes are likely to have, is now beyond dispute. Environmental security is becoming an even more important part of IR every year.

Other non-traditional issues that have received more attention in the post-Cold War period include energy security, food, and water security (not just in relation to climate change), and biosecurity. Energy security, in particular, is a concern that links a variety of other security concerns, both traditional non-traditional, as the case study below shows.

CASE STUDY
Securing Energy

On the eve of the First World War, Winston Churchill made a historic decision: to shift the power source of the British Navy from coal to oil, in order to make its ships faster than their German counterparts. However, the switch meant that the Royal Navy would rely not on coal from Wales but on insecure oil supplies from Persia (now Iran). Energy security thus became a question of national strategy. Since then, energy security has repeatedly emerged as a major concern.

This concern is not limited to oil. Power blackouts in the US, Europe, and Russia, and chronic shortages of electricity in the developing world, including China and India, cast doubt on the reliability of supply systems. Rising demand for limited supplies of natural gas also means that North America can no longer be self-sufficient. Thus the US is joining a new global market in natural gas that links countries, continents, and prices in an unprecedented way.

A new range of vulnerabilities also becomes more evident. Al-Qaeda has threatened to attack crucial elements of the world's economic infrastructure—of which energy is one. The world will increasingly depend on new sources of energy in places where security systems are underdeveloped, such as the oil and natural gas fields off the coast of West Africa and in the Caspian Sea.

SOURCE: Adapted from Daniel Yergin (2006), "Ensuring Energy Security," *Foreign Affairs* 86, 3 (March/April): 69.

17

Post-Cold War Conflicts

The end of the Cold War was hailed as a victory in many Western countries, including the US. But it unleashed a number of internal conflicts, as nationalist movements emerged in federal political entities such as Yugoslavia and the Soviet Union. In some cases, the internal conflicts were violent, with many casualties. What should the UN do? Should it sit back as thousands were massacred or grossly abused? The early 1990s saw ongoing conflicts across the developing world, from Africa to the Pacific, as well as in places such as Northern Ireland and Spain. In addition, the break-up of the former Soviet empire provoked a flurry of nationalist activity. Not all of this took a violent form. The Czech and Slovak Republics were formed peacefully from the former Czechoslovakia following a nation-wide referendum. The Baltic states also eventually negotiated a peaceful path to independence. The departure of Central Asian republics from the old Soviet Union was accompanied by relatively little violence.

Violence was evident in other cases, though. Leaders in Moscow, determined to keep the Russian Federation intact, were ruthless in their suppression of Chechen separatism. The Balkans also presented a particularly difficult case. Although the secession of Slovenia from Yugoslavia in 1991 was managed with relatively little violence (largely because Slovenia was ethnically homogeneous and had only a very small Serbian minority), the breakup of the rest of the Yugoslav state gave rise to serious conflict between Croats, Serbs, and Bosnian Muslims, as we saw in Chapter 16.

In the meantime, crises in Africa produced further challenges for an international community struggling to remain optimistic about the prospects for peace and security. As the Cold War receded into history, new fears were sparked by fragile and failing states and the associated human costs. The experience of Somalia, as we saw in Chapter 7, had a significant impact on American attitudes towards the deployment of US forces overseas. Clarke and Gosende (2003: 145) write that the "desperate failure of Somalia intruded deeply into the sensibilities of the US Government and public" and that the experience there had a profound effect on responses to other crises, especially in Rwanda, where the US (along with France) forced a reduction of UN forces immediately before the genocide of 1994. This event, in which some 800,000 Tutsis and moderate Hutus were massacred by extremist Hutu militia, is regarded as a product of the UN's monumental failure to take the decisive action necessary to prevent an internal conflict from turning into a large-scale tragedy. Yet it also speaks volumes about President Bill Clinton's reluctance to promote a humanitarian foreign policy. The US, as much as the UN, was to blame for this failure. Only three years after the successful conclusion of "Operation Desert Storm" (the Persian Gulf War of 1990–1), the disaster in Rwanda suggested that expectations regarding the UN's ability to keep the peace in the conditions of the post-Cold War world—a world very different from the one that emerged at the end of the Second World War—might have been inflated.

From State Security to Human Security

Another important manifestation of new thinking was contained in a UN-sponsored publication entitled the *Human Development Report: 1994* (UNDP, 1994). Produced in preparation for the World Summit for Social Development in 1995, it opened with this statement: "The world can never be at peace unless people have security in their daily lives" (ibid.: 1). It then contrasted the prosperity achieved by some with the deepening misery of so many others and set out a case for redefining security in "human" terms. This marked

17

a substantial shift away from the traditional understanding of state or national security. The "human" aspect would include health security, employment security, environmental security, and security from crime, and security itself was to be understood in the broadest possible terms as "safety from the constant threats of hunger, disease, crime and repression" and "protection from sudden and hurtful disruptions in the pattern of our daily lives—whether in our homes, in our jobs, in our communities or in our environment" (ibid.: 3).

Like previous UN reports, this one attracted both supporters and critics. A common objection was that if virtually everything came under the rubric of "security," the term would become meaningless and efforts to achieve security would be diluted. Which type of security counted more? Where should limited funds and attention be targeted? Furthermore, the broadening of the security agenda meant that the important focus on *international* security might be lost or downplayed. In theoretical terms, while realists were keen to maintain the international–domestic distinction as a matter of practical as well as conceptual importance, liberals and others subscribing to alternative ideas about security welcomed the conceptual shift and its implications for policy. As a result, concerted efforts have been made, by policy-makers and others, to address security issues at multiple levels, although these efforts have been somewhat overshadowed by the fallout from the events of 9/11.

Security and Insecurity After 9/11

The attacks on the World Trade Center and the Pentagon by al-Qaeda operatives led the US to invade two separate sovereign states. A few months later, in his 2002 State of the Union address George W. Bush famously claimed that Iraq, North Korea, and Iran constituted an "Axis of Evil." (Presumably North Korea and Iran were included because of their hostility to "the West" and their development of nuclear programs).

Official White House Photo by Pete Souza

PHOTO 17.4 Remembering 9/11 ten years later. Barack and Michelle Obama, and George W. and Laura Bush, commemorate the victims in New York (2011).

The attacks provoked tremendous outrage and fear in Washington, and US defence expenditures soon rose to Cold War-era levels. Secretary of Defense Donald Rumsfeld, in his foreword to the issue of the *Quadrennial Defense Review* published just weeks after the attacks, warned that an evil and united enemy was waging a war against "America's way of life," against "all that America holds dear," and indeed, "against freedom itself" (US Department of Defense, 2001: iii) For its part, the Defense Department described the international system as "increasingly complex and unpredictable" compared to the system of the Cold War era, when "the key geographic regions of competition were well defined" (US Department of Defense, 2001: 1; 6). As a result of the administration's interpretation of 9/11, the defence budget grew exponentially. In 2005, when adjusted for inflation, it was 12 per cent higher than the Cold War average (Bacevich, 2005: 17). By 2007 the budget had swollen to $425 billion, not including an extra $120 billion for Iraq and Afghanistan, more than over $100 billion in troop costs including pensions, medical costs and disability payments, $16.4 billion to cover nuclear weapons costs, and $12.2 billion under the Military Construction Appropriations Bill (Johnson, 2006: 7–8). The case study below, on the rise of al-Qaeda and "militant Islam," illustrates a number of twists and variations on the theme of security.

Al-Qaeda was the prime suspect in the 9/11 attacks. The Bush administration demanded that the Taliban government of Afghanistan hand over bin Laden to the US and the UN Security Council supported that demand. The Taliban refused, and four weeks later the US and its allies launched Operation Enduring Freedom. NATO members including Canada and Germany had already invoked Article 5 of NATO's charter, according to which an armed attack against one member is an attack against all NATO's International Security Assistance Force (ISAF) took responsibility for the area around Kabul in early 2002, and in 2003 expanded its mission to cover all of Afghanistan. A program of political reconstruction has seen elections held, a new government put in place, and a program of infrastructure development. Yet Afghanistan barely functions as a state and insecurity continues at multiple levels.

The ongoing problems in Afghanistan were partly overshadowed by the war in Iraq, launched in March 2003 as part of the Bush administration's war on terror with the backing of the UK, Italy, Spain, and Australia,. However, this intervention did not have the support of either NATO or the UN Security Council, where France, with the backing of Russia and China, took the lead in opposing any invasion. Although the "coalition of the willing"—countries that officially supported the war—at one stage numbered almost fifty, only Poland, Denmark, and Australia sent military contingents to Iraq. Troops from some other countries were deployed in attempts at peace-building, but operations were largely confined to US and UK forces. NATO and the UN played no major role in the Iraq War.

By almost any measure, the invasion and occupation of Iraq did not go well, except during the short period of euphoria in May 2003 when Saddam Hussein was driven from power. Hostilities continued until December 2011, when the US formally ended its mission. Although a government of national unity was formed after inconclusive elections in 2010, Iraq continues to teeter on the brink of civil war between Shia and Sunni factions, while many people in the northern Kurdish areas seek to create a state of their own. Furthermore, violent criminality has become widespread. Al-Qaeda had virtually no presence in Iraq before March 2003, but the chaos there opened the door for

17

CASE STUDY
The Rise of Al-Qaeda and Islamic Militancy

Islamic radicalism and militancy are deeply intertwined with politics in the Middle East region. They have been on the rise since at least the 1970s, although the background to that rise can be traced to the emergence of Zionist and Arab nationalist movements in the late nineteenth century.

The current Middle East geopolitical landscape has been shaped by the outcomes of the First and Second World Wars, colonialism, and the competing territorial claims of Palestinian and Jewish groups. These claims have taken on an increasingly religious character over the years, fuelling the emergence of extremist, politically driven fundamentalism in both communities. Today, however, Islamic fundamentalism is marked by opposition not simply to the state of Israel as a Jewish entity, but to "the West" more generally. According to Cassels (1996: 236), pan-Islamic ideology represents an extreme form of anti-colonialism in which anti-Western sentiments extend to pro-Western regimes in the Middle East. By contrast, radical Zionism is localized in Israel and tends to focus on demands for further settlement in the West Bank and Gaza, stricter immigration policies, or a harder line on trading land for peace.

It was in a more explicit Cold War theatre, that Osama bin Laden formed the organization called al-Qaeda ("the base"). Afghanistan, a country with strategic significance for the Soviet Union and a long history of political instability, had been a battleground for competing factions since the early 1970s. While the Soviets supported a Marxist government, the US, along with Pakistan, Saudi Arabia, China, the UK, and other countries, generally supported an insurrection led by the Mujahideen (guerilla fighters who take their name from *jihad*, "holy struggle"). Although the latter were initially energized by and partially united in opposition to the Soviet presence in Afghanistan, whatever coherence they had possessed dissipated after the Soviet withdrawal in 1989.

Violent conflict between contending factions as well as with the embattled central government continued until 1996, when the strongest of the resistance factions, the Taliban, gained control and imposed an uncompromising version of Islamic rule. Afghanistan thereafter became a haven for al-Qaeda, which had originated there in 1988–9, during the anti-Soviet struggle, but later moved to Sudan. In 1996, bin Laden returned to Afghanistan and from there planned attacks on two US embassies in East Africa in 1998, and a US Navy vessel in Yemen in 2000, before organizing the attacks of 11 September 2001.

17

its operatives. Now Iraq indeed has become a recruiting ground for both criminal and terrorist organizations; see **Box 17.5**.

One major lesson from the war on terror is that the use of conventional military tactics against a non-conventional enemy may not only be ineffectual in defeating that enemy, but may create a score of new problems: Osama bin Laden, al-Qaeda, and the Taliban have not been destroyed; a seemingly endless supply of suicide bombers poses a threat to civilian populations in countries around the world; and the prospects for peace and security for the people of both Afghanistan and Iraq remain bleak.

More than 2,000 years ago, the Chinese Taoist thinker and strategist Sun Tzu advised that the best victory of all is that which is gained without fighting. He pointed to various

KEY CONCEPT BOX 17.5
Bremer's "100 Orders" and the Occupation of Iraq

Why did the US fail so miserably in its efforts to restore law and order in Iraq? Part of the problem was the decision of the head of the US-led Coalition Provisional Authority, Paul Bremer, to disband both the Iraqi Security Forces and the former ruling party. Within four days of his arrival in late May 2003, soon after the fall of Baghdad in April, Bremer issued "100 Orders" drafted with little if any input from local Iraqi leaders. The decision to ban Ba'ath Party officials from public sector employment meant that senior civil servants from hospital administrators to university deans were stripped of their positions (Wright, 2008: 400–4). At the same time, in dissolving Iraq's security forces Bremer put 400,000 troops out of work and left their 2 million dependents with no legal means of support. These two moves alienated the major power centers in Iraq and singled out Sunnis for discrimination. Crucially, without the secular influence of the Ba'ath Party, which in the past had suppressed religious extremism, the big winners in the December 2005 elections were the sectarian Sunni and Shia religious parties (Wright, 2008: 403–6). This sudden mass unemployment may also have contributed to the escalation of crime, which soon became endemic in the country.

A further problem was the American failure to take control immediately. PA member and IR professor Larry Diamond has described the first few weeks of the occupation as "chaotic and ineffectual, as most of the infrastructure of the country was systematically looted, sabotaged, and destroyed while American troops stood by" (Diamond, 2005: 10). The country degenerated into lawlessness. Indeed, "Save for the oil ministry—protected by US troops—virtually every significant public building was methodically looted and gutted in the days and weeks following the fall of Baghdad" (2005: 13–14).

Additional problems were created by Bremer's infamous "Order 39," designed to open up the economy to 100 per cent foreign-owned corporations while privatizing Iraqi assets. "Order 39" laid out a blueprint for the equal recognition and protection of foreign, particularly American, businesses, at a time when Iraqis had virtually no input into the running of their country ("Coalition Provisional Authority Order Number 39: Foreign Investment"; www.cpa-iraq.org/regulations/). The Bremer orders had direct ramifications for the stability of the country. Hundreds of thousands of Iraqis were now out of work and resentful of the American presence. Secret assessments prepared for the White House showed that the rising insurgency could be traced directly to Bremer's ill-advised actions. The numbers of "enemy initiated attacks" rose from fewer than 300 each month in mid-2003 to more than 3,500 in May 2006 (Woodward, 2006: 206, 473).

17

strategies for achieving this end, including the use of spying and other forms of intelligence gathering (see Sun Tzu, 1963). Similarly, many modern commentators have argued that terrorism is best dealt with by civil law enforcement agencies and the strengthening of national and international intelligence networks dedicated to the task. Although they cannot guarantee complete security (they failed in the case of the London bombings of July 2005, for example), regular policing and intelligence operations have nonetheless succeeded in preventing numerous other attacks (see Peña, 2006: 289–306).

Military force is often a very blunt weapon, and its consequences tend to be both unpredictable and uncontrollable. This is what led one of the most famous commentators on war, the Prussian military strategist Carl von Clausewitz (1780–1831), to observe that the planning and execution of war necessarily take place in a kind of fog that distorts and obscures what is going on (see Clausewitz, 1993). The "fog of war" has become an increasingly common theme in IR as the long-term future of Iraq and its people remains shrouded in uncertainty.

Conclusion

As we have shown, security and insecurity in the realm of international politics are multi-faceted, both conceptually and in practical terms. Various institutions, practices, and policies have been developed over the years to cope with security challenges that range from *conventional* threats to international peace and security—that is, armed aggression by one or more states against others in the international system—to such *unconventional threats* as internal conflict, environmental security, energy security, and threats from non-state actors such as terrorist organizations. The fact that these non-conventional threats are among the most serious today should lead students and practitioners of IR to question how useful military responses really are. We need to ask what alternative policy approaches, attuned to the specific dynamics of specific threats, are possible.

? KEY QUESTIONS

- How does traditional IR theory treat the concept of security? How does this treatment reflect the Hobbesian image of the "state of nature"?
- How would you assess the UN's success in maintaining international peace and security since its creation in 1945?
- How relevant is the nation-state to the way security is conceptualized today?
- Does the concept of "human security" offer a superior framework for addressing issues in the contemporary period?
- How has the anti-nuclear movement challenged traditional militarist approaches to security?
- How has the agenda for international security changed in the post-Cold War period?
- In what ways does a gender perspective illuminate non-traditional security issues in IR?
- How do issues such as energy security link old and new concerns about security in IR?
- In what sense does the war on terror represent a non-traditional security threat?
- Were the problems that the US experienced in Iraq more the fault of military strategy or of civilian miscalculations?

📖 FURTHER READING

Dalby, Simon (2002). *Environmental Security*. Minneapolis: University of Minnesota Press.
A political theorist based at Carleton University, Dalby treats the issue of environmental security from a Critical Theory perspective, bringing in aspects of environmental history, identities and geopolitics, and relating problems of environmental security to industrialization and modernization.

Holzgrefe, Jeff L., and Robert O. Keohane, eds (2003). *Humanitarian Intervention: Ethical, Legal, and Political Dilemmas*. Cambridge: Cambridge University Press.
Experts from several disciplines examine the tensions between the principles of sovereignty and humanitarian intervention, and the dilemmas facing the UN in various cases.

17

Kaldor, Mary (2006). *New and Old Wars: Organized Violence in a Global Era*. 2nd edn. Cambridge: Polity Press,

> Despite the invasions of Afghanistan and Iraq, Kaldor argues that interstate war is actually becoming an anachronism. Instead, new kinds of organized violence—"new wars"—are emerging that combine traditional aspects of war with organized crime and involve actors at various levels.

Kaplan, Lawrence S. (2004). *NATO Divided, NATO United: The Evolution of an Alliance*. Westport, CT: Praeger.

> Tensions within the NATO alliance, especially between the US and its European partners, are long-standing and despite an initial show of solidarity after 9/11, have been exacerbated by the war on terror. An interesting and insightful study that encompasses the past, present, and possible futures for the Western alliance.

MacDonald, David B. (2009). *Thinking History, Fighting Evil: Neoconservatives and the Perils of Analogies in American Politics*. Lanham, MD: Lexington/Rowman & Littlefield.

> A study of the way American neoconservatives misapplied analogies from the Second World War to the war on terror.

Stoett, Peter (2000). *Human and Global Security: An Exploration of Terms*. Toronto: University of Toronto Press.

> An accessible study of the ways in which conceptions of global and human security have changed since the Cold War. The author, based at Concordia University, distinguishes four key security problems: state violence, the degradation of the environment, forced migration, ethnic-cleansing and genocide, and globalization.

WEB LINKS

www.international.gc.ca/indig-autoch/partnership-partenariat.aspx?lang=eng&view=d
> The website of Foreign Affairs and International Trade Canada offers links on human security.

www.un.org/en/peacekeeping/documents/factsheet.pdf
> Detailed factsheets on UN peacekeeping operations as of October 2011.

www.unac.org/en/about_us/index.asp
> Information on peacekeeping around the world. Formed in 1946, the United Nations Association in Canada is a non-profit organization that promotes knowledge of and support for the UN in Canada.

www.un.org/reform/
> Offers both an overview and details of reports and publications on the topic of UN reform.

www.un-instraw.org/
> The main UN-INSTRAW (International Research and Training Institute for the Advancement of Women) website offers a guide to numerous sections on gender issues; the section on gender and security sector reform provides a more specific range of resources and information.

www.envirosecurity.org
> The website of the Institute for Environmental Security (IES), an international non-profit non-government organization established in 2002 with headquarters in The Hague.

www.terrorism-research.com/
> A useful general website containing articles and information about terrorism.

www.nato.int/ and http://www.un.org/en/
> The general websites for the UN and NATO offer links to an enormous number of sub-sites with important documents and other interesting material.

18 Diplomacy and Foreign Policy

CHAPTER OVERVIEW

Diplomacy has been fundamental to relations between political communities for thousands of years. In the contemporary era, formal diplomacy is the job of fully professionalized state bureaucracies, but other types of actors may also have important roles to play, from NGOs to special envoys or third-party mediators tasked with special missions. In addition, there are special forms of diplomacy such as "summit diplomacy" and "public diplomacy." Foreign policy behaviour is a closely related but distinctive field of study focusing on the strategies that states adopt in their relations with each other, strategies that reflect the pressures that governments face in either the domestic or the international sphere. In this chapter we will also consider the foreign and security policy of the EU, which now has a role and an identity as an international actor in its own right. The EU is just one example of the other actors with which the state must now contend in the international system.

Diplomacy and Statecraft in International History

If IR in the conventional sense refers to the pattern of interactions between states in the international system of states, then diplomacy is the principal formal mechanism through which these interactions take place. **Statecraft** refers to the skilful conduct of state affairs or, as some put it, "steering the ship of state," usually in the context of external relations. The practice of diplomacy has a very long history, reaching back beyond the earliest written records. One author remarks that even though we can only imagine what ancient practices were really like, diplomacy must have begun when the first human societies decided it was more advantageous to hear the message than to devour the messenger (see Langthorne and Hamilton, 1994: 7). To this observation we should add that the possibility of sending the messenger back with a response, thereby establishing a basis for ongoing communications, would have represented another advantage. A specific recorded reference to the utility of envoys or messengers may be found in the ancient text called the *Arthashastra*: according to Kautilya, its author, the first principle of diplomacy is "Don't shoot the messenger"; see **Box 18.1**.

We know that diplomacy was practised in ancient China. Before they were conquered and unified in 221 BCE, relatively autonomous city-states (*guo*) formed a multi-state system with patterns of interstate relations and diplomacy comparable to those that developed many centuries later in early modern Europe (Hui, 2005: 4–5). Tansen (2003) has argued that Buddhism played an important role in the development of diplomacy and trade between India and China. Evidence has also been found for the practice of alliance

See Chapter 14, page 284, for a discussion of the history of international state system.

KEY QUOTE BOX 18.1

Kautilya on an Ancient Principle of Diplomacy

Messengers are the mouth-pieces of kings, not only of thyself, but of all; hence messengers who, in the face of weapons raised against them, have to express their mission as exactly as they are entrusted with do not, though outcasts, deserve death; where is then reason to put messengers of *Bráhman* caste to death? This is another's speech. This (i.e., delivery of that speech verbatim) is the duty of messengers.

SOURCE: Chapter XVI, "The Mission of Envoys" in Book I, "Concerning Discipline, Arthashastra of Kautilya"; www.sdstate.edu/projectsouthasia/upload/Book-I-Concerning-Discipline.pdf; accessed 6 March 2012.

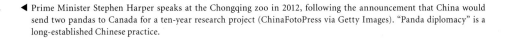

◀ Prime Minister Stephen Harper speaks at the Chongqing zoo in 2012, following the announcement that China would send two pandas to Canada for a ten-year research project (ChinaFotoPress via Getty Images). "Panda diplomacy" is a long-established Chinese practice.

diplomacy in the regions covered by the ancient Inca, Aztec, and Mayan empires (see Cioffi–Revilla and Landman, 1999: 559–98). Nevertheless, most analyses of diplomatic history have focused on developments in Europe, partly because the European state system has been so dominant, and partly because norms and negotiating practices in contemporary diplomacy largely reflect long-established European practices (including the use of English and French as the standard languages of diplomacy).

The first formal diplomatic practices in early modern Europe were developed in Italy, where resident embassies were established by the 1450s. Niccolò Machiavelli was among the most experienced diplomats of his time as well as one of the most famous commentators on statecraft. In addition to serving on bodies that oversaw the conduct of Florence's war efforts between 1500 and 1511, Machiavelli acted as a government envoy on 35 missions, including missions to France, the Papal Court, and the German Emperor (Miller, 1991: 303). The prime responsibility of an ambassador as a servant of the state was well understood by this time, as the well-known observation in **Box 18.2**, dating from the late fifteenth century, indicates.

KEY QUOTE BOX 18.2
The First Duty of an Ambassador

Ermolao Barbaro (1454–93) was a Venetian noble and scholar who served as ambassador at Naples and Rome. He believed it was his job to represent his government's position honestly and faithfully:

> The first duty of an ambassador is exactly the same as that of any other servant of a government, and that is, to do, say, advise, and think what may best serve the preservation and aggrandisement of his own state (cited in Langhorne, 2000: 35).

The practice of maintaining embassies quickly spread to other parts of Europe, where it became part and parcel of the sovereign state system (Mattingley, 1955: 10). In seventeenth-century France the administrative machinery for managing foreign policy took on a more advanced form under the guidance of one of diplomatic history's foremost figures, Cardinal de Richelieu (1585–1642). Richelieu famously established a system characterized by a continuous flow of information both in and out of Paris, careful record-keeping, and a unified system of management under his control. This type of bureaucratic centralization was largely absent elsewhere in Europe, where effective centralized government barely existed and foreign policy often depended "on the coming and going of court favourites, the whim of a monarch and accidents of administrative chaos—to name just three possibilities" (Langhorne, 2000: 37).

Another significant development was the consolidation of the notion of *raison d'état*. As we have seen, this notion reflected the idea that the state amounted to more than its ruler and that its needs should therefore come before the wishes of the king or (occasionally) queen (Craig and George, 1990: 5. The term subsequently became associated with realist ideas about *machtpolitik* (**power politics**), which also implied the irrelevance of morality in the conduct of international relations and the notion that "might is right." In the realist paradigm, *raison d'état* requires a statecraft attuned to the inevitability of conflict rather than one seeking justice and perpetual peace. It follows that however much we might agree that the latter are highly desirable political goods, the *reality* is that peace and justice in the international sphere can only ever be incidental or subordinate to the main business of diplomacy, statecraft, and foreign policy: the preservation of the state and the advancement of its interests by whatever means it is prudent to employ.

Amoral *raison d'état* was eventually absorbed into the ethically more acceptable notion of **national interest**, which is the face of power politics today. There is now much discussion of the concept of "normative power," a quality attributed to the EU that, according to its proponents, was developed precisely in order to escape "great power mentality" (Manners, 2006: 183).

In the wake of the Napoleonic wars, Europe achieved a relatively stable **balance of power** system, initially through the Congress of Vienna (1814–15) at which the great powers were represented mainly by ambassadors and their diplomatic aides. In agreeing to conduct regular meetings, the great powers established the **Concert of Europe**, an early attempt to institute a formal structure for conducting international relations. As Fry et al. note, Concert diplomacy, through which: the great powers "tried to avoid war, protect the status quo and, if this was impossible, to arrange for change by multilateral agreement" represented a high point in the history of diplomacy (Fry et al., 2002: 113). In the Concert system we see the first glimmerings of the kind of multilateralism that became the foundation of the League of Nations and the UN.

The Concert system declined gradually over the next half century, its failure evident in the Crimean War of 1854–6 and the Franco–Prussian War of 1870–1. Its demise may be attributed in part to the rise of the **nationalism** that was to become such as destructive force in the twentieth century. Nonetheless, the basic institutions of diplomacy and statecraft developed in Europe remained integral parts of the sovereign state system.

KEY POINTS

- Diplomacy and statecraft have been practised from the earliest times, appearing in various forms in different parts of the world.
- Traditional views of diplomacy and statecraft in international relations incorporate realist concepts such as *raison d'état* and *machtpolitik*.
- The methods of diplomacy and statecraft used today developed within the modern European state system, which provided the initial template for the current international system.

Diplomacy in the Contemporary World

Contemporary diplomatic processes cover virtually all aspects of a state's external or foreign relations, from trade to aid, negotiations about territorial borders, international treaties, the implementation of international law, the imposition of sanctions, the mediation of hostilities, the negotiation of disputed boundaries, fishing rights, and agreements on environmental protection. Diplomacy extends beyond the pursuit of a given state's own foreign policy objectives to encompass activities that range from third-party peace negotiations to Earth Summits involving a variety of actors in extensive multilateral diplomatic activity.

We have also seen the emergence of track two diplomacy: informal or unofficial diplomatic efforts undertaken by private citizens, business people, peace activists or NGOs as well as state actors. Informal diplomatic efforts are often helpful in peace negotiations,

18

preparing the ground for more formal talks by persuading the parties in conflict to agree to negotiate.

Heads of government are now often involved directly in diplomatic activities, as we shall see shortly, but the routine business of external affairs is still carried out by professional diplomatic services, which are usually located within foreign ministries (in Canada the Ministry of Foreign Affairs and International Trade; in Britain the Foreign and Commonwealth Office; in the US the Department of State). Whatever they are called, such departments run diplomatic missions, usually in the form of permanent embassies around the world. Within the Commonwealth, these are called High Commissions and the head of mission is the High Commissioner rather than the "ambassador"—one of the legacies of Britain's imperial system. Many small developing countries face particular problems in maintaining embassies or high commissions because of the cost of premises and personnel. This makes it very difficult for them to participate on an equal footing, even though the diplomatic "playing field" is in principle level. As in other spheres, the greater the resources, the greater the clout. For example, richer countries are able to fund consulates and trade missions in other cities, as well as cultural centres and other forms of diplomatic representation. This increases their profile, not only with diplomats in the host country, but also with business and cultural leaders.

In addition to regular diplomatic missions, special envoys may be appointed for particular purposes. Thus Tony Blair, immediately after his resignation as prime minister, was appointed to serve as a special peace envoy to the Middle East. Other special envoys are sometimes appointed by non-state actors such as religious leaders. Both the Archbishop of Canterbury and the Pope have appointed special envoys for various purposes—often in conflict situations or as special negotiators when people are being held hostage. Since the Vatican has its own special status as a sovereign entity, the appointment of envoys by the Pope may be seen as a regular function of state.

Special forms of diplomacy are sometimes used to resolve internal conflicts and problems. In 2000, ethnic conflict in the Solomon Islands, a former British colony in the Pacific, brought the state to the verge of collapse. With the assistance of Australia and New Zealand, approximately 150 representatives from the rival factions travelled to Townsville, Australia, for an "offshore" meeting, with mediators, This is an example of third-party mediation, which has become commonplace as conflicts within states, as well as between them, raise problems for regional and international order.

Styles of diplomacy vary depending on regional factors or considerations. The Association of Southeast Asian Nations (ASEAN) has promoted what it calls the "ASEAN Way" as a distinctive style of diplomacy marked by commitment to non-interference in the internal affairs of member states. It is true that member states of the EU have reduced the weight they give to state **sovereignty** in the interests of political and economic integration. They have also been known to openly criticize one other. However, to depict their different approaches to diplomacy as reflecting a great gulf of "cultural difference" between East and West would be misleading. The fact is that the doctrine of state sovereignty is itself a European invention, adopted elsewhere for its political efficacy, not because it was a good "cultural fit." As for "the West," this is not a coherent cultural entity in any case. The diplomatic style of the EU, for instance, stands in sharp contrast to the hawkish approach of the Bush administration in the US. (It's also worth noting that the principle of non-intervention has not prevented other ASEAN members from criticizing Burma's military regime in recent years.)

- Contemporary diplomacy may involve a broad range of actors, including professional diplomats, special envoys, heads of government, the UN, NGOs, and regional bodies such as the EU and ASEAN.
- Different countries or regions are said to possess certain diplomatic styles, which sometimes reflect cultural differences.
- "Track two diplomacy" is commonly deployed in peace negotiations and is an important adjunct to formal intergovernmental modes.

Cold War Diplomacy

Cold War diplomatic history is an eventful field of study. The Cuban missile crisis of 1962, for example, was the closest the world ever came to nuclear Armageddon. Triggered when the US discovered that the Soviets were building a base in Cuba from which they could launch nuclear missiles, the crisis was resolved largely because US President Kennedy and Soviet Premier Khrushchev both recognized that the consequences of a military confrontation would be disastrous. Strategic thinking subsequently produced a theory of deterrence known as "mutually assured destruction" (MAD). The idea that the key to preventing war is the ability to destroy any enemy remains an essential aspect of US foreign and security policy. Recent work on "nuclear diplomacy" during the Cold War has sought to determine whether the possession of nuclear weapons by both sides actually prevented a Third World War (Gaddis et al., 1999). Although there is no definitive answer to this question, it is clear that without diplomacy, however clumsy, the Cold War might well have become the "hottest" war ever. Where diplomacy often did fail was in relation to the developing countries, which bore the brunt of the fighting with conventional weaponry during the Cold War years. Many conflicts in Africa have stemmed from Cold War rivalries encouraged by the two superpowers. While some of these conflicts have been resolved, the proliferation of weapons has allowed others to continue.

Cold War diplomacy also introduced the concept of "**détente**" (French for "relaxation") in foreign policy. A key promoter of détente was Henry Kissinger, the US Secretary of State who orchestrated President Richard Nixon's ground-breaking trip to China in 1972. The easing of tensions that took place between 1969 and 1979 reflected a number of economic and geopolitical circumstances, including the recognition by Kissinger and Nixon that the Vietnam War was a fiasco, the development of closer relations between the US and the People's Republic of China, the huge cost of the arms race, the desire to devote more attention to domestic matters, and the souring of relations between China and the USSR, which feared that China and the US might form an alliance against it and therefore sought to improve its relations with the Americans. These factors led to the signing of the Strategic Arms Limitation Treaty (or SALT I) in 1972. As well, the Nuclear Non-Proliferation Treaty (NPT), which had been signed in 1968, was extended indefinitely. The NPT currently has a total of 190 signatories, including five nuclear-weapon states—the US, France, the UK, Russia, and China. But India and Pakistan, both of which possess nuclear weapons, have not signed; nor have Israel, which probably possesses nuclear weapons, and North Korea, which may well have a covert nuclear program.)

The NPT was complemented by other treaties and agreements including the second phase of the Strategic Arms Limitation Treaty (SALT II), which was negotiated between 1972 and 1979.

18

AP Photo/File

PHOTO 18.1 In February 1972, Richard Nixon launched a new era in world politics when he became the first US president to visit the communist People's Republic of China. Here he meets formally with Mao Zedong. Nixon's trip opened the way for the establishment of full diplomatic relations, and in 1979 the US formally recognized the PRC rather than the Republic of China (Taiwan) as the legitimate Chinese state.

However, the Soviet invasion of Afghanistan in 1979 took the Carter administration by surprise, and the policy of détente effectively collapsed. The Reagan administration withdrew from SALT I and adopted a more confrontational approach to the USSR. Nevertheless, international treaties and conventions concerning weapons remain a crucially important part of international diplomacy. The practices and procedures put in place during the Cold War continue as vital elements of contemporary diplomacy surrounding nuclear energy and weaponry, chemical and biological weapons, and the full range of conventional weapons, including small arms and land mines.

Other aspects of Cold War politics and diplomacy have become staples of popular culture, especially in fiction and film. Although the James Bond genre has been thoroughly reinvented for the post-Cold War world, its Cold War origins are unmistakable in its central theme of espionage. Real-life spy dramas were not uncommon during the Cold War, as intelligence agencies on both sides were prepared to do whatever it took to learn one another's secrets. Embassies and their diplomatic staff were prime targets, but even cabinet ministers were sometimes implicated in sexual and other intrigues. The Canadian Parliament was rocked by scandal in March 1966 when it was found that a junior cabinet minister had had an affair with a suspected spy. The scandal deepened as information came to light indicating how much Prime Minister Pearson knew about the affair; see **Box 18.3**.

18

KEY QUOTE BOX 18.3
The "Munsinger Affair" (1966)

The *Vancouver Sun* published this summary of the "Munsinger Affair" in 1997, following the release of Cabinet documents from the time.

Then Prime Minister Lester Pearson was so desperate to divert attention from the sensational Gerda Munsinger sex-and-spy scandal that he opened an explosive debate about capital punishment that led to the elimination of the death penalty. Cabinet documents released Wednesday show the Munsinger scandal dominated government business in March 1966, bringing Parliament to the brink of paralysis. . . .

Pearson told cabinet it was "imperative" for the Liberals to end debate on the issue, which threatened "to exacerbate an already dangerous and destructive Parliamentary situation." Seeking to douse the fevered debate in the Commons, Pearson agreed to a royal commission into Canada's first Parliamentary sex scandal. He also suggested the government close debate on the matter at once and start a new debate on the death penalty, also a hot subject as two Quebec separatists were on death row. . . .

The scandal erupted March 4, 1966 when justice minister Lucien Cardin—under attack for his handling of the Spencer spy case—lashed out at his Tory critics. Goaded mercilessly, Cardin shouted to Tory leader [John] Diefenbaker that he was the last man to be advising on security—given his performance in "the Munsinger case." Chaos ensued. Still angry, Cardin told reporters outside the Commons to ask Diefenbaker if they wanted the story, which he said was as serious as the 1963 Profumo sex-spy scandal in England [which nearly brought down Harold Macmillan's Conservative government]. As prime minister in the late 1950s, Diefenbaker retained [Pierre] Sévigny in cabinet even though the junior defence minister had an affair with Munsinger, a German immigrant US sources accused of being a security risk. . . .

When the scandal broke in Parliament, opposition members accused the government of mishandling an issue of national security. . . . The scandal escalated when Munsinger was found alive in Germany, after the government said she died of leukemia years before. After weeks of riotous debate in the House, cabinet decided to name Supreme Court Justice Wishart Spence to a narrowly defined inquiry, successfully burying the issue once and for all. Simultaneously, Pearson diverted attention from the scandal by introducing the debate on capital punishment. His gambit succeeded in calming one storm with another. Even though an initial vote retained the death penalty, the ensuing national debate led the government to abolish the death penalty in 1967 for a trial period of five years, except in cases where the victim was an off-duty police officer or a prison guard.

SOURCE: Brad Evenson and Andrew Duffy (1997), "Secret Papers Link Scandal, Death Penalty," *Vancouver Sun*, 28 Feb.; A4; http://www.walnet.org/csis/news/ottawa_97/vansun-970228.html.

A more recent debacle occurred in mid-2010 when the FBI purportedly discovered 11 Russian "sleeper" or "deep cover" agents who had been living and working in the US since the mid-1990s. Ten of the alleged spies appeared in a Manhattan court, suspected of trying to gather information on US foreign policy in the Middle East, nuclear weapons, and the activities of the CIA, among other matters. The court charges, 55 pages in total, were published by the *New York Times* (Adams, 2010). As the article quoted in **Box 18.4** (from the website of Germany's international broadcaster *Deutsche Welle*) suggests, the scandal brought to mind aspects of the Cold War.

KEY QUOTE BOX 18.4

New Spy Scandal Exhumes Cold War—Again

The initial reaction from the Russian government has been tough and outraged. A spokesman on Tuesday called American allegations that eleven people spied for Moscow over 20 years "baseless," and Deputy Justice Minister and parliament member Vladimir Kolesnikov quickly turned his attention to the US spies who may be operating in Russia. "It is after all no secret that agents of the US secret services work in Russia," Kolesnikov said in Moscow. . . . Russian Foreign Ministry spokesman Andrei Nesterenko said the scenario "resembles espionage scandals from the Cold War." . . .

The timing of the arrests could hardly be more sensitive. Russian President Dmitry Medvedev had barely returned from a trip to North America to sell Russia as an investor-friendly economy, and relations between the two old foes are better than they have been for many years, thanks largely to President Barack Obama's "reset" policy, following the suspicion of the Bush years. . . .

Nevertheless, the scandal says a lot about the old-fashioned paranoia still embedded in the secret services on both sides. The ingredients of this scandal have all been seen before—genteel suburban houses masking a world of deception, deep-cover identities and secret codes. With an incremental update in technology, spy scandals have returned regularly throughout the post-Cold War era. In almost all cases, these scandals have been characterized by tit-for-tat expulsions, with notable attention being paid to symmetry.

In May 1996, Moscow and London both ordered the expulsion of four diplomats from the other country following espionage allegations. Eleven Soviet citizens had previously been evicted from Britain in 1989 due to "irrefutable" evidence of spying. Moscow retorted with the expulsion of 11 British citizens.

Similarly in March 2001, Washington cracked down on up to 50 presumed Russian spies with diplomatic status. They were evicted, with US officials justifying the move by pointing to the unmasking of Moscow's FBI spy Robert Hanssen. . . .

Alex Nice points out that the logistics of international political espionage have barely changed since the Cold War. "The former head of MI5 remarked a few years ago that Russian espionage in Britain had reached Cold War levels," he said. "And another commentator pointed out that the US, unlike many other countries, has not wound down its domestic counter-espionage since the Cold War. Evidently these things still go on, and I'm sure they are not just conducted by Russia."

SOURCE: "New Spy Scandal Exhumes Cold War—Again," *Deutsche Welle*, 29 June 2010; http://www.dw-world.de/dw/article/0,,5743401,00.html.

- The Cold War was marked by crises in which diplomacy played a key role in preventing what might have been a Third World War waged with nuclear weapons.
- Cold War diplomacy also led to the negotiation of treaties and conventions that continue to play an important role in the ongoing effort to limit the production and distribution of a wide range of weapons.
- Although the end of the Cold War marked a major change in world politics, continuities have been evident in recent diplomatic dramas.

Summit Diplomacy

It is evident from the previous sections that diplomacy is practised by many different kinds of actors operating at different levels and in different capacities. In the early years of the Cold War, Winston Churchill coined the phrase "summit diplomacy" to refer to top-level meetings in which heads of government meet to negotiate over key issues. In the past such meetings were rare, but in recent years heads of government have met more regularly to discuss or negotiate directly (Melissen, 2003: 4). Summits come in many different kinds, from ad hoc bilateral meetings—which may include a third-party mediator if the issue in question involves a serious dispute—to global multilateral summits attended not only by heads of government and their teams but by leading figures from the UN; these major summits often include parallel meetings for NGOs.

Among the largest and best-known multilateral meetings have been the Earth Summits organized by the UN. In addition, regional or interregional summits are now regular features of the international scene; organizations such as the Asia-Pacific Economic forum (APEC), the Organization of American States (OAS) and the Asia-Europe Meeting process (ASEM) have become solidly institutionalized. The Commonwealth has reinvented itself in the postcolonial period as something of a diplomatic summit club: a Commonwealth Heads of Government Meeting (CHOGM) is held every two years to discuss matters of mutual interest and concern and formulate policies and initiatives at the highest level. Although such events are sometimes seen as little more than opportunities for international socializing (the acronym APEC, for example, has been amusingly recast as "A Perfect Excuse for a Chat"), their value should never be underestimated: diplomatic socialization at any level invariably contributes to building **international society**.

A summit of major historic importance was arranged by US President Jimmy Carter in 1978. The Camp David summit led to a peace accord between Egypt and Israel that has lasted to this day. Carter, acting as a mediator, demonstrated the efficacy of "shuttle diplomacy," keeping the principals largely apart and moving back and forth between them to broker an agreement; see the case study on the next page.

- Summit diplomacy has become a common feature of the international political landscape, both in ad hoc situations and at regularly scheduled events.
- Summit diplomacy has been used in situations that range from small bilateral meetings to large-scale multilateral negotiations over issues such as the environment.

- Summit events may help to promote the development of an "international society" by creating opportunities for personal interaction between world leaders.

CASE STUDY
Arab–Israeli Relations, Summit Diplomacy, and the Camp David Accords

Camp David, the presidential retreat north of Washington, DC, was the location for a summit meeting between President Anwar Sadat of Egypt and Prime Minister Menachem Begin of Israel in 1978, initiated by US President Jimmy Carter. Since the Six-Day War of 1967, Israel had occupied the Gaza Strip and the Sinai Peninsula, both former Egyptian territories. Sadat had been attempting to reclaim the Sinai since 1971, but negotiations had failed and fighting broke out again when Egypt and Syria, with the support of other Arab counties, launched a joint attack on Israel on the Jewish holy day of Yom Kippur in 1973. A UN ceasefire was organized on 24 October, followed by a peacekeeping operation. Further negotiations were held in which the US Secretary of State, Henry Kissinger, acted as a peace broker. In an interim agreement, signed in 1975, both Egypt and Israel agreed to renounce further military action. Several years of inaction followed until Sadat broke the stalemate with a visit to Jerusalem in 1977. Begin reciprocated six weeks later, travelling to the Egyptian city of Ismailia. These meetings constituted the main diplomatic prelude to the Camp David Summit.

Sadat believed that Gaza and the West Bank belonged to the Palestinians while the Sinai should be returned to Egypt. Begin insisted that God had given them to the Jews. After three days of direct negotiations, tensions had mounted to the point that Carter feared there was little chance of a lasting agreement. He then decided to separate the parties and act as a go-between. A single document was created and Carter worked individually with each leader to revise it, carrying proposals and counter-proposals back and forth over a two-week period. Although the negotiations almost broke down completely on several occasions, an accord was at last reached through Carter's non-stop "shuttle diplomacy." The Israeli–Palestinian dispute continues today despite the Oslo Accords of 1993 and a further summit at Camp David in 2000 mediated by President Clinton. However, there have been no hostilities between Egypt and Israel since 1978.

(For the text of the 1978 Camp David Accords see www.jimmycarterlibrary.org/documents/campdavid/accords.phtml.)

Public Diplomacy

The term "public diplomacy" refers primarily to the ways in which governments attempt to influence public opinion abroad. This activity has acquired increasing importance in recent years. It draws on the cultural power of ideas and the notion of "soft power" formulated by the American liberal academic Joseph Nye; see **Box 18.5**. In effect, the exercise of soft power amounts to winning "hearts and minds." Interestingly, this has some resonances with Antonio Gramsci's notion of cultural power and the way it supports **hegemony**. Yet the role of culture in diplomacy, foreign policy, and the broader field of international relations is highly contested; both "culturalists" and their critics have

KEY QUOTE BOX 18.5
Nye on "Soft Power"

Nye defines "soft power" as

> the ability to get what you want through attraction rather than coercion or payments. It arises from the attractiveness of a country's culture, political ideals, and policies. When our policies are seen as legitimate in the eyes of others, our soft power is enhanced. . . . When you can get others to admire your ideals and to want what you want, you do not have to spend as much on sticks and carrots to move them in your direction. Seduction is always more effective than coercion, and many values like democracy, human rights, and individual opportunity are deeply seductive. . . . But attraction can turn to repulsion if we act in an arrogant manner and destroy the real message of deeper values (Nye, 2004a: x).

produced an abundance of literature on the subject in recent years (see Gaenslen, 1997; Lawson, 2006).

In the UK, the Foreign and Commonwealth Office (FCO) has defined public diplomacy as "Work aiming to inform and engage individuals and organisations overseas, in order to improve understanding of and influence for the United Kingdom in a manner consistent with governmental medium and long term goals" (www.fco.gov.uk; accessed 17 Nov. 2011). Canada too promotes public diplomacy through Foreign Affairs and International Trade, which in addition to marketing Canada abroad seeks to promote "social cohesion" and "attachment and belonging to Canada" at home (http://www.international.gc.ca/about-a_propos/oig-big/2005/evaluation/diplomacy_program-programme_diplomatie.aspx?lang=eng; accessed 7 March 2012). The US State Department also has an Under Secretary dedicated to matters of public diplomacy and public affairs, as well as an advisory committee on public diplomacy. The office of the Under Secretary explains its purpose in terms of three strategic objectives:

1. offer people throughout the world a positive vision of hope and opportunity that is rooted in America's belief in freedom, justice, opportunity, and respect for all;
2. isolate and marginalize the violent extremists; confront their ideology of tyranny and hate; undermine their efforts to portray the west as in conflict with Islam by empowering mainstream voices and demonstrating respect for Muslim cultures and contributions; and
3. foster a sense of common interests and common values between Americans and people of different countries, cultures, and faiths throughout the world.

(SOURCE: www.state.gov/r/; accessed 20/07/07.)

Other countries promote their own brands of public diplomacy. In 2006, for example, the government of India created a public diplomacy division within its external affairs

State Dept Image/May 04, 2011

PHOTO 18.2 Public diplomacy in action. Here a US Assistant Secretary in the State Department gives a water pump to a beneficiary of a program jointly coordinated by the US, the UN, and the government of Sri Lanka.

ministry "to educate and influence global and domestic opinion on key policy issues and project a better image of the country commensurate with its rising international standing" (http://www.indiafutureofchange.com/initiativesParners_ExternalAffairs.htm; accessed 7 March 2012). And China has been proactive in raising its international profile through initiatives such as the international network of Confucius Institutes. Public diplomacy of this kind is all the more important for a country with a poor human rights record and serious international image problems. This was especially the case following the Tiananmen Square massacre of 1989, when large numbers of unarmed, peaceful pro-democracy protestors were killed by soldiers of the People's Liberation Army. The incident was televised internationally, and it is commonly believed that this was a major factor in the failure of China's bid to host the 2000 Olympic Games. However, the state took action to rehabilitate China's image, and its bid for the 2008 games succeeded despite ongoing human rights (and other) problems that sparked protests by individuals and groups around the world when the games were actually held.

So-called "pariah regimes" have used ad hoc acts of public diplomacy to attract favourable international attention. One example was Iranian President Mahmoud Ahmadinejad's release, amid much fanfare, of 15 British navy personnel captured in a waterway between Iraq and Iran in March 2007. In the same year the Palestinian movement Hamas took credit for gaining the release of British journalist Alan Johnston, who had been held hostage by the "Army of Islam" in Gaza for 114 days. Although public diplomacy is rarely a decisive factor in the success of particular foreign policy initiatives, some have argued that it serves an important ancillary function, especially today, when media and telecommunications have changed so radically. It has also been suggested that a new type of public diplomacy is developing in which the goal is not to indirectly influence other governments, which is still a state-to-state interaction, but rather to shape the attitudes of other societies in a more direct state-to-society interaction (Henriksen, 2006: 1). The need was especially acute for the US under the Bush administration, which had a serious image problem. In many places, attitudes towards the US improved rapidly when Barack Obama came to power. With the battle for hearts and minds so prominent in international affairs, it is clearly important for states seeking to play a prominent role on the world stage, or to attract support for their various causes, to invest in developing "soft power" through public diplomacy.

In 2007, the inventor of the term, Joseph Nye, co-chaired a bipartisan Congressional committee called the "Smart Power Commission" to improve the image of the US and, in his words, "move from exporting fear to inspiring optimism and hope." Nye even quoted Defense Secretary Robert Gates, who had observed that the budget of the State Department was a tiny fraction of his own department's much larger budget and called for "strengthening our capacity to use soft power and for better integrating it with hard power." Sadly, as Nye observed in mid-2011, Gates's plea for more State Department funding "was as odd as a man biting a dog, but these are not normal times." He went on to note that "Since then, the ratio of the budgets has become even more unbalanced" (Nye, 2011).

So what is the line between public diplomacy (usually perceived as a positive thing) and propaganda (usually perceived in negative terms)? Are they merely different sides of the same coin? Propaganda in a neutral sense simply denotes the dissemination or promotion of particular ideas and values through some means of communication. In a slightly more instrumental sense, it implies an attempt to influence beliefs and behaviour rather than an objective presentation of "the facts." Over time it has acquired more sinister overtones and often conjures up images of deceit, distortion of facts or even "brainwashing," perhaps because Nazi Germany actually had a ministry of propaganda, run by Joseph Goebbels. Contemporary variations on the theme of propaganda include "spin doctoring," otherwise known as "news management": a conscious strategy of minimizing negative images of either politicians or political events while maximizing positive images (see Jowett and O'Donnell, 2006: 2–3); although "spin" is most often directed to domestic audiences, it has an important place in the international sphere of diplomacy and **statecraft** as well.

KEY POINTS

- Public diplomacy at its most basic is the effort by a government to influence public opinion in other countries by promoting positive images of its country.

18

- Many acts of public diplomacy, from the release of hostages to the everyday activity of news management, involve elements of propaganda and "spin."
- Public diplomacy may be understood as an instrument of soft power, in contrast with the methods of power politics.

Foreign Policy

Foreign policy is generally framed in terms of the strategies that those in control of a state adopt in their dealings with other actors in the international system or with respect to relevant issues, such as the environment, aid to developing countries, trade regimes, and so on. Whatever particular issue is at stake, the study of foreign policy links the domestic and international spheres of politics. As Evans and Newnham (1998: 179) put it, foreign policy is often called a "boundary activity" because it effectively straddles the two spheres and mediates between them.

An important factor affecting a state's foreign policy behaviour is its regional or geopolitical location. For example, the history of US foreign policy shows the degree to which the country's location in the Americas has influenced its foreign policy behaviour. It was in the context of the establishment of independent states in South America, and the efforts of European powers to maintain colonial systems there, that the US enunciated the "Monroe Doctrine," named for its initiator, President James Monroe. After safely concluding the purchase of Florida from Spain, Monroe announced to Congress in 1823 that the US would focus on its interests in the Americas without necessarily respecting European interests. But this did not mean the US had unqualified respect for the sovereignty of the new states emerging in the Americas.

Rather, the Monroe Doctrine reflected the view that European powers should not intervene in the politics of Latin America because the latter was within the US sphere of influence. By contrast, as the dominant power in the region, the US itself was entitled to intervene whenever and wherever it felt it appropriate to do so. Subsequent interference by the US in the internal affairs of Central and South American politics—including the undermining or outright overthrow of leftist governments, whether democratically elected or not—may be seen as the logical outcome of the doctrine. The legacies of "Yanqui imperialism" continue to give the US a bad name in the region.

The foreign policy of the UK has followed a different trajectory in its historical development, shaped both by the dynamics of the European region and by its colonizing enterprises. In more recent years, it has become deeply enmeshed in "special relationships" that have been decisive for its foreign policy. The Anglo–American special relationship has ebbed and flowed depending on the nature of the salient issues in world politics as well as the personalities involved. The term "special relationship" actually dates from the time when Roosevelt and Churchill forged a close personal alliance during the Second World War. Another strong personal alliance developed between Margaret Thatcher and Ronald Reagan during the latter stages of the Cold War, assisted no doubt by their conservative dispositions and their shared loathing of communism.

A more recent special relationship was the one between former Prime Minister Tony Blair and President George W. Bush. Both men cast the invasion of Iraq as an integral part of the war on terror, even though there was no evidence linking Saddam Hussein with al-Qaeda or the events of 9/11. Blair came under much criticism at home for what seemed to be his uncritical endorsement of White House policy and his unwavering support for a war that turned out to lack any firm justification. More recently, President Obama, meeting with Prime Minister David Cameron in May 2011, had this to say of the special relationship between the US and UK:

> Yes, it is founded on a deep emotional connection, by sentiment and ties of people and culture. But the reason it thrives, the reason why this is such a natural partnership, is because it advances our common interests and shared values. It is a perfect alignment of what we both need and what we both believe. And the reason it remains strong is because it delivers time and again. Ours is not just a special relationship, it is an essential relationship—for us and for the world (Obama and Cameron, 2011).

KEY CONCEPT BOX 18.6
Canada's Special Relationship with the US

Like the UK, Canada has long had a special relationship with the US. Unlike the UK, however, Canada shares the world's largest undefended border with the world's only remaining superpower. The Canada–US relationship is interdependent and polyvalent. On the positive side, Carment, Hampson, and Hillmer note that the relationship has been "remarkably free of linkage, the practice of making threats and tying policy performance in one area to another." Indeed, "Canada has pursued its policies without fearing reprisals or sanctions from its neighbor when priorities clashed. The two countries shared values, interests, and goals during the long darkness of the Cold War and into the 1990s" (Carment, Hampson, and Hillmer, 2003: 12). Yet the relationship is also highly asymmetrical. The US accounts for 83 per cent of Canada's trade; 33 states claim Canada as their major export market, and another five states send more than 50 per cent of their goods north of the border (Carment, Hampson, and Hillmer, 2003: 16). Canadian provinces export more to the US than to the rest of Canada, and more to Home Depot in the US than to France. Four in ten Canadian jobs depend directly on trade with the US (Granatstein, 2007: 84). Militarily, the relationship is also close, with almost 90 treaty-level agreements as well as a Canada–US Bilateral Planning Group, established in 2002 in response to 9/11 (Bercuson, 2003: 122).

Some policy planners in both countries have mooted the idea of hemispheric integration on the model of the European Union. The project of creating common political and institutions is known as "deeper integration." Although some business elites welcome the idea, this is not necessarily the case with most Canadians, Americans, or Mexicans, since such a project would mean a loss of national sovereignty for all parties. As described to the Canadian Parliament by Robert Pastor, one of the key proponents of North American integration, the process would entail building common institutions as well as "an inclusive identity that would inspire citizens of all three countries to think of themselves also as North Americans" (Pastor, 2002: 2). Pastor proposes the formation of a "North American Commission" to develop "a continental plan for infrastructure and transportation, a plan for harmonizing regulatory policies, a customs union, a common currency"

18

and even suggests how a unified currency system based on the "Amero" could work (Pastor, 2002: 5–6).

Pastor's project is distrusted not only by many Canadian commentators, but also by many Americans, particularly conservative nationalists. He has been accused of anti-Americanism for proposing to relinquish American sovereignty and bind the US to a multinational framework in the same way that West Germany was bound to the European Coal and Steel Community (ECSC) and then later to NATO after the Second World War. Underlying deeper integration, one conservative commentator argued from a right of centre perspective, was Pastor's view of the US "as a North American bully that needs to be restrained, for the good of the region and possibly even for the good of the world" (Corsi, 2006).

Fears for Canada's independence may help to explain why Canadians have often been wary of US foreign policy. This was especially so during the Bush administration. It's interesting to note how Canada balances its special relationship with the US with another special relationship. Keeping the Queen as head of state, playing a key role in the Commonwealth, and maintaining certain British institutions and practices offsets the influence of "Americanization" and stakes out a distinctly Canadian identity. While forms of economic integration will no doubt continue, formal political union seems unlikely in the foreseeable future.

KEY POINTS

- "Foreign policy" generally refers to the strategies that governments adopt in their dealings with other actors in the international system.
- The foreign policy behaviour of states or other actors is influenced by size, capacity, geopolitical and historical circumstances.
- Canada also has a close relationship with the US, especially in trade matters. However many Canadians were distrustful of the US during the Bush era.

The EU's Common Foreign and Security Policy

The EU as a foreign policy actor represents a significant departure from the traditional sovereign state model, even though it was in Europe that the traditional model originated. In recent years, the EU has been working to develop a Common Foreign and Security Policy (CFSP) in which is also embedded a European Security and Defence Policy (ESDP). A major factor contributing to the development of the CFSP/ESDP, and indeed to the consolidation of the European movement itself, was the end of the Cold War and the perceived need for a coordinated approach to regional affairs in the wake of the Soviet collapse. Beyond the exigencies of these particular circumstances, it has also been suggested that the challenge for the European project was more fundamental: "From its origins, the ideal or 'vocation' of Europe has been to ensure peace between former warring European nation-states and to provide the conditions for geopolitical stability built on the foundations of a commitment to liberal democracy" (Dannreuther, 2004: 1–2).

The CSFP was embedded in the 1993 Treaty on European Union (also known as the Maastricht Treaty). It was subsequently refined in the 1999 Amsterdam Treaty and refined again in the Nice Treaty, which came into effect in 2003. The ESDP was given an operational capability in a 2001 meeting of the European Council. The CFSP's basic working profile is set out in **Box 18.7**.

These objectives clearly reflect a desire to export European political norms regarding human rights, democracy, and **good governance** to other parts of the world. During the Bush years, the EU consciously projected itself as a qualitatively different kind of actor in the international sphere than the US. In portraying itself as a "normative power," it staked a claim "to being a legitimate and thus a more effective international actor"

KEY CONCEPT BOX 18.7
EU Common Foreign and Security Policy: Objectives and Mechanisms

The Amsterdam Treaty spells out five fundamental objectives of the CFSP:

- to safeguard the common values, fundamental interests, independence and integrity of the Union in conformity with the principle of the United Nations Charter;
- to strengthen the security of the Union in all ways;
- to preserve peace and strengthen international security, in accordance with the principles of the United Nations Charter, as well as the principle of the Helsinki Final Act and the objectives of the Paris Charter, including those on external borders;
- to promote international cooperation;
- to develop and consolidate democracy and the rule of law, and respect for human rights and fundamental freedoms.

The treaty also identifies several ways in which these objectives are to be pursued:

- defining the principles and general guidelines for the common foreign and security policy.
- deciding on common strategies.
- adopting joint actions and common positions.

Additionally, mechanisms for regular political dialogue with a whole range of third countries have been set up, usually with troika meetings at ministerial, senior officials and working group level, summits and in some cases, meetings with all Member States and the Commission at ministerial or senior officials level. . . .

Outside these regular mechanisms, the EU maintains a political presence, particularly in areas of crisis or conflict. Special Representatives have been appointed to the Great Lakes (Africa), Middle East, Stability Pact, Former Yugoslav Republic of Macedonia, Ethiopia/Eritrea and Afghanistan. These Special Representatives provide a direct link to developments in these areas and allow the EU to have an active involvement in the search for lasting solutions.

SOURCE: http://www.deljpn.ec.europa.eu/union/showpage_en_union.cfsp.php; accessed 8 March 2012.

18

(Farrell, 2005: 453). With Obama in power, however, the differences between the EU and US seem far less stark.

Of course EU member states pursue their own foreign policies. The UK, Italy, and Spain supported the war in Iraq, for example, while France and Germany did not. Whether Turkey should enter the EU as a member is a current point of contention; whether to recognize the independence of Kosovo from Serbia is another. There are also disagreements in matters of trade and domestic policy. Among the areas in dispute are the Common Agricultural Policy (CAP), a European Constitution, immigration, and migration. Most prominently, there are fundamental divergences of opinion over the correct balance between EU institutions and national sovereignty.

The EU's future is especially unclear in light of the current economic crisis. Several EU members, notably Greece (and to a lesser extent Portugal, Spain, and Italy) face serious financial problems caused by a combination of bad debts, financial mismanagement, and corruption. In October 2011, Canada's finance minister, Jim Flaherty, bluntly described the European debt crisis as "the world's most immediate and pressing problem. It threatens Europe, and it is threatening to bring the world to the verge of another recession" (Whittington, 2011).

KEY POINTS

- The emergence of the EU as a foreign policy actor in its own right represents a significant departure from the traditional European state model.
- EU foreign policy is designed to project "normative power." The differences between EU and US approaches to foreign policy during the Bush years belied the notion that "the West" constitutes a coherent cultural/political entity in the international sphere.
- EU member states continue to make their own foreign policy decisions and often disagree on matters of domestic policy.

Conclusion

Diplomacy implies peaceful or at least non-violent interaction between political actors, and "diplomatic solutions" are frequently contrasted with military ones. By the mid-twentieth century diplomacy was generally understood as a means of maintaining an international order in the interests of peace and stability (Butterfield, 1966: 190), and our discussions of summit diplomacy and public diplomacy, in particular, reinforce the association of diplomacy with peace.

Yet diplomacy is not always a matter of negotiation between equals. States are not equal in their capacities or capabilities; stronger states are often in a superior bargaining position. In fact, diplomacy can also be aggressive and coercive; in "gunboat diplomacy," for instance, negotiations take place under the threat of force. Diplomacy can certainly be accompanied by sabre-rattling, and misunderstandings in negotiations can well lead to war. Still, diplomacy at its best is the opposite of war—a way of resolving conflicts and disagreements without resorting to violence. In the final analysis, peaceful diplomatic persuasion is much more likely to serve the "national interest" than the use of crude force.

18

← See Chapter 7, page 151, for a discussion of strong and weak states.

? KEY QUESTIONS

- What distinguishes diplomacy and statecraft from other forms of political activity?
- If states are no longer considered the only relevant actors in the international sphere, are they still the most effective when it comes to diplomatic activity?
- Are there genuinely different styles of diplomacy determined by cultural factors, or is the influence of culture in this respect sometimes exaggerated?
- What role did deterrence play in "nuclear diplomacy" during the Cold War?
- Under what circumstances is summit diplomacy likely to be effective?
- Would you agree with the critics who charge that public diplomacy is little more than propaganda on an international scale?
- Is the war on terror amenable to diplomatic solutions?
- In what ways does foreign diplomacy link the domestic and international spheres?
- What is the Monroe Doctrine and how does it illustrate the historic importance of geopolitics in US foreign policy?

📖 FURTHER READING

James, P., N. Michaud, and M.J. O'Reilly, eds (2006). *Handbook of Canadian Foreign Policy.* Lanham, MD: Lexington.

> A comprehensive introduction to nearly every aspect of Canadian diplomacy and foreign policy.

Berridge, G. R. (2005). *Diplomacy: Theory and Practice.* 3rd edn. Basingstoke: Palgrave Macmillan.

> This book combines theoretical and historical perspectives on various styles and modes of diplomacy, a theoretical treatise of primary characteristics of the modes of diplomacy, and includes discussion of key themes such as the art of negotiation, bilateral and multilateral diplomacy, summit diplomacy, and mediation.

Kennedy, Paul (1989). *The Rise and Fall of the Great Powers: Economic Change and Military Conflict from 1500 to 2000.* London: Fontana.

> A classic text in the general field of international history that provides valuable context for this chapter's themes of diplomacy, statecraft, and foreign policy.

Nathan, James (2002), *Soldiers, Statecraft, and History: Coercive Diplomacy and International Order.* Greenwood, CT: Praeger.

> A wide-ranging study that sets contemporary diplomatic practices against the historical backdrop of the rise of the modern state system, with particular emphasis on the use of force and coercion.

📱 WEB LINKS

www.international.gc.ca/international/index.aspx

> The official website of Foreign Affairs and International Trade Canada.

www.cdfai.org/

> The official website of the Canadian Defence & Foreign Affairs Institute (CDFAI), a right-of-centre policy institute based in Calgary.

www.state.gov/

> The official website of the US Department of State.

www.ec.europa.eu/external_relations

A section of the official EU website that provides a gateway into different aspects of the EU's external affairs.

www.foreignpolicy.com

The website of the US journal *Foreign Policy* makes available general information and short reports on issues in current foreign policy and provides partial access to its main articles.

http://english.chinese.cn/

The homepage of the Office of Chinese Language Council International provides information on the Confucius Institute project. For Canadian branches in Hamilton and Edmonton, see http://confucius.mcmaster.ca/ and http://www.confuciusedmonton.ca/.

International Organizations

19

CHAPTER OVERVIEW

In this chapter we look first at the nature of international organizations (IOs) and the ways in which they participate in international relations. We then review the rise of IOs from a historical perspective, with special reference to developments in Europe from the nineteenth century on. The chapter goes on to discuss the major intergovernmental institutions of the twentieth century that have played such important roles in shaping world order. We look briefly at the League of Nations before focusing on its successor, the United Nations, and its various appendages. Turning to the world of NGOs, we see that is populated with a bewildering variety of bodies: some have significant status in the international sphere, others have little relevance, and still others pose significant dangers. Finally, we consider ideas about social movements and international civil society and their relationship to the contemporary world of international organizations. In reviewing these institutions and actors we should keep in mind that proponents of liberal international theory, especially in the form of "liberal institutionalism," and international society consider robust international organizations to be essential building blocks of world order.

What Is an International Organization?

International organizations—from the United Nations down to voluntary organizations with members in just a few countries—operate in a sphere that transcends the state system. This does not mean that they are necessarily more powerful or more important than states; certainly realists would not see them that way. Like states, international organizations are tangible institutional products of social and political forces. Beyond that, though, they represent clusters of ideas and coalitions of interest that exist at a transnational level and actively work towards certain desired outcomes.

Such organizations may be public or private, depending on whether they are set up by state or non-state actors. Most are permanent, or at least aspire to be, even if many fall by the wayside. Their power varies enormously, depending on their size and the resources at their disposal. In short, they come in so many forms that it is very difficult to pin them down with a single definition.

A related concept is that of the **international regime**, which originated as a way of understanding international cooperation. Stephen Krasner (1983) is credited with popularizing the term, in an article in which he defined regimes as "implicit or explicit principles, norms, rules and decision-making procedures around which actors' expectations converge in a given area of international relations." As Keohane (1993: 23) explains, much of world politics is characterized by highly organized and systematic cooperation; yet there are few rules that are hierarchically enforced. Rather, the rules are followed voluntarily and cooperatively, becoming embedded in relations of reciprocity. An international regime, though not an organization as such, usually incorporates one or more international organizations focused on a particular issue or theme. The "international human rights regime" is a prime example, encompassing many organizations (including the UN, Human Rights Watch, and Amnesty International) that converge around a particular cluster of norms and principles (see Rittberger and Zangl, 2006: 6–7).

Although multinational corporations fit the general conception of the international organization, as for-profit enterprises they are usually considered to fall in a different category from government and non-profit organizations. We will discuss multinationals in the next chapter, on international political economy.

19

◀ Greenpeace volunteers at the UN's Durban Climate Change Conference in November 2011 (© Michelly Rall/Getty Images)

PHOTO 19.1 Activists protesting against climate change in Auckland, New Zealand, in 2009

Transnational criminal organizations (TCOs) are also excluded from most discussions of international organizations. However, it's worth noting that they are becoming increasingly important actors in international relations. They have been implicated very clearly in the "new wars" that Mary Kaldor (2006) describes as combining traditional aspects of war with organized crime and involving actors at many levels. Whereas in the past organized crime was mainly a concern for domestic policing agencies, the activities of TCOs—drug and weapons trafficking, money laundering, people smuggling—require international policing cooperation. Williams (1997) notes that the emergence of TCOs is at least in part a result of the same underlying changes in the international sphere that have favoured the spread of transnational corporations. Thus increased **interdependence** between states, developments in international travel and communications, and the globalization of international financial networks "have facilitated the emergence of what is, in effect, a single global market for both licit and illicit commodities" (Williams, 1997: 316). TCOs are also increasingly seen as threats to both national and international security. Even though they are primarily economic actors, they may facilitate the business of terror networks by providing money-laundering facilities, false documents, and weapons or other material for terrorist purposes. There may also be a growing convergence between some terrorist organizations and organized crime networks (see Sanderson, 2004: 49–61; Dishman, 2005: 237–52).

In the rest of this chapter we will focus mainly on two more conventional types of international organizations: those established by states through multilateral agreements,

19

sometimes called intergovernmental organizations or IGOs; and those established by non-state or non-government actors whose primary business is not strictly commercial (or illicit): the ubiquitous **non-government organizations** or NGOs. An important theme will be the interaction between different organizations in the international sphere—interaction that underlines how inadequate the traditional model of international relations (IR), based almost exclusively on individual sovereign states acting on their own initiative and in their own interest, has become. At the same time, it's essential to recognize that states continue to play crucial roles both in organizing their own affairs and in creating the very organizations that today may seem to be making states themselves less important. The quotation in **Box 19.1** suggests an approach that balances these views.

KEY POINTS

- International organizations come in such a variety of forms that they are difficult to define, both with respect to their relationship with states and the state system as well as in terms of their constituent elements.
- IR scholars interested in the contributions that international organizations make to the international system as a whole tend to focus on intergovernmental organizations and non-government organizations.
- Although multinational corporations and terrorist and other criminal organizations operating in the international sphere do constitute international organizations of a kind, they are usually treated separately.

KEY QUOTE BOX 19.1
Paul F. Diehl on International Organizations

There are two predominant views of international organizations among the general public. The first is a cynical view that emphasizes the dramatic rhetoric and seeming inability to deal with vital problems that are said to characterize international organizations and the UN in particular. According to this view, mirrored in some realist formulations, international organizations should be treated as insignificant actors on the international stage. The other view is an idealistic one. Those who hold this view envisage global solutions to the problems facing the world today, without recognition of the constraints imposed by state sovereignty. Most of the naive calls for world government are products of this view. An understanding of international organizations and global governance probably requires that neither view be accepted in its entirety, nor be wholly rejected. International organizations are neither irrelevant nor omnipotent in global politics. They play important roles in international relations, but their influence varies according to the issue area and situation confronted (Diehl, 2005: 3).

19

The Emergence of International Organizations

"History, prior to the nineteenth century, affords relatively few examples of international organizations" (Gerbet, 1981: 28). Although this is a widely accepted view, the international organizations we see today do have some analogues in the past. The structures, systems, activities, and ideas that are understood to characterize contemporary relations between political communities did not simply emerge out of nothing in Western Europe and then spread to the rest of the world. Just as recognizable diplomatic practices have been around in different times in different places, so too have recognizable international organizations. The earliest known examples appear to have been defensive leagues set up by groups of neighbouring states. This was the case between the seventh and the fifth centuries BCE in at least one part of China, where assemblies met to organize their defences; in ancient Greece, rudimentary international organizations were established to arbitrate on issues of mutual concern to a number of city-states (see, generally, Harle, 1998).

In North America, the Six Nations confederacy was a highly successful political and military alliance. As the Anishinaabe political scientist Dale Turner argues, the chiefs who made up the ruling Grand Council of the Confederacy consulted extensively with their people:

> The Grand Council, which was organized from the Confederacy, was not a European type of centralized government. Representation within the Grand Council consisted of fifty chiefs, or sachems, who represented the voices of their communities. The chiefs did not make decisions in consultation with other chiefs about the welfare of the community as a whole without *first* gaining the approval of their respective communities. This process was respected for every issue that affected the welfare of the Confederacy. This kind of democratic representation was grounded in the principles of reciprocity and renewal (Turner, 2006: 48–9).

See Chapter 3, page 64, for more on the Six Nations Confederacy.

In late medieval Europe, some fifty towns joined forces in the Hanseatic League to protection their trading interests, with representatives meeting in a general assembly to decide policy by majority voting. Although they were limited territorially, both the Swiss confederation, dating from the late 1200s, and the United Provinces of the Netherlands, formed in the sixteenth century, effectively started out as international organizations (Gerbet, 1981: 28–9; Klabbers, 2003: 16). The Catholic Church, which for centuries held sway throughout much of Europe, may be counted among the earliest international organizations. Exercising considerable political as well as cultural power, it established a presence that matched its name—"catholic" meaning "universal" in the sense of "all-embracing."

The scale of international organizations in earlier times was constrained by limitations on mobility and communications. As communications and transport technologies developed, so too did the capacity to form ongoing associations and, eventually, formal organizations that were intended to have a more or less permanent existence. With the rise of the modern state system and technological advances in transport and communications, diplomatic networks and practices developed, accompanied by organizations that were designed to facilitate the business of international relations as such. State actors may well have looked first to their own interests, but in many areas—especially trade—those interests were likely to be advanced by cooperation with other states.

19

← See Chapter 18, page 363, for a discussion of the Concert of Europe.

In post-Napoleonic Europe, the **Concert of Europe** or "Concert system" was not an international organization in the current sense of the term: it had no constitution, permanent secretariat, or headquarters, and did not meet on a regular basis (see Gerbet, 1981: 32). Nevertheless, it may be seen as a precursor of later developments in later years. Beginning with the 1815 Congress of Vienna, the Concert system allowed for interstate cooperation on setting international boundaries and managing waterways (vital for trade) on the continent as well as establishing certain diplomatic protocols. Subsequent conferences generated as part of the Concert system established a pattern of interaction that nurtured important ideas about collective responsibility and a mutual commitment to "concert together" against threats to the system. Above all, it established the idea that representatives of various states should not meet only to sign peace treaties at the end of a war, but should gather in times of peace to prevent war (Archer, 1983: 7).

Although the Concert system virtually ceased to exist after the mid-nineteenth century, the second half of the nineteenth century did see further ad hoc conferences held on important matters of mutual interest. Following the Russo–Turkish war of 1877–8, for example, when the Congress of Berlin met to settle issues in the Balkans, it brought together delegates from the major European powers, observers from several smaller European states with interests in the region, and representatives of the Ottoman Empire. Other treaties and conventions were required to deal with issues in colonial territories, such as navigation rights. The Hague Conferences of 1899 and 1907 gave the development of international law a significant boost by establishing the principle of compulsory arbitration of disputes.

It's worth noting that the 1815 Congress of Vienna was the first significant international forum to take a stand on a broad humanitarian issue, condemning the slave trade as contrary to universal morality (Butler and MacCoby, 2003: 353). It was no coincidence that this unusual event occurred around the time that private organizations, many with a specific philanthropic mission, were starting to make their presence felt on the international scene. The anti-slavery movement in Britain, already active domestically and a prime force behind the Congress resolution, gave rise to an early NGO when its supporters formed the Society for the Mitigation and Gradual Abolition of Slavery Throughout the British Dominions in 1823. Anti-Slavery International, which is still active today, was founded in 1839, and in 1840 a World Anti-Slavery Convention was held in London (see www.antislavery.org/). Anti-Slavery International is associated with the International Labor Organization (ILO), which itself was established by the Treaty of Versailles in 1919 with the status of an autonomous institution but in association with the League of Nations. It survived the demise of the League and is now a UN agency.

Early anti-slavery efforts were underpinned by concerted activism on the part of British women who had formed their own local anti-slavery societies and went on to forge international links, especially across the Atlantic. In these activities we can the beginnings of a women's movement that spread nationally and internationally to take up various causes, including women's own liberation (see, generally, Midgley, 1992).

Transport and communications technologies, so essential to both globalization and the emergence of functioning international organizations, were the most important subjects of international agreements and formal associations. The International Telegraph Union (now the International Telecommunications Union), for example, was founded in 1865,

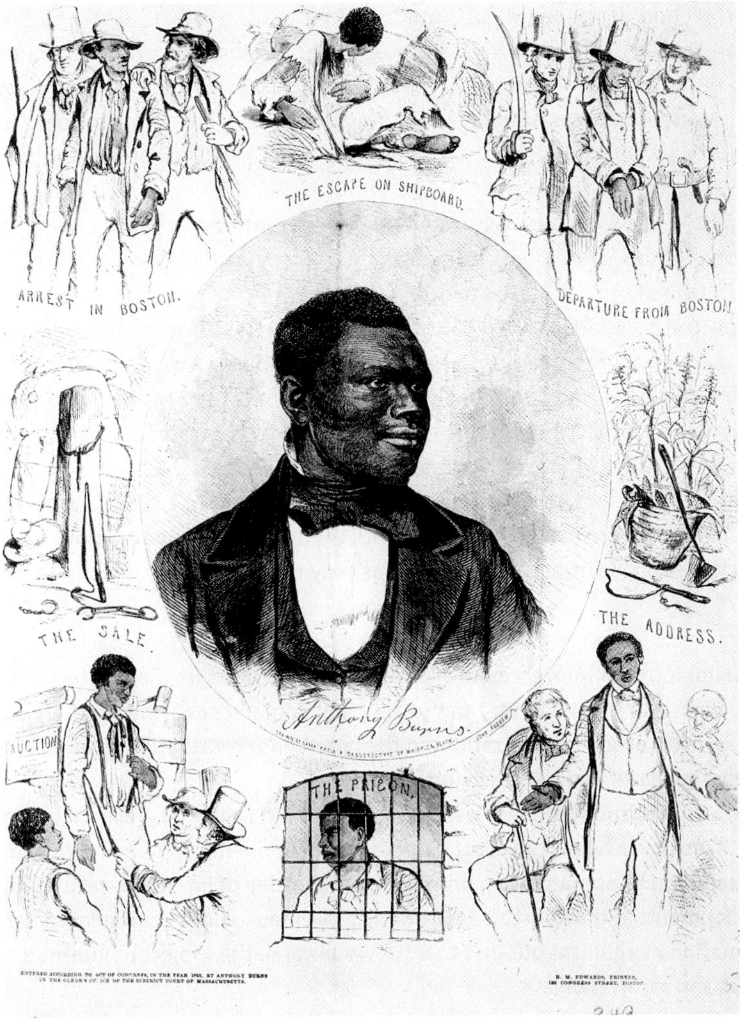

© HultonArchive/istockphoto.com

PHOTO 19.2 Anthony Burns (1834–62) surrounded by scenes from his life. Born a slave in Virginia, he had escaped to Boston and been arrested there under the Fugitive Slave Act. His case became a rallying point for anti-slavery activists, who stormed the jail and defended his case in court, but he was returned to Virginia. Ransomed by a group of African Americans in Boston the following year, he studied theology and became pastor of a Baptist church in St Catharines, Upper Canada (later Ontario), where he died of consumption at the age of 29.

the Universal Postal Union in 1874, and the International Union of Railway Freight Transportation in 1890 (see Klabbers, 2003: 18); the two former organizations are now UN specialized agencies. But improvements in transport technologies brought new problems, including the more rapid spread of disease. Concerns about international public health were reflected in the 1853 International Sanitary Convention, which was followed by additional conventions and the establishment of various international offices. Meanwhile, the rapid development of industry and trade saw the introduction of an International Bureau of Weights and Measures in 1875, and on the intellectual property front the Union for the Protection of the Rights of Authors over their Literary and Artistic Property was established in 1884. The development of private associations at an international level began to outstrip that of intergovernmental organizations in this period, accelerating the trend towards **internationalism**. Such associations were set up in connection with every kind of activity: humanitarian, religious, ideological, scientific, and technological (Gerbet 1981: 36).

At the first World Congress of International Organizations, held in Brussels in 1910, 132 international bodies and 13 governments were represented. A second world congress in Ghent and Brussels in 1913 attracted representatives from 169 international associations and 22 governments. The last world congress of this type (the seventh) was held in 1927, after which the League of Nations assumed responsibility (www.uia.org/ta/). The overall trend to internationalism before the outbreak of the First World War might have indicated that a new era of peaceful international relations was about to dawn. But other forces, including those of **nationalism**, were also at work. The death and destruction of 1914–18 was, for many key actors, the clarion call for a permanent intergovernmental organization designed to provide a strong framework for international law and, above all, to prevent further international conflict, a need that was only reinforced by the Second World War.

KEY POINTS

- Although forms of international organization existed before the nineteenth century, the Congress of Vienna in 1815 and subsequent conferences acted as catalysts for the rapid growth of such organizations in the nineteenth century; in the process a body of international law began to develop.
- Private organizations also achieved a significant international presence in the nineteenth and early twentieth centuries, those with philanthropic aims contributing to the development of humanitarian principles and the idea of international morality.
- Developments in transport and communications technologies stimulated the growth of international organizations and themselves became the subject of international agreements and associations.

Intergovernmental Organizations

← See Chapter 17, page 342, for more discussion of the history and structure of the UN.

The most important of all IGOs is the United Nations Organization. With a membership that encompasses virtually all of the world's states, it describes itself as a "global association of governments facilitating cooperation in international law, security, economic development, and social equity" (www.un.org accessed 06/08/07). Since we have already looked at its early development UN and the role of the Security Council, we will focus here on other aspects of the UN's history, structure, and mission.

First, it is useful to recall the key ideas behind the development of the UN's predecessor, the League of Nations. The preface to US President Woodrow Wilson's famous "Fourteen Points" address to the US Congress in January 1918 stands as one of the clearest statements of the idealist vision of world order in that period. The fourteenth point proposed the formation of a general association of nations, an idea given substance by the formation of the League of Nations in the immediate aftermath of the war. The idealists were to come under attack from realists in later years for their vision of a peaceful world order founded on strong institutions of **global governance** and their explicit emphasis on the need for

19

moral principles in the international sphere to curb naked self-interest. Realists were not opposed to the principles and norms that the UN advocated; they simply believed that such ideals were naïve and impossible to achieve.

The League, which was meant to function as a collective security organization, has sometimes been described as a failed experiment because it did not prevent the Second World War. It could also be argued that the failure began years before 1939, when the League chose not to take action against Japan for invading parts of China in 1931 and failed to prevent Italy from invading Ethiopia in 1935. These failures to act signalled that member states were too afraid of another world war to risk intervening to stop other acts of aggression. In effect, collective deterrence ceased to exist, and this cleared the way for Hitler. Preventing war would require a stronger organization (MacDonald, 2009: 26). Nevertheless, a number of key institutions and practices set up under the auspices of the League were enshrined in the present UN system, and the latter owes a great deal to the previous experiment in global governance, which in turn drew on models provided by the Concert system of the early to mid-1800s.

Building on the wartime cooperation among the major powers of the time, the UN became a more truly international body with a formal charter setting out the rights and obligations of members. The preamble to the Charter states the general principles and ideals on which the organization is based; see **Box 19.2**. The main organs of the UN are set

---

KEY QUOTE BOX 19.2

Preamble to the Charter of the United Nations

WE THE PEOPLES OF THE UNITED NATIONS DETERMINED

- to save succeeding generations from the scourge of war, which twice in our lifetime has brought untold sorrow to mankind, and
- to reaffirm faith in fundamental human rights, in the dignity and worth of the human person, in the equal rights of men and women and of nations large and small, and
- to establish conditions under which justice and respect for the obligations arising from treaties and other sources of international law can be maintained, and
- to promote social progress and better standards of life in larger freedom,

AND FOR THESE ENDS

- to practice tolerance and live together in peace with one another as good neighbours, and
- to unite our strength to maintain international peace and security, and
- to ensure, by the acceptance of principles and the institution of methods, that armed force shall not be used, save in the common interest, and
- to employ international machinery for the promotion of the economic and social advancement of all peoples,

HAVE RESOLVED TO COMBINE OUR EFFORTS TO ACCOMPLISH THESE AIMS.

SOURCE: www.un.org/aboutun/charter/index.html

19

out in the UN's official organizational chart at www.un.org/en/aboutun/structure/pdfs/
un_system_chart_colour_sm.pdf.

The business of the first organ, the Trusteeship Council, was to administer 11
non-self-governing trust territories that had formerly been League of Nations mandate
territories. Its role was terminated in 1994 when the last trust territory, administered
by the US, chose self-government and became an independent state. The second, and
most powerful, of the UN's organs is the Security Council, discussed in Chapter 17.
The third and largest is the General Assembly; some say this organ is also the weakest,
since it has no mechanism for enforcing the resolutions that it produces. This is the
fundamental difference between the UN General Assembly and a legislature: although
the Assembly's resolutions may guide policy and carry normative force, they cannot
have the legal status that legislation produced by a parliament has within the sphere
of the individual state. Nevertheless, to dismiss the General Assembly as nothing more
than a debating forum would be a mistake, for it is the one place where representatives
from all states can meet on a more or less equal footing, express views and debate the
full range of issues in international politics. Moreover, it is a key forum for both formal
and informal diplomacy and the formation of strategic alliances on issues that come
up for a vote.

The Economic and Social Council (ECOSOC) has a mandate to initiate studies and
reports. It can formulate policy recommendations regarding in an enormous range
of economic and social issues, from living standards and employment to international economic, social, and health problems; in so doing, it can facilitate international

UN Photo/Mark Garten

PHOTO 19.3 Gaining recognition as a state can be extremely difficult. Here Mahmoud
Abbas, President of the Palestinian Authority, waits to address the UN General Assembly in
September 2011. Ultimately, US President Obama promised that the US would veto any move
to admit the PA to the UN.

cultural and educational cooperation, and encourage universal respect for human rights and fundamental freedoms. Some of the best-known UN agencies, such as the World Health Organization (WHO), the Food and Agricultural Organization (FAO), the United Nations Educational, Scientific and Cultural Organization (UNESCO), and the World Bank group fall under its rubric. It has a major role in organizing the many major international conferences initiated by the UN and oversees the functional commissions, regional commissions, and other special bodies set out in the organizational chart. ECOSOC is by far the largest of the UN's principal organs and expends more than 70 per cent of the human and financial resources of the entire UN system (see www.un.org/ecosoc/about/).

One of ECOSOC's most controversial functional commissions has been the one dealing with human rights. A brief account of developments in this area illustrates just how problematic it is to achieve coherence in regimes of global governance. The establishment of a Human Rights Commission (HRC) was mandated by the UN's Charter, which reflected the members' abhorrence of the atrocities committed during the Second World War. Past wars had produced some appalling cases of cruelty, but the genocidal policies of Nazi Germany were unprecedented. Beginning with the Universal Declaration of Human Rights (UDHR; see **Box 19.3**), which was adopted by the General Assembly in 1948, the Commission has produced a series of human rights documents and treaties over the decades. Sadly, none of these have been able to guarantee that basic human rights will be respected or protected.

Another problem that has surfaced in many international debates since the Charter concerns two different types of rights: civil and political rights on the one hand, and economic, social, and cultural rights on the other. The former are sometimes seen as possessing a typically "Western" liberal character unsuited to the cultural context of non-Western countries. The most vocal proponents of this view have come from Muslim and African countries and parts of East Asia, especially China. In addition, it is often suggested that civil and political rights are less urgent concerns for the world's poorer countries than economic, social, and cultural rights. However, human rights activists in such countries generally do not support these arguments.

An early division of opinion on the two different clusters of rights led to the development of separate covenants for each. The International Covenant on Civil and Political Rights (ICCPR) and the International Covenant on Economic, Social, and Cultural Rights (ICESCR) both came into force in 1976. In addition to representing two broad approaches to rights, the covenants represent a significant attempt to advance the codification of human rights as such and to introduce an international legal framework to support their advancement. Member states are not obliged to sign on to the covenants, but those that do sign agree to accept their provisions as both legal and moral obligations.

More generally, the history of human rights issues in the UN has been plagued by competing conceptions of what the organization can and cannot, or should and should not, do to advance the protection of human rights around the world. On the one hand, the UN is committed to respect for state **sovereignty** and therefore to the notion that each state is entitled to conduct its own affairs free from external interference. On the other hand, it is committed to the universality of human rights, which implies that it is not only

19

KEY QUOTE BOX 19.3
The Universal Declaration of Human Rights (UDHR)

The General Assembly's adoption of the UDHR, on 10 December 1948, marked a moment in international history when all member states agreed, at least in principle, to a substantial list of human rights, beginning with the basic right to life and extending to a host of economic and social rights. All new members joining the UN must sign on to the UDHR.

The Preamble to the Declaration recognizes the "inherent dignity" and "the equal and inalienable rights of all members of the human family [as] the foundation of freedom, justice and peace in the world"; notes the extent to which "disregard and contempt for human rights have resulted in barbarous acts which have outraged the conscience of mankind"; and heralds "the advent of a world in which human beings shall enjoy freedom of speech and belief and freedom from fear and want has been proclaimed as the highest aspiration of the common people."

The Declaration itself contains 30 Articles, the first 10 of which are as follows:

Article 1 All human beings are born free and equal in dignity and rights. They are endowed with reason and conscience and should act towards one another in a spirit of brotherhood.

Article 2 Everyone is entitled to all the rights and freedoms set forth in this Declaration, without distinction of any kind, such as race, colour, sex, language, religion, political or other opinion, national or social origin, property, birth or other status. Furthermore, no distinction shall be made on the basis of the political, jurisdictional or international status of the country or territory to which a person belongs, whether it be independent, trust, non-self-governing or under any other limitation of sovereignty.

Article 3 Everyone has the right to life, liberty and security of person.

Article 4 No one shall be held in slavery or servitude; slavery and the slave trade shall be prohibited in all their forms.

Article 5 No one shall be subjected to torture or to cruel, inhuman or degrading treatment or punishment.

Article 6 Everyone has the right to recognition everywhere as a person before the law.

Article 7 All are equal before the law and are entitled without any discrimination to equal protection of the law. All are entitled to equal protection against any discrimination in violation of this Declaration and against any incitement to such discrimination.

Article 8 Everyone has the right to an effective remedy by the competent national tribunals for acts violating the fundamental rights granted him by the constitution or by law.

Article 9 No one shall be subjected to arbitrary arrest, detention or exile.

Article 10 Everyone is entitled in full equality to a fair and public hearing by an independent and impartial tribunal, in the determination of his rights and obligations and of any criminal charge against him.

SOURCE: www.un.org/Overview/rights.html; accessed 13/8/07.

entitled but obliged to take action to promote and protect human rights wherever and whenever necessary—action that may well be construed to violate the principle of state sovereignty. Unfortunately, some of the states represented on the Commission at various times were themselves associated with human rights abuses. Countries with poor human rights records—mainly outside "the West"—complained that they were being unfairly singled out for criticism, and the UN was accused of attempting to interfere in the internal affairs of sovereign states. By 2006 the HRC had been largely discredited as ineffectual. It was therefore replaced by a new Human Rights Council, which has new terms for membership and functions. Whether it can avoid the problems experienced in the past remains to be seen (see Alston, 2006).

The fifth major organ of the UN is the International Court of Justice (ICJ) located in The Hague. As with other parts of the UN system, its origins can be traced to much earlier periods and linked to the gradual development, in the course of the modern era, of methods of mediation and arbitration of disputes between states. Its immediate predecessor, the Permanent Court of International Justice (PCIJ), was part of the League of Nations system from 1922 until it was dissolved in 1946 to make way for the new UN court. The 15 judges of the ICJ are elected for nine-year terms by both the UN General Assembly and the Security Council. The ICJ functions as something of a world court with the jurisdiction to decide legal disputes submitted to it by states and to give advisory opinions on legal questions at the request of UN organs or authorized agencies. Between May 1947 and March 2012, 152 cases had been entered into its General List.

A recent example involved the application of the Genocide Convention in the case of Bosnia and Herzegovina *v*. Serbia and Montenegro. The 171-page judgment, delivered in February 2007, dealt with a number of issues, among them the massacre by Serb

See Chapter 8, page 169, for summaries of other social and economic rights included in the UDHR.

PHOTO 19.4 A member of the UN Security Council casts a vote during the election of the five members of the International Court of Justice in 2008.

forces of some 8,000 Bosnian Muslim men and boys. Although the court found Serbia and Montenegro not guilty of deliberately perpetrating genocide, it did find Serbia guilty of *failing to prevent* genocide and therefore in breach of their obligations in international law (see www.icj-cij.org). Another recent ICJ ruling concerned the legality of Kosovo's declaration of independence from Serbia under international law. The court ruled that the declaration was not illegal, and Kosovo is recognized by many Western countries, including the US, Canada, the UK, France, and Germany. However, many other countries (including Spain, Venezuela, China, and Russia) have backed Serbia in its refusal to recognize Kosovo's independence, fearful of setting a precedent for small ethnic groups seeking self-determination (see http://www.bbc.co.uk/news/world-europe-10734249, accessed 23/07/10). This issue became contentious in early 2012, when it led to a temporary delay in the European Union's decision to admit Serbia as a member.

KEY CONCEPT BOX 19.4
The Crime of Genocide in International Law

The term "genocide" was coined by Raphael Lemkin, a Polish Jewish lawyer, in the early 1940s to refer the deliberate attempt to annihilate a particular group. Specifically, Lemkin had in mind the attempted destruction of the Armenian people by the Ottoman Empire in 1915, and the ongoing extermination of European Jews by Nazi Germany. Genocide has been formally defined in international law, and codified in the United Nations Genocide Convention (1948). Article 2 defines genocide as follows:

Any of the following acts committed with intent to destroy, in whole or in part, a national, ethnical, racial or religious group, as such:

a. Killing members of the group:
b. Causing serious bodily or mental harm to members of the group;
c. Deliberately inflicting on the group conditions of life calculated to bring about its physical destruction in whole or in part;
d. Imposing measures intended to prevent births within the group;
e. Forcibly transferring children of the group to another group.

In recent years, the International Criminal Tribunals for Rwanda and the former Yugoslavia (ICTR and ICTY) have further refined the UN definition. Among the contributions of recent case law are judicial interpretations of how large a "part" of the target group must be killed for an act to be considered genocide. Other questions have concerned how clearly "intent" to commit genocide must be proven, and whether or not rape can be considered an act of genocide (in 1998 the ICTR ruled that it can be). While case law moves forward, this has not prevented acrimonious academic debate over whether the official definition is too broad or too narrow. Such debates are often politically charged, since a more expansive definition will allow more groups to reinterpret events in their past as acts of genocide. Conversely, a tighter definition might help certain states to excuse unsavoury parts of their past (MacDonald, 2008: 8).

19

Note that these cases were separate from the trial of former Serbian President Slobodan Milosevic, which was conducted by a special tribunal, the International Criminal Tribunal for the Former Yugoslavia (ICTY) established by a UN Security Council resolution. The ICTY has tried large numbers of suspected war criminals from all sides of the conflict, although Serbian defendants have featured predominantly. The trial had been running for four years when it came to a premature end with Milosevic's death in 2006. The case has been seen as a landmark because it marked the first time a former head of state had been put on trial before an international criminal tribunal.

The sixth and final major organ is the UN Secretariat, headed by the Secretary-General. The occupant of that office has an extremely demanding job. The Secretary-General seems to be expected to be everywhere at once, and must possess an encyclopaedic knowledge not only of the UN system itself, but of all the world's troubles, both current and potential. In practice, the Secretary-General will often appoint representatives for routine committee work. One particularly important role for the Secretary-General is to bring matters likely to affect international peace and security to the attention of the Security Council and to report regularly on operations that the UN is involved in. Although the Secretary-General has no authority beyond issuing formal warnings of trouble and delivering information, the importance of this function should not be underestimated.

The UN has also populated the sphere of international organizations with a plethora of agencies and special programs. The WHO, the FAO, UNICEF, and UNESCO have already been mentioned above and the UN's organizational chart lists many more. Some of these bodies, such as UNICEF, are well known; some, such as the United Nations Population Fund (UNFPA), less so. Others have emerged more recently to address problems unheard of in earlier periods, such as the joint UN Program on HIV/AIDS (UNAIDS). Then there are regional commissions and organizations. We have already mentioned the EU and ASEAN, but there are many others, from the African Union (AU) and the Pacific Islands Forum (PIF) to numerous trading blocs such as MERCOSUR in Latin America and of course NAFTA for Canada, the US, and Mexico (the richest of the trading blocs according to per capita income). These bodies reflect the trend to **regionalization**, which we will consider in more detail in Chapter 20. This trend, which has been gathering pace over the last few decades, is expected to have a significant impact in the future, though the organizations it gives rise to are more likely to complement the role of the UN than to compete directly with it. It points to a future in which intergovernmental organizations are likely to play an increasingly important role in world order rather than a diminishing one.

KEY POINTS

- The League of Nations is often seen as a failure, but it was an important forerunner to the UN, which has retained a number of its institutions.
- The UN is the largest single intergovernmental organization, with five functioning main organs and a plethora of programs, agencies, commissions, funds, courts, and tribunals involved in different aspects of global governance.
- Although the UN is the principal organ of global governance, it does not possess the characteristics of a "world government" since its constituent members maintain sovereign authority within their own realms and do not form a "world state."

19

Non-Governmental Organizations (NGOs)

Like international organizations in general, NGOs cannot be defined in a completely straightforward way. Still, most of them share the following characteristics: they are formal rather than ad hoc entities; they aspire to be self-governing according to their own constitutional rules; they are private in the sense that they operate independently from governments; and they do not make or distribute profits. This description applies to both national and international bodies, so for those that operate outside the national sphere, we should add that they have formal transnational links (see Gordenker and Weiss, 1996: 20).

Other organizations fall somewhere between the government and non-government spheres. Although they often claim to be NGOs, they don't really fit the description above. Gordenker and Weiss identify three significant types. The first are government-organized non-government organizations or GONGOs: entities created by governments, usually as front organizations for their own purposes. These were typically established by communist countries during the Cold War, but Western countries including the US had some as well. Today there is a wide variety of GONGOs, many of which serve dubious causes. The excerpt in **Box 19.5**, from an article published in *Foreign Policy* on the subject of GONGOs

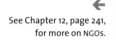

← See Chapter 12, page 241, for more on NGOs.

KEY QUOTE BOX 19.5

Moisés Naím on GONGOS

Naím's article "What Is a Gongo?" is subtitled "How government-sponsored groups masquerade as civil society":

> Behind this contradictory and almost laughable tongue twister ["gongo"] lies an important and growing global trend that deserves more scrutiny: governments funding and controlling nongovernmental organizations (NGOs), often stealthily. Some gongos are benign, others irrelevant. But many . . . are dangerous. Some act as the thuggish arm of repressive governments. Others use the practices of democracy to subtly undermine democracy at home. Abroad, the gongos of repressive regimes lobby the United Nations and other international institutions, often posing as representatives of citizen groups with lofty aims when, in fact, they are nothing but agents of the governments that fund them. Some governments embed their gongos deep in the societies of other countries and use them to advance their interests abroad. . . . The globalization and effectiveness of nongovernmental organizations will suffer if we don't find reliable ways of distinguishing organizations that truly represent democratic civil society from those that are tools of uncivil, undemocratic governments. . . .

SOURCE: Moisés Naím, "What Is a Gongo?" *Foreign Policy* May–June 2007; www.foreignpolicy.com/story/cms.php?story_id¼3818%26fpsrc¼ealert070430; accessed 16 Aug. 2007.

and the dangers that some of them pose, tells us something about their role in the sphere of international organizations.

A second special type is the quasi non-government organization or QUANGO, which typically receives its funding from government but operates autonomously. Unlike GONGOs, QUANGOs have a transparent relationship with government and no subterfuge is intended. The third type is the donor-organized NGO or DONGO. In this case, agencies such as the United Nations Development Program (UNDP) might organize and fund NGOs to coordinate or carry out projects (Gordenker and Weiss, 1996: 20–1). A significant number of other NGOs enjoy consultative status with the UN or, more specifically, one of its councils or agencies. The UN's Economic and Social Council, for example, accords consultative status of some kind to some 3500 NGOs ranging from the Adventist Development Relief Agency to the World Press Freedom Committee, each of which is allied with a specific UN agency such as UNESCO, the FAO, or the WHO (see the Council's list at www.un.org/esa/ coordination/ngo/pdf/INF_List.pdf).

The practice of giving UN consultative status to NGOs dates back to 1946, when ECOSOC granted such status to just over 40 NGOs. By 1992 there were more than 700 NGOs with consultative status, and now there are five times that number. Among the rules and criteria governing eligibility are the following:

1. The organization must have been in existence (officially registered with the appropriate government authorities as an NGO/non-profit) for at least two years.
2. It must have an established headquarters.
3. It must possess a democratically adopted constitution, authority to speak for its members, a representative structure, appropriate mechanisms of accountability and democratic and transparent decision-making processes.
4. Its basic resources must be derived mainly from contributions of the national affiliates or other components or from individual members.
5. It must not have been established by governments or intergovernmental agreements (see www.un.org/esa/coordination/ngo/).

Many NGOs have specific philanthropic or humanitarian purposes. Some are underpinned by religious beliefs and some are secular. Many are aligned with broader movements such as the environmental movement, the labour movement, the ecumenical movement, the peace movement, the indigenous rights movement, and the women's movement. We will say more about the role of these broader movements below.

Among the better-known NGOs are the Worldwide Fund for Nature, Greenpeace, the World Council of Churches, the World Peace Council, the International Women's Health Coalition, Médecins Sans Frontières, and Amnesty International, to name just a few. The case study of the Red Cross/Red Crescent Movement below outlines how one of the earliest NGOs operating in the international sphere grew to be the largest humanitarian organization in the world. It was also the prime mover behind the original Geneva Convention, which has become the most important international convention relating to the conduct of warfare.

CASE STUDY
The Origins and Development of the Red Cross/Red Crescent Movement

In 1859 Henry Dunant, a Swiss businessman travelling in what is now northern Italy, witnessed the aftermath of the battle of Solferino—one of the bloodiest battles of the nineteenth century, in which the French army under Napoleon III joined with local forces to drive out the Austrian army. Dunant subsequently published a small book in which he described not only the scene on the battlefield but the plight of the wounded and their desperate need for care. He went on to devise a plan for national relief societies to aid those wounded in war. In February 1863, the Société Genevoise d'Utilité Publique [Geneva Society for Public Welfare] appointed a committee of five, including Dunant, to consider how the plan could be put into action. This committee, which eventually founded the Red Cross, called for an international conference to pursue Dunant's basic objectives. Dunant put his own time and money into the project, travelling throughout much of Europe to persuade governments to send representatives. The conference was held in October 1863 with 39 delegates from 16 nations. Just under a year later, 12 nations signed an International Convention for the Amelioration of the Condition of the Wounded and Sick in Armed Forces in the Field, otherwise known as the Geneva Convention of 1864.

The convention provided for guaranteed neutrality for medical personnel and officially adopted as its emblem a red cross on a field of white (the red crescent was adopted in most Muslim countries). Three other conventions were later added to cover naval warfare, prisoners of war, and civilians. Revisions of these conventions have been made periodically, the most extensive, in 1949, relating to the treatment of prisoners of war. The International Committee of the Red Cross remains based in Geneva and the International Federation of Red Cross and Red Crescent Societies has national societies in 178 countries and a total membership of 115 million volunteers. In 1901 Henry Dunant was awarded the very first Nobel Peace Prize, and since then three additional Peace Prizes have been associated with the Red Cross. The Red Cross/Red Crescent is also instrumental in providing rescue assistance during civil conflicts and natural disasters.

© Niko Guido/istockphoto.com

PHOTO 19.5 Turkish women from Kovancilar village sit outside the temporary shelters provided by the Turkish Red Crescent after a 6.1 Mw earthquake in March 2010.

SOURCES: nobelprize.org/nobel_prizes/peace/laureates/1963/red-cross-history.html; www.redcross.int/en/history/not_nobel.asp, both accessed 07 Aug. 2007.

19

KEY POINTS

- Intergovernmental organizations, especially the UN and its agencies, often have close working relationships with NGOs and have established structures supporting the work of many NGOs.
- Not all NGOs are "good" in the sense that they make a positive contribution in the international sphere. Some are merely fronts for self-serving activities by dictatorial governments and may work actively to undermine the efforts of other organizations with respect to human rights issues and other matters.
- Many NGOs are also allied with broader movements, contributing to a complex web of relationships between different kinds of actors, both state and non-state, in the international sphere.

Social Movements and International Civil Society

As we noted above, many NGOs are involved in philanthropic or humanitarian causes, some of which are part of broader **social movements**. The term "social movement" usually refers to some kind of collective action, driven by a particular set of social concerns and emerging from society at large, without intervention on the part of the state. Indeed, many social movements have taken an adversarial position towards aspects of state or governmental activity. In this respect they are often seen as manifestations of grassroots democracy pursuing non-mainstream issues and agendas. Social movements often transcend the domestic sphere; an early example was the anti-slavery movement. When a movement achieves a transnational profile and popular following, it achieves the status of an international or global social movement. Such movements often reflect shifting coalitions of interests around issue-oriented activities. In one way or another, however, social movements and the NGOs associated with them usually represent a "cause" that very often involves a perceived injustice or danger: Third World poverty, environmental degradation, the oppression of indigenous communities, nuclear weapons, animal rights, and so on.

Together, international NGOs and social movements are said to constitute a kind of **international civil society** paralleling the domestic civil society we discussed in Chapter 12. Civil society is a sphere of human association not mediated by the state, or at least not directly, in which individuals participate in groups or collectives that have a private purpose—private in the sense that they are not part of the public realm of formal state or governmental activity. These groups or collectives include professional associations, charities, **interest groups**, businesses, and so on. Their freedom of organization and articulation of interests are widely seen as important ingredients in democracy, and any effort to repress them is likely to be perceived as a sign of **authoritarianism**. Many civil society groups are NGOs, but some do not fall easily into that definition. Also, not all NGOs are connected to social movements.

Like domestic civil society, international civil society stands apart from the formal, intergovernmental structures of global governance and sometimes locates itself in opposition to formal state-based or state-generated activities. Certainly, those who

See Chapter 12, page 239, for discussion of domestic civil society.

19

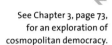

← See Chapter 3, page 73, for an exploration of cosmopolitan democracy.

look for democratic transformations in the international sphere and promote a form of **cosmopolitan democracy**—a project that, as we saw in Chapter 3, involves the extension of democratic accountability to the global sphere—are broadly supportive of the positive role that international civil society has to play in such a process.

Do social movements and international civil society present a serious challenge to the traditional state and the state system? This is an open question. As we have seen, many NGOs are closely associated with UN programs and agencies; so although we may distinguish the world of NGOs from the UN as such, they have come to form an important part of the UN system as a whole. Social movements and international civil society are thus at least partly enmeshed in the web of relations created by international organizations, including the more formal intergovernmental institutions of global governance.

KEY POINTS

- Global social movements form around particular sets of concerns regarding issues (such as the environment, indigenous rights, or arms control) that call for collective action on a global scale.
- International civil society, as a sphere of action and interaction standing apart from formal intergovernmental structures and sometimes in opposition to them, constitutes the space within which both international NGOs and international social movements operate.
- Social movements and international civil society are often seen as enhancing the space and substance of democratic activity at a supranational level.

Conclusion

Realist views of "the international" see states and the state system as the primary units around which almost everyone and everything else revolves. International activity of any real consequence is generated by state actors operating with state interests firmly in mind. It follows that the roles of virtually all other institutions and actors, including international organizations, are subordinate. Indeed, some realists dismiss the whole project of global governance as having little if any relevance in the "real world" of **power politics**. But realist views constitute only one perspective on how the international system works. Liberal views, especially those described as "liberal institutionalist," see international organizations as playing key roles in reducing the dangerous aspects of international **anarchy**. Thus liberals argue that all states have an interest in promoting greater interdependence. Both the League of Nations and the United Nations represent practical manifestations of liberal international theory. The fluid realm of NGOs, social movements, and international civil society may complement the more formal sphere of international organizations and global governance, often acting in concert with it but sometimes opposing and resisting its policies and practices. However we may regard them, international organizations have become such an integral part of the international system, and indeed of **international society**, that it is difficult to imagine a world without them.

? KEY QUESTIONS

- What are the key characteristics of international organizations?
- How does an international regime differ from an international organization?
- How and why did international organizations emerge in the modern period?
- Was the League of Nations a complete failure? What norms and practices were carried over into the UN?
- On what general principles was the UN founded?
- Is it possible for the UN to reconcile respect for state sovereignty and respect for universal human rights?
- Could the UN do more as an international organization, or is it expected to do too much as it is?
- What role do NGOs and social movements play in the international system?
- How can international civil society enhance opportunities for democratic expression?
- How can we deploy IR theory to interpret the role of international organizations in world order?

📖 FURTHER READING

Archibugi, Daniele, David Held, and Martin Köhler, eds (1998). *Re-Imagining Political Community: Studies in Cosmopolitan Democracy.* Cambridge: Polity Press.
> The editors of this collection argue that that the interstate system is increasingly challenged by new transnational forces and organizations: multinational companies, cross-border coalitions of social interest groups, global media, and numerous (and still multiplying) international agencies. This book looks at their impact on political life within and between communities, with a focus on the possibilities for democratizing the international sphere.

Bennett, A. Le Roy, and James K. Oliver (2001). *International Organizations: Principles and Issues.* 7th edn. Englewood Cliffs, NJ: Prentice Hall.
> The authors state that they are "normatively committed to the indispensability of global and regional, international and transnational organizations in an age when people and nation-states must adapt to a shrinking and increasingly interdependent globe and the growing demand for global governance." This book provides a very detailed and closely argued case for their view.

Gill, Stephen (2008). *Power and Resistance in the New World Order.* London: Palgrave Macmillan
> York University's Stephen Gill argues that as the world becomes more globalized, globalized resistance is also increasing. Gill is interested in how ordinary people are able to resist the forces of global capitalism, surveillance, and US military dominance.

Krasner, Stephen, ed. (1983). *International Regimes.* Ithaca, NY: Cornell University Press.
> A classic collection of essays by leading experts in the field that provides what is still one of the best formulations of the themes and issues around which the concept of "international regimes" revolves.

Robinson, Mary (2005). *A Voice for Human Rights.* Philadelphia: University of Pennsylvania Press.
> Mary Robinson was the President of Ireland during the 1990s, before serving as UN High Commissioner for Human Rights from 1997 to 2002—a period that included the events of 9/11 and the civil conflict in the Congo. The book is an edited collection of her speeches, but also provides an in-depth portrait of what the High Commissioner's office does to promote human rights and more moral foreign policies around the world.

19

Ruggie, John (1998). *Constructing the World Polity: Essays on International Institutionalization*, London: Routledge.

Ruggie made his name as a constructivist before becoming the UN Secretary-General's Special Representative for Business and Human Rights. This collection of his essays surveys the field of post-war IR theory and how constructivist theories of international organizations and institutions contribute to it.

WEB LINKS

www.libsci.sc.edu/bob/IGOs.htm#IGOS

Lists several hundred IGOs under different categories.

www.uia.org/extlinks/pub.php

Website of the Union of International Associations, self-described as the world's most comprehensive source of information on global civil society, with databases and publications covering many aspects of international organizations including their history and organization and the problems and methods with which they work.

http://portal.unesco.org/en/ev.php-URL_ID=32906%26URL_DO=DO_TOPIC%26URL_SECTION=201.html

A UNESCO portal that provides a gateway to numerous IGOs.

19

International Political Economy

20

CHAPTER OVERVIEW

This chapter builds on a number of themes introduced in earlier chapters. Theories of International Political Economy (IPE) are introduced from a historical perspective that we hope will help you appreciate how ideas, practices, and institutions develop and interact over time. Significant issues include international trade, international labour, the interaction of states and markets, the nexus between wealth and power, and the problems of development and underdevelopment in the global economy, with particular attention to the North–South divide. Concluding with the twin phenomena of globalization and regionalization, we examine how they are shaping the international economy and challenging the traditional role of the state. An underlying theme throughout the chapter is the relationship between economic and political power.

International Relations and the Study of IPE

The study of International Political Economy (IPE) has become a major focus in international relations since the 1970s. A significant impetus in this direction was provided by Susan Strange, who in 1970 published a seminal article entitled "International Relations and International Economics: A Case of Mutual Neglect." In it she argued that the two disciplines had been deliberately ignoring each other, and that as a result neither had been able to develop an adequate view of the world it studied. In the case of international relations, this neglect was traced to the discipline's almost exclusive preoccupation with the political and strategic relations between governments (Strange, 1970: 304). The study of IPE has grown enormously since that time, reflecting not only increased academic awareness of its importance but also the substantial changes that have taken place in the international sphere in recent decades.

As its name suggests, "political economy" (PE) is located at the intersection of political science and economics. International PE focuses on the interplay between political power and economic forces from the national level through to the international and global. We might define IPE as "the study of those international problems and issues that cannot adequately be addressed by recourse to economic, political, or sociological analysis alone," with a focus on "the elements of complex interdependence that define many of our most pressing problems today" (Balaam and Veseth, 2005: 3). Thus IPE, like politics and IR more generally, is not confined to the structural study of institutions or organizations but must also take into account the norms, values, and interests that they reflect. Any arrangement of the global system of production, distribution, and exchange reflects a mix of values and therefore, according to Strange, must be understood as "the result of human decisions taken in the context of manmade institutions and . . . self-set rules and customs" (Strange quoted in Balaam and Veseth, 2005: 5).

Many studies in IPE take the **state** and the market to be the two main entities involved. Indeed, it is the "parallel existence and mutual interaction" of the state and the market that create "political economy" (Gilpin, 1987: 8). The state embodies political forces, while the market, famously described by the liberal philosopher Adam Smith (1723–90) as an "invisible hand," is defined as "a coordinating mechanism" that allows "sellers and buyers [to] exchange goods and services at prices and output levels determined by supply and demand" (Cohn, 2005: 7). The relationship between states and markets is often depicted as one of permanent tension. Why? Because state actors are primarily concerned with preserving **sovereignty** and political unity, whereas markets thrive on openness and the absence of barriers to trade. Yet their relationship is also complementary: the market benefits from the services provided by the state (protection of property rights, provision of infrastructure, regulation of transactions), while the state benefits from a thriving

◀ A protest against the IMF-World Bank in Manila, Philippines, in 2004 (© AFP/Getty Images).

economy, which is often reflected in a strengthening of national political and military power (ibid).

Students of IPE are concerned mainly with the international sphere: the interactions between states, transnational corporations, international organizations, and so on. As in other fields of IR, however, the distinction between the domestic and the international is difficult to maintain. Indeed, the rise of IPE throughout the 1970s and 1980s was in part due to dissatisfaction with realist theories, including the sharp division between domestic and international spheres, which appeared to make little sense in an increasingly inter-dependent world (Crane and Amawi, 1991: 3–4).

One scholar has noted that IR continued to make artificial distinctions between military and economic policies well after many foreign ministries had begun renaming themselves Departments of Foreign Affairs *and* Trade (Pettman, 1996: 10), in recognition of their mutual importance. In Canada, for example, what had been the Department of External Affairs was renamed Foreign Affairs and International Trade (DFAIT) in 1993, reflecting the interweaving of diplomatic and economic concerns. DFAIT declared its priorities for 2011–12 to include

> bringing greater economic opportunity for Canada, building on a comprehensive strategy for relations with the Americas as well as a global strategy for relations with the United States, [and] asserting Canadian leadership in emerging global governance (http://www.international.gc.ca/about-a_propos/index.aspx?view=d; accessed 21 Oct. 2011).

Meanwhile, ministries that have kept their traditional names, such as the British Foreign and Commonwealth Office (FCO), have nevertheless developed substantial sections devoted to trade issues. The large size of the FCO's Trade and Investment section today—approximately 1,500 people—is a reflection of the fact that one in four jobs in the UK is linked to business overseas (www.fco.gov.uk). The interfaces between the national and the international, between politics and economy, are increasingly permeable. This particularly true within the EU, where extremely porous boundaries reflect the extent of European economic and political integration. This is an aspect of **regionalization**, which we will consider in more detail below.

KEY POINTS

- IPE sits at the intersection of international politics and economics. Incorporating insights from a variety of disciplines, it has become a major focus of study within the broader field of IR over the last four decades.
- Studies in IPE focus on states and markets. The relationship between them is a tangle of complex interactions, ranging from the cooperative to the hostile and involving important dynamics of power and wealth.

The Age of Mercantilism

Mercantilism (from the Latin for "merchant") is associated with political economy as both a theory and a system. Historically, it can be defined as the economic theory that trade generates wealth and hence that it is in the interest of government to promote exports and restrict imports; see **Box 20.1**. It is not a theory of IR as such, but its focus on advancing the interests of the state means that it complements **realism** in some respects. A basic premise

20

of classical mercantilism is that national wealth and military power form a virtuous circle: wealth enhances military (in early modern Europe, this often meant naval) power relative to other states; substantial wealth is acquired through trade; trade is protected by naval power; the wealth generated by trade further enhances naval capacity; and so on.

Thus the relentless pursuit of trade is justified by its positive contribution to national strength. However, the fundamental principle of the mercantilist system was **nationalism**, and therefore its logical accompaniment was **protectionism** rather than **free trade**. In the post-feudal age of state-building in Europe, mercantilism resonated with ideas about national greatness. It also went hand in hand with **colonialism**. From the seventeenth century onwards, the grounds for legitimate warfare were enlarged to encompass commercial and market considerations. Thus, for example, the Dutch and British East India companies (both of which were established in response to the Spanish monopolization of the spice trade in Asia) waged economic war against each other. Overall, the legacy of early mercantilist policies was "to concentrate physical wealth in a few European nation-states, and to create a network of global economic interdependence the remains of which can still be seen today" (Watson, 2004: 3).

Two notable sets of laws in Britain illustrate early mercantilist principles aimed at maximizing national profits. First, the Navigation Acts of the mid-seventeenth century required that any goods shipped to English colonies be carried by English ships and crews, and prohibited foreign ships from trading in the colonies altogether (other European countries followed similar policies). Second, the Corn Laws of 1815–46 created trade barriers, protecting the high prices charged for home-grown grain against cheaper foreign imports. Both sets of laws were part of a protectionist framework that encompassed shipping, the colonial empire, commercial activities, and the food supply. But this cumbersome system of tariffs and prohibitions frustrated bureaucrats as well as merchants, and in 1846, after centuries of protectionism, Britain abruptly changed course, repealing the Corn Laws and "seeking to lead the world towards a peaceful order based on free commercial exchange between individuals and nations" (Howe, 1997: 1–2).

BOX 20.1
The Rise of Mercantilism

Although the term "mercantilism" was rarely used until the mid- to late eighteenth century (first appearing in the work of the French economist Mirabeau), mercantilist ideas were expressed as early as 1664 in Thomas Mun's *England's Treasure by Foreign Trade*. Mun argued that to produce a favourable national outcome, one must observe a basic rule: "to sell more to strangers yearly than we consume of theirs in value" (quoted in Miller, 1991: 335). These ideas developed during an age of European imperialism when various countries were competing for raw materials to feed their emerging industries. England, which had significant land-based armed forces as well as effective control of the seas, was able to project itself almost anywhere in the world, ensuring its early pre-eminence as a global power (Watson, 2004: 2). Adam Smith was largely responsible for giving the term "mercantilism" its currency, along with the term "political economy."

Mercantilism was clearly at odds with emerging liberal ideas both in economics and in politics more generally. Conservative economic historians depicted mercantilism as *rightly* subordinating economic to political considerations of **national interest**, in line with their belief in "the subordination of the individual to the state and to the exaltation of vigorous nationalism characteristic of mercantilism" (Viner, 1949: 4). An early nineteenth-century defender of mercantilism argued along lines that recall classical realism: rejecting the "cosmopolitical" world view of economic liberals, which assumed peaceful relations in a politically stable environment, Friedrich List (1789–1846) argued that political economy must start from the premise that international relations are inherently conflictual, and that nationalist rivalries produce the dynamics with which political economy must grapple. Thus the "true political science" would consider a world characterized by free trade to be "a very unnatural one" (List, 1991: 54).

Mercantilist thinking declined following the rise of liberal thought but enjoyed a resurgence in the late nineteenth and early twentieth centuries, when nationalism became widespread. Liberal ideas supporting free trade accordingly suffered a decline, but it was only temporary. Cohn (2005: 71) suggests that the association of the extreme nationalism and trade protectionism of the interwar years with the Great Depression and the Second World War, gave liberal economic principles a boost in the post-war period even though mainstream IR thinking took a decidedly realist turn at the same time. Since realist theorists had little interest in economics, mercantilist ideas did not figure prominently in early post-war IR theorizing. Still, the cycle of ideas invariably turns, and "realist IPE"—a variation on a theme of neomercantilism—was to gather support in the 1970s, when the architecture of the liberal economic world appeared to be crumbling.

KEY POINTS

- Mercantilism is a theory of international political economy based on balance-of-trade principles. Historically, it contained nationalist, imperialist, and realist elements.
- Mercantilism opposes the ideology of the free market, favouring a strong state that not only provides security but actively intervenes in the economy by promoting protectionist measures.

The Rise of Liberal Political Economy

By the late eighteenth century mercantilism had been displaced by the liberal political economy of Adam Smith, who argued for free trade. In an unregulated international economy, Smith said, a state could specialize in the production of the goods that it was able to produce most cheaply; then it could trade with other states for the goods in which each of them had a similar absolute advantage. Smith's insight was further refined by David Ricardo (1772–1823), who argued that even if a particular state was not the best at producing a particular good, it could enjoy a *comparative* advantage in the production of that good if its "opportunity costs" were lower than those of a different state; see **Box 20.2**.

20

KEY QUOTE BOX 20.2
"Should Tiger Woods Mow His Own Lawn?"

In at least two editions of his textbook *Principles of Macroeconomics*, Gregory Mankiw used golfer Tiger Woods in an example illustrating the difference between the principles of absolute and comparative advantage. Following the 2009 scandal over Woods's marital infidelity, however, Mankiw replaced Woods with Tom Brady, a quarterback for the New England Patriots:

© Ola Dusegård/istockphoto.com

PHOTO 20.1 Should Tiger Woods mow his own lawn?

Tiger Woods spends a lot of time walking around on grass. One of the most talented golfers of all time, he can hit a drive and sink a putt in a way that most casual golfers only dream of doing. Most likely, he is talented at other activities too. For example, let's imagine that Woods can mow his lawn faster than anyone else. But just because he can mow his lawn fast, does this mean he should? To answer this question, we can use the concepts of opportunity cost and comparative advantage. Let's say that Woods can mow his lawn in 2 hours. In that same 2 hours, he could film a television commercial for Nike and earn $10,000. By contrast, Forrest Gump, the boy next door, can mow Woods's lawn in 4 hours. In that same 4 hours, he could work at McDonald's and earn $20. In this example, Woods's opportunity cost of mowing the lawn is $10,000 and Forrest's opportunity cost is $20. Woods has an absolute advantage in mowing lawns because he can do the work in less time. Yet Forrest has a comparative advantage in mowing lawns because he has the lower opportunity cost.

SOURCE: N. Gregory Mankiw (2004), *Principles of Macroeconomics* (Mason, OH: Thomson/South-Western): 54.

See Chapter 5, page 94, for a discussion of liberalism. ←

Another important concept underpinning early liberal political economy was laissez-faire (literally, "let it be") meaning that the state should give free rein to *individual initiative, competition, the pursuit of self-interest and the invisible hand of market forces*—all classic elements of liberal political economy. Although the pursuit of self-interest might seem to favour selfish individual ends, Smith and other liberals believed that, together, self-interested individual actions would add up to overall wealth and prosperity for the community. Liberalism thus described is a theory of the individual *in* society rather than a theory of individual, self-regarding action without reference to a wider social sphere. Because liberal theorists were opposed to mercantilist state practices, and to the abuse of state power generally, liberal thought had an anti-statist flavour from the beginning. Even so, most versions of liberalism recognize the necessity of the state for the organization of political life as well as for legislation to protect rights, especially property rights. In the course of explaining the principle of comparative advantage under a regime of free trade, David Ricardo very succinctly summed up classical liberal political economy ideas and their implications for the wider world; see **Box 20.3**.

The most prominent liberal thinker of the twentieth century was undoubtedly John Maynard Keynes (1883–1946). Unlike some other liberals, he took a fairly pro-state position, arguing that the state plays an essential role creating the social, political, and economic conditions necessary for human well-being. He also believed that rational individual actions did not always add up to a rational outcome at the collective level, and that therefore the state had to be able to step in and make adjustments. Certainly, to treat "the market" as the infallible source of all wisdom was a mistake. Keynes's legacy to IPE was embodied in the post-war economic order, and among the economists who promoted Keynsianism in the US was the Canadian-born John Kenneth Galbraith (1908–2006). Although Galbraith is not often cited in IPE literature, he was important in presenting a liberal case for state involvement in economy and society and warning against simplistic faith in the market: "the notion that [the market] is intrinsically and universally benign is an error of libertarians and unduly orthodox conservatives" (Galbraith, 1984: 39–42).

KEY QUOTE BOX 20.3
David Ricardo on Comparative Advantage

Under a system of perfectly free commerce, each country naturally devotes its capital and labour to such employments as are most beneficial to each. The pursuit of individual advantage is admirably connected with the universal good of the whole. By stimulating industry, by regarding ingenuity, and by using most efficaciously the peculiar powers bestowed by nature, it distributes labour most effectively and most economically: while, by increasing the general mass of production, it diffuses general benefit, and binds together, by one common tie of interest and intercourse, the universal society of nations throughout the civilized world (Ricardo, 1821: 99).

20

- Liberalism replaced mercantilism with the principles of free trade and comparative advantage.
- Liberal political economy promotes individual initiative, competition, the pursuit of self-interest, and the "invisible hand" of market forces. Liberals generally believe that the individual actions together add up to overall wealth and prosperity, although liberals such as Keynes and Galbraith were skeptical.

Marxism and Critical IPE

The third classical theory of political economy is Marxism. In theorizing such key matters as class struggle, exploitation, and **imperialism**, Marxism "contributes an essential critical approach to the operation of contemporary political economy" (Watson, 2004: 9–10). **Class analysis** and the distribution of wealth are implicit in dependency theory and world system analysis, as we saw in Chapter 16. Critical approaches to IPE in the contemporary period focus particular attention on the commodification of labour in international markets as part of the broader process of **globalization**. They are also sensitive to gender and race as well as traditional class analysis. But there is still a long way to go before these issues are brought into the mainstream of discussion. As Griffin (2007: 720) argues in relation to gender, a gendered IPE analysis is central to a proper understanding of the processes and practice of the global political economy, and much high-quality work has been done in this area in recent years; yet gender is still seen as a "women's issue" and therefore of marginal status relative to more traditional concerns.

Another critical study focuses on international labour migration. Goss and Lindquist argue that this is a massive "industry" with significant race and gender dimensions,

© Jessica Liu/istockphoto.com

PHOTO 20.2 Women working in a garment factory in Asia. The majority of workers engaged in sweatshop labour are women.

powered by wage inequalities between source and destination countries that are the result of highly uneven development (Goss and Lindquist, 1995: 317). Meanwhile, transnational corporations looking for ever-cheaper sources of labour are setting up manufacturing operations in developing countries—even in pariah dictatorships such as Burma (Myanmar). Supporters of the capitalist system argue that transnational manufacturing benefits the poor, but critics see it as perpetuating relations of exploitation.

CASE STUDY
Globalization, Labour Markets, and Gender

Ultimately, the global economy depends on the exploitation of labour, in particular cheap labour in less developed countries. Many cheap labour markets are heavily gendered. For example, Indonesian males are employed as migrant workers in construction projects in the Middle East, Singapore, and Malaysia, while Indonesian females are employed as domestic workers. Regulations protecting such migrants are often very weak, leaving many at the mercy of the companies that arrange the work contracts—an industry in itself—as well as their employers. Even less protected are illegal immigrant workers who are often "trafficked" into destination countries. "Illegals" are found around the world, wherever there is a demand for cheap labour, from the UK, France, and Germany to Dubai and Kuwait, Singapore, Malaysia, and Japan. Illegal immigrant labour is a significant part of the US economy as well (see Kaur, 2007).

Another growing phenomenon is the "feminization of labour." In a "global environment of open economies, new trade regimes, and competitive export industries, global accumulation relies heavily on the work of women, both waged and unwaged, in formal sectors and in the home, in manufacturing, and in public and private services" (Moghadam, 2005: 51). This trend is especially prominent in developing countries in Southeast and East Asia, parts of Latin America, the Caribbean, and North Africa, where increasing numbers of women work in labour-intensive, low-wage jobs in the textile and garment industries as well as in electronics and pharmaceuticals.

At the same time, as world trade in services has grown and global firms increasingly out-source service work, women's involvement in the services sector has grown as well. Valentine M. Moghadam observes: "Women around the world have made impressive inroads into professional services such as law, banking, accounting, computing, and architecture; in tourism-related occupations; and in the information services, including offshore airline booking, mail order, credit cards, word-processing for publishers, telephone operators, and so on" (Moghadam, 1999: 367–88).

At the other end of the spectrum is the increased trafficking of women made possible under conditions of globalization. According to a US immigration support website (www.usimmigrationsupport.org/illegal_immigration.html), young women from relatively poor countries are often deceived into thinking they have been promised a good job abroad, only to discover on arrival in the destination country that they have been brought in to work as prostitutes. Far from home, with no other means of support and nowhere to turn for help, many of them are effectively forced into sexual slavery. Although this kind of human trafficking is more common in the Middle East and Europe, it occurs in the US and Canada as well.

With the economic downturn in Europe and North America, citizen activism has become more pronounced. A key event in 2011 was the Occupy Wall Street movement, which began in New York and spread to cities around North America and Europe. The movement claimed to speak for the silent or silenced 99 per cent of the American population who had suffered from unemployment, failed mortgages, and the erosion of social services. Angry at corporate bailouts, they produced a newspaper called *The Occupied Wall Street Journal*. Canadian journalist and author Naomi Klein attended the Wall Street protests. She had been a vocal advocate for the rights of workers in the globalized economy, especially women, who are disproportionately exploited (see the case study for the very significant gender elements in international labour markets). She addressed the crowd in October, 2011:

If there is one thing I know, it is that the 1 percent loves a crisis. When people are panicked and desperate and no one seems to know what to do, that is the ideal time to push through their wish list of pro-corporate policies: privatizing education and social security, slashing public services, getting rid of the last constraints on corporate power. Amidst the economic crisis, this is happening the world over. And there is only one thing that can block this tactic, and fortunately, it's a very big thing: the 99 percent. And that 99 percent is taking to the streets from Madison to Madrid to say "No. We will not pay for your crisis."

SOURCE: Naomi Klein (2011), "Occupy Wall Street: The Most Important Thing in the World Now," The Nation, 6 Oct.; http://www.thenation.com/article/163844/occupy-wall-street-most-important-thing-world-now

© Mike Panic/istockphoto.com

PHOTO 20.3 October 2011: An Occupy Wall Street protester in New York wearing a gas mask and a bleak environmental message

We referred to the critical theory of Robert W. Cox in Chapter 16. Cox has also promoted a neo-Gramscian perspective on IPE, focusing on **hegemony** and the dynamics of domination and subordination, coercion, and consent. In a seminal article, Cox (1981) does not simply accept the international economic or political order as it is: he questions how it came into being and how it might be transformed into a more just and equitable one. The "new political economy" promoted by Cox and others in the critical tradition also rejects the methodological **positivism** of conventional realist and liberal IPE, which they see as constraining the capacity to think outside the parameters of conventional theory. A recent critical/feminist perspective also argues that IPE requires a radical rethinking of conventional theory (both realist and liberal) that questions the objectivist and rationalist **epistemology** on which they are based, and which has worked to marginalize issues concerning race, gender, and class in mainstream studies (Peterson, 2003: 21–2). Another scholar argues that the critical wing of global political economy (GPE), as he prefers to call the field, is multifaceted in its approach, incorporating gender perspectives and critiques of race and class in addition to analyzing institutions that range from the family, to the firm, the market, and the state. Above all, GPE scrutinizes much more thoroughly the exercise of power (Palan, 2000: 7–8).

KEY POINTS

- Class analysis remains relevant in an international sphere where low-cost labour migrates or, alternatively, manufacturing industries locate in countries offering cheap and more easily exploited labour. In either case, protection of workers' rights is often minimal or non-existent, further reducing costs.
- Critical IPE questions how the global political economy came into being, what interests support it (and are supported by it), and how it might be transformed. It is more sensitive than mainstream IPE to issues of class, race, and gender, incorporates a wider range of institutions into the analysis, and is attuned to issues of domination and subordination.

The Post-War International Economic Order

As the Second World War drew to an end, plans for a new international economic order that would free up access to markets and raw materials were developed alongside plans for new international political institutions. Delegates meeting at Bretton Woods, New Hampshire, in 1944 were also concerned to establish a system that would stabilize exchange rates and prevent any reoccurrence of the conditions that had triggered worldwide depression in the interwar years. However, competing national interests challenged pure liberal principles, and the system that emerged, which Ruggie has characterized as "embedded liberalism," reflected many compromises: "unlike the economic nationalism of the thirties it would be multilateral in character; unlike the liberalism of the gold standard and free trade, its multilateralism would be predicated on domestic interventionism" (Ruggie, 1982: 393).

Three major bodies were created to support the new international economic order, collectively dubbed the Bretton Woods institutions: the International Monetary Fund (IMF), the International Bank for Reconstruction and Development (IBRD; later the World Bank), and the General Agreement on Tariffs and Trade (GATT). The GATT was signed in 1947 as an interim measure until a more permanent institution could be worked out but it took until 1995 to establish the World Trade Organization (WTO) (see Wilkinson, 2000). In the intervening years, the GATT functioned to hold together whatever agreements could be reached on trade liberalization; see the case study below.

One success story in the early post-war years was the work of the IBRD in Europe. The US played a major role in its development. Fearing the influence of communism in a badly damaged Europe where millions of people were struggling, US policy-makers sought to contain the threat in part by rebuilding the economies of Western Europe via the Marshall Plan. Under this plan billions in US aid were distributed in ways compatible with securing Europe as a major trading and security partner. Meanwhile, the IMF was charged with maintaining a stable exchange rate mechanism and balance of payments regime. Opening for business in 1948 with fairly modest credit facilities, it did little in its first few years because the US focus was split between European reconstruction (mainly funded separately) and rebuilding Japan. By the early 1960s, though, the IMF's involvement in supplying credits was increasing, especially as decolonization progressed, and it became a major player in the economies of developing countries. The US continues to dominate both the IMF and the World Bank—a reflection of its early role as the major supplier of funds to international financial institutions. Both these institutions require the largest economies to contribute the most money, but in return those economies are given a heavily weighted vote in decisions on where the money will go and how it will be used.

CASE STUDY
The WTO and the Global Trading Regime

The WTO was officially established on 1 January 1995 as an organization dedicated to liberalizing trade, setting ground rules for the conduct of international commerce, and providing a forum for negotiating trade agreements and settling disputes. It consolidated and permanently institutionalized the rules of the trading system first established in 1948 by the GATT, which itself had evolved through several rounds of negotiations. The most important of these was the "Uruguay Round" of 1986, which finally led to the creation of the WTO. Whereas the GATT was principally concerned with trade in goods, the WTO expanded its scope to include trade both in services and in intellectual property (inventions, creations, and designs). It is based on principles of multilateralism, transparency, predictability, and equality of treatment. But it has some flexibility to accommodate special national circumstances through preferential treatment and regional free trade agreements (FTAs), and therefore is not a worldwide "free trade" organization as such. Significant rounds of negotiations have continued under the auspices of the WTO. The "Doha Round," which commenced in 2001, aims to eliminate unfair trading practices, especially those affecting poorer countries. Negotiations stalled at a meeting in Cancun in 2003 at which agreement on agriculture, among other key issues, failed to materialize. Among the main issues are the generous agricultural subsidies provided by rich countries at the expense of poorer countries. The EU's Common Agricultural Policy (CAP), for example, has long disadvantaged agricultural exports from the developing world. So too have the policies of most of the G8 countries, especially the US. There is broad agreement that the process should continue, but much depends on US leadership. (See, generally, www.wto.org.)

Although the Bretton Woods institutions remain an important part of international economic architecture, a breakdown occurred in the Bretton Woods exchange rate mechanism. As part of the 1944 agreement, currency values were fixed according to the price of gold (hence the "gold standard"). In earlier periods the British pound had served as a primary currency, but after 1945 only the US dollar could meet international demands for liquidity. The US agreed to convert dollars to gold at US$35.00 per ounce to facilitate the exchange rate mechanism. By the early 1970s, however, the US was faced with rising imports and a significant trade imbalance. Although the huge outflows of dollars providing liquidity for the international economy contributed to the country's considerable prosperity, they could not be sustained. Increased interdependence and the recovery of the European and Japanese economies, along with vastly increased financial flows, made it almost impossible to control currency values. The ongoing costs of the Vietnam War also weakened the US economy (see, generally, Spero and Hart, 1997: 16–21).

In 1971 the US abandoned the dollar gold standard and raised tariffs on imports. Other industrialized countries responded by strengthening their own protectionist measures. This flew in the face of GATT principles supporting free trade. Further trouble was in store with rising inflation and commodity shortages. These problems deepened when the world was hit by a series of "oil shocks" in the mid-1970s, when oil producers quadrupled the price of oil in a year. This had multiple consequences for the world economy, including recession. In 1975, seven leading industrial countries—the US, the UK, Canada, France, Germany, Italy, and Japan (later to become the G7)—met to discuss the problems of the international monetary system (Spero and Hart, 1997: 23).

By the early 1980s, in the wake of both international economic developments and the fiasco of the Vietnam War, America's status as the world's economic and military powerhouse was declining (Keohane, 2001). The global recession hit most countries, including the US, hard, and conservative commentators blamed liberal economics. One US-based commentator, William R. Hawkins, dismissed the liberal vision of world order based on free trade as "utopian" and advocated what he called "neomercantilism"—a form of economic conservatism based squarely on national interest (Hawkins, 1984: 25–39).

Five years later, with the collapse of communism and the apparent triumph of liberal democracy, capitalism, and free market ideology, the discourse of neoliberal globalization overshadowed neomercantilism and realist IPE. The new post-Cold War order proclaimed by liberal triumphalists such as Francis Fukuyama (1989) swept all before it in a wave of optimism about the global future. Hawkins's views nonetheless provide an interesting snapshot of neomercantilist thinking in the early 1980s, thinking that still resonates with realists and other conservative critics of the globalization thesis today.

See Chapter 6, page 116 for a further discussion of Fukuyama's "end of history" thesis.

Advocates of free trade, particularly libertarians, often claim that the interdependence produced by trade will usher in an era of world peace—a notion that has no foundation in either history or current events. This view was most popular just before World War I and again just after World War II. It accounts for much of the continued liberal-left support for free trade. . . . Technical advances in communications and transportation do seem to have brought the world closer together, but this is an illusion. The human element of competing values and ambitions has not changed. Nor has the fundamental economic assumption: at any point in time, resources are scarce relative to wants. Thus the technical advances have only provided nations with the means to carry out their rivalries on a global scale. World unity is not at hand (Hawkins, 1984: 29–30).

KEY POINTS

• The Bretton Woods monetary and exchange rate system was a compromise between liberalism and nationalism. Although the system itself had collapsed by the early 1970s, global economic governance is still underpinned by the institutions established to support it: the IMF, the World Bank (successor to the IBRD), and the WTO (successor to the GATT).

• Neomercantilism enjoyed a revival in response to the worldwide recession of the 1970s, but with the end of the Cold War a triumphant liberalism reasserted global economic openness as the basis for a prosperous new world order.

The North–South Gap

Since the early 1970s, the gap between the developed North and the developing South has only widened. The rising protectionism of the industrialized states (influenced by neomercantilism), together with soaring energy costs, inflation and increasing indebtedness, led to calls for meaningful reforms in aid, foreign investment regimes, the terms of trade, and financial arrangements, including loans, as well as a fairer overall monetary system. In the 1960s, developing countries had formed the Group of 77 (G77) to lobby as a bloc in global forums, especially the UN and the GATT, but it had limited success because neither the oil-producing nations (which formed their own Organization of Petroleum Exporting Countries [OPEC]) nor the countries of the industrialized North were prepared to make any significant concessions to ease the burden of poorer countries.

See Chapter 17, page 351, for a discussion of the Brandt report.

As we saw in Chapter 17, the UN's Brandt Commission attempted to put underdevelopment on the reform agenda in 1980, but no significant changes were made in response to its recommendations. In the meantime, the World Bank and IMF promoted **structural adjustment** programs for poor, underperforming countries. Inspired by neoliberal economic orthodoxies, these programs called for privatization of state resources and strict limits on public spending, including drastic cuts to the welfare state, and loans to the governments in question were made conditional on implementation of these measures. The effect in many cases was to limit access to health, education, and public utilities without either alleviating poverty or significantly improving overall economic performance.

See Chapter 16, page 319, for a discussion of dependency theory.

How do the various theories we have looked at "theorize" the North–South gap? In terms of dependency theory (introduced in Chapter 16), the post-war order with its mixture of liberal and mercantile/realist institutions and principles was a recipe for exploitation. World system analysis, for its part, proposes that underdevelopment and a global division of labour are actually necessary conditions for the maintenance of global capitalism. Liberal theory of course looks to other explanations for the poor performance of many Third World countries. Thus a World Bank report found that the best economic performance in sub-Saharan Africa had occurred in the two countries that had been able to maintain parliamentary democracy—Botswana and Mauritius—and blamed a "crisis of governance" for political, social, and economic woes elsewhere on the continent (cited in Williams and Young, 1994: 86). This report marked a watershed in World Bank thinking about the importance of **good governance** in countries with poor records (Williams and Young, 1994); see **Box 20.4**.

Yet the North–South gap in the distribution of the world's wealth has many causes, and the problems it generates cannot be resolved simply through the application of good

20

governance principles and practices, however important these are. In the developing world, poverty and instability often go hand-in-hand, generating humanitarian crises as well as wider security issues that impinge on developed countries. A question to be asked by any serious student of IPE is the extent to which this situation is attributable to a global economic architecture that favours those who designed it.

> ### KEY QUOTE BOX 20.4
> #### The World Bank on Good Governance
>
> The Governance group of the World Bank Institute (WBI) facilitates action-oriented and participatory programs to promote good governance and curb corruption in its client countries (http://go.worldbank.org/8CHK6P24S0).
>
> We define governance as the traditions and institutions by which authority in a country is exercised for the common good. This includes (i) the process by which those in authority are selected, monitored and replaced, (ii) the capacity of the government to effectively manage its resources and implement sound policies, and (iii) the respect of citizens and the state for the institutions that govern economic and social interactions among them (http://go.worldbank.org/MKOGR258V0).

← See Chapter 10, page 212, for a definition of good governance from UNESCAP.

KEY POINTS

- The North–South gap generates serious international political, economic, and social problems.
- Some programs inspired by neoliberal economic thinking and formulated by the World Bank and IMF, such as structural adjustment programs, have compounded the problems associated with the gap.

Globalization and Regionalization in the Post-Cold War World

Globalization

If globalization is defined as "the acceleration and intensification of mechanisms, processes, and activities . . . promoting global interdependence and perhaps, ultimately, global political and economic integration" (Griffiths and O'Callaghan, 2002: 126–7), then it must be a central concern for IPE. Indeed, some analyses focus almost exclusively on the economic dimensions of globalization positing global market forces as the central dynamic:

> the world economy has internationalized its basic dynamics, it is dominated by uncontrollable market forces, and it has as its principle economic actors and major agents of change truly transnational corporations that owe allegiance to no nation-state and locate wherever on the globe market advantage dictates (Hirst and Thompson, 1999: 1).

The phenomenon has other dimensions as well. As Tomlinson (1999) suggests, the cultural implications of new media and communication technologies and new transnational business and work practices in the global economy are far-reaching. The general direction of change will almost certainly be towards a more cosmopolitan culture, but what it will look like, and what it will mean in terms of social, political, and moral questions, is by no means certain.

Previous chapters have underlined the challenge that globalization—with its emphasis on interconnectedness and the transcendence of state boundaries and controls—presents to the traditional view of international order based on independent sovereign states. We have also seen in Chapter 7 how these trends are affecting states in the developed world. Even relatively strong developed states appear to be losing autonomy and regulatory capacity. What this means for states' ability to deliver a reasonable measure of prosperity and "human security" to their citizens is a particularly difficult question in the developing world, where structural adjustment programs have already had a negative impact on state capacity. Furthermore, the "market" is not geared to anything but producing profits. A strictly economistic approach to the dynamics of globalized markets cannot address issues of justice, either within or between states. As one observer has noted, globalization produces both winners and losers, and understanding it requires a multiperspectival approach incorporating markets, states, and people (Woods, 1998).

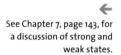

See Chapter 7, page 143, for a discussion of strong and weak states.

Another aspect of global economic development that has attracted very significant attention over the last two decades is the enormous growth in the economies of the Asia–Pacific region and the prospects for a "Pacific Century." Despite the financial crisis of the late 1990s, the Asia–Pacific boom is continuing, with the growth of China (see **Box 20.5**) and more recently India attracting particular attention. The fact that some governments have taken on a proactive role in creating the conditions for growth in the global economy is especially interesting. In these cases, states promote markets as part of a broader neoliberal developmental strategy. Although neoclassical (liberal) economic orthodoxy has attributed the spectacular growth in the region to laissez-faire principles, detailed studies show that it has been facilitated by direct government intervention in the form of macroeconomic planning (see Palat, 1996). Again, this suggests that strictly economistic approaches are far too narrow and need to be complemented with state-centred perspectives.

See Chapter 1, page 23, for a discussion of the developmental state.

Even so, studies urging attention to the continuing importance of the state have not deterred "hyperglobalists" from making extravagant claims about the future of the sovereign nation-state. A leading figure among the hyperglobalists is the Japanese economist Kenichi Ohmae, who as early as 1993 suggested that the nation-state was doomed to oblivion in the emerging borderless world (for a quotation, see **Box 20.6** on p. 422).

Regionalization

In the same paper in which he declared the demise of the nation-state, Ohmae proposed that the relevant unit now is what he called the "region-state" (1993: 78; see also **Box 20.6** on p. 422). This brings us to the second of the two phenomena we want to consider in this section. Regionalization resembles globalization in two ways: it is a complex process of integration, with cultural and social as well as political and economic dimensions, and

KEY CONCEPT BOX 20.5
China's Growing Influence in the Developing World

The Peoples' Republic of China has stocked up some $2.5 trillion in foreign reserves. This, as Rachman observes, is allowing China to compete with the US and its European allies in a variety of ways:

> China's economic prowess is already allowing Beijing to challenge American influence all over the world. The Chinese are the preferred partners of many African governments and the biggest trading partner of other emerging powers, such as Brazil and South Africa. China is also stepping in to buy the bonds of financially strapped members of the eurozone, such as Greece and Portugal. And China is only the largest part of a bigger story about the rise of new economic and political players. America's traditional allies in Europe—Britain, France, Italy, even Germany—are slipping down the economic ranks. New powers are on the rise: India, Brazil, Turkey. They each have their own foreign-policy preferences, which collectively constrain America's ability to shape the world. Think of how India and Brazil sided with China at the global climate-change talks. Or the votes by Turkey and Brazil against America at the United Nations on sanctions against Iran. That is just a taste of things to come (Rachman 2011).

Meanwhile, many people in Western countries are wondering what the rise of the Asian economies means for them. Is Asia rising at the expense of the West, or will its new powerful economies benefit everyone through techonological advances and cheaper prices? The latest survey by the Chicago Council on Global Affairs (Bouton et al., 2010) suggests that Americans have mixed feelings about globalization and are particularly worried that the US is in economic decline:

> While globalization is seen as "mostly good" for the United States by a majority of Americans, it is seen as bad for many aspects of American life, including the job security of American workers and creating jobs in the United States. Half of Americans now think it should be a goal of the United States to either try to slow globalization down or reverse it (Bouton et al., 2010).

its primary dynamic is usually considered to be economic. In addition, though, many regionalizing processes have an important security dimension. For example, the Association of Southeast Asian Nations (ASEAN), one of the longest-standing regional organizations outside Europe, was founded primarily to secure regional peace in the Cold War period and has only recently begun to concern itself with economic issues.

Though some have seen regionalization as leading to the formation of rival trading blocs and hence as a threat to "the multilateral order," others find it to be perfectly compatible with global integration (Haggard, 1997: 20). Indeed, in some parts of the world it is regarded as promoting participation in a globalized economy by creating opportunities for economic growth via free trade and other arrangements within a regional framework. From this perspective regionalization itself is part of the broader globalization process.

Regionalization is proceeding in Africa, the Americas, North Africa and the Middle East, in the regions of the former USSR, including Central Asia, South Asia, Southeast and East Asia, and in the Pacific and Caribbean. There are also organizations covering huge swathes of the globe. The Asia–Pacific Economic Cooperation (APEC) forum, for example, has grown from an initial membership of 12 when it was formed in 1989 to a current total of 21 (Australia, Brunei, Canada, Chile, China, Hong Kong, Indonesia, Japan, Malaysia, Mexico, New Zealand, Papua New Guinea, Peru, Philippines, Russia, Singapore, South Korea, Taiwan, Thailand, US, and Vietnam). Together these countries account for roughly 40 per cent of the world's population, 48 per cent of world trade, and almost 60 per cent of world GDP.

← See Chapter 18, page 363, for more on the history and structure of the EU.

While regionalization is clearly occurring in most parts of the world, the extent to which it has become institutionalized varies considerably. It is most advanced, though by no means complete, in the EU area, as we noted in Chapter 18. The EU itself has been a long time in the making—almost five decades passed from the time of the founding of the European Movement in 1943 to the Maastricht Treaty of 1992—and the process is not finished yet: the deepening and widening processes are ongoing, and the consequences of the current economic crisis are impossible to foresee.

Elsewhere in the world, experiments in regional integration are generally far less institutionalized: none approach the depth achieved by the EU. In fact, the EU model has found little support outside Europe. It may be that the circumstances in which it was created were unique: high levels of wealth, the glue of a Soviet "other" during the Cold War, US encouragement for integration, the need to prevent any repetition of the twentieth-century wars. States in other regions may cooperate closely on a range of matters, but any integration is fairly superficial. States that were still colonies only a generation ago guard their national sovereignty jealously, and many cling to an almost absolute principle of non-interference in their "sovereign affairs," especially when it comes to matters of human rights.

This is not to suggest that nationalism in the EU area is dead. Although it has not overwhelmed the European project, it continues to operate as a persistent low-level dynamic. Still, when nationalism interferes with Europe's liberal economic agenda, it can draw very pointed criticism from liberal quarters. In 2007 the European Economic Advisory Group (EEAG) argued that "Economic nationalism in the form of opposition to cross-border mergers, promotion of national champions and bailing out of domestic firms is a serious danger for economic efficiency." The group cited public ownership as a culprit, urging that it be "severely restricted"—a conclusion that flew in the face of Europe's long tradition of social democracy (European Economic Advisory Group, 2007). Little if anything has been done to implement this report, although governments have been forced to restrict spending in the wake of the 2008 financial crisis.

Another important development is interregionalism—a phenomenon that reinforces regionalization. A notable example is the Asia–Europe Meeting (ASEM) process established in the mid-1990s. Formed primarily to enhance economic relations, it has political and cultural pillars as well. The EU members comprise "Europe" for the purposes of the meeting process while the Asian members now include all the ASEAN countries plus China, Japan, and South Korea and, more recently, India, Mongolia, Pakistan, and the ASEAN Secretariat.

To summarize, although regional schemes have existed for decades, regionalization is clearly increasing in the post-Cold War period. It is driven primarily by economic factors, but virtually all of the regional associations seek closer social and political ties as well. The other observable pattern is the continuing development of an overarching tripolar economic system based on the "macroregions" of Europe, North America, and Asia—the power-houses of the global economy. The formation of ASEM is generally seen as strengthening the third leg of that system, balancing the already strong North American–European and North American–Asian legs. Seen from this perspective, globalization and regionalization are indeed complementary dynamics in the liberalization of the global economy.

At the same time, however, globalization and regionalization may also undermine the economic role and functions of the nation-state—the very foundation of traditional IR. Trade liberalization and financial deregulation are all about easing, if not eliminating, state-imposed restraints, even though in many cases the macroeconomic policy that responsible allowing such developments. Outside universities, dissent and critique emanate from broad social movements manifest in "anti-globalization" protests—now regular occurrences at global and regional forums. Most participants are peaceful pro-testers gathering under the banners of various NGOs with concerns ranging from labour rights to environmental issues, consumer protection, and peace advocacy. Others are self-described anarchists whose tactics range from civil disobedience to violence, mainly against commercial property and security personnel. An early manifestation of "global protest" was the "Battle for Seattle" in November 1999, when half a million demonstrators converged on a WTO ministerial meeting. The 2007 APEC meeting in Sydney saw the entire city centre locked down for several days to forestall the vigorous protests that had come to be expected. And in Toronto hundreds of protestors were arrested during the G-20 Summit of 2010, even though the vast majority were peaceful and well-intentioned. The same has been true of the Occupy Wall Street movement, as Naomi Klein told the protesters: "You have committed yourselves to non-violence. You have refused to give the media the images of broken windows and street fights it craves so desperately" (Klein, 2011).

Most anti-globalization protesters see the processes of globalization and regionaliza-tion as undermining the rights and interests of ordinary people in various ways. The fact that the issues they are concerned about—labour rights, consumer protection, environ-mental issues—were traditionally the preserve of the state has prompted debates on the role of the state, and indeed the future of sovereignty, in a globalizing world; see **Box 20.6**. As we have remarked elsewhere, the state will no doubt remain, but it is unlikely to be the sovereign nation-state of traditional IR theory (Lawson, 2002: 218).

KEY POINTS

- Globalization and regionalization are complex processes of integration, driven mainly by a liberal economic logic but also incorporating social and political dimensions. In general they are complementary rather than competitive processes. Some critical IPE approaches welcome the openings provided by globalization for new social movements while remaining critical of adverse economic consequences for marginalized groups.

- Both globalization and regionalization have been seen as undermining the tradi-tional role of the state. This development is unwelcome from the perspective of both neomercantilist/realist IPE and the traditional left, which fears negative impact on the state's ability to provision for social protection.

20

KEY QUOTE BOX 20.6

Ohmae on Globalism and the Demise of the Nation-State

The Nation-State has become an unnatural, even dysfunctional, unit for organizing human activity and managing economic endeavour in a borderless world. It represents no genuine, shared community of economic interests; it defines no meaningful flows of economic activity. In fact it overlooks the true linkages and synergies that exist among often disparate populations by combining important measures of human activity at the wrong level of analysis. . . . On the global economic map the lines that now matter are those defining what may be called "region states." The boundaries . . . are not imposed by political fiat. They are drawn by the deft but invisible hand of the global market for goods and services. They follow rather than precede, real flows of human activity, creating nothing new but ratifying existing patterns manifest in countless individual decisions (Ohmae, 1993: 78).

Conclusion

Although many students of politics and international relations tend to shy away from economics, understanding the relationships between states and markets, political and economic power, is now essential. Theories of IPE developed over the last few centuries parallel those in the more general fields of politics and international relations. Mercantilism and realism, together with doctrines of nationalism and sovereignty, form a theoretical cluster that, although not entirely coherent, supports a world-view in which the state is the ultimate repository of political, social, and economic life and should be defended as such. Many traditional social democrats and more conservative proponents of **communitarianism** would agree.

By contrast, liberal perspectives, while acknowledging the importance of states, generally support a world-view that centres on the overlapping ties between different political and economic communities. Aided by the revolutions in transport, communications, and other forms of technology, these ties have produced an interdependent world that can only benefit from a progressive softening of sovereign state boundaries to create a truly global market for goods and services. The twin phenomena of globalization and regionalization both reflect and support the liberal view of world order.

Critical IPE, for its part, challenges the assumptions of both realists and liberals, urging attention to the vested interests that lie behind them and the injustices they mask. Although levels of socioeconomic well-being also vary considerably within countries, critical IPE focuses on the North–South gap in the global economy as a standing indictment of both mercantilist and liberal approaches. The challenge is to move beyond incremental problem-solving and bring about major change in our theories and political practice, to help us probe the deeper historical development of opportunities and constraints and map out future trajectories. Critical IPE does not necessarily oppose all aspects of globalization;

some theorists welcome the challenge to sovereignty that it represents. It also welcomes the proliferation of global and regional social movements, seeing them as vehicles for positive change. Finally, critical IPE performs a useful role in providing an ongoing practical critique of both liberal and realist IPE.

? KEY QUESTIONS

- In what sense does classical mercantilism see national wealth and military power as forming a virtuous circle?
- Under what circumstances did liberalism first emerge as the dominant perspective in IPE?
- How does liberal theory justify the pursuit of economic self-interest?
- How relevant is class analysis to contemporary IPE?
- How can gender-sensitive studies contribute to IPE?
- What are the main features of critical IPE? How does it add to traditional Marxist perspectives?
- What does the North–South gap tell us about justice and injustice in the global economy?
- What do the terms "structural adjustment" and "good governance" mean? How do they reflect liberal political and economic principles?
- What are some of the concerns of the "global protest" movement?
- Do you regard globalization or regionalization as a genuine threat to the future of the nation-state as the foundation of world order?

📖 FURTHER READING

Breslin, Shaun, Christopher W. Hughes, Nicola Philips, and Ben Rosamund, eds (2002). *New Regionalisms in the Global Political Economy: Theories and Cases*. London: Routledge.
　　A comprehensive collection of essays by leading authors on regionalism and the issues it raises in terms of sovereignty, autonomy, identity, environmental concerns, and financial crises, set in a broad comparative perspective.

Cameron, David R., and Janice Gross Stein, eds (2002). *Street Protests and Fantasy Parks: Globalization, Culture, and the State*. Vancouver: University of British Columbia Press.
　　As globalization seems to be increasing in intensity, there has been serious debate about its impact on individuals and society in general. This book, edited by two political scientists at the University of Toronto, examines the social and cultural impacts of globalization and how the role of the state is changing in response to it. Rejecting Ohmae's dismissal of the nation-state, they argue that states still have the capacity to make very real choices and to wield considerable power.

McNally, David (2006). *Another World Is Possible: Globalization and Anti-Capitalism*. 2nd edn. Winnipeg: Arbeiter Ring Publishing.
　　David McNally of York University examines contemporary social activists from many countries, including Mexico, Korea, Bolivia, Indonesia, and Brazil,—why and how they organize, the types of political and economic orders they seek to resist—and contextualizes their protest in a world that is racialized, gendered, and imperialist.

Ravenhill, John, ed. (2008). *Global Political Economy*. 2nd edn. Oxford: Oxford University Press.
　　A detailed introduction to the subject matter of IPE, with 14 chapters by expert contributors covering theoretical approaches, global trade, finance and production, the implications of globalization for the state, and issues concerning the environment, the global south, and regionalism.

20

Scholte, Jan Aart (2005). *Globalization: A Critical Introduction*. 2nd edn. Basingstoke, Palgrave Macmillan.

Globalization for Scholte consists largely in deterritorialization, giving increasing significance to transborder global relations between people and organizations as communication and production are increasingly freed from geographic constraints. Thus the main focus is on the rise of supraterritoriality which is abundantly illustrated throughout the book.

WEB LINKS

http://europa.eu/index_en.htm

The English-language gateway to the EU website contains an enormous amount of information.

http://occupywallst.org

The official website for the Occupy Wall Street movement.

www.iisd.org

The website of the International Institute for Sustainable Development contains wide-ranging information on the developing world.

www.oecd.org

The Organization for Economic Cooperation and Development (OECD) is an invaluable source of statistical data.

www.ilo.org

The International Labour Organization (ILO) provides statistical data and more general information on international agreements and issues.

Note: Websites for all the regional organizations mentioned in this chapter can be easily found with a search engine.

Conclusion

CHAPTER OVERVIEW

In this concluding section we draw together the threads of several arguments that have run throughout the book. We begin by underlining the importance of the connections between our three main subject areas—political philosophy, political institutions, and international relations. We then turn to the impact of globalization and its consequences both for the state and for the study of politics. Finally, although much more has been written on Western political thought and political systems than other varieties, we argue that political science should be a genuinely international and comparative enterprise.

The Study of Politics in Context

We have divided this book into three parts—political philosophy, political institutions, and international relations—mainly for reasons of convenience, and because political science has evolved in this way. Clearly, though, the standard areas of specialization in political science have considerable overlap with one another and are not theoretically isolated. The study of normative political philosophy cannot be separated from the empirical study of political institutions; political institutions operate at both domestic and international levels; political rulers depend on ideas to gain the support of the people, educating or socializing citizens into believing that the system is legitimate; and so on. The latter is a clear example of the connection between the normative and empirical dimensions of politics.

We have discussed the concepts of "power" and "justice" in the context of both domestic political systems and the international arena. There are obvious connections between national political systems and the international system. The international system has developed on Westphalian principles, and assumes equality and equal sovereignty between nation-states. Among the Montevideo criteria for recognition as a state is the capacity of the national government to control all of the territory it claims. For many states, especially in the developing world, stability depends at least as much on a benign international environment as it does on domestic circumstances.

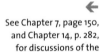
See Chapter 7, page 150, and Chapter 14, p. 282, for discussions of the Montevideo Convention.

The study of politics is eclectic, overlapping with other disciplines in terms of subject matter, theories, and methods. Political philosophy has traditionally been preoccupied with identifying the type of system best suited to let us to live the good life, and in this quest moral and political philosophy become largely inseparable. Similarly, one of the recurring themes of this volume has been the impact of history on the spread of both European-type states and the Westphalian state system around the world.

Economics is a discipline with a high degree of formal abstraction, yet there is increasing recognition that institutions play a key role in determining many economic outcomes. At the same time, economic abstractions form the basis of rational choice theories such as the economic theory of democracy, according to which political parties and voters, no less than businesses and consumers in the economic sphere, are utility-maximizers, bent on achieving the greatest possible benefits for themselves at the lowest possible cost. Political economy, both domestic and international, draws on methods from both politics and economics.

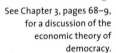
See Chapter 3, pages 68–9, for a discussion of the economic theory of democracy.

The overlap between sociology and politics is equally important. For example, social stratification plays a major role not only in determining voting patterns but in determining which individuals will become politicians. The studies of power that we examined in Chapter 2 used concepts and models of society developed by political sociologists. In Chapter 8 we emphasized how law and politics overlap in setting the rules that determine who gets what, when, and how in society. Psychology also overlaps with the study of politics: for example, in Chapter 11 we discussed how it can contribute to our understanding of voting behaviour. Many themes in political philosophy depend on assumptions concerning human nature, and policy studies often involve methods of analysis and data derived from disciplines outside the social sciences. Studies of environmental policy-making, for instance, often rely on information from the natural sciences; and policy analysis of all kinds often benefits from scientific or technological understanding. In short, a sophisticated understanding of political processes, whether national or international, will almost always reflect insights from other disciplines.

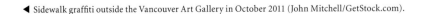
◀ Sidewalk graffiti outside the Vancouver Art Gallery in October 2011 (John Mitchell/GetStock.com).

The Impact of Globalization

The distinctions between domestic and international politics have been further eroded by trends associated with globalization. At the same time, the domestic politics of individual nation states are becoming more similar. Here are some examples:

1. It's becoming increasingly difficult to prevent economic crises in individual states from spreading to others. The most recent example was the 2011 eurozone crisis, which was in part a consequence of the 2008 "subprime" mortgage crisis in the US. These crises have forced millions of people on both sides of the Atlantic into unemployment and caused many banks in the US and Europe to seek government help. The global financial crisis has had a serious effect not only on international financial markets, but also on the economic policies of governments around the world. Although Canada has weathered the storm comparatively well, and no Canadian banks have failed, it is among the countries that have introduced significant stimulus programs.

2. There have been increasing flows of people across national borders in search of work or refuge. In Britain, the 2001 Census showed that 7.53 per cent of the population had been born outside the country, as compared with 5.75 per cent a decade earlier, and Canada and the US have some of the highest immigration rates in the world. Immigrants and their families often play significant roles in the political lives of both their new countries and the ones they left behind. This phenomenon is especially well-documented in the US and is increasingly frequent within the EU, but it can also be found in other countries around the world.

3. Concern for the environment has become a major global issue as states increasingly recognize the need to cooperatively move towards policies of sustainable development that will constrain their domestic choices.

4. Regional organizations, in which member states agree to pool elements of their sovereignty in exchange for the promise of coordinated policies and action, are on the rise. For centuries states have formed regional organizations in the form of military alliances; NATO is a fine example. What is new is the emergence of alliances with economic and non-military political objectives. The best example of this trend is the EU, which has the closest ties between its members of all regional organizations. Other regional organizations include ASEAN, Mercosur, and NAFTA.

See Chapter 20, page 417, for a discussion of regionalism.

5. Since the 1970s at least two waves of democratization have spread around the world. According to Freedom House, 40 per cent of states in the world (66) were electoral democracies in 1987; in 2007 this proportion rose to 63 per cent (121). The collapse of one authoritarian regime sometimes encourages opposition movements in others, as happened in Eastern Europe between 1989 and 1991 and during the "Arab spring" of 2011—hence the "wave"-like phenomenon. In these cases, political actors in one state look to their counterparts elsewhere for ideas regarding political organization, constitutional provisions, electoral arrangements, campaign strategies, reorganization of civil services, and so on. Democratic states will sometimes seek to promote the spread of democracy by offering assistance in the form of anything from training in the techniques used by professional politicians to outright intervention. We have seen this trend clearly in the Middle East, where a series of well-entrenched dictatorships were toppled by active citizen protests, often coordinated through social media such as

Facebook and Twitter. This may prove to be a third wave of democratization, although it is not yet clear what form the new regimes will take.

6. Ideas for the reform of policies in specific areas spread through international **epistemic communities** of specialists in various countries who share a particular set of skills and values and are able to offer advice on the most effective ways of delivering the policy objectives. Ideas for the reform of welfare policies, for example, spread from Canada and the US to Western Europe. Equally important has been the role of the Inter-governmental Panel on Climate Change, a group of climate scientists from around the world who have played a significant role in getting the issue of global warming onto the political agenda.

7. The proliferation and globalization of media institutions and sources of information, accelerated by the rise of the Internet and other forms of electronic communication have facilitated the beginnings of a global civil society, that is, transnational organizations of political activists. Organizations such as Greenpeace, Médecins sans Frontières, Amnesty International, Oxfam, Caritas, the Red Crescent, and the World Wildlife Fund, and events such as Live Aid concerts raise awareness of concerns beyond the level of the nation state.

←
See Chapter 12, page 249, for a discussion on the impact of the media.

Globalization presents enormous challenges to the academic study of politics. Above all, of course, it has made the study of international politics much more important. But it is also pushing political philosophy to broaden its focus beyond the nation-state whose character it has helped to shape since the days of Thomas Hobbes and John Locke. At the same time it is imposing new pressures on the state, complicating the activities of national governments.

If globalization challenges governments from above, another challenge comes from below. Kosovo's declaration of independence from Serbia and East Timor's successful bid for independence from Indonesia are recent examples of this trend towards decentraliza-tion, in which sub-units of nation-states demand greater autonomy or independence. The disintegration of the former Soviet Union and the former Yugoslavia in some cases gave rise to new sovereign states and in others restored sovereignty to formerly independent countries. Around the world, secessionist movements continue to demand independence in the Basque country, Scotland, Northern Cyprus, Tibet, the Philippines, Thailand, Canada, and the Kurdish regions of Turkey, Iraq, and Syria—to name just a few.

In Canada, Quebec separatists are not the only ones who have threatened to leave. Some Albertans articulated similar sentiments during the 1990s, even imagining a form of "deconfederation" (Bercuson and Cooper, 1991). Quebec separatism has important global dimensions. The fact that states are more interconnected financially and less bound by tariff barriers makes smaller states more viable economically. Yet separatists also argue that Quebec's cultural identity is threatened not only by English Canada, but by its status as a small francophone island in a continent dominated by English. The same porous borders that would improve the economic prospects for an independent Quebec could threaten its language and culture.

Another factor contributing to the erosion of the state is the spread of neoliberal market ideas that call for less government intervention in economic affairs, deregulation of banking, privatization of public enterprises, reductions in the size and scope of govern-ment services, and so on. Such measures curtail the state's ability to control the national economy. In some countries, as Rapley (2006) points out, criminal gangs have been able to carve out and control "statelets" of neighbourhoods that coexist in delicate, "often symbiotic" relationships with nation-states. Examples include the favelas of Brazil and the ganglands of Kingston, Jamaica. When these gangs are linked with broader networks of transnational crime, they challenge the traditional state from outside as well as within. In short, forces both above and below national governments are sucking the vitality from them and contributing to the "hollowing out" of the state. Some commentators argue that a new form of state activity is emerging at the international level, namely, transnationalism. Anne-Marie Slaughter (1997), for instance, has pointed to the development of new networks of cooperation between particular branches of different national governments, such as the growing webs of relations that link the courts and ministries of justice of individual states. This is encouraging them to cooperate on developing new approaches to solving problems such as what to do about war crimes being committed in other countries, or how to deal with issues such as piracy or human smuggling. Judges in one jurisdiction are increasingly aware of how judges in other jurisdictions are thinking about similar issues—and although this is most common in the EU, where a supranational court is closely integrated with national ones, it is happening elsewhere as well. As Slaughter sees it, "The state is not disappearing; it is disaggregating into its separate, functional distinct parts" (1997: 184).

See Chapters 1, page 41, and 10, page 211, for more on the "hollowing out" of the state.

The New Medievalism

The end of the Cold War transformed international relations. One approach to the changing international order—the most optimistic—was Francis Fukuyama's "end of history" thesis (1992), which proclaimed the victory of the West not just in material terms, but also on the level of ideology. The liberal democratic and capitalist model of politics and economics had prevailed over communist authoritarianism and fascism, and the future convergence of the rest of the world to the Western model seemed assured, although it would likely take some time. In fact, Eastern Europe has for the most part evolved in that direction, and most of Southeast Asia and East Asia have at least embraced the capitalist part of the model. Yet in other important parts of the world the expected convergence around the core values and practices of liberal democracy and capitalism has not occurred.

An alternative scenario is a form of a phenomenon that we encountered in Chapter 1. The term "new medievalism" refers to a world characterized by multiple overlapping international authorities and loyalties. This scenario has at least two variants. In one variant the hollowing-out of the nation-state leads to a breakdown of order—even anarchy—as traditional sources of stability erode and no adequate alternatives emerge to replace them. As we emphasized in Chapters 7 and 14, the nation-state has for decades tended to be relatively weak in the developing world, but now states the developed world are weakening as well. In other words, anarchy is increasingly evident not just in the international system, but also within individual states, as was supposedly the case in the Middle Ages.

The alternative version accepts the idea that traditional authority is eroding but argues that the Middle Ages were not as "dark" as many people believe, because there were sources of order and authority that restrained tendencies to anarchy. Advocates of this view generally focus on parallels from European history, emphasizing the influence of "universal" authorities such as the Catholic Church and the Holy Roman Empire. There was no organized international system in the modern sense, but neither was there anarchy

See Chapter 1, page 42, for a description of "new Medievalism."

in the sense that international relations theorists understand it. Conflict between various centres of power would erupt, spread, and then die down; life was not chaotic and violent all the time. Those who take this more positive view of the Middle Ages argue that it was a time of international pluralism in which conflict was restrained or moderated by overarching (mainly religious) ideologies. Admittedly, this view is Eurocentric, universalizing the European experience and taking no account of the many imperial systems, from Africa to China and the Americas, that we surveyed in Chapter 14.

Those who take this more positive view of the Middle Ages suggest that the situation today is similar, even if the poles of authority that prevent chaos are different. Jörg Friedrichs (2001), for instance, argues that just as the medieval world was held together by the competing universalistic claims of Empire and Church, so the post-international world is held together by various layers of authority, including the nation-state system, the transnational market economy, and international organizations such as the UN, IMF, and WTO. These different forms of authority claim legitimacy in a world that is becoming increasingly interconnected and interdependent.

Whether one believes that the world is becoming more anarchic or that it retains the capacity for self-stabilization, it is certainly clear that national boundaries are more porous and that national governments are more subject to influence by outside forces today than they were in the past. This reinforces both the connection between the study of domestic and international politics, and the need for political philosophers to theorize these developments.

The Rise of the Global South

Whether or not the new system is more anarchic, one political trend does seem to be emerging across the globe. This is the rise of new centres of power. Although the US continues unchallenged as the sole superpower, with an economy that will remain the most powerful in the world for the next two decades, with conventional and nuclear military resources that dwarf all others, the EU is now becoming a more powerful and cohesive player on the world stage. It offers a different approach to international politics, rooted in more on diplomacy and standards for law-based international behaviour. Despite the failure of its constitution in 2004, it has achieved its most basic objective of banishing war from the European continent, and the prospects that peace will continue are good. It has also managed to absorb many former satellite states of the Soviet Union: Poland, Hungary, and the Czech and Slovak Republics have all been granted EU member status. The gradual integration that has taken place across Europe has led to much greater prosperity. Despite the recent eurozone crisis, the EU remains a standard against which regional integration projects in other parts of the world are measured, even if they do not model themselves on it.

Certainly, the "West" appears just as powerful now as it has at any time since the end of the Second World War. Yet other actors in the world are gaining in confidence. Three states or groups of states exemplify the change. First are the powerful states in Asia. Japan has been an economic giant for some decades, but now China, and more recently India, have come into focus as both economic and military contenders for great power status. China is sometimes presented in the US as most likely challenge to the ascendancy of the US; former US Defense Secretary Donald Rumsfeld, for instance, has recently expressed fear

See Chapters 7, page 151, and 14, p. 296, for discussions of weak and weakening states.

See Chapter 14, page 284, for a discussion of states and empires in world history.

See Chapter 18, page 364, for a discussion of the different diplomatic styles of the US and EU.

that China constitutes a serious threat to future international stability (2011). Whether or not this turns out to be the case, the rise of China has become a standard topic of discussion and debate, both outside and inside China. Although China remains authoritarian, more Chinese people have lifted themselves out of poverty in the last generation than at any other time in world history. Similarly, India's economic take-off since the early 1990s signals a major shift in power to the developing world.

The second big change is the increasing self-confidence of the people in the so-called "Islamic world" and the growing sense of interconnectedness that has been facilitated by the Internet, social media, and global television, such as the Qatar-based channel Al Jazeera. Through the nineteenth and twentieth centuries, the Islamic world declined significantly vis-à-vis the West. The dissolution of its most powerful grouping—the Ottoman Empire—led both to military occupation by Western countries and a sense of inferiority in the face of Western technological modernity. Even the Arab OPEC members' use of the "oil card" as a weapon against the West in the 1970s did not essentially change anything. Now the situation is different. Younger generations of Muslims, it seems, feel more self-assured, and less deferential towards the West. The changes of government that followed the "Arab spring" also signal that the traditional view of the Arab states as a series of dictatorships will have to be rethought.

We must be very careful not to draw a simplistic dividing line between the "Islamic world" and "the West." There are many overlapping interests and alliances between these two generalized entities. After all, Turkey is a member of NATO—a largely "Western" alliance—as well as a candidate for EU membership. Many Islamic countries have been allies of the US in the war on terror, and many Arab states are now embracing more democratic systems of government. Furthermore, the West is increasingly attracting Muslim immigrants who are making important contributions to the cultures and politics of their new countries.

See Chapter 7, page 148, for a discussion of Turkey's radical reforms.

The third big change is the resurgence of Russia. In one sense this does not represent a major break with recent history: the Soviet Union was the rival superpower from the end of the Second World War until the Union's collapse in 1991. What is significant about the current situation is the disdain that the regime of Vladimir Putin shows for the West. Russia's democratic credentials are weak: there are major problems of corruption, electoral irregularities, and organized crime. Russia, more than any Asian or Islamic country, has the potential to be a destabilizing presence in the international system because of its large size and enormous resource base, its possession of nuclear weapons, and its authoritarian traditions.

This became especially obvious in late 2011, when then-Prime Minister Putin announced that he would run for a third term as president of Russia. Limited by law to two consecutive terms, Putin had run for prime minister in 2008 and handpicked Dmitry Medvedev as his successor in the president's office. In 2011 Putin proudly admitted that he planned this swap in order to maintain political control: Medvedev, it seems, was little more than a puppet. Putin, after securing the presidency in the 2012 elections, could remain in power until 2024; at age 58, he is young and healthy enough to see out another two terms in office (Arkhipov and Meyer, 2011).

The fact that these new actors are demanding greater respect reflects a wider change of attitude in other parts of the world. The West may still enjoy enviable levels of economic development and technological prowess, but it is no longer considered to be the only model of "modernity." Indeed, it is increasingly accused of being out of step with the movement towards new ethical priorities and more environmentally friendly development. Developing countries' refusal, despite enormous pressure from the US, to agree to binding commitments on reducing carbon emissions until they have the resources to cope with the consequences, is predicated on the idea that developed countries have been largely responsible for climate change and therefore should take responsibility for dealing with it.

This refusal resonates with two relatively new schools of political analysis. The first, "subaltern studies," rejects the idea of automatically according superiority to the "winners" with respect to economic development, whether elites within individual states or, at the international level, the developed countries. Instead, analysts should pay more attention to the "subalterns" or underdogs. Works such as Cornel West's 1991 article "Decentring Europe" and Dipak Chakrabarty's 2000 book *Provincializing Europe* illustrate how subaltern studies approach formerly "central" regions of the world.

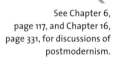

See Chapter 12, page 247, for a discussion of subaltern studies.

See Chapter 6, page 117, and Chapter 16, page 331, for discussions of postmodernism.

To some extent this approach parallels the approach taken by postmodern theorists, who reject the certainties of modernism, arguing that no "truth" is authoritative, and instead advocate pluralism. We share the subaltern theorists' view in that we do not believe that Western political systems are necessarily more worthy of respect and study than those in other parts of the world.

It is certainly true that, as we emphasized in the second section of this book, Western ideas and institutions have spread around the world and in many ways set the standard for "modern" political systems. This is not to disparage other systems of governance, such as the Six Nations Confederacy, that in many ways might have been superior to the Western system. "Political science" is primarily a Western academic discipline; and although critics continue to argue that "Western" institutions such as political parties are inappropriate for non-Western societies with different traditions, viable alternative forms of political organization have proved remarkably rare.

In the 1960s and 1970s, for instance, leaders of developing states such as Sukarno in Indonesia and Nyerere in Tanzania advocated forms of political organization and decision-making that were more in keeping with the traditions of village societies; but these alternative forms have not been particularly successful. To some extent their lack of success can be traced to other dimensions of modernization. For example, traditional rural forms of decision-making were not so well-suited to larger urban populations. Such forms of political organization also tended to encourage corruption and a certain degree of state violence. What began as two relatively legitimate forms of government lost legitimacy when their practitioners abused their newly acquired state powers. In part this had to do with the fact that the political culture spread by colonial regimes was one of corruption and inequality. The purpose of colonialism was not to spread democracy but to enrich the "mother" country. Although Britain and France were democratic at home, their empires certainly were not, and the indigenous elites that flourished under their colonial regimes were not necessarily attuned to their own traditions. Jawaharlal Nehru, India's first prime minister and a keen advocate of democracy, was also well aware of his upper-class British-style background. When meeting with the economist John Kenneth Galbraith, then serving as US ambassador, Nehru referred to himself as "the last Englishman to rule in India" (Dhani, 2008: 205).

It's worth repeating that, power aside, there is no obvious reason why forms of political organization developed in the West should take precedence over all other forms. Furthermore, the concepts underlying Western democratic forms are not always easily translated from their Western, especially anglophone, contexts to other parts of the world. Chapter 12, for example, suggested that the idea of "civil society" is based on assumptions that are not necessarily transferable to Arab or Asian societies. Yet many of us tend to judge political institutions in other countries through lenses that were formed by our own societies. The state, political parties, interest groups, federalism—these are just some of the key concepts of political discourse that may resist translation from one political system to another.

See Chapter 11, page 232, for a discussion of the problems facing parties.

←
See Chapter 12, page 239, for a discussion of civil society.

The Study of Politics in a Globalizing World

Political science has been a Western-dominated discipline since its birth, but times are changing and we now recognize that this problem needs to be corrected. Many political philosophers as well as IR scholars have acknowledged the need to engage more fully with the ideas underlying non-Western political practice. In his 2003 presidential address to the International Studies Association, Steve Smith suggested that the discipline of IR needed fundamental reform:

> The dominant accounts are white, male accounts and thus paint at best incomplete, and at worst totally distorted, pictures of international relations, ones that support existing forms of social power. Yet the discipline is rarely self-conscious about these biases, presenting itself as gender and colour blind (Smith, 2003).

Perhaps more important, as Smith and others have argued, non-Western studies of politics, society, and philosophy deserve a larger place in Western literature. Western scholars must increasingly engage with, encourage, and critique ideas from non-Western intellectual traditions, if the discipline of political science is to move beyond its current confines.

We have emphasized two key themes in this book: the declining importance of the sovereign state, and the growing significance of non-Western parts of the world in Western political science. Both present challenges for Western political analysts. The impact of globalization underlines the importance of studying international politics. Likewise, students of comparative politics and international relations must take into account the growing economic and political importance of the non-Western world. Finally, political philosophers too will have to reorient their traditional focus on the state and engage with the ideas underlying non-Western political practice. This does not mean that the state has eroded to the point that it is no longer an important concern. Nor does it mean that European and American politics will no longer be important. These political systems and the ideas underlying them will still attract wide interest, and when problems arise they will continue to offer each other possibilities for reform. What happens on both sides of the Atlantic will also have a major impact on world affairs for decades to come.

However, the former dominance of the state and Western theory and practice has been substantially eroded. This is a positive development, full of opportunity, because the great majority of the world's people do not live in either Europe or North America. As the dynamics of power and ideas change, the study of politics will continue to be exciting, invigorating, and unpredictable.

References

Introduction

Arneson, R. (2000). "The Priority of the Right Over the Good Rides Again." Pp. 60–86 in P. Kelly, ed. *Impartiality, Neutrality and Justice: Re-reading Brian Barry's Justice as Impartiality.* Edinburgh. Edinburgh University Press.

Ayer, A.J. (1971). *Language, Truth and Logic.* 2nd edn. Harmondsworth: Penguin.

Bell, D. (1960). *The End of Ideology.* Glencoe, IL: Free Press.

Berlin, I. (1969). *Four Essays on Liberty.* Oxford: Oxford University Press.

Bevir, R., and R.A.W. Rhodes (2002). "Interpretive Theory." Pp. 131–52 in D. Marsh and G. Stoker. *Theory and Methods in Political Science.* Basingstoke: Palgrave.

Crick, B. (1962). *In Defence of Politics.* London: Weidenfeld & Nicolson.

Dahl, R. (1991). *Modern Political Analysis.* 5th edn. Englewood Cliffs, NJ: Prentice-Hall.

Dworkin, R. (1987). *Taking Rights Seriously.* London: Duckworth.

Fukuyama, F. (1992). *The End of History and the Last Man.* Harmondsworth: Penguin.

Gallie, W. (1955–6). "Essentially Contested Concepts." *Proceedings of the Aristotelian Society* 56.

Gamble, A. (2000). *Politics and Fate.* Cambridge: Polity Press.

Garner, R. (2005). *The Political Theory of Animal Rights.* Manchester: Manchester University Press.

Gerth, H., and C. Wright Mills (1946). *From Max Weber: Essays in Sociology.* London: Routledge and Kegan Paul.

Goodwin, B. (2007). *Using Political Ideas.* 5th edn. Chichester: John Wiley & Sons,

Hay, C. (2002). *Political Analysis: A Critical Introduction,* Basingstoke: Palgrave.

Held, D. and A. Leftwich (1984). "A Discipline of Politics?" In A. Leftwich, ed. *What Is Politics? The Activity and its Study.* Oxford: Blackwell.

Heywood, A. (2004). *Political Theory: An Introduction.* 3rd edn. Basingstoke: Palgrave Macmillan.

Hoffman, J. (1995). *Beyond the State.* Cambridge: Polity Press.

Jamieson, D. (2002). *Morality's Progress: Essays on Humans, Other Animals and the Rest of Nature.* Oxford: Clarendon Press.

Laslett, P. (1956). "Introduction." *Philosophy, Politics and Society.* 1st series. Oxford: Blackwell.

Lasswell, H. (1936). *Politics: Who Gets What, When, How?* New York: McGraw-Hill.

Leftwich, A. (ed.) (1984). *What Is Politics? The Activity and its Study.* Oxford: Blackwell.

Marx, K., and F. Engels (1976 [1848]). *The Communist Manifesto.* Harmondsworth: Penguin.

Nagel, T. (1987). "Moral Conflict and Political Legitimacy." *Philosophy and Public Affairs* 16, 3: 215–40.

Rawls, J. (1971) *A Theory of Justice.* Cambridge, MA: Harvard University Press.

Stoker, G. (2006). *Why Politics Matter.* Basingstoke: Palgrave.
———, and D. Marsh (2002). "Introduction." Pp. 1–16 in Marsh and Stoker. *Theory and Methods in Political Science.* Basingstoke: Palgrave.

Thomas, G. (1993). *An Introduction to Ethics.* London: Duckworth.

Waldron, J. (1989). "Legislation and Moral Neutrality." Pp. 61–83. in R. Goodin and A. Reeve, eds. *Liberal Neutrality.* London: Routledge

Wolff, J. (1996). *An Introduction to Political Philosophy.* Oxford: Oxford University Press.

Part 1

Dahl, R. (1991). *Modern Political Analysis.* 5th edn. Englewood Cliffs, NJ: Prentice-Hall.

Horton, J. (1984). "Political Philosophy and Politics." Pp. 106–23 in A. Leftwich, ed. *What Is Politics? The Activity and its Study.* Oxford: Blackwell.

Chapter 1

Arblaster, A. (1984). *The Rise and Decline of Western Liberalism.* Oxford: Basil Blackwell.

Avineri, S. and A. de-Shalit, eds (1992). *Communitarianism and Individualism.* Oxford: Oxford University Press.

Bentham, J. (1948 [1789]). *An Introduction to the Principles of Morals and Legislation.* New York: Hafner Press.

Blom-Hansen, J. (2000). "Still Corporatism in Scandinavia?" *Scandinavian Political Studies* 23, 2: 157–78.

Brandt, R. (1992). *Morality, Utilitarianism, and Rights.* Cambridge: Cambridge University Press.

Britten, S. (1977). *The Economic Consequences of Democracy.* London: Temple Smith.

Burnham, J. (1941). *The Managerial Revolution.* New York: Day.

Carruthers, P. (1992). *The Animals Issue.* Cambridge: Cambridge University Press.

Cunningham, F. (2002). *Theories of Democracy.* London: Routledge.

Michael Curtis (1979). *Totalitarianism.* New Brunswick, NJ: Transaction Publishers.

Dahl, R. (1958). "A Critique of the Ruling Elite Model." *American Political Science Review* 52.
——— (1963). *Who Governs?* New Haven, CT: Yale University Press.
——— (1971). *Polyarchy.* New Haven, CT: Yale University Press.

Dearlove, J. and Saunders, P. (2000). *Introduction to British Politics.* 3rd edn. Cambridge: Polity Press.

Djilas, Milovan (1983). *The New Class: An Analysis of the Communist System.* London: Harcourt, Brace, Jovanovich.

Donner, J. (2011). "Nationalization." *The Canadian Encyclopedia.* www.thecanadianencyclopedia.com/index.cfm?PgNm=TCE&Params=A1ARTA0005639

Dunleavy, P., and B. O'Leary (1987). *Theories of the State.* Basingstoke: Macmillan.

Dworkin, R. (1978). *Taking Rights Seriously.* London: Duckworth.

Dye, T. (2000). *The Irony of Democracy.* Harcourt Brace.

Gallie, W. (1955/6). "Essentially Contested Concepts." *Proceedings of the Aristotelian Society* 56.

Gerth, H., and C. Wright Mills (1946). *From Max Weber: Essays in Sociology.* London: Routledge & Kegan Paul.

Hague, R. and M. Harrop (2007). *Comparative Government and Politics.* Basingstoke: Palgrave, 7th edn.

Heater, D. (1999). *What Is Citizenship?* Cambridge: Polity Press.

Hegel, G.W.F. (1942). *Philosophy of Right.* Oxford: Oxford University Press.

Held, David. (1989). *Political Theory and the Modern State.* Cambridge: Polity Press.

——— (2006). *Models of Democracy.* 2nd edn. Stanford, CA: Stanford University Press.

Hobbes, T. (1651/1992). *Leviathan.* Cambridge: Cambridge University Press.

Jessop, B. (1990). *State Theory.* Cambridge: Polity Press.

Johnson, C. (1995). *Japan: Who Governs? The Rise of the Developmental State.* New York: Norton.

Lijphart, A., and M. Crepaz (1991). "Corporatism and Consensus in Eighteen Countries: Conceptual and Empirical Linkages." *British Journal of Political Science* 21: 235–46.

Locke, J. (1690 [1988]). *Two Treatises of Government.* Cambridge: Cambridge University Press.

Tibor Machan (2005). "The Case for Libertarianism: Sovereign Individuals." In Craig Duncan and Tibor Machan, eds. *Libertarianism: For and Against.* Lanham, MD: Rowman & Littlefield.

MacIntyre, A. (1985). *After Virtue: A Study in Moral Theory.* 2nd edn. London: Duckworth.

Macpherson, C.B. (1962). *The Political Theory of Possessive Individualism.* Oxford: Oxford University Press.

Marquand, D. (1988). *The Unprincipled Society.* London: Jonathan Cape.

Michels, Robert (1962 [1911]). *Political Parties: A Sociological Study of the Oligarchical Tendencies of Modern Democracy.* With an introduction by Seymour M. Lipset. New York: Free Press.

Mills, C. Wright (1956). *The Power Elite.* New York: Oxford University Press.

Mulhall, S. and A. Swift (1996). *Liberals and Communitarians.* Oxford: Blackwell.

Mulroney, Brian (2009). Speech delivered in Beijing, China, 3 Sept.; excerpts at www.canadians.org/campaignblog/?p=1757; accessed 19 March 2012.

Münster, Cynthia, and Jeff Davis (2010). "Environmental Groups Losing Interest in Lobbying Prentice." *The Hill Times*, 1 Feb.

www.hilltimes.com/news/2010/02/01/environmental-groups-losing-interest-in-lobbying-prentice/23224./Niskanen, W. (1971). *Bureaucracy and Representative Government.* Chicago: Aldine.

Ohmae, K. (1995). *The End of the Nation State.* London: Harper Collins.

Pateman, Carole (1998). *The Sexual Contract.* Stanford, CA: Stanford University Press Plamenatz, J. (1963). *Man and Society.* Vol. 2. London: Longman.

Plant, R. (1991). *Modern Political Thought.* Oxford: Basil Blackwell.

Rawls, J. (1993). *Political Liberalism.* New York: Columbia University Press.

Robertson, R. (1992). *Globalization: Social Theory and Global Culture.* London: Sage.

Slaughter, A. (2003). *A New World Order.* Princeton, NJ: Princeton University Press.

Talos, E. and B. Kittel (2002). "Austria in the 1990s: The Routine of Social Partnership in Question." In S. Berger and H. Compston, eds. *Policy Concertation and Social Partnership in Western Europe.* New York: Berghahn Books.

Tickner, J. Ann (1992). *Gender in International Relations: Feminist Perspectives on Achieving Global Security.* New York: Columbia University Press.

Tilly, C. (1975). "Reflections on the History of European State-Making." In Tilly, ed. *The Formation of National States in Western Europe.* Princeton, NJ: Princeton University Press.

Walzer, M. (1990). "The Communitarian Critique of Liberalism." *Political Theory* 18, 1: 6–23.

Washington, Ellis (2008). *The Nuremberg Trials: Last Tragedy of the Holocaust.* Lanham, MD: University Press of America.

Watts, Ronald (1990). *Canada: The State of the Federation.* Kingston, ON: Institute of Intergovernmental Relations.

Wiarda, Howard (1997). *Corporatism and Comparative Politics: The Other Great "Ism."* Armonk, NY: M.E. Sharpe.

Chapter 2

Bachrach, Peter, and Morton Baratz (1962). "Two Faces of Power." *American Political Science Review* 56, 4 (December): 947–52.

——— (1963). "Decisions and Non-Decisions." *American Political Science Review* 57: 632–42.

——— (1970). *Power and Poverty: Theory and Practice.* New York: Oxford University Press.

Barry, N. (2000). *An Introduction to Modern Political Theory.* 4th edn. Basingstoke: Macmillan.

Blowers, A. (1984). *Something in the Air: Corporate Power and the Environment,* London: Harper & Row.

Crenson, M. (1971). *The Un-Politics of Air Pollution.* Baltimore, MD: Johns Hopkins University Press.

Dahl, R. (1963). *Who Governs?* New Haven, CT: Yale University Press.

Dearlove, J. and Saunders, P. (2000). *Introduction to British Politics.* Cambridge: Polity Press, 3rd edn.

Fleras, A., and J.L. Elliott (1999). *Unequal Relations: An Introduction to Race, Ethnic, and Aboriginal Dynamics in Canada.* 3rd ed. Scarborough, ON: Prentice Hall.

Foucault, M. (1977). *Discipline and Punishment.* Harmondsworth: Penguin.

Gerth, H., and C. Wright Mills (1946). *From Max Weber: Essays in Sociology.* London: Routledge & Kegan Paul.

Goodwin, B. (2007). *Using Political Ideas.* 5th edn. Chichester: John Wiley & Sons.

Gramsci, A. (1971). *Selections From Prison Notebooks.* London: Lawrence & Wishart.

Hay, C. (1997). "Divided by a Common Language: Political Theory and the Concept of Power." *Politics* 17, 1: 45–52.

——— (1999). "Marxism and the State." In A. Gamble, D. Marsh, and T. Tant, eds. *Marxism and Social Science.* London: Macmillan.

——— (2002). *Political Analysis: A Critical Introduction.* Basingstoke: Palgrave.

Hewitt, C. (1974). "Policy-Making in Postwar Britain: A National-Level Test of Elitist and Pluralist Hypotheses." *British Journal of Political Science* 4, 2: 187–216.

Heywood, A. (2004). *Political Theory: An Introduction.* Basingstoke: Palgrave Macmillan.

Hoffman, J. and P. Graham (2006). *Introduction to Political Theory.* Harlow: Pearson.

Lindblom, C. (1977). *Politics and Markets.* New York: Basic Books.

Lukes, S. (2005). *Power: A Radical View.* 2nd edn. Basingstoke: Palgrave Macmillan.

Marcuse, H. (1964). *One-Dimensional Man: Studies in the Ideology of Advanced Industrial Society.* Boston: Beacon.

McLellan, D. (1980). *The Thought of Karl Marx.* Basingstoke: Macmillan.

Miliband, R. (1978). *The State in Capitalist Society.* New York: Basic Books.

Mills, C. Wright (1956). *The Power Elite.* New York: Oxford University Press.

Polsby, N. (1980). *Community Power and Political Theory.* New Haven, CT: Yale University Press.

Poulantzas, N. (1973). *Political Power and Social Classes.* London: New Left Books.

——— (1976). "The Capitalist State: a Reply to Miliband and Laclau." *New Left Review* 95: 63–83.

Russell, B. (1938). *Power: A New Social Analysis.* London: Allen & Unwin.

Scott, J. (1990). *Domination and the Arts of Resistance.* New Haven, CT: Yale University Press.

Scruton, R. (2001). *The Meaning of Conservatism.* 3rd edn. Basingstoke: Palgrave Macmillan.

Westergaard, J., and H. Resler (1975). *Class in a Capitalist Society,* London: Heinemann.

Chapter 3

Arblaster, A. (2002). *Democracy.* Milton Keynes: Open University Press.

Bachrach, P. (1967). *The Theory of Democratic Elitism.* London: London University Press.

Barry, B. (1970). *Sociologists, Economics and Democracy.* Basingstoke: Collier Macmillan.

BBC News (2011). "Singapore calls general election." 19 April. www.bbc.co.uk/news/world-asia-pacific-13125905

Bessette, J. (1994). *The Mild Voice of Reason: Deliberative Democracy and American National Government.* Chicago: Chicago University Press.

Cunningham, F. (2002). *Theories of Democracy.* London: Routledge.

Dahl, R. (1971). *Polyarchy.* New Haven, CT: Yale University Press.

Downs, A. (1957). *An Economic Theory of Democracy.* New York: Harper & Row.

Dryzek, J. (2000). *Deliberative Democracy and Beyond.* Oxford: Oxford University Press.

Duncan, G., and S. Lukes (1964). "The New Democracy." In S. Lukes, ed. *Essays in Social Theory.* London: Macmillan.

Dunleavy, P., and H. Ward (1981). "Exogenous Voter Preferences and Parties with State Power: Some Internal Problems of Economic Theories of Party Competition." *British Journal of Political Science* 11: 351–80.

Hague, R. and M. Harrop (2007). *Comparative Government and Politics.* 7th edn. Basingstoke: Palgrave.

Held, D. (2006). *Models of Democracy.* 3rd edn. Cambridge: Polity Press.

Hoffman, J., and P. Graham (2006). *Introduction to Political Theory.* Harlow: Pearson.

Kornhauser, W. (1960). *The Politics of Mass Society,* Glencoe, IL: Free Press.

Levitsky, Steven, and Way Lucan (2002). "Assessing the Quality of Democracy." *Journal of Democracy* 13, 2 April: 51–65.

Lively, J. (1975). *Democracy.* Oxford: Blackwell.

Macpherson, C.B. (1966). *The Real World of Democracy.* Oxford: Oxford University Press.

——— (1977). *The Life and Times of Liberal Democracy.* Oxford: Oxford University Press.

Mauzy, D. and R. Milne (2002). *Singapore Politics: Under the People's Action Party.* London: Routledge.

Miliband R. (1972). *Parliamentary Socialism.* London: Merlin.

Pateman, C. (1970). *Participation and Democratic Theory.* Cambridge: Cambridge University Press.

Robertson, D. (1976). *A Theory of Party Competition.* London: Wiley.

Rousseau, J. (1913). *The Social Contract and Discourses.* London: Dent.

Schumpeter, J. (1961). *Capitalism, Socialism and Democracy.* New York: Harper & Row.

Stoker, G. (2006). *Why Politics Matter.* Basingstoke: Palgrave.

Stokes, D. (1963). "Spatial Models of Party Competition." *American Political Science Review* 57: 19–28.

Talmon, J. (1952). *The Origins of Totalitarian Democracy.* London: Secker & Warburg.

Wolff, R.P. (1970). In *Defence of Anarchism.* New York: Harper & Row.

Worthington, R. (2002). *Governance in Singapore.* London: Routledge/Curzon.

Wright, A. (1979). *G.D.H. Cole and Socialist Democracy.* Oxford: Clarendon Press.

Wright, R. (1992). *Stolen Continents: The "New World" Through Indian Eyes.* Toronto: Penguin.

Zakaria, F. (2003). *The Future of Freedom: Illiberal Democracy at Home and Abroad.* London: Norton.

Chapter 4

Barry, B. (1999). "Sustainability and Intergenerational Justice." In A. Dobson, ed. *Fairness and Futurity: Essays on Sustainability and Justice.* Oxford: Oxford University Press.

Barry, N. (2000). *An Introduction to Modern Political Thought.* 4th edn. Basingstoke: Macmillan,

Beitz, C. (1979). *Political Theory and International Relations.* Princeton, NJ: Princeton University Press.

Benn, S. (1971). "Privacy, Freedom and Respect for Persons." In J. Pennock and J. Chapman, eds. *Nomos XIII Privacy.* New York: Atherton.

Berlin, I. (1969). *Four Essays on Liberty.* Oxford: Oxford University Press.

Bramwell, A. (1989). *Ecology in the Twentieth Century.* New Haven, CT: Yale University Press.

Cohen, G. (1979). "Capitalism, Freedom and the Proletariat." In A. Ryan, ed. *The Idea of Freedom.* Oxford: Oxford University Press.

Cole, Juan (2005). "All the Vice President's Men." Salon.com. www.salon.com/2005/10/28/vice_president_2/.

Daniels, N. (1975). *Reading Rawls.* New York: Basic Books.

Devlin, P. (1965). *The Enforcement of Morals.* Oxford: Oxford University Press.

Dworkin, R. (1978). *Taking Rights Seriously.* London: Duckworth.

Forsythe, David (2009). *Encyclopedia of Human Rights.* Vol. 1. New York: Oxford University Press.

Fox, W. (1984). "Deep Ecology: A New Philosophy of our Times." *The Ecologist* 14, 5: 199–200.

Garner, R. (2005). *The Political Theory of Animal Rights.* Manchester: Manchester University Press.

Gray, T. (1991). *Freedom.* Atlantic Highlands, NJ: Humanities Press International.

Hart, H. (1967). "Are There any Natural Rights?" In A. Quinton, ed. *Political Philosophy.* Oxford: Oxford University Press.

Janda, Kenneth, Jeffrey M. Berry, and Jerry Goldman (2008). *The Challenge of Democracy: American Government in a Global World.* Independence, KY: Cengage Learning.

Jolly, David (2011). "Satirical Magazine Is Firebombed in Paris." *New York Times.* 2 Nov. www.nytimes.com/2011/11/03/world/europe/charlie-hebdo-magazine-in-paris-is-firebombed.html

Kukathas, C., and P. Pettit (1990). *Rawls: A Theory of Justice and its Critics.* Oxford: Polity Press.

Linklater, A. (2008). "Globalization and the Transformation of Political Community." In J. Baylis, S. Smith, and P. Owens, eds. *The Globalization of World Politics.* Oxford: Oxford University Press.

MacDonald, David B. (2008). *Identity Politics in the Age of Genocide: The Holocaust and Historical Representation.* London: Routledge.

———. (2009). *Thinking History, Fighting Evil: Neoconservatives and the Perils of Historical Analogy in American Politics.* Lanham, MD: Lexington/Rowman & Littlefield.

Mill, J.S. (1972). *Utilitarianism, On Liberty, and Considerations on Representative Government,* London: Dent.

Miller, D. (1976). *Social Justice.* Oxford: Clarendon Press.

Nozick, R. (1974). *Anarchy, State and Utopia.* Oxford: Blackwell.

Pogge, T. (1989). *Realizing Rawls.* Ithaca, NY: Cornell University Press.

Rawls, J. (1971). *A Theory of Justice.* Cambridge, MA: Harvard University Press.

———. (1999). *The Law of Peoples.* Cambridge, MA: Harvard University Press.

Ricci, Nino (2009). *Pierre Elliott Trudeau.* Toronto: Penguin.

Robertson, David (2004). *The Routledge Dictionary of Politics.* London: Routledge.

Singer, P. (2002). *One World: The Ethics of Globalization.* Melbourne: Text Publishing.

Taylor, P. (1986). *Respect for Nature.* Princeton, NJ: Princeton University Press.

Walzer, M. (1985). *Spheres of Justice.* New York: Basic Books.

———. (1994). *Thick and Thin: Moral Arguments at Home and Abroad.* Notre Dame, IN: University of Notre Dame Press.

Weir, Erica (2000). "Female Genital Mutilation." *Journal de l'Association Médicale Canadienne* 162, 9 (May).

Winter, Bronwyn (2008). *Hijab and the Republic: Uncovering the French Headscarf Debate.* Syracuse, NY: Syracuse University Press.

Wolff, J. (1996). *An Introduction to Political Philosophy.* Oxford: Oxford University Press.

Wolff, R. (1977). *Understanding Rawls.* Princeton, NJ: Princeton University Press.

Chapter 5

Alexander, E. (2001). "False Witness: The Irving-Lipstadt Trial and *The New Yorker.*" *Judaism: A Quarterly Journal of Jewish Life and Thought* 50, 4: 454.

Axworthy, L. (2005) "Missile Counter-Attack: An Open Letter to US Secretary of State." *Winnipeg Free Press.* 3 March.

Bauer, Y. (2001). *Rethinking the Holocaust.* New Haven: Yale University Press.

Bauman, Z. (1989). *Modernity and the Holocaust.* Cambridge: Polity Press.

Bernstein, E. (1961). *Evolutionary Socialism.* New York: Schocken Books.

Burke, E. [1790] (1968). *Reflections on the Revolution in France.* Harmondsworth: Penguin. Burleigh, M., and W. Wippermann

(1991). *The Racial State: Germany 1933–1945*. Cambridge: Cambridge University Press.

Crosland, C.A.R. (1980). *The Future of Socialism*. London: Jonathan Cape.

Festenstein, M., and M. Kenny (2005). *Political Ideologies*. Oxford: Oxford University Press.

Freeden, M. (1996). *Ideologies and Political Theory*. Oxford: Oxford University Press.

Gamble, A. (1994). *The Free Economy and the Strong State*. 2nd edn. London: Macmillan.

Gellner, E. (1983) *Nations and Nationalism*. Oxford: Blackwell.

Gobineau, J.A. (1967). *Essai sur l'inégalité des races humaines*. Paris: Éditions Pierre Belfond.

Goodwin, B. (2007). *Using Political Ideas*. 5th edn. Chichester: John Wiley & Sons.

Greenfeld, L. (1993) *Nationalism: Five Roads to Modernity*. Cambridge, MA: Harvard University Press.

P. Haas (1992). *Morality After Auschwitz: The Radical Challenge of the Nazi Ethic*. Philadelphia: Fortress Press.

Hitler, A. (1969 [1926]). *Mein Kampf*. London: Hutchinson.

Hoffman, J. (1995). *Beyond the State*. Cambridge: Polity Press.

———, and P. Graham (2006). *Introduction to Political Theory*. Harlow: Pearson.

Ignatieff, M. (1994). *Blood and Belonging*. London: Vintage.

Kitchen, M. (1976). *Fascism*. Basingstoke: Macmillan.

Kohn, H. (1944). *The Idea of Nationalism*. London: Macmillan.

Koonz, C. (2003). *The Nazi Conscience*. Cambridge, MA: Belknap Press/Harvard University Press.

Kristol, Irving (2003). "The Neoconservative Persuasion." *Weekly Standard*. 25 Aug. www.weeklystandard.com/Content/Public/Articles/000/000/003/000tzmlw.asp.

Lifton, R.J. (1986). *The Nazi Doctors: Medical Killing and the Psychology of Genocide*. New York: Basic Books.

Lipstadt, D. (1993). *Denying the Holocaust: The Growing Assault on Truth and Memory*. New York: Free Press.

MacDonald, David B. (2008). *Identity Politics in the Age of Genocide: The Holocaust and Historical Representation*. London: Routledge.

———. (2009). *Thinking History, Fighting Evil: Neoconservatives and the Perils of Historical Analogy in American Politics*. Lanham, MD: Lexington/Rowman & Littlefield.

Macpherson, C.B. (1962). *The Political Theory of Possessive Individualism*. Oxford: Oxford University Press.

Marx, K., and F. Engels (1976 [1848]). *The Communist Manifesto*. Harmondsworth: Penguin.

Miller, D. (1990). *Market, State and Community: Theoretical Foundations to Market Socialism*. Oxford: Clarendon Press.

Miller, S. (1995). "Denial of the Holocaust." *Social Education* 59, 6.

Najarian, J. (1997). "Gnawing at History: The Rhetoric of Holocaust Denial." *The Midwest Quarterly* 39, 1.

Oakeshott, M. (1962). *Rationalism in Politics and Other Essays*, New York: Routledge, Chapman & Hall.

Ozkirimli, U. (2000). *Theories of Nationalism: A Critical Introduction*. London: Macmillan.

Popper, K. (1962). *The Open Society and its Enemies*. Vol. II. *Hegel and Marx*. London: Routledge & Kegan Paul.

Proctor, R. (1988). *Racial Hygiene: Medicine Under the Nazis*. Cambridge, MA: Harvard University Press.

Schain, M., A. Zolberg, and P. Hossay (eds) (2002). *Shadows Over Europe: The Development and Impact of the Extreme Right in Western Europe*. Basingstoke: Palgrave Macmillan.

Shermer, M., and A. Grobman (2000). *Denying History: Who Says the Holocaust Never Happened and Why Do They Say It?* Berkeley: University of California Press.

Smith, A.D. (1990). *National Identity*. London: Penguin.

——— (1996). "The 'Golden Age' and National Renewal." In G. Hosking and G. Schöpflin, eds. *Myths and Nationhood*. London: C. Hurst and Co.

——— (1998). *Nationalism and Modernism: A Critical Survey of Recent Theories of Nations and Nationalism*. London: Routledge.

——— (2001). "Authenticity, Antiquity and Archaeology." *Nations and Nationalism* 7, 1.

——— (2010). *Nationalism*. Cambridge: Polity.

Trevor Roper, H. (1947). *The Last Days of Hitler*. London: Macmillan.

Vincent, A. (1995). *Modern Political Ideologies*. 2nd edn. Oxford: Blackwell,

Wright, A. (1996). *Socialisms: Old and New*. London: Routledge.

Chapter 6

Ali, T. (2002). *The Clash of Fundamentalisms*. London: Verso.

Barrett, M. (1988). *Women's Oppression Today*. London: Verso.

Barry, B. (2001). *Culture and Equality: An Egalitarian Critique of Multiculturalism*. Cambridge: Polity Press.

Barry, J. (1999). *Rethinking Green Politics*. London: Sage.

Bell, D. (1960). *The End of Ideology*. Glencoe, IL: Free Press.

Andy Blatchford (2011). "Burka Ban at Canadian Citizenship Ceremonies Prompts Debate amongst Muslims." *Winnipeg Free Press*. 12 Dec. www.winnipegfreepress.com/canada/breakingnews/burqa-ban-no-more-face-covering-when-new-canadians-take-oath-of-citizenship-135440883.html

Bookchin, M. (1971). *Post Scarcity Anarchism*. Berkeley, CA: Ramparts.

Borrows, John (2008). "Seven Generations, Seven Teachings: Ending the Indian Act." Research Paper for the National Centre for First Nations Governance. May.

Bramwell, A. (1989). *Ecology in the Twentieth Century*. New Haven, CT: Yale University Press.

Bryson, V. (1999). *Feminist Debates*. 4th edn. Basingstoke: Macmillan.

Dobson, A. (2007). *Green Political Thought*. London: Unwin Hyman,

Dworkin, A. (1981). *Pornography: Men Possessing Women*. London: Women's Press.

Eckersley, R. (1992). *Environmentalism and Political Theory*. London: UCL Press.

Firestone, S. (1972). *The Dialectic of Sex*. London: Paladin.

Fox, W. (1995). *Toward a Transpersonal Ecology: Developing New Foundations for Environmentalism*. Totnes: Resurgence.

Frey, R.K. (1983). *Rights, Killing and Suffering*. Oxford: Clarendon Press.

Fukuyama, F. (1992). *The End of History and the Last Man*. Harmondsworth: Penguin.

Gamble, A. (2000). *Politics and Fate*. Cambridge: Polity Press.

Goodin, R. (1992). *Green Political Theory*. Cambridge: Polity Press.

Goodwin, B. (2007). *Using Political Ideas*. 5th edn. Chichester: John Wiley & Sons.

Gorz, A. (1985). *Paths to Paradise*, London: Pluto.

Graveline, F.J. (1998). *Circle Works: Transforming Eurocentric Consciousness*. Halifax: Fernwood.

Greer, G. (1970). *The Female Eunuch*. New York: McGraw-Hill.

Hajer, M. (1997). *The Politics of Environmental Discourse*. Oxford: Clarendon Press.

Hardin, G. (1968). "The Tragedy of the Commons." *Science* 162: 1243–8.

Hay, C. (2002). *Political Analysis: A Critical Introduction*. Basingstoke: Palgrave.

Heilbroner, R. (1974). *An Inquiry into the Human Prospect*. New York: Norton.

Heywood, A. (2007). *Political Ideologies: An Introduction*. Basingstoke: Palgrave.

Hoffman, J., and P. Graham (2006). *Introduction to Political Theory*. Harlow: Pearson.

Huntington, S. (1996). *The Clash of Civilizations*. New York: Simon & Schuster.

Jaggar, A. (1983). *Feminist Politics and Human Nature*. Lanham, MD: Rowman & Littlefield.

Kidwell, C.S., Noley. H., & Tinker, G.E. (2001). *A Native American Theology*. Maryknoll, NY: Orbis.

Kymlicka, W. (1995). *Multicultural Citizenship: A Liberal Theory of Minority Rights*. Oxford: Oxford University Press.

——— (2002). *Contemporary Political Philosophy*. Oxford: Oxford University Press, 2nd edn.

Leopold, A. (1949). *A Sand County Almanac*. Oxford: Oxford University Press.

MacDonald, David B. (2009). *Thinking History, Fighting Evil: Neoconservatives and the Perils of Historical Analogy in American Politics*. Lanham, MD: Lexington/Rowman & Littlefield.

MacKinnon, C. (1989). *Towards a Feminist Theory of the State*, London: Harvard University Press.

Marshall, T.H. (1950). *Citizenship and Social Class, and other Essays*. Cambridge: Cambridge University Press.

Martell, L. (1994). *Ecology and Society*. Cambridge: Polity Press.

McElroy, W. (1995). *A Woman's Right to Pornography*. New York: St. Martin's Press.

McIntosh, M. (1978). "The State and the Oppression of Women." In A. Kuhn and A. Wolpe, eds. *Feminism and Materialism: Women and Modes of Production*. London: Routledge & Kegan Paul.

Meadows, D., et al. (1972). *The Limits to Growth*. New York: Universe.

Mill, J.S. (1970). *The Subjection of Women*. Cambridge, MA: MIT Press.

Millett, K. (1971). *Sexual Politics*. New York: Granada Publishing.

Mitchell, J. (1971). *Woman's Estate*. Harmondsworth: Penguin.

Ophuls, W. (1973). "Leviathan or Oblivion." Pp. 215–30 in H. Daly, ed. *Toward a Steady State Economy*. San Francisco, CA: Freeman.

Parekh, B. (2000). *Rethinking Multiculturalism: Cultural Diversity and Political Theory*. Cambridge, MA: Harvard University Press.

Pateman, C. (1988). *The Sexual Contract*. Oxford: Polity Press.

——— (1989). *The Disorder of Women*. Oxford: Polity Press.

Pepper, D. (1993). *Eco-Socialism: From Deep Ecology to Social Justice*. London: Routledge.

Porritt, J. (1984). *Seeing Green*. Oxford: Basil Blackwell.

Rawls, J. (1993). *Political Liberalism*. New York: Columbia University Press.

Schechter, Danny (2003). *Media Wars: News at a Time of Terror*. Lanham, MD: Rowman & Littlefield.

Schumacher, E. (1973). *Small Is Beautiful: Economics as if People Mattered*. London: Blond and Briggs.

Stoker, G., and Marsh, D. (2002). "Introduction." Pp. 1–16 in Marsh and Stoker, eds. *Theory and Methods in Political Science*. Basingstoke: Palgrave.

Trudeau, Pierre Elliott (1971). "Announcement of Implementation of Policy of Multiculturalism Within Bilingual Framework." *House of Commons Debates*. 8 Oct. www.abheritage.ca/albertans/speeches/trudeau.html

Vincent, A. (1995). *Modern Political Ideologies*. 2nd edn. Oxford: Blackwell.

Wissenburg, M. (1993). "The Idea of Nature and the Nature of Distributive Justice." Pp. 3–20 in A. Dobson and P. Lucardie, eds. *The Politics of Nature: Explorations in Green Political Thought*. London: Routledge.

Wollstonecraft, M. (1978 [1792]). *A Vindication of the Rights of Women*. Harmondsworth: Penguin.

World Commission on Environment and Development (1987). *Our Common Future*. Oxford: Oxford University Press.

Chapter 7

Anderson, Benedict (1990). *Language and Power: Exploring Political Cultures in Indonesia*. Ithaca, NY: Cornell University Press.

Bayart, Jean-François (1993). *The State in Africa: The Politics of the Belly*. London: Longman.

Bell, Daniel A., David Brown, Kanishka Jayasuriya, and David Martin Jones (1995). *Towards Illiberal Democracy in Pacific Asia*. Basingstoke: Macmillan.

Buzan, Barry (1991). *People, States and Fear*. 2nd edn. London: Harvester Wheatsheaf.

Chabal, Patrick, and Jean-Pascal Daloz (1999). *Africa Works: Disorder as Political Instrument*. Oxford: International Africa Institute in association with James Currey.

Clapham, Christopher (1996). *Africa and the International System: The Politics of State Survival*. Cambridge: Cambridge University Press.

Coronil, Fernando (1997). *The Magical State: Nature, Money, and Modernity in Venezuela*. Chicago: Chicago University Press.

Dudden, Alexis (2006). *Japan's Colonization of Korea: Discourse and Power*. University of Hawaii Press.

Edelman, Murray (1964). *The Symbolic Uses of Politics*. Urbana: University of Illinois Press.

Finer, S.E. (1997). *The History of Government from the Earliest Times*. Vol. 3. *Empires, Monarchies and the Modern State*. Oxford: Oxford University Press.

Fulbrook, Mary (2005). *The People's State: East German Society from Hitler to Honecker*. New Haven, CT, and London: Yale University Press.

Giddens, Anthony (1979). *Central Problems in Social Theory: Action, Structure and Contradiction in Social Analysis*. Basingstoke: Macmillan.

Gill, Graeme (2003). *The Nature and Development of the Modern State*. Basingstoke: Palgrave.

International IDEA (2002a). *Handbook on Democracy Assessment*. The Hague: Kluwer.

——— (2002b). *The State of Democracy*. The Hague: Kluwer.

Jackson, Robert H. (1990). *Quasi-States: Sovereignty, International Relations and the Third World*. Cambridge: Cambridge University Press.

Little, Peter D. (2003). *Somalia: Economy Without State*. Oxford: International African Institute in association with James Currey.

MacDonald, David B. (2009). *Thinking History, Fighting Evil: Neoconservatives and the Perils of Historical Analogy in American Politics*. Lanham, MD: Lexington/Rowman & Littlefield.

MacDonald, David B., Brendon O'Connor, and Peter J. Katzenstein (2008). "Anti-Americanism among the Antipodes: Australia and New Zealand." Paper presented to the International Studies Association. San Francisco. 26–29 March.

Marsh, David, Nicola J. Smith, and Nicola Hothi (2006). "Globalization and the State." Pp. 172–89 in Colin Hay, Michael Lister, and David Marsh, eds. *The State: Theories and Issues*. Basingstoke: Palgrave.

Menkhaus, Ken (2007). "Governance without Government in Somalia." *International Security* 31, 3: 74–106.

Paley, Julia (2002). "Toward an Anthropology of Democracy." *Annual Review of Anthropology* 31: 469–96.

Peterson, Scott (2000). *Me Against My Brother: At War in Somalia, Sudan, and Rwanda*. New York and London: Routledge.

Rotberg, Robert I. (ed.) (2004). *When States Fail: Causes and Consequences*. Princeton, NJ: Princeton University Press.

Sky News (2009). "Clinton: 2000 Poll 'Like Nigeria Corruption.'" 13 Aug. http://news.sky.com/skynews/Home/World-News/US-Secretary-Of-State-Hillary-Clinton-Compares-2000-US-Election-Corruption-To-Nigeria-Rigged-Votes/Article/2009 08215359933?lpos=World_News_Article_Related_Content_Region_2&lid=ARTICLE_15359933_US_Secretary_Of_State_Hillary_Clinton_Compares_2000_US_Election_Corruption_To_Nigeria_Rigged_Votes

Starr, June (1992). *Law as Metaphor: From Islamic Courts to the Palace of Justice*. Albany: State University of New York Press.

Steinmo, S. (2001). "Institutionalism." Pp. 7554–8 in Neil J. Smelser and Paul Baltes, eds. *International Encyclopedia of the Social and Behavioral Sciences*. Vol. 11. Amsterdam: Elsevier.

Suwannathat-Pian, Kobkua (1988). *Thai–Malay Relations*. Oxford: Oxford University Press.

Tanzi, Vito, and Ludger Schuknecht (2000). *Public Spending in the Twentieth Century*. Cambridge: Cambridge University Press.

Tilly, Charles (1975). *The Formation of National States in Europe*. Princeton, NJ: Princeton University Press.

——— (1990). *Coercion, Capital and European States, AD 990–1990*. Oxford: Blackwell.

van Creveld, Martin (1999). *The Rise and Decline of the State*. Cambridge: Cambridge University Press.

Wang, Shaoguang (1995). "Rise of the Regions: Fiscal Reform and the Decline of Central State Capacity in China." In Walder, Andrew G., editor *The Waning of the Communist State: Economic Origins of Political Decline in China and Hungary*. Berkeley: University of California Press.

Terry, Edith (2002). *How Asia Got Rich: Japan, China and the Asian Miracle*. M.E. Sharpe.

Weber, Max (1968). *Economy and Society: An Outline of Interpretive Sociology*. Edited by Guenther Roth and Claus Wittich. Vol. 3. New York: Bedminster Press.

White Paper on Political Democracy (2005). www.china.org.cn/english/features/book/145941.htm.

Chapter 8

Bonnett, Alastair (2004). *The Idea of the West: Culture, Politics and History*. Basingstoke: Palgrave.

Buxbaum, R.M. (2004). "Law, Diffusion of." Pp. 1–7 in Neil J. Smelser and Paul B. Baltes, eds. *International Encyclopedia of the Social and Behavioral Sciences*. Amsterdam: Elsevier.

Colomer, Josep M. (2007). *Great Empires, Small Nations: The Uncertain Future of the Sovereign State*. London: Routledge.

Dahl, Robert A. (2001). *How Democratic Is the American Constitution?* New Haven, CT: Yale University Press.

Epp, Charles B. (1998). *The Rights Revolution: Lawyers, Activists, and Supreme Courts in Comparative Perspective*. Chicago: Chicago University Press.

Fuller, Lon L. (1969). *The Morality of Law*. Rev. edn. New Haven, CT: Yale University Press.

Hallaq, Wael B. (2005). *The Origins and Evolution of Islamic Law*. Cambridge: Cambridge University Press.

King, Anthony (2001). "Distrust of Government: Explaining American Exceptionalism." Pp. 74–98 in Susan J. Pharr and Robert D. Putnam, eds. *Disaffected Democracies: What's Troubling the Trilateral Countries?* Princeton, NJ: Princeton University Press.

——— (2007). *The British Constitution*. Oxford: Oxford University Press.

Lewis, Bernard (2005). "Freedom and Justice in the Modern Middle East." *Foreign Affairs* 84, 3: 36–51.

Lieberman, J.K. (2001). "Legalization." Pp. 8693–7 in Neil J. Smelser and Paul B. Baltes, eds. *International Encyclopedia of the Social and Behavioral Sciences*. Amsterdam: Elsevier.

Lijphart, Arend (1977). *Democracy in Plural Societies: A Comparative Explanation*. New Haven, CT: Yale University Press.

———— (1999). *Patterns of Democracy: Government Forms and Performance in Thirty-Six Countries*, New Haven, CT: Yale University Press.

Lombardi, Clark Benner (1998). "Islamic Law as a Source of Constitutional Law in Egypt: The Constitutionalization of the Sharia in a Modern Arab State." *Columbia Journal of Transnational Law* 37, 1: 81–123.

Menski, Werner (2006). *Comparative Law in a Global Context: the Legal Systems of Asia and Africa*. Cambridge: Cambridge University Press.

Montada, L. (2001). "Justice and its Many Faces: Cultural Concerns." Pp. 8037–42 in Neil J. Smelser and Paul B. Baltes, eds. *International Encyclopedia of the Social and Behavioral Sciences*, Amsterdam: Elsevier.

Moten, Abdul Rashid (1996). *Political Science: An Islamic Perspective*. Basingstoke: Macmillan.

Ramet, Sabrina P. (2005). *Thinking About Yugoslavia: Scholarly Debates about the Yugoslav Breakup and the Wars in Bosnia and Kosovo*. Cambridge: Cambridge University Press.

Robertson, David (1993). *The Penguin Dictionary of Politics*. Harmondsworth: Penguin.

Rosen, Lawrence (1989). *The Anthropology of Justice: Law as Culture in Islamic Society*. Cambridge: Cambridge University Press.Statistics Canada (2011). "Quebec's Population Clock": 1 July. www.statcan.gc.ca/ig-gi/pop-qc-eng.htm.

Stepan, Alfred (2004). "Federalism and Democracy: Beyond the US Model." Pp. 441–56 in Ugo Amoretti and Nancy Bermeo, eds. *Federalism and Territorial Cleavages*. Baltimore, MD: Johns Hopkins University Press.

Twining, William (2000). *Globalisation and Legal Theory*. London: Butterworth.

Watt, W. Montgomery (1968). *Islamic Political Thought*, Edinburgh: Edinburgh University Press.

Yilmaz, Ihsan (2005). *Muslim Laws, Politics and Society in Modern Nation States: Dynamic Legal Pluralisms in England Turkey and Pakistan*. Aldershot: Ashgate.

Zakaria, Fareed (1997). "The Rise of Illiberal Democracy." *Foreign Affairs* 76, 6 (Nov.–Dec.): 22–43.

Chapter 9

Arora, Balveer (2003). "The Indian Parliament and Democracy." Pp.14–37 in Ajay K. Mehra and Gert W. Kueck, eds. *The Indian Parliament: A Comparative Perspective*. Delhi: Konarck Publishers.

Asa-El, Amotz (2008). "Israel's Electoral Complex", *Azure* 31 (Winter). www.azure.org.il/magazine/magazine.asp?id = 410.

Baktiari, Bahman (1996). *Parliamentary Politics in Iran: The Institutionalization of Factional Politics*. Gainesville, FL: Florida University Press.

Bayart, Jean-François (1993). *The State in Africa: The Politics of the Belly*. London: Longman.

Borchert, Jens, and Jürgen Zeiss (2003). *The Political Class in Advanced Democracies*. Oxford: Oxford University Press.

Boundary Commission for England (2007). *Fifth Periodical Report*. London: HMSO, cm7032, vol. 1.

Burke, Edmund (1996). *The Writings and Speeches of Edmund Burke*. Edited by W.M. Elofson with John A. Woods. Vol. 3. Oxford: Clarendon Press.

Chabal, Patrick, and Jean-Pascal Daloz (1999). *Africa Works: Disorder as Political Instrument*. Oxford: International African Institute in association with James Currey.

Cheibub, Jose Antonio (2007). *Presidentialism, Parliamentarianism and Democracy*. Cambridge: Cambridge University Press.

Coronel, Sheila S., Yvonne T. Chua, Luz and Cruz Rimban, and B. Booma (2004). *The Rulemakers: How the Wealthy and Well-Born Dominate Congress*. Quezon City: Philippine Center for Investigative Journalism.

Cracknell, Richard (2005). "Social Background of MPs." www.parliament.uk/commons/lib/research/notes/snsg-01528.pdf.

Dahlerup, Drude (2005). "Increasing Women's Political Representation: New Trends in Gender Quotas." Pp. 141–53 in Julie Ballington and Azza Karam, eds. *Women in Parliament: Beyond Numbers*. Rev. edn. Stockholm: International IDEA.

Fitzpatrick, Meagan (2011). "Senate Reform Bill Proposes 9-Year Terms." *CBC News*. 21 June. www.cbc.ca/news/canada/story/2011/06/21/pol-senate-reform-bill.html.

Gallagher, Michael, Michael March, and Paul Mitchell, eds. (2003). *How Ireland Voted 2002*. Basingstoke: Palgrave.

Gamm, Gerald, and John Huber (2002). "Legislatures as Political Institutions: Beyond the Contemporary Congress." Pp. 313–41 in Ira Katznelson and Helen V. Milner, eds. *Political Science: State of the Discipline*. New York: Norton for the American Political Science Association.

Inglehart, Ronald, Miguel Basáñez, Jaime Diéz-Madrano, Loek Halman, and Ruud Luijkx, eds (2004). *Human Beliefs and Values*. Mexico: Siglo XXI Editores.

Jacobson, Gary C. (1997). *The Politics of Congressional Elections*. 4th edn. New York: Longman.

Linz, Juan J. (1992). "The Perils of Presidentialism." Pp. 118–27 in Arend Lijphart, ed. *Parliamentary Versus Presidential Government*. Oxford: Oxford University Press.

Mainwaring, Scott (2006). "State Deficiencies, Party Competition, and Confidence in Democratic Representation in the Andes." Pp. 295–345 in Scott Mainwaring, Ana María Bejarano, and Eduardo Pizarro LeongÓmez, eds. *The Crisis of Democratic Representation in the Andes*. Stanford, CA: Stanford University Press.

Matland, Richard E. (2005). "Enhancing Women's Political Participation: Legislative Recruitment and Electoral Systems." Pp. 93–111 in Julie Ballington and Azza Kazam, eds. *Women in Parliament: Beyond Numbers*. Rev. edn. Stockholm: International IDEA.

Mezey, Michael (1990). "Classifying Legislatures." Pp. 149–76 in Philip Norton, ed. *Legislatures*. Oxford: Oxford University Press.

Miller, Vaughne (2007). "EU Legislation." www.parliament.uk/commons/lib/research/notes/snia-02888.pdf.

Norton, Philip, ed. (1998). *Parliaments and Governments in Western Europe.* Vol. 1. London: Cass.

Oborne, Peter (2007). *The Triumph of the Political Class.* London: Simon & Schuster.

Rizzo, Sergio, and Gian Antonio Stella (2007). *La casta: così i politici italiani sono diventati intoccabili.* Milan: Rizzoli.

O'Donnell, Guillermo (2003). "Horizontal Accountability: The Legal Institutionalization of Mistrust." Pp. 34–54 in Scott Mainwaring and Christopher Welna, eds. *Democratic Accountability in Latin America.* Oxford: Oxford University Press.

Olson, David M. (1994). *Democratic Legislative Institutions: A Comparative View.* New York: M.E. Sharpe.

Patterson, Samuel C., and Anthony Mughan (eds) (1999). *Senates: Bicameralism in the Contemporary World*, Columbus, OH: Ohio State University Press.

Pitkin, Hanna (1967). *The Concept of Representation.* Berkeley: University of California Press.

Rüland, Jürgen (2003). "Constitutional Debates in the Philippines: From Presidentialism to Parliamentarianism?" *Asian Survey* 43, 3: 461–84.

———, Clemens Jürgenmeyer, Michael H. Nelson, and Patrick Ziegenhain (2005). *Parliaments and Political Change in Asia.* Singapore: ISEAS.

Stockwin, J.A.A. (1999). *Governing Japan.* 3rd edn. Oxford: Blackwell.

Sutherland, Keith (2004). *The Party's Over: Blueprint for a Very English Revolution.* Exeter: Imprint Academic.

"Transparency International 2010 Corruption Perceptions Index" (2010). www.transparency.org/policy_research/surveys_indices/cpi/2010/results.

Tremblay, Manon, and Réjean Pelletier (2000). "More Feminists or More Women?" *International Political Science Review* 21, 4: 381–4.

Tsebelis, George, and Jeannette Money (1997). *Bicameralism.* Cambridge: Cambridge University Press.

Uhr, John. "Bicameralism" (2008). In R.A.W. Rhodes, Sarah A. Binder, and Bert A. Rockman, eds. *The Oxford Handbook of Political Institutions.* Usui, Chikako, and Richard A. Colignon (2004). "Continuity and Change in Paths to High Political Office: Ex-Bureaucrats and Hereditary Politicians." *Asian Business and Management* 3, 4: 395–416.

Chapter 10

Abord de Chatillon, Renaud (1994). *La politique des transports en France.* Paris: Eds Eska.

Adamolekun, Ladipo (2007). "Africa: Rehabilitating Civil Service Institutions—Main Issues and Implementation Progress." Pp. 82–99 in Jos C.N. Raadschelders, Teho A.J. Toonen, and Frits M. Van der Meer, eds. *The Civil Service in the 21st Century: Comparative Perspectives.* Basingstoke: Palgrave.

Allison, Graham T. (1971). *Essence of Decision: Explaining the Cuban Missile Crisis.* Boston: Little Brown.

Barber, Michael (2007). *Instruction to Deliver: Tony Blair, Public Services and the Challenge of Achieving Targets.* London: Politico's.

Bevir, Mark, and Rhodes, R.A.W. (2006). *Governance Stories* London: Routledge.

Calder, Kent E. (1993). *Strategic Capitalism: Private Business and Public Purpose in Japanese Industrial Finance.* Princeton, NJ: Princeton University Press.

Bobbitt, Philip (2003). *The Shield of Achilles: War, Peace and the Course of History.* London: Penguin.

Castells, Manuel (1998). *The End of Millennium, The Information Age: Economy, Society and Culture.* Vol. 3. Oxford: Blackwell.

Eddington Transport Report. December (2006). www.dft.gov.uk/162259/187604/206711/executivesummary.

Evans, Peter B. (1995). *Embedded Autonomy: States and Industrial Transformation.* Princeton, NJ: Princeton University Press.

Ginsborg, Paul (2001). *Italy and Its Discontents.* London: Allen Lane, Penguin.

Glaister, Stephen, Jane Burnham, Handley Stevens, and Tony Travers (1998). *Transport Policy in Britain.* Basingstoke: Macmillan.

———, Jane Burnham, Handley Stevens, and Tony Travers (2006). *Transport Policy in Britain.* 2nd edn. Basingstoke: Palgrave.

Hall, Peter A., and David Soskice, eds. (2001). *Varieties of Capitalism: The Institutional Foundations of Comparative Advantage.* Oxford: Oxford University Press.

Héritier, Adrienne, and Christoph Knill (2001). "Differential Responses to European Policies: A Comparison." Pp. 257–94 in Héritier, Dieter Kerwer, Christoph Knill, Dirk Lehmkuhl, Michael Teutsch, and Anne-Cécile Douillet (2001). *Differential Europe: The European Union Impact on National Policy-Making.* Lanham, MD: Rowman & Littlefield:

Johnson, Chalmers A. (1982). MITI *and the Japanese Miracle.* Stanford, CA: Stanford University Press.

Kamarck, Elaine C. (2007). *The End of Government . . . As We Know It: Making Public Policy Work*, Boulder, CO: Lynne Rienner.

Kayizzi-Mugerwa, Steve (2003). "Introduction." In Steve Kayizzi-Mugerwa, ed. *Reforming Africa's Institutions: Ownership, Incentives, and Capabilities.* Tokyo, New York, Paris: UNUP and UNU WIDER.

Kim, Wangsik (2006). "Government Executive and Policy Reform in Japan." *International Review of Public Administration* 10, 2: 21–35.

Kohli, Atul (2004). *State-Directed Development: Political Power and Industrialization in the Global Periphery.* Cambridge: Cambridge University Press.

Landier, Augustin, and Thesmar, David (2007). *Le grand méchant marché.* Paris: Flammarion.

Lynn, Laurence E. (2006). *Public Management: Old and New.* Abingdon: Routledge.

Neiertz, Nicolas (1999). *La coordination des transports en France: de 1918 à nos jours.* Paris: CHEEF.

Olsen, Johan P. (2003). "Towards a European Administrative Space?" *Journal of European Public Policy* 10, 4: 506–31.

Ourzik, Abdelouahad (2000). "Public Service in Africa: New Challenges." Pp. 43–9 in *African Public Service: New Challenges, Professionalism and Ethics.* New York: United Nations.

Pierre, Jon, and Guy B. Peters (2000). *Governance, Politics and the State.* Basingstoke: Macmillan.

Rhodes, R.A.W. (1997). *Understanding Governance: Policy Networks, Governance, Reflexivity and Accountability.* Buckingham: Open University Press.

Richards, David (2008). *New Labour and the Civil Service: Reconstituting the Whitehall Model.* Basingstoke: Palgrave.

Salisu, Mohammed (2003). "Incentive Structure, Civil Service Efficiency and the Hidden Economy in Nigeria." In Steve Kayizzi-Mugerwa, ed. *Reforming Africa's Institutions: Ownership, Incentives, and Capabilities.* Tokyo, New York, Paris: UNUP and UNU/WIDER.

Talbot, Colin (2004). "The Agency Idea: Sometimes Old, Sometimes New, Sometimes Borrowed, Sometimes Untrue." Pp. 3–21 in Christopher Pollitt and Colin Talbot. eds. *Unbundled Government: A Critical Analysis of the Global Trend to Agencies, Quangos and Contractualisation.* Abingdon: Routledge.

Thatcher, M. (2001). "Issue Networks: Iron Triangles, Subgovernments, and Policy Communities." Pp. 7940–2 in Neil J. Smelser and Paul B. Baltes, eds. *International Encyclopedia of the Social and Behavioral Sciences.* Amsterdam: Elsevier.

Toonen, Theo A.J. (2001). "The Comparative Dimension of Administrative Reform: Creating Open Villages and Redesigning the Politics of Administration." Pp. 183–201 in B. Guy Peters and Jon Pierre, eds. *Politicians, Bureaucrats and Administrative Reform.* Abingdon: Routledge.

UN Economic and Social Commission for Asia and the Pacific. "What Is Good Governance?" www.unescap.org/pdd/prs/ProjectActivities/Ongoing/gg/governance.asp; accessed 23 Jan. 2012. Weber, Max (1968). *Economy and Society: An Outline of Interpretive Sociology.* Vol. 3. New York: Bedminster Press.

Weiss, Linda (1998). *The Myth of the Powerless State: Governing the Economy in a Global Era.* Cambridge: Polity Press.

Chapter 11

Aldrich, John H. (1995). *Why Parties? The Origin and Transformation of Political Parties in America.* Chicago: Chicago University Press.

Beyme, Klaus von (1985). *Political Parties in Western Democracies.* Aldershot: Gower.

Biezen, Ingrid van (2003). *Political Parties in New Democracies: Party Organization in Southern and East-Central Europe.* Basingstoke: Palgrave.

Carothers, Thomas (2006). *Confronting the Weakest Link: Aiding Political Parties in New Democracies.* Washington, DC: Carnegie Endowment.

Colomer, Josep M. (ed.) (2004). "The Strategy and History of Electoral System Choice." Pp. 1–73 in Josep M. Colomer, ed. *Handbook of Electoral System Choice.* Basingstoke: Palgrave.

Coppedge, Michael (2002). "Venezuela: Popular Sovereignty Versus Liberal Democracy. Pp. 165–92" in Jorge I. Dominguez and Michael Shifter, eds. *Constructing Democratic Governance.* 2nd edn. Baltimore: Johns Hopkins University Press.

Corrales, Javier and Michael Penfold (2007). "Venezuela: Crowding Out the Opposition." *Journal of Democracy* 18, 2 (April): 99–113.

Doorenspleet, Renske (2003). "Political Parties, Party Systems and Democracy in Sub-Saharan Africa." Pp. 169–87 in M.A. Mohamed Salih, ed. *African Political Parties.* London: Pluto.

Dunleavy, Patrick (2005). "Facing Up to Multi-Party Politics: How Partisan Dealignment and PR Voting Have Fundamentally Changed Britain's Party System." *Parliamentary Affairs* 58, 3: 503–32.

Duverger, Maurice (1964). *Political Parties.* 3rd edn. London: Methuen.

Farrell, David M. (2001). *Electoral Systems: A Comparative Introduction.* Basingstoke: Palgrave.

Federal Election Commission (2009). "Party Financial Activity Summarized for the 2008 Election Cycle: Party Support For Candidates Increases." 28 May. www.fec.gov/press/press2009/05282009Party/20090528Party.shtml.

Fiorina, Morris P. (2002). "Parties, Participation, and Representation in America: Old Theories Face New Realities." In Ira N. Katznelson and Helen V. Milner, eds. *Political Science: State of the Discipline.* New York: Norton, for the American Political Science Association.

"First Deliberative Polling for Candidate Selection in Marousi, Greece: A Summary." (2006). http://cdd.stanford.edu/polls/greece/2006/ marousisummary.pdf.

Gambetta, Diego, and Steven Warner (2004). "Italy: Lofty Ambitions and Unintended Consequences." Pp. 237–52 in Josep M. Colomer, ed. *Handbook of Electoral System Choice.* Basingstoke: Palgrave.

Gott, Richard (2005). *Hugo Chavez and the Bolivarian Revolution.* London: Verso.

Gunther, Richard, and Diamond, Larry (2003). "Species of Political Parties: A New Typology." *Party Politics* 9, 2: 167–99.

Hale, Henry E. (2006). *Why Not Parties in Russia? Democracy, Federalism, and the State.* Cambridge: Cambridge University Press.

International IDEA (2003). *Funding of Political Parties and Election Campaigns.* Stockholm.

International IDEA (2007). *Electoral System Design,* Stockholm.

Inter-Parliamentary Union (1997). *Universal Declaration on Democracy.* www.ipu.org/cnl-e/161-dem.htm.

Levitsky, Steven and Maxwell A. Cameron (2003). "Democracy Without Parties? Political Parties and Regime Change in Fujimori's Peru." *Latin American Politics and Society* 45, 3: 1–33.

Lipset, Seymour Martin, and Stein Rokkan, eds (1967). *Party Systems and Voter Alignments: Cross National Perspectives.* New York: Free Press.

McCoy, Jennifer L., and David L. Myers, eds (2004). *The Unravelling of Representative Democracy in Venezuela.* Baltimore, MD: Johns Hopkins University Press.

Mair, Peter (2005). "Democracy Beyond Parties." *Center for the Study of Democracy*. University of California, Irvine. http://repositories.cdlib.org/csd/05–06.

————, and Ingrid van Biezen (2001). "Party Membership in Twenty European Democracies, 1980–2000." *Party Politics* 7, 1: 5–21.

Meredith, Martin (2005). *The Fate of Africa: A History of Fifty Years of Independence*. New York: Public Affairs.

Mugaju, Justus, and J. Oloka-Onyango, eds (2000). *No-Party Democracy in Uganda: Myths and Realities*. Kampala: Fountain Publishers.

Power Inquiry (2006). *Power to the People*. www.makeitanissue.org.uk/2007/01/power_commission_archive.php#more.

Reeve, David (1985). *Golkar of Indonesia: An Alternative to the Party System*. Singapore: Oxford University Press.

Riker, William H. (1982). *Liberalism Against Populism: A Confrontation Between the Theory of Democracy and the Theory of Social Choice*. San Francisco: Freeman.

Rosenbluth, Frances and Mark Ramseyer (1993). *Japan's Political Marketplace*. Cambridge, MA: Harvard University Press.

Saari, Donald G. (2001). *Chaotic Elections! A Mathematician Looks at Voting*. Providence, RI: American Mathematical Society.

Sartori, Giovanni (1976). *Parties and Party Systems: A Framework for Analysis*. Cambridge: Cambridge University Press.

Ware, Alan (1996). *Political Parties and Party Systems*. Oxford: Oxford University Press.

Chapter 12

Asking the Right Questions About Electronic Voting (2005). http://books.nap.edu/openbook.php?record_id = 11449&page.

Barber, Benjamin (1984). *Strong Democracy: Participatory Politics for a New Age*. Berkeley: University of California Press.

———— (1998). "Three Scenarios for the Future of Technology and Strong Democracy." *Political Science Quarterly* 113: 573–89.

Baso, Ahmad (1999). *Civil Society versus Masyarakat Madani: Arkeologi Pemikiran "Civil Society" dalam Islam Indonesia*. Bandung: Pustaka Hidayah.

Becker, Ted, and Christa Daryl Slaton (2000). *The Future of Teledemocracy*. Westport, CT: Praeger.

Bruce, Iain, ed. (2004). *The Porto Alegre Alternative: Direct Democracy in Action*. London: Pluto Press.

Budge, Ian (1996). *The New Challenge of Direct Democracy*. Cambridge: Polity Press.

Castells, Manuel (1996). *The Rise of the Network Society*. Oxford: Blackwell.

Chabal, Patrick, and Jean-Pascal Daloz (1999). *Africa Works: Disorder as Political Instrument*. Oxford: International Africa Institute in association with James Currey.

Chandhoke, Neera (2003). *The Conceits of Civil Society*. New Delhi: Oxford University Press.

Chatterjee, P. (2001). "Subaltern History." Pp. 15237–41 in Neil J. Smelser and Paul B. Baltes, eds. *International Encyclopedia of the Social and Behavioral Sciences*. Amsterdam: Elsevier.

Comaroff, John L., and Jean Comaroff, eds (1999). *Civil Society and the Political Imagination in Africa: Critical Perspectives*. Chicago: Chicago University Press.

Doronila, Amando (2001). *The Fall of Joseph Estrada: The Inside Story*. Pasig City: Anvil Publishing and Philippine Daily Inquirer.

Edwards, Michael (2004). *Civil Society*. Cambridge: Polity Press.

Eickelman, Dale F. (1996). "Foreword." Pp. ix–xiv in Augustus Richard Norton, ed. *Civil Society in the Middle East*. Vol. 2. Leiden: E.J. Brill.

Fleras, Augie, and Jean Leonard Elliott (2006). *Unequal Relations: An Introduction to Race, Ethnic, and Aboriginal Dynamics in Canada*. 3rd edn. Scarborough, ON: Prentice Hall Canada.

Franklin, Bob (2004). *Packaging Politics: Political Communications in Britain's Media Democracy*. London: Hodder Headline.

Ginsborg, Paul (2001). *Italy and its Discontents 1980–2001*. London: Allen Lane, Penguin.

Gledhill, John (1994). *Power and Its Disguises: Anthropological Perspectives on Politics*. London: Pluto.

Gupta, Akhil (2006). "Blurred Boundaries: The Discourse of Corruption, the Culture of Politics and the Imagined State." Pp. 211–42 in Aradhana Sharma and Akhil Gupta, eds. *The Anthropology of the State: A Reader*. Oxford: Blackwell.

Gustin, Sam (2011). "Social Media Sparked, Accelerated Egypt's Revolutionary Fire." *Wired*. 11 Feb. www.wired.com/epicenter/2011/02/egypts-revolutionary-fire/.

Hahm, Chaihark (2004). "Disputing Civil Society in a Confucian Context." *Korea Observer* 35, 3 (Autumn): 433–62.

Hale, Geoffrey (2006). *Uneasy Partnership: The Politics of Business and Government in Canada*. Toronto: University of Toronto Press.

Hill, Annette (2005). *Reality TV: Audiences and Popular Factual Television*. New York: Routledge.

Hoexter, Miriam (2002). "The Waqf and the Public Sphere." Pp. 19–38 in Miriam Hoexter, Shmuel N. Eisenstadt, and Nehemia Levtzion, eds. *The Public Sphere in Muslim Societies*. Albany: State University of New York Press.

Ibrahim, Saad Eddin (1995). "Civil Society and Prospects of Democratization in the Arab World." Pp. 27–54 in Augustus Richard Norton, ed. *Civil Society in the Middle East*. Vol. 1. Leiden: E.J. Brill.

Jenkins, Rob (2005). "Civil Society: Active or Passive?—India." Pp. 275–85 in Peter Burnell and Vicky Randall, eds. *Politics in the Developing World*. Oxford: Oxford University Press.

Jordan, Grant, and Maloney, William A. (2007). *Democracy and Interest Groups: Enhancing Participation*? Basingstoke: Palgrave.

Kenney, Padraic (2002). *A Carnival of Revolution: Central Europe, 1989*. Princeton, NJ: Princeton University Press.

Lehmbruch, Gerhard (2001). "Corporatism." Pp. 2813–16 in Neil J. Smelser and Paul R. Baltes, eds. *International Encyclopedia of the Social and Behavioral Sciences*. Amsterdam: Elsevier.

Leifer, Michael (1995). *Dictionary of the Modern Politics of South-East Asia*. London: Routledge.

McLean, Iain (1989). *Democracy and New Technology.* Cambridge: Polity Press.

Migdal, Joel S. (2001). *State in Society: Studying How States and Societies Transform and Constitute One Another.* Cambridge: Cambridge University Press.

Puhle, H.-J. (2001). "History of Interest Groups." Pp. 7703–8 in Neil J. Smelser and Paul B. Baltes, eds. *International Encyclopedia of the Social and Behavioral Sciences.* Amsterdam: Elsevier.

Reporters Without Borders (2006). "Press Freedom Round-up 2006." http://en.rsf.org/press-freedom-round-up-2006-31-12-2006,20286.html.

Rheingold, Howard (2002). *Smart Mobs: The Next Social Revolution.* Cambridge, MA: Perseus.

Robertson, David (1993). *The Penguin Dictionary of Politics.* Harmondsworth: Penguin.

Saeki, Keishi (1997). *Gendai minshushugino by ri,* Tokyo: NHK Books.

Schlozman, K.L. (2001). "Interest Groups." Pp. 7700–3 in Neil J. Smelser and Paul B. Baltes, eds. *International Encyclopedia of the Social and Behavioral Sciences.* Amsterdam: Elsevier.

Schmitter, Philippe (1980). "Modes of Interest Intermediation and Models of Societal Change in Western Europe." Pp. 63–94 in Philippe Schmitter and Gerhard Lehmbruch, eds. *Trends Towards Corporatist Intermediation.* Beverly Hills, CA: Sage.

Scott, James (1990). *Domination and the Arts of Resistance: Hidden Transcripts.* New Haven: Yale University Press.

Swanson, Judith A. (1992). *The Public and the Private in Aristotle's Political Philosophy.* Ithaca, NY: Cornell University Press.

Chapter 13

Alesina, Alberto, and Edward L. Glaeser (2004). *Fighting Poverty in the US and Europe: A World of Difference.* Oxford: Oxford University Press.

Almond, Gabriel A, and Sidney Verba (1965). *The Civic Culture.* Boston: Little Brown.

———, eds (1989). *The Civic Culture Revisited.* Newbury Park, CA: Sage.

Aronoff, M.J. (2001). "Political Culture." Pp. 640–4 in Neil J. Smelser and Paul H. Baltes, eds. *International Encyclopedia of the Social and Behavioral Sciences.* Amsterdam: Elsevier.

Banfield, Edward C. (1958). *The Moral Basis of a Backward Society.* Glencoe, IL: Chicago University Press.

Baregu, Mwesiga (1997). "Political Culture and the Party-State in Tanzania." In Research for Democracy in Tanzania Project, *Political Culture and Popular Participation in Tanzania.* Dar es Salaam: Dept. of Political Science and Public Administration, University of Dar es Salaam.

Chaligha, Amon, Robert Mattes, Michael Bratton, and Yul Derek Davids (2002). "Uncritical Citizens or Patient Trustees? Tanzanians' Views of Economic and Political Reform." *Afrobarometer Working Paper No. 18.*

Commission for Racial Equality (2005). *Citizenship and Belonging: What Is Britishness?* London. at http://ethnos.co.uk/what_is_britishness_CRE.pdf; accessed 14 Feb. 2012.

Dahl, Robert (1961). *Who Governs? Democracy and Power in an American City.* New Haven, CT: Yale University Press.

Emmerson, Donald, K. (1995). "Singapore and the 'Asian Values' Debate." *Journal of Democracy* 6, 4: 95–105.

Esping-Andersen, Gøsta (1990). *The Three Worlds of Welfare Capitalism.* Cambridge: Polity Press.

Fischer, David Hackett (1989). *Albion's Seed: Four British Folkways in America.* New York: Oxford University Press.

Fish, M. Steven (2005). *Democracy Derailed in Russia: The Failure of Open Politics.* Cambridge: Cambridge University Press.

Fukuyama, Francis (1995). "Confucianism and Democracy." *Journal of Democracy,* 6, 2 (April): 20–33.

Giscard d'Estaing, Valéry (2004). "A Better European Bridge to Turkey." *Financial Times.* 24 Nov. at www.ft.com/intl/cms/s/1/263d9778-3e4b-11d9-a9d7-00000e2511c8.html#axzz1mINapr7l; accessed 13 Feb. 2012.

Greenfeld, Liah (1992). *Nationalism: Five Roads to Modernity.* Cambridge, MA and London : Harvard University Press.

Home Office (2007). *Life in the UK: A Journey to Citizenship 2007.* London: HMSO.

Humayun, Syed (1995). "Pakistan: One State, two Nations: An Analysis of Political Anatomy of United Pakistan." Pp. 593–613 in Verinder Grover and Ranjana Arora, eds. *Political System in Pakistan.* Vol. 3.c New Delhi: Deep and Deep.

Huntington, Samuel (1996). *The Clash of Civilizations and the Re-making of World Order.,* New York: Simon & Schuster.

Inglehart, Ronald, and Pippa Norris (2003). "The True Clash of Civilizations., *Foreign Policy.* March–April: 67–74.

Inglehart, Ronald, Michael Basañez, Jaime Diéz-Medrano, Loek Halman, and Ruud Luijkx (2004). *Human Beliefs and Values: A Cross-Cultural Sourcebook Based on the 1999–2002 Values Surveys..* Mexico: Siglo XXI Editores.

Jackman, Robert W., and Ross A. Miller (2004). *Before Norms: Institutions and Civic Culture,* Ann Arbor: University of Michigan Press.

Jenner, W.J.F. (1992). *The Tyranny of History: The Roots of China's Crisis.* Harmondsworth: Allen Lane.

Kaplan, Robert D. (2005). *Balkan Ghosts: A Journey Through History.* New York: Picador.

Kyogoku, Jin-ichi (1987). *The Political Dynamics of Japan.* Tokyo: Tokyo University Press.

Leoussi, Athena, and Stephen Grosby, eds (2006). *Nationalism and Ethnosymbolism: History, Culture and Ethnicity in the Formation of Nations.* Edinburgh: Edinburgh University Press.

Lind, Michael (2002). *Made in Texas: George W. Bush and the Southern Takeover of American Politics.* New York: Basic Books.

Robertson, David (1993). *The Penguin Dictionary of Politics.* Harmondsworth: Penguin.

Malik, Yogendra K., and V.B. Singh (1995). *Hindu Nationalists in India: The Rise of the Bharatiya Janata Party.* New Delhi: Vistaar Publications.

Martin, Denis C. (1988). *Tanzania:L'Invention d'une culture politique*. Paris: Presses de la Fondation Nationale de Science Politique et Karthala.

Mock, Steven (2011). *Symbols of Defeat in the Construction of National Identity*. Cambridge: Cambridge University Press.

Putnam, Robert, with Robert Leonardi and Raffaella Y. Nanetti (1993). *Making Democracy Work: Civic Traditions in Modern Italy*. Princeton, NJ: Princeton University Press.

Pye, Lucian W. (1985). *Asian Power and Politics: The Cultural Dimensions of Authority*. Cambridge, MA: Belknap Press.

Pye, Lucian W., and Sidney Verba, eds (1965). *Political Culture and Political Development*. Princeton, NJ: Princeton University Press.

Sodaro, Michael (2008). *Comparative Politics: A Global Introduction*. 3rd edn. Boston: McGraw Hill.

de Tocqueville, Alexis (2000). *Democracy in America*. Chicago: Chicago University Press.

Waldron, Arthur (1993). "Representing China: the Great Wall and Cultural Nationalism in the Twentieth Century." Pp. 36–60 in Harumi Befu, ed. *Cultural Nationalism in East Asia: Representation and Identity*. Berkeley, CA: Research Papers and Policy Studies, Institute of East Asia Studies.

Yilmaz, Ihsan (2005). *Muslim Laws, Politics and Society in Modern Nation States: Dynamic Legal Pluralisms in England Turkey and Pakistan*. Aldershot: Ashgate.

Zakaria, Fareed (2002). "The Dustbin of History: Asian Values." 1 Nov. www.foreignpolicy.com/articles/2002/11/01/ the_dustbin_of_history_asian_values?page=full

Chapter 14

Aristotle (1981). *The Politics*. Trans. T.A. Sinclair. Rev. T.J. Saunders. London: Penguin.

Boesche, Roger (2002). "Moderate Machiavelli? Contrasting The Prince with the Arthashastra of Kautilya." *Critical Horizons* 3, 2: 253–76.

Boucher, David (1998). *Political Theories of International Relations: From Thucydides to the Present*. Oxford: Oxford University Press.

Cassels, Alan (1996). *Ideology and International Relations in the Modern World*. London: Routledge.

Clarke, Ian (2005). *Legitimacy and International Society*. Oxford: Oxford University Press.

Dunn, Frederick S. (1948). "The Scope of International Relations." *World Politics* 1, 1: 142–6.

Evans, Graham, and Jeffrey Newnham (1998). *The Penguin Dictionary of International Relations*. London: Penguin.

Ferguson, Niall (2003a). "Hegemony or Empire." *Foreign Affairs* 82, 5 (Sept.–Oct.): 154.

——— (2003b). *Empire: How Britain Made the Modern World*. London: Allen Lane.

Hall, John (ed.) (1986). *States in History*, Oxford: Basil Blackwell.

Hardt, Michael, and Negri Antonio (2000). *Empire*. Cambridge, MA: Harvard University Press.

Jackson, Robert H. (1990). *Quasi-States: Sovereignty, International Relations, and the Third World*. Cambridge: Cambridge University Press.

Kennedy, Paul (1989). *The Rise and Fall of the Great Powers: Economic Change and Military Conflict from 1500 to 2000*. London: Fontana.

King, Preston (1999). *The Ideology of Order: A Comparative Analysis of Jean Bodin and Thomas Hobbes*. London: Frank Cass.

Lawson, Stephanie (2002). *The New Agenda for International Relations: From Polarization to Globalization in World Politics?* Cambridge: Polity Press.

——— (2003). *International Relations*. Cambridge: Polity Press.

——— (2006). *Culture and Context in World Politics*. London: Palgrave Macmillan.

Migdal, Joel S. (1988). *Strong Societies and Weak States: State–Society Relations and State Capabilities in the Third World*. Princeton, NJ: Princeton University Press.

Miller, David (ed.) (1991). *The Blackwell Encyclopaedia of Political Thought*. Oxford: Blackwell Publishers.

Montevideo Convention on the Rights and Duties of States (1933). at www.molossia.org/montevideo.html; accessed 17 Nov. 2007.

Perkins, John (2007). *The Secret History of the American Empire: Economic Hit Men, Jackals, and the Truth About Global Corruption*. New York: Dutton.

Rotberg, Robert I., ed. (2003). "Failed States, Collapsed State, Weak States: Causes and Indicators." in Robert I. Rotberg, ed. *State Failure and State Weakness in a Time of Terror*. Cambridge, MA, and Washington, DC: World Peace Foundation and Brookings Institution Press.

Singer, Peter (2002). *One World: The Ethics of Globalisation*. Melbourne: Text Publishing.

Stern, Geoffrey (2000). *The Structure of International Society*. London: Pinter.

Chapter 15

Brown, Chris (2001). *Understanding International Relations*. London: Macmillan.

———, Terry Nardin, and Nicholas Rengger, eds (2002). *International Relations in Political Thought: Texts from the Ancient Greeks to the First World War*. Cambridge: Cambridge University Press.

Bull, Hedley (1997). *The Anarchical Society: A Study of Order in World Politics*. 2nd edn. Basingstoke: Macmillan.

Buzan, Barry (2004). *From International Society to World Society: English School Theory and the Social Structure of Globalisation*. Cambridge: Cambridge University Press.

Carr, Edward Hallett (1948 [1939]). *The Twenty Years' Crisis 1919–1939: An Introduction to the Study of International Relations*. London: Macmillan.

Clark, Ian (2005). *Legitimacy in International Society*. Oxford: Oxford University Press.

Dunne, Tim (1998). *Inventing English Society: A History of the English School*. Basingstoke: Macmillan.

Evans, Graham, and Jeffrey Newnham (1998). *The Penguin Dictionary of International Relations*. London: Penguin.

Grieco, Joseph M. (1988). "Anarchy and the Limits of Cooperation: A Realist Critique of the Newest Liberal Institutionalism." *International Organization* 42, 3: 485–507.

Herz, John M. (1950). "Idealist Internationalism and the Security Dilemma." *World Politics* 3, 2: 157–80.

Hochstrasser, T.J. (2000). *Natural Law Theories in the Early Enlightenment*. Cambridge: Cambridge University Press.

Kaplan, Morton A. (2005). *System and Process in International Politics*. Colchester: ECPR Press.

Keohane, Robert (1984). *After Hegemony: Cooperation and Discord in the World Political Economy*. Princeton, NJ: Princeton University Press.

———, and Joseph S. Nye (1977). *Power and Interdependence: World Politics in Transition*. Boston, MA: Little, Brown.

Kerr, John (2003). *Germany, 1918–39*. N.p.: Heinemann.

Lawson, Stephanie (2003). *International Relations*. Cambridge: Polity Press.

Lebow, Richard Ned (2007). "Classical Realism." Pp. 52–70 in Tim Dunne, Milja Kurki, and Steve Smith, eds. *International Relations Theories: Discipline and Diversity*. Oxford: Oxford University Press.

Linklater, Andrew, and Hidemi Suganami (2006). *The English School of International Relations: A Reassessment*. Cambridge: Cambridge University Press.

Little, Richard (1996). "The Growing Relevance of Pluralism?" In Steve Smith, Ken Booth, and Marysia Zalewski, eds. *International Theory: Positivism and Beyond*. Cambridge: Cambridge University Press.

MacDonald, David B. (2005). "Forgetting and Denying: Iris Chang, the Holocaust and the Challenge of Nanking", *International Politics* 42, 403–28.

Machiavelli, Niccolò (2005). *The Prince*. Trans. George Bull. London: Penguin.

Mearsheimer, John J. (2007). "Structural Realism." In Tim Dunne, Milja Kurki, and Steve Smith, eds. *Theories of International Relations: Discipline and Diversity*. Oxford: Oxford University Press.

Michalak, Stanley J. (2001). *A Primer in Power Politics*. Lanham, MD: Rowman & Littlefield.

Morgenthau, Hans J. (1948). *Politics Among Nations: The Struggle for Power and Peace*. New York: Alfred A. Knopf.

Nye, Joseph S., Jr (2005). *Understanding International Conflicts: An Introduction to Theory and History*. New York: Pearson Longman, 5th edn.

Rose, Gideon (1998). "Neoclassical Realism and Theories of Foreign Policy." *World Politics* 51, 1: 144–72.

Smith, Steve, Ken Booth, and Marysia Zalewski, eds (1996). *International Theory: Positivism and Beyond*. Cambridge: Cambridge University Press.

Thucydides (1972). *History of the Peloponnesian War*. Trans. Rex Warner. London: Penguin.

Waltz, Kenneth (1959). *Man, State and War*. New York: Colombia University Press.

——— (1979). *Theory of International Politics*. London: Addison Wesley.

Wheeler. Nicholas J. (2002). *Saving Strangers: Humanitarian Intervention in International Society*. Oxford: Oxford University Press.

Wight, Martin (1966). "Why Is There No International Theory?" In Martin Wight and Herbert Butterfield, eds. *Diplomatic Investigations: Essays in the Theory of International Politics*. London: Allen & Unwin.

Wight, Martin, and Herbert Butterfield, eds (1966). Diplomatic Investigations: *Essays in the Theory of International Politics*. London: Allen & Unwin.

Zimmern, Alfred (1997). *Prospects of Democracy and Other Essays*. London: Ayer Publishing.

Chapter 16

Adler, Emmanuel (1997). "Seizing the Middle Ground: Constructivism in World Politics." *European Journal of International Relations* 3, 3: 319–63.

Agathangelou, Anna, and Lily Ling (2004). "The House of IR: From Family Power Politics to the *Poisies* of Worldism." *International Studies Review* 6, 1: 21–49.

Barkawi, Tarak, and Mark Laffey (2006). "The Postcolonial Moment in Security Studies." *Review of International Studies* 32, 2: 329–52.

Berger, Peter L., and Thomas Luckman (1966). *The Social Construction of Reality: A Treatise in the Sociology of Knowledge*. New York: Anchor Books.

Blanchard, Eric M. (2003). "Gender, International Relations, and the Development of Feminist Security Theory." *Signs*: *Journal of Women in Culture and Society* 28: 1289–312.

Booth, Ken (1991). "Security and Emancipation." *Review of International Studies* 17, 4 (October).

———, ed. (2005). *Critical Security Studies and World Politics*. Boulder, CO, and London: Lynne Rienner.

Connell, R.W. (2005). *Masculinities*. 2nd edn. Cambridge: Polity Press.

Cox, Robert (1981). "Social Forces, States and World Orders: Beyond International Relations Theory." *Millennium Journal of International Studies* 10, 2: 126–55.

Dunne, Tim (1998). *Inventing International Society: A History of the English School*. London: Macmillan.

Dunne, Tim, Milja Kurki, and Steve Smith (eds) (2007). *Theories of International Relations: Discipline and Diversity*. Oxford: Oxford University Press.

Enloe, Cynthia (1983). *Does Khaki Become You?* London: Pluto Press.

——— (1993). "Bananas, Beaches and Bases." Pp. 441–64 in Linda S. Kauffman, ed. *American Feminist Thought at Century's End: A Reader*. Cambridge, MA: Blackwell Publishing.

———, and Marysia Zalewski (1999). "Feminist Theorizing from Bananas to Maneuvers: A Conversation with Cynthia Enloe." *International Feminist Journal of Politics* 1, 1: 138–46.

Foucault, Michel (1980). *Power/Knowledge: Selected Interviews and Other Writings*. Ed. and trans. Colin Gordon. Brighton: Harvester Press.

Frank, Andre Gunder (1967). *Capitalism and Underdevelopment in Latin America: Historical Studies of Chile and Brazil.* New York: Monthly Review Press.

——, and Barry K. Gills, eds (1996). *The World System: Five Hundred Years or Five Thousand?* London: Routledge.

Goldstein, Joshua S. (2001). *War and Gender: How Gender Shapes the War System and Vice Versa.* Cambridge: Cambridge University Press.

Gramsci, Antonio (1967). *The Modern Prince, and Other Writings.* New York: International Publishers.

Habermas, Jürgen (2003). "Toward a Cosmopolitan Europe." *Journal of Democracy* 14, 4: 86–100.

International Criminal Tribunal for Former Yugoslavia ICTY) (2004). *Appeals Chamber Judgement in the Case of the Prosecutor v. Radislav Krstic.* ICTY. 19 April. www.un.org/ icty/krstic/ Appeal/judgement/krs-aj040419e.pdf; accessed 13 Nov. 2007.

Katzenstein Peter J. (1996). *Cultural Norms and National Security: Police and Military in Postwar Japan.* Ithaca, NY: Cornell University Press.

Lapid, Yosef and Friedrich Kratochwil (eds) (1996). *The Return of Culture and Identity in IR Theory.* Boulder, CO: Lynne Rienner.

Lawson, Stephanie (2006). *Culture and Context in World Politics.* Basingstoke, Palgrave Macmillan.

Lenin, V. I. (1986). *Imperialism: The Highest Stage of Capitalism.* Moscow: Progress Publishers.

Linklater, Andrew (1998). *The Transformation of Political Community: Ethical Foundations of the Post-Westphalian Era.* Cambridge: Polity Press.

MacDonald, David B. (2002). *Balkan Holocausts? Serbian and Croatian Victim Centred Propaganda and the War in Yugoslavia.* Manchester: Manchester University Press.

Milbank, Dana and Claudia Deane (2003). "Hussein Link to 9/11 Lingers in Many Minds." *Washington Post.* 6 September: A1.

Mosse, George L. (1996). *The Image of Man: The Creation of Modern Masculinity.* New York: Oxford University Press.

Onuf, Nicholas (1989). *World of Our Making: Rules and Rule in Social Theory and International Relations.* Columbia: University of South Carolina Press.

Ruggie, John Gerard (1998). *Constructing the World Polity: Essays on International Institutionalization.* London: Routledge.

Smith, Steve (1996). "Positivism and Beyond." Pp. 11–44 in Steve Smith, Ken Booth, and Marysia Zalewski, eds. *International Theory: Positivism and Beyond.* Cambridge: Cambridge University Press.

—— (2000). "The Discipline of International Relations: Still an American Social Science?" *British Journal of Politics and International Relations* 2, 3: 374–402.

Tickner, Arlene (2003). "Seeing IR Differently: Notes from the Third World." *Millennium* 32, 2: 295–324.

Tickner, J. Ann (1992). *Gender in International Relations: Feminist Perspectives on Achieving Global Security,* New York: Columbia University Press.

—— and Laura Sjoberg (2007). "Feminism." Pp. 185–202 in Dunne, Kurki, and Smith, eds. *Theories of International Relations: Discipline and Diversity.* Oxford: Oxford University Press.

True, Jacquie (2005). "Feminism." Pp. 213–34 in Scott Burchill et al. *Theories of International Relations.* 3rd edn. Basingstoke: Palgrave Macmillan.

Wallerstein, Immanuel (1976). *The Modern World-System: Capitalist Agriculture and the Origins of the European World-Economy in the Sixteenth Century,* New York: Academic Press.

—— (2001). *Unthinking Social Science: The Limits of Nineteenth-Century Paradigms.* 2nd edn. Philadelphia: Temple University Press.

Wendt, Alexander (1992). "Anarchy Is What States Make of It: The Social Construction of Power Politics." *International Organization* 46, 2: 391–425.

—— (1996). "Identity and Structural Change in International Politics. Pp. 47–64 in Yosef Lapid and Friedrich Kratochwil, eds. *The Return of Culture and Identity in IR Theory.* Boulder, CO: Lynne Rienner.

Chapter 17

Best, Anthony, Jussi M. Hanhimaki, Kirsten E. Schulze, and Joseph A. Maiolo (2004). *An International History of the Twentieth Century.* London: Routledge.

Boutros-Ghali, Boutros (1992). *An Agenda for Peace.* Report of the Secretary-General pursuant to the statement adopted by the Summit Meeting of the Security Council on 31 January. New York: United Nations.

Cassels, Alan (1996). *Ideology and International Relations in the Modern World.* London: Routledge.

Clarke, Walter S., and Robert Gosende (2003). "Somalia: Can a Collapsed State Reconstitute Itself?" Pp. 129–58 in Robert I. Rotberg, ed. *State Failure and State Weakness in a Time of Terror.* Cambridge and Washington: World Peace Foundation and Brookings Institution Press.

Clausewitz, Carl von (1993). *On War.* Rev. edn. Trans. Michael Howard and Peter Paret. New York: Alfred A. Knopf.

Dunne, Tim, Milja Kurki, and Steve Smith (eds) (2007). *Theories of International Relations: Discipline and Diversity.* Oxford: Oxford University Press.

Evans, Graham, and Jeffrey Newnham (1998). *The Penguin Dictionary of International Relations.* London: Penguin.

Feldman, Linda (2003). "The Impact of Bush Linking 9/11 and Iraq." *Christian Science Monitor.* Online edn. 14 March. www.csmonitor.com/2003/0314/p02s01-woiq.html; accessed 9 June 2007.

Galtung, Johan (1969). "Violence, Peace, and Peace Research." *Journal of Peace Research* 6, 3: 167–91.

Independent Commission on International Development Issues (1980). *North–South: A Programme for Survival.* Report of the Independent Commission on International Development Issues. Boston: MIT Press.

Kent, John, and John W. Young (2003). *International Relations Since 1945: A Global History.* Oxford: Oxford University Press.

Lawson, Stephanie (ed.) (1995). *The New Agenda for International Security: Cooperating For Peace and Beyond.* St Leonards: Allen & Unwin.

MacDonald, David B. (2005). "Regionalism: New Zealand, Asia, the Pacific, and Australia" in Robert G. Patman and Chris Rudd (eds) *Sovereignty Under Siege? The Case of New Zealand*. London: Ashgate Press, 171–192

Mearsheimer, John J. (2007). "Structural Realism." In Tim Dunne, Milja Kurki, and Steve Smith, eds. *Theories of International Relations: Discipline and Diversity*. Oxford: Oxford University Press.

———, and Stephen S. Walt (2002). *Can Saddam Be Contained? History Says Yes*. Cambridge, MA: Harvard University. Belfer Center for Science and International Affairs International Security Program Occasional Paper. November.

Peña, Charles V. (2006). "A Smaller Military to Fight the War on Terror." *Orbis* 50, 2: 289–306.

Rotberg, Robert I. (ed.) (2003). *State Failure and State Weakness in a Time of Terror*. Cambridge and Washington: World Peace Foundation and Brookings Institution Press.

Shimko, Keither L. (2005). *International Relations: Themes and Perspectives*. Boston: Houghton Mifflin.

Sun Tzu (1963). *The Art of War*. Trans. Samuel B. Griffith. Oxford: Clarendon Press.

United Nations (1945). Preamble to the Charter, as adopted 26 June. www.un.org/en/documents/charter/preamble.shtml.

United Nations Development Program (1994). *Human Development Report: 1994*. New York: United Nations.

US Department of Defense (2001). *Quadrennial Defense Review*.

Weiss, Thomas G. (2003). "The Illusion of UN Security Council Reform." *Washington Quarterly* 26, 4: 147–61.

Yergin, Daniel (2006). "Ensuring Energy Security." *Foreign Affairs* 86, 3 (March–April): 69–82.

Young, John W., and John Kent (2004). *International Relations Since 1945: A Global History*. Oxford: Oxford University Press.

Chapter 18

Butterfield, Herbert (1966). "The New Diplomacy and Historical Diplomacy" in Butterfield and Wight (1966): 181–92.

———, and Martin Wight, eds (1966). *Diplomatic Investigation: Essays in the Theory of International Politics*. London: George Allen & Unwin.

Bercuson, David (2003)."Canada–US Defence Relations Post-11 September." In Carment, Hampson, and Hillmer, eds (2003). *Coping with the American Colossus*. Toronto: Oxford University Press.

Carment, David, Fen Hampson, and Norman Hillmer (2003), *Coping with the American Colossus*. Toronto: Oxford University Press.

Cioffi-Revilla, Claudio and Todd Landman (1999). "Evolution of Maya Polities in the Ancient Mesoamerican System." *International Studies Quarterly* 43, 4: 559–98.

Corsi, Jerome (2006). "Meet Robert Pastor: Father of the North American Union." 25 July. www.humanevents.com/article.php?id=16189.

Craig, Gordon A., and Alexander L. George (1990). *Force and Statecraft: Diplomatic Problems of Our Times*. 2nd edn. New York: Oxford University Press.

Dannreuther, Roland (ed.) (2004). *European Union Foreign and Security Policy: Towards a Neighbourhood Strategy*. London: Routledge.

——— (2004). "Introduction: Setting the Framework." Pp. 1–11 in Dannreuther, ed. *European Union Foreign and Security Policy: Towards a Neighbourhood Strategy*. London: Routledge.

Evans, Graham, and Jeffrey Newnham (1988). *Penguin Dictionary of International Relations*. London: Penguin.

Farrell, Mary (2005). "EU External Relations: Exporting the EU Model of Governance." *European Foreign Affairs Review* 10, 4: 451–62.

Freedman, Lawrence (2006). "The Special Relationship: Then and Now." *Foreign Affairs* 85, 3 (May–June): 61–74.

Gaddis, John Lewis, Philip H. Gordon, Ernest R. May, and Jonathan Rosenberg, eds (1999). *Cold War Statesmen Confront the Bomb: Nuclear Diplomacy Since 1945*. New York: Oxford University Press.

Gaenslen, Fritz (1997). "Advancing Cultural Explanations." Pp. 265–79 in Valerie M. Hudson, ed. *Culture and Foreign Policy*. Boulder, Co: Lynne Reinner.

Granatstein, J.L (2007). *Whose War Is It?: How Canada Can Survive in the Post-9/11 World*. Toronto: HarperCollins.

Henriksen, Alan K. (2006). *What Can Public Diplomacy Achieve?* Discussion Papers in Diplomacy. The Hague: Institute of International Relations. www.clingendael.nl/publications/2006/20060900_cdsp_ paper_dip_b.pdf ; accessed 20 July 2007.

Howard, Michael (1966). "War as an Instrument of Policy." Pp. 193–205 in Herbert Butterfield and Martin Wight, eds. *Diplomatic Investigation: Essays in the Theory of International Politics*. London: George Allen & Unwin.

Hudson, Valerie M., ed. (1997). *Culture and Foreign Policy*. Boulder, CO: Lynne Reinner.

Hui, Victoria Tin-bor (2005). *War and State Formation in Ancient China and Early Modern Europe*. Cambridge: Cambridge University Press.

Jowett, Garth S., and Victoria O'Donnell (2006). *Propaganda and Persuasion*. Thousand Oaks, CA: Sage.

Kautilya (n.d.). *Arthashastra*. www.mssu.edu/projectsouthasia/history/ primarydocs/Arthashastra/BookI.htm.

Langhorne, Richard (2000). "Full Circle: New Principals and Old Consequences in the Modern Diplomatic System." *Diplomacy and Statecraft* 11, 1: 33–46.

Lawson, Stephanie (2006). *Culture and Context in World Politics*. Basingstoke: Palgrave Macmillan.

Manners, Ian (2006). "Normative Power Europe Reconsidered: Be-yond the Crossroads. *Journal of European Public Policy* 13, 2: 182–99.

Mattingley, Garrett (1955). *Renaissance Diplomacy*. Boston, MA: Houghton Mifflin.

Melissen, Jan (2003). *Summit Diplomacy Coming of Age* (Discussion Papers in Diplomacy). The Hague, Netherlands Institute of International Relations. www.nbiz.nl/publications/2003/20030500_cli_paper_dip_issue86.pdf; accessed 15 July 2007.

Miller, David (ed.) (1991). *The Blackwell Encyclopaedia of Political Thought*. Oxford: Blackwell Publishers.

Mockaitis, Thomas R. (2003). "Winning Hearts and Minds in the 'War on Terrorism.'" *Small Wars and Insurgencies* 14, 1: 21–38.

Nye, Joseph S. Jr (2004). *Soft Power: The Means to Success in World Politics*. New York: Public Affairs.

———— (2011). "The War on Soft Power." *Foreign Policy*. 12 April; http://www.foreignpolicy.com/articles/2011/04/12/the_war_on_soft_power?page=full.

Obama, Barack, and Cameron, David (2011). "Shoulder to Shoulder Against Terror." *The Australian*. 25 May.

Pastor, Robert (2002). "A North American Community." A Background Paper for The Trilateral Commission. Toronto. 1–2 Nov. www.trilateral.org/download/file/FNAI/pastor02.pdf.

Tansen, San (2003). *Buddhism, Diplomacy and Trade: The Realignment of Sino-Indian Relations 600–1400*. Honolulu: University of Hawaii Press.

Whittington, Les (2011). "Investors Bail Out After Germany Says No Silver Bullet for Europe's Debt Mess." *Toronto Star*. 17 Oct.

Web:

ec.europa.eu/external_relations/cfsp/intro/index.htm

www.jimmycarterlibrary.org/documents/campdavid/accords. phtml

www.mi5.gov.uk/output/Page244.html

www.mssu.edu/projectsouthasia/history/primarydocs/ Artha-shastra/BookI.htm

www.yale.edu/lawweb/avalon/monroe.htm

Chapter 19

Abi-Saab, Georges, ed. (1981). *The Concept of International Organization*. Paris: UNESCO.

Alston, Philip (2006). "Reconceiving The UN Human Rights Regime: Challenges Confronting the New UN Human Rights Council." *Melbourne Journal of International Law* 7, 1. bar. austlii.edu.au/au/journals/MelbJIL/2006/.

Archer, Clive (1983). *International Organizations*. London: Allen & Unwin.

Butler, Geoffrey G., and Simon MacCoby (2003). *Development of International Law*. Union, NJ: Lawbook Exchange.

Diehl, Paul F., ed. (2005). *The Politics of Global Governance: International Organizations in an Interdependent World*. 3rd edn. Boulder, CO: Lynne Rienner.

———— (2005). "Introduction." Pp. 3–8 in *The Politics of Global Governance: International Organizations in an Interdependent World*. Boulder, CO: Lynne Rienner.

Dishman, Chris (2005). "The Leaderless Nexus: When Crime and Terror Converge." *Studies in Conflict and Terrorism* 28, 3: 237–52.

Gerbet, Pierre (1981). "Rise and Development of International Organizations." Pp. 27–49 in Georges Abi-Saab, ed. *The Concept of International Organization*. Paris: UNESCO.

Gordenker, Leon (2005). *The UN Secretary-General and Secretariat*. London: Routledge.

————, and Thomas G. Weiss (1996). "Pluralizing Global Governance: Analytical Approaches and Dimensions."

In Thomas G. Weiss and Leon Gordenker, eds. *NGOs, the UN and Global Governance*. Boulder, CO: Lynne Rienner.

Haas, Ernst B. (1990). *When Knowledge Is Power: Three Models of Change in International Organizations*. Berkeley: University of California Press.

Harle, Vilho (1998). *Ideas of Social Order in the Ancient World*. Westport, CT: Greenwood Press.

Kaldor, Mary (2006). *New and Old Wars: Organized Violence in a Global Era*. 2nd edn. Cambridge: Polity Press.

Keohane, Robert O. (1993). "The Analysis of International Regimes: Towards a European-American Research Programme." In Volker Rittberger and Peter Mayer, eds. *International Regime Theory*. Oxford: Oxford University Press.

Klabbers, Jan (2003). *An Introduction to International Institutional Law*. Cambridge: Cambridge University Press.

Krasner, Stephen (1983). "Structural Causes and Regime Consequences: Regimes as Intervening Variables." In Krasner, ed. *International Regimes*. Ithaca: Cornell University Press.

MacDonald, David B. (2008). *Identity Politics in the Age of Genocide: The Holocaust and Historical Representation*, London: Routledge.

———— (2009). *Thinking History, Fighting Evil: Neoconservatives and the Perils of Historical Analogy in American Politics*. Lanham, MD: Lexington/Rowman & Littlefield.

Midgley, Claire (1992). *Women Against Slavery: The British Campaigns, 1780–1870*. London: Routledge.

Naím, Moisés (2007). "What Is a Gongo?" *Foreign Policy* May–June www.foreignpolicy.com/story/cms.php?story_id¼ 3818&fpsrc¼ ealert070430.

Sanderson, Thomas M. (2004). "Transnational Terror and Organized Crime: Blurring the Lines." *SAIS Review* 24, 1: 49–61.

Rittberger, Volker, and Bernhard Zangl (2006). *International Organization: Polity, Politics and Policies*, Basingstoke: Palgrave.

————, and Peter Mayer, eds (1993). *International Regime Theory*. Oxford: Oxford University Press.

Turner, Dale (2006). *This is Not a Peace Pipe*. Toronto: University of Toronto Press.

Union of International Associations (2006). *Yearbook of International Organizations 2005/2006*, 12th edn. www.uia.org/statistics/organizations/types-2004.pdf.

Weiss, Thomas G., and Leon Gordenker, eds. *NGOs, the UN and Global Governance*. Boulder, CO: Lynne Rienner.

Williams, Phil (1997). "Transnational Criminal Organizations and International Security." Pp. 315–37 in John Arquilla and David Ronfeldt, eds. *In Athena's Camp: Preparing for Conflict in the Information Age*. Santa Monica, CA: Rand Corporation.

Web:

nobelprize.org/nobel_prizes/peace/laureates/1963/red-cross-history.html

www.antislavery.org/

www.icj-cij.org

www.redcross.int/en/history/not_nobel.asp

www.un.org

Chapter 20

David N. Balaam and Michael Veseth (2005). *Introduction to International Political Economy.* 3rd edn. Upper Saddle River, NJ: Pearson Education.

Bouton, Marshall M., et al. (2010). *Constrained Internationalism: Adapting to New Realities.* Chicago: Chicago Council on Global Affairs.

Cohn, Theodore H. (2005). *Global Political Economy: Theory and Practice.* 3rd edn. New York: Pearson Longman.

Cox, Robert W. (1981). "Social Forces, States and World Orders: Beyond International Relations Theory." *Millennium: Journal of International Studies* 10: 126–55.

Crane, George T., and Abla Amawi, eds (1991). *The Theoretical Evolution of International Political Economy: A Reader.* Oxford: Oxford University Press.

European Economic Advisory Group (2007). *Report on the European Economy.* Press release at www.cesifo-group.de/portal/page/portal/ifoHome/e-pr/e1pz/_generic_press_item_detail?p_itemid=4485615; accessed 4 April 2012.

Flynn, Dennis O. and Arturo Giráldez (1995). "Born with a 'Silver Spoon': The Origin of World Trade in 1571." *Journal of World History* 6: 201–21.

Galbraith, J.K. (1984). "Comment." *National Review* 36, 6: 39–42.

Gilpin, Robert, with Jean M. Gilpin (1987). *The Political Economy of International Relations.* Princeton, NJ: Princeton University Press.

Goss, Joss, and Bruce Lindquist (1995). "Conceptualizing International Labor Migration: A Structuration Perspective." *International Migration Review* 29, 2: 317–51.

Griffin, Penny (2007). "Refashioning IPE: What and How Gender Analysis Teaches International (Global) Political Economy." *Review of International Political Economy* 14, 4: 719–36.

Griffiths, Martin, and Terry O'Callaghan (2002). *International Relations: The Key Concepts.* London: Routledge.

Haggard, Stephan (1997). "The Political Economy of Regionalism in Asia and the Americas." Pp. 2049 in Edward D. Mansfield and Helen V. Milner, eds. *The Political Economy of Regionalism.* New York: Columbia University Press.

Hawkins, William R. (1984). "Neomercantilism: Is There a Case for Tariffs?" *National Review* 36, 6: 25–39.

Hirst, Paul, and Graeme Thompson (1999). *Globalization in Question.* 2nd edn. Cambridge: Polity Press.

Howe, Anthony (1997). *Free Trade and Liberal England 1846–1946.* Oxford: Oxford University Press.

Kaur, Amarjit (2007). "International Labour Migration in Southeast Asia: Governance of Migration and Women Domestic Workers." *Intersections: Gender, History and Culture in the Asian Context* 15 (May).

Keohane, Robert O. (2001). *After Hegemony: Cooperation and Discord in the World Political Economy.* Princeton, NJ: Prince-ton University Press.

Lawson, Stephanie (2002). "After the Fall: International Theory and the State." In Stephanie Lawson, ed. *The New Agenda for International Relations.* Cambridge: Polity Press.

———, ed. (2002). *The New Agenda for International Relations.* Cambridge: Polity Press.

List, Frederich (1991). "Political and Cosmopolitical Economy" in George T. Crane and Abla Amawi, eds. "Introduction: Theories of International Political Economy." Pp. 48–54 in *The Theoretical Evolution of International Political Economy: A Reader.* Oxford: Oxford University Press.

Lawler, Kevin, and Hamid Seddighi (2001). *International Economics: Theories, Themes and Debates.* Harlow: Pearson Education.

Magnusson, Lars (1994). *Mercantilism: The Shaping of an Economic Language.* London: Routledge.

Miller, David, ed. (1991). *The Blackwell Encyclopaedia of Political Thought.* Oxford: Blackwell Publishers.

Moghadan, Valentine M. (2005). *Globalizing Women: Transnational Feminist Networks.* Baltimore, MD: Johns Hopkins University Press.

——— (1999). "Gender and Globalization: Female Labor and Women's Mobilization." *Journal of World-Systems Research* 5, 2: 367–88.

O'Brien, Robert, Anne Marie Goetz, Jan Aart Scholte, and Marc Williams (2000). *Contesting Global Governance: Multilateral Economic Institutions and Global Social Movements.* Cambridge, Cambridge University Press.

Ohmae, Kenichi (1993). "The Rise of the Region-State." *Foreign Affairs* 72, 2: 78–87.

Palan, Ronen (2000). "New Trends in Global Political Economy." Pp. 7–18 in Ronen Palan, ed. *Global Political Economy: Contemporary Theories.* London: Routledge.

Palat, Ravi Arvind (1996). "Pacific Century: Myth or Reality." *Theory and Society* 25, 3: 303–47.

Peterson, V. Spike (2003). *A Critical Rewriting of Global Political Economy: Integrating Reproductive, Productive and Virtual Economies.* London: Routledge.

Pettman, Ralph (1996). *Understanding International Political Economy: With Readings for the Fatigued.* Boulder, Co: Lynne Rienner.

Rachman, Gideon (2011). "Think Again: American Decline." *Foreign Policy* January–February. www.foreignpolicy.com/articles/2011/01/02/think_again_american_decline?page=0,0

Ricardo, David (1821). *On the Principles of Political Economy and Taxation.* 3rd edn. London: John Murray.

Ronen Palan (ed.) (2000). *Global Political Economy: Contemporary Theories.* London: Routledge.

Ruggie, John Gerard (1982). "International Regimes, Transactions, and Change: Embedded Liberalism in the Postwar Economic Order." *International Organization* 36: 379–415.

Spero, Joan E. and Jeffrey A. Hart (1997). *The Politics of International Economic Relations.* 5th edn. New York: St Martin's Press.

Strange, Susan (1970). "International Relations and International Economics: A Case of Mutual Neglect." *International Affairs* 46, 2: 304–15.

Tomlinson, John (1999). *Globalization and Culture.* Chicago: Chicago University Press.

Viner, Jacob (1949). "Power Versus Plenty as Objectives of Foreign Policy in the Seventeenth and Eighteenth Centuries. *World Politics* 1, 2: 1–29.

Watson, Alison M.S. (2004). *An Introduction to International Political Economy.* London: Continuum.

Wilkinson, Rorden (2000). *Multilateralism and the World Trade Organisation: The Architecture and Extension of International Trade Regulation.* London: Routledge.

Williams, David, and Tom Young (1994). "Governance, the World, Bank and Liberal Theory." *Political Studies* 42, 1: 84–100.

Woods, Ngaire (1998). "Editorial Introduction: Globalization: Definitions, Debates and Implications." *Oxford Development Studies* 26, 1: 5–13.

Web:

www.fco.gov.uk
www.brettonwoods.org/institutions.html

Conclusion

Arkhipov, Ilya, and Henry Meyer (2011). "Putin Seeks Russian Presidency, Eyes Job Swap With Medvedev." *Business Week.* 25 Sept.; www.businessweek.com/news/2011-09-25/putin-seeks-russian-presidency-eyes-job-swap-with-medvedev.html.

Bercuson, David, and Barry Cooper (1991). *Deconfederation : Canada without Quebec.* Toronto: Key Porter Books.

Chakrabarty, Dipak (2000). *Provincializing Europe.* Princeton, NJ: Princeton University Press.

Dhani, S.L. (2008). *Value Education: Based on all the Religions of the World.* Gyan Publishing House.

Friedrichs, Jörg (2001). "The Meaning of New Medievalism." *European Journal of International Relations* 7, 4: 475–502.

Fukuyama, Francis (1992). *The End of History and the Last Man.* London: Penguin.

Rapley, John (2006). "The New Middle Ages." *Foreign Affairs* 85, 3: 95–103.

Scholte, Jan Art (2005). *Globalization: A Critical Introduction.* 2nd edn. Basingstoke: Palgrave.

Slaughter, Anne-Marie (1997). "The Real New World Order." *Foreign Affairs* 76, 5 (Sept.–Oct.): 183–97.

Smith, Steve (2004). "Singing Our World into Existence: International Relations Theory and September 11." *International Studies Quarterly* 48, 3: 499–515.

West, Cornel (1991). "Decentring Europe: A Memorial Lecture for James Snead." *Critical Quarterly* 33, 1.

Glossary

Agency In social science literature, "agency" is used to refer both to the human action that makes something happen and to the capacity for such action. The idea of agency is often contrasted with the idea of impersonal causes (historical, economic, etc.) over which human actors have little control. Hence the frequent use of the combined term "structure-agency" in situations where it not clear whether the primary causes are impersonal background factors or human actions.

Alternative member model A hybrid voting system that combines the strengths of **majoritarianism** and **proportional representation**: votes are cast both for individual candidates within a constituency and for a general list of candidates from separate parties.

Amoral familism The promotion of family interests above all other moral considerations; the term was coined by Banfield to describe social relations in Sicily and was later used by Putnam.

Anarchy The absence of political rule or sovereign authority. In realist and neorealist IR theory, the international sphere is considered anarchic because there is no sovereign authority standing above the individual states that make up the sphere. States therefore have no choice but to defend themselves.

Anthropocentric Human-centred, prioritizing the interests of humans over those of all other life forms.

Arrow's impossibility theorem A mathematical theorem, formulated by the economist Kenneth Arrow, that shows the impossibility of determining the "optimal" ranking of preferences when none of the options voted on receives an absolute majority of the votes.

Authoritarian A form of rule that restricts personal liberty and is not accountable to the public.

Authority Legitimate power, in the sense that the individual or group exercising it is regarded as having the right to do so.

Balance of power A system of relations between states in which the goal is to maintain an equilibrium of power (usually military and economic), thus preventing the dominance of any one state.

Behaviouralism An approach to the study of social phenomena based on the methods used in the natural sciences. Objective measurement of the social world was the goal, and values were considered to have no place in social enquiry.

Bicameralism A system of government in which the legislature is divided between two separate chambers. Examples include Canada (House of Commons and Senate), the US (House of Representatives and Senate), and the UK (House of Commons and House of Lords).

Bipolarity In international politics, a situation in which two states possess a preponderance of economic, military, and political power and influence either internationally or in a particular region. During the Cold War the two "poles" were the US and the USSR.

Bourgeoisie Term associated with Marxist analysis, referring to the merchant and/or propertied class that possesses essential economic power and therefore has control over the working class or proletariat.

Cartel party A type of political party that has a relatively limited membership and is dominated by professional politicians; compare **mass party**.

Citizenship The state of being a citizen, with the social and political rights required to participate in state decision-making.

Civic culture The particular set of attitudes that allow citizens to feel capable of taking an active part in politics.

Civic nationalism Loyalty to the institutions and values of a particular political community; sometimes presented as a more moderate form of nationalism.

Civil society Broadly, the community of citizens; today, however, the term is often used specifically to refer to institutions such as interest groups and non-governmental organizations, which stand in an intermediary position between the individual and the state. See also **International civil society.**

Civilization The largest possible grouping of individuals with shared religious, linguistic, or cultural features.

Class analysis Analysis that centres on socio-economic class (proletariat, peasantry, bourgeoisie, aristocracy); the type of political analysis associated with traditional Marxism.

Cold War A term for the states system as it existed between the end of the Second World War in 1945 and the collapse of Soviet communism in the early 1990s. On one side was the US, the dominant power in the West; on the other, the Soviet Union, the dominant power in the East.

Colonialism A mode of domination involving the subjugation of one population group and their territory to another, usually established by settling the territory with sufficient people from the colonizing group to impose direct or indirect rule over the indigenous population and to maintain control over resources and external relations. Colonialism is a common manifestation of **imperialism** but is not identical with it.

Communitarianism A school of thought that emphasizes the individual's particular community as the source of his or her identity, rights, and duties; often contrasted with **cosmopolitanism.**

Concert of Europe A largely informal agreement among the major powers of nineteenth-century Europe to act together on matters of mutual concern. It developed following the Congress of Vienna (1814–15) after the defeat of Napoleon Bonaparte, and generally took the form of diplomatic meetings and conferences aimed at the peaceful resolution of differences.

Consociational democracy A form of rule practised in some divided societies whereby the elites of different communities within the society share power.

Constituency An electoral district.

Constitution The body of principles governing relations between a state and its population, including the understandings that are involved. In most countries these principles are codified in a single document.

Constitutionalism The principle that assigns a special significance to constitutions and rule of law in national life.

Constructivism The notion that the "reality" of the world around us is constructed intersubjectively, through social interaction that gives meaning to material objects and practices; thus "reality" is not simply an objective truth detached from a social base. Sometimes called "social constructivism."

Coordinated market economies (organized capitalism) Economies in which the state plays a larger role in the coordination of market activities than it does in liberal Anglo-American economies; typically found in continental Europe.

Corporatism Traditionally, "corporatism" has referred to a top-down model (e.g., fascism) in which the state incorporates economic interests in order to control them and civil society in general. "Modern corporatism" refers to a more recent model in which governments incorporate key economic interests—notably trade unions and business groups—into the decision-making process.

Cosmopolitan democracy A system based on popular control of supranational institutions and processes.

Cosmopolitanism The idea that humans ought to be regarded as a single moral community to which universal principles apply, irrespective of national boundaries.

Cultural pluralism The existence in a single society of different behavioural norms determined by culture. From a normative perspective, cultural pluralism may be either desirable or undesirable.

Deliberative democracy A model of democracy based on the principle that discussion and debate among citizens lead to rational, legitimate, and altruistic decision-making.

Democracy A political system based on elected, representative self-government by citizens. Normally democracy also includes changes of government through regular elections, various institutional checks and balances, and some form of civil society capable of articulating the people's political and social preferences.

Democratic elitism A model of democracy in which voters have the opportunity to choose between competing teams of leaders; an attempt, most closely associated with Joseph Schumpeter, to reconcile elitism with democracy.

Détente The easing of tensions between the US and USSR that began with the Nixon presidency in 1969 and continued until 1979; from the French for "relaxation."

Deterrence The theory that the possession of powerful weapons will deter aggression by other countries. During the Cold War, nuclear deterrence was a widely accepted military strategy.

Developmental state A state that gives priority to rapid economic development and uses carrots and sticks to induce private economic institutions to comply; Japan is a classic example.

Direct democracy A system in which the people rule directly (not through representatives).

Duverger's Law The idea (proposed by the French political scientist Maurice Duverger) that first-past-the-post electoral systems lead to two-party systems.

Ecocentrism An ethic that removes humans from the centre of the moral universe and accords intrinsic value to non-human parts of nature.

Ecological modernization A version of the "sustainable development" principle according to which liberal capitalist societies can be reformed in an environmentally sustainable way.

Ecologism An ideology that stresses the interdependence of all forms of life; often connotes the moral dethroning of humans.

Elitism In a normative sense, the rule of the most able; in an empirical sense, rule by a group that is beyond popular control.

Emancipation which denotes a normative aspiration to liberate people from unfair economic, social and political conditions; a common theme in Critical Theory.

Embedded autonomy A term used to describe the position of state economic policy-makers in **developmental states,** who are insulated from short-term pressures but sufficiently embedded in the society to be aware of its needs and priorities.

Empire A system in which one country or centre of power directly or indirectly dominates and controls other, weaker countries.

Empirical analysis Analysis of factual **information** (what is, as opposed to what ought to be).

Enlightenment The European intellectual and cultural movement that emphasized the use of reason in the search for knowledge and human progress.

Epistemology A theory of knowledge concerned with establishing what can be known about what exists.

Ethnic cleansing A term coined during the breakup of the former Yugoslavia to refer to efforts to "cleanse" (i.e., rid) a particular area of people from a certain ethnic group either by driving them out or by murdering them.

Ethnic nationalism Loyalty to a shared inheritance based on culture, language, or religion.

Ethnocentricity The tendency to see and interpret the world primarily from the perspective of one's own cultural, ethnic, or national group; often entails a tendency to regard one's own culture as superior, or at least preferable, to others.

False consciousness A belief or perspective that prevents someone from assessing the true nature of a situation. The concept reflects the Marxist idea that capitalism makes it impossible for most people living within the system to see the true nature of their exploitation. Power theorists such as Steven Lukes have also used it to refer to a more general inability to understand one's circumstances.

Federalism The principle that different territorial units within a state have the authority to make certain policies without interference from the centre.

First Nations One of three officially recognized Aboriginal peoples of Canada, alongside Inuit and Métis.

Fordism A form of large-scale mass-production that was homogeneous both in terms of the products made and also in terms of the repetitive jobs that it required workers to perform.

General will The concept, associated with Rousseau, that the state ought to promote an altruistic morality rather than the selfish interests of individuals.

Global governance An extension of the concept of **governance**, referring; loosely to the "architecture" constituted by various authoritative political, social, and economic structures and actors that interconnect and interact in the absence of actual "government" in the global sphere.

Global justice The application of principles of justice at a global (as opposed to national) level.

Global South A term for the poorer, underdeveloped countries of the world (most of which lie south of the equator), more or less corresponding to what used to be called the "Third World." Its counterpart is the "North"—a term that is sometimes used as an alternative designation for "the West."

Globalization The ongoing movement towards economic, political, social, and cultural interdependence that has, for good or ill, reduced the autonomy of sovereign states.

Good governance A set of principles formulated by international financial institutions to make the government of developing states fair, effective, and free from corruption.

Governance A term often preferred now to "government" since it reflects the broader nature of modern government which includes not just the traditional institutions of government but also the many other factors that may influence the decisions that steer society, such as subnational and supranational institutions, the workings of the market, and the role of interest groups.

Harm principle The principle, associated with John Stuart Mill, that all actions should be allowed unless they harm others.

Hegemony Political, social, and economic domination. In IR "hegemony" may refer to the general dominance of a particular country over others. The concept was developed by Antonio Gramsci and is used to theorize relations of domination and subordination in both domestic and international spheres.

Human nature A general term for innate and immutable human characteristics. Hobbes believed that the competitive and self-serving nature of humans necessitated an all-powerful state, while Marx suggested that human character was shaped by the social and economic structure of society.

Humanitarian intervention Direct intervention by one country, or a group of countries, in the internal affairs of another country, for humanitarian reasons (e.g., to prevent genocide). See also **Intervention.**

Idealism This term has invited numerous interpretations in philosophy, politics, and International Relations. In IR it is usually taken to refer to a particular school of liberal thought that emerged in the wake of the First World War and sought positive change in world affairs, including the elimination of warfare. It remains an appropriate designation for any school of thought in IR that envisions a world order in which peace and justice are the norm.

Illiberal democracy A state in which elections are held but there is relatively little protection of rights and liberties, and state control over the means of communication means that the party in power generally remains there.

Imperialism The exercise of power by one group over another; from a Latin verb meaning literally "to command." "Imperialism" is sometimes used as a synonym for **colonialism**, but is broader because it does not necessarily involve actual physical occupation of the territory in question or direct rule over the subjugated people.

Insider groups Interest groups that enjoy a privileged relationship with government.

Institutions Regular patterns of behaviour that provide stability and regularity in social life; sometimes these patterns are given organizational form with specific rules of membership and behaviour.

Interdependence In IR, the (primarily liberal) notion that states are increasingly interconnected through a web of relations, especially in the economic field, and that this makes warfare less desirable as a foreign policy strategy. The concept of **complex interdependence** simply introduces more variables to the equation, deepening the complexity of interdependence and strengthening the case for a more pluralistic approach to IR than neorealist thought allows for.

Interest groups Groups within civil society that seek to press specific interests on governments (also known as pressure groups).

Intergenerational justice Principles of justice relating to non-contemporaries; e.g., between parents and children, or those living now and those still to be born.

International civil society Broadly, the realm of non-state actors, including interest groups and voluntary associations, in the international sphere.

International regime The principles, norms, rules, and procedures around which groups of actors in certain areas of international relations converge. An example is the international human rights regime. The concept was developed by Stephen Krasner.

International society A society of states characterized by peaceful working relations; a concept associated with the English School of International Relations, which proposed that the anarchic nature of the international sphere did not preclude cooperation.

Internationalism Belief in the benefits of international political and economic cooperation; may also refer to a movement that advocates practical action in support of such cooperation.

Intervention In IR, usually refers to direct intervention by one or more states in the internal affairs of another, by either military or non-military means. Humanitarian intervention is claimed to have a primarily *humanitarian* purpose, such as intervening to prevent genocide.

Intragenerational justice Principles of justice relating to contemporaries, that is, people who are living at the same time.

Iron triangles Groups of politicians, officials, and outside experts who regularly formulate government policy in particular issue areas to the exclusion of wider social groups.

Issue networks Looser groups of officials and outsiders who regularly share ideas in particular policy areas.

Legal positivism A form of legal theory according to which law is simply what the state says it is.

Liberal democracy A state characterized by free and fair elections, universal suffrage, a relatively high degree of personal liberty, and protection of individual rights.

Liberal institutionalism Focuses attention on the ability of international institutions to alleviate the negative effects of anarchy in the international system.

Machtpolitik See **Power politics**.

Mass parties Political parties (typical of the first half of the twentieth century) that attracted millions of grass-roots members.

Mercantilism The economic theory that trade generates wealth and hence that it is in the interest of government to promote exports and restrict imports; from the Latin for "merchant."

Meritocratic theory of justice A theory that advocates distributing resources to those who display some merit, such as innate ability, or willingness to work, and therefore deserve to be rewarded.

Metanarrative A "grand narrative," a comprehensive philosophical or historical explanation of the social and political world presented as ultimate truth.

Methodology A particular way in which knowledge is produced. Methodologies vary considerably depending on the field—history, anthropology, language, biology, medicine, etc. Different methodologies invariably incorporate a particular set of assumptions and rationales about the nature of knowledge, although these are not always stated explicitly.

Modernity A temporal and cultural phenomenon linked in part to the rise of industrialization in Europe and North America and in part to profound changes in social and political thought associated with the intellectual movement known as the Enlightenment.

Monism The view that there are no fundamental divisions in phenomena.

Nation A named community, often referred to as "a people," usually occupying a homeland and sharing one or more cultural elements, such as a common history, language, religion, or set of customs. Nations may or may not have states of their own.

Nation-building The process in which a state is created and then its leaders attempt to mould its sometimes quite diverse groups of inhabitants into a coherent, functional "nation."

National interest The concept (closely associated with *raison d'état* and power politics) that the interests of the state (or at least of one's own state) take precedence over any other consideration in the international sphere. Although it is a foundational concept in realist approaches, "national interest" is just as easily used to justify idealist approaches; this suggests that what is actually in the national interest may be highly contested.

Nationalism In politics and IR, the doctrine or ideology according to which "the nation" is entitled to political autonomy, usually in a state of its own.

Natural law Law conceived as both universal and eternal, applying to all people in all places and at all times because it derives from either "nature" or God (as opposed to local laws created within specific communities).

Natural rights Rights that all humans are said to possess, irrespective of the particular legal and political systems under which they live.

Negative liberty Liberty that can be increased by removing external obstacles, such as physical constraints or legal prohibitions.

New liberalism A version of liberalism that advocates a more positive role for the state than classical liberalism. Argues that the state, in correcting the inequities of the market, can increase liberty by creating greater opportunities for individuals to achieve their goals.

New medievalism A system of governance recalling Europe in the Middle Ages, in an overlapping array of local, national, and supranational institutions compete for authority.

New Public Management An approach to the reform of government bureaucracies, introduced in the 1990s, that sought to apply the market-oriented methods of business administration to the public sector.

Night-watchman state A model in which the state concentrates on ensuring security (external and internal), playing little role in civil society and allowing the economic market to operate relatively unhindered.

Non-governmental organizations (NGOs) Organizations that are independent of government, whether at the local, national, or international level.

Normative analysis The basis of political philosophy. Normative analysis is concerned with what "ought to be," as opposed to what "is." Thus instead of asking whether democracy, or freedom, or a pluralist state exists, it asks whether these things are desirable.

Ontology The study of what exists, of what there is to know. For example, is there a political world out there that is capable of being observed? Or is the reality, at least to some degree, created by the meanings or ideas that we impose on it?

Organized capitalism See **Coordinated market economies**.

Original position A term used by John Rawls to denote a hypothetical situation in which individuals under a "veil of ignorance" as to their personal circumstances would decide which rules of justice should govern the society in which they will live.

Outsider groups Interest groups that enjoy no special relationship with the government and thus seek to press their case from the outside.

Parliamentarianism The principle that governments are formed by prime ministers (as opposed to heads of state) and are therefore primarily responsible to parliament.

Paternalism The practice, often associated with conservatism, of restricting individuals' liberty "for their own good."

Patriarchy Male domination and oppression of women.

Patrimonial state A state in which power flows directly from the leader and political elites take advantage of their connections to enrich themselves and their clients.

Perestroika The attempted restructuring of the Soviet political system under President Mikhail Gorbachev in the late 1980s.

Pluralism Originated as a normative argument against monism or sameness. In political theory it is usually associated with a theory of the state according to which political power is diffuse, all organized groups having some influence on state outputs. In IR it is associated both with the "English School" and with neoliberal theory highlighting the multiplicity, or plurality, of forces at work in the international system.

Plurality A simple majority of votes (as in "first-past-the-post wins"), as distinct from an absolute majority (i.e., 50 per cent plus one).

Policy community The community of officials, experts, and interest groups with a stake in a particular policy area whose regular interaction leads to a convergence of views that is reflected in policy-making.

Political culture The aggregate attitudes of members of a society towards the institutions of rule and how they should operate.

Political obligation The question of what, if anything, obliges individuals to obey the state; a central preoccupation of political theorists. Answers to this question range from the ancient notion that monarchs have a "divine right" to rule to the modern notion that democracy is the basis of authority.

Political party A group of political activists who aspire to form or be part of the government on the basis of a program of policies.

Political system The totality of institutions within a state and all the connections between them.

Polyarchy A term coined by Robert Dahl to refer to a society where government outcomes are the product of the competition between groups. The rule of minorities, not majorities, is postulated as the normal condition of pluralist democracies.

Positive discrimination The practice of discriminating in favour of certain disadvantaged groups on the grounds that they would remain disadvantaged unless affirmative action is taken in their favour.

Positive liberty Liberty that can be increased either by state action or by removing internal obstacles such as immorality or irrationality.

Positivism A school of thought that believes it is possible to generate empirical statements without any evaluative or normative connotations. At the extreme, so-called logical positivists argue that only empirical statements and tautologies (statements that are true by definition) are meaningful.

Postmodernism A multi-faceted theoretical approach that challenges the certainties and dualisms of modernism and promotes pluralism and difference.

Power The ability to make others do something that they would not have chosen to do.

Power politics (*machtpolitik*) A view of politics, predicated on the notion that "might is right," that generally takes morality and justice to be irrelevant to the conduct of international relations; associated with realism.

Presidentialism The principle that the president of a republic is the head of the government.

Principal–agent relations A term for the relationship between the person who gives instructions (usually a government administrator) and the person who implements then.

Procedural justice The fairness of the process by which an outcome is reached, regardless of what the outcome actually is.

Proportional representation Any of various voting systems designed to achieve a close approximation between the number of votes received by each party and the number of seats into which those totals translate in parliament.

Protectionism An economic strategy, usually associated with a national policy of trade restriction in the form of tariffs and quotas, that attempts to protect domestic industries, businesses, and jobs from foreign competition.

Public space The arena (real or virtual) in which any member of society is free to express views on any issue of interest to the public. Sometimes associated with the German philosopher Habermas, who stressed its key importance for democracy and the difficulty of maintaining it under capitalism.

Rational choice theory The theory (borrowed from economics) that humans are self-interested and rational beings and therefore will analyze the costs and benefits of their choices in order to maximize gains and minimize losses. At the same time, however, the theory recognizes that preferences will be determined in part by context (class, job, gender, and so on), as well as cultural, religious, or other factors. Thus a belief in the value of altruism, or the hereafter, or some other standard of behavior, may lead individuals to act in ways that appear non-egotistical or self-serving. Rational choice theorists call these influences "institutional constraints" and factor them into individual decision-making processes.

Realism A school of thought in the human sciences, especially philosophy, sociology, politics, and international relations. In the latter, it refers to a general approach that takes concepts such as power politics and national interest to be the foundations of action; realists oppose what they see as the idealism of liberal and critical theories.

Raison d'état (reason of state) See **National interest**.

Rechtsstaat Literally, a law-based state, as distinct from a state where the executive is free to change policies as it sees fit.

Regionalization A process in which a number of states in a given geographical area come together for mutual benefit, often forming a regional association. Some, like the EU, are highly institutionalized and have myriad economic, social, and political interconnections, while others have minimal rules and less ambitious purposes.

Representative democracy A system in which the people choose others to represent their interests, instead of making decisions themselves.

Rule of law The principle that everyone in a state, including the executive, is subject to the same impersonal laws.

Secularism In political terms, the principle that religion does not enjoy a privileged position in the state.

Security dilemma A concept in IR, developed principally in realist thought, in which the anarchy of the system forces states to engage in self-regarding behaviour in order to survive. The dilemma arises when efforts by one state to enhance its own security (such as acquiring superior weaponry) provokes insecurity in another state, which may then respond by building up its own military capacity.

Self-determination The principle (embodying elements of both democracy and nationalism) that "peoples" (nations) have the right to determine their own political future.

Semantic analysis Analysis focusing on the meaning of the concepts we use, where they came from, and why and how we use them.

Social capital The aggregate of attitudes and networks that enable members of a society to cooperate in joint projects.

Social contract The idea that individuals in the **state of nature** (i.e., society before any form of government has been established) have voluntarily agreed to accept certain limits on their freedom in return for the benefits that government will provide; a device used by a number of political thinkers, most recently John Rawls, to justify a particular form of state.

Social constructivism See **Constructivism**.

Social Darwinism Darwin's theory of natural selection as applied to social life; the idea that it is a law of nature that individuals or groups with the characteristics best suited to a particular environment will survive to reproduce, while those less well suited will die out. This theory was used to justify a laissez-faire approach to social policy.

Social democracy Originally, a movement for a peaceful, non-revolutionary transition from capitalism to socialism; after the Russian Revolution in 1917 it came to be associated with liberal democracies that adopted redistributive policies and created a welfare state.

Social justice The principle that goods ought to be distributed according to need, merit, or the principle of equality.

Social movement A broad-based, largely informal movement composed of groups and individuals coalescing around a key issue area on a voluntary and often spontaneous basis. Examples include the environmental, women's, peace, and anti-globalization movements.

Solidarism A branch of thought in English School IR theory that promotes solidarity among humans and argues that the obligation to protect human rights can override the right of states to non-intervention in domestic politics.

Sovereignty The principle of self-government; to say a state is sovereign is to claim that it has a monopoly of force over the people and institutions in a given territorial area.

State A two-level concept: either (a) the government executive of a country (often referred to as a nation-state); or (b) the whole structure of political authority in a country.

Statecraft The skillful conduct of state affairs, usually in the context of external relations.

State of nature A hypothetical vision of how people lived before the institution of civil government and society; a concept with a long history in political and social thought. There are different versions of the state of nature, some thinkers emphasizing its dangers and others seeing it in a more positive light.

Structural adjustment A term for the deficit-reducing economic policies imposed by the World Bank and the International Monetary Fund on countries—usually poor and under-developed—seeking loans from them. Specific policies have included privatization, cuts in government spending on public services, currency devaluation, tariff cuts, and so on.

Structuration A concept derived from the sociologist Anthony Giddens, referring to all the factors that at once constrain a political system and provide the resources required for it to function.

Sustainable development The (contested) notion that economic growth is not incompatible with environmental protection and therefore can be sustained indefinitely.

Totalitarianism An extreme version of authoritarian rule, in which the state controls all aspects of social and economic life.

Track two diplomacy Informal or unofficial diplomatic efforts undertaken by private citizens, businesspeople, peace activists, or NGOs, as well as state actors.

Unicameralism A form of government in which the parliament consists of just one chamber.

Utilitarianism The ethical theory that the behaviour of individuals and governments should be judged by the degree to which their actions maximize pleasure or happiness.

Utopia An ideal state of affairs that does not exist but can be aimed for. Some see the search for utopias as a worthwhile exercise to expand the limits of human imagination; others see it as a recipe for illiberal, authoritarian, and even totalitarian societies.

Welfare state A political system in which the government takes responsibility for the basic physical and economic well-being of the people.

Credits

Grateful acknowledgement is made for permission to reprint the following:

Page 37, Key Quote Box 1.5: J. Ann Tickner (1992), *Gender in International Relations: Feminist Perspectives on Achieving Global Security*, New York: Columbia University Press, 62–3.

Pages 64 and 65: Excerpts from *Stolen Continents* by Ronald Wright. Copyright © Ronald Wright, 1992. Reprinted by permission of Penguin Group Canada, a Division of Pearson Canada Inc.

Pages 105–6: Excerpt from Michael Ignatieff, *Blood and Belonging: Journeys into the New Nationalism*, Farrar, Straus and Giroux (September 30, 1995).

Pages 161–2, Key Quote Box 8.1: Excerpt from Alfred, T., *Peace, Power, Righteousness: An Indigenous Manifesto* 2nd ed, Copyright © Oxford University Press Canada 2009. Reprinted by permission of the publisher.

Page 186, Key Quote Box 9.2: Excerpt from Burke, Edmund (1996), *The Writings and Speeches of Edmund Burke*, Vol. 3 (edited by W.M. Elofson with John A. Woods), Oxford: Clarendon Press. By permission of Oxford University Press.

Page 190, Key Quote Box 9.3: Excerpt from Linz, Juan J. (1992), "The Perils of Presidentialism" in Arend Lijphart (ed.), *Parliamentary Versus Presidential Government*, Oxford: Oxford University Press: 118–27. By permission of Oxford University Press.

Page 245, Key Quote Box 12.2: Excerpt from Ken Georgetti, *National Post*, Thu Sep 29 2011, Page: FP13: "Who finances Fraser's anti-union agenda?" Reprinted with permission.

Page 304, Key Quote Box 15.2: Excerpt from Thucydides (1972), *History of the Peloponnesian War*, London: Penguin. © Rex Warner, 1954. Introduction and Appendices © M.I. Finley, 1972.

Page 367, Key Quote Box 18.3: Excerpt from Brad Evenson and Andrew Duffy, "Secret papers link scandal, death penalty" *Vancouver Sun*, February 28, 1997, p. A4. Material reprinted with the express permission of Postmedia News, a division of Postmedia Network Inc.

Page 384, Key Quote Box 19.1: From *The Politics of Global Governance*, 3rd edition, edited by Paul F. Diehl. Copyright © 2005 by Lynne Rienner Publishers, Inc. Used with permission by the publisher.

Page 408, Key Quote Box 20.2: From Mankiw, *Brief Principles of Macroeconomics*, 3E. © 2004 South-Western, a part of Cengage Learning, Inc. Reproduced by permission. www.cengage.com/permissions.

Index

Lehmbruch, Gerhard, 246

Lemkin, Raphael, 394

Lenin, V.I., 57, 96, 97–8, 318

Leuchter, Fred, 112

Leviathan, 9, 12, 35, 294

Lewis, Bernard, 149, 171

"Lewis Doctrine," 149

liberal institutionalism, 341, 456

liberalism, 22–3, 39, 93, 94–6, 136, 321, 409; classical,
   84, 94–5; critique of, 305; eco-, 128; equality and, 96;
   historical development of, 94–5; individuals in, 95–6, 409;
   international relations and, 300–2; limited state interference, 38;
   multiculturalism and, 130; new, 84, 457; peace and, 313;
   thought, 95–6

Liberal parties, 94, 228; Canada, 2, 72, 94, 137;
   United Kingdom, 95, 188

liberal political economy, 407–9

liberal social contract tradition, 35–8

liberty, 77; negative, 79, 95, 457; positive, 79, 95, 458;
   see also freedom

Libya, 253; 2011 revolution, 140, 141

Lifton, R.J., 111

Lijphart, Arendt, 177, 178

Limits to Growth, The, 125

Lincoln, Abraham, 219

Lindblom, Charles, 53

Linklater, Andrew, 321

Linz, Juan, 189–90, 190

Lipset, Seymour Martin, 103

Lipset, Seymour Martin and Stein Rokkan, 235

List, Friedrich, 407

Lively, J., 69, 70

Locke, John, 32, 35, 36, 38, 63, 78, 95, 428

log-rolling, 224

lottizzazione ("parcelling out"), 207

Lukes, Steven, 49–50, 56–7, 78; three dimensions or
   "faces" of power, 50–4

Lynn, Laurence E., 209

Maastricht Treaty, 377, 420

Macapagal-Arroyo, Gloria, 190, 253

McCain, John, 235

McClellan, Scott, 334

Macdonald, John A., 103

Machiavelli, Niccolò, 288, 294, 305, 306, 362

machtpolitik. See power politics

MacKinnon, C., 122

Macpherson, C.B., 36, 66

Madison, James, 65, 224

Mainwaring, Scott, 202

majoritarianism, 72, 74; *see also* democracy

Making Democracy Work, 263

Malaysia, 23, 24

Man, the State and War, 313–14

Mankiw, Gregory, 408

Mannheim, Karl, 322

Mao Zedong, 265, 274, *366*

March of the Living, *111*

Marcos, Ferdinand, 191, 239

Marcuse, Herbert, 57

market (the), 404, 418; state and, 404–5

Marshall, George, 347

Marshall, T.H., 129

Marshall Plan, 347

Marx, Karl, 3, 30, 40, 57–8, 96, 97, 318; vision of
   communism, 97

Marxism, 3, 30, 33, 43; on capitalism, 31; and critical
   IPE, 410–13; power and, 57–8, 66; the state and,
   30–1, 151

masculinity, 325, 327

mass parties, 224, 456

Matland, Richard E., 185

Mauritius, 416

Mearsheimer, John, 314, 315, 340

Medbedev, Dmitry, 431

Médecins Sans Frontières, 397, 428

media, 24; bloggers and, 254–5; encoding and decoding of
   messages, 251; formation of public attitudes, 193;
   globalization of, 428; impact of, 248–51; models of, 251;
   new technologies, 252–6; political affiliation and, 249;
   politicians and, 250–1; war on terror and, 334;
   watchdog function, 249

Mein Kampf, 109

Melian Dialogue, 304

members of parliament (MPs), 200; constituents
   and, 186

Menkhaus, Ken, 155

mercantilism, 405–7, 422, 456

MERCOSUR, 395, 427

Merkel, Angela, 329

metanarratives, 332, 456

methodology, 51, 308, 456

Mezey, Michael, 195–6

Michels, Robert, 30

Middle Ages: positive view of, 429–30

Middle East: democratization in, 427–8;
   Islamic militancy in, 356

migration, international, 410–11

Milbank, Dana and Claudia Deane, 333–5

Miliband, Ralph, 58, 66

Military Construction Appropriations Bill, 355

Mill, James, 65, 80

Mill, John Stuart, 2, 39, 69, 83–4, 95, 119;
   on liberty, 80–1, 81–3

Millett, Kate, 122

Mills, C. Wright, 28, 30

Milosevic, Slobodan, 176–7, 330, 395

minority governments, 188

modernity, 118, 291, 319, 321, 456

Moghadam, Valentine M., 411